The Complete Grants Sourcebook for Higher Education

THE COMPLETE GRANTS

SOURCEBOOK FOR

HIGHER EDUCATION

Third Edition

by
David G. Bauer

AMERICAN COUNCIL ON EDUCATION ★
ORYX PRESS ★
Series on Higher Education
1995

*The rare Arabian Oryx is believed to have inspired the myth of the unicorn. This desert
antelope became virtually extinct in the early 1960s. At that time several groups of
international conservationists arranged to have 9 animals sent to the Phoenix Zoo
to be the nucleus of a captive breeding herd. Today the Oryx population
is over 800 and nearly 400 have been returned to reserves
in the Middle East.*

© 1996 by American Council on Education and The Oryx Press
Published by The Oryx Press
4041 North Central at Indian School Road
Phoenix, Arizona 85012-3397

Published simultaneously in Canada
Printed and Bound in the United States of America

♾ The paper used in this publication meets the minimum requirements of
American National Standard for Information Science—Permanence of Paper
for Printed Library Materials, ANSI Z39.48, 1984.

Library of Congress Cataloging-in-Publication Data

Bauer, David G.
    The complete grants sourcebook for higher education / by David G.
Bauer.—3rd ed.
        p. cm.
    Includes indexes.
    ISBN 0-89774-821-2 (alk. paper)
    1. Endowments—United States—Directories. 2. Universities and
colleges—United States—Finance—Directories. I. Title.
LB2336.B38 1995
378'.02—dc20   95-47018
                                                                CIP

CONTENTS

PREFACE

The third edition of *The Complete Grants Sourcebook for Higher Education* has been extensively revised. However, its goal remains the same: to provide faculty members, administrators, and researchers with the most complete and accurate information available on the best foundation, corporate, and government funding sources for higher education.

This book differs from other sourcebooks, directories, and computer-based information retrieval systems in that the government grantors have been contacted, information on past granting patterns has been analyzed, and, when possible, anticipated changes have been forecast. The information is not a direct reprint of the *Catalog of Federal Domestic Assistance* or the *Foundation Directory*, and the entries have not been prepared by grantors.

The "how-to" format is retained in this edition of the *Sourcebook*. This approach encourages readers to utilize the research provided and to take further steps to increase their knowledge of the grantor's funding interests, application requirements, review process, and so on.

Successful grantseeking calls for an approach tailored to each grantor. The information in this book shows the grantseeker how to do this and will help them match their project to the "right" grantor.

The pressure to pursue and obtain resources from outside of your college or university has never been greater. Each year more and more faculty are finding that their evaluation, merit raise, or promotion system is based more and more on sponsored research or extramural grant funding and less on teaching proficiency. This book does not seek to address this issue, but instead provides the higher education professional with research on major education funding sources and a process for approaching each type of grantor.

The benefits of successful grantseeking are far greater than securing funds and merit raises. Successful grantseeking can have a tremendous impact on an institution by improving

- institutional image
- faculty/staff morale
- student education and success
- college/university facilities and equipment
- the ability to attract top professionals

In addition, successful grantseeking enhances the image of *all* educational institutions and increases the ability of higher education to attract a greater portion of the support available from the grants marketplace.

Now more than ever, higher education proponents are finding that they cannot rely on their past records to attract grant moneys. For example, when the first edition of this book was published in 1982, education received 42.5 percent of foundation grant dollars. By 1993 this figure dropped to 24 percent. Since 1988 foundations have been increasing their support of precollege programs. In 1990 precollege programs received only 3.9 percent of foundation funds. By 1993 this figure had increased to 6 percent. In other words, the competition is increasing and higher education's portion of foundation grant dollars will erode unless we make a strong case for continued and increased grant support and develop innovative approaches such as consortium projects with precollege programs.

This document was conceived and produced to move toward this goal of continued benefits to higher education. The staff of Bauer Associates who prepared the *Sourcebook* hope you will take advantage of the hundreds of hours of research that went in to determining the best funding sources for higher education. David Bauer, author, and research associates Donna Macrini-Bauer and Janet Salmons wish you much success in your grantseeking endeavors.

INTRODUCTION

■

During the last half of the current decade (1995–2000), higher education will increasingly have to justify the continued investment of billions of federal dollars for college- and university-initiated, sponsored projects and research. Efforts to limit or reduce the role of the federal government and to move toward federalized programs in which the states set their own priorities will test the adaptation skills of the higher education grantseeker. In an attempt to balance the federal budget, programs that are discretionary (such as the Higher Education Act) are likely to be hit harder than entitlements (such as Social Security) since discretionary programs must be periodically re-enacted and appropriated annually. *All* grant programs that provide colleges and universities with grant funds will be scrutinized, but the Department of Education will be exposed to a continued drive to eliminate or reduce its education programs.

Do not let the news media, politicians, or appropriations and budget cuts mislead you into thinking that applying for grant funds is futile. Even when a program experiences a 20 percent cut, it will still have 80 percent of its original funding. This book and its "how-to" section will help you capitalize on the facts, not the emotions, of the grants marketplace. Use the techniques and tips presented to help you collect accurate data on prospective grantors and to ascertain true levels of funding and numbers and types of awards.

Foundation and corporate grants support for higher education will also experience fluctuations over the next few years. Again, do not overreact to temporary or widely publicized reductions in the marketplace. Only a careful review of the actual statistics and the use of pre-proposal contact to validate and expand your knowledge of the funding source will provide you with the confidence that identifies a true grant winner.

HOW TO USE THIS BOOK

This document is divided into four sections:

    I How to Increase Your Grants Success

   II Sources of Foundation Funding for Higher Education

 III Sources of Corporate Funding for Higher Education

 IV Sources of Government Funding for Higher Education

Sections II, III, and IV each contain a detailed introduction to help you use the funding source information provided as efficiently as possible.

Section I: How to Increase Your Grants Success

As a grants seminar instructor, I have administered a preseminar quiz on the grants marketplace to thousands of college and university personnel. On the average, only 10 percent of the educators surveyed answer one-half of the questions correctly. Read Section I to increase your knowledge of the grants marketplace and to better enable you to determine which of the marketplaces is "best" for your project.

In addition to marketplace information, Section I contains specific strategies for increasing your grants success. This section provides you with valuable information on how to

- develop a proactive grantseeking system
- use timesaving techniques to organize your grants effort
- redefine your proposal ideas to find more funding sources
- use advocates and volunteers
- contact funding sources
- develop and negotiate a realistic budget
- write a letter proposal
- deal with the funder's decision

Use the worksheets in Section I to develop a tailored approach to each funder that positions your institution/department as a credible grantee. (Permission is given for photocopying these worksheets for individual use.)

Section II: Sources of Foundation Funding for Higher Education

Section II provides detailed information on private foundations and the amounts of money they have contributed to higher education, as well as instruction on how to use the research provided to maximize your foundation grants success.

In this section you will find current profiles on foundation funding sources that include

- addresses and telephone numbers
- areas of interest
- funding analysis
- eligibility requirements

- policy statements
- trustees and officers
- financial profiles
- application procedures
- sample grants

Section III: Sources of Corporate Funding for Higher Education

This section presents research on corporate foundations and corporate giving programs that support higher education. In addition to information on specific funding sources, this section provides the reader with insight into how to find local corporations with foundations or giving programs too small to be included in this sourcebook.

This section will be a valuable resource for learning how to

- locate corporations that give
- research on what they fund
- make pre-proposal contact and proceed in your grants quest

Section IV: Sources of Government Funding for Higher Education

Section IV contains information on federal agency programs that support higher education. Although every program that makes grants to higher education is not included, the reader is presented with information on many of the major programs and with techniques for locating less obvious government funders and programs that may prove to be excellent choices for particular projects. In addition, this section provides techniques for locating new sources that may have been created since this edition went to press and tips on how to identify changes in the programs listed.

This document is based upon the same practical "how-to" format that made the author, David Bauer, one of the best-known grants consultants in the United States. Improving your approach to grantseeking is as valuable as the time savings that the research in this sourcebook represents to your grants success.

For more valuable techniques that will save you time and improve your grants effort, consult *The "How To" Grants Manual* by David Bauer. This manual is part of the American Council on Education's Series on Higher Education (Oryx Press, 1995) and can be used with the American Council on Education's video cassette series, Winning Grants. (For ordering information call Bauer Associates at 800-836-0732.)

SECTION

How to Increase Your

Grants Success

HOW TO INCREASE YOUR GRANTS SUCCESS

A successful grant proposal follows a win-win-win-win approach. The grantor wins because the proposal meets their needs and reinforces their values. The proposal developer or grantseeker wins because they have the opportunity to conduct the research or implement the project they have developed. The grantseeker's college or university wins because it receives positive recognition by being the recipient or host agent. And finally the field of interest, clients, or subjects that stand to benefit from the knowledge that the project will expand or validate, win.

Your objective is to develop a proposal that will produce the greatest return for your investment. Grantors want to read well-organized proposals that take their needs into consideration and demonstrate that the applicant is knowledgeable of the grantor's most recent priorities and their commitment to those priorities as evidenced by their granting pattern and financial profile. By using your time efficiently to tailor your proposal to the prospective grantor, you have a greater chance of being funded and, hence, an increased likelihood of

- boosting the grant acceptance rate at your college or university
- projecting a good image for your project and your institution

What you do not want to do is waste time and effort sending your proposal to grantors who are only vaguely interested in it. This will position your organization as a member of the "grantseeker's shotgun club"—a group that believes if you "shoot out" enough proposals, you are bound to hit something. By taking this approach you waste not only your time, but the grantors' as well, and you reduce your chances of being funded when you do have a proposal that meets their needs.

The key to getting the most out of this sourcebook is to understand that successful grantseeking requires matching what the funding source wants with what your project and institution can provide. Remember that not many funders care about what *your* needs or wants are unless they match with *theirs*.

This section of the sourcebook (Section I) will help you organize your proposal ideas and develop strategies to match the interests of funders in projects or grants that would benefit both of you. This requires a thorough analysis of prospective grantors before writing your proposal and the tailoring of your proposal to each funding source. The result is well worth it. Rather than investing time in a grants effort that generates a 10 percent success rate, you can obtain a 50 to 80 percent success rate through this systematic approach. The "secret ingredient" in this system is confidence in knowing that you can and will meet the grantor's needs.

Your grants interests may be very self-focused (a summer stipend or fellowship), institutionally based (cross-curricular interests), or specific to your research and career interests. You may be interested in producing one proposal or many. No matter how involved in grants you may wish to be, the steps outlined in this section will assist you in organizing a successful approach that will work for you on the occasional proposal or hundreds of proposals. The research section will save you hours you could spend uncovering the interests of particular funders and identifying previous grantees, average grant size, application guidelines, and so on.

Much of the work required in developing a grant-winning proposal is done *before* the proposal is written. In fact, successful grantseeking can be largely attributed to doing your "homework" and using the research data contained in this book to view your approach from the grantor's perspective. This section provides techniques and tips for gathering as much information as you can on prospective grantors and for doing the work of grantseeking in as time efficient a manner as possible. Several worksheets have been included to assist you in your quest for funds. These worksheets have been selected from *The "How To" Grants Manual* (Oryx Press, 1995).

One of your first steps in grantseeking should be to check with your office of sponsored projects and research or the grants office at your campus to become knowledgeable about your institutions's existing grants system. Many universities are decentralizing their grant support functions to assist faculty at the department level. By contacting the appropriate office early in the grantseeking process, you may discover valuable proposal preparation assistance and find it easier to obtain the signatures your proposal will require at submittal time. You may even be pleasantly surprised to find that there are travel funds available to help grantseekers visit funding sources. In addition, your college may have sanctions governing what sources you are allowed to contact or who coordinates contacts with funding sources. Contact with your grants office may help you avoid asking to have your proposal submitted to a grantor who is also being approached by other grantseekers from your institution.

THE MARKETPLACE: WHO HAS THE MONEY? HOW MUCH DO THEY HAVE? HOW MUCH DO THEY GIVE TO HIGHER EDUCATION?

Before you rush to the index to uncover specific grantors who share your values and needs, test your "Grants

IQ" by reviewing the following grants marketplace information. Keep in mind that a successful grants strategy requires the careful examination of each of the grants marketplaces and a realistic appraisal of the potential each marketplace holds for you and your project/research.

Public Funding Sources

The federal government is the largest single grantor to colleges and universities. Tracking and researching the federal agencies that fund higher education is difficult because there are so many. Approximately 3,000 colleges and universities apply to over 1,100 federal programs across the full spectrum of federal agencies including, but not limited to

- Department of Education
- Department of Labor
- National Endowment for the Humanities
- National Endowment for the Arts
- National Science Foundation
- Department of Health and Human Services
- Department of Energy

Not only does the federal government disseminate $80 to $90 billion through the competitive grants process, but there are additional billions of dollars worth of federal funds distributed through the competitive bidding process (although the scope of this book does not include these funds).

The federal grants marketplace is the first place to look for grant funds because it is approximately five times larger than the $15 billion foundation and corporate grants marketplace. Furthermore, foundation and corporate funding officials expect grantseekers to research federal granting programs before approaching them for their much more limited resources. In fact, being rejected by a federal agency because you do not have enough preliminary data may actually help you secure a grant from a private funding source. While federal granting agencies may not be as open to new and untried approaches as many grantseekers believe, foundation and corporate grantors often fund less expensive trials and the development of models with the understanding that once the potential viability of the project is documented, even on a preliminary basis, the grantee will be in a better position to get money from the federal government for continuation and expansion of the project.

The ultimate question is not how much of the total federal grants marketplace is awarded to institutions of higher education, but rather

- which federal granting programs are suited to your particular project or research
- who and how your proposal will be reviewed
- how successful other colleges and universities have been in securing grant funds from this agency for your type of proposal

The federal grants marketplace will receive close scrutiny as Congress and the executive branch seek to put their fiscal policies in place. Appropriations for federal grant programs will change. Do not be tempted to base your appraisal of your potential success in this marketplace on media announcements of cuts and changes in federal spending. Instead, use the research in this document and other factual data you gather. You need to know how federal agencies will use their appropriations to support new awards as well as continue existing grants in multiple-year award cycles.

Foundation Grants to Higher Education

By law every foundation must report the grants it makes on an annual IRS tax return known as a 990. However, much of the data available on grants made by individual foundations comes from voluntary information provided by the foundations themselves. The foundation data provided in this sourcebook comes from analysis of individual foundation tax returns and represents the highest degree of accuracy possible, considering that many tax returns are one to two years old before they are made available for analysis.

In 1994 an estimated $9.91 billion in grants was awarded by 37,571 foundations. These foundations held over $182 billion in assets and were required by law to donate a minimum of 5 percent of their assets to 487,000 eligible nonprofit organizations.

The entire field of education received about 24 percent of all foundation grant dollars in 1993. While elementary and secondary schools have made significant gains in foundation support, colleges and universities continue to be the prime recipients, as illustrated in the following figures:

- higher education (undergraduate, graduate, and professional)—15 percent
- elementary and secondary education—6 percent

- other education—3 percent
- total—24 percent

There are many more grants involving colleges and universities than the 15 percent reported here. For example, grants awarded to institutions of higher education in subject areas such as medical research, the environment, human services, science and technology may be categorized and counted under the specific subject area rather than higher education. This may add as much as 10 percent or approximately $1 billion to the actual amount of foundation grant dollars awarded to higher education.

There are also many misconceptions about foundation giving. In general, foundation grants are not as large as many people believe they are, nor do foundations prefer to fund the types of projects grant-seekers think they do. For example, 1993 estimates show 13,000 foundation grants of $10,000 or more awarded to colleges and universities, graduate schools, and junior/community colleges, for a total of approximately $1.5 billion. In addition, capital grants (building, renovations, endowments, etc.) account for little over 22 percent of all foundation grants dollars, though most grantseekers believe that foundations prefer to support this type of project. The real interest of foundations is program support, including program development, faculty/staff development, seed money, and curriculum development. As a matter of fact, in 1993 program support received over 44 percent of the total $9.2 billion awarded in foundation grants. General support received 12.3 percent, research 10.5 percent, and student aid funds 5.8 percent.

Although faculty and staff in higher education have the programs and research interests that move the purse strings of foundations, the percentage of foundation grant support going to higher education has actually dropped substantially from the 1982 level of 42.5 percent. One of the reasons for this decline may be higher education's inability to stay in touch with and focus on *what* motivates the *grantor* instead of what higher education would like to have funded.

Another factor in the downward trend may be the grantseeker's lack of desire to perform the research necessary to prepare a quality proposal tailored to the prospective grantor's needs and granting patterns. Many applicants only hear about large grant awards and therefore, do not consider requesting small- or average-sized grants.

Selecting a Foundation

Before you can select the correct foundation for your proposal, you must understand each of the five major types of foundations:

- community foundations
- national general purpose foundations
- special purpose foundations
- family foundations
- corporate foundations

Community Foundations

These are grant-making foundations created by philanthropic individuals to fund a specific geographic area. The size of the area may vary from a community or city to an entire state, but the purpose is limited to making grants in the specified area.

This fast-growing segment of the foundations marketplace has $9 billion in assets. Initially, most support for community foundations came from bequests or deferred giving, but gifts from public-spirited, living individuals now constitute 82 percent of the support. Typically, the community foundation holds funds from local, philanthropic individuals, with the average foundation handling over 383 separately named funds.

Higher education attracts 20 percent of community foundation grant funds. The types of projects or programs supported varies dramatically by donor interests and wishes, but always includes a geographic parameter. Some examples of projects funded by community foundations are

- scholarships for local students
- needs assessment for local problems
- replication of a project proven to be effective in other communities

Community foundations prefer to fund projects that impact their restricted view of community. Innovative, model projects or research are considered "risky" and generally do not receive a favored response.

The Cleveland Foundation was the first community foundation established and has served as a model for most community foundations in the United States. In 1992 it awarded 51 grants to higher education for a total of $3,692,960 or approximately 11 percent of its total grant expenditures.

National General Purpose Foundations

This is the type of foundation that most educators think of when they use the word "foundation." While this group numbers only a few hundred out of the total of 37,571 foundations, national general purpose foundations hold two-thirds of all foundation assets and account for 50 percent of all the grants awarded to all areas of interest. It is a major influence in foundation giving to education in particular. This group prefers to fund proposals that are innovative, have the potential of focusing national attention on an important program or area, and can be replicated by others.

The Ford Foundation is an example of a national general purpose foundation. In the year ending September 30, 1992, Ford awarded 1,482 grants totaling $259,966,848. However, it is not the *amount* of giving but the scope that makes Ford a national general purpose foundation. In 1992, Ford's grant funds were distributed to 25 areas of interest, including higher education. In fact, in 1992 it gave to 418 higher education institutions and organizations throughout the United States and around the world, for a total $83,072,419.

Special Purpose Foundations

Depending on how "special purpose" is defined, several thousand foundations fall into this category. In this publication, special purpose foundations include those whose funding record consistently supports higher education and represents a significant contribution to higher education. This definition reduces the number to several hundred.

The Robert Wood Johnson Foundation is an example of a special purpose foundation. In 1992 it awarded 180 grants in higher education totaling $76,454,081. The well-defined purpose of these grants dealt with improving the health and health care of Americans and containing escalating health care expenditures.

The approaches to meet the special purpose of the Robert Wood Johnson Foundation varied widely in 1992, but the underlying goals and objectives remained constant. From fellowships in health policy planning to the funding of special projects evaluating health services for those with chronic health conditions, many recipients were colleges and universities, and their proposals were all ultimately related to improving the American health care delivery system.

Family Foundations

There are over 30,000 foundations in this category. Their interests represent the values of family groups or members, friends, and the foundations' boards. Since many family foundations were set up as trusts to honor or memorialize a deceased family member, their giving often patterns the life and goals of the deceased. When researching a family foundation, look up the memorialized individual's obituary in the newspaper archives of your library.

Most family foundations have geographic preferences and may act as small scale special purpose foundations. Many are operated by family members who can redirect their foundation's giving patterns and funding priorities at any time.

Family foundations are most susceptible to the influence of board members, their friends, and popular "causes." Therefore, your ability to link your project or college/university to "friends" of the foundation is very important. Since these family foundations can and do change their priorities, it is helpful to have a contact who keeps you informed of the foundation's current funding priorities.

The Connelly Foundation is an example of a family foundation. In 1992 it funded 16 grants in higher education for a total of $5,861,282. Grants were made for scholarship funds, capital campaigns, endowment funds, operating budgets, renovation projects, and special projects. The foundation favored the Philadelphia, Pennsylvania, and Delaware Valley areas. In coming years they may provide funding for other types of activities, but the value they place on higher education is likely to continue.

Corporate Foundations

The total corporate support to all nonprofit organizations in 1993 was estimated at $6.11 billion, only 1 percent higher than in 1992. This marks the sixth year in a row that increases in corporate contributions did not keep pace with the cost of living.

Many colleges and universities have misconceptions about this limited, but valuable resource. The corporate foundation marketplace is much different than the would-be grantee believes. First, most grantseekers mistakenly believe that corporate support to nonprofits is far greater than the facts reveal. In reality this is the smallest of the three grant sources (federal, foundation, and corporate).

Second, higher education does not attract all of the six billion corporate dollars as some colleges and universities believe it does. For instance, the breakdown of corporate funding in 1993 was as follows:

- education projects (including higher education *and* all other education)—43 percent
- health and human services projects—30 percent
- civic and community projects—12 percent
- culture and arts projects—12 percent
- other projects—3 percent

It is true, however, that of the portion going to education, higher education has historically received the greatest percentage. It is estimated that in 1993

- higher education received 72.7 percent of corporate funds going to education (up from 70.3 percent in 1992)
- precollege education received 14.9 percent
- other education programs and educational organizations received 7.1 percent (down from 7.5 percent in 1992)
- scholarships and fellowships received 5.2 percent (down from 6.3 percent in 1992)

While colleges and universities have been maintaining their market share, there have been significant changes in the precollege area. Corporate grant dollars to precollege education as a percent of total corporate grant dollars to all education has grown from 3 percent in 1961 to 14.9 percent in 1993. A 1989 survey of corporate contributions conducted by the Council for Aid to Education (CFAE) showed that 64 percent of the responding corporations planned to increase support to precollege education in the future. Sixty-six percent reported that the increase would come through an increase in their overall education budgets, while 11 percent planned to shift dollars from higher education-related giving. Twenty-three percent reported that they were planning to increase their support of precollege education by doing both—increasing their education grants budget *and* shifting some money from higher education.

Many colleges and universities are aware of this growing support to precollege education and are taking an active role in developing consortia projects with precollege grantees. Those institutions are learning firsthand that working together can pay off handsomely.

The data presented in the preceding paragraphs shows that higher education attracts approximately three-fourths of the total corporate support given to education. A breakdown by type of higher education institution shows a marked increase over the past 10 years of support for public colleges and universities. Most experts agree that this increase has come, at least in part, at the expense of private education. Surveys performed by the CFAE show that corporate support for private four-year institutions has been declining for several years. Exhibit 1.1 from CFAE's booklet *Corporate Support of Education 1993*[1] illustrates this decline.

While the change appears dramatic, keep in mind that growth in the number of students in public higher education is much greater than in private higher education. Exhibit 1.2 from CFAE's booklet shows that in corporate contributions per student, private institutions lead public institutions for every type of college except "specialized public." Therefore, the comparison of corporate support for public institutions versus private must be evaluated not only by type of institution, but by how many students are impacted as well.

Specialized public colleges and universities fare four times better than private institutions but are the only public institutions who garner more dollars per student than private higher education institutions. The growth of the specialized category, which includes many of the technology and engineering related areas, demonstrates the "this for that" attitude that pervades today's corporate support for nonprofits. Prospective grantees that can demonstrate a return on a corporation's investment will continue to attract its support. Therefore, to successfully access the corporate marketplace, higher education must focus on what the prospective corporate grantor wants from them and not what they want from the corporate marketplace.

Corporations have traditionally supported those universities that provide them with an educated work force, product development, and research. In 1993 public doctoral institutions received 80 percent of all corporate support to public higher education, while their counterparts on the private side received 64 percent. Support for both of these groups declined by 3 and 4 percent respectively from 1992 estimates. However, it is too early to tell how seriously this de-

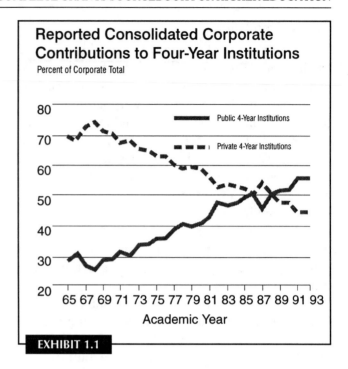

Reported Consolidated Corporate Contributions to Four-Year Institutions
Percent of Corporate Total

EXHIBIT 1.1

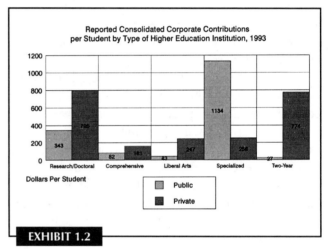

Reported Consolidated Corporate Contributions per Student by Type of Higher Education Institution, 1993

Dollars Per Student

EXHIBIT 1.2

crease should be considered when planning your corporate grants strategy.

What should be considered is that corporate grantors support a variety of activities related to higher education and that corporate support should not be restricted to development office programs only. While it is true that in 1993 capital support projects (including buildings, equipment, property, and endowments) accounted for 28.6 percent of corporate funding to higher education, research accounted for 27.1 percent, 17.6 percent was given for restricted support, 14 percent for proposals supporting academic divisions, 7.5 percent for unrestricted support, and 5 percent for student financial aid. What this shows is that while coordinating the solicitation of corporate

[1] Council for Aid to Education, *Corporate Support of Education 1993* (New York: Council for Aid to Education, 1994). Reproduced with permission of the CFAE.

grantors is very important in maintaining a college or university's image and mission, it is short-sighted to restrict an institution's grantseekers from seeking corporate grants support.

Forces at Work in the Corporate Marketplace. Since the last edition of this book, many changes have occurred in corporate philanthropy. In previous years there was a direct correlation between profitability and corporate philanthropy. But in the 1990s, the profits of many corporations have gone up while their corporate contributions have remained flat or gone down. For example, in 1992 corporate pretax net income increased 9 percent while charitable contributions decreased 2 percent. Although corporate pretax net income was up 14 percent in 1993, charitable contributions were up by only 2 percent.

One theory about this paradigm shift is that companies are using their profits to replace the assets that were depleted from their foundations in the 1980s in an effort to keep corporate giving at constant levels. The facts demonstrate that corporate foundations have continued to donate more than each dollar received from the parent company.

When analyzing the corporate grants marketplace, the grantee must consider contributions made through corporate giving programs as well as those made through corporate foundations. While the motivations of both sources are quite similar (many times the corporate foundation board members and the corporate contributions committee members are identical), the facts are that

- approximately 30 percent of corporate support comes from corporate foundations
- the remaining 70 percent comes from corporate profits distributed by corporate contributions committees comprised of trustees, management, and in a number of cases, employee representatives

IRS 990 tax returns reveal corporate foundation granting patterns. However, the 70 percent of corporate contributions that come from corporate profits are not subject to public information laws and are nonverifiable. The information that companies make available is done so as a courtesy or as a result of surveys developed by nonprofit, data-gathering organizations such as the CFAE, Conference Board, and AAFRS Trust for Philanthropy.

Although cash gifts declined by 5 percent between 1992 and 1993, cash is still the leading type of support from corporations to higher education and accounted for 84 percent of the gifts reported in 1993.

In the most recent survey conducted by the CFAE, reported gifts of company products rose from 12.5 percent in 1992 to 13.2 percent in 1993, while the category of "other property" rose from .6 percent to 6.7 percent.

Does the 1993 $6.11 billion figure represent all corporate support to nonprofits? The answer is no. This figure represents only those contributions that fall within the allowable 10 percent of pretax earnings that companies can take as deductions under current IRS rules.

While it is difficult to verify corporate cash contributions, estimating the amount of company support not taken as deductions is nearly impossible. A decade ago companies were surveyed by the Conference Board and the CFAE to ascertain the extent of nondeductible support. Of the 344 companies who indicated that they made deductible contributions, 184 reported that they also made expenditures not reported as charitable deductions. These expenditures consisted of

- $100 million in cash
- $19 million in loaned personnel
- $46 million in products and property
- $14.5 million in donated use of corporate facilities
- $7.9 million in loans at below market yields
- $41.4 million in administrative costs for contribution functions

When this survey is repeated it is likely that there will be hundreds of millions (if not billions) of dollars of nondeducted donations reported. The survey data is mixed, but a trend toward donations of corporate products to many types of nonprofit recipients and especially colleges and universities is evident.

Why would profit-making companies not take advantage of every deduction possible? Deductions must be reported to the IRS and therefore subject the company to the possibility of an audit and questions regarding the "charitable nature" of the gift. In many cases the corporation may have acquired a distinct benefit by making the contribution. As a corporate executive once remarked to me: "Let's call the gift to your college a marketing expense. That way I will not be required to get approval from the North American headquarters and it will not appear on our tax return. Besides if I take it out of my marketing budget it will not be subject to tax since it will be considered a cost of doing business."

No one knows the total commitment of the 2.5 million U.S. corporations to higher education because a considerable amount of "support" comes as contracts for services. From drug testing to product development, there are many more opportunities for corporate support than appear in this book. Grantseekers are limited only by their own creativity and ability to relate their projects' benefits to companies who value those same benefits.

Remember that the only constant in the corporate marketplace is change. The corporate marketplace is also much more unpredictable than the foundation or government marketplace. For example, mergers have, in the long run, had a negative impact on corporate giving because they have eroded decision making at the plant and local levels. However, in the short run, they have led some companies to increase their philanthropy in hopes that their "giving" will influence the government regulators overseeing the merger.

Many companies are insisting that their employees be committed, through volunteer activities, to the nonprofit organizations the company supports. The companies generally feel that it is the nonprofit organization's responsibility to demonstrate employee involvement before asking for the investment. This is particularly true as companies downsize and are wary that giving away the fruits of their labor may appear unfair when corporate cutbacks have forced employee layoffs.

As with the foundation and federal grants marketplaces, success in the corporate arena (both in grants and gifts) requires that you coordinate your approach with your appropriate college/university body and that you initiate pre-proposal contact.

DEVELOPING A PROACTIVE GRANTSEEKING SYSTEM

Many well-intended grantseekers begin the proposal development process in a reactive manner by chasing after deadlines and submitting their proposals at the last minute. Reactive grantseekers wait for a colleague or college staff person to place a federal or state request for a proposal (RFP) or a request for application (RFA) on their desks and then react to the impending deadline. They approach foundation and corporate grants in a similar manner. Even when they discover that there is no deadline, they put off preparing and submitting their proposal until right before the proposed project is scheduled to begin. Neither approach is a good way to do business, since reactive grantseeking, as illustrated by these examples, leaves prospective funding sources with negative impressions.

The correct course of action is to initiate a proactive grantseeking system that strives to keep the proposal preparation process orderly and under control. One way to do this is to use a "swiss cheese book." Allen Lakein suggests in his classic publication *How to Get Control of Your Time and Your Life*[2], that a complex task is best approached when divided into smaller parts. The example he uses is a mouse faced with the overwhelming task of moving a large piece of cheese. To move the cheese the mouse must nibble at it, reducing it in size and turning it into swiss cheese. By applying this concept to the task of proposal preparation, the overburdened grantseeker can save 50 percent of the time it takes to create a tailored proposal and find the "spare" time to take the proactive steps suggested throughout this section.

To make a swiss cheese book, begin with a ring binder with three one-and-a-half- or two-inch rings and a clear plastic pouch on the front. Write a short statement of the problem area that you are seeking to impact, then slip it into the pouch as the title of your swiss cheese book. Do not use your preferred solution as the title since several solutions and several proposals will eventually come from this binder. For example, a binder designated "Problems of Predelinquent Youth" might contain various proposal ideas, such as after-school enrichment programs, organized evening recreation, an adopt-a-teen program, and so on.

The binder should be divided into tabbed sections, with each tab identifying the information contained in that section. In essence, the tabs divide the full-scale proposal process into achievable tasks and allow the grantseeker to address each task one at a time. To follow the above example, when the grantseeker reads a research article on the problems of predelinquent youth, he or she makes a copy of it (or writes a summary) and places it in the section tabbed "Docu-

[2] Allen Lakein, *How to Get Control of Your Time and Your Life* (New York: New American Library, 1974).

menting Need." Likewise, as he or she gathers information on solutions, reads more articles, and conducts needs assessments, he or she places each article in the appropriate section of the swiss cheese book.

You may create your own tabs or purchase preprinted swiss cheese tabs from Bauer Associates. (To order call 800-836-0732.) The following is a list of suggested tabs. Please note that these tabs follow the chapters in David G. Bauer's *The "How To" Grants Manual.*[3]

1. Introduction
2. Documenting Need
3. Organizing the Process
4. Developing Ideas
5. Redefining Ideas
6. Uniquenesses
7. Advisory Committees and Advocacy
8. Choosing the Marketplace

In addition to these general tabs, you will need tabs to organize the information you collect within the specific marketplace you choose. For government funding sources, consider using the following tabs:

9. Researching Government Marketplace
10. Characteristics: Government Grants
11. Contacting Government Sources
12. Planning Federal Proposals
13. Improving Federal Proposals
14. Submission: Public Sources
15. Decision: Public Sources
16. Follow-Up: Government Sources

For private funding sources, you may include these additional tabs:

17. Differences: Public versus Private Sources
18. Recording Research
19. Foundation Research Tools
20. Researching Corporate Grants
21. Contacting Private Sources
22. Letter Proposal
23. Submission: Private Sources
24. Decision: Private Sources
25. Follow-Up: Private Sources

Your proposal development workbook acts as a file for your proposal ideas. A potential funding source will be impressed with your organizational skills if you respond to a question by referring to your proposal development workbook instead of a tattered pile of file folders and loose pages of notes. The grantor wants to believe that you will be equally as organized when taking care of their grant funds.

One grantseeker using this process recalled a potential funder who asked her, "Why should we give the money to your college when there are many others asking for this grant?" She opened her proposal development workbook to the tab on uniquenesses and presented a list of 50 reasons why her college was uniquely suited to carry out the proposed project, with the five best reasons circled.

Proposal preparation requires an organized approach that utilizes your time wisely and provides support to the mission and the image of your institution. The use of a proposal development workbook is one technique for accomplishing this.

By making grantseeking a more controlled, manageable process you will avoid waiting until the last minute to prepare your proposal. Just remember, grantseekers who prepare proposals overnight generally create chaos in their offices and promote disdain for proposal preparation among colleagues and staff. In addition, one hastily written proposal with budget transpositions and typographical errors can have a possibly permanent negative impact on an institution's image.

In summary, organizing a proposal development workbook is a process that, once initiated, promotes

- clearer vision of the additional information required to develop a credible proposal
- more thorough development of project ideas
- more organized proposals
- confidence when making pre-proposal contact with prospective grantors

REDEFINING PROPOSAL IDEAS TO FIND MORE FUNDING SOURCES

Many grantseekers have a myopic view of their proposal ideas. They have tunnel vision and define their ideas narrowly. What these grantseekers fail to see is that they could make their projects appeal to many

---

[3] David G. Bauer, *The "How To" Grants Manual*, 3rd edition (Phoenix: ACE/Oryx Press, 1995).

more funding sources by just broadening their perspective. This sourcebook represents billions of dollars in funding opportunities for your project. Locating the best—the one most likely to fund you—is a function of how flexible and creative you are in describing and designing your project.

To expand your funding horizons, think of your project in as many ways as possible. Carefully examine each of the following categories. Each time you look at your project from another subject area, constituency group, grant type, or geographic boundary, you may uncover additional funding sources interested in supporting your work.

1. Subject area: To what subject areas can you relate your project/research?

2. Constituency group: What constituencies or target groups could benefit from the project/research?

3. Type of grant: Could your proposal be considered a needs assessment? Pilot project? Model project? Research?

4. Project location: What are the geographic boundaries of your project as currently conceived? Could they be expanded to attract more or different funding sources?

Review the following worksheets on redefining your project (see exhibits 1.3–1.7). Put a check mark next to the subcategories that might apply to your project and use the space provided to explain how your project could be related to these subcategories. The subject areas and constituency groups you identify will become key words in your search for potential funding sources. You will use these key words when working with the subject index of this book and to assist you when searching computer databases and the indexes of other grants research books. The more key words you use, the more potential funders you will uncover. By expanding your universe of funders and selecting the best choices for pre-proposal contact, you will increase your chances of locating the grantor who is most likely to support your proposal.

Those grantseekers who thought this book would immediately lead them to one grantor for their narrowly defined project may be a bit frustrated at this point. Yes, I am suggesting that you redefine your project to increase the number of potential grantors, but do not despair. I can assure you that the steps you take now to redefine your project will pay off when you search for the best funding source for your project.

HOW TO USE ADVOCATES AND VOLUNTEERS TO INCREASE YOUR SUCCESS RATE

The Grants Advisory Committee

One effective way to involve volunteers in your grants quest is to establish a grants advisory committee focused on the need or problem your grant proposal addresses. Think of this committee as an informal affiliation of individuals you have invited to take part in attracting grant funds to the problem area you have chosen. You will survey these individuals to determine their willingness to supply resources and play an advocacy role.

Begin by checking with your department chair, dean, or grants office for possible rules and regulations governing advisory committees. Once you have explained how you will use this group, approval is much easier to get and in some cases your department chair may suggest involving a standing committee that is not currently being used in this manner.

Invite fellow professionals, individuals from other colleges or the community, and corporate members who are interested in the area you have identified to be on your committee. By inviting a cross section of individuals, you will develop a wider base from which to draw support. Ask yourself who would care if you developed grants resources to solve a particular problem. Develop a list of individuals, groups, and organizations you think would volunteer a little of their time to be instrumental in making progress in the problem area. Be sure to include

- individuals who might know foundation, government, or corporate grantors
- colleagues who may have previously prepared proposals for the grantors you will be approaching or who may have acted as grant reviewers

Also consider current and past employees and board of trustees members.

Grant Resources/Skills

After you have identified individuals or groups who would be interested in seeing change in the area identified, make a list of skills and resources that would help you develop your proposal. Match these with the individuals who may possess them. Your list of skills and resources may provide you with some ideas about who you should recruit for your grants advisory

REDEFINING YOUR PROJECT

1. List the words that describe the subject areas your project/research is directly related to.

   _____   _____
   _____   _____
   _____   _____

2. What changes could you make in your project/research that would allow you to relate it to other subject areas?

   _____
   _____
   _____
   _____

3. The following nonexhaustive list of subject areas is designed to encourage you to explore other possible areas for which you may find grant funds. (By changing your focus and/or including other beneficiary groups, you can redefine your project and make it applicable to more interest areas). The subject areas in exhibit 1.4 will get you started. Add your own terms to the list.

4. Many grantors identify their granting interests according to the constituency groups that are involved or benefit as the target population. Review exhibit 1.5 for groups your project could focus on and add others to the list.

5. The type of support you seek will narrow your focus dramatically. Review exhibit 1.6 to explore other types of support you might apply for.

6. You can also change your proposal's focus by adding "partners" who will share in the proposed work and improve your chances for grants success. List other organizations whose involvement would add depth to your project and increase your credibility with the funding source.

   Partner   Advantage

   _____   _____
   _____   _____
   _____   _____

7. Most grantors have particular geographic interests. By developing a consortia relationship with a compatible partner in another section of the United States or in another country you may be able to reveal additional funders. Review exhibit 1.7.

EXHIBIT 1.3

Subject Areas

Project:

____ Adult Education	____ Natural Science
____ Aging	____ Nutrition
____ Agriculture	____ Physical Education
____ Alcoholism	____ Physics
____ Archaeology	____ Political Science
____ Architecture	____ Pollution
____ Asian Studies	____ Population
____ Astronomy	____ Psychology
____ Behavioral Research	____ Robotics
____ Biology	____ Rural Education
____ Business	____ Science
____ Career	____ Social Welfare
____ Chemistry	____ Sociology
____ Computer Science	____ Technology
____ Criminal Justice	____ Theater
____ Dance	____ Undergraduate Education
____ Dentistry	____ Vocational Education
____ Drug Abuse	____ Water
____ Economic Development	____ _____
____ Educational Research	____ _____
____ Engineering	____ _____
____ Environment	____ _____
____ Equipment	____ _____
____ Faculty Development	____ _____
____ Foreign Language	____ _____
____ Graduate Education	____ _____
____ Health	____ _____
____ History	____ _____
____ Humanities	____ _____
____ Information Science	____ _____
____ Labor Relations	____ _____
____ Law Libraries	____ _____
____ Literacy	____ _____
____ Math	____ _____
____ Media	____ _____
____ Medical Education	____ _____
____ Mental Health	____ _____
____ Museums	____ _____

Relationship/Connection to Your Project:

EXHIBIT 1.4

Constituency Groups

Project:

____ Adolescents
____ African Americans
____ Asians
____ Children
____ Delinquents
____ Drop-Outs
____ Elderly
____ Faculty
____ Families
____ Gifted
____ Handicapped
____ Hearing Impaired
____ Hispanics
____ Homeless
____ Ill
____ Indigent
____ Men
____ Mentally Ill
____ Minorities
____ Native Americans
____ Students
____ Teachers
____ Visually Impaired
____ Women
____ Youth

____ _____
____ _____
____ _____
____ _____

Relationship/Connection to Your Project:

EXHIBIT 1.5

Types of Support

Project:
_____ Annual Campaigns
_____ Building/Construction
_____ Capital Campaigns/Improvements
_____ Challenge Grants
_____ Conferences, Seminars, Workshops
_____ Consortia
_____ Consulting Services
_____ Continuing Support
_____ Deficit Financing
_____ Documentaries
_____ Emergency Funds
_____ Endowments
_____ Equipment
_____ Fellowships
_____ Films
_____ Financial Aid
_____ Fund Raising
_____ General Operating Support
_____ In-Kind Contributions
_____ Internships
_____ Land Acquisitions
_____ Lectureships
_____ Loaned Executives
_____ Loans
_____ Matching Grants
_____ Model Project
_____ Needs Assessment
_____ Product Development
_____ Professorships
_____ Publications
_____ Renovations
_____ Research
_____ Scholarships
_____ Seed Money
_____ Special Projects
_____ Student Aid
_____ Training

_____ _____
_____ _____
_____ _____
_____ _____

EXHIBIT 1.6

Geographic Interests

Project:

____ Local (in your city/town)
____ County
____ Region (list states)

_____

_____

_____

_____

_____

_____

_____

_____

____ National
____ International (list countries)

_____

_____

_____

_____

_____

_____

_____

Other Geographic Interests:
____ Appalachia
____ Arctic
____ Rural
____ Urban

____ _____

____ _____

____ _____

____ _____

____ _____

____ _____

____ _____

____ _____

____ _____

____ _____

____ _____

EXHIBIT 1.7

committee. Consider the skills, resources, and types of individuals who would be useful in

- preparing your proposal (writers; experts in evaluation, design, or statistics; individuals with skills in the areas of computer programming, printing, graphics, or photocopying)
- making pre-proposal contact (individuals with sales and marketing skills, people who travel frequently, volunteers who could provide long-distance phone support)
- developing consortia or cooperative relationships and subcontracts (individuals who belong to other nonprofit groups with similar concerns)

Review the grants resources inventory (exhibit 1.8) for those resources and skills your volunteers may be able to provide.

Advocacy Roles

Consider these specific activities in relation to the advocacy roles of the individuals on your list:

- writing endorsement letters
- talking to funding sources and setting up appointments
- providing expertise in particular areas (finance, marketing, etc.)
- accompanying you to meetings with potential funders or visiting a funding source without you if the advocate has separate plans to travel to the funding source's locale

Use the advocacy planning sheet (exhibit 1.9) to help you organize your approach.

Advocacy, Webbing, and Linkages

Another way to involve your advocates is to present them with the names of grantors that are most likely to be interested in your proposal and ask them whether they know any of the grantors' key individuals, such as board members. Although this approach is reactive in nature, it may be necessary if your advocates are reluctant to reveal all of their contacts and are holding back to see how serious you are about researching potential grantors.

The proactive approach to using advocates involves asking your supporters to trust you with a comprehensive list of their contacts. This includes asking your committee members to reflect on their ability to con-

tact a variety of potential grantors. To take a proactive approach, follow these steps:

1. Explain the advocacy concept to the individuals you have identified as possible advocates and how the information they provide will be used. This may be done in a group or individually. Ask each participant to complete an advocacy/webbing worksheet (see exhibit 1.10) and return it to you. When introducing the advocacy concept for the first time, some institutions find they have better results when they relate the concept to a major project at the institution that has widespread support.

2. Distribute the advocacy/webbing worksheet to the individuals you have identified as possible advocates. This may be done in a group or individually.

3. Input the advocacy information you collect in your computer or file it. Keep all completed advocacy/webbing worksheets on file and update them periodically. This is a good activity for volunteers. Be aware, however, that advocacy data should be considered privileged information. You must not allow open access to the data or you will be violating your advocates' trust. Using a central computing facility to store this information greatly reduces security. Instead, use a personal computer system and store a copy of your program in a safe place. Winning Links, an inexpensive software program designed especially for this purpose, is available from Bauer Associates. (For ordering information, see the list of computer research services and resources at the end of the book.)

4. When a potential funding source is identified, search your database to determine whether any of your advocates has a relationship to the potential funding source. You may have an advocate who

   - is a member of both your organization and the funding source's board
   - has worked for the grantor or has been a reviewer for the funder's grant program

When a match between a potential funder and advocate is made, call your advocate and discuss the possiblity of having him or her

GRANTS RESOURCES INVENTORY

Please indicate those resource areas you would be willing to help us with. At the end of the list provide more detailed information on exactly what you can provide. In addition, if you are willing to meet with funding sources for us please list the geographic areas you travel to frequently.

____ Evaluation of Projects

____ Computer Equipment

____ Computer Programming

____ Layout and Design Work

____ Printing

____ Budgeting, Accounting, Developing Cash Flow, Auditing

____ Audiovisual Assistance (equipment, videotaping, etc.)

____ Purchasing Assistance

____ Long Distance Telephone Calls

____ Travel

____ Writing/Editing

____ Searching for Funding Sources

____ Other Equipment/Materials

____ Other

Description of Resources: _____

_____

_____

_____

Areas Frequently Visited: _____

_____

_____

EXHIBIT 1.8

ADVOCACY PLANNING SHEET

Project Title: _____   Project Director: _____

Select from the following list the ways you can use advocates to advance your project.

- Endorsement Letters
- Testimonials
- Letters of Introduction

- Set up your appointment
- Accompany you to see funding source
- Go see funder for you

Techniques for This Project	Advocate to Be Used	Who Will Contact Advocate & When	Desired Outcome	Date Completed

EXHIBIT 1.9

ADVOCACY/WEBBING WORKSHEET

Our organization's ability to attract grant funds is increased substantially if we can talk informally with a funding official (or board member) before we submit our formal proposal. However, it is sometimes difficult to make preproposal contact without having a link to the funding source. We need your help. By completing this worksheet, you will identify any links that you may have with potential grantors and possibly open up an oasis of opportunities for our organization.

If you have a link with a funding source that our research indicates may be interested in supporting one of our projects, we will contact you to explain the project and discuss possible ways you could help us. For example, you could write an endorsement letter, arrange an appointment, or accompany us to see the funding source. Even a simple phone call could result in our proposal actually being read and not just being left in a pile. No matter what the case may be, you can rest assured that we will obtain your complete approval before any action is taken and that we will never use your name or link without your consent.

Links to foundation, corporation, and government funding sources are worth hundreds of thousands of dollars per year and your assistance can ultimately help us continue our vital mission. Thank you for your cooperation.

Your Name: _____ Phone No.:_____

Address: _____

1. What foundation or corporate boards are you or your spouse on?

2. Do you know anyone who is on a foundation or corporate board? If so, whom and what board?

3. Does your spouse know anyone on a foundation or corporate board? If so, whom and what board?

4. Have you served on any government committees? If so, please list.

5. Do you know any government funding contacts? If so, please list.

6. Please list any fraternal groups, social clubs, and/or service organizations you or your spouse are members of.

EXHIBIT 1.10

- arrange an appointment for you with the funder
- write a letter to a "friend" on the funding source's board

INCREASE YOUR ACCEPTANCE RATE BY CONTACTING THE GRANTOR BEFORE WRITING YOUR PROPOSAL

The profile of each grantor in this sourcebook is as complete as possible, though each profile is subject to availability of reliable data and currency of information. This sourcebook helps you to develop a historical perspective of the funding source's granting interests. Your knowledge of this history sets you apart from the average grantseeker. It allows you to ask the funding source questions that

- update this information and help you to gain insight into their current grants agenda as well as future changes
- test which of your approaches is most compatible with the grantor's agenda

There are vast differences in how each of the major types of grantors (government, foundation, and corporate) should be approached and what information you should request. Studies have demonstrated that you can increase the likelihood of your success with government grantors three times and private grantors five times by making an information gathering contact before writing your proposal. Increasing your knowledge of who will review your grant, their background(s), the criteria used in evaluation, and the time each reviewer spends reading each proposal will allow you to write toward the reviewer/decision maker.

Contacting Public Funding Sources

Contacting federal grantors at the right time is crucial. Each of the 1,000-plus federal programs has its own time frame and sequence of events. Review the diagram of the federal grants clock whenever you need to determine where a particular federal agency or program is in the grants process (see exhibit 1.11).

The federal grants clock can be thought of as a five-step cycle or process.

1. The first step involves the dissemination of and comment on the rules and regulations governing the program. Federal regulations mandate that the rules governing each program be made available for review by any interested party and comments encouraged. The comments are published, the final rules are determined, and the deadlines are announced in such publications as the Federal Register, the NIH Guide, and the National Science Foundation Bulletin.

2. The federal program officer then develops the application package, referred to as the Request for Proposal (RFP) or the Request for Application (RFA), and mails it to prospective grantees who have requested it.

3. The deadline for submission occurs.

4. Submitted proposals are sent to peer reviewers for evaluation. The reviewers must follow the agency's evaluation system and distribute points to each proposal according to the published guidelines.

5. The notices of award and rejection are made, and the cycle starts again.

Establishing pre-proposal contact for the next funding cycle is most productive when initiated after the notices of award or rejection have been given (step 5) for the previous cycle and before the application packages are sent out (step 2) for the new cycle. Use the techniques outlined in this section to maximize the benefits of pre-proposal contact and gain the insight you need to prepare a grant-winning proposal.

Contacting Past Grantees

Use the sample letter in exhibit 1.12 to request a list of past grantees, guidelines, and an application package when it becomes available. Enclose a return label or self-addressed, stamped envelope with your letter for the funding source's convenience.

Access to the list of past grantees is your right. If you have trouble getting the list, call the funding source and let them know that you are aware that you are entitled to this list under the Freedom of Information Act. If all else fails you may be able to get this information from the public information office of the appropriate branch of government, or you can ask your congressperson to get the list for you. By law, federal employees must respond to a congressperson's request. Be aware, however, that program officers may react negatively to the intervention of elected officials.

THE FEDERAL GRANTS CLOCK

Award/Rejection

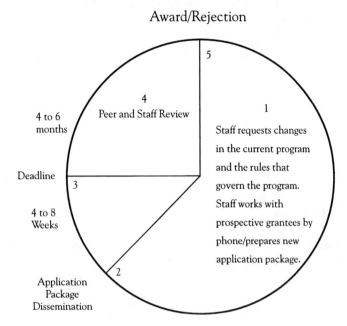

4 to 6 months

Deadline

4 to 8 Weeks

Application Package Dissemination

4 — Peer and Staff Review

5

1 — Staff requests changes in the current program and the rules that govern the program. Staff works with prospective grantees by phone/prepares new application package.

3

2

The clock operates 365 days per year. The federal government's year begins on October 1 and ends September 30.

EXHIBIT 1.11

With this list in hand you are ready to analyze your chances for success. Complete the federal funding source evaluation worksheet (exhibit 1.13) and analyze the information contained in the list of grantees. When this worksheet is completed you will be able to approach the grantor with knowledge and insight into its granting program.

Next, select a grantee to call. A grantee closer to your institution may be more reluctant to share information than one farther away. However, most successful grant recipients will be happy to share information with you. There is usually no competition between you because you are seeking first-year funding and they are seeking second-year. Tell the grantee how you got his or her name, congratulate him or her on the award, and then ask to speak to the director or person who worked on the proposal.

Following is a list of suggested questions to ask the person who worked on the proposal. However, don't hesitate to ask any other questions that you think will help you learn about the funding source.

- Did you call or visit the funding source before writing the proposal?

- Whom on the funding source's staff did you find most helpful?
- How did you use your advocates or congresspeople?
- Did the funding source review your idea or proposal before submission?
- Did you use consultants to help prepare the proposal?
- Was there a hidden agenda to the program's guidelines?
- When did you begin developing your application?
- When did you first contact the funding source?
- What materials did you find most helpful in developing your proposal?
- Did a representative or representatives from the funding source come to see you? Before or after the proposal was awarded? Who came? What did they wear? Would you characterize them as conservative, moderate, or liberal? Did anything surprise you during their visit?

SAMPLE LETTER TO A FEDERAL AGENCY REQUESTING INFORMATION AND GUIDELINES

Date

Name
Title
Address

Dear (Contact Person):

I am interested in receiving information on (CFDA # and Program Title). I am particularly interested in receiving application forms, program guidelines, and any materials you think would be helpful to me.

In order to increase my understanding of your program, I am also requesting a list of last year's grant recipients. I have enclosed a label to assist you in forwarding the requested items. Thank you.

Sincerely,

Name/Title
Phone Number

EXHIBIT 1.12

- How close was your initial budget to the awarded amount? (You can check the answer to this question by looking at the proposal when you visit the funding source. The Freedom of Information Act allows you to see any proposal funded by government money.)
- Who on the funding source's staff negotiated the budget?
- What would you do differently next time?

Understanding the Proposal Review Process

To prepare the best possible proposal, you must know who will be reading it and how it will be reviewed. Request a list of last year's reviewers in writing, then follow up by phone or in person if necessary. Exhibit 1.14 is a sample letter you may use.

Once you have the list, contact the reviewers to discuss what they look for when reviewing proposals. Also, ask them questions that will help you determine their expertise, reading level, biases, etc.

Some federal programs use the same reviewers each year and may be reluctant to give you their names. If this is the case, explain to your contact that you would like to know at least the general background and credentials of the reviewers so that you can write to their level of expertise. You ultimately want to know the organizations the reviewers come from, their titles and degrees, and, if possible, why they were selected as reviewers. This may also be a good opportunity to tell the program officer that you would like to become a reviewer. Whether the reviewers meet in Washington, D.C., or review proposals at home, you would learn a great deal about the evaluation process and the grantor by being a member of a peer review committee.

If a system that the reviewers must adhere to has been published in the Federal Register or an agency publication, request a copy or find out the date of publication so you can locate the publication in a federal depository library. (A federal depository library is

FEDERAL FUNDING SOURCE EVALUATION WORKSHEET

1. Award Size

   • What was the largest award granted?

   • For what type of project?

   • What was the smallest award granted?

   • For what type of project?

   • Based on last year's grantees, what would be your project's likely award size?

2. Grantor Type

   • What characteristics or similarities can be drawn from last year's list of grant recipients?

   • Size or type of grantee organization

   • Geographic spread (preferences/concentrations)

3. Project Director/Principal Investigator

   • What titles or degrees appear most frequently on the list of last year's recipients?

   • Does there seem to be a relationship between award size and project director degree?

4. From the list of last year's grantees, select two to contact for more information. Select ones that you may have a link with and/or organizations that you are familiar with.

5. Based on the information gathered in questions 1 through 4, rate how well your proposal idea/concept matches the prospective grantor's profile.
   _____ very well
   _____ good
   _____ fair
   _____ not well

EXHIBIT 1.13

SAMPLE LETTER TO A FEDERAL AGENCY TO REQUEST A LIST OF REVIEWERS

Date

Name
Title
Address

Dear _____:

    I am presently developing a proposal under your _____ program. I would find it very helpful if you could send me a list of last year's reviewers and information on the makeup of this year's review committee.

    The list of last year's reviewers and information on the composition of this year's committee will help me prepare a quality proposal based upon the level, expertise, and diversity of the reviewers.

    I have enclosed a self-addressed stamped envelope for your convenience in responding to this request. I will use the materials you send, and I thank you for your consideration in providing them.

Sincerely,

Name
Title
Phone Number

EXHIBIT 1.14

---

one designated by the government to receive copies of all federal documents.) Let the funding source know that a mock review of your proposal will be conducted before submission and that you would like it to mirror the actual review process as closely as possible.

Contacting Past Reviewers

As you examine the list of reviewers, look for any links you could use when contacting them. If there are none, call any reviewer. Explain that you understand he or she was a reviewer for the program you are interested in and that you would like to ask a few questions about his or her experience. Select a few questions from the following list, or make up your own.

- How did you get to be a reviewer?
- Did you review proposals at a funding source location or at home?
- Did you meet other reviewers?
- How many proposals were you given to read?

- How much time did you have to read them?
- What training or instruction did the funding source give you?
- Did you follow a point system? Which one? How did it work?
- How did the funding source handle discrepancies in point assignments?
- What were you told to look for in each proposal?
- Did a staff review follow your review?
- What did the staff members of the funding source wear, say, and do during the review process?
- How would you write a proposal differently now that you have been a reviewer?
- What were the most common mistakes you saw?

Calling Federal and State Funding Sources

Initial calls to public funding sources seldom yield the name and phone number of the best individual to handle a particular request. (The federal programs listed in this book have been contacted and names and phone numbers are as up-to-date as possible.) Call the number you have and ask who could best help you. After several referrals, you should locate the office that administers the funds for the program you want. Find out who the program officer is.

The best approach is to go see the program officer in person. Use the techniques outlined in the following section to make an appointment.

If you cannot visit the funding source, try to gather information over the phone. Since it may be difficult for the program officer to discuss your ideas and approaches without seeing a written description of your project, ask if you could mail or fax a one-page concept paper. Set up a time for a return call and ask the same types of questions you would ask if you were meeting with the officer in person.

Although it may be difficult for you to "read" over the phone what the program officer is really saying, at least try to uncover any hidden agenda so that you can meet the grantor's needs and increase your chance of success. Review the list of questions in the section, "Questions to Ask Program Officers" (page 28).

Making Appointments with Public Funding Source Officials

Your objective is to get an interview with an administrator of the program you are interested in. Start by sending a letter requesting an appointment, such as the sample letter in exhibit 1.15. In most cases, you will not get a response to this letter. It is intended to show that you mean business. Then follow these steps.

SAMPLE LETTER TO A FEDERAL AGENCY REQUESTING AN APPOINTMENT

Date

Name
Title
Address
Dear _____ :

My research on your funding program indicates that a project we have developed would be appropriate for consideration by your agency for funding under _____.

I would appreciate five to ten minutes of your time to discuss my project. Your insights, knowledge, and information on any grants that have been funded using a similar approach would be invaluable.

My travel plans call for me to be in your area on _____. I will phone to confirm the possibility of a brief meeting during that time to discuss this important proposal.

Sincerely,

Name
Title
Phone Number

EXHIBIT 1.15

1. Call and ask to speak to the program officer or information contact.

2. If you get the person's assistant, ask when his or her boss can be reached. (Keep in mind that some federal employees are on flextime or come in and leave at odd hours to cope with traffic.)

3. Call back. Try person-to-person, and if that fails, ask the assistant whether anyone else can answer technical questions about the program. You may get an appointment with an individual whose job it is to screen you from the boss, but this is still better than nothing.

4. When you get the program person on the phone, introduce yourself and give a brief (10-word) description of your organization. Explain that

   • the need to deal with the specific problem your project addresses is extreme

   • your organization is uniquely suited to deal with this problem

   • you understand that the grantor's program deals with this need

   • you would like to make an appointment to talk about program priorities and your approach

Once the program person makes an appointment with you, stop and hang up. If it is impossible for the person to see you, tell him or her that you have some questions and would like to schedule a 10-minute phone call. If a callback is not possible, ask if he or she could take the time to answer your questions now.

Visiting Public Funding Sources

A pre-proposal visit to the public funding source is an important step toward getting the input you need to prepare a proposal tailored to the funding source. It will also allow you to update the information you have about the funding source.

The objective of the pre-proposal visit is to find out as much as possible about the funding source and how it perceives its role in the awarding of grants. You will use this information to produce a proposal that reflects a sensitivity to the funding source's needs and an understanding of its mission.

In general, the greater the differences between what the funding source expects a grantseeker to be like and what the grantseeker is actually like, the greater the problems with communication, agreement, and acceptance. The grantseeker wants the funder to love him or her, so he or she must strive to produce as little dissonance as possible by looking and talking as the funder "thinks" he or she should. (If you do not know the funding source's expectations on dress, play it safe and read the *New Dress for Success* by John T. Malloy.[4])

Plan Your Visit. When making a personal visit, it is better to send two people than just one, and an advocate, advisory committee member, or graduate of your program has more credibility than a paid staff member. In deciding who to send, try to match the age, interests, and other characteristics of your people with any information you have on the funding official. Before the visit, role-play your presentation with your team members and decide who will take responsibility for various parts of the presentation.

What to Take. It may be helpful to bring the following items with you on the visit:

• your proposal development workbook (swiss cheese book)

• materials that help demonstrate the need for your project

• audiovisual aids that document the need, such as pictures or a brief (three-to-five minute) filmstrip, videotape, slide presentation, or cassette tape. Be sure you can operate all equipment with ease, and that you know how to replace bulbs and batteries. Bring extension cords, two- or three-prong plug adapters, and whatever other peripheral equipment you may need.

• information about your institution/program/department that you can leave with the funding official. (Never leave a copy of the proposal.)

Questions to Ask Program Officers

The following is a list of possible questions to ask a program officer:

• Do you agree that the need addressed by our project is important?

---

[4]John T. Malloy, *New Dress for Success* (New York: Warner Books, 1988).

- In _____, your average award to higher education institutions/programs/departments like ours was $_____. Do you expect that average amount to change?

- How will successful grantees from last year affect the chances for new applicants? Will last year's grantees compete with new grantees, or have their funds been set aside? If their funds have been set aside, how much is left for new grants?

- Are there any unannounced program or unsolicited proposal funds in your agency to support an important project like ours?

- The required matching portion is _____ percent. Would it improve our chances for funding if we provided a greater portion than this?

- If no match is required, would it help our proposal if we volunteered to share costs?

- What is the most common mistake or flaw in the proposals you receive?

- Are there any areas you would like to see addressed in a proposal that may have been overlooked by the other grantees or applicants?

- We have developed several approaches to this needs area. You may know whether one of our approaches has already been tried. Could you review our concept paper and give us any guidance?

- Would you review or critique our proposal if we got it to you early?

- Would you recommend a previously funded proposal for us to read for format and style? (Remember, you are entitled to see funded proposals, but don't be too pushy.)

- What changes do you expect in type or number of awards given this year? For example, do you expect fewer new awards than continuing awards?

- Is there a relationship between the type of project or proposal and the amount awarded? Is there a sequence or progression in the type of grant awarded? For example, do you have to get a consultant grant before you can receive a demonstration grant or an evaluation grant? Is there a hidden agenda?

- Is it okay to use tabs or dividers in my proposal?

- The guidelines call for _____ copies of the proposal. Could you use more? (New guidelines developed to reduce paperwork sometimes restrict the number of proposal copies an agency can request, though the agency may really need more copies and will be pleased if you volunteer to send extras.)

Immediately after your visit, record any information you have gathered about the funder on the funding source staff profile (exhibit 1.16). Record the results of your visit on the public funding source contact summary sheet (exhibit 1.17).

Deciding Which Federal Grant Program to Pursue

So far you have not invested a tremendous amount of time in writing your proposal. Instead, you have taken time to gather data and contact potential grantors. Now you must use that data to decide to which federal grant program you will apply.

Your best prospect is the grant program that provides the closest match between the program you want to implement, your institution, and the profile you have developed of the grantor. There is seldom a perfect fit between your project and the grantor's program, and some tailoring and changes in your program will likely add to your chance of success. Use the tailoring worksheet (exhibit 1.18) to analyze each grant program you are interested in and to select your first choice.

Contacting Private Funding Sources

It is much more difficult to make contact with foundation and corporate funding sources than government grantors for two main reasons. First, there are only 2,000 professionals and a few thousand support staff working in the 37,571 foundations that grant over $9 billion a year. Second, these funding sources are not paid by you, the taxpayer, and therefore do not have to be as available or responsive as public funding sources.

The sequence of steps for contacting private funding sources is the same as for contacting government sources. The differences occur in how you contact the source and the materials you request. Review the following worksheets and use them when you pursue one of the foundations or corporations in this book or any others you uncover in your research.

Exhibit 1.19 is a sample inquiry letter to a private funding source. This letter can be used to obtain an

FUNDING SOURCE STAFF PROFILE

Before each visit to a funding source, review this sheet to be sure you are taking the correct materials, advocates, and staff.

Agency Director: _____

Program Director: _____

Contact Person: _____

Birthdate: _____ Birthplace: _____

Education:

College: _____

Postgraduate: _____

Work Experience: _____

Military Service: _____

Service Clubs: _____

Religious Affiliations: _____

Interests/Hobbies: _____

Publications: _____

Comments: _____

_____

_____

Note: Do not ask the staff person direct questions related to these areas. Instead, record information that has been volunteered or gathered from the comments or observations made in the office.

EXHIBIT 1.16

PUBLIC FUNDING SOURCE CONTACT SUMMARY SHEET

Project Title: _____

Add to this sheet each time you contact a public funding source.

Agency Name: _____

Program Officer: _____

Contacted On (Date): _____

By Whom: _____

Contacted By: Letter: _____ Phone: _____

Personal: _____

Staff or Advocate Present: _____

Discussed: _____

_____

_____

Results: _____

_____

_____

EXHIBIT 1.17

TAILORING WORKSHEET

Federal Program: Prospect Rating _____

                Amount Requested _____

                % Match/In-kind _____

1. How does your grant request match with the average award size to your
    *   type of organization? _____
    *   size of organization? _____
    *   location of organization? _____
    *   proposal focus? _____

2. What was the number of applications received versus the number of grants awarded in your area of interest?
    *   applications received _____
    *   grants awarded _____

3. How would you rate the funding staff's interest in your concept?
    *   very interested ____
    *   interested ____
    *   not interested ____
    *   unknown ____

4. From the information you obtained on the reviewers and the review process, what should your writing strategy include?

5. Based on the information you obtained on the review process, how will the points be distributed in the funding source's evaluation process?

Area	Point Value
_____	_____
_____	_____
_____	_____
_____	_____
_____	_____
_____	_____
_____	_____
_____	_____
_____	_____
_____	_____
_____	_____
_____	_____

EXHIBIT 1.18

SAMPLE INQUIRY LETTER TO A PRIVATE FUNDING SOURCE

Date

Name
Title
Address

Dear:

I am developing a project that deals with _____ and provides benefits to (or in) _____. My research indicates that this area is an important concern of the <u>(name of foundation/funding source)</u>.

Please use the enclosed label to send me your current priority statement and information on your desired format for proposals or other guidelines. I would also appreciate it if you could add us to your mailing list so that we could receive your annual reports, newsletters, and any other materials you think might be useful to us as we work on this and related projects.

Thank you for your cooperation.

Sincerely,

Name/Title
Organization
Address

EXHIBIT 1.19

---

application and any other available information. Many foundations and corporations will state that an application form is available but not required.

Calling Private Funding Sources

The chances of your research yielding the right phone number is much greater for private funding sources than for public ones. But what do you say when you call?

1. Ask for the funding official by name if possible.

2. Tell the official you will be in the area and would like to meet with him or her briefly to discuss a project that your research indicates they would be interested in.

3. If one of your advocates has contacted one of the funding source's board members, let the funding official know. This will encourage him or her to talk with you.

4. Ask for an appointment. If he or she makes an appointment with you, get off the phone and start preparing for your visit.

In many cases, foundation/corporation policy dictates that no appointment is possible. In fact, your research may have already indicated that the funding source does not make appointments. Many private grantors, however, will be willing to take a few minutes to talk with you on the telephone to determine if they are interested in your project. Ask if it would be best to talk to them now or better to set up a phone interview for a later date.

If a phone interview is granted, ask the same questions you would in a face-to-face meeting. (See "Questions to Ask at the First Meeting," page 33.) Let your approach reflect your knowledge of the funder, and collect or validate the following information:

- the organization's current granting priorities and changes from past priorities

- specific information on how you should change your project and/or proposal to make it more attractive to the funding source
- desired proposal format (Although foundations may not have formal guidelines, they or their board members may have preferences.)
- the best grant size to request
- the number of years over which to spread your request

If the foundation/corporation seems interested in your project, ask the funding official if he or she would like to visit your campus.

If the foundation/corporation is not interested in your project, ask

- why not. However, be aware that changes in the interests of funding sources often occur
- if they agree that your proposal addresses an important need
- who else might be interested. Funding sources know one another and who is doing what

If you cannot get through to the funding official

- use the intermediaries or screens and ask them intelligent questions concerning the foundation/corporation's funding priorities, cycle, and preferred proposal format
- let them know *you* will call back to speak to the funding official at another time. (Most grantseekers try once and give up.)

Visiting Private Funding Sources

Visiting in person is the best way to get to know a funding source, but an in-person visit is also difficult to arrange. Foundations may not have anyone who can see you, and corporate people are occupied with important corporate jobs that provide the profits they must generate. You are fortunate if your request to visit is granted, and in many cases your invitation will come only after you have submitted your letter proposal and the funding source has reviewed it. In either case, it is important that you know who should go to the meeting, what to wear, and what materials to bring. Keep in mind the following:

- Your credibility will be higher if you take a volunteer representative with you. An articulate, impressive advocate or advisory committee member is an excellent choice. Use the information you collected from your webbing and linkage to choose a match close to the funding official's profile. Consider age, education, club affiliations, etc.
- Dress according to the information you have about the funding source, or follow suggestions in Malloy's *New Dress for Success*.
- Bring your proposal development workbook (swiss cheese book), as well as any other materials you feel will document the need for your project in an interesting or vivid manner. Use visual and audio-visual aids to demonstrate the need for your project/research, not just to document your solution/approach. However, make sure that the audio-visual aids are in balance with your request. (A $250,000 request, for instance, can justify a short videotape while a $5,000 request can not.) Be ready to use parts of your swiss cheese book to answer questions such as, "Why should we give the money to your institution instead of some other college or university?"

Questions to Ask at the First Meeting

Review the following questions to determine which would be best to ask based on your situation and your current knowledge about the funding source. You may want to assign questions to those attending the meeting and role-play answers.

- We have developed several approaches to our request for funding. Please tell us which seems most interesting to you or to the board.
- Last year, the amount of funds given by your organization to our kind of project was $___, and the average grant was $___. Is that consistent with this year's goals?
- Our research indicates that your deadlines were ___ and ___ last year. Will they be the same this year?
- Are there any advantages to submitting proposals early? Do early proposals receive more favorable treatment?
- How are proposals reviewed and who reviews them? Outside experts? Board members? Staff?
- Are these your current granting priorities? (Provide the funding source with a copy of your research on their priorities or relay this information to them.)

- Is it okay for us to submit more than one proposal per funding cycle?
- Is our budget estimate in keeping with your current goals?
- Would you look over our proposal if we finished it early?
- Can you suggest other funders appropriate for this project?
- May we see a proposal you have funded or one you feel is well written?

Private Funding Source Report Form

Each time a member of your staff contacts a funder in person or over the phone, he or she should fill out a private funding source report form (exhibit 1.20) and file it electronically or in printed form. This simple procedure has a number of important benefits. It will keep you from damaging your credibility by repeating the same questions or having the funder say, "I already gave that information to someone in your office. Don't you people ever talk to each other?" Also, it will allow another person from your organization to pick up where you left off.

Funding Executive Research Worksheet

In addition to the research you conduct on grant-making organizations, you should also uncover and record as much data as possible on the decision makers in those organizations. The funding executive research worksheet (exhibit 1.21) is designed to help you record this data.

You can find information on private funding officials in books such as Dun & Bradstreet's *Reference Book of Corporate Managements*[5] and the *Who's Who*[6] publications. You should also check periodical indexes, libraries, and newspapers. The data you record can help you in two ways:

1. It can help you determine preferences and biases you may encounter during an interview.
2. It makes it easier to identify "linkages" between your organization and a funding source.

Note: It is not absolutely necessary that you have this information to consider a source for a proposal, but it helps. The more information you gather the greater your chances of success.

HOW TO ORGANIZE YOUR PROPOSAL

Many overzealous grantseekers make the mistake of requesting an unrealistic grant amount. Then they compound the problem by presenting an inadequate budget and, in negotiation, accepting an unrealistically low grant award to do all the work outlined in their original proposal. The research in this book will help you keep your grant request in line with the funder's history. Pre-proposal contact will allow you to focus on the grantor's level of interest and likely award size. But what you also need is a technique or resource to help you plan your project and develop your budget and time frames.

Project Planner

Consider using a project planner (exhibit 1.22) to develop your initial budget and to negotiate your final, agreed upon grant award size. The project planner, developed throughout 20 years of work in grant and contract preparation and now adaptable to several software programs with spreadsheet functions, will help you relate activities to specific budgetary line items and come to a final budget agreement that is logical and realistic. The use of a project planner will help you minimize your chances of making mistakes such as accepting $80,000 for a project that cannot be done for less than $100,000. The project planner would make it possible for you to "see" if and where you could eliminate $20,000 worth of activities from your project so that you would be accountable for only those activities you were paid to carry out. Use the following explanations to help you review the project planner in exhibit 1.22:

1. List your objectives or tasks in Column A/B. Some contracts may require tasks or enabling objectives.
2. Also in Column A/B, list the methods necessary to meet the objectives. These are the tasks you have decided upon and are your approach to meeting the need. State objective A and list methods as A-1, A-2, etc. Repeat for Objective B, etc.

[5]*Reference Book of Corporate Managements: America's Corporate Leaders*, 4 vols. (Parsippany, NJ: Dun and Bradstreet Information Services, 1993).
[6]*Who's Who in America* (New Providence, NJ: Reed Reference Publishing, 1995).

PRIVATE FUNDING SOURCE REPORT FORM

Complete one of these forms after each contact with a private funding source.

Funding Source: _____

Funding Source Address: _____

_____

Funding Source Contact Person: _____

Telephone Number: _____

Contacted On (Date): _____

Contacted By (Name): _____

Type of Contact: Phone _____ Visit _____

Objective of Contact: _____

_____

_____

Results of Contact: _____

_____

_____

_____

_____

_____

_____

_____

_____

_____

_____

_____

Follow-Up: _____

_____

_____

_____

_____

_____

_____

_____

_____

_____

_____

_____

EXHIBIT 1.20

FUNDING EXECUTIVE RESEARCH WORKSHEET

Source & Date:

1. Funding Source Name: _____

2. Name of Contributions Officer: _____

3. Title: _____ Birthdate: _____

4. Business Address: _____
   _____

5. Home Address: _____
   _____

6. Education: _____
   _____
          Secondary _____
          College _____
          Postgraduate _____

7. Military Service: _____
   _____

8. Clubs/Affiliations: _____
   _____
   _____
   _____

9. Corporate Board Memberships: _____
   _____
   _____
   _____

10. Business History (Promotions, Other Firms, etc.): _____
    _____
    _____
    _____

11. Religious Affiliation: _____

12. Other Philanthropic Activities: _____
    _____
    _____

13. Recent Articles/Publications: _____
    _____
    _____
    _____

14. Awards/Honors: _____
    _____

15. Newspaper/Magazine Clippings Attached: yes___ no ___

16. Contacts in Our Organization: _____
    _____
    _____

EXHIBIT 1.21

PROJECT PLANNER™
PROJECT TITLE: _____

A. List Project objectives or outcomes A. B. B. List Methods to accomplish each objectives as A-1, A-2, A-3 . . . B-1 . . .	MONTH		TIME	PROJECT PERSONNEL	PERSONNEL COSTS		
	BEGIN	END			SALARIES & WAGES	FRINGE BENEFITS	TOTAL
	C/D		E	F	G	H	I

TOTAL DIRECT COSTS OR COSTS REQUESTED FROM FUNDER ▶ ___

MATCHING FUNDS, IN-KIND CONTRIBUTIONS, OR DONATED COSTS ▶ ___

TOTAL COSTS ▶ ___

EXHIBIT 1.22

Proposal Developed for

PROJECT DIRECTOR: _____   Proposed starting date_____ Proposal Year _____

CONSULTANTS • CONTRACT SERVICES			NON-PERSONNEL RESOURCES NEEDED SUPPLIES • EQUIPMENT • MATERIALS				SUB-TOTAL COST FOR ACTIVITY	MILESTONES PROGRESS INDICATORS	
TIME	COST/WEEK	TOTAL	ITEM	COST/ITEM	QUANTITY	TOT.COST	TOTAL I.L.P	ITEM	DATE
J	K	L	M	N	O	P	Q	R	S

T

◄ % OF TOTAL

◄

100% ◄

EXHIBIT 1.22 *(continued)*

3. In column C/D write the date you will begin each activity and its projected completion date.

4. In column E designate the number of person-weeks (or use hours or months) needed to accomplish each task.

5. Use column F to designate the key personnel who will put in measurable or significant amounts of time on each activity or the accomplishment of each objective. The designation of key personnel is a critical step in developing a job description for each individual. If you list the activities each person is responsible for and the minimum qualifications or background required to do the job, you will have a rough job description. Then call a placement agency to get an estimate of the salary needed to fill the position. The number of weeks or months necessary to complete the task will determine full- or part-time classification. Note: This step also allows you to see how many hours of work are required in a given period. If you find that a task requires a key person to work more than 160 hours per month, you may want to increase the number of weeks in column E. Or you may want to reschedule activities or shift responsibility to another staff member.

6. List personnel costs in columns G, H, and I. Calculate the salaries and fringe benefits for those individuals who will be paid under the grant. Special consideration should be given to staff who will be donated by your organization. This in-kind contribution may be a requirement of your grant, or you may want to provide it to appear to the funding source to be a better investment. In either case, remember that you may be audited; be prepared to document this contribution. Put an asterisk (*) by each person you donate to the project. Be sure to include the value of fringe benefits as well as wages in your donation. As you complete the remaining columns, put an asterisk by anything else you donate. The total costs designated with an asterisk will appear at the bottom of the column I under "Matching Funds, In-Kind Contributions, or Donated Costs."

7. Consultants and contract services are listed in columns J, K, and L. These three columns are for the individuals and services supplied by individuals not normally in your employ. You will not pay fringe benefits to consultants or contract workers.

8. In columns M, N, O, and P, list any nonpersonnel resources, such as supplies, equipment, and materials, needed to complete each activity and achieve your objective. Many grantseekers underestimate the cost of materials and supplies necessary for their project. Some miss opportunities for funding or donated or matching items because they do not ask themselves what they need to complete each activity.

9. Column Q is the subtotal of columns I, L, and P and can be completed in two ways. Either subtotal each activity or add the totals for several activities and come up with a subtotal for each objective.

10. Columns R and S are for milestones or progress indicators. Column R is used to record what the funding source will receive as indicators of progress toward your objectives. In column S are listed the dates when the funding source will receive each milestone or progress indicator.

Pads of the Project Planner are available from Bauer Associates (800-836-0732).

Indirect Costs

Federal grants contain a cost reimbursement concept that is critically important but poorly understood by many grantseekers. The concept, known as indirect costs, involves repaying the recipient of a federal grant for costs that are difficult to break down individually but are indirectly attributable to performing the federal grant, such as heat, electricity, and office space. Other indirect costs include upkeep on the building where the office is located, maintenance staff, personnel, and administrative support. You calculate indirect costs by using a formula provided by the Federal Regional Controller's Office. It is a percentage of the total amount requested from the funding source and represented by the total in column Q of the project planner or of the people on the grant (represented under salaries and wages and fringe benefits or columns G, H, and I of the project planner).

When the grantseeker or the college administration does not understand the basis for indirect costs, these costs can cause unnecessary friction between them. Indirect costs are paid to the institution because it houses the grant and pays the people who take care of everything from payroll transactions to janitorial services. How these indirect cost funds are handled and dispersed is different at each institution. Some institutions share a percentage with the proposal initiator, and some do not. The important point, however, is that indirect costs are not the property of the grantseeker and, invariably, the actual costs incurred by accepting the grant are greater than the indirect costs received by the institution. Check with your grants office, development office, or your fiscal officer to get your current rate.

Do not ask foundations or corporations for indirect costs. If you do, they are likely to get very upset and think you are asking for money to take their money. In many cases you can request 8 to 12 percent for administrative costs (not indirect costs), but the amount you receive will not be anything close to your federal indirect cost rate.

The government feels that colleges and universities should collect the same rate of indirect costs from *all* project sponsors and that they are unfairly charged when corporate and foundation funding sources do not pay the same amount as they do. As you become more and more involved in proposal preparation, you are likely to hear a considerable amount about this issue from both sides—public and private.

HOW TO WRITE A LETTER PROPOSAL

Historically, private sources have used the letter proposal format as the primary component of their application process. In general, you will find that your initial contact with smaller foundations with limited geographic perspectives and/or no staff must be "in writing." Federal and state granting programs are also showing a shift in this direction, and many have instituted a pre-application process that is similar to creating a letter proposal. Public funding sources may call the letter proposal a pre-proposal concept paper or letter of intent. In some cases they will not send a prospective grantee an application package unless they like the approach outlined in this paper or letter. Although this pre-proposal screening may sound burdensome at first, it is valuable because it prevents grantseekers from completing a 50- to 100-page ap-

plication for a project that the prospective grantor has little interest in reviewing or funding.

Foundations and corporations use the letter proposal format simply because they do not have the time or staff to read long, complex proposals. They want short, concise letters and grant billions of dollars each year based on these two to three page documents.

Letter proposals are often read by board members during relatively brief meetings. A recent survey of foundations revealed that most foundations meet one to three times a year for an average of one to three hours each time. Within this short time frame, they must read an overwhelming number of letter proposals; therefore, it is imperative that your proposal attract and retain their interest.

Constructing a Letter Proposal

The main components of a letter proposal are:

- introductory paragraph stating the reason you are writing
- paragraph explaining why you chose this grantor
- needs paragraph
- solution paragraph
- uniqueness paragraph
- request for funds paragraph
- closing paragraph
- signatures
- attachments, if allowed

Introductory Paragraph

Begin by stating your reason for writing to the funding source and mention any link you have to the grantor. In some cases your advocate may prefer to remain anonymous and endorse your proposal at a board meeting. In other instances your advocate may actually instruct you to refer to him or her in your proposal. If so, you could say something like this:

> Susan Clarendon [a former board member, trustee, or staff member of the foundation or corporation] and I have discussed the mutual concerns of the Cross Foundation [the funding source] and my research on the remedial needs of the disadvantaged student [subject area or problem].

If your prospective funding source is a corporation, you can use a link or demonstrate a volunteer connection to the company. Many corporations will not invest in a local nonprofit organization unless their

employees are voluntarily involved with it. Therefore, your opening paragraph should refer to the commitment of the corporation's employees to your cause.
For example:

> Hank Felder, your region four supervisor, and I have
> discussed Strawberry Computer's role in increasing
> the performance and proficiency of our community
> college students through the use of applied technol-
> ogy. As chairperson of our advisory committee, Mr.
> Felder has donated over 100 hours of his time and
> has been instrumental in making our computer lab a
> reality and a success.

Why You Chose this Grantor

If you cannot mention a link or the commitment of
the funding source's employees in your introductory
paragraph, begin your letter proposal with the next
most important factor—why you chose this grantor
for solicitation or how you knew they would be interested in your proposal.

Foremost in the reader's mind is why he or she
should be spending time on your proposal. This is your
opportunity to position yourself and your organization as winners that do their homework. You want
the prospective funding source to know you are not
operating a hit-or-miss grantseeking operation or blan-
keting the foundation and corporate world with a "one
proposal fits all" approach. What you need to make
clear in this paragraph is that, based on what you have
discovered through your research, you believe the
funding source is very likely to find your proposal interesting. The data in this sourcebook allows you to
focus on the higher education areas and values of the
grantor. Instead of saying "We hope you will find our
proposal of interest," you should be able to say something like: "Our research indicates that your foundation is committed to the support of humanities in
undergraduate education." In this example you could
also refer to the percentage of the funding source's
total grant dollars that went to supporting humanities for undergraduate education or mention a major
or significant accomplishment made in this area
through a previously awarded grant.

This paragraph need not be long. You just want to
demonstrate that you have taken the time to research
the funding source's needs and that your proposal will
address an issue that has been a concern of the
grantor's. By doing so, your proposal will command
the respect of the reader and warrant the time he or
she will take to review it.

To keep the reader interested you must present a
proposal that reinforces his or her values and feelings
of worth and importance. Seek to align your college,
department, or program with the values of the grantor
by adding something like "It is because of our mutual
concern for [or commitment to] the support of the
humanities that we come to you with this proposal."

Needs Paragraph

If you have constructed a proposal development workbook (swiss cheese book) as suggested, you have already gathered statistics, case studies, quotes, and
articles to document a need for action. The main dif-
ference between stating the need in a letter proposal
to a foundation or corporation and stating it in a federal grant application is that you have the opportunity to present the more human side of the problem
to the private grantor. The challenge is to portray a
compelling need without overusing either the facts
(by quoting too many research articles) or the human interest aspects of the problem.

Select the components of the need that are most
likely to convince the grantor that the gap between
what is and what ought to be must be closed immediately. Use what you have learned about the values
and perspective of the grantor to tailor your argument
to each particular funding source.

In a few paragraphs, your letter proposal must

- include a few well-chosen statistics
- exhibit sensitivity to the geographic perspective of the grantor
- portray the human side of the problem

Whether your proposal is for research, a service
model, technology transfer, or product development,
your statement of need must be more compelling than
those of your competitors. Those reviewing your proposal must have a desire to read the rest of it to discover what you are going to do about closing the gap
you have so eloquently and succinctly documented.

Many novice grantseekers overlook or underestimate the importance of the needs section of their letter proposal; they assume readers already know about
the need since they have granted funds to this area
in the past. This assumption is a mistake. Even if grantors do know about the need, they expect you to command their respect by proving your expertise in the
field.

Solution Paragraph

What will you do to close the gap you have just documented? The solution section of your proposal calls for a brief description of the approach you will use to solve the problem. In most cases your approach will not totally eliminate the problem, but you must describe how much of the gap you will close (your objective or specific aim). While describing how you will close the gap, include the measurement indicator you will use to evaluate the success of your approach. In a research proposal, include your hypothesis and specific aims but be sure your explanation is written so that a board member can understand the significance of the work proposed and not feel intimidated by jargon or overly complex explanations.

Depending on the number of pages allowed, you may have to limit this section to one or two paragraphs of five to seven lines. While you need to have a legitimate plan, you must guard against making the methodology too elaborate. Since you are the content expert, you may have difficulty viewing your proposal from the reader's point of view. Ask yourself the following questions:

- How much does the reader really need to know?
- Will the reader understand my plan?
- Will the words used in the description of my solution be familiar to the reader?
- Is all of the information included necessary to convince the funder that I have a sound, worthwhile plan, or am I including some extraneous information?

Remember that while you are concerned with how you will solve the problem, grantors are concerned with what will be different after their money is spent. If possible, use this section to summarize your approach and objectives and refer the funder to your project planner for more information, as in the following example:

> What can we do in Smithville to promote the sharing of responsibility for education between schools, parents, and children? With assistance from the West State University College of Education, Smithville Elementary School has developed a unique approach. Our program is designed to increase responsible education behavior and encourage parental involvement in the classroom and at home. Teachers will actually work with parents and students to develop tailored,

individual contracts to produce increases in all levels of education and the quality of coursework.

> The attached project planner outlines each objective and the activities that will foster the changes we desire. West State professors and graduate students will evaluate the involvement of parents in their children's responsible use of out-of-school time. Our program will provide the catalyst for decreasing the television viewing of students, increasing the completion of homework assignments, and improving test scores.

Uniqueness Paragraph

In the uniqueness paragraph you want to assure the grantor that your institution is the best choice for implementing the solution. Assuming you have held the reader's interest up to this point, he or she knows

- why you have selected the funding source
- that there is a compelling need
- that you have a plan to address this need

The key question in the grantor's mind at this critical moment is whether your college or university is the right one to address the problem.

Include your uniquenesses and, if appropriate, the unique advantages of your college, department, and/or consortia members. Choose credibility builders that will convince the grantor that you have the commitment, staff, skill, buildings, and equipment to do the job. For example, you could say something like this:

> In 1994 our Minority Engineering Advancement Center received a citation of excellence from our state's Commission of Higher Education. The citation was accompanied by a $50,000 grant from the Texas Technology Company for providing them with more of their minority engineers than any other college.

Request for Funds Paragraph

You must make a precise request for money. If you want to demonstrate that you have done your homework, refer to the fact that your request is (or is close to) the grantor's average size award for your area of interest.

If your request from this grantor does not cover the entire cost of the project, mention other sources that have already given support or others you will be approaching. In general it is easier to attract corporate support if you already have one corporate sponsor or at least one other credible grantor. This makes the grantor you are approaching feel as if it is investing in a blue-chip stock rather than a risky junk bond.

You can summarize the budget categories that make up your total request or you can provide prospective grantors with the portion of the budget that you would like them to fund. Since you are working under a severe space limitation, your budget summary should be arranged in paragraph form or in several short columns. If you submit your project planner with your proposal, refer to the column subtotals in your planner. For example:

The salary and wages, including fringe benefits, total $24,000. The work of the project director and other employees called for in this proposal is documented on page 3 in columns G, H, and I of the project planner.

To keep the focus on the value of the project and the results that you are seeking, you may want to divide the cost of the project by the number of people who will benefit from it. Consider the effect your project may have over several years, and calculate a cost per person served or affected by the project. For example:

In the next five years the equipment that you provide under this grant will touch the lives of approximately 5,000 students at a cost of $5.63 per person served.

Closing Paragraph

Many grantseekers close their letter proposals with a statement reflecting their willingness to meet with the prospective grantor to discuss their proposal. Unless the prospective grantor is a large foundation with a staff, any reference to such a meeting is usually futile. Instead, use the closing to underscore your willingness to provide any further documentation or information the funding source may desire.

This brings up the question of who from your institution will be the best person to communicate with the prospective grantor. While you may have written the proposal, you probably will not be the individual to sign it. Therefore, in your closing paragraph request that the prospective grantor contact you (or the individual responsible for the project) for more information or to answer any questions. For example:

I encourage you to telephone me at my office or to call Ms. Connors directly at_____. She will be able to respond to technical questions or supply additional information.

Be sure to include a telephone number and extension and test the line that will be used to ascertain that it is answered by a courteous and knowledgeable representative of your institution.

The closing paragraph is also the appropriate place to include your institution's designation as a 501(c)3 nonprofit organization.

Signatures

Your college/university's grants or development office will be able to assist you in the sign-off process. Since this is a grant application and constitutes an agreement between your college or university and the grantor if it is accepted, the administrator who holds rank and responsibility should sign it. If the link to the grantor is not your chief administrator, there is no reason why the link and the administrator cannot sign the proposal. Remember that the purpose of the signature is to provide the proposal with legal commitment and credibility.

Attachments, if Allowed

Most foundations and corporations do not encourage prospective grantees to submit any additional materials with their proposals. This includes attachments as well as videotapes, audiotapes, compact discs, and so on.

Whenever possible include your project planner as a page in your proposal rather than as an attachment, and be sure to always refer to it by page number. In general, your proposal should give the impression that you have more information you are willing to share with the prospective grantor. Including too much with the proposal, however, may reduce the likelihood that it will be read.

The letter proposal follows an orderly progression that focuses on the needs and interests of the funding source. As you gain insight into your prospective grantor, you will develop the ability to write grant-winning foundation proposals.

SECTION

II

Sources of Foundation Funding for Higher Education

FOUNDATION FUNDING FOR HIGHER EDUCATION

HOW TO MAXIMIZE YOUR FOUNDATION GRANTS SUCCESS

The foundation grants section of this book contains information on 91 foundations selected from the 37,571 grant-making foundations in the United States, listed in alphabetical order. Those included in the book have consistently designated a significant portion of their grant funds to higher education. While the majority of the foundations selected demonstrate a widespread geographical giving pattern, there are some with limited geographic preferences (giving in a particular state or region only) that were included because of their extensive giving and broad interest in the field of higher education.

The foundation research included in this section is derived from foundation tax returns (990 PF), annual reports, newsletters, and directories. By reviewing this data you will be taking the first step toward focusing on a potential foundation grantor for your project. Please note that this data will not give you the complete picture of a foundation's current granting interests since it only reflects the foundation's past granting patterns. Income tax returns and annual reports are recent history at best. The data you find in this book, as well as through other means, provides you with a historical perspective and allows you to develop insight into how a grantor has preferred to fund higher education in the past.

As with corporate and federal grantors, the optimal way to determine how well your proposal idea matches a foundation's current priorities is through the establishment of pre-proposal contact. Section I of this book details the importance of and techniques for making pre-proposal contact. The data in this section provides you with the background necessary to ask questions during pre-proposal contact that demonstrate your knowledge of the grantor's past interests and reflect your intent to create a proposal and a relationship with the funding source that is based upon meeting their needs as well as yours. Not only will your homework on the grantor pay off by commanding their respect during pre-proposal contact, but it will also help you create the best possible letter proposal tailored to the funding source.

HOW TO USE THE FOUNDATIONS SECTION

Three indexes at the end of this book will help you locate the most appropriate funding sources for your project.

After you have redefined your project and developed your list of key search words, proceed to the Subject Index (see page 293), which lists areas of interest commonly related to higher education. By matching the subject areas in the Index with your key words you can locate those foundations that have an expressed interest in your subject area.

The Index of Foundations and Corporate Foundations by State (see page 321) allows you to determine which foundations from your state have been included in this book. Since some foundations only give or prefer to give in their geographic area, this index is helpful in determining which foundations to examine first. However, many of the foundations included do give nationally to higher education. Therefore, it is imperative that you read the descriptions of all the foundations that have an interest in your subject area to determine which, if any, have specific geographic giving patterns or limitations.

The Index of Additional Foundations (see page 331) provides abbreviated descriptions of foundations that do not have full entries in this book but may be worthwhile for you to pursue. Use this index as you would the Index of Foundations and Corporate Foundations by State.

Each foundation description contains the following information:

1. Name and Address of Foundation: This includes the full legal name of the foundation and the street address, city, state, and zip code of its principal office. (You will note that some foundation entries also list an additional, separate geographically-based application address.)

2. Program Description: This section describes the purpose and funding interests of the foundation. The interests identified in this section were used to compile the subject index and, as already mentioned, can be matched with your key words to locate potential funding sources for your project.

3. Assistance Types: This section highlights the activities the foundation prefers to support. For example, the Ahmanson Foundation provides funds for building, equipment, land acquisition, and so on.

4. Restrictions: This section lists geographic restrictions when applicable, as well as restrictions on the types of activities and recipients eligible for support. Note that if you fall outside of the geographic area listed, are an ineligible recipient, or are in search of a type of support that is not funded by the foundation, your chances of attracting funds are not good.

5. Officers and Trustees: These sections contain the names and titles, when appropriate, of the officers and trustees. Use this information with your advocates for webbing and linkage. You can find more information on these private funding officials in books such as *Who's Who in America.*[1]

6. Staff: This information will provide you with an indication of whether pre-proposal contact is likely. In general, the more staff a foundation has, the greater the likelihood for pre-proposal contact.

7. Financial Profile: This section provides you with the information you need to determine whether the request size you are considering fits the funder's giving pattern. In those instances when more than one year of giving is listed, you may also be able to identify any potentially important trends such as significant decreases or increases from year to year.

8. Application Process: This section provides you with a contact name and telephone number, deadlines, board meeting dates, processing time, publications, and guidelines. Review the information listed but consider it preliminary. If guidelines or other publications are available, obtain them to ensure that you have the most current application information. If the information states that personal contact is not allowed, do not call the foundation. However, remember you can use your advocates and linkages to make informal contact with board members.

9. Sample Grants: Sample grants provide you with more knowledge about the types of activities funded by the foundation in the recent past and who some of the recipients were. You may also use this information to contact a past recipient to find out how they got their grant. Since many foundations do not fund the same institutions each year, you may be surprised at the help you receive.

10. Comments/Analysis: When possible, this section provides more in-depth information on the foundation's giving pattern, interests, and so on.

---

[1] *Who's Who in America* (New Providence, NJ: Reed Reference Publishing, 1995).

FOUNDATION FUNDING SOURCES

1

Ahmanson Foundation
9215 Wilshire Boulevard
Beverly Hills, CA   90210

Areas of Interest

Program Description: Support for elementary, secondary, and higher education; the arts and humanities; medical sciences; health and health services; human service programs; and youth organizations. Areas of interest also include museums, fine arts, minority education, literacy, libraries, social services, homeless, disadvantaged, mental health and substance abuse.
Assistance Types: Building funds, equipment, land acquisition, endowment funds, matching funds, scholarship funds, special projects, renovation projects, capital campaigns, medical research

Eligibility

Restrictions: No grants to individuals or for continuing support, annual campaigns, deficit financing, professorships, internships, fellowships, film production, underwriting, exchange programs; no loans. Giving primarily in southern California with an emphasis on Los Angeles.

Personnel

Officers: Robert H. Ahmanson, President; Lee E. Walcott, VP and Managing Director; William H. Ahmanson, VP; Karen A. Hoffman, Secy.; Donald B. Stark, Treas.
Trustees/Directors: Howard F. Ahmanson Jr., Daniel N. Belin, Lloyd E. Cotsen, Robert M. DeKruif, Robert F. Erburu, Franklin D. Murphy
Staff: Eight full-time professional, one part-time professional

Financial Profile

Assets: In 1992, $472,345,000; 1993, $545,776,500
High Grant: $1,000,000
Low Grant: $500
Ave. Grant: $10,000-$25,000

Total Grants: In 1992, 433 grants totaling $21,050,925; 1993, 463 grants totaling $19,530,770
High Grant Higher Ed.: $750,000
Low Grant Higher Ed.: $10,000
Ave. Grant Higher Ed.: $20,000-$100,000
Total Grants Higher Ed.: 79 grants totaling $5,565,250

Application Process

Contact: Lee E. Walcott, VP and Managing Director, (310) 278-0770
Deadline: None
Board Meeting: Four times annually
Processing Time: 30 to 60 days
Publications: Application guide, grants list, and annual report
Guidelines: The initial approach should be a letter of inquiry. Application form not required. Proposals should include the history and mission of organization, description of project and amount of request, additional sources of funding, timetable of project, budget, annual report and financial report, names and affiliations of board members and trustees, and IRS letter of determination.

Sample Grants

Otis Art Institute of Parsons School of Design in Los Angeles, California, received two grants totaling $55,000 for scholarship support.

California Institute of the Arts in Valencia received $30,000 toward the IntraSchool and InterSchool Projects and $13,000 toward the Real Post Office Exhibition.

Hebrew Union College-Jewish Institute of Religion in Los Angeles, California, received $12,000 for conservation activities at the Skirball Museum.

Nebraska Wesleyan University in Lincoln received $17,000 for scholarship support.

Santa Monica City College Foundation in California received $20,000 toward a library automation project.

California State University at Los Angeles Foundation received $30,000 for the 1992 Institute for Youth Services with 30 scholarships dedicated to law enforcement officers.

University of California at Los Angeles Foundation School of Medicine received a $150,000, three-year grant for the growth and development of the UCLA AIDS Institute.

University of Southern California Norris Cancer Center in Los Angeles received $1,000,000 toward a cancer pharmacology laboratory suite in the new research tower of the Kenneth Norris Jr. Comprehensive Cancer Center.

Comments/Analysis

Education is the foundation's top area of interest, and colleges and universities are its major recipients of funds. Since the foundation is also interested in the arts and humanities, it funds scholarships, exhibitions, and projects in these areas at institutions of higher education, as well as at other organizations. Medicine and health receive significant funding for medical research, mental health, and substance abuse with some of these grants going to colleges and universities.

2
George I. Alden Trust
370 Main Street, Suite 1250
Worcester, MA   01608

Areas of Interest

Program Description: To support education in schools, colleges, and other educational institutions, with an emphasis on vocational, technical, and professional education. The foundation also supports cultural programs, programs related to youth, historical programs, and the Young Men's Christian Association.
Assistance Types: Seed money, emergency funds, building funds, equipment, land acquisition, research, publications, conferences and seminars, scholarships, renovations, professorships, matching funds, and endowments

Eligibility

Restrictions: Giving primarily in Northeast with an emphasis on Worcester, Massachusetts; no loans or grants to individuals

Personnel

Officers: Francis H. Dewey III, Chair; Robert G. Hess, Vice-Chair; Warner S. Fletcher, Secy.; Harry G. Bayliss, Treas.
Staff: None

Financial Profile

Assets: In 1993, $103,237,384
High Grant: $600,000
Low Grant: $1,000
Ave. Grant: $5,000-$50,000
Total Grants: 142 grants totaling of $4,415,000
High Grant Higher Ed.: $150,00
Low Grant Higher Ed.: $1,500
Ave. Grant Higher Ed.: $25,000-$50,000
Total Grants Higher Ed.: In 1992, 59 grants totaling $1,340,000

Application Process

Contact: Francis H. Dewey III, (508) 798-8621
Deadline: None
Board Meeting: Bimonthly, beginning in February
Processing Time: Two months
Publications: Annual report, informational brochure, including application guidelines
Guidelines: Application form is not required. Submit one copy of proposal, including signature and title of chief executive officer, organizational/project budget, annual report/financial statement/990, IRS letter of determination, detailed description of project and amount requested, and results expected from project.

Sample Grants

Alice Lloyd College in Pippa Passes, Kentucky, was granted $35,000 for capital support for new construction.
Keuka College in Keuka Park, New York, was awarded $25,000 for scholarship endowment.
Kings College in Wilkes-Barre, Pennsylvania, received $15,000 for capital repairs and renovation.
Simmons College in Boston, Massachusetts, was awarded $25,000 for equipment acquisition and repair.
Endicott College in Beverly, Massachusetts, was awarded $30,000 for designated program support.
Northeastern University in Boston, Massachusetts, received $50,000 for capital support for new construction.
Oberlin College in Oberlin, Ohio, was awarded $50,000 for equipment acquisition, repair and upkeep.
Russell Sage College in Troy, New York, received $25,000 for scholarship endowment.

Comments/Analysis

Historically, higher education received approximately 49 percent of the awards made by the foundation, and graduate and professional education an additional 5 percent. Education is the foundation's greatest area of interest, followed by human services and arts and culture. The top recipients of funds are colleges and universities, followed by human service agencies, museums, and historical societies. The largest categories of funding to higher education are capital support, including building and renovation, and student aid. The foundation has a particular interest in supporting projects that benefit women and girls.

3
Annenberg Foundation
150 Radnor-Chester Road, Suite A-200
Saint Davids Center
Saint Davids, PA   19087

Areas of Interest

Program Description: To advance well-being through improved communication. The foundation is particularly interested in projects that develop more effective ways to share ideas and knowledge. Areas of interest include childhood, elementary, secondary, and higher education; culture; and health.

Assistance Types: Seed money, special projects, program support, capital campaigns, endowments, professorships, scholarships

Eligibility

Restrictions: No grants to individuals or for basic research or capital construction

Personnel

Officers: Walter H. Annenberg, Chair and President; Leonore A. Annenberg, Vice-Chair and VP; Wallis Annenberg, VP; William J. Heinrich Jr., Secy.
Trustees/Directors: Lauren Weingarten Bon, Charles Weingarten, Gregory Weingarten
Staff: Three full-time professional, four full-time support

Financial Profile

Assets: In 1993, $1,654,401,774
High Grant: $72,665,141
Low Grant: $100
Ave. Grant: $1,000-$300,000
Total Grants: 358 grants totaling $136,595,763
High Grant Higher Ed.: $7,879,832
Low Grant Higher Ed.: $10,000
Ave. Grant Higher Ed.: $25,000-$500,000
Total Grants Higher Ed.: 35 grants totaling $27,248,343

Application Process

Contact: Dr. Gail C. Levin, Program Officer, (610) 341-9066
Board Meeting: April and November
Processing Time: Within six months
Publications: Application guidelines
Guidelines: Proposals should include description of project and amount of request, history and mission of organization, additional sources of funding and amount, how project will be sustained after grant period, annual report and financial report, and IRS letter of determination.

Sample Grants

Moore College of Art in Philadelphia, Pennsylvania, received $10,000.
University of Reading in Reading, England, received $50,000.
Eton College in Windsor, England, received $16,500.
Northwestern University in Evanston, Illinois, received $3,531,048 for program support for the Annenberg/Washington Program and general support.
United Negro College Fund in New York City received $5,000,000 for its capital campaign.
University of Pennsylvania in Philadelphia received $7,879,832 for capital campaign, program support, professorships, scholarships, and general support for the Annenberg School for Communication.

University of Southern California in Los Angeles received $4,829,167 for endowment, scholarships, research, and general operating support for the Annenberg School for Communication.
Pine Manor College in Chestnut Hill, Massachusetts, received $15,000.
Wake Forest University in Winston-Salem, North Carolina, received $250,000.

Comments/Analysis

Colleges and universities receive the greatest funds. Museums and historical societies are the next highest recipients. The top type of support is capital, including building and renovations, capital campaigns, and endowment funds. The second type of funding given is general support, followed by program support. The foundation is particularly interested in projects that serve African Americans, immigrants and refugees, and women and girls.

4
Arnold and Mabel Beckman Foundation
100 Academy Drive
Irvine, CA   92715

Areas of Interest

Program Description: To support nonprofit research institutions that promote research in chemistry and life sciences and foster the invention of methods and materials that will lead to innovation in science research. Particular areas of interest include chemistry, biochemistry, biological sciences, medical sciences, physical sciences, marine science, physics, ophthalmology, medical research, science and technology, AIDS, cancer, and heart disease.

Eligibility

Restrictions: No grants to individuals; no loans

Personnel

Officers: Harold Brown, Chair; George L. Argyros, Vice-Chair and CFO; Donald Strauss, VP and Secy.
Trustees/Directors: Arnold O. Beckman, Arnold W. Beckman, Theodore L. Brown, Harry B. Gray, Gary H. Hunt, Donald Shields
Staff: One full-time professional

Financial Profile

Assets: In 1993, $233,745,710
High Grant: $1,000,000
Low Grant: $82,500
Ave. Grant: $82,500-$600,000
Total Grants: 37 grants totaling $7,959,500
Total Grants Higher Ed.: 31 grants totaling $7,302,500

Application Process

Contact: Ron Henderson, Administrator, (714) 721-2222
Deadline: July 1
Board Meeting: December or January and July or August
Processing Time: Decisions made in April or May
Publications: Grant policy statement including application information
Guidelines: An application form is not required. Initial approach should be made by a letter proposal not longer than three pages.

Sample Grants

The California Institute of Technology in Pasadena received $920,000 for chemical synthesis equipment, $1,000,000 for matching trustee pledge, $400,000 for hearing research, and $600,000 for its Beckman Institute for Medical Research.

Michigan State University in East Lansing was granted $82,500 for a project entitled Intercalated Conductive Polymers: Structured-Property Relationships.

Stanford University Beckman Center for Molecular and Genetic Medicine in Stanford, California, received $400,000 for medical research.

University of Illinois Beckman Institute in Advanced Science and Technology in Champaign was awarded $600,000 for medical research.

Comments/Analysis

Historically, science is the top area of interest and is granted the greatest number of grants as well as the highest amount of funds. The second area of interest is education, and the third, medical research. Colleges and universities receive the largest amount of support, followed by hospitals and medical research institutes.

5
H.N. and Frances C. Berger Foundation
PO Box 3064
Arcadia, CA   91006-0966

Areas of Interest

Program Description: To support higher education, cultural programs, public health organizations, and hospitals. The foundation funds arts and culture, crime and justice programs, employment programs, housing shelter and human services, disaster relief, and science and technology.
Assistance Types: Scholarships, fellowships, equipment, construction

Eligibility

Restrictions: Giving primarily in California; no grants to individuals

Personnel

Officers: Ronald Auen, President; Shirley Allen, VP and Treas.; John N. Berger, VP; Christopher McGuire, VP; Lewis Webb Jr., VP; Joan Auen, Secy.
Trustees/Directors: Robert M. Barton, James Kuhn, Douglas Vance

Financial Profile

Assets: In 1993, $147,583,000
Total Grants: $2,365,400
High Grant Higher Ed.: $1,002,000
Low Grant Higher Ed.: $12,500
Ave. Grant Higher Ed.: $20,000-$100,000

Application Process

Contact: Christopher McGuire, VP, (818) 447-3551
Deadline: None
Board Meeting: Semiannually and as needed
Publications: None
Guidelines: The initial approach should be by letter.

Sample Grants

University of Arizona at Tucson was granted $1,380,000 for endowment for scholarships for its entrepreneurship program and Plus Scholarships.

College of the Ozarks in Point Lookout, Missouri, received $52,204 for a scholarship fund.

Pasadena City College Foundation in, Pasadena, California, received $100,000 for the construction of a new library.

California Western School of Law in San Diego received $28,000 for Berger Scholarships.

Cumberland College in Williamsburg, Kentucky, received $375,000 for the expansion of its existing library.

University of Southern California Thornton Kidney Research Foundation in Los Angeles received $51,000 for equipment.

Stanford University Department of Dermatology, Psoriasis Research Institute, in Stanford, California, received $20,000 for a one-year fellowship and one full-time investigator for psoriasis.

Comments/Analysis

The foundation is committed to long-term support of its presently funded grantees. Although the foundation's grants are primarily distributed to institutions in the state of California, projects in the foundation's interests from other states have received support.

6

Corella and Bertram Bonner Foundation, Inc.
Box 712
22 Chambers Street
Princeton, NJ   08542

Areas of Interest

Program Description: The foundation is interested in supporting higher education and other education including educational programs for minorities. Funding is also provided for religious organizations, including those operating missionary programs and welfare programs; social service and hunger programs; hospitals; medical research; and ophthalmology.
Assistance Types: Scholarship funds, continuing support

Eligibility

Restrictions: Giving limited to domestic programs in the United States; no grants to individuals, or for capital improvements, endowments, operating budgets, building funds, or renovations

Personnel

Officers: Corella A. Bonner, VP
Staff: Four full-time professional, five full-time support

Financial Profile

Assets: In 1993, $48,715,001
High Grant: $125,000
Low Grant: $1,000
Ave. Grant: $1,000-$25,000
Total Grants: 380 grants for a total of $6,677,494
High Grant Higher Ed.: $49,600
Low Grant Higher Ed.: $10,000
Ave. Grant Higher Ed.: $10,000-$25,000
Total Grants Higher Ed.: In 1992, 60 grants totaling $1,409,400

Application Process

Contact: Wayne Meisel, Exec. Director, (609) 924-6663
Deadline: August 15
Publications: Informational brochure
Guidelines: An application form is required. The application may be requested by telephone.

Sample Grants

Ferrum College in Ferrum, Virginia, was awarded five grants totaling $98,800, ranging $10,000-$23,125.
College of the Ozarks in Point Lookout, Missouri, received five grants totaling $113,600, ranging $10,000-$27,750.
Berea College in Berea, Kentucky, was awarded five grants totaling $197,725, ranging $26,685-$49,600.

Comments/Analysis

The foundation seems to award certain institutions of higher education multiple grants annually. These institutions include Berea College in Kentucky, Berry College in Georgia, Carson-Newman College in Tennessee, College of the Ozarks in Missouri, Concord College in West Virginia, Davidson College in North Carolina, Emory and Henry College in Virginia, Ferrum College in Virginia, Guilford College in North Carolina, Mars Hill College in North Carolina, Maryville College in Tennessee, and Wofford College in South Carolina.

7

Helen Brach Foundation
55 W Wacker Drive, Suite 701
Chicago, IL   60601

Areas of Interest

Program Description: To support the prevention of cruelty to animals; programs that test public safety; child welfare and family services; and projects that benefit the homeless, aged, youth, women, the disabled, and the disadvantaged. The foundation also supports secondary, higher, and other education, as well as the arts, health and hospitals, law and justice, hunger, conservation of the environment, and citizenship.
Assistance Types: Annual campaigns, building and renovations, general purposes, operating budgets, special projects, publications, research

Eligibility

Restrictions: No grants to individuals

Personnel

Officers: Charles M. Vorhees, Chair; Raymond F. Simon, President; James J. O'Connor, VP; John J. Sheridan, Secy.-Treas.
Trustees/Directors: R. Matthew Simon, Charles A. Vorhees
Staff: One full-time support

Financial Profile

Assets: In 1992, $63,496,233
High Grant: $25,000
Low Grant: $135
Ave. Grant: $5,000-$25,000
Total Grants: 130 grants totaling $212,691
High Grant Higher Ed.: $75,000
Low Grant Higher Ed.: $10,000
Ave. Grant Higher Ed.: $10,000-$75,000
Total Grants Higher Ed.: Five grants totaling $180,000

Application Process

Contact: Raymond F. Simon, President, (312) 372-4417

Deadline: December 31
Board Meeting: Quarterly
Processing Time: March notification
Publications: Annual report, application guidelines
Guidelines: The initial approach should be by letter. An application form is required.

Sample Grants

Loyola University in Chicago, Illinois, was granted $75,000 to support a crisis intervention and family counseling program.

Thomas Aquinas College in Santa Paula, California, received $25,000 for student aid.

Illinois Benedictine College in Lisle was awarded $20,000 to continue the expansion of the Jurica Natural History Museum.

Barat College in Lake Forest, Illinois, received $10,000 for scholarships and program support.

DePaul University in Chicago, Illinois, was awarded $50,000 toward the construction of a new library on their Lincoln Park campus.

Comments/Analysis

The foundation's first priority is the support of organizations that protect and educate the public about animals and wildlife. Human services giving to community-based organizations is their next priority, followed by secondary and higher education, museums, and cultural organizations.

8
Buffet Foundation
222 Kiewit Plaza
Omaha, NE   68131

Areas of Interest

Program Description: To support family planning programs.
Assistance Types: General purposes

Eligibility

Restrictions: Unsolicited applications are not accepted.

Personnel

Officers: Susan T. Buffet, President; Warren E. Buffet, VP and Treas.; Gladys Kaiser, Secy.
Trustees/Directors: Susan Greenberg, Carol Loomis, Thomas S. Murphy
Staff: One full-time professional, one part-time professional

Financial Profile

Assets: In 1993, $21,699,655
High Grant: $500,000
Low Grant: $250

Ave. Grant: $1,000-$100,000
Total Grants: In 1992, 74 grants totaling $2,025,079, plus 18 grants to individuals at $10,000 each
High Grant Higher Ed.: $207,000
Low Grant Higher Ed.: $25,916
Ave. Grant Higher Ed.: $25,000-$45,000
Total Grants Higher Ed.: Five grants totaling $422,564

Application Process

Contact: Allen Greenberg, (402) 345-9168
Deadline: None
Publications: None
Guidelines: Prospective applicants should contact the foundation.

Sample Grants

University of Nebraska in Lincoln received $40,418 for scholarships.

University of Nebraska in Omaha received $42,608 for scholarships.

John Hopkins University, School of Hygiene and Public Health, in Baltimore, Maryland, was awarded a $207,000 grant.

University of California in San Francisco received $106,622 for fellowships and clinical trials.

Wayne State College in Wayne, Nebraska, was awarded $25,916 for scholarships.

Comments/Analysis

The foundation's primary area of interest is family planning as it relates to medicine, education, and international affairs and development. Hospitals and medical facilities are the top recipients of funds, followed by international organizations, colleges, and universities.

9
Bush Foundation
332 Minnesota Street
E-900 First National Bank Building
Saint Paul, MN   55101

Areas of Interest

Program Description: Support for higher and other education, arts and humanities, delivery of health care, leadership development, minority opportunity, and women and girls. Operates the Bush Leadership Fellows Program, the Bush Fellowships for Artists, and the Bush Medical Fellows Program. Other areas of interest include fine arts, music, minority education, performing arts, museums, language and literature, humanities, media and communication, social services, and science and technology.
Assistance Types: Fellowships, matching funds, endowment funds, special projects, seed money, capital campaigns, renovation projects, faculty development

Eligibility

Restrictions: Giving primarily in Minnesota, North Dakota, and South Dakota; no support for private foundations; no grants to individuals (except for fellowships) or for research in biomedical and health sciences; generally no grants for continuing operating support, for building construction of hospitals or medical facilities, church sanctuaries, individual day-care centers, municipal buildings, and buildings in public colleges and universities; no covering of operating deficits or to retire mortgages or other debts; no loans

Personnel

Officers: Thomas E. Holloran, Chair; Frank B. Wilderson Jr., First Vice-Chair; Anita M. Pampusch, Second Vice-Chair; Humphrey Doermann, President; Sharon Sayles Belton, Secy.; Richard D. McFarland, Treas.

Trustees/Directors: Merlin E. Dewing, Phyllis B. France, Ellen Z. Green, Beatrix A. Hamburg, John A. McHugh, Diane E. Murphy, Kennon V. Rothchild, W. Richard West Jr., C. Angus Wurtele, Ann Wynia

Staff: Eight full-time professional, four full-time support, four part-time support

Financial Profile

Assets: In 1992, $450,143,909; 1993, $469,007,588
High Grant: In 1992, $1,000,000; 1993, $875,000
Low Grant: In 1992, $4,470; 1993, $5,000
Ave. Grant: $25,000-$50,000
Total Grants: In 1992, 253 grants totaling $18,560,085, plus 66 grants to individuals totaling $41,641,022; 1993, 238 grants totaling $16,683,525
Total Grants Higher Ed.: In 1992, $10,334,629

Application Process

Contact: Humphrey Doermann, President, (612) 227-0891
Deadline: Four months before board meetings
Board Meeting: February, April (odd numbered years only), June, and October
Processing Time: 10 days after board meeting
Publications: Annual report, application guide, program policy statement, financial statement
Guidelines: The initial approach can take the form of a letter or telephone call. Applications should include the following: name, IRS letter of determination, signature of the chief executive officer, history and mission of the organization, names and affiliations of board members, qualifications of key personnel, description of the project and amount of request, annual report and financial report, additional documentation or program materials, organization or project budget, and how the project will be measured or evaluated.

Sample Grants

Claflin College in Orangeburg, South Carolina, received a three-year grant for $102,000 for faculty development.

Sioux Falls College in Sioux Falls, South Dakota, was awarded $150,000 toward the completion of its library and computer improvement projects in its capital fund drive.

Fort Peck Community College in Poplar, Montana, received $25,000 for their faculty development program.

Bethel College and Seminary in Saint Paul, Minnesota, received $440,000 toward building a new Center for Community Life.

Johnson C. Smith University in Charlotte, North Carolina, received a two-and-a-half-year grant for $1,000,000 toward building and endowment projects in its capital fund drive.

Comments/Analysis

Education is the foundation's highest priority. Its second priority area is arts and culture. Colleges and universities are its top recipients of funds.

10
Louis Calder Foundation
230 Park Avenue, Room 1530
New York, NY   10169

Areas of Interest

Program Description: To support programs that best promote the health, education, and welfare of New York City residents and enhance the potential and increase the self sufficiency of children, youth, and their families. Related areas of interest include higher education, the disadvantaged, social services, and family services.

Assistance Types: Operating budgets, equipment, special projects, scholarship funds, general purposes, challenge grants, matching grants, medical research, financial aid

Eligibility

Restrictions: Giving primarily in New York City. No support for publicly operated educational or medical institutions, governmental organizations, or private foundations; cultural grants only to well-known established organizations. No grants to individuals; no grants for building or endowment funds, capital development, or continuing support.

Personnel

Officers: Barbara Sommer, Grant Program Manager
Trustees/Directors: Paul R. Brenner, Peter D. Calder, Chemical Bank
Staff: Two full-time support

Financial Profile

Assets: In 1992, $115,297,278; 1994, $117,850,232
High Grant: In 1992, $200,000; 1994, $200,000
Low Grant: In 1992, $2,000; 1994, $3,000
Ave. Grant: $15,000-$50,000

Total Grants: In 1992, 48 grants totaling $5,174,750; 1994, 126 grants totaling $4,260,400
Ave. Grant Higher Ed.: $20,000-$475,000
Total Grants Higher Ed.: In 1992, 28 grants totaling $1,632,500

Application Process

Contact: The Trustees, (212) 687-1680
Deadline: Submit one copy of proposal between November 1 and March 31; deadline five months prior to end of organization's fiscal year or March 31, whichever is earliest.
Board Meeting: As required
Processing Time: Notification is July 31
Publications: Annual report, including application guidelines
Guidelines: The New York Regional Association of Grantmaker's Common Application Form is accepted. However, an application form is not required. Submit a one- to three-page letter proposal between November 1st and March 31st and include the history and mission of organization, names and affiliations of board members, budget, IRS letter of determination, additional sources of funding and amounts, and description of project and amount requested.

Sample Grants

Mount Holyoke College in South Hadley, Massachusetts, received $15,000 for a financial aid program to assist students from New York City who have shown high academic promise and whose families have demonstrated financial need.

Fordham University in Bronx, New York, received $212,500 as the final installment of a matching grant to assist in the renovation of the main house at the Calder Center in Armonk, New York.

Independent College Fund of New York in New York City received $25,000 for a college work-study program for New York City students, and to raise additional money from New York City area funding.

New York University in New York City received $50,000 for the New York City operations of the Reading Recovery Program for first grade public school students.

Rockfeller University, Laboratory of Biochemical Genetics and Metabolism in New York City was awarded $200,000 for heart disease research.

Comments/Analysis

The foundation's top area of interest is education, the second is other, and the third is the arts. The top recipients of funds are human service organizations, followed by colleges and universities and performing arts groups.

11
Carnegie Corporation of New York
437 Madison Avenue
New York, NY   10022

Areas of Interest

Program Description: To advance knowledge and understanding among the people of the United States and of certain countries that are or have been members of the British Overseas Commonwealth. The foundation's present goals are education and health; development of children and youth, including early childhood health and development, early adolescence educational achievement and health, science education, and education reform; strengthening human resources in developing countries; and cooperative security, which seeks to avoid catastrophic conflict among nations. Other areas of interest include minorities, race relations, literacy, minority education, educational associations, educational research, science and technology, drug abuse, public policy, international affairs, international development, peace, arms control, and foreign policy.
Assistance Types: Seed money, continuing support, special projects, research, publications, conferences and seminars, exchange programs, general purposes

Eligibility

Restrictions: Giving primarily in the United States. Some grants in sub-Saharan Africa, South Africa, and the Caribbean. No support for facilities of educational or human services institutions. No grants for scholarships, fellowships, travel, basic operating expenses or endowments; no program-related investments.

Personnel

Officers: Newton M. Minow, Chair; Eugene H. Cota-Robles, Vice-Chair; David A. Hamburg, President; Barbara D. Findberg, Exec.VP and Prog. Chair, Special Projects; Dorothy Wills Knapp, Secy.; Cynthia E. Merritt, Assoc. Secy; Jeanmarie C. Grisi, Treas.
Trustees/Directors: Caryl P. Haskins, Honorary Trustee; Richard I. Beattie; Richard F. Celeste; James P. Corner; Teresa F. Heinz; James A. Johnson; Helene L. Kaplan; Thomas H. Kean; Shirley M. Malcolm; Mary Patterson McPherson; Henry Muller; Lawrence A. Tisch; James D. Watkins
Staff: 54 full-time professional, 10 part-time professional, 21 full-time support, two part-time support.

Financial Profile

Assets: In 1992, $1,051,666,391; in 1993, $1,180,442,588
High Grant: $1,600,000
Low Grant: $975
Ave. Grant: $25,000-$250,000; for foundation-administered programs, $25,000-$2,334,672
Total Grants: In 1992, $43,892,989 for grants and $4,893,876 for foundation-administered programs. In 1993, a total of $51,205,167 was awarded.

High Grant Higher Ed.: $1,141,000
Low Grant Higher Ed.: $10,000
Ave. Grant Higher Ed.: $25,000-$250,000
Total Grants Higher Ed.: In 1992, 94 grants totaling $15,965,450; 1993, 77 grants totaling $15,672,400

Application Process

Contact: Dorothy Wills Knapp, Secy., (212) 371-3200
Deadline: None
Board Meeting: October, January, April, and June
Processing Time: Six months
Publications: Annual report, informational brochure, newsletter, grants list, occasional report
Guidelines: The initial approach should be by letter. Proposals should include the following: description of project and amount requested, statement of the problem the project will address, anticipated results, and qualifications of key personnel.

Sample Grants

Association of American Universities in Washington, DC, received $79,800 for a study on the role of the university in society.

Vanderbilt University in Nashville, Tennessee, received two grants totaling $50,000 for papers on effective ways to promote positive interracial and interethnic relations among youth.

Stanford University in Stanford, California, received two grants: a three-year, $499,700 grant for the development of curriculum in human biology for middle grades and teacher training materials; and $230,000 for a working group to study federal education programs for limited-English-proficient children.

Columbia University in New York City received three grants in the general health area: $300,000 for research and training on maternal health in sub-Saharan Africa, $150,400 toward meetings on school-based health centers, and $25,000 toward health care reform briefing for journalists.

Mahidol University in Bangkok, Thailand, received $53,000 toward establishing an international organization on school and health sciences.

Carnegie-Mellon University in Pittsburgh, Pennsylvania, received $25,000 for the assessment of a United Nations Special Commission on the demilitarization of Iraq.

University of Cape Town in Rondebosch, South Africa, was awarded $24,200 to plan a women's leadership institute.

Duke University in Durham, North Carolina, received $97,350 for planning a center for the study of children and youth.

Georgetown University in Washington, DC, received a two-year $295,000 grant toward research and analysis on science in the former Soviet Union.

Comments/Analysis

The foundation prefers to support programs. Its second priority is research. The top recipients of its funds are colleges and universities, followed by professional societies and associations.

12
E. Rhodes & Leona B. Carpenter Foundation
c/o Joseph A. O'Connor Jr., Morgan, Lewis & Bockius
2000 One Logan Square
Philadelphia, PA   19102-8880

Areas of Interest

Program Description: To support the arts, performing arts, museums, education, graduate theological education, and health.
Assistance Types: Program support, scholarships, art and literature acquisition

Eligibility

Restrictions: No grants to individuals or for support for local church congregations or parishes, private secondary education, or large public charities. Giving mainly in areas east of the Mississippi River.

Personnel

Officers: Ann B. Day, President; Paul B. Day Jr., VP and Secy.-Treas.

Financial Profile

Assets: In 1993, $137,755,313
High Grant: $1,500,000
Low Grant: $825
Ave. Grant: $10,000-$50,000

Application Process

Contact: M.H. Reinhart, Director, (215) 963-5212
Deadline: None
Guidelines: The initial approach should be by letter. The letter should include a brief description of the history and mission of the organization, description of the project and amount requested, copy of current year organization or project budget, and copy of IRS determination letter. Applications should be sent to PO Box 58880, Philadelphia, Pennsylvania 19102-8880.

Sample Grants

University of Kansas, Spencer Museum of Art, in Lawrence received $12,000 for the purchase of a Chinese painting.

Andover Newton Theological School in Newton Centre, Massachusetts, received two grants totaling $84,500 for a South Africa church leadership project.

John Hopkins University, School of Nursing in Baltimore, Maryland, was awarded $500,000 for a scholarship in the memory of Leona B. Carpenter.

Duke University in Durham, North Carolina, received $500,000 to purchase a collection of American and English literature for its library.

Mary Baldwin College in Staunton, Virginia, received two grants: $174,600 for a program in health care administration and $25,000 for a ministry scholarship.

Union Theological Seminary in Richmond, Virginia, received $48,000 for an Appalachian program.

Comments/Analysis

Priority is given to education, followed by arts and culture. In the past, education received 40 percent of the grants distributed by the foundation, while arts and culture received 33 percent. Graduate and professional education was included in the 40 percent allocated to education and accounted for 24 percent of the total funds distributed by the foundation.

13

Ben B. Cheney Foundation Inc.
1201 Pacific Avenue, Suite 1600
Tacoma, WA   98402

Areas of Interest

Program Description: To support education, secondary and higher education, health, hospitals, social services, and cultural programs. Other areas of interest include the elderly, youth, the disabled, recreational facilities, and museums.

Assistance Types: Seed money, equipment and building, general purposes, scholarship funds, special projects, emergency funds

Eligibility

Restrictions: Giving limited to Washington, Oregon, and the seven counties of northern California. No giving for religious purposes, for operating budgets or basic research, endowment funds, conferences, or for book, or media productions; no loans.

Personnel

Officers: R. Gene Grant, President; Elgin E. Olrogg, VP; John F. Hansler, Secy.; Bradbury F. Cheney, Treas.

Trustees/Directors: William O. Rieke

Staff: One full-time support

Financial Profile

Assets: In 1992, $63,389,326; 1993, $66,966,136
High Grant: In 1992, $350,000; 1993, $100,000
Low Grant: $1,000
Ave. Grant: $1,500-$25,000
Total Grants: In 1992, 152 grants totaling $4,216,450; 1993, 167 grants totaling $2,475,900
High Grant Higher Ed.: $35,000
Low Grant Higher Ed.: $20,000
Ave. Grant Higher Ed.: $10,000-$25,000
Total Grants Higher Ed.: In 1992, 15 grants totaling $607,500

Application Process

Contact: William O. Rieke, Exec. Director, (206) 572-2442
Deadline: Four weeks prior to board meeting
Board Meeting: May, September, and December
Processing Time: Three months
Publications: Informational brochure, including application guidelines
Guidelines: The initial approach should be by letter. Application form is required.

Sample Grants

Pacific Lutheran University in Tacoma, Washington, received $35,000 for a energy-dispersive X-ray spectrometer.

Linfield College in McMinnville, Oregon, received $20,000 in support of a scholarship program.

Tacoma Community College in Tacoma, Washington, received $25,000 to create an endowment fund in support of literacy services.

Heritage College in Toppenish, Washington, received $25,000 to build a library and learning center.

Pacific University in Forest Grove, Oregon, was awarded $20,000 for a scholarship program.

Seattle Pacific University in Seattle, Washington, received $20,000 for a scholarship program.

Comments/Analysis

The foundation divides its giving fairly equally across its areas of interest, giving grants of a similar size to secondary and higher education, community organizations, and museums. The foundation has a particular interest in projects that serve the elderly, the disabled, and youth.

14

Edna McConnell Clark Foundation
150 Park Avenue, Room 900
New York, NY   10177-0026

Areas of Interest

Program Description: To support programs in five interest areas: children—reducing unnecessary removal of children from their homes; disadvantaged youth—improving middle schools to improve educational opportunities; justice—creating a more humane and effective criminal justice system; tropical disease research—reducing deadly illnesses in the poorest countries; and homelessness—assisting families in New York City to move from temporary, emergency housing into permanent housing.

Assistance Types: Consulting services, research, seed money, technical assistance, special projects

Eligibility

Restrictions: No grants to individuals or for construction, equipment, endowments, scholarships, annual appeals, or loans. Some programs have geographic limitations.

Personnel

Officers: Hays Clark, Chair; Peter Bell, President; Carol B. Einiger, VP and CFO

Trustees/Directors: James McConnell Clark Jr., John M. Emery, Lucy H. Nesbeda, Mary E. Proctor, Edward C. Schmults, Ruth A. Wooden

Staff: 16 full-time professional, 10 full-time support, three part-time support

Financial Profile

Assets: In 1993, $520,603,931
High Grant: $1,000,000
Low Grant: $5,000
Ave. Grant: $25,000-$250,000
Total Grants: 275 grants totaling $20,000,504
High Grant Higher Ed.: $737,000
Low Grant Higher Ed.: $50,000
Ave. Grant Higher Ed.: $50,000-$220,000
Total Grants Higher Ed.: 27 grants totaling $2,907,500

Application Process

Contact: Carol B. Einiger, VP and CFO, (212) 551-9100
Deadline: None
Board Meeting: March, May, June, September, and December
Processing Time: One month for rejections, two to three months for approval
Publications: Annual report, informational brochure (including application guidelines), grants list, occasional report
Guidelines: The initial approach should be by letter. Application form is not required. Proposals should include a statement of the problem project will address; copy of annual report, audited financial statement, or 990; IRS letter of determination; names and affiliations of board members, trustees, and other key people; list of other sources of support, amounts, and names of other sources to which application is being submitted; qualifications of key personnel; detailed description of the project and the funding requested; current organization or project budget; anticipated results; timetable for implementation and evaluation; how project will be measured or evaluated; how project will be sustained after grant period; and plans for cooperation with other organizations.

Sample Grants

University of Massachusetts at Amherst was awarded $170,000 for a two-year grant to its Department of Microbiology.

University of California, San Francisco, received $50,000 to characterize and produce 12 antigens for onchocerciasis vaccine in the next year using the yeast method.

Bank Street College of Education in New York City received $123,000 to continue to organize training, convene monthly

agency meetings, and offer on-site technical assistance to Partners for Success, a group of organizations developing and implementing family support and parent education programs.

University of Minnesota in Minneapolis received $198,000 for 12 Pennsylvania judges and prosecutors to take part in a judicial education workshop.

University of Southampton, England, received a $120,000 one-and-a half-year grant to develop a user-friendly computerized system that simulates the epidemiology and transmission dynamics of trachoma.

The State University of Iowa at Iowa City was awarded $85,000 for a three-year grant.

Comments/Analysis

Action-oriented projects are preferred. The largest subject area supported by the foundation is medical research, followed by education and human services. The greatest amount of funds are granted to colleges and universities, primarily for medical research. In 1993, medical research received 28 percent of all grants. The foundation also has a strong interest in children and youth, which is reflected in their giving pattern. K-12 education received 25 percent of the grants awarded by the foundation in 1993.

15
Commonwealth Fund
One E 75th Street
New York, NY   10021-2962

Areas of Interest

Program Description: To support opportunities to improve the health and well-being of Americans and to assist specific groups of Americans who have serious and neglected problems. The fund's five major programs strive to improve the efficacy and appropriateness of clinical care through patient's perceptions; help develop ways to enable senior Americans to participate more fully; help build a climate of respect and opportunity for skilled work training within the American education system and help non-college-bound youth shape a vision; and foster further examination of urban life and ways to improve it. Harkness Fellowships are awarded by selection committees in each country to citizens and potential leaders from the United Kingdom, Australia, and New Zealand for study and research in the United States. Other areas of interest include minority medical education, advanced management training for nurses, public policy, and drug abuse.

Assistance Types: Research, special projects

Eligibility

Restrictions: No grants to individuals (except for Harkness Fellowships) or for building or endowment funds; general support; capital funds; construction or renovation of facilities; purchase of equipment; or assistance with operating budgets or deficits of established programs or institutions, scholarships, or matching gifts; no loans. Grants are awarded to nonprofit organizations to support service, educational, and research activities.

Personnel

Officers: C. Sims Farr, Chair; Margaret E. Mahoney, President; Karen Davis, Exec. VP; John Craig, VP and Treas.
Trustees/Directors: Lewis Bernard, Lawrence S. Huntington, Helene Kaplan, Robert M. O'Neil, Roswell B. Perkins, Dr. Charles A. Sanders, Alfred R. Stern, Blenda J. Wilson
Staff: 14 full-time professional, 15 full-time support, two part-time support

Financial Profile

Assets: In 1992, $339,932,193; in 1993, $365,083,964
High Grant: $400,000
Low Grant: $1,000
Ave. Grant: $5,000-$40,000
Total Grants: In 1992, 146 grants totaling $9,936,297; 1993, 125 grants totaling $8,232,891
High Grant Higher Ed.: $500,000
Low Grant Higher Ed.: $12,500
Ave. Grant Higher Ed.: $25,000-$100,000
Total Grants Higher Ed.: In 1992, 15 grants totaling $1,381,079; in 1993, 28 grants totaling $1,873,545

Application Process

Contact: Adrienne A. Fisher, Grants Manager, (212) 535-0400
Deadline: None
Board Meeting: April, July, and November
Processing Time: Immediately following board meeting
Publications: Annual report, application guidelines
Guidelines: The initial approach should come as a letter or proposal.

Sample Grants

New York University Robert Wagner Graduate School of Public Service in New York City received $25,000 to develop a drug abuse prevention program for ex-offenders.

George Washington University Intergovernment Health Policy Project in Washington, DC, received $61,932 for monitoring changes in state health policy and $13,500 to publish a summary of the National Health Policy Forum's 20th anniversary session on Pressures for Reform.

William Carey College in Hattiesberg, Mississippi, received $100,000 to establish the Career Beginnings Project.

University of Michigan, School of Business Administration in Ann Arbor received $185,000 for a project entitled New Era of Corporate Involvement with Pressing Community Problems.

Harvard University School of Public Health in Cambridge, Massachusetts, received two grants: $88,727 for Social Marketing, Phase Two: A Case Study of the Partnership for a Drug-Free America, and $27,250 for Comparison of Treatment Approaches Used in Industrial Alcoholism Programs: Further Analysis of the Data.

University of California Department of General Internal Medicine in Los Angeles received $97,381 for a study on the utilization of angiography by minority patients.

Comments/Analysis

The Commonwealth Fund's highest priority for support is general and rehabilitative medicine. Historically, this area has received approximately 60 percent of the total funds distributed by the foundation.

16
Compton Foundation, Inc.
545 Middlefield Road, Suite 178
Menlo Park, CA   94025

Areas of Interest

Program Description: To support community, national, and international programs in peace, world order, population studies, and the environment. The foundation's interests include equal education opportunity, community welfare, social justice, culture and the arts, family planning, foreign policy, arms control, conservation, and minority education.
Assistance Types: Endowment funds, fellowships, general purposes, matching funds, operating budgets, continuing support, annual campaigns, special projects, consulting services, land acquisition

Eligibility

Restrictions: No grants for capital or building funds; no grants to individuals; no loans

Personnel

Officers: James R. Compton, President; Ann C. Stephens, VP and Secy.; Michael P. Todaro, Treas.
Trustees/Directors: Randolph O. Compton, W. Danforth Compton, Lee Etta Powell, Kenneth W. Thompson, Laurie Wayburn
Staff: Two full-time professional, two part-time support

Financial Profile

Assets: In 1992, $73,671,846; 1993, $71,536,564
Ave. Grant: $500-$40,000
Total Grants: In 1992, 411 grants totaling $3,612,020; 1993, 451 grants totaling $3,909,058
High Grant Higher Ed.: $25,000
Low Grant Higher Ed.: $10,000
Ave. Grant Higher Ed.: $500-$40,000
Total Grants Higher Ed.: In 1992, 20 grants totaling $711,000

Application Process

Contact: Edith T. Eddy, Exec. Director, (415) 328-0101
Deadline: May 1 to October 1
Board Meeting: May and December
Processing Time: Six months
Publications: Biennial report, informational brochure

Guidelines: Submit one copy of a three- to four-page proposal. If the foundation is interested in considering the project, a proposal outline form will be sent. Application form not required. Proposal should include a detailed description of project and amount of funding requested, how project will be evaluated or measured, qualifications of key personnel, listing of additional sources and amount of support, copy of current year's organizational budget and/or project budget, and copy of IRS letter of determination.

Sample Grants

Brown University in Providence, Rhode Island, received a $52,000, two-year grant to enhance training in a population of students from developing countries.

The University of North Carolina in Chapel Hill received $21,415 for a project entitled Impact of Human Populations on the Environment: Deforestation in the Equadorian Amazon.

Columbia University in New York City received two grants: $25,000 for family planning and teenage pregnancy prevention programs in New York City and $10,000 for general support.

Meharry Medical College in Nashville, Tennessee, was awarded $75,000 for renewal of general operating support.

Dominican College of San Rafael in California received $10,000 for its graduate program in Pacific Basin Studies.

Comments/Analysis

International affairs, peace, security, and arms control are top areas of priority for the foundation. Environmental protection and natural resources are the second areas of interest. The foundation supports graduate-level training in environment and sustainable development and fellowships and scholarships that promote equal educational postsecondary opportunities for low-income and minority students. Education grants are initiated by the foundation.

17
Jessie B. Cox Charitable Trust
c/o Grants Management Associates
230 Congress Street, 3rd Floor
Boston, MA   02110

Areas of Interest

Program Description: To support education, health, protection of the environment, conservation, and the development of philanthropy. Other areas of interest include minority education.

Assistance Types: Seed money, special projects

Eligibility

Restrictions: Giving primarily in New England; no support for sectarian religious activities or for efforts usually supported by the general public; no grants to individuals; no support for capital or building funds, equipment and materials, land acquisition, reno-

vation, operating budgets, deficit financing, annual campaigns, general endowments, or loans

Personnel

Trustees/Directors: William C. Cox Jr., Roy A. Hammer, Jane Cox MacElree, George T. Shaw

Staff: Four part-time professional, one part-time support

Financial Profile

Assets: In 1993, $55,000,000
High Grant: $100,000
Low Grant: $1,000
Ave. Grant: $20,000-$60,000
Total Grants: 81 grants totaling $3,059,230
Total Grants Higher Ed.: In 1992, 15 grants totaling $605,000

Application Process

Contact: Michealle Larkins, Foundation Asst., (617) 426-7172
Deadline: January 15, April 15, July 15, and October 15
Board Meeting: March, June, September, and December
Processing Time: Within three months of deadline
Publications: Annual report, informational brochure, application guidelines
Guidelines: The initial approach should be a brief concept paper. Applications should include a history and description of the organization, description of the project and amount requested, statement of the problem to be addressed by the proposed project, anticipated results from the project, why the foundation is the appropriate donor, population served by the project, qualification of key personnel, other organizations that will cooperate, timeline for the project, how the project will be sustained after the grant period, how the project will be measured or evaluated, names and affiliations of board members or trustees, and IRS letter of determination.

Sample Grants

University of Maine in Orono received $45,000 toward a scientific survey documenting the extent of hunger among Maine's low-income families with children.

University of Massachusetts Department of Pediatrics in Worcester received $25,000 for a final grant for a pilot project to test ways to help local pediatricians in central Massachusetts provide health services for children with chronic illnesses and special health needs.

Bryant College of Business Administration in Smithfield, Rhode Island, received $25,000 for Project Venture, an early intervention education program for at-risk minority eighth graders.

University of New England Community Internship Center in Biddeford, Maine, received $20,000 for a final grant to provide for-credit internships and volunteer opportunities for students.

Arnold Arboretum of Harvard University in Jamaica Plain, Massachusetts, was awarded $27,508 toward teacher training and followup activities for LEAP, an environmental education project.

Mount Holyoke College in South Hadley, Massachusetts, received $25,000 for continued support for a model magnet middle school partnership project.

Comments/Analysis

The trustees are inclined to support organizations that have not received prior funding, along with innovative approaches different from previously funded projects. Historically, the top area of funding has been the environment, followed by other and education. The top recipients are environmental organizations, with colleges and universities the second largest recipients.

18

Charles E. Culpeper Foundation, Inc.
695 E Main Street
Financial Centre, Suite 404
Stamford, CT   06901-2138

Areas of Interest

Program Description: To support organizations concerned with health, medical and higher education, arts and culture, and the administration of justice.
Assistance Types: Research, general purposes, seed money, special projects

Eligibility

Restrictions: The foundation rarely supports endowments, building funds, operating budgets, conferences or travel; no loans.

Personnel

Officers: Francis McNamara Jr., President; Philip M. Drake, VP and Secy.-Treas.; Linda E. Jacobs, VP for Programs
Trustees/Directors: Colin G. Campbell, Joseph F. Fahey Jr., John Morning, John C. Rose
Staff: Five full-time professional, one part-time professional, one full-time support

Financial Profile

Assets: In 1993, $217,667,158
High Grant: $150,000
Low Grant: $500
Ave. Grant: $15,000-$50,000
Total Grants: 125 grants totaling $5,646,365
High Grant Higher Ed.: $324,000
Low Grant Higher Ed.: $10,000
Total Grants Higher Ed.: In 1992, 26 grants totaling $3,417,525; 1993, 25 grants totaling $3,927,395

Application Process

Contact: Linda E. Jacobs, VP for Programs, (203) 975-1240; fax: (203) 975-1847
Deadline: None
Board Meeting: Quarterly
Publications: Informational brochure, including application guidelines, annual report
Guidelines: A letter of inquiry should be submitted first, and should include a description of project and amount requested, current budget, history and mission of organization, listing of additional sources of funding and amounts, and IRS letter of determination. Applicant will later be asked to provide name of contact person, names and affiliations of board members and key people, anticipated results, annual report and 990, qualifications of key personnel, and timetable for implementation and evaluation of project.

Sample Grants

Dillard University in New Orleans, Louisiana, was awarded $72,320 to support a foreign language learning center.
Amherst College in Amherst, Massachusetts, was awarded $121,000 to build and equip a lab and hire a full-time conservator.
Lehigh University in Bethlehem, Pennsylvania, was awarded $200,000 to support a multimedia language instruction project.
Columbia University in New York City received two grants: $225,000 toward a program for teaching professional medical ethics and $85,408 toward research on the pathophysiology of pulmonary hypertension.
Yale University in New Haven, Connecticut, received $75,000 toward preserving an exhibit on the history of cardiovascular surgery and creating a permanent exhibit area.
University of California in La Jolla; Stanford University in Stanford, California; and John Hopkins University in Baltimore, Maryland, each received $324,000 for their Medical Science Scholars programs.
Harvard University in Cambridge, Massachusetts; University of Michigan in Ann Arbor; and Vanderbilt University in Nashville, Tennessee, each received $97,200 for their Medical Humanities Scholars programs.

Comments/Analysis

The foundation's highest funding priority is education, which accounted for 57 percent of all grants distributed by the foundation in 1993. This figure includes graduate and professional education, which received 44 percent of all grants distributed by the foundation and libraries, which received 8 percent. Arts and culture are the foundation's second priority, receiving approximately 26 percent of all awards.

19

Nathan Cummings Foundation, Inc.
1926 Broadway, Suite 600
New York, NY   10023

Areas of Interest

Program Description: The foundation support projects that improve the environment on a global scale, multicultural arts and access to the arts, health-delivery systems for the poor, and relations between Jews and non-Jews.
Assistance Types: Annual campaigns, building funds, capital campaigns, consulting services, general purposes, special projects, seed money, operating budgets, conferences and seminars

Eligibility

Restrictions: Giving primarily in the United States.

Personnel

Officers: Robert N. Mayer, Chair; James K. Cummings, Vice-Chair; Ruth Cummings Sorensen, Vice-Chair; Charles R. Halpern, President and CEO; Diane Cummings, Secy.; Bevis Longstreth, Treas.
Trustees/Directors: Mark H. Cummings, Karyn Cummings, Michael Cummings, Reynold Levy, Beatrice Cummings Mayer
Staff: 10 full-time professional, seven full-time support, one part-time support

Financial Profile

Assets: In 1992, $274,179,917; 1993, $302,602,870
High Grant: In 1992, $200,000; 1993, $300,000
Low Grant: In 1992, $2,000; 1993, $1,000
Ave. Grant: $10,000-$75,000
Total Grants: In 1992, 304 grants totaling $10,995,009; 1993, 296 grants totaling $10,865,134
High Grant Higher Ed.: $92,000
Low Grant Higher Ed.: $10,000
Ave. Grant Higher Ed.: $15,000-$30,000
Total Grants Higher Ed.: In 1992, 32 grants totaling $1,483,226

Application Process

Contact: Charles Halpern, President, (212) 787-7300
Deadline: None
Board Meeting: Twice yearly
Processing Time: Not available
Publications: Grants list, application guidelines, annual report
Guidelines: The initial approach should be by letter. Application form is not required. One copy of the proposal should include a detailed description of project and amount requested, names and affiliations of board members and key people, organizational/project budget, history and mission of organization, IRS letter of determination, contact person, statement of problem project will address, timetable for implementation and evaluation, qualifications of key personnel, and listing of additional sources and amount of support.

Sample Grants

Arizona State University in Tempe received $10,000 in general operating support.
Hebrew Union College, Jewish Institute of Religion in Los Angeles was awarded $30,000 for consultation with leading experts on the restructuring of congregational schools.
Cleveland College of Jewish Studies in Beachwood, Ohio, received $30,000 toward a Jewish teacher training program conducted by the Cleveland College of Jewish Studies in Kiev.
Oberlin College in Oberlin, Ohio, was awarded $10,000 for a conference on rethinking the role of educational institutions in the transition process toward sustainability.
University of Louisville School of Medicine in Kentucky received $60,000 to develop a medical school curricula on mind/body techniques and to encourage professional careers in mind/body medicine.

Comments/Analysis

The foundation gives top priority to arts and culture, including visual, performing, and literary. Support focuses on arts education for at-risk youth, arts advocacy, and projects that assist arts institutions to be more accessible to the elderly, minorities, and persons with disabilities. The environment is the foundation's second priority, including support for projects in transportation, and a sustainable agriculture and economy. Health, the third priority, focuses on projects that promote health among underserved children and their families and the development of patient-centered approaches. In addition, the foundation is particularly interested in Jewish giving and Jewish welfare.

20

Charles A. Dana Foundation, Inc.
745 Fifth Avenue, Suite 700
New York, NY   10151

Areas of Interest

Program Description: The foundation is primarily interested in education and medicine. In education, it prefers to support precollegiate education and has a strong interest in mathematics and science education. In health, the foundation supports projects that focus on understanding the brain and treating related diseases. The foundation administers the Charles A. Dana Awards for Pioneering Achievements in Health and Education. These awards aim to call attention to innovative and effective ideas and to encourage dissemination. Applications for the Charles A. Dana Awards are by nomination only. The foundation also supports cultural and civic projects in New York City.
Assistance Types: Fellowships, general purpose, medical research

Eligibility

Restrictions: Grants require matching support from applicant organizations. No support for projects outside of the United States, professional organizations, for capital campaigns, continuing support, building or emergency funds, publications, conferences, or demonstration projects.

Personnel

Officers: David J. Mahoney, Chair; Stephen A. Foster, Exec. VP; Walter G. Corcoran, VP; Clark M. Whittemore Jr., Secy.-Treas.
Trustees/Directors: Edwards C. Andrews Jr., Wallace L. Cook, Charles A. Dana Jr., Donald B. Marron, Carlos D. Moseley, L. Guy Palmer II, William L. Safire
Staff: 10 full-time professional, five full-time support

Financial Profile

Assets: In 1992, $222,598,489; 1993, $238,648,541
High Grant: In 1992, $1,837,000; 1993, $5,167,080
Low Grant: In 1992, $2,000; 1993, $2,500
Ave. Grant: $50,000-$300,000
Total Grants: In 1992, 56 grants totaling $5,522,850; 1993, 113 grants totaling $11,807,847
High Grant Higher Ed.: $1,837,000
Ave. Grant Higher Ed.: $14,800-$300,000
Total Grants Higher Ed.: In 1992, 14 grants totaling $13,713,800

Application Process

Contact: Walter Donway, education; Stephen A. Foster, health; Cynthia Read, Dana Awards, (212) 223-4040
Deadline: None
Board Meeting: April, June, October, and December
Processing Time: Two to three months
Publications: Annual report, application guidelines, newsletters, informational brochure
Guidelines: The initial approach should be a letter of not more than two pages. Application form is not required. Applicants should submit a statement of problem the project will address, detailed description of project and amount requested, explanation of why the foundation is an appropriate donor, and qualifications of key personnel.

Sample Grants

Duke University in Durham, North Carolina, received $31,000 in support of a summer program and conference as part of the Preparing Minorities for Academic Careers Program.

Harvard University in Cambridge, Massachusetts, received $1,837,000 for medical research.

University of Texas at Austin received a four-year grant for $1,216,000 to support the Dana Center for Innovations in Mathematics and Science Education.

University of California at Berkeley was awarded $190,000 to create and disseminate math curriculum programs for middle and junior high schools.

New School of Social Research in New York City received $80,000 to complete the design and testing of a new teacher education program aimed at meeting the shortage of school teachers in New York.

Comments/Analysis

The foundation's top subject area of interest is medicine and medical research. The second area of foundation interest is education. Colleges, universities, and graduate schools are by far the largest recipients of funds. Libraries and public and research institutes also receive significant funds. Elementary and secondary education is also a strong interest. The majority of grants to higher education, outside of the area of medicine, support research or the creation of projects to serve K-12 education.

21
Danforth Foundation
231 S Bemiston Avenue, Suite 1080
Saint Louis, MO   63105-1996

Areas of Interest

Program Description: To enhance the humane dimensions of life by improving the quality of teaching and learning. The foundation supports early childhood education, precollegiate education, school and community partnerships, and administrators and legislators who formulate public policy on secondary public education. Other areas of interest include child development and minority education.
Assistance Types: Consulting services, technical assistance, special projects, fellowships

Eligibility

Restrictions: No grants to colleges and universities except for programs administered by the foundation, or for projects in elementary and secondary education.

Personnel

Officers: William H. Danforth, Chair; James R. Compton, Vice-Chair and Secy.; Bruce J. Anderson, President; Melvin C. Bahle, Treas.; Janet Levy, Prog. Director; Kathryn Nelson, Prog. Director; Peter Wilson, Prog. Director
Trustees/Directors: John H. Biggs, Virginia S. Brown, Donald C. Danforth Jr., Charles Geggenheim, George E. Pake, P. Roy Vagelos
Staff: Four full-time professional, three full-time support

Financial Profile

Assets: In 1993, $217,667,158
High Grant: $645,500
Low Grant: $190
Ave. Grant: $20,000-$105,000
Total Grants: 125 grants totaling $5,646,365

High Grant Higher Ed.: $105,000
Low Grant Higher Ed.: $15,000
Ave. Grant Higher Ed.: $25,000-$100,000
Total Grants Higher Ed.: In 1992, 29 grants totaling $2,352,682;
1993, 23 grants totaling $1,975,220

Application Process

Contact: Bruce J. Anderson, President, (314) 862-6200
Deadline: None
Board Meeting: May, November, and as required
Processing Time: Four weeks
Publications: Annual report, informational brochure, application
guidelines, financial statement, grants list
Guidelines: Application form is not needed. Proposals should
include an IRS letter of determination; qualifications of key personnel; budget; anticipated results; timetable; name, address, and
phone number of contact person; description of project and
amount requested; and how project will be measured or evaluated.

Sample Grants

Brown University in Providence, Rhode Island, was awarded
$48,000 for professional and support staff for the National
Faculty for the Coalition of Essential Schools.

City College of the City University of New York was awarded
$79,465 for model teacher education programs in secondary
school reform.

Vanderbilt University in Nashville, Tennessee, was awarded
$44,000 for a training and dissemination project, Problem-
Based Learning and School Leadership Development.

San Diego State University in California received $11,700 for an
administrator preparation program through partnership with
San Diego Unified School, San Diego County Office of Education, and various community agencies.

Comments/Analysis

Education, as a top foundation priority, received 53 percent of all
grants in 1993, with 41 percent of all grants to K-12 and 11 percent
to graduate and professional education. In respect to higher education, the foundation sponsors a Dorothy Danforth Compton
Minority Fellowship Program to support minority PhD candidates
preparing for careers in college and university teaching. In 1994,
these $105,000 fellowships were awarded to Brown University,
Columbia University, Howard University, Stanford University,
University of California at Los Angeles, University of Chicago,
University of Texas at Austin, University of Washington, Vanderbilt University, and Yale University.

22
Arthur Vining Davis Foundation
111 Riverside Avenue, Suite 130
Jacksonville, FL   32202-4921

Areas of Interest

Program Description: To support private higher education, hos-
pices, health care, public television, and graduate theological
education. Other areas of interest include medical sciences, media
and communications, film, and library acquisitions and improvement.
Assistance Types: Building funds, continuing support, endowment
funds, internships and fellowships, lectureships, publications, technical assistance, special projects, faculty development, curriculum
development

Eligibility

Restrictions: No grants to individuals or to colleges supported by
public funds; no loans; no support for projects incurring obligations
extending over many years; giving limited to the United States and
its possessions and territories

Personnel

Officers: Nathanial V. Davis, Chair
Trustees/Directors: Holbrook R. Davis, J.H. Dow Davis, Joel P.
Davis, Maynard K. Davis, Atwood Dunwoody, Davis Given,
Serena Davis Hall, John L. Kee Jr., William Kee, W.R. Wright
Staff: Four full-time professional, one part-time professional, three
full-time support

Financial Profile

Assets: In 1993, $145,716,418
High Grant: $375,000
Low Grant: $50,000
Ave. Grant: $75,000-$125,000
Total Grants: 74 grants totaling $5,757,112
High Grant Higher Ed.: $200,000
Low Grant Higher Ed.: $16,000
Ave. Grant Higher Ed.: $100,000-$125,000
Total Grants Higher Ed.: In 1992, 44 grants totaling $4,383,000;
1993, 40 grants totaling $4,353,000

Application Process

Contact: Max Morris, Exec. Director, (904) 359-0670
Deadline: None
Board Meeting: Spring, fall, winter
Processing Time: 10 to 15 months for approvals; eight months for
rejections
Publications: Annual report, including application guidelines, in-
formational brochure
Guidelines: The initial approach should be a letter. Application
forms are not required. Proposals should include a brief history of

the organization and description of its mission, detailed description of the project and amount of funding requested, copy of the previous year's organizational budget and/or project budget, and signature and title of chief executive officer.

Sample Grants

Bethune-Cookman College in Daytona Beach, Florida, received $125,000 for building construction.

Washington College in Chestertown, Maryland, was awarded $125,000 for junior faculty fellowships.

Coker College in Hartsville, South Carolina, received $100,000 for library acquisitions.

Johnson C. Smith University in Charlotte, North Carolina, received $100,000 for curriculum improvement.

Episcopal Theological Seminary of the Southwest in Austin, Texas, was awarded $120,000 for library automation.

Oklahoma Christian University in Oklahoma City received $100,000 for a residence hall computer network.

Comments/Analysis

The foundation is particularly interested in supporting institutions with outstanding records of teaching and learning in the liberal arts. The foundation will support projects that college presidents have placed at the top of their respective institution's priorities.

23
Ira W. DeCamp Foundation
c/o Mudge Rose Guthrie Alexander & Ferdon
630 Fifth Avenue, Suite 1650
New York, NY   10011

Areas of Interest

Program Description: To support health care facilities and equipment and medical research and education, including AIDS and alcoholism research.

Assistance Types: Building funds, equipment, seed money, research, special projects, capital campaigns, endowments, challenge grants, general support

Eligibility

Restrictions: No support for government affiliated institutions, land acquisition, publications, conferences, operating funds, emergency funds, deficit financing, continuing support or annual campaigns; no support for research on live animals except rats and mice; no grants to individuals

Personnel

Trustees/Directors: Herbert H. Faber, Chemical Bank
Staff: None

Financial Profile

Assets: In 1992, $62,654,618
High Grant: $300,000
Low Grant: $5,000
Ave. Grant: $25,000-$100,000
Total Grants: In 1993, 63 grants totaling $3,720,000

Application Process

Contact: Arthur Mahon, (212) 332-1613
Deadline: None
Board Meeting: Quarterly
Processing Time: Three months
Guidelines: Initial approach should be by letter. Application form is not required; proposals should include a description of project and amount requested, statement of problem the project will address, and anticipated results.

Sample Grants

Fairfield University in Fairfield, Connecticut, received $300,000 for a challenge grant for financial aid and scientific equipment.

Fordham University School of Law in New York City received two grants of $50,000 each for an endowment for the position of pro-bono coordinator.

Saint Michaels College in Winooski, Vermont, received $10,000 for its capital campaign.

Yale University School of Medicine in New Haven, Connecticut, received $100,000 for the construction of its Center for Molecular Medicine and for a medical informatics program.

Georgetown University in Washington, DC, received $25,000 for an endowment.

Marymount Manhattan College in New York City received $50,000 for a scholarship endowment fund.

Comments/Analysis

The top priority for the foundation is general and rehabilitative medicine, which received 43 percent of its funds. The second is education, which received 24 percent. This includes 17 percent of the foundation's total disbursements going to higher education and another 6 percent to graduate and professional education.

24
Joseph Drown Foundation
1999 Avenue of the Stars, No. 1930
Los Angeles, CA   90067

Areas of Interest

Program Description: To support health services and education including early childhood education, elementary education, and minority education.

Assistance Types: Scholarship funds, general purposes, matching funds, seed money, operating budgets, medical research, special projects, loans

Eligibility

Restrictions: Giving primarily in California; no support for religious purposes or for building funds, seminars or conferences

Personnel

Officers: Milton F. Fillius Jr., Chair; Norman Obrow, President; Wendy Wachtell Scine, VP and Program Director; Thomas Marshal, VP; Philip S. Margaram, Secy.-Treas.
Trustees/Directors: Harry C. Cogan, Benton C. Coit, Elaine Mahoney
Staff: Two full-time professional, one full-time support

Financial Profile

Assets: In 1993, $70,156,194
High Grant: $200,000
Low Grant: $5,000
Ave. Grant: $10,000-$25,000
Total Grants: 131 grants totaling $3,497,188

Application Process

Contact: Norman Obrow, President, (310) 277-4488
Deadline: January 15, April 15, July 15, and October 15
Board Meeting: Quarterly
Processing Time: Immediately after board meeting
Publications: Informational brochure, including application guidelines
Guidelines: Initial approach should be by letter with one copy of proposal. Formal application not required; proposals should include copy of IRS letter of determination, annual report and audited financial statement/990, current organization and/or project budget, names and affiliations of board and other key people, and detailed description of project and funding request.

Sample Grants

Pitzer College in Claremont, California, received $25,000 for an interest-free student loan fund.
Hamilton College in Clinton, New York, was awarded $100,000 for the Joseph Drown Loan Fund.
Cornell University School of Hotel Administration in Ithaca, New York, received $20,000 for the Joseph Drown Foundation Prize.
University of California School of Medicine in Los Angeles received $100,000 for the Frontiers of Medical Science Program at the Center for Health Sciences.
Sierra Nevada College in Incline Village, Nevada, received $30,000 for scholarships.
University of California College of Letters and Science in Los Angeles received $35,000 for an academic advancement program.

Comments/Analysis

The subject area of highest priority to the foundation is education. Forty-two percent of all grants awarded in 1993 went to education. The foundation provides various types of support to higher education including awards under the categories of the Joseph Drown Foundation Prize and the Joseph Drown Loan Fund. Medical research is also a priority and was awarded 10 percent of all grants. Colleges and universities are the foundation's top recipients of funds, followed by schools and hospitals.

25
Earhart Foundation
2200 Green Road, Suite H
Ann Arbor, MI   48105

Areas of Interest

Program Description: To support educational and research organizations and to grant research fellowships to faculty members for projects in economics, history, international affairs, and political science. H.B. Earhart Fellowships for graduate study are also awarded, but through a special nominating process only.
Assistance Types: Professorships, fellowships, research, publications, conferences and seminars, grants to individuals

Eligibility

Restrictions: No grants for capital, building, or endowment funds; operating or continuing support; seed money; emergency or deficit funding; or matching gifts; no loans

Personnel

Officers: Dennis L. Bark, Chair; William D. Laurie Jr., Vice-Chair; David B. Kennedy, President; Antony T. Sullivan, Secy. and Director of Progs.; Edward H. Sichler III, Treas.
Trustees/Directors: Thomas J. Bray, Earl I. Heenan, Willa Ann Johnson, Paul W. McCracken, Robert L. Queller, Richard A. Ware
Staff: Two full-time professional, two full-time support

Financial Profile

Assets: In 1992, $56,275,594; 1993, $58,512,299
High Grant: $50,000
Low Grant: $1,000
Ave. Grant: $1,000-$30,000
Total Grants: In 1992, 120 grants totaling $1,194,116; 1993, $127 grants totaling $1,270,077
High Grant Higher Ed.: $59,000
Low Grant Higher Ed.: $1,000
Ave. Grant Higher Ed.: $5,000-$20,000
Total Grants Higher Ed.: In 1992, 26 grants totaling $422,708

Application Process

Contact: David B. Kennedy, President, (313) 761-8592
Deadline: None
Board Meeting: Monthly, with the exception of August
Processing Time: Minimum 120 days
Publications: Annual report, including application guidelines
Guidelines: The initial approach should be by letter. An application form is not required. Proposals should include a brief history and mission of organization, IRS letter of determination, annual report/audited financial statement/990, listing of other sources of support and amounts, detailed description of project and amount of funding requested, organization/ project budget, timetable for implementation and evaluation of project, how project's results will be measured or evaluated, and how project will be sustained after foundation support is completed.

Sample Grants

George Mason University in Fairfax, Virginia, was awarded two grants totaling $42,500, including $30,000 for the general support of an international institute and $12,500 for the preparation of a book.

The University of Chicago in Illinois received four grants totaling $59,000 for social science projects including a post-doctoral fellowship, a conference, and the preparation of books and articles.

University of Virginia Law School Foundation in Charlottesville received $16,600 for fellowships for graduate students and/or visiting scholars from Eastern Europe.

New York University Department of Economics in New York City received $12,600 for the general support of an Austrian economics colloquium.

Yale University in New Haven, Connecticut, received $15,000 for a research and documentation project on Cambodian genocide.

Comments/Analysis

The foundation's top area of support is the social sciences, followed by education. Colleges and universities are recipients of the most grant dollars and the largest number of awards. Public policy institutes are second, followed by social science organizations. Grants to individuals are the largest support type, followed by program support, which includes publications, conferences, faculty/staff development, and program development.

26
Educational Foundation of America
35 Church Lane
Westport, CT   06880-3589

Areas of Interest

Program Description: To support the arts; education; energy and the environment; reproductive health and rights; family planning;

and programs benefiting Native Americans, children and youth, and women and girls.
Assistance Types: Seed money, matching funds, special projects

Eligibility

Restrictions: No grants to individuals, or for capital or endowment funds, no loans; giving in the United States only

Personnel

Officers: Lynn P. Babicka, President; Diane M. Allison, Exec. Director
Trustees/Directors: Sharon Ettinger, Richard P. Ettinger Jr., Wendy P. Ettinger, Elaine P. Hapgood, Heidi Landesman, David Orr, John P. Powers, W. Richard West
Staff: Two full-time professional, two part-time professional, one full-time support

Financial Profile

Assets: In 1993, $141,334,884
High Grant: $200,000
Low Grant: $3,600
Ave. Grant: $10,000-$150,000
Total Grants: In 1993, 100 grants totaling $5,719,828
High Grant Higher Ed.: $350,000
Low Grant Higher Ed.: $10,000
Ave. Grant Higher Ed.: $10,000-$50,000
Total Grants Higher Ed.: In 1992, 15 grants totaling $1,008,231; 1993, higher education received $662,379

Application Process

Contact: Diane M. Allison, Exec. Director, (203) 226-6498
Deadline: None
Board Meeting: Varies
Processing Time: Six to nine months
Publications: Annual report, application guidelines
Guidelines: Initial approach should be by letter of inquiry. An application form is not required. The foundation will notify applicant about whether a full proposal should be submitted. If invited to apply, submit six copies of the proposal and include a brief history of organization and description of mission, descriptive literature about the organization, signature and title of chief executive officer, anticipated results, timetable for implementation and evaluation, detailed description of project and amount of funding requested, and copy of IRS letter of determination.

Sample Grants

The University of Massachusetts at Boston was awarded $159,460 for a two-year grant for a project entitled Public School Science Education: A Rainforest Collaboration.

The University of New Mexico at Albuquerque School of Medicine was awarded $98,535 for a two-year grant supporting a position on the adolescent medicine faculty.

Norfolk Community College Foundation in Norwalk, Connecticut, was awarded $29,000 to develop strategies for educating a multicultural population.

Harvard University in Cambridge, Massachusetts, received a $171,171, two-year grant to support Native American leadership.

Comments/Analysis

The foundation's top area of interest is environmental protection, followed by education. Colleges and universities are the foundation's top recipients of funds, followed by environmental agencies and schools. Program support is the most frequent type of giving, including program development, publications, media projects, conferences, and curriculum development. General support is the second most frequent type of giving, followed by student aid funds.

27
Lettie Pate Evans Foundation, Inc.
50 Hurt Plaza, Suite 1200
Atlanta, GA   30303

Areas of Interest

Program Description: To support higher education, education associations, social services, and arts and culture.
Assistance Types: Building and renovation, equipment, endowments, land acquisition, seed money, capital campaigns

Eligibility

Restrictions: Giving primarily in Atlanta; no support for individuals, operating expenses, research, scholarships, fellowships, or matching gifts; no loans

Personnel

Officers: J.W. Jones, Chair; Hughes Spalding Jr., Vice-Chair; Charles H. McTier, President; P. Russell Hardin, Secy.-Treas.
Trustees/Directors: Roberto C. Goizueta, James M. Sibley, James B. Williams
Staff: Nine staff shared with the Joseph B. Whitehead Foundation

Financial Profile

Assets: In 1992, $152,035,932; 1993, $156,970,024
High Grant: $1,500,000
Low Grant: $15,000
Ave. Grant: $50,000-$250,000
Total Grants: In 1992, 30 grants totaling $5,995,000; 1993 total $7,195,000
High Grant Higher Ed.: $700,000
Low Grant Higher Ed.: $100,000
Ave. Grant Higher Ed.: $100,000-$250,000
Total Grants Higher Ed.: In 1992, 12 grants totaling $3,350,000

Application Process

Contact: Charles H. McTier, President, (404) 522-6755
Deadline: February 1, September 1
Board Meeting: April and November
Processing Time: 30 days after board meeting
Publications: Application guidelines
Guidelines: Initial approach should be made by letter of inquiry followed by proposal. An application form is not required.

Sample Grants

Mercer University in Macon, Georgia, received $500,000 to establish the Ferrol A. Sams Endowed Chair of English.

University of Georgia Foundation in Atlanta received $100,000 for the restoration of the Seney-Stovall Chapel at the Old Lucy Cobb Institute.

Berry College in Mount Berry, Georgia, received $700,000 for the endowment for the Bonner Scholarship Program, computer system enhancements, and the installation of an elevator in Evans Hall.

Oglethorpe University in Atlanta, Georgia, received $100,000 for the endowment of the Charles L. Weltner Sr. Scholarship Fund to benefit African American students from Georgia.

Comments/Analysis

The foundation prefers to fund one-time capital projects of established organizations.

28
Sherman Fairchild Foundation, Inc.
71 Arch Street
Greenwich, CT   06830

Areas of Interest

Program Description: To support higher education, fine arts and cultural institutions, medical research, and social welfare.
Assistance Types: Fellowships, student aid, equipment, medical research

Personnel

Officers: Walter Burke, President; Bonnie Himmelman, Exec. VP; Patricia A. Lydon, VP
Trustees/Directors: Walter Burke III, William Elfers, Robert P. Henderson, Michele Myers, Paul D. Paganucci, Agnar Pytte, James Wright
Staff: One full-time support, one part-time support

Financial Profile

Assets: In 1992, $225,259,036; 1993, $247,816,427
High Grant: In 1992, $1,750,000; 1993, $1,000,000
Low Grant: $10,000

Ave. Grant: $50,000-$500,000
Total Grants: In 1992, 48 grants totaling $11,122,542; 1993, 60 grants totaling $9,737,600
Ave. Grant Higher Ed.: $100,000-$500,000
Total Grants Higher Ed.: In 1992, 18 grants totaling $9,353,670

Application Process

Contact: Patricia A. Lydon, VP, (203) 661-9360
Deadline: None
Guidelines: Initial approach should be made by a proposal describing the project and the amount of funding requested.

Sample Grants

The University of California at San Francisco was awarded $1,350,000 for research into degenerative diseases.

California Institute of Technology in Pasadena received two grants totaling $914,000: $864,000 for postdoctoral fellowships and $50,000 for the design of the Engineering Center.

Earlham College in Richmond, Indiana, was granted $350,000 for scientific equipment.

Case Western Reserve University in Cleveland, Ohio, received $364,515 for the Bachelor of Science in Nursing Bolton Scholars Program.

University of Minnesota Law School in Minneapolis received $20,000 for its minority student fund.

Columbia University in New York City was awarded $500,000 for college core curriculum.

Northeastern University in Boston, Massachusetts, received $280,000 for the support of minority engineering students.

Comments/Analysis

Education, a high priority for the foundation, received 50 percent of all grants made in 1993. This includes grants to libraries, which accounted for 30 percent of all funds distributed by the foundation, and awards to graduate or professional programs which accounted for 18 percent. The foundation's second priority was science, with 37 percent of all grants awarded, and the third, medical research, which received 10 percent of all grants awarded by the foundation.

29
Ford Foundation
320 E 43rd Street
New York, NY   10017

Areas of Interest

Program Description: To advance the public well-being by identifying and contributing to the solution of problems of national and international importance. Giving is in the United States as well as Europe, Africa, the Middle East, Asia, and Latin America. Grants to institutions are primarily aimed at experimental, demonstration, and development efforts that are likely to produce significant advances in the fields of urban poverty, rural poverty and resources, rights and social justice, governance and public policy, education and culture, international affairs, and reproductive health and population. Other areas of interest include community development, welfare, youth, environment, agriculture, minorities, women, immigration, legal services, government, public policy, secondary and higher education, arts and culture, museums, music, foreign policy, Eastern Europe, and AIDS.

Assistance Types: Conferences and seminars, consulting services, exchange programs, general purposes, matching funds, professorships, program-related investments, publications, research, seed money, special projects, technical assistance, continuing support, endowment funds, fellowships, and grants to individuals

Eligibility

Restrictions: No support for projects for which substantial government support is available; no grants for routine operating costs, undergraduate scholarships, local needs, religious sectarian activities, construction, or building maintenance

Personnel

Officers: Henry B. Schacht, Chair; Franklin A. Thomas, President; Barron M. Tenny, VP, General Counsel, and Secy.; Linda B. Stumpf, VP and Chief Investment Officer; Susan V. Berresford, VP; Barry D. Gaberman, Deputy VP; Nicholas Gabriell, Deputy VP

Staff: 246 full-time professional staff, one part-time professional, 335 full-time support, eight part-time support

Financial Profile

Assets: In 1992, $6,470,502,994
High Grant: $5,300,000
Low Grant: $600
Ave. Grant: $15,000-$1,500,000
Total Grants: In 1992, 1,482 grants totaling $259,966,848
High Grant Higher Ed.: $1,500,000
Low Grant Higher Ed.: $16,000
Ave. Grant Higher Ed.: $25,000-$200,000
Total Grants Higher Ed.: In 1992, 418 grants totaling $83,072,419; 1993, 447 grants totaling $79,549,884

Application Process

Contact: Barron M. Tenny, Secy., (212) 573-5000
Deadline: None
Board Meeting: December, March, June, and September
Processing Time: Initial notice about whether program falls within program interests, within one month
Publications: Annual report, newsletter, program policy statement, application guidelines, occasional report
Guidelines: The initial approach may be by telephone, letter, or proposal. Proposals should include the following: statement of problem the project will address, anticipated results, detailed description of project and amount requested, qualifications of key personnel, copy of current organizational and/or project budget, principal past support for project, list of additional sources of support, and amount requested.

Sample Grants

Bemidji State University in Bemidji, Minnesota, received $236,000 to improve race relations and address diversity issues at residential colleges and universities.

Cornell University in Ithaca, New York, received $366,000 for minority undergraduate summer research fellowships at Cornell, Princeton, Stanford, University of California Berkeley, UCLA, and Yale.

Evergreen State College in Olympia, Washington, was awarded $280,000 for efforts to mainstream research on women in liberal arts courses at community and tribally controlled colleges.

University of Zimbabwe in Harare, Zimbabwe, received $16,600 for a study on the university's staff development program and staff retention problems.

University of Massachusetts Foundation in Boston received $70,000 for an ethnographic study of urban community colleges that are successful in working with underprepared transfer students.

National Law School of India University in India received $500,000 for institutional support of innovative legal education and community outreach on human rights issues.

China College for Women Administrators received $74,000 for staff training and training workshops.

Birzeit University in Jordan received $175,000 for community outreach and development programs.

Comments/Analysis

In the past, 35 percent of all grants distributed by the foundation were awarded to education. Higher education received 21 percent of the foundation's grants, elementary and secondary received 11 percent, other education received 3 percent, and 1 percent went to education in the form of small grants of less than $10,000. The top area of interest for the foundation is education, the second is arts and culture, and the third is medicine. The foundation's top recipients include museums and historical societies, followed by educational organizations and institutions and government agencies.

30
Francis Families Foundation
800 W 47th Street, Suite 604
Kansas City, MO   64112

Areas of Interest

Program Description: To support medical fellowships in pulmonary medicine and anesthesiology, and to support education, higher education, and the performing arts in the greater Kansas City area.

Assistance Types: Fellowships, capital campaigns, special projects, continuing support, medical research, general support

Eligibility

Restrictions: Giving is limited to the United States for fellowship support and to the local area for support of educational and cultural institutions

Personnel

Officers: John B. Francis, President; Mary Harris Francis, VP; Linda K. French, Secy.-Treas.

Trustees/Directors: Mary Shaw Branton, Charles Curran, David V. Francis, Robert J. Reintjes, James P. Sunderland, Robert West

Staff: Two part-time support

Financial Profile

Assets: In 1993, $67,935,465
High Grant: $524,242
Low Grant: $350
Ave. Grant: $20,000-$100,000
Total Grants: 100 grants totaling $2,964,347
High Grant Higher Ed.: $225,000
Low Grant Higher Ed.: $15,000
Ave. Grant Higher Ed.: $20,000-$50,000
Total Grants Higher Ed.: In 1992, 44 grants totaling $1,568,865; 1993, 38 grants totaling $1,238,615

Application Process

Contact: Linda K. French, Secy.-Treas., (816) 531-0077. Applications should be sent to Dr. Donald F. Tierney, Director of Fellowship Programs, Department of Medicine, UCLA, Los Angeles, California 90024-1690, (213) 825-5316

Deadline: October 1 for grants; October 11 for fellowships
Board Meeting: May and January
Processing Time: Notification is made in December
Publications: Annual report, informational brochure
Guidelines: An application form is required for the fellowship program. Institutions will need to describe the resident activities and opportunities and summarize accomplishments.

Sample Grants

Louisiana State University Section of Pulmonary and Critical Care in New Orleans received $32,000 to support fellowship in the field of pulmonary medicine.

The University of Maryland at Baltimore Division of Pulmonary and Critical Care received $32,000 to support fellowships in the field of pulmonary medicine.

The University of California at San Francisco received $34,000 for anesthesiology investigatorships.

Avila College in Kansas City, Missouri, received $20,000 for general support.

Donnelly College in Kansas City, Kansas, received $20,000 for general support.

University of Missouri School of Education in Kansas City was awarded $40,000 for general support.

Comments/Analysis

Medical research is the top priority for the foundation's national work, with 56 percent of its grants going for that purpose in 1993. The vast majority of its medical research grants are for $34,000 and support medical fellowships in pulmonary medicine at schools of medicine throughout the United States.

31

Charles A. Frueauff Foundation, Inc.
307 E Seventh Avenue
Tallahassee, FL   32303

Areas of Interest

Program Description: To support health and mental health, welfare, including services to children, the indigent and disabled, and higher education.
Assistance Types: Operating budgets, annual and capital campaigns, building funds, equipment, emergency funds, endowments and scholarship funds, matching funds

Eligibility

Restrictions: No grants for research; no loans; support for projects in the United States only.

Personnel

Officers: A.C. McCully, President; Charles T. Klein, VP; David A. Frueauff, Secy.
Trustees/Directors: James P. Fallon, Karl P. Fanning, Margaret Perry Fanning, Sue M. Frueauff
Staff: One full-time support, three part-time support

Financial Profile

Assets: In 1992, $75,061,481; 1993, $77,802,284
High Grant: In 1992, $100,000; 1993, $50,000
Low Grant: In 1992, $1,000; 1993, $4,000
Ave. Grant: $10,000-$50,000
Total Grants: In 1992, 145 grants totaling $3,733,500; 1993, 144 grants totaling $3,874,500
High Grant Higher Ed.: $50,000
Low Grant Higher Ed.: $1,000
Ave. Grant Higher Ed.: $25,000-$50,000
Total Grants Higher Ed.: In 1992, 47 grants totaling $1,490,000

Application Process

Contact: David A. Frueauff, Secy., (904) 561-3508
Deadline: March 15; proposals should be submitted between September and March.
Board Meeting: May
Processing Time: After annual meeting
Publications: Program policy statement, annual report

Guidelines: The initial inquiry may be by telephone or letter, or applicants can request an interview. The foundation does not acknowledge receipt of materials. Applicants may submit a proposal, which should include IRS letter of determination, annual report, and statement of problem.

Sample Grants

Moravian College in Bethlehem, Pennsylvania, received $25,000 for its financial aid program.
Westminster College in Salt Lake City, Utah, received $50,000 for its annual campaign fund.
Arkansas College in Batesville received $25,000 for a scholarship endowment.
Oglethorpe University in Atlanta, Georgia, was granted $35,000 for construction and renovation of its library.
Alice Lloyd College in Pippa Passes, Kentucky, received $30,000 for a work-study program.
Stetson University in DeLand, Florida, received $25,000 for equipment.
Saint Andrews Presbyterian College in Laurinburg, North Carolina, received $35,000 for its program for the physically disabled.

Comments/Analysis

Education is the foundation's major area of interest, and historically, has approximated 43 percent of all grants distributed, with 27 percent going to higher education and 8 percent going to graduate and professional education. Colleges and universities are the foundation's top recipients of funds. Human services is the foundation's second greatest area of interest with human services agencies receiving the second largest amount of funds. Capital support is the type of support most often given by the foundation, followed by program support and student aid.

32

Helene Fuld Health Trust
c/o Townley & Updike
405 Lexington Avenue
New York, NY   10174

Areas of Interest

Program Description: To support nursing education at state-accredited nursing schools affiliated with accredited hospitals. The foundation is interested in integrating interactive computer technology into the teaching of nurses, establishing a national database for students, and starting a new nursing doctorate degree. The foundation is also interested in projects that analyze major health care issues and their effect on the educational needs of student nurses.
Assistance Types: Equipment, publications, special projects

Eligibility

Restrictions: No support for matching funds, endowment funds, operating expenses or general purposes; no loans; no grants to individuals

Personnel

Officers: Marine Midland Bank, N.A.
Staff: One full-time professional, five part-time professionals

Financial Profile

Assets: In 1992, $86,541,253
High Grant: $1,407,900
Low Grant: $5,030
Ave. Grant: $10,000-$100,000
Total Grants: 144 grants totaling $6,496,078
High Grant Higher Ed.: $100,000
Low Grant Higher Ed.: $10,000
Ave. Grant Higher Ed.: $15,000-$30,000
Total Grants Higher Ed.: 124 grants totaling $3,626,096

Application Process

Contact: Robert C. Miller, Counsel, or Arlene J. Kennare, Grants Office Administrator, (212) 973-6859
Deadline: October 31
Board Meeting: March, June, September, and December
Processing Time: Eight months
Publications: Annual report, including application guidelines, grants list, financial statement
Guidelines: Application form is required. The initial approach should be by a written request for an application form; telephone and facsimile requests will not be filled. The application form is revised annually and available in August.

Sample Grants

Bellin College of Nursing in Green Bay, Wisconsin, received $25,000 for interactive video and computer equipment.

Frederick Community College in Frederick, Maryland, was granted $21,134 for interactive video and computer-assisted instruction equipment for nursing education.

Comments/Analysis

Applicants must operate an accredited nursing school or nursing education program, and have graduated at least three classes of nursing students. Historically, education has received 98 percent of the grants awarded by the foundation, including 96 percent for graduate and professional training.

33
Joyce Mertz-Gilmore Foundation
218 E 18th Street
New York, NY   10003

Areas of Interest

Program Description: To support concerns in human rights; the environment; world security issues; and cultural, social, and civic concerns in New York City. Other areas of interest include international affairs and law, AIDS, community improvement and development, and crime.
Assistance Types: Operating budgets, general purposes, special projects, technical assistance, continuing support, seed money, and program-related investments

Eligibility

Restrictions: No grants for capital or endowment funds, building construction or maintenance, annual campaigns, conferences, travel, publications, film or television production, scholarships, fellowships or matching gifts; no loans

Personnel

Officers: Larry E. Condon, President; Elizabeth Burke-Gilmore, Secy.; Charles Bloomstein, Treas.
Trustees/Directors: Harlan Cleveland, Hal Harvey, C. Virgil Martin, Patricia Ramsay, Denise Nix Thompson, Franklin W. Wallin
Staff: Eight full-time professional, two part-time professional, six full-time support, two part-time support

Financial Profile

Assets: In 1992, $63,120,387; 1993, $66,684,992
High Grant: $300,000
Low Grant: $500
Ave. Grant: $5,000-$125,000
Total Grants: In 1992, 529 grants totaling $8,327,470; 1993, 526 grants totaling $10,907,926
High Grant Higher Ed.: $50,000
Low Grant Higher Ed.: $10,000
Ave. Grant Higher Ed.: $10,000-$50,000
Total Grants Higher Ed.: In 1992, 13 grants totaling $335,000

Application Process

Contact: Robert Crane, VP, Programs, or Penny Fujiko Willgerodt, Program Officer, (212) 475-1137
Deadline: None
Board Meeting: April and November
Processing Time: Three weeks after meeting
Publications: Biennial report, application guidelines, informational brochure, grants list
Guidelines: The initial approach should be a two-page letter of inquiry. If the foundation judges the project to be within its guidelines, an application form will be sent to the applicant.

Applicants should submit the following: statement of problem project will address, copy of most recent annual report/audited financial statement/990, copy of current year's organizational budget and/or project budget, copy of IRS letter of determination, names and affiliations of board and other key people, and additional materials/documentation.

Sample Grants

Pace University in New York City was awarded $30,000 to support a project on energy policies at its School of Law.

The Monterey Institute of International Studies in California was granted $20,000 to establish a database on environmental developments in the former Soviet Union.

Hunter College of the City University of New York received $15,000 for Latin American and Caribbean Studies Program internships for students of color, immigrants, and low-income students. Interns work for one year with human rights organizations focusing on Latin America and the Caribbean.

New York University Center for War, Peace, and the News Media in New York City received $20,000 to establish the Moscow Press and Information Center to help the journalist community in the former Soviet Union play its role as an indispensable component of democracy.

Columbia University Institute for Not-For-Profit Management in New York City received $10,000 for scholarships for executives of community groups to study general management disciplines and create strategic plans for their agencies.

Comments/Analysis

The foundation's top area of interest is environmental protection. Energy efficiency, and efforts to change public policy to promote energy efficiency, are important to the foundation. Projects to protect natural resources receive approximately one-fourth of all grants distributed by the foundation. Human rights is a strong area of interest for the foundation, including international law and efforts to maintain a free flow of information between countries. Domestic human rights, including protection of the rights of immigrants and gay men and lesbians is also an interest.

34
Florence Gould Foundation
c/o Cahill, Gordon and Reindel
80 Pine Street
New York, NY   10005

Areas of Interest

Program Description: To promote understanding and goodwill between France and the United States, to support the arts in the United States and France, and to support higher education and museums in the United States.

Eligibility

Restrictions: Giving primarily in the United States and France

Personnel

Officers: John R. Young, President; William E. Hegarty, VP and Secy.; Daniel Davison, VP and Treas.; Daniel Wildenstein, VP
Trustees/Directors: Walter C. Cliff
Staff: None

Financial Profile

Assets: In 1992, $76,440,522
High Grant: $1,614,052
Low Grant: $1,500
Ave. Grant: $5,000-$100,000
High Grant Higher Ed.: $100,000
Low Grant Higher Ed.: $15,000
Ave. Grant Higher Ed.: $5,000-$100,000
Total Grants Higher Ed.: In 1992, 18 grants totaling $691,722

Application Process

Contact: John R. Young, President, (212) 701-3400
Deadline: None
Board Meeting: As necessary
Processing Time: Varies
Publications: None
Guidelines: Application form is not required.

Sample Grants

Bryn Mawr College in Bryn Mawr, Pennsylvania, was awarded $50,000.

The American University in Paris, France, received $100,000.

Rice University in Houston, Texas, received $22,060.

Wayne State University in Detroit, Michigan, received $10,000.

University of California in Los Angeles received $18,790.

Massachusetts Institute of Technology in Cambridge received $54,598 for an Athena Language Learning Project.

City University of New York in New York City received $25,000 for CUNY-TV.

Comments/Analysis

The foundation's top area of interest is arts and culture, followed by education and general and rehabilitative medicine. In the past, 13 percent of the funds distributed by the foundation went to higher education. The top recipients of funds are museums and historical societies, followed by colleges and universities and the arts and humanities.

35
William T. Grant Foundation
515 Madison Avenue, 6th Floor
New York, NY   10022-5403

Areas of Interest

Program Description: To support research in any medical or social-behavioral scientific discipline and the development of school-age children, adolescents, and youth. Particular focus is on interdisciplinary research using multiple methods to research several problems simultaneously. The foundation is interested in public policy, race relations, delinquency prevention, and education for minorities. Support is given in four forms: research grants, evaluations of innovative community-based inventions, Faculty Scholars Program for junior investigators, and a limited number of small one-time grants for community service projects for children in the New York City metropolitan area.
Assistance Types: Special projects, research

Eligibility

Restrictions: Limited to the metropolitan New York City area for community service grants. No grants to individuals, except for the Faculty Scholars Program, or for annual fundraising campaigns, equipment and materials, land acquisition, or building or renovation projects. Application to Faculty Scholars Program by nomination only.

Personnel

Officers: Robert P. Patterson Jr., Chair; Dr. Beatrix A. Hamburg, President; Lonnie R. Sherrod, VP for Prog.; Mary Goodley-Thomas, VP for Finance and Administration; William H. Chisholm, Treas.; Eileen Dorannm, Controller
Trustees/Directors: Ellis T. Gravette Jr., Martha L. Minow, Richard Price, Henry W. Riecken, Kenneth S. Rolland, Rivington R. Winant
Staff: Five full-time professional, 10 part-time support

Financial Profile

Assets: In 1992, $180,574,410; 1993, $187,000,000
Total Grants: In 1992, 335 grants totaling $5,561,318; 1993, $6,000,000
High Grant Higher Ed.: $200,000
Low Grant Higher Ed.: $10,000
Ave. Grant Higher Ed.: $25,000-$100,000
Total Grants Higher Ed.: In 1992, 33 grants totaling $4,228,963

Application Process

Contact: Dr. Beatrix A. Hamburg, President, (212) 752-0071
Deadline: July 1st for Faculty Scholars Program nominations, no set deadline for grants

Board Meeting: February, June, October, and December
Processing Time: Immediately following board meeting; March for Faculty Scholars Program
Publications: Annual report, informational brochure, application guidelines, newsletter
Guidelines: Grant applicants should initially submit a letter. Proposals should include the following: description of the problem to be addressed by the project and amount requested, qualifications of key personnel, how project will be measured or evaluated, description of what distinguishes the proposed project from others in the field, annual report and financial report, and IRS letter of determination.

Sample Grants

Smith College in Northampton, Massachusetts, received $10,000 for a study on the effects of movement and music on learning.
University of Vermont in Burlington received $59,925 for Depression in Childhood and Adolescence, a consortium that meets twice yearly.
The University of California in Irvine received $119,808 for a study on unemployment and self-esteem in the school-to-work transition.
University of Colorado in Boulder received $352,637 for study on transition to adulthood.
University of Rochester in Rochester, New York, received $394,609 for a program entitled Transforming Educational Communities To Meet the Needs of Youth: A Model for Linking Research and Educational Reform.

Comments/Analysis

Colleges and universities are the foundation's top recipients for grant funds, followed by hospitals and medical research institutions. The foundation's top funding interest includes projects in the social sciences, followed by medical research.

36
Harry Frank Guggenheim Foundation
527 Madison Avenue, 15th Floor
New York, NY   10022-4304

Areas of Interest

Program Description: To support research projects aimed at providing a better understanding of violence, aggression, and dominance. Areas of interest include anthropology, biological sciences, history, political science, psychology, archaeology, social sciences, delinquency, crime and law enforcement, law and justice, intercultural relations, government, public policy, urban affairs, international affairs, and higher education.
Assistance Types: Research, seed money, grants to individuals, fellowships, employee matching gifts

Eligibility

Restrictions: No grants for capital or endowment funds, matching gifts or loans, indirect costs, travel, or conferences

Personnel

Officers: Peter O. Lawson-Johnston, Chair; James M. Hester, President; Mary-Alice Yates, Secy.; Joseph A. Koenigsberger, Treas.; Karen Colvard, Senior Prog. Officer

Trustees/Directors: William O. Baker, Josiah Bunting III, Peyton Cochran Jr., James B. Edwards, George J. Fountaine, Donald R. Griffin, Carol Langstaff, Peter Lawson-Johnston II, Theodore D. Lockwood, Alan Pifer, Floyd Ratliff, Lois Dickerson Rice, Rudy L. Ruggles Jr., Roger W. Strauss Jr., Joan G. Van de Maele, William C. Westmoreland

Staff: Five full-time professional, one part-time professional

Financial Profile

Assets: In 1992, $49,242,002
High Grant: $100,000
Low Grant: $100
Ave. Grant: $10,000-$50,000
Total Grants: 37 grants totaling $793,210, and 27 grants to individuals totaling $556,425
High Grant Higher Ed.: $34,975
Low Grant Higher Ed.: $10,000
Ave. Grant Higher Ed.: $10,000-$20,000
Total Grants Higher Ed.: 15 grants totaling $407,173

Application Process

Contact: Karen Colvard, Senior Program Officer or Joel Wallman, Program Officer, (212) 644-4907
Deadline: February 1 for PhD support; August 1 and February 1 for research grants
Board Meeting: June and December
Processing Time: Three days after meeting
Publications: Biennial report, application guidelines
Guidelines: The initial approach should be by proposal and include a curriculum vitae of the researcher.

Sample Grants

The University of Virginia at Charlottesville was awarded $63,778 for two studies: Assessment of Instrumental and Reactive Aggression in Violent Criminal Defendants; and Mothers Aggression before Marriage and Children's Aggression after Divorce.

The University of Illinois in Chicago was awarded $30,386 for a study entitled Punishing the Conscionable: Democracy, Dissent, and Tolerance.

The University of New Mexico at Albuquerque was awarded $34,523 for a study entitled Race and Violent Crime in Postwar America, 1946-1990.

Comments/Analysis

The foundation has a special program that awards fellowships for dissertation writing. In addition, grants are awarded for postdoctoral research. Colleges and universities are the top recipients of funds and are awarded the greatest number of grants by the foundation. The second most favored recipient type are museums and historical societies, followed by science organizations. The subject area receiving the greatest amount of support is the social sciences. The top support type is research, followed by grants to individuals.

37
George Gund Foundation
45 Prospect Avenue W
1845 Guildhall Bldg
Cleveland, OH   44115

Areas of Interest

Program Description: Assistance to education research and projects, with emphasis on new concepts and methods of teaching and learning in elementary, secondary, and higher education; opportunities for the disadvantaged; projects supporting employment, neighborhood development, improvement of human services, housing for minority and low-income groups, ecology, civics, and the arts. Other areas of interest include women, youth, AIDS, conservation, child welfare, crime and law enforcement, urban development, race relations, and urban affairs.

Assistance Types: Operating budgets, continuing support, seed money, emergency funds, land acquisition, matching funds, internships, scholarship funds, special projects, publications, conferences and seminars, program-related investments, exchange programs, research

Eligibility

Restrictions: Generally no grants to individuals, building or endowment funds, equipment, or renovation projects. Giving primarily to northeastern Ohio organizations and universities.

Personnel

Trustees/Directors: Frederick K. Cox, Geoffrey Gund, Ann L. Gund, David Bergholz, Kathleen L. Barber, George Gund III, Llura A. Gund
Staff: Five full-time professional, five full-time support

Financial Profile

Assets: In 1992, $505,847,312; in 1993, $407,483,893
High Grant: $250,000
Low Grant: $10,000
Ave. Grant: $10,000-$100,000

Total Grants: In 1992, $18,363,850 was awarded for grants and $975,000 for four program-related investments; 1993, 154 grants totaling $22,144,958
Ave. Grant Higher Ed.: $20,000-$100,000
Total Grants Higher Ed.: 34 grants totaling $1,735,477

Application Process

Contact: David Bergholz, Exec. Director, (216) 241-3114
Deadline: Send one copy of proposal by January 15, March 30, June 30, and September 30
Board Meeting: March, June, September, and December
Processing Time: Eight weeks
Publications: Annual report, including application guide
Guidelines: A proposal should be submitted, an application form is not required. Proposals should include a description of the project and amount requested, history and mission of organization, organization or project budget, IRS letter of determination, annual and financial report, additional sources of funding and amounts expected, qualifications of key personnel, how project will be measured or evaluated, timetable, and names and affiliations of board members.

Sample Grants

The Cleveland State University Development Foundation in Ohio was awarded two grants: a $214,583, three-year grant for support services for minority students and a $45,000 grant to recruit administrators.
Kenyon College in Gambier, Ohio, received $100,000 for a presidential discretionary fund.
Mount Union College in Alliance, Ohio, was awarded a $193,391, three-year grant for a minority retention and multicultural sensitivity program.
Lorain County Community College Foundation in Elyria, Ohio, received a $150,000, three-year grant for financial assistance for minority and nontraditional students.

Comments/Analysis

The foundation's top area of interest is education, the second is other projects, and the third is environmental issues. The top recipients of funds are colleges and universities.

38
Hearst Foundation, Inc.
888 Seventh Avenue, 45th Floor
New York, NY   10106-0057

Areas of Interest

Program Description: To support programs to aid poverty-level and minority groups, higher education and private secondary education, health delivery systems, and culture. Other areas of interest include nursing education and minority education.

Assistance Types: Special projects, scholarship funds, endowment funds, general purposes, operating budgets, research

Eligibility

Restrictions: Giving limited to the United States and its possessions. No support for political purposes. No grants to individuals or private foundations or for the purchase of tickets, tables, or advertising for fundraising events. Organizations serving larger geographic areas are generally favored over those serving community areas.

Personnel

Officers: George R. Hearst Jr., President; Harvey L. Lipton, VP; Robert M. Frehse Jr., VP and Exec. Director; Thomas Eastham, VP and Western Director; Frank A. Bennack Jr., VP; Millicent Boudjakdji, VP; John G. Conomikes, VP; Richard E. Deems, VP; John R. Hearst Jr., VP; Randolph A. Hearst, VP; J. Kingsbury-Smith, VP; Frank Massi, VP; Gilbert C. Maurer, VP; Raymond J. Petersen, VP; Victor F. Ganzi, Secy.; Ralph J. Cuomo, Treas.
Staff: 10 full-time professional, three full-time support, two part-time support; 12 staff are shared with the William Randolph Hearst Foundation.

Financial Profile

Assets: In 1992, $165,926,419; 1993, $195,276,150
High Grant: In 1992, $786,000; 1993, $100,000
Low Grant: In 1992, $50,000; 1993, $15,000
Ave. Grant: $10,000-$35,000
Total Grants: In 1992, 237 grants totaling $5,993,786; 1993, 252 grants totaling $7,635,000
High Grant Higher Ed.: $35,000
Low Grant Higher Ed.: $10,000
Ave. Grant Higher Ed.: $20,000-$35,000
Total Grants Higher Ed.: In 1992, 69 grants totaling $1,838,000; 1993, 83 grants totaling $2,545,000

Application Process

Contact: East of the Mississippi River, Robert Frehse Jr., (212) 586-5404; west of the Mississippi River, Thomas Eastham, (415) 543-0400. Address to be used by applicants west of the Mississippi River: 90 New Montgomery Street, Suite 1212, San Francisco, CA 94105.
Deadline: None
Board Meeting: March, June, September, and December
Processing Time: Four to six weeks
Guidelines: Only fully documented appeals will be considered. The NYRAG common application form is accepted. Applicants should include the following: detailed description of project and amount of funding requested; organization or project budget; listing of board of directors, trustees, officers, and other key people; brief history of organization and description of its mission; copy of most recent annual report/audited financial statement/990; copy of IRS determination letter; listing of additional sources and amount of support; and additional supporting materials.

Sample Grants

Dillard University in New Orleans, Louisiana, received $28,000 for the third year of a program on preparing minorities for academic careers.

University of California in Berkeley received $25,000 toward the renovation of North Gate Hall.

University of San Francisco, College of Professional Studies in California was awarded $25,000 toward a California nonprofit database.

Catholic University of America in Washington, DC, received $35,000 to establish the William Randolph Hearst Endowed Scholarship Fund for Minority Nursing Students.

Bethel College and Seminary in Saint Paul, Minnesota, received $35,000 to establish a William Randolph Hearst Endowed Scholarship Fund for students demonstrating financial need.

Temple University in Philadelphia, Pennsylvania, received $25,000 to complete the William Randolph Hearst Endowed Scholarship Fund for nontraditional students.

Bacone College in Muskogee, Oklahoma, received $25,000 toward a capital campaign to increase the college's endowment for scholarship support.

Comments/Analysis

The foundation's top subject area is education, followed by other projects and human services. In the past, education received 43 percent of all grants awarded, with 19 percent going to higher education, 12 percent to K-12, and 12 percent to other education. Colleges and universities are the largest recipients, followed by human service agencies and schools. Much of the funds distributed to institutions of higher education are for William Randolph Hearst Endowed Scholarship Funds for minority students, nontraditional students, students demonstrating financial need, students from rural areas, and minority nursing students.

39
William Randolph Hearst Foundation
888 Seventh Avenue, 45th Floor
New York, NY   10106-0057

Areas of Interest

Program Description: To support programs to aid poverty-level and minority groups, higher education, private secondary education, health delivery systems, and culture. Other areas of interest include minority education, minority engineering education, and minority nursing education. The foundation also supports two independent scholarship programs: the Journalism Awards Program and the United States Senate Youth Program.

Assistance Types: Special projects, scholarship funds, endowment funds, general purposes, operating budgets, and research

Eligibility

Restrictions: Giving limited to the United States and its possessions. No support for political purposes. No grants to individuals or private foundations or for the purchase of tickets, tables, or advertising for fundraising events. Organizations serving larger geographic areas are given priority over those serving one locality.

Personnel

Officers: Randolph A. Hearst, President; Harvey Lipton, VP; Robert M. Frese Jr., VP and Exec. Director; Thomas Eastham, VP and Western Director; Frank A. Bennack Jr., VP; Millicent Boudjakdji, VP; John G. Conomikes, VP; Richard E. Deems, VP; George R. Hearst Jr., VP; John R. Hearst Jr., VP; William Hearst III, VP; J. Kingsbury-Smith, VP; Frank Massi, VP; Gilbert C. Maurer, VP; Raymond J. Peterson, VP; Victor F. Ganzi, Secy.; Ralph J. Cuomo, Treas.

Staff: 14 full-time professional, three full-time support, two part-time support; 12 staff are shared with the Hearst Foundation.

Financial Profile

Assets: In 1992, $362,853,208; 1993, $406,192,268
High Grant: In 1992, $800,000; 1993, $250,000
Low Grant: $10,000
Ave. Grant: $25,000-$50,000
Total Grants: In 1992, 312 grants totaling $13,575,214; 1993, 265 grants totaling $12,910,000
High Grant Higher Ed.: $250,000
Low Grant Higher Ed.: $10,000
Ave. Grant Higher Ed.: $25,000-$50,000
Total Grants Higher Ed.: In 1992, 105 grants totaling $4,025,500

Application Process

Contact: East of the Mississippi River, Robert Frehse Jr., (212) 586-5404; west of the Mississippi River, Thomas Eastham, (415) 543-0400. Address to be used for applicants west of the Mississippi River: Thomas Eastham, VP and Western Director, 90 New Montgomery Street, Suite 1212, San Francisco, CA 94105
Deadline: None
Board Meeting: March, June, September, and December
Processing Time: The foundation acknowledges receipt in four to six weeks
Guidelines: Only fully documented appeals will be considered. The NYRAG Common application Form is accepted. Applicants should include the following: detailed description of project and amount of request; organization or project budget; list of board of directors, trustees, officers, and other key people; description of organization's history and mission; copy of most recent annual report/audited financial statement/990; copy of IRS determination letter; listing of additional sources and amount of support; and list of additional materials.

Sample Grants

National Hispanic University in San Jose, California, received $60,000 to upgrade its library to accreditation standards.

Vanderbilt University School of Nursing in Nashville, Tennessee, received $35,000 toward the William Randolph Hearst Endowed Scholarship Fund for nursing students.

University of Pennsylvania in Philadelphia received $30,000 to complete the William Randolph Hearst Endowment for a tutor coordinator fellowship, as part of their program to enhance minority permanence.

University of Arkansas in Fayetteville was awarded $30,000 to complete the William Randolph Hearst Endowment for Ph.D. Fellowships in engineering for women or minority students.

Silver Lake College of the Holy Family in Manitowoc, Wisconsin, received $25,000 toward the William Randolph Hearst Scholarship Endowment Fund to aid low-income single parents.

Drew University in Madison, New Jersey, received $35,000 toward the William Randolph Hearst Endowment Fund for graduate education of minority students seeking teaching careers in higher education.

Comments/Analysis

Top priority is given to education, by dollars as well as numbers of grants. Historically, education has received 35 percent of the foundation's total funding; of this 14 percent went to higher education, 9 percent to graduate and professional, 8 percent to elementary and secondary, and 4 percent to other. Colleges and universities were the top recipients of funds, with hospitals and medical care facilities second and human service agencies third. Much of the funds distributed to institutions of higher education are for William Randolph Hearst Endowed Scholarship Funds for nontraditional students, minority students, students with financial need, ethnic/minority students, minority engineering students, and minority nursing students.

40

Herrick Foundation
150 W Jefferson, Suite 2500
Detroit, MI   48226

Areas of Interest

Program Description: The foundation supports higher education and secondary education, churches and religion, youth and youth agencies, hospitals and health services, social services, and libraries.
Assistance Types: Building funds, equipment, research, scholarship funds, special projects, capital campaigns, renovation projects

Eligibility

Restrictions: Giving primarily in Michigan, as well as Indiana, Kentucky, Mississippi, Tennessee, and Wisconsin; no grants to individuals.

Personnel

Officers: Kenneth G. Herrick, President and Treas.; John W. Gelder, VP and Secy.; Todd W. Herrick, VP
Trustees/Directors: Catherine R. Cobb

Staff: None

Financial Profile

Assets: In 1993, $204,119,607
High Grant: $525,000
Low Grant: $300
Ave. Grant: $5,000-$50,000
Total Grants: In 1993, 159 grants totaling $5,280,569
High Grant Higher Ed.: $100,000
Low Grant Higher Ed.: $10,000
Ave. Grant Higher Ed.: $50,000-$100,000
Total Grants Higher Ed.: In 1992, 25 grants to higher education totaling $2,164,000

Application Process

Contact: Dolores de Galleford, (313) 496-7656
Deadline: None
Board Meeting: Every two to four months
Guidelines: Initial approach should be by a letter of not more than three pages. An application form is not required. Proposals should include the following: description of project and amount of funding requested, IRS letter of determination, and name and address of contact person.

Sample Grants

Adrian College in Adrian, Michigan, received two grants: $100,000 for a central heating system and $25,000 for general support.

Cumberland College in Williamsburg, Kentucky, received $50,000 for its capital improvement fund.

Purdue University in West Lafayette, Indiana, was awarded $200,000 for the Herrick Professor of Engineering Endowment Fund.

Defiance College in Defiance, Ohio, received $50,000 toward the construction of a new library.

Washburn University of Topeka, Kansas, received $25,000 for scholarships for part-time students.

Comments/Analysis

Education is the foundation's top priority, receiving 41 percent of its funds in 1993. Programs in medicine followed, receiving 17 percent of the foundation's grant disbursements.

41

William and Flora Hewlett Foundation
525 Middlefield Road, Suite 200
Menlo Park, CA   94025

Areas of Interest

Program Description: To provide support for conflict resolution, the environment, college-level performing arts, higher education, arts education, family planning and population studies, community development, youth services, child welfare, and a regional grants program. Other areas of interest include public policy, arms control, international studies, Mexico, video services, dance, theater, film, music, minority education, leadership development, homeless, AIDS, urban development, and urban affairs.

Assistance Types: Operating budgets, general purposes, continuing support, seed money, emergency funds, land acquisition, special projects, matching funds, employee matching gifts, endowment funds

Eligibility

Restrictions: Giving limited to the San Francisco Bay Area for the regional grants program; performing arts partially limited to the Bay Area. No support for medicine and health-related projects; law, criminal justice, and related fields; juvenile delinquency; drug and alcohol addiction; problems of the elderly and the handicapped; or television or radio projects. No grants to individuals, or for building funds, basic research, equipment, scholarships, or fellowships; no loans.

Personnel

Officers: William R. Hewlett, Chair; Walter B. Hewlett, Vice-Chair; David P. Gardner, President; Marianne Pallotti, VP and Corp. Secy.; William F. Nichols, Treas.
Trustees/Directors: Robert F. Erburu, Eleanor H. Gimon, Roger W. Heyns, Mary H. Jaffe, Dr. Herant Katchdourian, Arjay Miller, Loret M. Ruppe
Staff: Nine full-time professional, six full-time support, three part-time support

Financial Profile

Assets: In 1992, $819,596,000; 1993, $875,286,675
Ave. Grant: $25,000-$100,000
Total Grants: In 1993, $45,216,000 was allocated for grants and $2,000,000 for one program-related investment
High Grant Higher Ed.: $600,000
Low Grant Higher Ed.: $20,000
Ave. Grant Higher Ed.: $20,000-$250,000
Total Grants Higher Ed.: In 1992, 53 grants totaling $12,137,000

Application Process

Contact: David P. Gardner, President, (415) 329-1070
Deadline: January 1, music; April 1, theater; July 1, dance, film, and video service organizations; no deadlines for other programs
Board Meeting: January, April, July, and October
Processing Time: Two to three months
Publications: Annual report, program policy statement, application guidelines, informational brochure
Guidelines: The initial approach should take the form of a letter. Proposals should include the following information: description of the problem to be addressed by the project and amount requested, description of what distinguishes the proposed project from others in the field, organization and/or project budget, qualifications of key personnel, names of board members and trustees and affili-

ations, IRS letter of determination, signature and title of chief operating officer, and additional materials and documentation.

Sample Grants

American Association for Higher Education in Washington, DC, received a $230,000, two-year grant for a project on peer review of teaching in universities.
Occidental College in Los Angeles received $23,000 for a summer project.
University of California at Berkeley Office of the President in received $25,000 for the distribution of a book entitled In Pursuit of Ideas.
Connecticut College in New London was awarded a three-year, $250,000 grant to supplement the presidential discretionary endowment established under the Hewlett-Mellon Program.
Independent Colleges of Northern California in San Francisco received $50,000 for general support.

Comments/Analysis

Historically, 23 percent of the foundation's grants have been awarded to education, including 12 percent to higher education. Education was the top area of funding, and colleges and universities were the top recipients of awards. In 1993 several institutions of higher education received three-year, $250,000 grants to supplement the presidential discretionary fund endowment established under the Hewlett-Mellon Program including Albion College, Amherst College, Barnard College, Connecticut College, Mills College, Oberlin College, Vassar College, and Wells College.

42
Conrad N. Hilton Foundation
100 W Liberty Street, Suite 840
Reno, NV   89501

Areas of Interest

Program Description: To support major, long-term projects in the areas of drug abuse prevention, early intervention services for disabled children, hotel administration education, and Catholic welfare.
Assistance Types: Building funds, endowment funds, equipment, publications, scholarship funds, seed money operating budgets, technical assistance, and continuing support

Eligibility

Restrictions: No support for medical research, the arts, the elderly, political lobbying, fundraising events, travel, or surveys

Personnel

Officers: Donald Hubbs, President; Steven M. Hilton, VP; Patrick Modugno, VP; Jean Van Sickle, Secy.; Deborah Kerr, Treas.

Trustees/Directors: Dr. Robert Buckley, William H. Edwards, James R. Galbraith, Robert A. Groves, Barron Hilton, Barry Hilton, Eric M. Hilton
Staff: Seven full-time professional, three full-time support

Financial Profile

Assets: In 1993, $494,150,303
High Grant: $3,600,000
Low Grant: $75
Ave. Grant: $5,000-$100,000
Total Grants: 174 grants totaling $21,651,191
High Grant Higher Ed.: $2,197,500
Low Grant Higher Ed.: $5,000
Ave. Grant Higher Ed.: $5,000-$42,500
Total Grants Higher Ed.: In 1992, 10 grants totaling $2,749,500; 1993, 16 grants totaling $3,341,175

Application Process

Contact: Donald Hubbs, President, (702) 323-4221
Deadline: None
Board Meeting: Quarterly
Processing Time: 30 days
Publications: Annual report, application guidelines, informational brochure
Guidelines: An initial letter of one to two pages should include a detailed description of project and amount requested, brief history of organization and description of mission, and copy of the IRS letter of determination. If invited to submit a full application, the following items will be required: plans for cooperation with other organizations; how results will be measured or evaluated; how project will be sustained after grant period; qualifications of key personnel; names and affiliations of key board members; annual report/audited financial statement/990; copy of organizational/project report; and list of additional funding sources and amounts.

Sample Grants

University of California in San Diego received $25,000 for its Medicine Education Research Foundation.

Loyola University of Chicago in Illinois was awarded $15,000 for program support.

University of Houston, Conrad N. Hilton College of Hotel and Restaurant Management, received $2,197,500.

Saint Paul Seminary in Saint Paul, Minnesota, received $37,000 for program support.

University of Southern California in Los Angeles received $15,000 for its Law Center.

Comments/Analysis

The area of highest priority to the foundation is human services, followed by education and medicine. In 1993, 29 percent of the foundation's grants went to education. Graduate and professional education received 11 percent of all grants for a total of $2,274,500. Human services agencies were the top recipients of funds, followed by mental health agencies and schools.

43

Independence Foundation
2500 Philadelphia National Bank Building
Philadelphia, PA   19107-3493

Areas of Interest

Program Description: The foundation supports educational and cultural programs and programs that address the problems of the needy. The foundation has a strong interest in nursing and nurse-operated health care projects.
Assistance Types: Endowment funds, general purposes, scholarship funds, professorships, and fellowships

Eligibility

Restrictions: Giving is primarily in the Delaware Valley area. No grants to individuals or for building, travel, research, publications, or matching gifts

Personnel

Officers: Theodore K. Warner Jr., President; Frederick H. Donner, VP; Susan E. Sherman, Secy.; Madeline M. Nuss, Treas.
Staff: Three full-time professional

Financial Profile

Assets: In 1993, $86,950,102
High Grant: $400,000
Low Grant: $1,000
Ave. Grant: $10,000-$30,000
Total Grants: 89 grants totaling $4,764,986
High Grant Higher Ed.: $250,000
Low Grant Higher Ed.: $5,000
Ave. Grant Higher Ed.: $100,000
Total Grants Higher Ed.: 19 grants totaling $3,450,000

Application Process

Contact: Theodore K. Warner Jr., President, (215) 563-8105; fax: (215) 563-8105
Deadline: Three weeks prior to board meetings
Board Meeting: March, June, September, December
Processing Time: Three to six weeks
Publications: Annual report, including application guidelines
Guidelines: The initial approach should be by letter. If the foundation is interested in the proposal, interviews with the board may be arranged. Application form is not required. Proposals should include detailed description of the project and amount requested, anticipated results, current year's organizational and/or project budget, and copy of IRS letter of determination.

Sample Grants

Vanderbilt University School of Nursing in Nashville, Tennessee, received $100,000 for scholarship and loan funds.

Case-Western Reserve University School of Nursing in Cleveland, Ohio, received $250,000 for teaching endowments.

Emory University School of Nursing in Atlanta, Georgia, received $250,000 for teaching endowments.

University of Pennsylvania School of Nursing in Philadelphia received two grants: $250,000 for teaching endowments and $100,000 for scholarship and loan funds.

Comments/Analysis

Historically, schools of nursing have been the foundation's top recipients of higher education funds with several schools receiving $100,000 for scholarship and loan funds and/or $250,000 for teaching endowments.

44
James Irvine Foundation
One Market, Spear Tower, Suite 1715
San Francisco, CA   94105

Areas of Interest

Program Description: To support community service, community development, intercultural relations, leadership development, arts, culture, health and health services, higher education, and youth. Other areas of interest include rural development, public policy, volunteerism, immigration, fine arts, dance, music performing arts, theater, AIDS, literacy, child development, child welfare, social services, family planning, family services, minorities, homeless, women, housing, disadvantaged, citizenship, minority education, employment and race relations.

Assistance Types: Seed money, equipment, special projects, renovation projects, technical assistance, program-related investments

Eligibility

Restrictions: Giving is limited to California. No support for primary or secondary schools, agencies receiving substantial government support, or sectarian religious activities. No grants to individuals or for operating budgets, continuing support, annual campaigns, deficit financing, endowment funds, research, scholarships, publications, films, conferences, or debt reduction.

Personnel

Officers: Myron Du Bain, Chair
Trustees/Directors: Samuel H. Armacost, Angela G. Blackwell, Camilla C. Frost, James C. Gaither, Walter B. Gerken, Roger W. Heyns, Joan F. Lane, Donn B. Miller, Forrest N. Shumway, Kathryn L. Wheeler, Dr. Edward Zapanta
Staff: 10 full-time professional, 11 full-time support, two part-time support staff

Financial Profile

Assets: In 1992, $626,228,757; 1993, $680,264,425

High Grant: In 1992, $1,200,000; 1993, $1,400,000
Low Grant: In 1992, $500; 1993, $350
Ave. Grant: $25,000-$200,000
Total Grants: In 1992, 473 grants totaling $25,079,693; 1993, $27,080,103 for grants and $900,000 for two program-related investments
Total Grants Higher Ed.: In 1992, $9,895,000

Application Process

Contact: Luiz A. Vega, Director of Grants Programs, (415) 777-2244; Southern CA office: 777 South Figueroa Street, Suite 740, Los Angeles, California 90017-5430, (213) 236-0552
Deadline: None
Board Meeting: March, June, September, October, and December
Processing Time: Three to six months
Publications: Annual report, guidelines for application, and informational brochure
Guidelines: Applicants should submit a letter and proposal. Proposals should include the following: annual and financial reports, description of project and amount requested, organization or project budget, timetable for project, IRS letter of determination, signature of chief executive officer, names and affiliation of boards, description of problem to be addressed by project, and how project will be evaluated or measured.

Sample Grants

California Institute of Technology in Pasadena received $1,000,000 for the continuation of the Irvine Postdoctoral and Graduate Fellowship Program for Underrepresented Minorities and the Dean's Fund for Community Outreach and Service.

Loyola Marymount University in Los Angeles was awarded $600,000 for faculty and curriculum development on multicultural issues.

University of San Francisco in California received $500,000 for a Multicultural Action Plan (MAP).

Art Center College of Design in Pasadena, California, received $500,000 for recruitment costs and financial aid for underrepresented minority students.

Occidental College in Los Angeles was awarded $1,000,000 for the Irvine leaders/scholars program for outstanding minority students from Los Angeles inner-city high schools.

University of Southern California in Los Angeles received $80,000 toward the implementation of the Inter-Professional Initiative, a collaboration between six professional schools and five service organizations to improve preparation of human service professionals.

Comments/Analysis

The James Irvine Foundation has a history of support for community service and has now taken the lead in California's implementation of the National Community Service Trust Act. The foundation supports collaborations of nonprofit agencies, schools and colleges, with a focus in two areas: capacity-building and quality assurance. In terms of higher education, the foundation appears to be particularly interested in supporting programs aimed at underrepresented minorities.

45
Robert Wood Johnson Foundation
PO Box 2316
Princeton, NJ   08543-2316

Areas of Interest

Program Description: To support projects to improve the health and health care of Americans and to identify and pursue new opportunities to respond to persistent and emerging health problems. The foundation's three basic goals are to assure that Americans of all ages have access to health care; to improve the way that services are organized and provided to people with chronic health conditions; and to prevent harm caused by substance abuse, including AIDS. The foundation is concerned about the health issues of the homeless, minorities, children and youth, and is interested in improving hospitals, mental health, dentistry, and medical education. It is also interested in addressing projects that address the problem of escalating health care expenditures. Other areas of interest include nursing, the aged, child development, and minority education.
Assistance Types: Seed money, research, special projects, fellowships, program-related investments. and matching funds

Eligibility

Restrictions: Giving limited to the United States; no grants to individuals or for general operating funds, endowment funds or capital costs; no support for programs or institutions concerned solely with a specific disease or basic biomedical research

Personnel

Officers: Sidney F. Wentz, Chair; Dr. Steven Schroeder, President; Dr. Richard C. Reynolds, Exec. VP; J. Warren Wood III, VP, General Counsel, and Secy.; Andrew R. Greene, VP and Treas.; Peter Goodwin, VP, Financial Monitoring; Frank Karel III, VP, Communications; Paul Jellinek, VP; Nancy J. Kaufman, VP; James R. Knickman, VP; Lewis G. Sandy, VP; William C. Imhof, Chief Investment Officer
Trustees/Directors: Dr. Edward C. Andrews Jr., James E. Burke, David R. Clare, Rheba de Tronyay, Lawrence G. Foster, John J. Heldrich, Leonard F. Hill, Frank Hoenemeyer, John J. Horan, Thomas H. Kean, Jank W. Owen, Franklin D. Raines, Dr. Norman Rosenberg, Richard B. Sellars, John H. Steele
Staff: 43 full-time professional, 79 full-time support, five part-time support

Financial Profile

Assets: In 1992, $3,734,939,414; 1993, $3,461,378,272
High Grant: In 1992, $3,464,255; 1993, $1,030,403
Low Grant: In 1992, $10,000; 1993, $82

Total Grants: In 1992, $176,054,270 was distributed: 763 grants totaling $102,977,206, $45,436,751 for set-asides, 188 employee matching gifts totaling $146,814, and four program-related investments totaling $6,500,000; in 1993, 269 grants totaling $105,611,050, $28,769,909 for set-asides, 235 employee matching gifts totaling $5,222,546, four foundation-administered programs totaling $4,217,769, and $500,000 for one program-related investment
High Grant Higher Ed.: $1,173,334
Low Grant Higher Ed.: $15,000
Ave. Grant Higher Ed.: $15,000-$150,000
Total Grants Higher Ed.: In 1992, 180 grants totaling $76,454,081

Application Process

Contact: Edward H. Robbins, Proposal Manager, (609) 452-8701
Deadline: None
Board Meeting: Quarterly
Processing Time: Six to 12 months
Publications: Annual report, informational brochure, application guidelines, occasional report, newsletter
Guidelines: Application form not required. Initial approach should be made by letter requesting application guidelines.

Sample Grants

Kean College of New Jersey Foundation in Union, New Jersey, received a $711,923, four-year grant for an educational consortium to increase minority nurses in New Jersey.

Vanderbilt University School of Medicine in Nashville, Tennessee, was awarded a $163,005, two-year grant for a minority medical faculty development program.

University of Wisconsin Medical School in Madison received a $368,518, two-year grant for policy studies on the generalist-specialist physician mix.

University of Washington School of Medicine in Seattle was awarded a $1,353,135, three-year grant for a clinical scholars program.

Johns Hopkins University School of Medicine in Baltimore, Maryland, received a $2,494,358, four-and-one-third-year grant for the program, Preparing Physicians for the Future: A Program in Medical Education.

American College of Nurse-Midwives Foundation in Washington, DC, received $49,841 for the development of a plan to increase the number of nurse midwives.

University of New England College of Osteopathic Medicine in Biddeford, Maine, received a $149,954, one-and-one-half-year grant for a generalist physician initiative.

Georgetown University School of Medicine in Washington, DC, received $332,580 for technical assistance and direction for a generalist faculty scholars program.

Comments/Analysis

The most frequent type of support funded by the foundation is program support, followed by research. The top recipients of funds are institutions of higher education, with an emphasis on schools and colleges of medicine. Most of the support provided to schools and colleges of medicine is given for minority medical faculty development programs, generalist physician initiatives, generalist faculty scholars programs, clinical scholars programs, and programs in medical education preparing physicians for the future.

46

Fletcher Jones Foundation
624 S Grand Avenue
One Wilshire Building, Suite 1210
Los Angeles, CA   90017-9843

Areas of Interest

Program Description: To support private colleges and universities primarily in California, cultural programs, social services, health and hospitals, and organizations promoting law and justice and citizenship.
Assistance Types: Building funds, equipment, professorships, special projects, endowment funds, scholarship funds, renovation projects

Eligibility

Restrictions: No support for secondary schools; no grants to individuals or for operating funds, deficit financing, conferences, travel exhibits, surveys, or projects supported by government organizations

Personnel

Officers: John P. Pollock, President; Robert F. Erburu, VP; Houston Flournoy, VP; Chancey J. Medberry III, VP; Dickinson C. Ross, VP; Jess C. Wilson Jr., VP; Jack Pettker, Secy.; John W. Smythe, Treas. and Exec. Director
Trustees/Directors: Parker S. Kennedy, Rudy J. Munzer, Donald E. Nickelson
Staff: One part-time professional, one part-time support

Financial Profile

Assets: In 1992, $92,839,651; 1993, $115,907,398
High Grant: In 1992, $250,000; 1993, $1,500,000
Low Grant: In 1992, $10,000; 1993, $2,500
Total Grants: In 1992, 55 grants totaling $5,031,202; 1993, $5,805,037
High Grant Higher Ed.: $1,500,000
Low Grant Higher Ed.: $10,000
Total Grants Higher Ed.: In 1992, 15 grants totaling $3,207,000

Application Process

Contact: John W. Smythe, Exec. Director, (213) 689-9292
Deadline: One month prior to board meeting
Board Meeting: March, May, September, and November
Processing Time: Three to six months
Publications: Annual report, including grant guidelines

Guidelines: The initial approach should be a letter. Proposals should include a history and mission of the organization, description of project and amount requested, qualifications of key personnel, budget, additional sources of support and amount anticipated, how project will be measured or evaluated, IRS letter of determination, and names and affiliations of board.

Sample Grants

University of the Pacific in Stockton, California, received $1,500,000 for the Fletcher Jones Chair in Entrepreneurship.
Washington University Center for the Study of American Business in Saint Louis, Missouri, received $10,000 for research.
Claremont University Center and Graduate School in Claremont, California, received a $500,000, two-year grant for computer upgrades.
Saint Marys College in Notre Dame, Indiana, received $160,869 for library automation.
Deep Springs College in Deep Springs, California, was awarded $22,000 to upgrade its telephone system.

Comments/Analysis

The foundation's first interest is the social sciences, followed by education and science. The top recipients are colleges and universities, followed by human services agencies. Historically, private institutions of higher education in California have received over 90 percent of the funds distributed by the foundation. In the past, several large grants have been awarded to colleges and universities for computer equipment and upgrades and library automation.

47

W. Alton Jones Foundation, Inc.
232 E High Street
Charlottesville, VA   22902-5178

Areas of Interest

Program Description: To protect the earth's life-support systems from environmental harm and to eliminate the possibility of nuclear warfare. Areas of interest include peace, conservation, arms control, and ecology.
Assistance Types: Special projects, general purposes, research, seed money, matching funds, operating budgets

Eligibility

Restrictions: No funding through conduit organizations; no grants to individuals or for building construction, endowment funds, general support, basic research, scholarships, conferences, or international exchanges. Proposals only accepted for programs in environmental protection and arms control.

Personnel

Officers: Patricia Jones Edgerton, President; Bradford W. Edgerton, VP; Diane Edgerton Miller, Secy.; Bernard F. Curry, Treas.
Trustees/Directors: James S. Bennett, James R. Cameron, William A. Edgerton, William A. McDonough, Scott McVay
Staff: Eight full-time professional, six full-time support

Financial Profile

Assets: In 1992, $215,203,561; 1993, $258,749,776
High Grant: In 1992, $250,000; 1993, $200,000
Low Grant: In 1992, $1,500; 1993, $1,000
Ave. Grant: $5,000-$100,000
Total Grants: In 1992, 199 grants totaling $13,890,605; 1993, 305 grants totaling $15,764,096 and $100,000 for one program-related investment
High Grant Higher Ed.: $200,000
Low Grant Higher Ed.: $20,000
Ave. Grant Higher Ed.: $20,000-$50,000
Total Grants Higher Ed.: In 1991, 26 grants totaling $1,371,500; 1992, 17 grants totaling $1,184,687

Application Process

Contact: Dr. J.P. Myers, Director, (804) 295-2134
Deadline: None
Board Meeting: Quarterly
Processing Time: Variable; applicants must wait one year after a grant is approved or declined before submitting another application.
Publications: Annual report, application guidelines, informational brochure, newsletter
Guidelines: The initial approach should be a letter of inquiry describing the goals of the project, summarizing how goals will be met, and stating the amount requested. The letter of inquiry should not be more than two pages long. An application form is not required. Proposals should include a detailed description of project and amount requested, timetable for implementation and evaluation, organizational/project budget, IRS letter of determination, and how project will be measured or evaluated.

Sample Grants

University of Maryland Center for Global Change in College Park received $120,000 to analyze and disseminate educational information about options for a carbon tax and impact on global climate change.

Harvard University John F. Kennedy School of Government in Cambridge, Massachusetts, received $40,000 for the production and dissemination of educational materials related to market incentives for environmental protection.

Princeton University in Princeton, New Jersey, received three grants: a $200,000, two-year grant for the analysis of renewable energy options available to the United States and the developing world; $30,000 to produce and disseminate findings from a symposium on state leadership in industrial pollution prevention policy; and $27,180 to organize a summer school in China on arms control and environment and energy

for young public interest scientists in the United States, former Soviet Republics, and China.

University of Georgia Center for East-West Trade Policy in Athens, Georgia, received $50,000 to promote multilateral cooperation on nonproliferation export controls of former Soviet bloc weapons and technology.

Comments/Analysis

The foundation supports two major programs: the Sustainable Society Program, including environmental protection, particularly natural resources and pollution control; and the Secure Society Program, focusing on international affairs, including peace, security, and arms control. Environmental agencies are the top recipient of funds, followed by professional societies and associations, international organizations, research institutes, and colleges and universities. A limited amount of the foundation's funding is also provided for arts and culture.

48
Joyce Foundation
135 S LaSalle Street, Suite 4010
Chicago, IL   60603

Areas of Interest

Program Description: To address issues of critical importance to the midwest, including conservation of natural resources, improvement of urban elementary and secondary educational systems, economic development, revitalization of the electoral process, issues of cultural diversity, and the disadvantaged. Other areas of interest include arts and culture, employment, minority education, vocational education, public policy, community development, and public affairs.
Assistance Types: Operating budgets, continuing support, seed money, emergency funds, matching funds, special projects and project-related investments, loans, publications, conferences and seminars, employee matching gifts, general purposes

Eligibility

Restrictions: Giving primarily to midwestern states, including Illinois, Indiana, Iowa, Michigan, Minnesota, Ohio, and Wisconsin; conservation grants to North Dakota, South Dakota, Kansas, Missouri, and Nebraska; culture grants only to Chicago metropolitan area. No funds for endowment or building funds, annual campaigns, deficit financing, research, or land acquisition.

Personnel

Officers: John T. Anderson, Chair; Raymond Wearing, Vice-Chair; Deborah Leff, President; Linda K. Schelinski, VP for Administration and Treas.; Joel Getzendanner, VP Programs and Secy.

Trustees/Directors: Cushman B. Bissell Jr., Lewis H. Butler, Charles U. Daly, Richard K. Donahue, Roger R. Fross, Carlton L. Guthrie, Marion T. Hall, Craig Kennnedy, Paula Wolff
Staff: 10 full-time professional, three full-time support

Financial Profile

Assets: In 1992, $417,925,222; 1993, $489,007,578
High Grant: $200,000
Low Grant: $750
Ave. Grant: $5,000-$60,000
Total Grants: In 1992, 361 grants totaling $16,335,059; 1993, 351 grants totaling $17,603,374
High Grant Higher Ed.: $330,000
Low Grant Higher Ed.: $10,000
Ave. Grant Higher Ed.: $20,000-$100,000
Total Grants Higher Ed.: In 1992, 45 grants totaling $3,877,977

Application Process

Contact: Deborah Leff, President, (312) 782-2464
Deadline: November 15 for Education and Economic Development; March 15 for Conservation; July 15 for Culture and Elections
Board Meeting: April or May, July or August, and twice in November
Processing Time: Three weeks following meeting
Publications: Annual report (including application guidelines), informational brochure, financial statement, newsletter
Guidelines: Initial approach should take the form of a letter. Application guidelines are reviewed each November; application form is required.

Sample Grants

Chicago State University in Illinois received $45,850 for a collaborative effort between the Colleges of Education and Art Sciences to complete the planning and begin the implementation of a mentoring program for new teachers.

University of Wisconsin School of Education in Milwaukee received a $227,000, two-year grant for the continued evaluation of the progress of an African American Immersion Schools Project in Milwaukee public schools.

Northwestern University J.L. Kellogg Graduate School of Management in Evanston, Illinois, received $75,000 to work with three Chicago public schools to use principles of continuous improvement to manage their efforts at reform.

Queens College Center for the Biology of Natural Systems in Flushing, New York, was awarded $108,647 for the first phase of a project to identify industrial sources and uses of chlorine in the Greats Lake basin and suggest ways of phasing them out without harming the overall level of economic activity in the region.

Comments/Analysis

The foundation's first priority is the environment, which received 32 percent of its grants in 1993. Its second priority is education, which received 26 percent, with K-12 receiving 21 percent and others receiving 5 percent. Public affairs and community development both received 10 percent of all grants awarded.

49
Max Kade Foundation, Inc.
100 Church Street, Room 1604
New York, NY 10007

Areas of Interest

Program Description: To support higher education institutions, with an emphasis on postdoctoral research exchange programs between the United States and Europe in medicine and natural and physical sciences. The foundation also supports visiting faculty exchange programs and the training of language teachers. Additional areas of interest include the biological sciences, chemistry, engineering, literature, and Germany.
Assistance Types: Exchange programs, special projects, language equipment, international conferences

Eligibility

Restrictions: Giving primarily in the United States and Europe. No grants for operating budgets, development campaigns, endowments funds; no loans. Foreign scholars and scientists are selected by the sponsoring universities upon nomination by the respective academy of sciences.

Personnel

Officers: Erich H. Michel, President; Reimer Koch-Weser, VP; Berteline Dale Baier, Secy.; Hans G. Hachman, Treas.
Trustees/Directors: Dr. Fritz Kade Jr.
Staff: Four full-time professional

Financial Profile

Assets: In 1992, $54,522,344; 1993, $54,355,347
High Grant: In 1992, $500,000; 1993, $66,500
Low Grant: In 1992, $1,000; 1993, $1,000
Ave. Grant: $9,000-$30,000
Total Grants: In 1992, 110 grants totaling $2,466,597; 1993, 115 grants totaling $1,866,687
High Grant Higher Ed.: $500,000
Low Grant Higher Ed.: $1,000
Ave. Grant Higher Ed.: $9,000-$30,000
Total Grants Higher Ed.: 1992, 73 grants totaling $2,232,575

Application Process

Contact: Dr. Erich Markel, President, (212) 964-7980
Deadline: None
Board Meeting: As required
Publications: Occasional report

Guidelines: The initial approach can be by letter or proposal. Applications should include a detailed description of project and amount requested and qualifications of key personnel.

Sample Grants

University of Florida in Gainesville received $31,400 for postdoctoral research exchange programs in medicine.

Technical University of Dresden in Dresden, Germany, received $500,000 for equipment for Max Kade Language Centers and for other charitable activities.

Dartmouth College in Hanover, New Hampshire, received $12,000 for visiting faculty exchange programs.

Indiana University in Bloomington was awarded three grants: $66,500 for the training of language teachers, graduate study abroad, and international conferences; $13,750 for postdoctoral research exchange programs in medicine; and $50,000 for equipment for the Max Kade Language Centers and for other charitable activities.

University of Wisconsin Foundation in Madison received $10,000 for the training of language teachers, graduate study abroad, and international conferences.

Comments/Analysis

Education is the foundation's top area of interest, followed by science. Colleges and universities receive the largest number of grants and the greatest amount of funds. Hospitals and medical care facilities receive the second largest amount of funds, followed by graduate schools. The foundation gives primarily in the area of program support, including program development, faculty development, and conferences and seminars. Historically, institutions of higher education have received grants for postdoctoral research exchange programs in medicine; visiting faculty exchange programs; equipment for Max Kade Language Centers; and the training of language teachers, graduate study abroad, and international conferences.

50
W. M. Keck Foundation
555 S Flower Street, Suite 3230
Los Angeles, CA   90071

Areas of Interest

Program Description: National giving is primarily devoted to studies in biological and earth sciences involving the development of natural resources, and engineering, medical research, education, liberal arts, law and legal administration, and science and technology. Some support is also provided for health care, arts and culture, civic and community services, and precollegiate education in southern California.

Assistance Types: Building and renovation, seed money, equipment, special projects, research, fellowships, endowments, professorships, scholarships

Eligibility

Restrictions: No support for conduit organizations or for organizations that do not have a tax-exempt ruling determination. No grants to individuals, or for routine expenses, general endowments, deficit reduction, fund-raising events, dinners, mass mailings, conferences, seminars, publications, films, or public policy research. Unsolicited proposals are not accepted.

Personnel

Officers: Howard B. Keck, President and CEO; Greg R. Ryan, VP and Secy.; Robert Day, VP; Walter B. Gerken, VP; Dorothea A. Harris, Treas.

Trustees/Directors: Lew Allen Jr., Norm Baker Jr., Marsha A. Cooper, Naurice G. Cummings, Howard M. Day, Tammis M. Day, Theodore J. Day, Bob Rawls, Thomas P. Ford, Erin A. Keck, Howard B. Keck Jr., John E. Kolb, Max R. Lents, James P. Lower, Kerry K. Mott, Simon Rano, Arthur Smith Jr., David A. Thomas, C. William Verity Jr.

Staff: Six full-time professional, eight full-time support

Financial Profile

Assets: In 1993, $876,602,003
High Grant: $3,700,000
Low Grant: $25,000
Ave. Grant: $100,000-$750,000
Total Grants: In 1993, 68 grants totaling $41,217,000
High Grant Higher Ed.: $3,700,000
Low Grant Higher Ed.: $100,000
Ave. Grant Higher Ed.: $100,000-$350,000
Total Grants Higher Ed.: 46 grants totaling $23,775,000

Application Process

Contact: Sandra A. Glass, science, engineering, and liberal arts; Joan Du Bois, medical research, medical education, law and legal administration, arts and culture, health care, precollegiate education, and community services: (213) 680-3833

Deadline: Letters of inquiry are accepted year round; proposals are due September 15 and March 15

Board Meeting: June and December

Processing Time: June and December

Publications: Annual report, informational brochure, application guidelines

Guidelines: The initial approach should be by letter of inquiry. Organizations should not complete the required applicant information form unless they receive an invitation to submit a proposal.

Sample Grants

Stanford University Law School in Stanford, California, received $300,000 to establish a program in legal ethics and the legal profession.

Calvin College in Grand Rapids, Michigan, received $150,000 to equip a classroom/laboratory for engineering instruction.

Lawrence University in Appleton, Wisconsin, received $250,000 for the enhancement of an advanced theoretical and experimental physics course.

Vanderbilt University in Nashville, Tennessee, was awarded a two-year grant for $3,700,000 to expand its Free-Electron Laser Center for biophysical and materials research.

Brandeis University in Waltham, Massachusetts, received $1,000,000 for the construction of a center for complex systems for biomedical research on higher brain function.

University of Colorado in Boulder received $200,000 for research in RNA biochemistry.

Holy Names College in Oakland, California, received $150,000 for an endowment for its CORE Programs in Humanistic Studies.

College of Holy Cross in Worcester, Massachusetts, received $350,000 to develop a language resource center.

Comments/Analysis

The foundation's priority area is science, with medical research its second priority. The top recipients of funds are colleges and universities, medical schools, law schools, and major independent medical research institutions.

51
W.K. Kellogg Foundation
One Michigan Avenue E
Battle Creek, MI   49017-4058

Areas of Interest

Program Description: The foundation focuses on the area of education, preferring to support projects based on existing knowledge rather than research, and pilot projects that can be replicated in other communities or organizations. Priorities include projects to improve human well-being in the areas of elementary, secondary, and higher education; youth, leadership, community-based health services, food systems and agriculture, rural development, community development, philanthropy and volunteerism, and ground water resources. The following areas receive limited funding, but may become major interests in the future: families, neighborhoods, and human resources for the management of information systems. Other areas of interest include the aged, minorities, Southern Africa, Latin America, the Caribbean, and conservation.

Assistance Types: Seed money, fellowships

Eligibility

Restrictions: No support for religious purposes, no grants to individuals, or for building, endowment funds, research, operating budgets, annual campaigns, emergency funds, deficit financing, land acquisition, renovation, development campaigns, film equipment, publications, conferences, radio or television programs; no loans

Personnel

Officers: Russell Mawby, Chair and CEO; Norman A. Brown, President and COO; Laura A. Davis, VP, Corporate Affairs and Corporate Secy.; William Fritz, VP, Finance and Treas.; Helen K. Grace, VP, Progs.; Dan E. Moore, VP, Progs.; Valora Washington, VP, Progs.; Karen Holleneck, VP, Admin.; Katherine L. Sageon, Asst. VP, Finance

Trustees/Directors: Shirley D. Bowser, Chris T. Christ, Dorothy A. Johnson, William E. La Mothe, Wenda Weeks Moore, Robert L. Raun, Fred Sheriff, Howard F. Sims, and Jonathon T. Walton

Staff: 71 full-time professional, one part-time professional, 155 full-time support, two part-time support

Financial Profile

Assets: In 1992, $6,446,933,666; 1993, $5,046,557,137
High Grant: $12,044,822
Low Grant: $1,000
Ave. Grant: $75,000-$250,000
Total Grants: In 1993, 1,456 grants totaling $223,479,263
High Grant Higher Ed.: $3,000,000
Low Grant Higher Ed.: $10,691
Ave. Grant Higher Ed.: $25,000-$250,000
Total Grants Higher Ed.: 1992, 234 grants totaling $76,546,223; 1993, 213 grants totaling $98,718,266

Application Process

Contact: Nancy A. Sims, Exec. Asst., Programming, (616) 968-1611; fax: (616) 968-0413
Deadline: None
Board Meeting: Monthly
Processing Time: Monthly
Publications: Annual report, including application guidelines, informational brochure, newsletter, occasional report
Guidelines: The initial approach should be a preproposal letter of one to two pages including a statement of problem, description of project and amount of funding, results expected from the project, timetable for implementation and evaluation, qualifications of key personnel, budget for organization and project, additional sources of support anticipated and amount, plans for cooperation with other organizations, and IRS letter of determination. Full proposals must conform to specified program priorities.

Sample Grants

Indiana University in Bloomington received a $426,000, three-year grant to strengthen classroom instruction by helping schools improve their selection of educational technology and training educators in its use.

Central Michigan University in Mount Pleasant received a $905,000, three-year grant to improve effectiveness of middle school personnel through preservice and inservice teacher training and implementation of a teacher certification program.

Henry Ford Community College in Dearborn, Michigan, was awarded $34,920 to increase state residents access to community college services through a statewide telecommunications network.

Morehouse College in Atlanta, Georgia, received a $3,000,000 three-and-three-quarter-year grant to establish a center for business leadership development.

University of Natal in Durban, South Africa, received two grants totaling $252,237 to improve black African leadership by providing scholarships to undergraduates to pursue degrees in agriculture, business, and public administration.

Florida A&M University in Tallahassee received a $65,290, two-and-one-quarter-year grant to strengthen nursing and allied health education programs at historically black colleges and universities through a program of faculty and curriculum development.

Iowa State University of Science and Technology in Ames received a $41,000, two-year grant to assist existing multicommunity rural development organizations through an educational network.

State University of New York in Binghamton received $129,378 to help residents of small rural communities improve their decision making skills through a leadership development program and evaluation.

Comments/Analysis

Education received 38 percent of foundation awards. Graduate and professional awards accounted for 20 percent; other, 11 percent; and adult and continuing education, 7 percent. The top type of interest is program support followed by student aid. In 1993, numerous grants were made to Michigan community colleges and four-year higher education institutions to increase state residents' access to college services through a statewide telecommunications network. In addition, several universities in South Africa received awards to improve black African leadership by providing scholarships to undergraduates to pursue degrees in various fields including agriculture, health, business, public administration, education, commerce, and veterinary science.

52

F.M. Kirby Foundation, Inc.
PO Box 151
17 DeHart Street
Morristown, NJ   07963-0151

Areas of Interest

Program Description: To support higher and secondary education; health, including AIDS, family planning, and hospitals; community programs; performing arts; historic preservation; churches and religion; social services; conservation; and public policy organizations. Additional areas of interest include business education, youth, recreation, economics, and leadership development.

Assistance Types: Operating budgets, special projects, general purposes, equipment, renovations, seed money, annual campaigns, research, continuing support

Eligibility

Restrictions: Giving primarily in New York, New Jersey, Pennsylvania, and North Carolina; no grants to individuals or for fundraising; no loans or pledges

Personnel

Officers: F.M. Kirby, President; Walter D. Kirby, VP; Thomas J. Bianchini, Secy.-Treas.; Paul B. Mott Jr., Exec. Director
Trustees/Directors: Alice Kirby Horton, Fred M. Kirby III, Jefferson W. Kirby, S. Dillard Kirby
Staff: Two part-time professional, two part-time support

Financial Profile

Assets: In 1993, $269,025,549
High Grant: $1,500,000
Low Grant: $1,000
Ave. Grant: $15,000-$25,000
Total Grants: In 1993, 200 grants totaling $8,968,743
High Grant Higher Ed.: $162,000
Low Grant Higher Ed.: $10,000
Ave. Grant Higher Ed.: $10,000-$30,000
Total Grants Higher Ed.: In 1992, 22 grants totaling $1,269,667

Application Process

Contact: F.M. Kirby, President, (201) 538-4800
Deadline: Ongoing; proposals received after October 31 are reviewed the following year.
Board Meeting: Quarterly
Processing Time: Notification is made monthly for grant approvals
Publications: Informational brochure, including application guidelines
Guidelines: The initial approach should include a cover letter and one copy of the proposal. An application form is not needed. Applicants should submit a description of the project and amount requested, names and affiliations of board members and other key people, IRS letter of determination, annual report and 990, and signature and title of chief executive officer.

Sample Grants

The University of Medicine and Dentistry of New Jersey Foundation in Newark was granted $10,000 for a capital campaign for E.O.H.S.I.

Columbia University in New York City received $10,000 for internships for F.M. Kirby Foundation Summer Fellows.

The Harvard Business School Fund in Boston, Massachusetts, received $10,000.

Hahnemann University in Philadelphia, Pennsylvania, received $20,000 for Parkinson's Disease research.

Lafayette College in Easton, Pennsylvania, received $15,000 for a special endowment fund for unforeseen athletic needs.

Duke University in Durham, North Carolina, received $10,000 for the Duke Athletic Fund.

Comments/Analysis

The foundation's top area of funding is medical research, which received 35 percent of all grants in 1993. Higher education received 10 percent.

53

Kresge Foundation
PO Box 3151
3215 W Big Beaver Road
Troy, MI   48007-3151

Areas of Interest

Program Description: To support challenge grants for building construction or renovation projects, major capital equipment, and real estate purchases of at least $75,000. Applications are also accepted for the Kresge Foundation Science Initiative, a special grant program upgrading and endowing scientific equipment and laboratories in colleges and universities, teaching hospitals, medical schools, and research institutions. Areas of interest include higher education, health and long-term care, social services, science, environment, arts, humanities and public affairs.
Assistance Types: Building funds, equipment, land acquisition, matching funds, renovation projects

Eligibility

Restrictions: No support for elementary or secondary schools. No grants to individuals, operating or special project budgets, furnishings, conferences, seminars, church building projects, endowment funds, student aid, scholarships, fellowships, research, debt retirement, completed projects, or general purposes; no loans.

Personnel

Officers: Alfred H. Taylor Jr., Chair and CEO; John E. Marshall III, President and Secy.; Edward M. Hunia, VP and Treas.; Bruce A. Kresge, VP; Miguel A. Satut, VP
Trustees/Directors: Jill K. Conway, George D. Langdon Jr., Robert C. Larson, David K. Page, Margaret T. Smith, Robert D. Storey
Staff: Nine full-time professional, 11 full-time support

Financial Profile

Assets: In 1992, $1,456,852,521; 1993 $1,543,183,104
High Grant: $3,278,400
Low Grant: $20,000
Ave. Grant: $100,000-$500,000
Total Grants: In 1992, 178 grants totaling $67,592,400; 1993, 159 grants totaling $59,303,626
High Grant Higher Ed.: $1,000,000
Low Grant Higher Ed.: $150,000
Ave. Grant Higher Ed.: $150,000-$500,000
Total Grants Higher Ed.: 1992, 56 grants totaling $29,972,000; 1993, 60 grants totaling $25,712,000

Application Process

Contact: Alfred H. Taylor Jr., Chair, (313) 643-9630
Deadline: None
Board Meeting: Monthly
Processing Time: Generally within five months; grants announced February through June and September through December for approvals; throughout the year for rejections.
Publications: Annual report, informational brochure (including application guidelines)
Guidelines: An application form can be requested by letter or telephone. The application form is required.

Sample Grants

Brenau University in Gainesville, Georgia, received $300,000 toward the purchase and renovation of its Business and Communication Arts Building.
Union College in Schenectady, New York, received $750,000 toward the restoration and renovation of its Nott Memorial Hall.
Drake University in Des Moines, Iowa, received $250,000 toward the creation of a restricted endowment fund.
Saint Johns University in Collegeville, Minnesota, received $500,000 toward construction of the Sexton Commons Student Center and renovation of Saint Mary Hall.
Defiance College in Defiance, Ohio, received $400,000 toward construction of a new library.
University of Miami in Coral Gables, Florida, received $500,000 toward the phase I completion of shelled space in the Anne Bates Leach Eye Hospital.

Comments/Analysis

The foundation's top area of funding is education, with colleges and universities its top recipients of funds.

54

Robert Lehman Foundation, Inc.
c/o Hertz, Herson & Co.
Two Park Avenue
New York, NY   10016

Areas of Interest

Program Description: To support cultural programs and higher education, with a focus on visual and fine arts and related teaching activities and publications. The foundation is also interested in projects that benefit women and girls and children and youth.
Assistance Types: Program-related grants

Eligibility

Restrictions: Giving primarily in the northeastern United States, with an emphasis on New York City

Personnel

Officers: Philip H. Isles, President; Edwin L. Weisl Jr., VP; Paul C. Guth, Exec. Secy.; Robert A. Bernhard, Treas.
Trustees/Directors: James M. Hester, Michael M. Thomas
Staff: None

Financial Profile

Assets: In 1992, $50,916,396
High Grant: $994,682
Low Grant: $1,000
Ave. Grant: $5,000-$100,000
Total Grants: 29 grants totaling $2,295,013
High Grant Higher Ed.: $255,000
Low Grant Higher Ed.: $35,000
Ave. Grant Higher Ed.: $5,000-$50,000
Total Grants Higher Ed.: In 1992, five grants totaling $450,496

Application Process

Contact: Paul C. Guth, Exec. Secy., (212) 808-7946
Deadline: None
Board Meeting: As required
Publications: None
Guidelines: Prospective applicants should initially submit a letter of inquiry. Unsolicited applications are generally not accepted.

Sample Grants

Cooper Union for the Advancement of Science and Art in New York City received $50,000.
Vassar College in Poughkeepsie, New York, received $125,000.
New York University in New York City was awarded $220,496 for its Institute of Fine Arts.

Comments/Analysis

The foundation is a significant contributor to the visual arts. The top recipients are museums and historical societies, the second, colleges and universities, and the third, arts and humanities organizations.

55
Lilly Endowment, Inc.
2801 N Meridian Street
Indianapolis, IN   46208

Areas of Interest

Program Description: To support religion, education, and community development through the funding of programs that benefit youth, promote leadership, and develop state-of-the-art fundraising to help nonprofit organizations become more self-sustaining. Other areas of interest include culture and arts, historic preservation, community funds, disadvantaged, social services, economic education, and public policy research.
Assistance Types: Seed money, research, fellowships, matching funds, special projects, conferences and seminars, employee matching gifts, scholarship funds, student aid, technical assistance, capital campaigns, general purposes, operating budgets, renovation projects

Eligibility

Restrictions: Giving limited to Indiana with emphasis on Indianapolis for community development projects, elementary and secondary education, undergraduate scholarship funds, and university libraries. No support for health care, biological science projects, endowed chairs, or media grants. No grants to individuals, except for fellowships. Giving primarily to charitable organizations that depend on private support, with a limited number of grants to government institutions and tax-supported programs.

Personnel

Officers: Thomas M. Lofton, Chair and President; William C. Bonifield, VP, Education; Craig R. Dykstra, VP, Religion; N. Clay Robbins, VP, Community Development; Charles A. Johnson, VP, Development; William M. Goodwin, Secy.-Treas.
Staff: 35 full-time professional, 32 full-time support

Financial Profile

Assets: In 1992, $2,607,538,024; 1993, $2,798,848,224
Total Grants: In 1992, 1,856 grants totaling $117,424,863; 1993, 1,826 grants totaling $131,084,221
High Grant Higher Ed.: $1,996,474
Low Grant Higher Ed.: $10,000
Ave. Grant Higher Ed.: $20,000-$300,000
Total Grants Higher Ed.: In 1992, 189 grants totaling $50,607,697; 1993, 109 grants totaling $17,062,815

Application Process

Contact: Gretchen Wolfram, Communications Director, (317) 924-5471
Deadline: None
Board Meeting: February, April, June, September, and November. Officers' Committee approves requests of $7,500-$500,000 in March, May, October, and December.
Processing Time: Three to six months
Publications: Annual report including application guidelines, informational brochure, program policy statement, occasional report, newsletter
Guidelines: Initial approach should consist of a one- to two-page letter. An application form is not required. Applications should include a description of project and amount of funding requested, list of additional funding sources and amounts, qualifications of key personnel, statement of problem, population served, timetable for implementation and evaluation, copy of organization and or project budget, how project will be measured or evaluated, how project will be sustained after grant period, IRS letter of determination, and history and mission of organization.

Sample Grants

Rutgers University in Piscataway, New Jersey, received $150,000 for the Lilly Teaching Fellows Program.

Holy Cross College in Notre Dame, Indiana, received $61,000 for an institutional development program.

Colorado College in Colorado Springs, Colorado, received $234,147 for continued support of its annual workshop on liberal arts.

Butler University in Indianapolis, Indiana, received $10,000 for assistance with the implementation of an institutional ethics program.

Indiana Institute of Technology in Fort Wayne received two grants: $75,000 for a three-year grant for faculty development and $45,325 for curriculum development.

Indiana University and Indiana University Foundation in Bloomington received six grants: $19,315 for a weekly media series of faculty development programs on long-distance education; $1,700,000 for continued support of the Indiana Education Policy Center; $530,000 for phase III of the Urban Teacher Education Project to provide training programs for undergraduate students to teach in elementary, middle, and high schools and for a graduate program that prepares non-education majors for state teacher certification; $46,004 for development program for the Institute for Religious Studies; and $20,000 for assistance with the implementation of an institutional ethics program (two grants for $10,000 each).

Auburn Theological Seminar in New York City received $314,712 for the continued support for the establishment of the Auburn Center for the Study of Theological Education.

University of Pittsburgh in Pennsylvania received a three-year, $430,201 grant to continue an evaluation program that analyzes foundation grants to education and their impact in the area.

Comments/Analysis

Although education programs are geographically targeted on a regional or invitational basis, higher education is a primary interest of the foundation. In 1993, several institutions of higher education received grants for institutional development programs, institutional ethics programs, and Lilly Teaching Fellows. The foundation's priority giving area is program support, followed by research.

56
Henry Luce Foundation, Inc.
111 W 50th Street, Room 3710
New York, NY 10020

Areas of Interest

Program Description: To support projects in Asian affairs, higher education and scholarship, theology, American arts, and public affairs. The foundation sponsors the following programs: the Luce Scholars Program for study in Asia; Henry R. Luce Professorship Program, supporting integrative academic programs; Program in American Art for various artistic projects and research; US-China Cooperative Research Program, encouraging joint research projects; and the Clare Boothe Luce Program to support science careers for women. Additional areas of interest include international studies, social sciences, humanities, fine arts, museums, leadership development, engineering, and science and technology.

Assistance Types: Special projects, research professorships, internships, scholarship funds, employee matching gifts, fellowships

Eligibility

Restrictions: International activities are supported only in East and Southeast Asia. No support for journalism or commercial media projects. No grants to individuals (except for Luce scholars program), or for endowment or domestic building funds, general operating support, annual fund drives; no loans. Nominees for Luce Scholars Program accepted from institutions only; Clare Boothe Luce Programs by invitation to institutions only; individual applications cannot be considered.

Personnel

Officers: Henry Luce III, Chair and CEO; John Wesley Cook, President; Mrs. Maurice T. Moore, VP; John C. Evans, VP and Treas.; Irwin Skolnick, VP and Controller

Trustees/Directors: Robert E. Armstrong, Margaret Boles Fitzgerald, Jane G. Irwin, James T. Laney, H. Christopher Luce, Thomas L. Pulling, David V. Ragone, Charles C. Tillinghast Jr.

Staff: Six full-time professional, seven full-time support

Financial Profile

Assets: In 1992, $450,761,381; 1993, $534,690,161

High Grant: $500,000

Low Grant: $10,000

Ave. Grant: $10,000-$500,000; for individuals: $18,000-$22,000

Total Grants: In 1992, 239 grants totaling $17,156,871; 18 grants to individuals totaling $528,408; 136 employee matching gifts totaling $220,074. In 1993, a total of $20,031,655 was awarded in all areas.

Total Grants Higher Ed.: In 1992, 58 grants totaling $10,195,687; 1993, 69 grants totaling $12,138,707

Application Process

Contact: John Wesley Cook, President, (212) 489-7700

Deadline: Henry R. Luce Professorship, April 1; Program in American Art, June 15; Luce Scholar nominations, first Monday in December; all others, no specific deadlines

Board Meeting: June, October, and December

Publications: Biannual report, including application guidelines and informational brochure

Guidelines: The initial approach should be by letter. Application form is not required.

Sample Grants

Marietta College McDonough Center for Leadership and Business in Marietta, Ohio, received a $80,000, two-year grant for conferences on leadership and the liberal arts.

Princeton Theological Seminar in Princeton, New Jersey, received $1,000,000 for a two-year grant for the completion of the Henry Luce III Library.

New York University in New York City received a $315,000, three-year grant for an extension of the Henry R. Luce Professorship in Architecture, Urbanism, and History.

Huazhong Agricultural University in Wuhan, China, received a $120,000, three-year grant for a research center on the history of Christian universities and Christianity in China.

Boston College in Chestnut Hill, Massachusetts, received a $525,000, five-year grant for a Henry R. Luce Professorship in nursing ethics.

University of Akron in Ohio was awarded $30,000 to initiate a project entitled Urbanization from Below: The Growth of Towns in Post-Mao China, through a US-China Cooperative Research Program.

Connecticut College in New London, Connecticut, was awarded a $225,000, three-year grant for its Center for International Studies and Liberal Arts.

Comments/Analysis

Historically, the top area of funding has been the social sciences, followed by arts and culture. The top recipients have been colleges and universities, followed by museums.

57
J.E. and L.E. Mabee Foundation, Inc.
3000 Mid-Continent Tower
Tulsa, OK   74103

Areas of Interest

Program Description: The foundation supports Christian education and research into the discovery, treatment, and care of diseases. Grants are awarded to Christian religious organizations, charitable organizations, institutions of higher learning, hospitals, and other agencies and institutions engaged in medical research.

Assistance Types: Building funds, capital campaign, renovation projects

Eligibility

Restrictions: Giving limited to Oklahoma, Texas, Kansas, Arizona, Missouri, and New Mexico. No support for secondary or elementary education or tax-supported institutions. No grants to individuals, or for research endowment funds, scholarships, fellowships, or operating expenses; no loans.

Personnel

Officers: Guy R. Mabee, Chair; John H. Conway Jr., Vice-Chair and Secy.-Treas.; John W. Cox, Vice-Chair; Joe Mabee, Vice-Chair

Trustees/Directors: James L. Houghton, H. Alan Nelson

Staff: One full-time professional, six part-time professional, seven full-time support

Financial Profile

Assets: In 1992, $562,497,780; 1993, $579,643,537
High Grant: In 1992, $1,500,000; 1993, $2,000,000
Low Grant: In 1992, $4,000; 1993, $5,000
Ave. Grant: $30,000-$500,000
Total Grants: In 1992, 111 grants totaling $31,046,750; 1993, 99 grants totaling $26,857,592
High Grant Higher Ed.: $1,000,000
Low Grant Higher Ed.: $200,000
Ave. Grant Higher Ed.: $200,000-$500,000
Total Grants Higher Ed.: In 1992, 23 grants totaling $13,700,000; 1993, 19 grants totaling $8,142,000

Application Process

Contact: John H. Conway Jr., Vice-Chair, (918) 584-4286
Deadline: March 1, June 1, September 1, and December 1
Board Meeting: January, April, July, and October
Processing Time: After board meetings
Publications: Program policy statement and application guidelines
Guidelines: The initial approach should be by proposal. Proposals should include IRS letter of determination, annual and financial reports, description of project and amount requested, timetable for implementation, organization and project budget, and descriptive literature.

Sample Grants

Arkansas College in Batesville received $750,000 to build a dormitory.

Saint Gregorys College in Shawnee, Oklahoma, received $82,000 for renovations to academic/classroom buildings.

College of the Ozarks in Point Lookout, Missouri, received $1,000,000 for building renovation.

West Texas State University Catholic Student Center in Canyon, Texas, received $75,000 to build a student center.

Manhattan Christian College in Manhattan, Kansas, received $200,000 to build a dormitory.

Baylor College of Medicine, Research Division, in Houston, Texas, received $500,000 for building support.

Comments/Analysis

The foundation's top area of interest is education, followed by human services. The top recipients of funds are colleges and universities. Historically, 40 percent of the funds dispersed by the foundation have gone to education, with 35 percent going to higher education and 5 percent to other education. Most grants awarded to institutions of higher education are for building and renovation projects.

58
John D. and Catherine T. MacArthur Foundation
140 S Dearborn Street
Chicago, IL   60603

Areas of Interest

Program Description: The foundation supports a fellows program for talented individuals in any field who are chosen in a foundation initiated effort; a general grants program that funds a changing array of purposes; a health program, primarily supporting rehabilitation parasitology, aging, and research in mental health; a community initiatives program, which supports projects in the Chicago area; a program on peace and international cooperation; a world environment and resources program; an education program focusing on literacy; and a population program. Additional areas of interest include biological sciences; AIDS; media and communications; foreign policy; international affairs; government, law, and justice; arms control; conservation; ecology; and reproductive health.

Assistance Types: Matching funds, funds for general purposes, special projects, research, fellowships, program-related investments, and employee matching gifts

Eligibility

Restrictions: No support for churches or religious programs, political activities or campaigns, or other foundations or institutions. No grants for capital or endowment funds, equipment purchases, plant construction, conferences, publications, media productions, debt retirement, development campaigns, fundraising appeals, scholarships, or fellowships (other than those sponsored by the foundation). Although the foundation gives nationally and internationally, the emphasis is on Chicago and Palm Beach, Florida.

Personnel

Officers: Elizabeth Jane McCormack, Chair; Adele Simmons, President; Victor Rabinowitch, Senior VP; Lawrence L. Landry, VP and CFO; William Lowry, VP; Rebecca Riley, VP; Woodward A. Wickham, VP; Nancy B. Ewing, Secy.; Philip M. Grace, Treas. *Trustees/Directors:* John E. Corbally, Robert P. Ewing, Dr. William H. Foege, James M. Furman, Alan M. Hallene, Paul Harvey, John P. Hildren, Shirley Mount Hufstedler, Sara Lawrence Lightfoot, Margaret E. Mahoney, George A. Ranney Jr., Dr. Jonas Salk, Jerome B. Weisner
Staff: 121 full-time professional, three part-time professional, 75 full-time support, six part-time support

Financial Profile

Assets: In 1992, $2,948,361,000; 1993, $3,098,880,225

High Grant: $10,000,000
Low Grant: $4,700
Ave. Grant: $10,000-$300,000
Total Grants: In 1992, 804 grants totaling $127,357,804; 1993, $134,400,000 for program-related investments
High Grant Higher Ed.: $10,000,000
Low Grant Higher Ed.: $10,000
Total Grants Higher Ed.: In 1992, 154 grants totaling $23,941,291; 1993, 146 grants totaling $41,941,455

Application Process

Contact: Richard Kaplan, Director, Grants Management, Research and Information, (312) 726-8000
Deadline: February 1 and August 1
Board Meeting: Monthly, except January, July, August, and September
Publications: Annual report, program policy statement, application guidelines, informational brochure, newsletter.
Guidelines: The board is taking an increased role in initiating grants. Initial approach should by a letter; application form is not required. Proposals should include a description of the organization and project budget, name, address, phone number, statement of proposal, project timetable, expected results, list of additional services, and amount requested.

Sample Grants

Columbia University, Department of Anthropology, in New York City received a $175,000, three-year grant for a research and training program in conservation genetics for Indonesian scientists that will increase the local capacity for research on the distribution and preservation of biological diversity.

University of Illinois Department of Economics in Chicago received a $75,000, two-year grant for a workshop on market-based approaches to environmental policy that will publish papers on issues in environmental economics.

University of South Pacific in Suva, Fuji, received $210,000 for a project to design and implement a community-based biodiversity conservation program in Fije, Vanuatu, New Caledonia, and the Solomon Islands.

Hampshire College Civil Liberties and Public Policy Program in Amherst, Massachusetts, received $28,000 for public education on international population policies.

University of Ibadan in Nigeria received a $370,000, three-year grant for a multicenter research and intervention program on sexual behavior, sexually transmitted diseases, and the use of barrier contraceptives among young adults.

University of Wisconsin, Central Asian Studies Program, in Madison, Wisconsin, received $50,000 for a conference on democratization in Central Asia.

Virginia Tech Foundation in Blacksburg, Virginia, received $13,000 to develop a support system for private farming in the former Soviet Union.

Brown University Options Program in Providence, Rhode Island, received $25,000 for the evaluation of a community education project on US foreign policy in preparation for the development of a similar project at the national level.

Comments/Analysis

International affairs and development are the foundation's primary focus, followed by environmental protection and peace.

59
John and Mary R. Markle Foundation
75 Rockefeller Plaza, Suite 1800
New York, NY   10019-6908

Areas of Interest

Program Description: To improve mass media communications by supporting projects and services growing out of new technologies for the transfer of information. Other areas of interest include computer science, social science, and public policy.
Assistance Types: Research, special projects, program-related investments

Eligibility

Restrictions: No grants for general support, annual campaigns, seed money, equipment, land acquisition, renovations, capital or endowment funds, publications, media production, or scholarships or fellowships.

Personnel

Officers: Joel L. Fleishman, Chair; Lloyd N. Morrisett, President; Dolores E. Miller, Secy.; Karen D. Byers, Director, Finance and Operations
Trustees/Directors: Michael L. Ainslie, David O. Beim, Raymond C. Clevenger III, Michael Collins, D. Ronald Daniel, Stephen W. Fillo, John G. Heimann, Gertrude G. Michelson, Diana T. Murray, Stanley S. Shuman, George B. Weiksner
Staff: Five full-time professional, six full-time support, one part-time support

Financial Profile

Assets: In 1992, $104,435,226; 1993, $111,205,740
High Grant: In 1992, $1,751,000; 1993, $1,748,775
Low Grant: $3,000
Ave. Grant: $3,000-$100,000
Total Grants: In 1992, 49 grants totaling $1,940,666; 1993, 49 grants totaling $4,676,655
High Grant Higher Ed.: $252,767
Low Grant Higher Ed.: $20,000
Ave. Grant Higher Ed.: $25,000-$75,000
Total Grants Higher Ed.: In 1992, 15 grants totaling, $1,146,507

Application Process

Contact: Lloyd N. Morrisett, President, (212) 489-6655; fax: (212) 765-9690
Deadline: Six weeks prior to board meetings

Board Meeting: March, June, and November
Processing Time: Two weeks to two months
Publications: Annual report, application guidelines, informational brochure
Guidelines: The initial approach should be by letter.

Sample Grants

Carnegie-Mellon University School of Computer Sciences in Pittsburgh, Pennsylvania, received two grants totaling $343,767 to continue research on computer-based models of cognition and interactive media.

University of Kansas Center for Research on the Influences of Television on Children, in Lawrence, Kansas, received $40,000 to study the long-term effects of television viewing on educational attainment and motivation.

University of Massachusetts, Department of Psychology, in Amherst was awarded $50,000 to study the long-term effects of television viewing on educational attainment and motivation.

Harvard University John F. Kennedy School of Government in Cambridge, Massachusetts, received two grants: $60,000 for research examining issues related to broadening public access to Internet and $25,000 to expand an information infrastructure project to include publishing and public access issues.

New York University Tisch School of the Arts in New York City received $20,000 for the development of standards to counteract digital manipulation of imagery in the press.

Rutgers University, Center for Culture and Politics of Democracy, in New Brunswick, New Jersey, received $20,000 for research on measures of civic participation.

Comments/Analysis

The foundation is particularly interested in supporting projects in the following areas: the uses of the media to inform and facilitate political participation, the role of information technology in the lives of older people; advances in interactive communications technology; and the development of telecommunications policy that serves the public interest.

60
G. Harold and Leila Y. Mathers Charitable Foundation
103 S Bedford Road, Suite 101
Mount Kisco, NY   10549-3440

Areas of Interest

Program Description: Support primarily for basic medical research and biological sciences
Assistance Types: Medical research, general support

Eligibility

Restrictions: No grants to individuals

Personnel

Officers: Donald E. Handelman, President; William R. Handelman, VP; John Hay, VP; Don Fizer, Secy.; Joseph W. Handelman, Treas.
Trustees/Directors: John R. Young
Staff: One full-time professional, one full-time support

Financial Profile

Assets: In 1993, $125,000,000
High Grant: $666,667
Low Grant: $5,000
Ave. Grant: $5,000-$305,646
Total Grants: 95 grants totaling $9,113,966
High Grant Higher Ed.: $600,000
Low Grant Higher Ed.: $25,000
Ave. Grant Higher Ed.: $50,000-$200,000

Application Process

Contact: James H. Handelman, Exec. Director, (914) 242-0465
Deadline: None
Board Meeting: Two to three times a year
Processing Time: Variable
Publications: None
Guidelines: The initial approach should include a letter and one copy of a research proposal. Applicants should include a brief history of organization and description of mission, organizational/project budget, and listing of additional sources and amount of support.

Sample Grants

New York University Stern School of Business in New York City received $50,000 for general support.
University of Paris in France received $110,000 for medical research.
University of Tennessee College of Veterinary Medicine in Knoxville received $39,700 for medical research.
Harvard University School of Public Health in Cambridge, Massachusetts, received two grants totaling $581,334 for medical research.
University of Nevada School of Medicine in Reno received $99,850 for medical research.

Comments/Analysis

The foundation's top area of interest is medical research. Hospitals and medical care facilities received the highest amount of funds, followed by colleges and universities and medical research institutes. The majority of funds distributed to institutions of higher education goes to schools and colleges of medicine.

61
Andrew W. Mellon Foundation
140 E 62nd Street
New York, NY   10021

Areas of Interest

Program Description: The foundation supports higher education and cultural affairs, including the humanities, art conservation, museums, and performing arts. The foundation is also interested in population issues, the environment, and public policy and affairs.
Assistance Types: Endowment funds, continuing support, research, internships, fellowships, matching funds, special projects

Eligibility

Restrictions: No support for primarily local programs; no grants for individuals

Personnel

Officers: John C. Whitehead, Chair; William G. Bowen, President; T. Dennis Sullivan, Financial VP; Harriet Zucherman, VP; Richard Ekman, Secy.; Eileen M. Scott, Treas.
Trustees/Directors: Charles E. Exley Jr., Hanna Holburn Gray, Timothy Mellon, Frank H.T. Rhodes, Charles A. Ryskamp, John R. Stevenson
Staff: 13 full-time professional, 20 full-time support

Financial Profile

Assets: In 1992, $2,063,235,543; 1993, $2,330,432,410
High Grant: In 1992, $2,000,000; 1993, $6,280,000
Low Grant: In 1992, $20,000; 1993, $3,500
Ave. Grant: $15,000-$600,000
Total Grants: In 1992, 156 grants totaling $95,865,156; 1993, 396 grants totaling $93,989,549
High Grant Higher Ed.: $2,010,000
Low Grant Higher Ed.: $20,000
Ave. Grant Higher Ed.: $50,000-$200,000
Total Grants Higher Ed.: In 1992, 176 grants totaling $54,052,150; 1993, 154 grants totaling $50,522,050

Application Process

Contact: Richard Ekman, Secy., (212) 838-8400
Deadline: None
Board Meeting: March, June, October, and December
Processing Time: After board meetings
Publications: Annual report, which includes application guidelines
Guidelines: The initial approach should be a descriptive letter or proposal. Proposals should include the history and mission of organization, names and affiliations of board members and trustees, description of project and amount requested, statement of problem to be addressed by project, timetable for implementation

and evaluation, anticipated results, how project will be measured or evaluated, the population served, qualifications of key personnel, additional sources of funds, how the project will be sustained after the grant period, organization and project budget, annual report and financial statement, descriptive literature, IRS letter of determination, and signature of chief executive officer.

Sample Grants

Cornell University in Ithaca, New York, received three grants under the category of higher education: $491,000 toward establishing a master's program in agricultural economics and management at the University of Agriculture at Nitra, Slovakia; $400,000 toward assisting institutions in the Czech Republic and Slovakia in efforts teach human resource management and industrial relations in a market context; and $366,000 for use by six universities for a minority summer research exchange program.

Sheldon Jackson College in Sitka, Alaska, received $42,700 for a study of the college's alumni.

University of Maryland in Baltimore received $50,000 toward planning programs in immigrant education.

University of Puget Sound in Tacoma, Washington, was awarded $250,000 to improve educational effectiveness and efficiency through curricular and administrative consolidation.

Connecticut College in New London received $50,000 for a project to expand ways in which technology can strengthen instruction in several fields of study.

Estovos Lorand University in Budapest, Hungary, received $75,000 toward completing high-speed computer connections among academic institutions in Budapest.

American Council of Learned Societies Devoted to Humanistic Studies in New York City received three grants: $350,000 toward the Darwin Correspondence Project; $300,000 to establish a database for the humanities and for studies of these disciplines; and $25,000 toward publishing and distributing a summary of a conference cosponsored by three other organizations.

Emory University Art Museum in Atlanta, Georgia, received $195,000 to enhance the educational role of its collections and programs.

Yale University in New Haven, Connecticut, received two grants in the area of arts and culture: $450,000 for its School of Drama and its repertory theater to initiate changes in faculty, curriculum, and administrative structure; and $40,000 toward editorial costs of the project, The Works of Jonathan Edwards.

Clemson University in Clemson, South Carolina, received $130,000 toward ecological research and training.

University of Chicago, Irving B. Harris Graduate School of Public Policy, received $1,500,000 for a matching endowment to support training, research, and policy analysis.

Comments/Analysis

In 1993, several grants were awarded to colleges and universities to advance educational effectiveness and financial efficiencies through curricular and/or administrative consolidation. In the area of the environment, numerous academic institutions received grants for ecological research and training.

62
John Merck Fund
11 Beacon Street, Suite 1230
Boston, MA   02108

Areas of Interest

Program Description: To support medical teaching hospitals for research on developmental disabilities in children, to preserve environmental quality both in rural New England and globally, to promote nonproliferation of weapons of mass destruction and conventional arms, to support control policy and planning, and to advance international human rights. Other areas of interest include family planning and conservation.

Assistance Types: Research, publications, special projects, operating budgets, conferences and seminars, program-related investments

Eligibility

Restrictions: The foundation discourages applications from large, well-established organizations. No grants to individuals or for endowment or capital fund projects. Grants are usually made at the initiation of the fund.

Personnel

Officers: Francis W. Hatch, Chair; Huyler C. Held, Treas.
Trustees/Directors: Sherman B. Altchuler, Judith M. Buechner, Oliva H. Farr, Serena M. Hatch, Arnold Hiatt, Robert M. Pennoyer
Staff: Two full-time professional

Financial Profile

Assets: In 1992, $113,459,938; 1993, $95,843,704
High Grant: $250,000
Low Grant: $600
Ave. Grant: $25,000-$60,000
Total Grants: In 1992, 136 grants totaling $5,561,870; 1993, 131 grants totaling $4,828,579
Total Grants Higher Ed.: In 1992, 25 grants totaling $948,480; 1993, 19 grants totaling $818,000

Application Process

Contact: Ruth G. Hennig, Administrator, (617) 723-2932
Deadline: None
Board Meeting: Monthly
Publications: Grants list, informational brochure
Guidelines: Applicants should provide a copy of most recent annual report/ audited financial report/990, and a copy of the IRS letter of determination.

Sample Grants

Columbia University in New York City received $60,000 for research on the role of nitric oxide in childhood hypoxic-ischemic injury.

Dartmouth College in Hanover, New Hampshire, received $25,000 for research on the production of ethanol fuel from cellulosic biomass.

Georgia Institute of Technology in Atlanta was awarded $10,000 to produce videotaped messages from world leaders attesting to the urgent need for strong government commitments to environmental protection.

Comments/Analysis

International affairs and international organizations receive the greatest amount of funds and the greatest number of grants from the fund, followed by support for environmental protection and colleges and universities. The fund concentrates on program development and support, including conferences, faculty development, curriculum development, and publications. The foundation's secondary area of support is medical research. Medical research grants made to institutions of higher education are made as part of the John Merck Scholars Program in the Biology of Developmental Disabilities in Children. The fund is also interested in projects that benefit women and girls and the economically disadvantaged. In addition, its giving pattern historically reflects its support of projects related to reproductive freedom.

63
Ambrose Monell Foundation
c/o Fulton, Duncombe and Rowe
30 Rockefeller Plaza, Room 3217
New York, NY   10112

Areas of Interest

Program Description: To promote projects that improve the physical, mental, and moral condition of humanity throughout the world. The foundation supports health, hospitals, and mental health services; medical and scientific research, including AIDS research; arts, performing arts, and museum and cultural programs; aid to the disabled and aged; higher and secondary education; animal welfare; and research in the social sciences, physical sciences, and political science.

Assistance Types: General purposes, research, building funds, endowment funds, continuing support

Eligibility

Restrictions: No grants to individuals

Personnel

Officers: George Rowe Jr., VP and Secy.
Trustees/Directors: Eugene P. Griasanti, Henry G. Walter Jr.

Financial Profile

Assets: In 1992, $167,684,586; 1993, $173,459,205
High Grant: In 1992, $650,000; 1993, $1,500,000
Low Grant: $1,000
Ave. Grant: $5,000-$100,000
Total Grants: In 1992, 80 grants totaling $7,210,000; 1993, 76 grants totaling $8,581,000
High Grant Higher Ed.: $500,000
Low Grant Higher Ed.: $20,000
Ave. Grant Higher Ed.: $25,000-$70,000
Total Grants Higher Ed.: In 1992, seven grants totaling $964,000

Application Process

Contact: (212) 586-0700
Deadline: December 1
Board Meeting: December
Publications: None
Guidelines: The initial approach should be by proposal. One copy, not to exceed 10 pages, should be submitted. No application form is needed. Applicants should include an annual report and an organizational budget.

Sample Grants

The Foundation for Teaching Economics in San Francisco received $15,000 for general support.

Harvard University School of Public Health in Cambridge, Massachusetts, received $100,000 for general support of the Department of Tropical Medicine and $500,000 for immunology research.

Mannes College of Music in New York City received $50,000 for general support.

Johns Hopkins University in Baltimore, Maryland, was granted $44,000 for general support.

The United Negro College Fund in New York City was granted $200,000 for general support.

The School of American Ballet in New York City was granted $50,000 for general support.

The Institute for Advanced Study in Princeton, New Jersey, was granted $350,000 for general support of its social sciences programs.

Comments/Analysis

The foundation awards grants to hospitals, educational institutions, performing arts groups, and human service agencies. The top area of funding is medical research, followed by arts and culture. In the past, education received 8 percent of all grants distributed by the foundation. The top type of funding awarded is general support, followed by research and continuing support. The foundation is particularly interested in projects that serve the mentally disabled, minorities, and youth.

64

Charles Stewart Mott Foundation
1200 Mott Foundation Building
Office of Proposal Entry
Flint, MI   48502-1851

Areas of Interest

Program Description: Support for community improvement through grants for expressing individuality, expanding personal horizons, citizenship, volunteer activities, counteracting alienation, community identity and stability, community renewal, environmental management, fostering institutional openness, improved delivery of services, and training in and improving practices of leadership. Additional areas of interest include early childhood; secondary, vocational, and minority education; rural and urban development; family services; delinquency; disadvantaged; youth; environment; conservation; southern Africa; and welfare and employment.

Assistance Types: Conferences and seminars, continuing support, loans, matching funds, operating budgets, program-related investments, publications, seed money, special projects, technical assistance, general purposes

Eligibility

Restrictions: No support for religious organizations or purposes. No grants to individuals or generally for building or endowment funds, research, scholarships, or fellowships.

Personnel

Officers: William S. White, Chair, President, and CEO; William H. Piper, Vice-Chair, Richard K. Rappleye, VP and Secy.-Treas.; Judy Y. Samelson, VP, Communications; Robert E. Swaney Jr., VP and Chief Inv. Officer; Maureen H. Smyth, VP, Progs.

Trustees/Directors: Alonzo A. Crim, Katherine Fanning, Rushworth M. Kidder, Webb F. Martin, C.S. Harding Mott II, Maryanne Mott, Willa B. Player, John W. Porter

Staff: 38 full-time professional, three part-time professional, 18 full-time support

Financial Profile

Assets: In 1992, $1,164,407,915; 1993, $1,273,305,723
High Grant: $6,000,000
Low Grant: $2,500
Ave. Grant: $20,000-$200,000
Total Grants: In 1992, 430 grants totaling $41,614,586; 1993, 452 grants totaling $46,281,668
Total Grants Higher Ed.: In 1992, 37 grants totaling $2,210,482; 1993, 37 grants totaling $8,428,736

Application Process

Contact: (313) 238-5651
Deadline: None

Board Meeting: March, June, September, and December
Processing Time: 60 to 90 days
Publications: Annual report, newsletter, informational brochure, program policy statement, financial statement
Guidelines: Proposals should include the following information: description of the problem to be addressed by the project and amount requested, population served, organization and/or project budget, annual and financial reports, history and mission of organization, IRS letter of determination, timetable for implementation of project, and how the project will be measured or evaluated.

Sample Grants

Michigan State University in East Lansing received $112,896 for community models for early life poverty prevention among infants and young children in the African American communities of North Flint and Beecher.

Bakers College in Flint Michigan received $200,000 for library expansion.

United Negro College Fund in New York City received two grants: $2,000,000 for its Campaign 2000 capital campaign and a $100,000, two-year grant toward its planned giving program.

University of the Witwatersrand Foundation in Johannesburg, South Africa, received a two-year, $180,000 grant for a community-based development program.

Johns Hopkins University in Baltimore, Maryland, received three grants in the area of community improvement and development: a $300,000, two-year grant for an Eastern European nonprofit sector training program; a $97,000 one-and-one-half-year grant for a global nonprofit sector awareness project; and $25,000 for organizational support for the International Society for Third Sector Research.

University of Arizona Foundation in Tucson received $100,000 for the redesigning of education for at-risk children.

University of Texas in Austin was awarded $50,000 for the second national conference on school reform.

University of California in Riverside received $18,816 for a People of Color Environmental Directory.

Howard University in Washington, DC, received a two-year, $300,000 grant for the documentary, Living on the Edge, which will examine poverty issues related to America's central cities and explore debilitating conditions facing their residents.

Comments/Analysis

The priority area of interest for the foundation is community improvement and development, the second is environmental protection, and third, public affairs. The foundation is committed to supporting efforts to increase citizenship, volunteer action, and leadership development, and community renewal and identity.

65

M.J. Murdock Charitable Trust
703 Broadway, Suite 710
Vancouver, WA 98660

Areas of Interest

Program Description: To support projects or programs of private, nonprofit charitable organizations aimed at the solution or prevention of significant problems with implications beyond the immediate geographic area and able to continue after initial funding. Interests include education, higher education, social services, science and technology, medical research, and the physical sciences.
Assistance Types: Seed money, building funds, equipment, research, special projects

Eligibility

Restrictions: Giving focused primarily in the Pacific Northwest, (Washington, Oregon, Idaho, Montana, and Alaska). Support for community projects only in the Portland, Oregon, and Vancouver, Washington, areas. No support for government programs; projects common to many organizations without distinguishing merit; sectarian or religious organizations whose principal activities benefit their own members; or agencies served by United Way of Columbia-Wilmette, except for approved projects. No grants to individuals, or for annual campaigns, general support, continuing support, deficit financing, endowment funds, operating budgets, emergency funds, scholarships, fellowships, or matching gifts; no loans.

Personnel

Officers: Ford A. Anderson II, Exec. Director
Trustees/Directors: James B. Castles, Walter P. Dyke, Lynwood W. Swanson
Staff: Four full-time professional, one part-time professional, six full-time support

Financial Profile

Assets: In 1992, $263,699,731; 1993, $285,541,345
High Grant: In 1992, $1,000,000; 1993, $1,250,000
Low Grant: In 1992, $5,000; 1993, $1,500
Ave. Grant: $20,000-$150,000
Total Grants: In 1992, 101 grants totaling $13,900,673; 1993, 137 totaling $16,764,325
High Grant Higher Ed.: $2,000,000
Low Grant Higher Ed.: $25,000
Ave. Grant Higher Ed.: $50,000-$150,000
Total Grants Higher Ed.: In 1992, 32 grants totaling $9,155,740; 1993, 25 grants totaling $7,529,100

Application Process

Contact: Ford A. Anderson II, Exec. Director, (503) 285-4085; mailing address: PO Box 1618, Vancouver, Washington 98668
Deadline: None

Board Meeting: Monthly
Processing Time: Three to six months
Publications: Both the annual report and informational brochure include application guidelines; newsletter
Guidelines: Send letter to request required application form.

Sample Grants

Southern Oregon State College Foundation in Ashland received $33,500 for enhancements to scanning electron microscopy.
Northern Montana College in Havre received $67,500 for a library automation project.
Oregon Health Sciences University Foundation in Portland received $272,500 for its Frontier Delivery Baccalaureate Nursing Program.
Willamette University in Salem, Oregon, was awarded $326,000 for library automation.
Carroll College Foundation in Helena, Montana, received $275,000 to strengthen its mathematics, science, and engineering programs.
Montana State University in Bozeman received $475,000 for instrumentation for a surface and image analysis facility.
Northwest Nazarene College in Nampa, Idaho, was awarded $59,500 for undergraduate research in biology and chemistry.
Oregon Graduate Institute of Science and Technology in Portland received $2,000,000 for its Center for Lifelong Learning and computer science and engineering facilities.

Comments/Analysis

In the past, 13 percent of the funds awarded by the trust have gone to education, with colleges and universities the top recipients, followed by graduate schools. Science and technology was the trust's top area of interest.

66

Charlotte W. Newcombe Foundation
35 Park Place
Princeton, NJ 08542

Areas of Interest

Program Description: Support is provided to colleges and universities in the form of scholarships and fellowships for the physically disabled, the disadvantaged, doctoral candidates in the humanities, and second-career women.
Assistance Types: Scholarship funds, fellowships

Eligibility

Restrictions: No additional support given to colleges outside of scholarship and fellowship programs; no grants to individuals, for staffing, program development, or building funds; no loans or postdoctoral fellowships. Scholarships restricted to four-year schools in Pennsylvania, New Jersey, New York, Maryland, Delaware, and Washington, DC; no second career women scholarships to two-year colleges, professional schools, or seminaries; scholarships for the disadvantaged only awarded to students attending colleges affiliated with the Presbyterian Church.

Personnel

Officers: Janet A. Fearon, Exec. Director
Trustees/Directors: Robert M. Adams, K. Roald Bergethon, Aaron E. Gast, Thomas P. Glassmoyer
Staff: Two full-time professional, one part-time support

Financial Profile

Assets: In 1992, $34,031,047; 1993, $34,880,125
High Grant: In 1992, $545,600; 1993, $587,950
Low Grant: $1,750
Ave. Grant: $5,000-$45,000
Total Grants: In 1992, 59 grants totaling $1,496,450; 1993, 56 grants totaling $1,539,200
High Grant Higher Ed.: $545,600
Low Grant Higher Ed.: $1,750
Ave. Grant Higher Ed.: $3,000-$45,000
Total Grants Higher Ed.: In 1993, 52 grants totaling $1,549,650

Application Process

Contact: Janet A. Fearon, Exec. Director, (609) 924-4666
Deadline: November 1 for scholarship programs; November 15 for fellowships
Board Meeting: February, April, June, October, and December.
Processing Time: April for fellowships beginning in June; May for scholarships beginning in July
Publications: Annual report, including application guidelines
Guidelines: Applications are available from mid-June to mid-October for physically disabled students and mature women students. Presbyterian Colleges should inquire to the foundation regarding scholarships. Selection of scholarship recipients is the responsibility of the academic institution. Fellowship applicants should request applications by November 15 from the Woodrow Wilson National Fellowship Foundation at the following address: Newcombe Fellowships, Woodrow Wilson National Fellowship Foundation, PO Box 642, Princeton, NJ 08542.

Sample Grants

West Chester University of Pennsylvania in West Chester received $10,000 for scholarships to mature second career women who have completed half of the credits required for their degrees.

Warren Wilson College in Swannanoa, North Carolina, received $10,000 to provide Newcombe scholarships to economically disadvantaged and/or minority students from the area.

Tusculum College in Greenville, Tennessee, received $20,000 to provide Newcombe Scholarships to economically disadvantaged and/or minority students from the area.

New York University in New York City received $40,000 to provide scholarships to physically disabled students.

Comments/Analysis

The top area of interest for the foundation is student aid; the second is capital funds. The top recipients are colleges and universities; the second is educational support services; third, graduate schools.

67
Samuel Roberts Noble Foundation, Inc.
PO Box 2180
2510 State Highway, 199 E
Ardmore, OK   73402

Areas of Interest

Program Description: To support higher education, health research pertaining to cancer and degenerative diseases, and for health delivery systems. The foundation operates two programs: plant research, particularly genetic engineering; and agricultural research and wildlife management.
Assistance Types: Research, seed money, building funds, equipment, endowment and matching funds, capital campaigns

Eligibility

Restrictions: Giving primarily in the southwest, in particular, Oklahoma

Personnel

Officers: Michael A. Cawley, President; Larry Pulliam, Senior VP, CFO, and Treas.; Elizabeth A. Aldridge, Secy.
Trustees/Directors: Ann Noble Brown, David R. Brown, Vivan N. Dubose, William R. Goddard, Shelley Mullins, Edward E. Noble, Mary Hane Noble, John F. Snodgrass
Staff: 50 full-time professional, 90 full-time support

Financial Profile

Assets: In 1993, $567,299,890
High Grant: $1,414,051
Low Grant: $280
Ave. Grant: $5,000-$150,000
Total Grants: In 1993, 68 grants totaling $45,257,462
High Grant Higher Ed.: $500,000
Low Grant Higher Ed.: $10,000
Ave. Grant Higher Ed.: $20,000-$100,000
Total Grants Higher Ed.: In 1992, 20 grants totaling $1,898,869; 1993, 10 grants totaling $804,637

Application Process

Contact: Michael A. Cawley, President, (405) 223-5810
Deadline: Six weeks prior to board meetings

Board Meeting: Usually in January, April, July, and October
Processing Time: Two weeks after board meeting
Publications: Annual report, application guidelines, informational brochure
Guidelines: Initial approach should be by letter. An application form is required. Proposals should include the history and mission of the organization, a description of the project, and amount of funding requested.

Sample Grants

Oglethorpe University in Atlanta, Georgia, was awarded $20,000 for the scholarship fund.

Oklahoma State University Foundation in Stillwater was granted $118,500 for purchase of high technology instructional equipment.

The Medical College of Wisconsin in Milwaukee was granted $10,000 for a bone marrow transplant registry.

Comments/Analysis

Education is the top area of foundation funding, receiving 30 percent of all grants in 1993. Higher education received 13 percent, graduate and professional education, 8 percent. Other grants, including arts, culture, and recreation was the secondary priority for the foundation. Science was the third priority for funding in 1993, receiving 17 percent of all grants.

68

John M. Olin Foundation, Inc.
100 Park Avenue, Suite 2701
New York, NY 10017

Areas of Interest

Program Description: Support for public policy, research, strategic and international studies, studies of American political institutions, and law and the legal system, with an emphasis on the application of the fundamental American principles of freedom and justice. Additional areas of interest include higher education, economics, media and communications, political science, government, journalism and leadership development.
Assistance Types: Seed money, research, special projects, publications, conferences and seminars, general purposes, professorships, fellowships, continuing support, lectureships

Eligibility

Restrictions: No support for programs not significantly important to national affairs. No grants to individuals or for annual campaigns, operating budgets, or building or endowment funds; no loans.

Personnel

Officers: William E. Simon, President; George J. Gillespie III, Secy.-Treas.; James Piereson, Exec. Director
Trustees/Directors: Peter Flanigan, Richard M. Furlaud, Charles F. Knight, Eugene F. Williams Jr.
Staff: Four full-time staff, one part-time professional, one full-time support, and one part-time support

Financial Profile

Assets: In 1992, $57,571,966; 1993, $45,258,167
High Grant: In 1992, $1,770,376; 1993, $2,729,624
Low Grant: In 1992, $2,000; 1993, $976
Ave. Grant: $10,000-$200,000
Total Grants: In 1992, 188 grants totaling $415,272,569; 1993, 184 grants totaling $14,584,299
High Grant Higher Ed.: $3,398,460
Low Grant Higher Ed.: $10,000
Ave. Grant Higher Ed.: $20,000-$125,000
Total Grants Higher Ed.: In 1992, 108 grants totaling $12,856,568; 1993, 100 grants totaling $10,206,902

Application Process

Contact: James Piereson, Exec. Director, (212) 661-2670
Deadline: None
Board Meeting: Four times a year
Processing Time: Usually within 90 days
Publications: Annual report, application guidelines
Guidelines: The initial approach should be a proposal.

Sample Grants

Intercollegiate Studies Institute in Bryn Mawr, Pennsylvania, received $30,000 for its student newspaper.

Cambridge University Peterhouse College in Cambridge, England, received $25,000 for work on religion and public doctrine in modern England and other research projects.

University of Toronto, Faculty of Law in Toronto, Canada, received $94,000 for a program in law and economics.

Georgetown University Department of Government in Washington, DC, received $123,011 for a John M. Olin Professorship.

Washington University in Saint Louis, Missouri, received $3,398,460 to establish the John M. Olin Graduate School of Business Administration.

Comments/Analysis

The foundation's top areas of interest are education and student aid. Its top recipients of funds are colleges and universities.

69

David and Lucile Packard Foundation
300 Second Street, Suite 200
Los Altos, CA 94022

Areas of Interest

Program Description: Primary areas of support include child development and welfare; early, elementary, and secondary education; the environment and conservation; family planning; marine sciences; and population studies. Local support is also given for the performing arts, employment and job training, food, shelter, and youth. Funding also for management assistance; archaeology; and Pueblo, Colorado. Additional areas of interest include science and technology, minority education, educational research, the disadvantaged, homeless, community and urban development, ecology, and Latin America.

Assistance Types: Building funds, general purposes, equipment, land acquisition, research, internships, matching funds, program-related investments, consulting services, technical assistance, loans, operating budgets, capital campaigns, seed money, renovation projects, emergency funds, conferences and seminars

Eligibility

Restrictions: Giving for the arts and community development primarily in Santa Clara, San Mateo, Santa Cruz, and Monterey Counties, California, with some support also in the Pueblo, Colorado area; national giving for child health and education; national and international giving in Latin America for population and the environment. No support for religious purposes. No grants to individuals; generally no grants for endowment funds.

Personnel

Officers: David Packard, Chair; Susan Packard Orr, President; David Woodley Packard, VP; Barbara P. Wright, Secy.; Edwin E. Van Bronkhorst, Treas.; Colburn S. Wilbur, Exec. Director

Trustees/Directors: Nancy Packard Burnett, Robin Chandler Duke, Dr. Robert Glaser, Dean O. Morton, Julie E. Packard, Frank Roberts

Staff: 12 full-time professional, two part-time professional, 24 full-time support, three part-time support

Financial Profile

Assets: In 1992, $871,261,000; 1993, $1,279,828,472
High Grant: In 1992, $18,130,000; 1993, $10,000,000
Low Grant: In 1992, $5,000; 1993, $720
Ave. Grant: $5,000-$50,000
Total Grants: 413 grants totaling $35,113,000, plus $1,908,924 for foundation-administered programs and $870,000 for four program-related investments; 1993, 651 grants totaling $55,561,180, plus $2,453,201 for three foundation-administered programs and $3,031,000 for three program-related investments
High Grant Higher Ed.: $500,000
Low Grant Higher Ed.: $10,000
Ave. Grant Higher Ed.: $15,000-$100,000

Total Grants Higher Ed.: In 1992, 73 grants totaling $14,473,996; 1993, 68 grants totaling $19,451,912

Application Process

Contact: Colburn S. Wilburn, Exec. Director, (415) 948-7658
Deadline: December 15, March 15, June 15, and September 15
Board Meeting: March, June, September, and December
Processing Time: Immediately after board meetings
Publications: Annual report (including application guidelines), grants list, occasional report, informational brochure, and program policy statement
Guidelines: Applicants should approach the foundation with a proposal. Proposals should include a description of the project and amount requested, name and address of applicant, history and mission of organization, problem addressed by proposed project, population served, geographic area served, timetable, anticipated results, qualifications of key personnel, how project will be measured or evaluated, names and qualifications of board, organization or project budget, annual and financial reports, IRS letter of determination, additional funding expected from other sources, and program materials or documentation.

Sample Grants

San Diego State University in California was awarded $20,000 for a child care health and safety telephone hotline.

University of California Center for Reproductive Health Policy in San Francisco received $20,000 for a study of the family planning program in the state of Queretaro, Mexico.

Cabrillo College in Aptos, California, received $10,130 for Cabrillo Strings/Suzuki music program.

University of California at Santa Cruz Foundation received $30,000 for general support for performing arts.

University of California at Berkeley received $25,000 to disseminate information on the school voucher initiative.

California Institute of Technology in Pasadena received $1,000,000 for an endowed graduate fellowship.

University of Colorado Foundation in Boulder was awarded a $1,000,000, four-year grant for the construction of an integrated teaching laboratory.

Native American Scholarship Fund in Albuquerque, New Mexico, received $25,000 for 10 scholarships to Native American students majoring in engineering.

Boston University in Massachusetts received $65,340 to study the effects of managed care on medicaid recipients and on public institutions.

Comments/Analysis

The foundation's priority area is science. The top recipients of funds are colleges and universities. In 1993, institutions of higher education received grants for support of Historically Black Colleges and Universities Science Program; Packard Scholars Program for Chemistry, Physics, and Math Award; and for fellowships in chemistry, physics, zoology, biology, astronomy, microbiology, mathematics, electrical engineering, and genetics.

70

Ralph M. Parsons Foundation
1055 Wilshire Boulevard, Suite 1701
Los Angeles, CA   90017

Areas of Interest

Program Description: To support higher and precollegiate education, particularly engineering, science, technology, and medicine, including health services for disadvantaged populations and AIDS. The foundation also supports cultural and civic projects and projects aimed at social needs, including assistance for children, women, elderly, and families. Additional areas of interest include community development, homeless, housing, engineering, science and technology, and computer science.

Assistance Types: Seed money, equipment, matching and scholarship funds, internships and fellowships, renovation projects, research, operating budgets

Eligibility

Restrictions: Giving primarily in Los Angeles County, except for higher education grants. No support for annual campaigns, emergency or endowment funds, land acquisition, workshops, exhibits, surveys, or conferences.

Personnel

Officers: Joseph G. Hurley, President; Albert A. Dorskind, VP and CFO; Leroy B. Houghton, VP; Edgar R. Jackson, VP; Everett B. Laybourne, VP; Christine Sisley, Exec. Director
Trustees/Directors: Ira J. Blanco, Robert F. Erburu, James A. Thomas
Staff: Three full-time professional, three full-time support

Financial Profile

Assets: In 1992, $190,578,218; 1993, $197,386,397
Ave. Grant: $10,000-$75,000
Total Grants: In 1992, 172 grants totaling $48,307,687; 1993, 171 totaling $8,809,755
High Grant Higher Ed.: $1,000,000
Low Grant Higher Ed.: $1,000
Ave. Grant Higher Ed.: $50,000-$150,000
Total Grants Higher Ed.: In 1992, 12 grants totaling $2,837,422; 1993, 18 grants totaling $2,624,839

Application Process

Contact: Christine Sisley, (213) 482-3185
Deadline: None
Board Meeting: Bimonthly, beginning in January
Processing Time: Six months
Publications: Annual report
Guidelines: Initial approach should be by letter. Application form is not required; applicants should submit the following items: description of project and amount requested; statement of problem project will address; history and mission of organization; IRS letter of determination; signature and title of chief executive officer; qualifications of key personnel; how results will be evaluated; annual report; and names and affiliations of board, trustees, and other key people.

Sample Grants

Thomas Aquinas College in Santa Paula, California, received $150,000 for its financial aid fund.
Pacific Oaks College in Pasadena, California, received $70,000 for a study to improve the coordination of child care provider recruitment, training, and retention in California.
California State University at Long Beach Foundation was awarded $93,549 for a summer orientation institute of the minority engineering program.
Los Angeles Mission College in San Fernando, California, was awarded $120,000 for computer and other equipment needed in the Ralph M. Parsons Engineering Lab and Materials Testing Lab.
Heritage College in Toppenish, Washington, was awarded $120,000 for computer labs in the new library and learning center.

Comments/Analysis

Historically, education has been the foundation's top priority area, accounting for approximately 22 percent of all grants distributed. Higher education receives 7 percent; K-12, 7 percent; graduate and professional, 5 percent; and other education, 3 percent.

71

Pew Charitable Trusts
2005 Market Street
One Commerce Square, Suite 1700
Philadelphia, PA   19103-7017

Areas of Interest

Program Description: To develop leadership through giving in arts and performing arts, culture, secondary and higher education, health and medical sciences, human services, conservation and the environment, public and foreign policy, religion and theology, and a newly formed interdisciplinary fund. Additional areas of interest include missionary programs, international affairs and relief, citizenship, immigration, minorities, volunteerism, social services, child development, youth, family services, employment, disadvantaged, aged, handicapped, educational associations, mental health, and substance abuse.

Assistance Types: Seed money, matching funds, continuing support, renovation projects, research, operating budgets, special projects, general purposes, internships, technical assistance, exchange programs, program-related investments, fellowships, publications, seminars

Eligibility

Restrictions: No grants to individuals or for endowment funds, deficit financing, scholarships, or fellowships (except those identified by the trust).

Personnel

Officers: Rebecca W. Rimel, President; Micheal Rubinger, Exec. VP

Trustees/Directors: Susan W. Catherwood, Robert G. Dunlop, Robert E. McDonald, Howard Pew II, J.N. Pew III, Dr. Joseph N. Pew IV, R. Anderson Pew, William C. Richardson

Staff: 66 full-time professionals, 34 full-time support

Financial Profile

Assets: In 1992, $3,337,295,049; 1993, $3,512,044,823

High Grant: $2,250,000

Low Grant: $1,500

Ave. Grant: $50,000-$200,000

Total Grants: In 1992, 605 grants totaling $143,537,605; 1993, a total of $143,385,679 awarded in all categories

High Grant Higher Ed.: $7,900,000

Low Grant Higher Ed.: $18,000

Ave. Grant Higher Ed.: $45,000-$300,000

Total Grants Higher Ed.: In 1992, 170 grants totaling $80,218,261

Application Process

Contact: Rebecca W. Rimel, President, (215) 575-9050

Board Meeting: March, June, September, and December

Processing Time: Approximately three weeks after board meetings

Publications: Annual report, grants list, occasional report, informational brochure, including application guidelines

Guidelines: Contact the foundation for brochure on specific guidelines and limitations in each program area. An application form is required. A letter of inquiry (two to three pages) should be sent to obtain an application.

Sample Grants

Heritage College Research Center for the Teaching of Math and Applied Sciences in Toppenish, Washington, received a $300,000, three-year grant to improve the teaching of mathematics and applied sciences in rural school districts that serve Hispanic and Native American populations.

Columbia University Teachers College in New York City received two grants: a $45,000, two-year grant for technical assistance to Community Compacts for Students Success sites to help strengthen the focus on teaching and learning in participating schools; and a $480,000, three-year grant to the National Center for Restructuring Education, Schools, and Teaching to document the development and implementation of a New York School Quality Review Process.

Syracuse University, Center for Instructional Development in Syracuse, New York, received $45,000 for a national study on the perceived balance between research and teaching at colleges and universities.

Montana State University Foundation, Yellowstone Center for Mountain Environments in Bozeman, Montana, received $40,000 for a two-year grant for research on the impact of different types of disturbances on the region's forest ecosystem and for an annual symposium.

Delaware County Community College Educational Foundation in Media, Pennsylvania, received a $200,000, three-year grant for professional development programs for faculty.

Saint Charles Borromeo Seminary in Philadelphia, Pennsylvania, received $300,000 to construct and equip a special collections area in the Ryan Memorial Library.

Temple University College of Arts and Sciences in Philadelphia, Pennsylvania, received a $3,000,000, three-year grant for construction of a new classroom building.

Comments/Analysis

The trusts' focus on education is in helping secondary schools, enabling colleges and universities to enhance the performance and success of disadvantages students, promoting fundamental changes in the structure and management of institutions, up-grading teacher quality, and linking employee training to secondary and higher education institutions.

72
Carl and Lily Pforzheimer Foundation, Inc.
650 Madison Avenue
New York, NY   10022

Areas of Interest

Program Description: To support higher and secondary education; libraries and literacy; civic and cultural programs; public administration; arts, performing arts, and theater; literature and language; health care, hospitals, and nursing; and government.

Assistance Types: Seed money, professorships, internships, scholarships, endowment funds, matching funds, program-related investments, publications, and special projects

Eligibility

Restrictions: No building funds or loans

Personnel

Officers: Carl H. Pforzheimer Jr., President; Carl H. Pforzheimer III, VP and Treas.; Martin F. Richman, Secy., Anthony L. Ferranti, Controller

Trustees/Directors: Nancy P. Aronson, Richard W. Couper, George L.K. Frelinghuysen, Carl A. Pforzheimer, Carol K. Pforzheimer, Allison A. Sherman

Staff: Three full-time professional, two full-time support

Financial Profile

Assets: In 1992, $37,816,271; 1993, $38,969,688

High Grant: In 1992, $288,935; 1993, $400,000
Low Grant: In 1992, $3,000; 1993, $2,000
Ave. Grant: $10,000-$50,000
Total Grants: In 1992, 31 grants totaling $1,473,498; 1993, 36 grants totaling $2,003,057
High Grant Higher Ed.: $150,000
Low Grant Higher Ed.: $25,000
Ave. Grant Higher Ed.: $50,000-$100,000
Total Grants Higher Ed.: In 1992, eight grants totaling $673,000

Application Process

Contact: Carl H. Pforzheimer Jr., President, (212) 223-6500
Deadline: None
Board Meeting: April, June, October, and December
Processing Time: Immediately following board meeting at which the proposal is reviewed
Guidelines: The initial approach may be either a letter or a proposal. Applications should include the history and mission of the organization, detailed description of project and amount of request, and qualifications of key personnel.

Sample Grants

Wilberforce University in Wilberforce, Ohio, was awarded $125,000.
Bank Street College of Education in New York City received $100,000.
Harvard University in Cambridge, Massachusetts, received $150,000.
Barnard College in New York City was granted $50,000.
Pace University in New York City was awarded $73,000.
Wellesley College in Wellesley, Massachusetts, received $100,000.
University of California in Riverside received $25,000.

Comments/Analysis

The foundation's top subject area of interest is education, followed by general and rehabilitative medicine, and arts and culture. Colleges and universities are the top recipients of funds and receive the largest number of grants. The second are hospitals and medical care facilities, followed by graduate schools. The foundation is interested in projects that benefit women, minorities, and children and youth.

73
Plumsock Fund
9292 N Meridian Street, Suite 312
Indianapolis, IN   46260

Areas of Interest

Program Description: To support higher and secondary education, cultural programs, anthropology, youth agencies, health and welfare. The foundation has a special interest in Latin America and publishes a Spanish Language journal.

Assistance Types: General purpose, special projects

Eligibility

Restrictions: Giving primarily in the United States. The foundation does not support fellowships or scholarships, no grants to individuals, no loans.

Personnel

Officers: Edwin Fancher, President; Daniel A. Wolf, VP; John G. Rauch Jr., Secy.-Treas.
Trustees/Directors: Kenneth Chapman, Christopher H. Lutz
Staff: None

Financial Profile

Assets: In 1992, $4,560,958; 1993, $4,454,563
High Grant: In 1992, $239,110; 1993, $148,500
Low Grant: $100
Ave. Grant: $500-$25,000
Total Grants: In 1992, 139 grants totaling $1,438,799; 1993, 140 totaling $1,461,665
High Grant Higher Ed.: $48,000
Low Grant Higher Ed.: $800
Ave. Grant Higher Ed.: $5,000-$20,000
Total Grants Higher Ed.: In 1992, eight grants totaling $261,000; 1993, six grants totaling $162,000

Application Process

Contact: John G. Rauch Jr., Secy.-Treas., (317) 846-8115
Deadline: None
Board Meeting: Annually
Publications: None
Guidelines: The initial approach should be by letter. Three copies of the proposal should be submitted.

Sample Grants

Oglala Lakota College in Kyle, South Dakota, received $24,000 for general support.
United States Foundation of the University of the Valley of Guatemala in Ithaca, New York, received $96,000 for a chair in history.
University of California in Berkeley received $12,000 to subsidize one student internship in Latin America.
Dartmouth College Thayer School of Engineering in Hanover, New Hampshire, received $10,000 for the course, Engineering Concepts for the High School Classroom.

Comments/Analysis

The fund's top subject of interest is arts and culture, followed by social sciences and education.

74

Public Welfare Foundation
2600 Virginia Avenue NW, Room 505
Washington, DC   20037-1977

Areas of Interest

Program Description: To support programs that meet the needs of and advocate more effective services and delivery systems for low-income populations, and organizations in the United States and abroad that address problems in the areas of the environment, including threats to the health and safety of low-income communities, environmentally sound agricultural, and economic efforts; health, including access to health care and good nutrition; criminal justice, including alternatives to incarceration and public education about criminal justice issues; disadvantaged elderly and youth; and population programs, including family planning and AIDS prevention, education, and care.
Assistance Types: Matching funds, seed money, special projects, operating budgets

Eligibility

Restrictions: No support for religious purposes, endowments, research, scholarships, graduate or foreign study, capital improvements, conferences or workshops, consulting services, annual campaigns, or deficit financing; no grants to individuals and no loans

Personnel

Officers: Donald T. Warner, Chair; Linda Campbell, Secy.
Trustees/Directors: Veronica T. Keating, Antoinette Haskell, Robert H. Haskell, Myrtis H. Powell, Thomas W. Scoville, Jerome W.D. Stokes, C.E. Warner
Staff: 12 full-time professional, five full-time support, one part-time support

Financial Profile

Assets: In 1993, $300,303,054
High Grant: $250,000
Low Grant: $10,000
Ave. Grant: $15,000-$250,00
Total Grants: 445 grants totaling $17,434,500
High Grant Higher Ed.: $250,000
Low Grant Higher Ed.: $24,000
Ave. Grant Higher Ed.: $20,000-$50,000
Total Grants Higher Ed.: In 1992, 14 grants totaling $701,600; 1993, 15 grants totaling $813,600

Application Process

Contact: Larry Kressley, Exec. Director, (202) 965-1800
Deadline: None

Board Meeting: Board or committee meets eight times per year
Processing Time: Three to four months
Publications: Annual report, including application guidelines, and grants list
Guidelines: Application form is not required; however, guidelines should be consulted. The initial approach should be a proposal with a summary sheet. One copy should be submitted. Applicants should include the following in the proposal: name, address, and phone number of organization; contact person; brief history of organization and mission; detailed description of project and amount requested; copy of organizational/ project budget; copy of most recent annual report/audited financial statement; timetable for implementation and evaluation; qualifications of key personnel; names and affiliations of board members and key people; population project will serve; listing of additional sources and amount of funding; how project's results will be evaluated or measured; and copy of IRS letter of determination.

Sample Grants

Warren Wilson College in Swannanoa, North Carolina, was awarded a four-year grant of $250,000 for the start-up of a scholarship program and for the completion of renovations on the common areas of Sunderland Hall.

University of North Carolina Public Health Foundation in Chapel Hill was awarded $30,000 for a community childhood hunger identification project in North Carolina.

Skidmore College in Saratoga Springs, New York, received $25,000 for an ex-offender transition program which will provide coordinated services for inmates in the University Without Walls Prison Program as they graduate, achieve parole, or are transferred.

Vanderbilt University in Nashville, Tennessee, received $21,000 for a final grant for Service Training for its Environmental Progress (STEP) Program, providing technical assistance to community groups working on environmental health problems.

Columbia University Health Sciences Department in New York City received $59,000 for a cooperative program between the Columbia and Mexican family planning agency, Descosal, through which reproductive health education and family planning services are made available to women factory workers and gang members in Saltillo, Mexico.

Comments/Analysis

The top subject area of foundation interest is health and medicine; the second largest is environment; the third, crime, courts, and legal services. Historically, human services agencies have received the most funds, followed by professional societies and associations, and environmental agencies. Research and public policy institutes and educational support agencies received significant funding support. In the past the top form of support has been program support, including faculty/staff development, program development, seed money, and film/television/radio. The second has been general support, and the third, capital support, particularly building, renovations, and capital campaigns. The foundation generally supports higher education projects that are either linked with a grassroots community effort or that provide education or training to those engaged in efforts to meet community needs.

75
Research Corporation
101 N Wilmot Road, Suite 250
Tucson, AZ   85711-1119

Areas of Interest

Program Description: To support academic science and technology through an awards programs that includes the Cottrell College Science Program, research opportunity awards, the Partners in Science program, and general foundation grants.
Assistance Types: Research, special projects

Eligibility

Restrictions: No grants to individuals, or for building or endowment funds, indirect costs, common supplies and services, tuitions, research leave to begin new projects, faculty academic year salaries, postdoctoral or graduate student stipends, secretarial assistance, general support, scholarships, fellowships, publications, travel expenses to scientific meetings or research facilities, or matching gifts; no loans.

Personnel

Officers: John P. Schaefer, President; Brian H. Andreen, VP; Helen Dacy, Secy.; Suzanne D. Jaffe, Treas.
Trustees/Directors: Stuart B. Crampton, Michael P. Doyle, Robert M. Gavin, John W. Johnstone Jr., Joan Selverstone Valentine, G. King Walters, Laurel L. Wilkening
Staff: Three full-time professional, four part-time professional, five full-time support

Financial Profile

Assets: In 1992, $90,289,218; 1993, $94,905,353
Ave. Grant: $13,000-$30,000
Total Grants: 1992, 310 grants totaling $2,833,566, plus $223,000 for two foundation-administered programs; 1993, $3,734,038 for grants
High Grant Higher Ed.: $33,000
Low Grant Higher Ed.: $10,874
Ave. Grant Higher Ed.: $15,000-$30,000
Total Grants Higher Ed.: In 1992, 129 grants totaling $2,758,476; 1993, 167 grants totaling $44,234,781

Application Process

Contact: Brian H. Andreen, VP, (602) 571-1111; fax: (602) 571-1119

Deadline: Cottrell College Science Awards target dates, May 15 and November 15; research opportunity awards nominations, May 1 and October 1; Partners in Science, November 1 and December 1; no deadline for general awards
Board Meeting: November and April
Processing Time: 10 months
Publications: Annual report, application guidelines, newsletter, occasional report
Guidelines: Applicants should request an application form. Proposals should include description of the project and the amount of the request, qualifications of key personnel, how project will be measured or evaluated, what distinguishes project from others in the field, annual report and financial report, and IRS letter of determination.

Sample Grants

Colby College in Waterville, Maine, was awarded $31,080 for a research project on the determination of quantum yields for fe(III) photoreduction in well-defined electrolyte solutions.

Erskine College in Due West, South Carolina, received $11,378 for a research project on the synthesis of alkaloids by cyclization of w-halonitriles with grignard reagents.

New Jersey Institute of Technology in Newark received $23,300 for an optical and electrical study of photo-induced superconductivity.

Oregon Graduate Institute of Science and Technology received three $14,000 Partner in Science Awards.

Pepperdine University in Malibu, California, received $31,450 for a mechanistic and kinetic study of sulfer dioxide oxidation on metal oxide surfaces.

Comments/Analysis

Support is given to basic research in the physical sciences (physics, chemistry, and astronomy). The transfer of useful inventions from universities and other nonprofit research institutions to industry is encouraged. Since the foundation's primary interest is science, colleges and universities are the top recipients, followed by research and science organizations.

76
Rockefeller Brothers Fund
1290 Avenue of the Americas
New York, NY   10104-0233

Areas of Interest

Program Description: To support efforts in the United States and abroad to develop leaders and to assist institutions in the transition to global interdependence by encouraging cooperation, trade, and economic growth; arms restraint; and conservation. The five major giving categories are the following: One World, with two major components: sustainable resource use and world security, including issues related to arms control, international relations, development, trade, and finance; New York City; the nonprofit sector; education; and South Africa. Additional areas of interest include the environment, intercultural relations, agriculture, urban development, AIDS, education, and minority education.

Assistance Types: Seed money, general purposes, special projects, conferences and seminars, internships, exchange programs, matching funds, consulting services, continuing support, research, technical assistance

Eligibility

Restrictions: No support for churches, hospitals, or community centers. No grants to individuals, including research, graduate study, or the writing of books or dissertations, with two exceptions: the RBF Fellowships and the Program for Asia projects; no grants for land acquisitions or building funds; no loans

Personnel

Officers: Abby M. O'Neill, Chair; Steven C. Rockefeller, Vice-Chair; Colin G. Campbell, President; Russel A. Phillips Jr., Exec. VP; Benjamin R. Shute Jr., Secy.-Treas.; Leora E. Landmesser, Comptroller

Trustees/Directors: Catherine O. Broderick, Jonathan F. Fanton, Neva R. Goodwin, T. George Harris, Kenneth Lipper, William H. Luers, Jessica Tuchman Mathews, Richard D. Parsons, David Rockefeller Jr., Richard G. Rockefeller, Rodman C. Rockefeller, S. Frederick Starr.

Staff: Five full-time professional, two part-time professional, 16 full-time support, one part-time support

Financial Profile

Assets: In 1992, $342,426,742; 1993, $374,329,834
High Grant: $440,000
Low Grant: $1,000
Ave. Grant: $25,000-$300,000
Total Grants: In 1992, 191 grants totaling $11,042,604, plus $17,252 in employee matching gifts; 1993, 337 grants totaling $11,611,740
High Grant Higher Ed.: $224,984
Low Grant Higher Ed.: $15,000
Ave. Grant Higher Ed.: $20,000-$75,000
Total Grants Higher Ed.: In 1992, 24 grants totaling $1,884,590; 1993, 31 grants totaling $2,780,184

Application Process

Contact: Benjamin R. Shute Jr., Secy.-Treas., (212) 373-4200
Deadline: None
Board Meeting: February, June, and November
Processing Time: Three months
Publications: Annual report, guidelines for application
Guidelines: Initial approach should be a letter of no more than two to three pages. Proposals should include the following information: description of proposed project and amount requested, history and mission of organization, description of what distinguishes the proposed project from others in the field, statement of problem to be addressed in the project, anticipated results, timetable for implementation of project, qualifications of key personnel, organization and/or project budget, names and affiliations of board members

and trustees, IRS letter of determination, and annual and financial reports.

Sample Grants

Yale University School of Forestry in New Haven, Connecticut, received $55,000 to develop a network of researchers in the field of political ecology in Southeast Asia.

Harvard University John F. Kennedy School of Government and Center for Science and International Affairs in Cambridge, Massachusetts, received $150,000 to examine and improve the effectiveness of international transfers of financial resources for environmental protection.

York University in Toronto, Canada, received $25,000 for an assessment of Asia-Pacific security studies and related exchange activities.

Massachusetts Institute of Technology in Cambridge received $50,000 toward a project, Nuclear Arms Control in the Middle East.

Yonsei University, College of Business and Economics, in Seoul, South Korea, received $117,500 toward a project on structural transition and industrial cooperation in Northeast Asia.

Catholic University of America Columbus School of Law in Washington, DC, received $15,000 to study Poland's laws on foundations.

Claremont University Center and Graduate School in Claremont, California, received $150,000 for a multi-ethnic teacher mentoring project to increase the number of minority students within their teacher education program.

Princeton University in Princeton, New Jersey, received $224,984 toward a summer institute in history, a workshop for social studies teachers led by the department of history faculty with assistance from undergraduates in the teacher preparation program.

Comments/Analysis

The foundation's top area of interest in 1993 was the environment, followed by international affairs and development and higher education.

77
Rockefeller Foundation
1133 Avenue of the Americas
New York, NY   10036

Areas of Interest

Program Description: The foundation primarily supports three areas: international science-based development, the arts and humanities, and equal opportunities. Scientific emphases are on the global environment; on the agricultural, health and population sciences; and on a limited number of African initiatives. Smaller grant programs focus on international security and US school reform.

Assistance Types: Fellowships, research, publications, conferences and seminars, special projects, grants to individuals, program-related investments, employee matching gifts, seed money, technical assistance

Eligibility

Restrictions: No support for establishment of local hospitals, churches, schools, libraries, or welfare agencies or their building or operating funds; financing altruistic movements involving private profit; or attempts to influence legislation. No grants for personal aid to individuals or for capital or endowment funds, general support or scholarships; no loans, except program-related investments.

Personnel

Officers: John R. Evans, Chair; Peter C. Goldmark Jr., President; Kenneth Prewitt Sr., VP; Danielle Parris, Acting VP for Communications; Hugh B. Price, VP; Lynda Mullen, Secy.; David A. White, Treas.; Sally Ferris, Director for Administration
Trustees/Directors: Allan Alda, Ela R. Bhatt, Johnetta Cole, Peggy Dulany, Frances FitzGerald, Daniel P. Garcia, Ronald E. Goldsberry, W. David Hopper, Karen N. Horn, Alice Stone Ilchman, Richard H. Jenrette, Robert C. Maynard, Alvaro Umana, Frank G. Wells, Harry Woolf.
Staff: 73 full-time professional, one part-time professional, 65 full-time support, three part-time support

Financial Profile

Assets: In 1992, $2,138,585,815; 1993, $2,364,552,922
High Grant: In 1992, $1,400,000; 1993, $2,400,000
Low Grant: In 1992, $316; 1993, $98
Ave. Grant: $20,000-$100,000
Total Grants: In 1992, 1,115 grants totaling $78,754,297, plus 463 grants to individuals totaling $8,090,348; 1993, 961 grants totaling $75,845,843, plus 352 grants to individuals totaling $6,939,973
High Grant Higher Ed.: $592,900
Low Grant Higher Ed.: $10,000
Ave. Grant Higher Ed.: $20,000-$100,000
Total Grants Higher Ed.: In 1992, 257 grants totaling $27,797,932; 1993, 254 grants totaling $21,470,130

Application Process

Contact: Lynda Mullen, Secy., (212) 869-8500
Deadline: None unless specified in special notices for certain programs and fellowships
Board Meeting: Usually in March, June, September, and December
Publications: Annual report, program policy statement, application guidelines
Guidelines: Application forms are required for certain programs and fellowships. Applicants may be asked to supply information on their affirmative action efforts, including data on the gender and minority composition of the institution's leaders. The initial approach should be a letter or proposal including description of project and amount of request, how project will be sustained after grant period, additional sources of funding and amount, history and mission of organization, and qualifications of key personnel.

Sample Grants

College Art Association in New York City received $40,000 toward a mentoring program enabling minority scholars of art history to attend the annual conference in their field.

Columbia College Center for Black Music Research in Chicago, Illinois, received $20,000 toward the National Conference on Black Music Research.

Lakehead University Native Philosophy Project in Thunder Bay, Canada, received $250,000 toward a program of Rockefeller Foundation Resident Fellowships.

University of Pittsburgh College of General Studies International Center for Culture and Development in Pennsylvania was awarded $12,000 toward seminars on culture and development.

Texas A&M University Center for Biotechnology Policy and Ethics at College Station, Texas, received $15,000 toward the development of a program, A New Agenda for the Humanities in Development.

El Colegio de Mexico in Mexico City received $184,060 for a program entitled Leadership for Environment and Development (LEAD).

North Carolina State University in Raleigh was awarded $500,000 to develop sustainable agroforestry systems for the western Amazon as a way of slowing continuous deforestation in the region.

Stanford University Institute for International Studies in Stanford, California, received $70,000 toward a conference on herbicide use in Asian rice production.

Case Western Reserve University in Cleveland, Ohio, received four grants totaling $525,850 for continued and final funding of the Women for Women's Health Initiative in Uganda.

University of Buenos Aires Faculty of Pharmacy and Biochemistry in Argentina received $35,000 for a study on oxidative damage to sperm and its relevance to human fertility.

University of the Philippines in Manila was awarded $175,000 for training responsibilities within the International Clinical Epidemiology Network (INCLEN).

Purdue University in West Lafayette, Indiana, received two grants: $90,000 for research on integrated biotechnological approaches to the control of striga, a parasitic weed that causes serious losses in small farmers' sorghum and millet crops in Africa and India; and $31,000 for research on the genetic transformation of indica rice.

Michigan State University in East Lansing received $13,500 for research on the genetic analysis of brown planthopper biotypes.

Comments/Analysis

The foundation's top area of interest in 1993 was arts and culture, followed by health, science and technology, and the environment. Colleges and universities are the greatest recipients of funds, followed by professional associations.

78

Sarah Scaife Foundation, Inc.
525 William Penn Place
Three Mellon Bank Center, Suite 3900
Pittsburgh, PA   15219-1708

Areas of Interest

Program Description: To support public policy programs that address major international and domestic issues. Areas of interest include government; higher education; economics; international law, affairs, and studies; political science; crime and law enforcement; and social sciences.

Assistance Types: Operating support, continuing support, seed money, matching funds, fellowships, research, special projects, continuing support, publication support

Eligibility

Restrictions: No support for scholarships; no loans

Personnel

Officers: Richard M. Scaife, Chair; Richard M. Larry, President; Donald C. Sipp, VP, Investment and Treas.; Barbara L. Slaney, VP; Daniel McMichael, Secy.

Trustees/Directors: William J. Bennett, Anthony J.A. Bryan, T. Kenneth Cribb Jr., Edwin J. Feulner Jr., Allan H. Meltzer, James M. Walton

Staff: Six

Financial Profile

Assets: In 1993, $120,016,859
High Grant: $1,000,000
Low Grant: $1,000
Ave. Grant: $25,000-$150,000
Total Grants: In 1993, 107 grants totaling $6,896,340
High Grant Higher Ed.: $350,000
Low Grant Higher Ed.: $20,000
Ave. Grant Higher Ed.: $25,000-$150,000
Total Grants Higher Ed.: In 1992, 31 grants totaling $3,720,000; 1993, 29 grants totaling $4,061,000

Application Process

Contact: William R. Fitz, (415) 565-5803
Deadline: None
Board Meeting: February, May, September, and November
Processing Time: Two to four weeks
Publications: Annual report, including application guidelines
Guidelines: The initial approach may be by either letter or proposal. The initial letter should be signed by the organization's president. Application form is not required; proposals should include a description of project and amount of funding requested; organizational budget; annual report; IRS letter of determination; and names and affiliations of board, trustees, and other key people.

Sample Grants

Stanford University in California was granted $350,000 for international studies, security affairs, and domestic studies programs (grant shared with the Hoover Institution on War, Revolution, and Peace).

Claremont McKenna College in Claremont, California, received $89,000 for research and publication support.

Tufts University Fletcher School of Law and Diplomacy in Medford, Massachusetts, received $225,000.

University of California in Santa Cruz received $15,000 for publication support.

Foundation for Research in Economics and Education (FREE) in Los Angeles received $100,000 for research at the University of California, Los Angeles, Graduate School of Management.

Southwest Missouri State University Foundation, Center for Defense and Strategic Studies in Springfield, Missouri, received $85,000.

University of Virginia Law School Foundation, Center for National Security Law in Charlottesville, Virginia, received $250,000.

George Mason University Foundation, Center for the Study of Public Choice in Fairfax, Virginia, was awarded $132,000.

University of California at Irvine Foundation received $50,000 for graduate fellowships in public choice theory.

Comments/Analysis

The foundation's top priority is human services, receiving 25 percent of its grants in 1993; its second priority is education at 17 percent.

79

Florence and John Schumann Foundation
33 Park Street
Montclair, NJ   07042

Areas of Interest

Program Description: To support programs in effective governance, the environment, and international relations. Other areas of interest include education, foreign policy, public policy, citizenship, community improvement and development, and human services.

Assistance Types: Operating budgets, continuing support, seed money, matching funds, special projects

Eligibility

Restrictions: No grants to individuals, or for annual campaigns equipment, land acquisition, or endowment funds

Personnel

Officers: Robert F. Schumann, Chair; Bill Moyers, President; Howard D. Brundage, VP, Finance; Caroline S. Mark, VP; David S. Bate, Secy.-Treas.

Trustees/Directors: Edwin D. Etherington, John C. Whitehead
Staff: Two full-time professional, two full-time support

Financial Profile

Assets: In 1993, $78,543,614
High Grant: $1,000,000
Low Grant: $2,500
Ave. Grant: $10,000-$50,000
Total Grants: In 1993, 80 grants totaling $7,001,600
High Grant Higher Ed.: $340,426
Low Grant Higher Ed.: $15,000
Total Grants Higher Ed.: In 1992, seven grants totaling $1,195,000; 1993, five grants totaling $595,426

Application Process

Contact: Patricia McCarthy, (201) 783-6660
Deadline: January 15, April 15, and August 15
Board Meeting: February, June, and October
Processing Time: Two to three months
Publications: Biennial report, including application guidelines
Guidelines: The initial approach should be a two- to three-page letter. An application form is not required. Proposals should include the following items: brief history and mission of the organization, detailed description of the project and amount requested, copy of annual report/audited financial report/990, organizational/project budget, timetable for implementation and evaluation of project, and copy of IRS letter of determination.

Sample Grants

Columbia University Graduate School of Journalism in New York City received $340,426 for the training of promising minority students in their pursuit of advanced level careers in electronic journalism.

University of Minnesota Foundation in Minneapolis received $50,000 for a challenge grant for the Solomon Project.

College of the Atlantic in Bar Harbor, Maine, was awarded $15,000 for the distribution and coordination of citizen action with a mini-documentary on rivers.

Pace University School of Law, Center for Environmental Legal Studies, in White Plains, New York, received a $90,000, three-year grant for the Pace Energy Project.

University of Pennsylvania Annenberg School for Communication in Philadelphia, Pennsylvania, received $100,000 for regular analysis of presidential campaign discourse in 1992.

Comments/Analysis

The foundation's uppermost area of interest is the environment, followed by public affairs/government and community improvement and development. The foundation favors video and media projects as a medium for public information about public affairs issues. Professional societies and associations are the top recipients of funds, followed by human services agencies and technical assistance centers.

80
Seaver Institute
800 W Sixth Street, Suite 1410
Los Angeles, CA   90017

Areas of Interest

Program Description: To support projects in the arts, the community, education, health, and science. Other areas of interest include music, educational research, medical sciences, and medical research.
Assistance Types: Matching funds, research, special projects

Eligibility

Restrictions: No support for operating budgets or continuing support, annual campaigns, scholarships, capital or building funds, publications, or conferences; no loans.

Personnel

Officers: Richard C. Seaver, Vice-Chair; Richard W. Call, President; John F. Hall, VP and Treas.; Christopher Seaver, Secy.
Trustees/Directors: David Alexander, Richard Archer, Camron Cooper, Myron E. Harpole, Leroy Hood, Raymond Jallow, Martha Seaver, Victoria Seaver
Staff: Two full-time professional, three part-time professional

Financial Profile

Assets: In 1993, $36,600,196
High Grant: $159,360
Low Grant: $50
Ave. Grant: $1,000-$50,000
Total Grants: In 1993, 79 grants totaling $1,378,415
High Grant Higher Ed.: $400,000
Low Grant Higher Ed.: $10,000
Ave. Grant Higher Ed.: $1,000-$15,000
Total Grants Higher Ed.: In 1992, six grants totaling $775,090

Application Process

Contact: Richard Call, President, (213) 688-7550
Deadline: None
Board Meeting: December and June
Publications: Informational brochure, including application guidelines
Guidelines: Interested applicants should contact the foundation for application guidelines. The foundation generally initiates projects.

Sample Grants

The California Institute of Technology in Pasadena was granted $400,000 for its Doctor Hood project.

The Massachusetts Institute of Technology in Cambridge received $150,000 for research on silicon retinal implants.

Princeton University in Princeton, New Jersey, received $100,000 for a study on superconductivity.

Johns Hopkins University in Baltimore, Maryland, received $65,090 for a study on public policy.

Comments/Analysis

The foundation's top interest is higher education, followed by medical research and arts and culture, in particular the performing arts. Colleges and universities are the top recipients, followed by social science organizations and medical research institutes.

81
Alfred P. Sloan Foundation
630 Fifth Avenue, Suite 2550
New York, NY   10111-0242

Areas of Interest

Program Description: The foundation supports science and technology; education in science, technology, and management; economic growth and industrial competitiveness; and selected national issues. Additional areas of interest include higher education, mathematics, physical sciences, social sciences, and engineering.

Assistance Types: Research, fellowships, conferences and seminars, special projects

Eligibility

Restrictions: No support for the creative or performing arts, humanities, medical research, religion, or primary or secondary education. No grants to individuals directly, or for endowment or building funds, or equipment not related directly to foundation supported-projects; no loans.

Personnel

Officers: Howard W. Johnson, Chair; Ralph E. Gomory, President; Stewart F. Campbell, Financial VP and Secy.; Arthur L. Singer, Jr., VP
Trustees/Directors: Lucy Wilson Benson, Stephen L. Brown, Lloyd C. Elam, S. Parker Gilbert, Howard H. Kehrl, Donald N. Langengerg, Cathleen Synge Morawetz, Frank Press, Lewis T. Preston, Harold T. Shapiro, Roger B. Smith, Roger M. Solow
Staff: 19

Financial Profile

Assets: In 1992, $775,698,874; 1993, $849,741,304
High Grant: $3,500,000
Low Grant: $1,500
Ave. Grant: $15,000-$100,000
Total Grants: In 1992, 207 grants totaling $28,622,466

High Grant Higher Ed.: $3,361,760
Low Grant Higher Ed.: $10,000
Ave. Grant Higher Ed.: $20,000-$150,000
Total Grants Higher Ed.: In 1992, 63 grants totaling $17,169,422; 1993, 100 grants totaling $18,366,315

Application Process

Contact: Stewart F. Campbell, VP, (212) 649-1649
Deadline: September 15 for fellowship program; no deadline for other programs
Board Meeting: Grants of $30,000 or less, throughout the year; grants over $30,000, five times a year
Processing Time: Early in year for research fellowships; within three months for others
Publications: Informational brochure (including application deadlines), annual report, newsletter
Guidelines: Nomination forms available for fellowship candidates; direct applications not accepted. Application form not required for other proposals. The initial approach should be by letter of inquiry. Proposals should include description of program and amount of request, qualifications, timetable of project, IRS letter of determination, and results anticipated from project.

Sample Grants

Appalachian State University in Boone, North Carolina, received $29,933 for the study of an existing data set on what works for minority students in developmental education programs at different types of institutions.

Mississippi Community College Foundation in Raymond received $27,246 for a community college-based experiment in foreign marketing.

University of Maryland in College Park was awarded $84,962 for a pilot study of the causes and consequences of departure from doctoral programs before completing degrees.

Drexel University in Philadelphia, Pennsylvania, received $750,000 to develop the project, Self-Paced Local and Remote Instruction for Information Systems and Software Design.

Wellesley College in Wellesley, Massachusetts, received $334,630 for further support for the second and final phase of a research project on women in science.

Research Foundation of the City University of New York in New York City received $333,000 for renewal of the Program for Retention of Engineering Students (PRES).

University of Montana Foundation Division of Biological Sciences in Missoula received $36,841 for a sabbatical supplement award in molecular studies of evolution.

University of Colorado Foundation in Boulder received $80,500 for postdoctoral fellowship in molecular studies of evolution.

University of California in Los Angeles received $99,830 for research on immigrant and native engineers in California.

University of Arkansas in Fayetteville received $30,000 for a program on poultry research productivity.

Cornell University in Ithaca, New York, received $27,484 for a conference on the technical workforce.

Swathmore College in Swathmore, Pennsylvania, was awarded $30,000 for the development of a project, Evolution of US Economic Institutions.

Comments/Analysis

The foundation's top interest is science, followed by the social sciences. The foundation is particularly interested in projects that benefit women, immigrants, and minorities. The majority of higher education awards are distributed in the areas of science and technology and social science. In 1993, several colleges and universities received sabbatical supplement awards and postdoctoral fellowships in molecular studies of evolution.

82
Spencer Foundation
900 N Michigan Avenue, Suite 2800
Chicago, IL   60611

Areas of Interest

Program Description: To support research aimed at expanding the knowledge, understanding, and practice of education.
Assistance Types: Research and fellowships

Eligibility

Restrictions: No support for capital funds, general purposes, operating support and continuing support, sabbatical supplements, work in instructional or curriculum development, training programs, scholarships, travel funds, endowments, predoctoral research or matching gifts; no loans

Personnel

Officers: David Tatel, Chair; William Jukius Wilson, Vice-Chair; Patricia Alberg Graham, President; John H. Barcroft, VP and Secy.; Linda M. Schumacher, Treas.
Trustees/Directors: Frank L. Bixby, Linda Darling-Hammond, Robert A. LeVine, Mary Patterson McPherson, George M. Pullman, George A. Ranney Jr., John S. Reed, Albert Shanker, Lee S. Shulman
Staff: Five full-time professional, one part-time professional, five full-time support, three part-time support

Financial Profile

Assets: In 1993, $246,176,000
High Grant: $500,000
Low Grant: $12,000
Ave. Grant: $25,000-$300,000
Total Grants: 80 grants totaling $4,600,000
High Grant Higher Ed.: $496,100
Low Grant Higher Ed.: $25,000
Ave. Grant Higher Ed.: $50,000-$200,000
Total Grants Higher Ed.: 28 grants totaling $6,081,775

Application Process

Contact: Rebecca Barr, Research Grants; Catherine Lacey, Fellowships, (312) 337-7000
Deadline: No deadline for preliminary proposal
Board Meeting: January, April, July, and October
Processing Time: After meeting
Publications: Annual report, application guidelines, informational brochure, newsletter
Guidelines: Prospective applicants should send a letter or preliminary proposal; the foundation will request full proposal if interested. Preliminary proposal should include a detailed description of project and amount of funding requested, summary of research methodologies, modes of analysis, and/or instruments project will employ; and full curriculum vitae for key personnel. Information and application form for the Spencer Postdoctoral Fellowships should be requested from the National Academy of Education, Stanford University School of Education, CREAS-507G, Stanford, California 94305-3084, (415) 725-1003.

Sample Grants

Roosevelt University Institute for Metropolitan Affairs in Chicago, Illinois, received $25,000 for a project entitled Chicago Public Schools: At the Crossroads.

Arizona State University in Tempe received a $86,520, two-year grant for a study entitled Black Scientists and Engineers on Postsecondary Faculties: Organizational Barriers to Recruitment and Equity in Academic Rewards.

Pennyslvania State University in University Park received $42,750 for a study entitled Dynamics of Institutional Change in Higher Education: American Colleges and Universities in the Nineteenth Century.

University of Southern California in Los Angeles received $25,000 toward a study entitled Technology Teaching and Scholarship: A National Survey About Faculty Use of Information Technology.

Syracuse University in Syracuse, New York, received $116,000 for a one-and-one-third-year grant on the study of new roles for teachers.

University of Chicago in Illinois was awarded $429,000 for a three-year study, Talking Aloud during Reading Comprehension.

Duke University in Durham, North Carolina, received a $129,000, two-and-three-quarter-year grant for a study entitled Comparative Analysis of Ability Grouping: Extension and Clarification.

University of Washington Institute for Public Policy and Management in Seattle received a $350,000, five-year grant for long-term inquiry into the hidden curricula of K-12 schools.

Comments/Analysis

The foundation's top subject area is education; the second is social science. Colleges and universities receive the largest number of grants and the largest amount of funds. Educational support agencies are the second largest recipients, followed by public policy institutes.

83
Starr Foundation
70 Pine Street
New York, NY   10270

Areas of Interest

Program Description: Primarily to support elementary, secondary, higher, and other education, including scholarships under specific programs. Other areas of interest include culture, health, welfare, social sciences, and social services.
Assistance Types: Continuing support, endowment funds, professorships, student aid, scholarship funds, fellowships, general purposes, research

Eligibility

Restrictions: No grants to individuals, except through the foundation's scholarship program, or for matching gifts; no loans.

Personnel

Officers: Maurice R. Greenberg, Chair; Ta Chun Hsu, President; Marion I. Breen, VP; Gladys Thomas, VP; Ida E. Galler, Secy.; Frank R. Tengi, Treas.
Trustees/Directors: Houghton Freeman, Edwin A.G. Manton, John J. Roberts, Ernest E. Stempel
Staff: Two full-time professionals, three full-time support

Financial Profile

Assets: In 1992, $893,229,359; 1993, $893,216,217
Ave. Grant: $1,000-$25,000
Total Grants: In 1992, $40,436,495; 1993, $40,150,209
High Grant Higher Ed.: $5,000,000
Low Grant Higher Ed.: $10,000
Ave. Grant Higher Ed.: $50,000-$100,000
Total Grants Higher Ed.: In 1992, 60 grants totaling $20,374,656; 1993, 44 grants totaling $6,237,276

Application Process

Contact: Ta Chun Hsu, President, (212) 770-6882
Deadline: None
Board Meeting: February and September
Processing Time: Varies
Publications: 990-PF
Guidelines: A letter of inquiry should be the initial approach. An application form is not required.

Sample Grants

Amherst College in Amherst, Massachusetts, received $50,000 toward the C.V. Starr Scholarship Fund.
Haverford College in Haverford, Pennsylvania, received $200,000 toward the Starr Scholarship Fund.

University of Washington Foundation, Center for International Business Education and Research, in Seattle received a $450,000, three-year grant for the Chinese track of the International Management Fellows (IMF) Program.
Wells College in Aurora, New York, was awarded a $45,000, three-year grant for its Corporate Affiliates Internship and Investment Program.
Harvard University Business School in Cambridge, Massachusetts, received a $300,000, three-year grant for its Global Financial System Project.
New York University, Gallatin Division, in New York City received $95,000 for continued support of its Public Policy Series.
Brooklyn College of the City University of New York received a $300,000, three-year grant to establish a Starr English as a Second Language (ESL) Learning Center.
Cornell University Medical College Cardiovascular Center in New York City received $50,000 for renewed support of research programs and activities.
New York University in New York City received a $1,500,000, five-year grant to endow a Starr Foundation Chair and Endowed Fellowships in Medical and Molecular Parasitology.

Comments/Analysis

Many of the foundation's grants to higher education go toward the C.V. Starr Scholarship Fund and the Starr Scholarship Fund.

84
Hatton W. Sumners Foundation
325 N Saint Paul, Suite 3333
NCNB Center, Tower III
Dallas, TX   75201

Areas of Interest

Program Description: To support higher education for the study and teaching of the science of self-government; also support for youth organizations.
Assistance Types: Endowment funds, financial aid, scholarships, program support, capital, conferences, faculty and staff development

Eligibility

Restrictions: The foundation primarily supports projects in Texas and the southwestern states.

Personnel

Officers: James Cleo Thompson Jr., Chair; William C. Pannell, Secy.; Thomas S. Walker, Treas.; Gordon R. Carpenter, Exec. Director
Trustees/Directors: David Bourne Long, Alfred Paul Murah Jr.
Staff: Two

Financial Profile

Assets: In 1992, $38,452,871; 1993, $37,375,544
High Grant: In 1992, $244,687; 1993, $308,396
Low Grant: In 1992, $3,500; 1993, $2,000
Ave. Grant: $5,000-$50,000
Total Grants: In 1992, 41 grants totaling $1,440,187; 1993, $1,706,396
High Grant Higher Ed.: $200,000
Low Grant Higher Ed.: $5,000
Ave. Grant Higher Ed.: $5,000-$15,000
Total Grants Higher Ed.: In 1992, 14 grants totaling $888,000

Application Process

Contact: Gordon R. Carpenter, Exec. Director, (214) 220-2128
Deadline: None
Board Meeting: Varies
Processing Time: Usually in the fall
Publications: None
Guidelines: The initial approach should be by letter.

Sample Grants

Schreiner College in Kerrville, Texas, was awarded two grants: $200,000 for a Sumners Scholarship Endowment and $10,000 for a library fund.

Oklahoma City University in Oklahoma City, Oklahoma, received three grants: $100,000 for a building fund, $50,000 for a library fund, and $30,000 for the Native American Legal Center.

Texas A & M University in College Station received $10,000 for its Wiley Lecture Series.

Southern Methodist University in Dallas, Texas, received $148,000 for partial tuition grants and $10,000 for a scholarship program development.

Comments/Analysis

Education is the top area of interest, receiving both the largest amount of funds and the largest number of grants. The top recipients of funds are colleges and universities, followed by educational support agencies and human services agencies. The top form of support is program support, including program development, conferences, and faculty/staff development. Secondary priority is given to student aid funds, followed by capital support.

85
Teagle Foundation, Inc.
30 Rockefeller Plaza, Room 2835
New York, NY   10112

Areas of Interest

Program Description: To support higher education through general and project grants. Scholarships for children of employees of Exxon Corporation and its affiliates. Limited support for youth activities sponsored by New York City community organizations. Direct assistance grants to needy employees, annuitants, and widows of deceased employees of Exxon Corporation.

Assistance Types: Employee-related scholarships, continuing support, matching funds, special projects, employee matching gifts, general purposes, seed money

Eligibility

Restrictions: Giving limited to the United States and (for Exxon scholarships only) Canada. No grants to community organizations outside of New York City. No grants to US organizations for foreign projects. No grants to individuals not connected to Exxon Corporation; no loans.

Personnel

Officers: Donald M. Cox, Chair; Richard W. Kimball, President and CEO; Margaret B. Sullivan, Secy.; James C. Anderson, Treas.
Trustees/Directors: George Bugliarello, Elliot R. Cattarula, John S. Chalsty, Peter O. Crisp, Richard L. Morrill, Walter C. Teagle III
Staff: Two full-time professional, one part-time professional, two full-time support

Financial Profile

Assets: In 1992, $105,999,014; in 1993, $106,007,921
High Grant: $150,000
Low Grant: $4,625
Ave. Grant: $25,000-$75,000
Total Grants: In 1992, 80 grants totaling $4,664,528; in 1993, 79 grants totaling $4,664,528
High Grant Higher Ed.: $100,000
Low Grant Higher Ed.: $12,000
Ave. Grant Higher Ed.: $20,000-$90,000
Total Grants Higher Ed.: 1992, 62 grants totaling $2,906,700

Application Process

Contact: Richard W. Kimball, President, (212) 247-1946
Deadline: Applications for Exxon scholarships due November 1 at the college scholarship service; no deadline for other grants.
Board Meeting: February, May, and November
Processing Time: Promptly after decision
Publications: Annual report, guidelines
Guidelines: The initial approach should take the form of a letter. Application form is not required.

Sample Grants

Milikin University in Decatur, Illinois, received $19,000 for a faculty-student internship program.

Applachian Ministries Educational Resource Center in Berea, Kentucky, received $44,000 to recruit clergy for service in Appalachia.

Union College in Barbourville, Kentucky, received $50,000 for computer laboratory for teaching of English.

The Salvation Army of Greater New York in New York City received $65,000 for officer's children's college scholarships.

Hampton University in Hampton, Virginia, received $90,000 for nursing education.

86
Thrasher Research Fund
50 E North Temple Street, 7th Floor
Salt Lake City, UT   84150

Areas of Interest

Program Description: To support research that has the potential to improve the health of children throughout the world. Areas of interest include child welfare, medical sciences, nutrition, and health and medical research.
Assistance Types: Research

Eligibility

Restrictions: No support for conferences, general operations, construction or renovation, or scholarships. The foundation does not support research in the areas of abortion, contraceptive technology, sexually transmitted diseases, or reproductive physiology.

Personnel

Officers: Richard C. Edgley, Chair; E.W. Thrasher, Vice-Chair
Trustees/Directors: Victor L. Brown, Aileen H. Clyde, Isaac C. Ferguson, Clayton S. Huber, John M. Matsen, Keith B. McMullin, Mary Ann Q. Wood
Staff: One full-time professional, two part-time professional, one full-time support, one part-time support

Financial Profile

Assets: In 1993, $38,046,765
High Grant: $105,976
Low Grant: $1,000
Ave. Grant: $60,000-$150,000
Total Grants: 60 grants totaling $1,883,317
High Grant Higher Ed.: $147,485
Low Grant Higher Ed.: $44,405
Ave. Grant Higher Ed.: $45,000-$100,000
Total Grants Higher Ed.: Nine grants totaling $694,593

Application Process

Contact: Robert M. Briem, Assoc. Director, (801) 240-4753; fax: (801) 240-1417
Deadline: None
Board Meeting: May and November
Processing Time: Six to nine months
Publications: Biennial report, including application guidelines, informational brochure

Guidelines: Prospective applicants are encouraged to consult the foundation by telephone or letter. The next step should be a four-page prospectus. The foundation will review the prospectus and notify applicants whether a full proposal should be submitted. An application form is required and will be provided once the prospectus has been approved.

Sample Grants

Johns Hopkins University in Baltimore, Maryland, received two grants: $47,289 to the Department of International Health for a study on the efficacy of iodine supplementation in conjunction with the World Health Organization's Expanded Programme on Immunization; and $147,485 to the Department of Pediatrics for a three-year grant to study the immunogenicity of the Pneumococcal-Protein Conjugate vaccine in infants with Sickle Cell Disease.

McGill University School of Dietetics and Human Nutrition in Montreal, Canada, received a $94,100, two-and-three-quarter-year grant to investigate the effect of iron supplementation on the growth and morbidity of children six months to five years of age in rural Ethiopia.

Texas A & M University Institute of Biosciences and Technology in Houston was awarded $55,666 to continue work on a novel approach to vaccine development and delivery.

University of Alabama Department of Public Health Sciences in Birmingham received a $99,947, two-year grant to study the effect of infection on urinary excretion, serum level, and body depletion of vitamin A.

Comments/Analysis

The foundation's top area of interest is medical research; the second is medicine; the third, food, nutrition, and agriculture.

87
Tinker Foundation, Inc.
55 E 59th Street
New York, NY   10022

Areas of Interest

Program Description: The foundation supports efforts to promote better understanding among the peoples of the United States, Portugal, Spain, and Latin America. It is particularly interested in projects that promote the exchange of information and activities with strong public policy implications and that benefit immigrants and refugees. Areas of interest include social science, foreign policy, economics, international affairs, marine science, political science, environment, ecology, and higher education.
Assistance Types: Special projects, research, conferences and seminars, matching and seed funds, lectureships, exchange programs

Eligibility

Restrictions: No support for the arts, media projects, humanities, or health or medical activities; no support for building, endowment, operating budgets, equipment, annual campaigns or appeals, or community funds

Personnel

Officers: Martha T. Muse, Chair, President, and CEO; Grayson Kirk, VP; Raymond L. Brittenham, Secy.; Gordon T. Wallis, Treas.; Renate Rennie, Exec. Director
Trustees/Directors: William R. Chanet, John N. Irwin II, John A. Luke Jr., Charles C. Mathias, W. Clarke Wescoe
Staff: Five full-time professional, three full-time support

Financial Profile

Assets: In 1993, $60,423,517
High Grant: $150,000
Low Grant: $2,700
Ave. Grant: $25,000-$50,000
Total Grants: 59 grants totaling $2,287,200
High Grant Higher Ed.: $150,000
Low Grant Higher Ed.: $15,000
Ave. Grant Higher Ed.: $15,000-$50,000
Total Grants Higher Ed.: 19 grants totaling $1,129,350

Application Process

Contact: Martha T. Muse, Chair, (212) 421-6858
Deadline: Institutional grants, March and October; field research grants, October 1
Board Meeting: Institutional grants, June and December; field research grants, December
Processing Time: Two weeks after board meeting
Publications: Annual report, grants list, application guidelines
Guidelines: The initial approach should be by letter. Required application form and two copies of the proposal should be submitted. Proposals should include a description of the project and amount requested, names and affiliations of board members, qualifications of key personnel, results anticipated, population served, name, address and phone number, organization/project budget, IRS letter of determination, annual report/990, history and mission of organization, and additional materials.

Sample Grants

Duke University Center for Tropical Conservation in Durham, North Carolina, received a $125,000, three-year grant to strengthen Latin American training activities.
Mississippi State University in Mississippi State, Mississippi, received $50,000 toward a two-day meeting on US-Mexican Environmental Cooperation and North American Economic Integration: Security, Ecology, and NAFTA.
University of California Energy and Resources Group in Berkeley received a $90,000, two-year grant for two training sessions on the management of coastal wetlands in the tropical Americas.

University of Toronto Center for International Studies in Toronto, Canada, received a $150,000, two-year grant for a comparative study of the consequences of trade policy restructuring for labor markets in Chile, Columbia, Mexico, and Costa Rica.
Tulane Education Fund in New Orleans, Louisiana, received a $150,000, two-year grant toward its program in Mexico policy studies.

Comments/Analysis

The foundation's funding priority is program support, followed by research. The top subject areas of interest are social sciences and interdisciplinary studies, environmental protection, and animals and wildlife. Colleges and universities are the top recipients of funds, followed by environmental agencies and social science organizations.

88
Dewitt Wallace-Reader's Digest Fund, Inc.
261 Madison Avenue, 24th Floor
New York, NY　10016

Areas of Interest

Program Description: This fund works to provide opportunities for youth to fulfill their educational and career aspirations. The fund invests in nationwide efforts to improve elementary and secondary schools, strengthen organizations and programs that serve youth, encourage ties between schools and communities, and increase career, service, and education opportunities for youth. Generally, its grants are designed to build the staff and management capacity of schools and organizations that serve youth, develop and institutionalize nationwide model programs, and support public policy that promotes youth development.
Assistance Types: Operating budgets, continuing support, internships, scholarship funds, special projects, fellowships, technical assistance

Eligibility

Restrictions: No support for public television, film, or media projects; local chapter or national organizations; religious, fraternal, or veteran's organizations; government and public policy organizations; private organizations; or private foundations; no grants to individuals or for annual campaigns, endowments, emergency or capital funds, deficit financing, or scholarly research; no loans

Personnel

Officers: George V. Grune, Chair; M. Christine DeVitam, President; Jessica Chao, VP and Secy.; Rob D. Nagel, Treas. and CFO
Trustees/Directors: William G. Bowen, Melvin R. Laird, Laraine S. Rothenberg, James P. Schadt, Walter V. Shipley, C.J. (Pete) Silas
Staff: Nine

Financial Profile

Assets: In 1992, $1,133,580,423; 1993, $1,010,511,992
High Grant: $3,290,000
Low Grant: $6,000
Ave. Grant: $50,000-$850,000
Total Grants: In 1992, 163 grants totaling $72,324,761; in 1993, 156 grants totaling $140,726,265
Total Grants Higher Ed.: In 1992, 20 grants totaling $13,728,300

Application Process

Contact: Jane Quinn, Prog. Director, (212) 953-1201; fax: (212) 953-1279
Deadline: None
Board Meeting: Four times a year
Processing Time: 12 weeks
Publications: Annual report, which includes application guidelines
Guidelines: The initial approach should be by a letter of not more than two pages. Proposals should include annual and financial reports, organization and project budget, qualifications of key personnel, names and affiliations of board members, additional sources of funding and amount anticipated, IRS letter of determination, and how project will be measured or evaluated.

Sample Grants

Florida Memorial College in Miami received a $612,000, four-year grant for scholarship and other support services aimed at helping paraprofessionals obtain four-year college degrees and meet other state certification requirements and for a teacher training curriculum model that addresses issues of poor academic preparation and language barriers.

Barnard College in New York City received a $2,957,600, five-year grant to recruit and train undergraduate students at 16 private liberal arts colleges to become teachers and provide a new model for training undergraduates to work in middle grades.

Wellesley College Center for Research on Women in Wellesley, Massachusetts, received $160,000 for a planning grant for a school-age child care project to assess need and potential market demand for college-level degree and nondegree programs of study for school-age child care providers and to design a pilot career preparation program for school-age child care providers.

Comments/Analysis

The fund's priority giving area is education, followed by programs for youth. The top recipient of its funds are educational institutions and support agencies. DeWitt Wallace-Reader's Digest Fund is the nation's largest private funder of service-learning programs aimed at improving schools and involving young people in community service. Of the $7.6 million the foundation has invested since 1990, 48 percent has been allocated to support training, networking, and information services for practitioners and policy-makers; 36 percent to direct service; and the remaining 16 percent to combinations of direct services and capacity-building for the field. Historically, scholarship support has been provided to several

institutions of higher education for returning Peace Corps volunteers who want to become fully certified teachers and for continued participation in the Peace Corps Fellows/USA program.

89
Weatherhead Foundation
1801 E Ninth Street
730 Ohio Savings Plaza
Cleveland, OH   44114

Areas of Interest

Program Description: To support universities and research organizations.
Assistance Types: Endowment funds, special projects, research, operating budgets

Eligibility

Restrictions: No support for religious purposes or for churches or denominational institutions; no grants to individuals

Personnel

Officers: Albert J. Weatherhead III, President; Don K. Price, VP; Henry Rosovsky, VP; Charles E. Sheedy, VP; Celia Weatherhead, VP; Dwight S. Weatherhead, VP; John P. Weatherhead, VP Michael H. Weatherhead, VP; Frank M. Rasmussen, Secy.; Thomas F. Allen, Treas.
Staff: One full-time professional

Financial Profile

Assets: In 1993, $4,484,334
High Grant: $1,900,000
Low Grant: $5,000
Ave. Grant: $20,000-$400,000
Total Grants: 10 grants totaling $2,650,000
High Grant Higher Ed.: $1,100,000
Low Grant Higher Ed.: $17,500
Total Grants Higher Ed.: Five grants totaling $2,389,500

Application Process

Contact: Thomas F. Allen, Treas., (216) 771-4000; fax: (216) 771-0422
Deadline: None
Board Meeting: Spring, fall, additional as needed
Publications: Annual report, application guidelines, informational brochure
Guidelines: The initial approach should be by letter. Proposals should include a timetable for implementation and evaluation, organizational budget, history and mission of organization, and how project will be measured or evaluated.

Sample Grants

Case Western Reserve University in Cleveland, Ohio, received two grants totaling $922,000.

Columbia University in New York City received $350,000.

Harvard University in Cambridge, Massachusetts, was awarded $1,100,000.

Macalester College in Saint Paul, Minnesota, received $17,500.

Comments/Analysis

Over 90 percent of the foundation's funds were allocated to education in 1993. Colleges and universities were the top recipients.

90

Del E. Webb Foundation
PO Box 20519
2023 W Wickenburg Way
Wickenburg, AZ   83558

Areas of Interest

Program Description: To improve and expand medical services and medical research.

Assistance Types: Research, special projects, fellowships, building funds

Eligibility

Restrictions: Giving primarily in Arizona, Nevada, and California. No support for government agencies, religious organizations, or for deficit financing or indirect costs.

Personnel

Officers: Robert H. Johnson, President; Owens F. Childress, VP; Marjorie Klinefelter, Secy.; Del V. Werderman, Treas.

Staff: One

Financial Profile

Assets: In 1992, $48,497,974; 1993, $48,815,613

High Grant: In 1992, $2,000,000; 1993, $1,000,000

Low Grant: $5,000

Ave. Grant: $5,000-$100,000

Total Grants: In 1992, 19 grants totaling $3,046,100; 1993, 21 grants totaling $2,888,000

High Grant Higher Ed.: $2,000,000

Low Grant Higher Ed.: $28,000

Ave. Grant Higher Ed.: $50,000-$100,000

Total Grants Higher Ed.: In 1992, four grants totaling $2,303,000

Application Process

Contact: Marjorie Klinefleter, Secy., (602) 684-7223

Deadline: March 31 and October 31

Board Meeting: May and December

Processing Time: Following each meeting

Publications: None

Guidelines: The initial approach should be by letter. An application form is required. Four copies of the proposal should be submitted. Applicants should include organization's charter and by-laws, copy of IRS letter of determination, annual report/audited financial statement/990, signature and title of chief executive officer, names and affiliations of board members and other key people, organization/project budget, timetable for implementation and evaluation of project, detailed description of project and amount of funding requested, statement of problem to be addressed by project, and anticipated results.

Sample Grants

Northern Arizona University in Flagstaff was granted $28,000 to support the Department of Dental Hygiene's dental care program for homebound elderly and disabled people.

Arizona State University in Tempe received $2,000,000 toward the creation of the Del E. Webb School of Construction.

California Institute of Technology in Pasadena received $75,000 for postdoctoral fellows in neurology.

University of Southern California in Los Angeles received $200,000 for a laboratory suite in the USC Center for Molecular Medicine.

Comments/Analysis

Medicine and medical research are the priority areas of interest for the foundation. Hospitals and medical research institutes are top recipients of funds, followed by colleges and universities.

91

E.L. Wiegand Foundation
165 W Liberty Street
Wiegand Center
Reno, NV   89501

Areas of Interest

Program Description: To provide grants for education, including K-12 and higher education; health, hospitals, and medical research; and to support public, civic, and community affairs; arts and culture, including fine arts, music, theater, performing arts, and museums; and Roman Catholic institutions. Additional areas of interest include legal, medical, and business education; cancer, heart disease, chemistry, biology, biochemistry, ophthalmology, aged, and community development.

Assistance Types: Equipment, special projects, program support

Eligibility

Restrictions: Giving primarily in Nevada and neighboring states: California, Arizona, Oregon, Idaho, and Utah. Public affairs grants primarily given to California; Washington, DC; and New York City. No support for endowments or fundraising campaigns, emergency funds, film or media projects, or operating funds. No loans and no support for organizations receiving significant funding from United Way or public tax funds.

Personnel

Officers: Raymond C. Avansino Jr., Chair; Kristen A. Avansino, President and Exec. Director; Michael J. Melarkey, VP and Secy.; Joanne C. Hildahl, VP, Grants Program; James T. Carrico, Treas.
Trustees/Directors: Frank J. Fahrenhopf Jr., Harvey C. Fruehauf Jr., Mario J. Gabelli
Staff: None

Financial Profile

Assets: In 1993, $83,253,674
High Grant: $336,877
Low Grant: $500
Ave. Grant: $4,000-$100,000
Total Grants: 80 grants totaling $4,266,185
High Grant Higher Ed.: $115,000
Low Grant Higher Ed.: $2,000
Ave. Grant Higher Ed.: $20,000-$50,000
Total Grants Higher Ed.: 15 grants totaling $1,066,980

Application Process

Contact: Kristen A. Avansino, President and Exec. Director, (702) 333-0310
Deadline: None

Board Meeting: February, June, and October
Processing Time: Within 30 days of the meeting at which the application is reviewed
Publications: Informational brochure, application guidelines
Guidelines: The initial approach should be by letter. Applicant organizations must be in operation a minimum of five years. In addition to the required application form, applicants should submit the IRS letter of determination, description of program, and annual report/990.

Sample Grants

Santa Clara University Media Center in Santa Clara, California, received $115,000 for equipment.

Westmont College in Santa Barbara, California, received $60,000 for theatrical lighting.

Dominican College of San Rafael in California received $78,000 for a laboratory for the nursing program.

Holy Names College Raskob Learning Center in Oakland, California, received $15,200 for computer equipment.

University of San Francisco School of Law in California received $100,000 for building acquisition.

Gonzaga University in Spokane, Washington, received $74,000 for science equipment.

Westminster College in Salt Lake City, Utah, received $26,800 for science laboratory enhancement.

Comments/Analysis

The foundation places education at the top of its priorities, with the sciences second, and human services third. Schools are the top recipients of funds, followed by hospitals. Capital support is the top type of support given, followed by program support. The foundation has an interest in projects that benefit children and youth.

SECTION

Sources of Corporate Funding for Higher Education

CORPORATE FUNDING FOR HIGHER EDUCATION

HOW TO MAXIMIZE YOUR CHANCES OF CORPORATE GRANTS SUCCESS

There are two parts to this introduction to the corporate grants section of *The Complete Grants Sourcebook for Higher Education*. Part one discusses corporate foundation grants, and part two describes support obtained through corporate giving programs. Corporations provide support to nonprofit organizations through corporate foundations, corporate giving programs, or both. In general, corporate foundations maintain small endowments and rely on contributions from their parent company to support their giving program, which reflects their company's interests. In addition, corporate foundations must follow specific IRS regulations. Corporate giving programs are less regulated by the IRS, and gifts made through this avenue are not required to be publicized.

CORPORATE FOUNDATION GRANTS

The ability to determine which of 35,765 U.S. foundations provides significant support to the nation's colleges and universities is possible because of the Internal Revenue Service's requirement that foundations make their tax returns public. Corporations that want to take advantage of current rules that allow profit-making companies to donate up to 10 percent of their pretax profits to their own charitable entity can form a corporate foundation to receive and distribute these donations. In exchange for this tax benefit, the corporation's foundation must donate at least 5 percent of its assets to eligible nonprofit organizations each year.

Corporations see at least two advantages when they form a foundation. First, the foundation is a buffer between grantseekers and the corporation. ("Our corporation would love to support your project but the decision concerning who and what to support is made by our corporate foundation's board.") Second, the foundation's asset base provides a source of funds that the company can use to maintain levels of giving when profits are low or nonexistent.

In the 1980s, many corporate foundations reduced their asset base to keep corporate grant levels equal to previous years. Although the asset bases of many foundations were decreased, having a source of funds during problematic times helped to stabilize corporate support to nonprofits. In the 1990s, numerous corporate foundations are in a position to begin replenishing this valuable source of support.

Many college and university grantseekers are not aware that corporate foundation grants account for only 27 percent of corporate support. Of the $5.9 billion in corporate grants, only $1.6 billion comes from corporate foundations. However, the only corporate giving that is required to be made public is that of corporate foundations. Hence, most corporate giving data reflects only the small percentage of corporate support made through corporate foundations. For example, the Foundation Center's *The National Directory of Corporate Giving*[1] contains information on 2,050 corporate granting programs, 85 percent of which are corporate foundations.

This section of *The Complete Grants Sourcebook* contains the profiles of 78 corporate foundations that have demonstrated a strong commitment to colleges and universities and whose giving patterns reflect a national or at least regional distribution of funding. Begin your quest for corporate grants by reading through this section and using the indexes to locate corporate foundations that may be interested in your project. Expand your search beyond this book by visiting the nearest Foundation Center Cooperative Collection (see Appendix A) and reviewing its collection of resources. Of particular interest is *The Guide to US Foundations, Their Trustees, Officers, and Donors*,[2] which lists all foundations (corporate and other types) from most to least grants awarded. By reviewing this list, foundation addresses, and geographic limitations you will be able to identify those foundations that are in proximity to your institution. Since most corporate foundations "give where they live," you are likely to uncover some interesting prospects that will take you beyond those selected for inclusion in this book.

CORPORATE GIVING PROGRAMS

While we can rely on corporate tax returns to determine information on contributions, gifts, and grants paid through corporate foundations, support provided through corporate giving programs is not as accessible. No one, not even stockholders, can gain access to the tax returns of the four to five million U.S. corporations. This lack of information is particularly unfortunate since corporate giving programs account for 73 percent of all corporate support to nonprofits.

The problem that this lack of access to verifiable data creates can be seen in many of the companion grants tools to this book. For example, the Foundation Center's *National Directory of Corporate Giving* provides information on 2,360 corporate grant sources, but only 621 deal with corporate giving programs. That book, like many others, is forced to focus on corporate foundations because more data about them is available. The Foundation Center reports that they have encountered the same problem as many grantseekers when researching corporate giving—most corporations view our research as an intrusion into what they (correctly) perceive as their business. The Foundation Center reported that 157 of the corporations with entries in *The National Directory of Corporate Giving* would not verify or provide any data, and only 46 of the 621 corporate giving programs would provide *any* sample grants. Those that did generally provided "conservative" or "safe" grants. Corporations are very sensitive about how their stockholders and employees perceive the management's distribution of profits (whether the funds were realized from tax savings or not) and hence, most of the sample grants selected for public review are for United Way grants and grants to noncontroversial organizations and projects. Remember that there is no way to verify if the grants provided by this small percentage of corporations are accurate or representative of their funding patterns.

A random review of corporate giving programs reveals that corporate awards matching gifts made by employees to nonprofit organizations (including colleges and universities) account for 10 percent to 25 percent of the contributions reported. Since many corporations prefer to fund organizations that have already attracted financial support from their employees, it is important for you to determine whether the companies you solicit for a grant have an employee matching gift program and if your department or college has benefited from it.

The best way to get dependable information on a corporation's giving program is from corporate officials.

Targeting Your Corporate Giving Prospects

Corporate interest in your program or research is a function of the following variables:

- Your organization's proximity to the corporate facility. Since companies "give where they live," get a list of the corporations in your area

---

[1]*The National Directory of Corporate Giving*, 3rd edition (New York: The Foundation Center, 1993).
[2]*The Guide to US Foundations, Their Trustees, Officers, and Donors*, (New York: The Foundation Center, 1994).

from your corporate development office or chamber of commerce.

- The corporation's employee training policies. What, if anything, does your institution, program, department, etc., do to upgrade the skills of the corporation's employees or supply the corporation with skilled employees? Check with your continuing education office and off-campus programs.

- The corporation's product development plans. Will your project provide information that the corporation can use to develop new products or improve existing products?

- The corporation's product positioning. Will your project or research involve familiarizing potential purchasers, including undergraduate and graduate students, with the company's products or services?

The more of these variables you can relate to a local corporation, the better your chances are of securing funds. Your ability to extend your corporate search outside of your geographic area is directly related to the last three variables, but particularly to the last two.

As you move into product-related grantseeking, use *The Standard Industrial Classification Manual,*[3] found in your university library, to help you identify potential corporate funding sources. This manual indexes corporations by the products they produce and is instrumental in locating the manufacturers of products that you can relate to your research or project.

At a recent conference, a panel of corporate grantors expressed their preference for involvement with colleges and universities. The corporations suggested that they should no longer be looked at as "cash cows" (F. Pat Foy, Ph.D., Intel Corp.) and that pre-proposal contact should include intimate involvement with the interested and affected partners in the companies from which support is sought. Contact can come in the form of a phone call to anyone—the heads of sales, engineering, operations, manufacturing, materials, etc.—in the corporation that realizes that working together will provide mutual benefits.

One key to securing corporate grants is to involve corporations in the development of your programs and projects. The old idea that higher education and corporations should "collaborate" is out and "co-creation" is in. When your project involves curriculum, "articulation" is out and "co-curriculum involvement" is in. Co-creation is not possible when the grantseeker sends the proposal idea to a corporation in a letter proposal requesting support. There must be sharing and brainstorming.

In order to develop the proper basis for a productive corporate relationship, you must know and understand the corporation's organizational structure, culture, and products. This is a shift away from research that consists solely of obtaining the address of a corporation's contributions officer and a copy of its application guidelines. The corporate marketplace is constantly changing. One of the major problems that colleges and universities have in dealing with the "new" corporate marketplace is understanding the way today's corporate management and workers operate. Many of the most successful corporations (especially the high-tech ones) display a flat structure that encourages shared decision making and team involvement. They have moved away from the rigid hierarchial structure still found in many colleges and universities. They expect your college/department to practice in a similar fashion, even though cross-divisional and disciplinary cooperation and team work is not the norm on many campuses.

Your chances of success with corporate grantors are enhanced when you have access to current information on their products, sales, profitability, and marketplace position. One way to obtain this information for publicly held corporations is to purchase a share of its stock. By doing so you will receive the most current information on and annual reports from the company, as well as a dividend check to help you determine its current level of profitability. Information you gather from corporate reference books, such as *Dun and Bradstreet's Million Dollar Directory*[4] and *Standard and Poor's Register of Corporations, Directors and Executives,*[5] will be more useful than books on corporate giving. Of particular importance is knowledge of your corporate prospect's divisions and subsidiaries. This information can be found in *Directory of Corporate Affiliations.*[6]

---

[3]*The Standard Industrial Classification Manual* (Springfield, VA: National Technical Information Service, 1987).

[4]*Dun and Bradstreet's Million Dollar Directory,* 5 vols. (Parsippany, NJ: Dun and Bradstreet Information Services, 1995).

[5]*Standard and Poor's Register of Corporations, Directors and Executives,* 3 vols. (New York: Standard and Poor's Corporation, 1995).

[6]*Directory of Corporate Affiliations,* 6 vols. (New Providence, RI: Reed Reference Publishing, 1995).

After reading this section you will agree that merely printing and indexing the paucity of information available on corporate grants is of questionable value. Instead, put the information and suggestions presented in this section to work for you in developing productive relationships with corporations that result in grants.

HOW TO USE THE CORPORATE FOUNDATION SECTION

The indexes at the end of this book will help you determine which of the corporate foundations included in this book have demonstrated an interest in your area of concern. To help you develop an expanded list of key search words, refer to Section I, pages 11–17. The corporate foundation entries follow the same format as the foundation entries. Refer to page 48 for an explanation of the format.

Each corporate foundation entry contains the following information:

- Name and address of the corporate foundation
- Program description
- Assistance types
- Restrictions
- Officers and trustees or directors
- Staff
- Financial profile
- Application process
- Sample grants
- Comments/Analysis

CORPORATE FOUNDATION FUNDING SOURCES

92
Aetna Foundation, Inc.
151 Farmington Avenue
Hartford, CT   06156-3180

Areas of Interest

Program Description: Primarily to support immunization and health care for children and minority higher education.
Assistance Types: Special projects, seed money, scholarships, employee matching gifts, employee-related scholarships, program support, continuing support

Eligibility

Restrictions: No grants to individuals or to religious organizations for religious purposes. No support for sporting events, endowments, medical research, capital, building/renovation, or computer hardware. No loans. No support for annual operating funds for colleges, universities, secondary schools, social services agencies, museums, or hospitals.

Personnel

Officers: Ronald E. Compton, President and Director; Michael C. Alexander, VP and Exec. Director; Stephen B. Middlebrook, VP; Jean M. Waggett, Secy.; Timothy A. Holt, Treas.; Robert A. Morse, Comptroller and Director
Trustees/Directors: Wallace Barnes, Marian Wright Edelman, Edward K. Hamilton, Frank R. O'Keefe Jr.
Staff: Nine full-time professional, four full-time support

Financial Profile

Assets: In 1992, $30,219,121; 1993, $29,978,352
High Grant: In 1992, $1,350,000; 1993 $1,300,000
Low Grant: In 1992, $500; 1993, $300
Ave. Grant: $5,000-$25,000

Total Grants: In 1992, 200 grants totaling $7,385,376, plus $940,862 for employee matching gifts; 1993, 400 grants totaling $7,378,677, plus $966,856 for 4,581 employee matching gifts

Application Process

Contact: Diana Kinosh, Management Information Supervisor, (203) 273-1932
Deadline: None
Board Meeting: March, July, September, and November
Processing Time: Two months
Publications: Annual report; corporate giving report, including application guidelines; program policy statement; informational brochure
Guidelines: Application form required for FOCUS grants, Dollars for Doers, and matching gifts. All other applicants should submit a letter proposal including a brief history of the organization and its mission, a copy of the organization's IRS determination letter, a detailed description of the project and the amount of funding requested, a copy of the organization's budget and the project budget, and a summary of how the project results will be evaluated or measured. If interested, the foundation will request that a formal proposal be submitted with additional information.

Sample Grants

Bejing University in Bejing, China, received $25,000 for scholarships for Chinese business students.
Trinity College in Hartford, Connecticut, received $25,000 for a challenge grant for a summer enrichment program for at-risk women and minorities entering a freshman class.
University of Virginia, McIntire School of Commerce, in Charlottesville, Virginia, received $14,500 for minority student retention and recruitment programs.
National Merit Scholarship Corporation in Evanston, Illinois, received $20,743 for a scholarship program for children of Aetna employees.
University of Hartford in West Hartford, Connecticut, received $20,000 to connect public school educators at all levels and to articulate essential knowledge and skills expectations for students from K through university level.

Illinois State University in Normal, Illinois, received $12,071 for an insurance education enrichment program for talented minority students from inner-city Chicago.

National Judicial College in Reno, Nevada, received $30,000 for judicial education programs.

Comments/Analysis

The foundation has four specified areas of interest or programs: Employee Field Office programs, which encourage employee participation in community affairs and include regional and FOCUS grants that serve Hartford and other cities where Aetna has offices and a Dollars for Doers program in which employees may apply for grants for organizations in which they volunteer; Immunization/Child Health, aimed at meeting the Surgeon General's goal for immunizing young children and to use immunizations as a point of entry into the health care system; minority education, focused on increasing the successful participation of minorities in higher education; and employee matching gifts to junior and community colleges, four-year colleges and universities, graduate and professional schools, and seminaries and theological schools. Although the foundation gives on a broad geographic basis, New England and the South Atlantic receive the greatest number of grants and the greatest amount of grant dollars.

93
Air Products Foundation
7201 Hamilton Boulevard
Allentown, PA   18195-1501

Areas of Interest

Program Description: To support higher education, welfare, community investment, and culture and art. Specific areas of interest in higher education include engineering, mechanical engineering, chemical engineering, chemistry, business, and management.

Assistance Types: General support, unrestricted operating support, symposiums, equipment, building and renovation, scholarships, capital campaigns, fellowships, professorships, continuing support, seed money, emergency funds, special projects

Eligibility

Restrictions: No grants to individuals, sectarian or denominational organizations, political organizations, veterans organizations, service clubs, labor groups, elementary or secondary schools, or organizations receiving support from United Way. No grants for national capital campaigns of health organizations, or hospital capital campaigns or operating expenses. No loans. Support primarily for activities that benefit communities in which a significant number of employees live and work.

Personnel

Officers: D.T. Shire, Chair and Trustee; C.P. Powell, Vice-Chair; J.H. Agger, Secy.; D.H. Kelly, Treas.; C.M. Walker, Administrator of Philanthropy

Trustees/Directors: P.L. Thibaut Brian, R.M. Davis, R.F. Dee, Walter F. Light, Harold A. Wagner

Staff: None

Financial Profile

Assets: For fiscal year ending September, 1993, $2,914,648
High Grant: $150,000
Total Grants: One grant totaling $150,000
High Grant Higher Ed.: $50,000
Low Grant Higher Ed.: $500
Ave. Grant Higher Ed.: $500-$5,000
Total Grants Higher Ed.: In 1992, 142 grants totaling $689,500

Application Process

Contact: Charlotte Walker, Contributions Officer, (215) 481-8079
Deadline: None
Board Meeting: Monthly
Processing Time: Three months
Publications: Informational brochure including application guidelines
Guidelines: Application form is not required. Requests must be in writing and include a brief description of the organization including history, activities, purpose, who is served, and governing board; a description of the purpose for which the grant is requested; specific details on how this purpose will be achieved; total amount of the fund-raising campaign; total amount being requested and the project budget; a copy of the most recent audited financial statement; a copy of the organization's IRS determination letter and most recent 990 tax return; a copy of the organization's operating budget for the current fiscal year; and a list of current contributions or commitment received including amounts; and the amounts of assured or anticipated support, including names of donors.

Sample Grants

Villanova University in Villanova, Pennsylvania, received $40,000 for a chemical engineering professorship.

Columbia University in New York City received $500 for its AIChE Chapter; $2,000 for its Higher Education Opportunity Program; $2,500 for unrestricted support of its Chemical Engineering Department; and $5,000 for laboratory equipment.

Carnegie Mellon University in Pittsburgh, Pennsylvania, received $7,500 for unrestricted support of its graduate business school; $10,000 for unrestricted support of its Chemical Engineering Department; $3,500 for its Minority Engineering Program; $2,000 for unrestricted support of its Mechanical Engineering Department; $500 for its AIChE Chapter; and $500 for a chemical engineering symposium.

The Foundation for Independent Colleges, Inc. in Harrisburg, Pennsylvania, was awarded $12,500 for unrestricted operating support.

Lehigh University in Bethlehem, Pennsylvania, received $2,500 for its Challenge for Success Program.

Moravian College in Bethlehem, Pennsylvania, received $10,000 for its athletic complex and $2,500 for unrestricted general support.

National Academy of Engineers in Washington, DC, received two $20,000 grants: one for a library capital campaign and the other for unrestricted operating support.

National Consortium for Graduate Degrees for Minorities in Engineering and Science in Notre Dame, Indiana, received $25,000 for scholarships.

Princeton University in Princeton, New Jersey, received a $4,000 unrestricted support grant for its Chemistry Department.

Pennsylvania State University in University Park, Pennsylvania, received $50,000 for a capital campaign for its Center for Advanced Materials.

University of Michigan in Ann Arbor, Michigan, was awarded $5,000 for minority fellowships for graduate study in management.

Comments/Analysis

Historically, higher education has received 52 percent of the funds distributed by the foundation, followed by health and welfare (36 percent), community (8 percent), and culture and art (4 percent). The majority of the grants to colleges and universities have been awarded to departments of chemical and mechanical engineering for general and unrestricted operating support. There have been also many $500 awards made in support of chapters of engineering associations such as AIChE and ASME. The foundation is also a frequent supporter of minority engineering programs and awards many of its higher education grants to institutions in Pennsylvania. Please note that in 1993 only one grant was awarded.

94
Alcoa Foundation
2202 Alcoa Building
425 Sixth Avenue
Pittsburgh, PA   15219-1850

Areas of Interest

Program Description: To support higher education, arts and culture, health and hospitals, welfare, community development, civic affairs, and youth. A specific area of interest in higher education is engineering.

Assistance Types: Employee-related scholarships, scholarship funds, building, renovation, equipment, annual campaigns, conferences, seminars, continuing support, emergency funds, fellowships, matching funds, operating budgets, research, seed money, capital campaigns, general purposes, special projects

Eligibility

Restrictions: No grants to individuals except for employee related scholarships; sectarian or religious organizations; or elementary or secondary schools. No support for political purposes, endowment funds, deficit reduction, documentaries, videos, tickets, souvenir programs, advertising, golf outings, trips, tours, or student exchange programs. Giving mainly in areas of company operations including Davenport, Iowa; Knoxville, Tennessee; Massena, New York; Pittsburgh, Pennsylvania; Evansville, Indiana; Cleveland, Ohio; and Rockdale, Texas.

Personnel

Officers: F. Worth Hobbs, President and Director; Kathleen W. Buechel, VP; Kathleen R. Burgan, Secy. and Treas.
Trustees/Directors: Mary Lou Ambrose, John L. Diederich, Ernest J. Edwards, Richard L. Fischer, Ronald R. Hoffman, Vincent R. Scorsone
Staff: Three full-time professional, one part-time professional, three full-time support

Financial Profile

Assets: In 1992, $268,583,194; 1993, $272,600,287
Ave. Grant: $100-$20,000
Total Grants: In 1992, 2,550 grants totaling $10,205,329, plus $424,000 for grants to individuals and $1,462,066 for employee matching gifts; 1993, 1,186 grants totaling $10,372,839, plus $438,000 for grants to individuals and $1,461,447 for employee matching gifts

Application Process

Contact: F. Worth Hobbs, President, (412) 553-2343
Deadline: None
Board Meeting: Monthly
Processing Time: One to four months
Publications: Annual report, informational brochure including application guidelines
Guidelines: Application form is not required. Initial approach should be by letter.

Sample Grants

National Action Council for Minorities in Engineering in New York City received $40,000.

Pittsburgh Regional Engineering Program in Pittsburgh, Pennsylvania, received $15,000.

United Negro College Fund in New York City received $70,000.

Bowling Green State University in Bowling Green, Ohio, received $12,000.

Clark Community College Foundation in Vancouver, Washington, received $25,000.

Galludet University in Washington, DC, received two $10,000 grants.

McKendree College in Lebanon, Illinois, received $12,500.

Pennsylvania State University in University Park, Pennsylvania, received five grants totaling $66,496.

University of Tennessee in Knoxville, Tennessee, received seven grants totaling $123,600.

Pittsburgh Theological Seminary in Pittsburgh, Pennsylvania, received $10,000.

Wheeling College in Wheeling, West Virginia, received $10,000. University of Nevada in Reno, Nevada, received $13,000.

Comments/Analysis

In the past, 22 percent of the foundation's grant funds have gone to education with approximately half of the education dollars distributed for grants of under $10,000. Historically, the top subject area by dollars has been education and the top recipient type by dollars has been colleges and universities. Institutions of higher education also have been the top recipient type by number of grants awarded.

95

Allied Signal Foundation
PO Box 2245
101 Columbia Road
Morristown, NJ   07962-2245

Areas of Interest

Program Description: To support education, community funds, health, aging, human services, youth, urban affairs, culture, social services, and science and technology. Specific areas of interest in higher education include business, engineering, and minority education.

Assistance Types: Fellowships, scholarship funds, employee matching gifts, renovation, building, operating budgets, continuing support, annual campaigns, seed money

Eligibility

Restrictions: In general, no grants to religious organizations, special interest groups, political organizations, or individuals. No support for endowments. No loans. Giving mainly in areas of company operations.

Personnel

Officers: Lawrence A. Bossidy, Chair and Director; David G. Powell, President and Director; Alan S. Painter, VP and Exec. Director; Peter M. Kreindler, V.P and Director; Heather M. Mullett, Secy.; G. Peter D'Aloia, Treas.

Trustees/Directors: Issac R. Barpal, John W. Barter, Alan Belzer, Daniel P. Burnham, Fred M. Poses, Ralph E. Reins, Paul R. Schindler, James E. Sierk

Staff: None

Financial Profile

High Grant: $150,000
Ave. Grant: $2,000-$15,000
Total Grants: In 1993, 600 grants totaling $7,629,757, plus $1,352,431 for 6,906 employee matching gifts and $100,000 for one foundation-administered program

Application Process

Contact: Alan S. Painter, VP and Exec. Director, (201) 455-5877
Deadline: September 1
Board Meeting: December
Publications: Informational brochure including application guidelines, annual report
Guidelines: Application form is not required. Initial approach should be made by letter. All proposals must be submitted through and recommended by an Allied Signal Plant location. Corporate locations are in New Jersey, Arizona, California, Florida, Indiana, Maryland, Michigan, Missouri, South Carolina, Tennessee, and Virginia.

Sample Grants

Arizona State University in Tempe, Arizona, received $85,000 for an Engineering Excellence Program.

Drew University in Madison, New Jersey, received $10,000 for minority scholarships and $10,000 for capital campaign.

Fairleigh Dickinson University in Teaneck, New Jersey, received $65,500 for electrical engineering lab renovation, $25,000 for scholarships for minorities in engineering, and $10,000 for master of science in taxation program.

Polytechnic University in Brooklyn, New York, received $30,000 for faculty enhancement.

University of North Carolina, School of Business and Economics in Greensboro, North Carolina, received $10,000 for an endowed chair.

Pellissippi State Technical Community College in Knoxville, Tennessee, received $10,000 for a scholarship program.

Ohio Foundation of Independent Colleges in Columbus, Ohio, received $14,000.

United Negro College Fund in New York City received $50,000.

Comments/Analysis

In the past, education received 27 percent of the grant dollars paid by the foundation, other received 22 percent, community improvement and development received 21 percent, arts and culture received 9 percent, science received 6 percent, and employee matching gifts to education, arts and culture received 15 percent. Historically, education is the top subject area by dollars and colleges and universities are the top recipients by dollars. In recent years, several colleges and universities received $10,000 grants for the Allied Signal Scholars Program including New Jersey Institute of Technology; Prairie View A&M University; Purdue University, Calumet; Stevens Institute of Technology; and University of California at Los Angeles Foundation.

96

Ameritech Foundation
30 S Wacker Drive, 34th Floor
Chicago, IL   60606

Areas of Interest

Program Description: To support economics, education, and culture in the Great Lakes region and research and projects aimed at using communication to improve society. Specific areas of interest include information and technology, communications, and public policy as related to the telecommunications industry.
Assistance Types: Employee matching gifts, special projects, conferences and seminars, research, endowed chairs, minority scholarships, fellowships

Eligibility

Restrictions: No grants to individuals, religious organizations, national or international organizations with limited relationships to local company operations, affiliates of labor organizations, local chapters of national organizations, veterans or military organizations, discriminary organizations, political groups, athletics, or health organization focusing on research in and the treatment of one specific disease. No grants for start-up funds, advertising, or for the purchase of tickets for benefits and fund raising events. Giving primarily in Illinois, Wisconsin, Indiana, Michigan, and Ohio.

Personnel

Officers: Richard H. Brown, President and Director; Robert J. Kolbe, VP and CFO; Michael E.Kuhlin, Secy. and Director; Connie L. Lindsey, Treas.; Ronald G. Pippin, Comptroller
Trustees/Directors: Ronald L. Blake, Hanna Holburn Gray, James A. Henderson, Martha L. Thornton, William L. Weiss, Bernard M. Windon
Staff: One full-time professional, one part-time support

Financial Profile

Assets: In 1993, $67,308,940
High Grant: $515,000
Low Grant: $2,000
Ave. Grant: $10,000-$25,000
Total Grants: $8,503,916
High Grant Higher Ed.: $500,000
Low Grant Higher Ed.: $5,000
Ave. Grant Higher Ed.: $10,000-$60,000
Total Grants Higher Ed.: Approximately 26 grants totaling $3,105,000, plus $110,951 in matching gifts

Application Process

Contact: Michael E. Kuhlin, Director
Deadline: None; applications may be submitted throughout the year

Board Meeting: March, June, August, and December
Processing Time: Three months
Publications: Informational brochure including application guidelines
Guidelines: Application form not required. Initial approach should be made by letter. Proposals should include a brief history of organization and description of its mission, detailed description of project and amount being requested, list of additional sources and amount of support, description of population and geographic area to be served, IRS determination letter, and organizational budget and/or project budget.

Sample Grants

Association of Governing Boards of Universities and Colleges in Washington, DC, received $5,000 in support of college governance programs.
Council for Aid to Education in New York City received $20,000 to increase the amount and effectiveness of private sector aid to education.
Michigan State University in East Lansing was awarded $150,000 for Ameritech Graduate Fellowship in Information Technology.
National Council for Minorities in Engineering in New York City received $30,000 to support programs in the midwest that foster minority participation in engineering programs at colleges and universities.
Ohio State University in Columbus received $200,000 for the first payment on a $1 million pledge to support using telecommunications to improve education, health care, and international communication.
Purdue University in West Lafayette, Indiana, was awarded $240,000 for the first payment on a $1.2 million pledge to support enhanced teaching and learning effectiveness using technology-based delivery.
University of Illinois in Champaign received a total of $200,000: $150,000 to fund the Ameritech Fellowship Minority Assistance Program and $50,000 for the first payment on a $100,000 pledge to support the Regional Economic Applications Laboratory.
Pennsylvania State University in University Park was awarded $500,000 for the first payment on a $1.5 million pledge to endow the William L. Weiss Chair in Information and Communications Technology.

Comments/Analysis

In 1993, higher education received approximately 38 percent of the dollars distributed by the Ameritech Foundation. Arts and culture received 25 percent, followed by elementary and secondary education at 14 percent, civic and community programs at 13 percent, and health and human services at 10 percent. In terms of higher education, Ameritech awarded $110,951 in employee matching gifts to colleges and universities. It also awarded five $60,000 grants to independent college associations and foundations to enhance the value of independent higher education. Recipients of these Partnership Awards included Associated Colleges of Illinois, Independent Colleges of Indiana Foundation, Michigan Colleges Foundation, Ohio Foundation of Independent

Colleges, and Wisconsin Foundation of Independent Colleges. Several colleges and universities received large payments ($240,000-$500,000) toward multiyear pledges to endow chairs in areas such as regional economics, economic development, information technology, information and communication technology, and public policy.

97

Amoco Foundation, Inc.
200 E Randolph Drive
Chicago, IL   60601

Areas of Interest

Program Description: To support precollege education and higher education, community development, urban affairs, energy conservation, culture, social services, youth, medical research, and civic affairs. Specific areas of interest in higher education include science, science and technology, engineering, and minorities in engineering and science.

Assistance Types: Scholarship funds, fellowships, special projects, general purposes, capital campaigns, employee matching gifts, operating budgets, continuing support, annual campaigns, seed money, emergency funds, building, equipment

Eligibility

Restrictions: No support for individuals; endowments; research; publications; conferences; primary or secondary schools; religious, fraternal, social, or athletic organizations; or United Way-supported organizations.

Personnel

Officers: R. Wayne Anderson, Chair; Frederick S. Addy, President and Director; Patricia D. Wright, Secy.and Exec. Director; John S. Ruey, Treas.
Trustees/Directors: Jerry M. Brown, Richard E. Evans, J.M. Griffith, Arthur R. McCaughan, George S. Spindler
Staff: Six full-time professional, five full-time support, two part-time support

Financial Profile

Assets: In 1992, $68,816,244; 1993, $73,886,279
High Grant: In 1992, $220,813; 1993, $1,005,000
Low Grant: $100
Ave. Grant: $2,000-$100,000
Total Grants: In 1992, 1,090 grants totaling $23,702,088, plus $1,416,480 for two program-related investments; 1993, 764 grants totaling $18,125,397, plus $2,228,962 for 1,098 employee matching gifts and $1,653,818 for one program-related investment

Application Process

Contact: Patricia D. Wright, Secy. and Exec. Director, (312) 856-6305
Deadline: None
Board Meeting: March, June, September, and December; contributions committee meets monthly
Processing Time: Four to six weeks
Publications: Annual report including application guidelines
Guidelines: An application form is not required. Submit a letter or proposal including a history of organization and description of its mission; description of project and amount requested; explanation of how project results will be measured; project budget; most recent annual report, audited financial statement, or 990; and list of board of directors, trustees, officers and other key people.

Sample Grants

Illinois Institute of Technology in Chicago, Illinois, received $370,370.
Lamar University in Beaumont, Texas, received $99,822.

Comments/Analysis

The foundation is a strong supporter of higher education on a national level. It is particularly interested in improving the quality of science and engineering education by supporting programs that help to relieve the shortage of US PhD engineering faculty and graduates; providing grants for science and engineering laboratory equipment; and supporting the National Council for Minorities in Engineering and the Historically Black College Science and Engineering Advancement Program.

98

Anheuser-Busch Foundation
c/o Anheuser-Busch Companies, Inc.
One Busch Place
Saint Louis, MO   63118

Areas of Interest

Program Description: To support higher education, youth, community development and community funds, United Way, health, and the arts.
Assistance Types: Employee matching gifts, matching funds, building funds, capital campaigns, continuing support

Eligibility

Restrictions: No grants to individuals; no support for religious, social, fraternal, or athletic groups; no grants for hospital operating budgets; giving mainly in areas of company operations

Personnel

Trustees/Directors: August A. Busch III, Jerry Ritter, JoBeth Brown, Boatmen's Trust Company
Staff: 71

Financial Profile

Assets: In 1992, $76,722,825; 1993, $73,330,936
High Grant: $1,500,000
Low Grant: $1,000
Ave. Grant: $1,000-$25,000
Total Grants: In 1992, $8,606,827; 1993, 488 grants totaling $8,971,752
High Grant Higher Ed.: $400,000
Low Grant Higher Ed.: $1,000
Ave. Grant Higher Ed.: $25,000-$100,000 (excluding matching gifts)
Total Grants Higher Ed.: In 1992, approximately 65 grants totaling $2,380,105, including matching gifts

Application Process

Contact: JoBeth Brown, (314) 577-2453
Deadline: None
Board Meeting: Approximately every two months
Processing Time: Following board meetings
Publications: Application guidelines
Guidelines: Application form required. Applications must be written and include information concerning the organization and the purpose for which the grant is requested.

Sample Grants

Fontbonne College in Saint Louis, Missouri, received $25,000.
Lindenwood College in Saint Charles, Missouri, received $25,000.
Northwestern University in Evanston, Illinois, received $50,000.
Ranken Technical Institute in Saint Louis, Missouri, received $50,000.
Colorado State University in Fort Collins was awarded $25,000.
Washington University in Saint Louis, Missouri, was awarded $400,000.
United States Business School in Prague received $250,000.
University of Texas at San Antonio received two grants for $100,000 each.
University of Missouri in Saint Louis was awarded $200,000.

Comments/Analysis

In the past, higher education has received approximately 28 percent of the contributions distributed by the foundation. The foundation is historically a strong supporter of colleges and universities in the Saint Louis, Missouri, area.

99
Archer-Daniels-Midland Foundation
PO Box 1470
Decatur, IL   62525

Areas of Interest

Program Description: To support higher education, minorities, culture, hospitals, youth, community funds, public policy, child welfare, animal welfare, international affairs, and media and communications.
Assistance Types: Program support

Personnel

Officers: John H. Daniels, Chair and Director; Lowell W. Andreas, President and Director; Roy L. Erickson, Secy.-Treas.; Richard E. Burket, Manager

Financial Profile

Assets: In 1993, $7,424,107
High Grant: $1,000,000
Low Grant: $25
Ave. Grant: $500-$25,000
Total Grants: 236 grants totaling $3,771,629, plus $515,598 for 776 employee matching gifts

Application Process

Contact: Ken Struttmaann, General Auditor, (217) 424-5200
Deadline: None
Board Meeting: As needed
Processing Time: Notification upon acceptance; notification of negative decisions is not made
Guidelines: Initial approach should be made by letter.

Sample Grants

University of Minnesota Foundation in Minneapolis, Minnesota, received a $50,000 grant and a $25,000 grant.
Dana College in Blair, Nebraska, received $25,000.
Harvard University School of Public Health in Cambridge, Massachusetts, received $15,000.
Kansas State University Foundation in Manhattan, Kansas, received $100,000.
University of Illinois Foundation in Urbana, Illinois, received $13,000.
Minnesota Private College Fund in Saint Paul, Minnesota, received $15,000.
Columbia University in New York City received $10,000.
Mount Mercy College in Cedar Rapids, Iowa, received $15,000.
Emory University in Atlanta, Georgia, received $25,000.

Comments/Analysis

Historically, other has received 26 percent of the grant dollars distributed by the foundation; arts and culture, 19 percent; education, 19 percent; international affairs, development and peace, 12 percent; public affairs, 11 percent; community improvement and development, 7 percent; and social science, 6 percent. Colleges and universities are generally the top recipient type by dollars, while the top population group served by foundation dollars is children and youth.

100

Ashland Oil Foundation, Inc.
PO Box 391
Ashland, KY   41105

Areas of Interest

Program Description: Primarily to support higher, adult, early childhood, elementary, and minority education in areas of major company operations. Other fields of interest include engineering, business, economics, environment, and community funds.
Assistance Types: Employee matching gifts, scholarship funds

Eligibility

Restrictions: No support for individuals, building, or endowment funds. Giving mainly in Kentucky, West Virginia, Ohio, and Minnesota.

Personnel

Officers: Harry M. Zachem, Chair and Trustee; Judy B. Thomas, President and Trustee; Franklin P. Justice Jr., V.P and Trustee; J. Marvin Quinn, VP and Trustee; Frederick M. Greenwood, Secy.; Ruth E. Davis, Treas.; George W. McKnight, Asst. Treas.; Terry L. McKinley, Asst. Secy.; Thomas L. Fenzell, Asst. Secy.
Trustees/Directors: John A. Brothers, Rick E. Music, Robert C. Ball, Paul W. Chellgren
Staff: Two full-time professional, three full-time support, three part-time support

Financial Profile

Assets: In 1993, $593
High Grant: $263,500 (excluding matching gifts)
Low Grant: $500 (excluding matching gifts)
Ave. Grant: $1,000-$10,000
Total Grants: $4,745,965
High Grant Higher Ed.: $207,500
Low Grant Higher Ed.: $500 (excluding matching gifts)
Ave. Grant Higher Ed.: $1,000-$25,000
Total Grants Higher Ed.: Approximately 35 grants totaling $1,201,645, plus $734,175 in matching gifts

Application Process

Contact: Judy B. Thomas, President, (606) 329-4525
Deadline: None
Board Meeting: February
Processing Time: Varies
Publications: Informational brochure including application guidelines
Guidelines: Application form is not required. Applicants should submit a short narrative letter and include a description of the project, the specific amount requested, the project budget, and a list of directors and key staff.

Sample Grants

Midway College in Midway, Kentucky, received $10,000.
Transylvania University in Lexington, Kentucky, received $150,000.
Business Higher Education Forum in Washington, DC, was awarded $11,250.
College of Business and Economics in Lexington, Kentucky, was awarded $200,000.
Georgia Foundation for Independent Colleges in Atlanta received $2,500.
Marshall University in Huntington, West Virginia, received $38,255, plus $207,500 for its foundation and $10,700 for its research corporation.
Morehead State University Foundation in Morehead, Kentucky, was awarded $75,000.
National Merit Scholarship Corporation in Evanston, Illinois, received $4,340.
Ohio State University in Columbus received $15,000.

Comments/Analysis

In 1993, the foundation awarded 50 percent of its contribution dollars to educational organizations, 15 percent for matching gifts to education, 13 percent for matching gifts to United Funds and community chests, 4 percent to civic causes, 4 percent to public policy and economics education, 2 percent to health and welfare, and 3 percent to other. Of the $2,362,288 awarded to educational organizations, approximately 51 percent was given to institutions of higher education and higher education related associations.

101

AT&T Foundation
1301 Avenue of the Americas, Room 3100
New York, NY   10019

Areas of Interest

Program Description: To support higher education, arts and culture, health, international affairs, public policy, and social action. Specific areas of interest in higher eduction include science, engineering, and minority education.
Assistance Types: Matching funds, employee matching gifts, special projects, research, annual campaigns, endowments, operating

budgets, technical assistance, capital campaigns, scholarships funds, faculty development, facilities improvements

Eligibility

Restrictions: Giving is on a national basis. No support for individuals, religious organizations, local chapters of national organizations; social or health sciences programs, medical or nursing schools, junior or community colleges, industrial affiliate programs or technical trade associations, or disease related health associations. No grants for medical research, emergency funds, deficit financing, land acquisition, fellowships, publications, conferences, operating expenses or capital campaigns of local health and human service agencies (other than hospitals), sports, teams, or athletic competitions. The foundation does not purchase advertisements or sponsorships and does not donate equipment.

Personnel

Officers: Marilyn Laurie, Chair and Trustee; Reynold Levy, President and Trustee; Anne Alexander, VP, Education Programs; Gary Doran, VP, International and Public Policy Programs; Timothy J. McClimon, VP, Arts and Culture Program; Liza Parker, VP, Policy and Administration; Milton J. Little Jr., VP, Health and Social Action Programs; Laura Abbott, Secy.; Robert E. Angelica, Treas.; Sarah Jepsen, Exec. Director

Trustees/Directors: Curtis R. Artis, Harold W. Burlingame, W. Frank Cobbin, Curtis J. Crawford, John C. Guerra Jr., Robert M. Kavner, Judity A. Maynes, Thomas H. Norris, C. Kumar, N. Patel, Robert J. Ranalli, Yvonne M. Shepard, M. Kent Takeda, Frederic S. Topor, Thomas C. Wajnert, Doreen S. Yochum

Staff: 12 full-time professional, two part-time professional, four full-time support, three part-time support

Financial Profile

Assets: In 1993, $128,925,271
High Grant: $1,800,000
Low Grant: $5,000
Ave. Grant: $5,000-$50,000
Total Grants: 835 grants totaling $27,660,750

Application Process

Contact: Laura Abbott, Secy., (212) 841-4747
Deadline: January, April, June, and September
Board Meeting: March, June, September, and December
Processing Time: 90 Days
Publications: Biennial report, informational brochure including application guidelines. Address for guidelines and report: PO Box 45284, Dept. FC, Jacksonville, Florida 32232-5284
Guidelines: Application form is not required. Initial approach should be by written request for guidelines. Guidelines contain program limitations and addresses of regional contributions managers.

Sample Grants

American Association of Colleges for Teacher Education received two $25,000 grants for the Teachers for Tomorrow program.

California Institute of Technology in Pasadena, California, received six grants totaling $189,001 and ranging from $19,968-$42,372 for Ph.D. scholarships; $20,637 for a special purpose grant for the chemistry and chemical engineering department; a $20,000 special purpose grant for the division of physics, math, and astronomy; $25,000 for a special purpose grant for the electrical engineering department; and a $24,363 special purpose grant for the mechanical engineering department.

Jackson State University in Jackson, Mississippi, received $50,000 for Historically Black Colleges and Universities Engineering and Computer Science Programs.

Foundation For Independent Colleges in Harrisburg, Florida, received $45,000 for program support.

Hispanic Association of Colleges and Universities in San Antonio, Texas, received two grants totaling $40,000 for operating support.

Hobart and William Smith Colleges in Geneva, New York, received $50,000 for liberal arts education.

Rensselaer Polytechnic Institute in Troy, New York, received $100,000 for undergraduate curriculum.

University of Puerto Rico, Institute of Statistics in Rio Piedras, Puerto Rico, received $15,000 for a special purpose grant.

University of Texas in Richardson, Texas, received $50,000 for a Hispanic Mother/Daughter program.

University of Massachusetts in Amherst received $12,500 for AT&T minority achievement awards.

Birmingham Southern College in Birmingham, Alabama, received $12,500 to improve science education at the secondary level.

Merrimack College in North Andover, Massachusetts, received $25,000 to upgrade its microscale laboratory.

Monmouth College in West Long Branch, New Jersey, received a $25,000 special purpose grant for its computer science department.

Arizona State University Manufacturing and Industrial Technology Departments in Tempe, Arizona, received $65,000 for a manufacturing technology grant.

Comments/Analysis

In higher education, the AT&T Foundation is particularly interested in funding development and projects grants supporting junior faculty, minorities and women in the study of business and engineering, excellence in liberal arts, and the development of America's workforce. The foundation is also interested in fostering programs that require collaboration between parents and educators to reform public schools and improve teacher preparation. In addition, the foundation supports higher education science and engineering through four specific programs in which participation is by invitation only. The types of grants awarded under these programs include special purpose grants for science and engineering designated for research, curriculum development, or other departmental needs in electrical engineering, computer science, materials science, chemistry, and physics.; manufacturing technology grants aimed at strengthening applied engineering disciplines essential to manufacturing productivity and industrial competitiveness; AT&T Bell Laboratories PhD scholarships in selected science and engineering disciplines; and grants to Historically Black Colleges and Universities and other universities with engineering and computer science programs aimed at increasing the number of minorities in the engineering and science professions. The foundation also operates an employee matching gifts program for higher education and cultural institutions. Historically, community improvement and development has received 22 percent of the grant dollars distributed by the foundation; science, 21 percent; education, 18 percent; other, 14 percent; arts and culture, 13 percent; and employee matching gifts 12 percent. Many of the grants awarded in both the education and the science category are given to colleges and universities. Many of the education grants for $10,000 or more have been awarded for the Teachers for Tomorrow Program, PhD scholarships, program support for state independent college funds, the Hispanic Mother/Daughter Program, and special purpose grants.

102

Bank of Boston Corporation Charitable Foundation
c/o Bank of Boston, 100 Federal Street
Government & Community Affairs Department
Boston, MA   02110

Areas of Interest

Program Description: To support health and welfare, education, culture and art, and civic and community. Specific areas of interest include hospitals, neighborhood health centers, youth, families, the aged, visual and performing arts, museums, arts service organizations, housing, community and economic development, employment and training, justice and law, and the environment.
Assistance Types: Operating expenses, program support, capital campaigns, employee matching gifts, building and renovation, annual campaigns, endowments, equipment, scholarship funds

Eligibility

Restrictions: No grants to individuals, religious programs, or national health organizations; no support for research, fellowships, fundraising events, conferences, or forums; no loans. Strong preference is given to organizations/institutions in New England with emphasis on Suffolk County, Massachusetts, and the metropolitan Boston area

Personnel

Trustees/Directors: Ira Stepanion, Charles K. Gifford, Eliot N. Vestner, Bank of Boston
Staff: Two full-time professional, one full-time support

Financial Profile

Assets: In 1992, $8,875,695; 1993, $5,700,000
High Grant: In 1992, $640,000; 1993, $100,000
Low Grant: In 1992, $25; 1993, $500

Ave. Grant: $2,500-$25,000
Total Grants: In 1993, 2,000 grants totaling $4,700,000
High Grant Higher Ed.: $50,000
Low Grant Higher Ed.: $25
Ave. Grant Higher Ed.: $100-$10,000
Total Grants Higher Ed.: In 1992, approximately 449 grants totaling $671,233

Application Process

Contact: Judith Kidd, Coordinator, Corporate Contributions; questions and requests for additional information should be directed to staff of the Community Investment Department: (617) 434-2189
Deadline: At least 30 days before meetings
Board Meeting: Third week of March, July, November, and January
Processing Time: Two months
Publications: Application guidelines
Guidelines: Requests should be submitted in writing and include the following: a brief history and description of the organization; specific amount and purpose of grant request; organization's budget for current and previous years (or current and proposed budgets), including sources and amounts of support for the most recent completed year; total project budget (if request is for a project); financial statements (audited if available); evidence of tax-exempt status; and names and affiliations of the board of directors and/or trustees. Repeat requests are not considered within any calendar year. Generally, multiyear grants are limited to capital campaigns and usually for no more than three years. A two-year period is required to elapse before a new capital and/or multiyear request will be considered.

Sample Grants

Boston College in Chestnut Hill, Massachusetts, received $30,000.
Boston University in Boston, Massachusetts, received $33,334 for the Chelsea Project.
Northeastern University in Boston, Massachusetts, received $50,000.
Tufts University Management and Community Development Institute in Medford, Massachusetts, was awarded two grants totaling $32,500.
University of Maine in Orono, Maine, received $40,000.
Wentworth Institute of Technology in Boston, Massachusetts, was awarded $25,000.
Berklee College of Music in Boston, Massachusetts, was awarded $10,000.
Salve Regina University in Newport, Rhode Island, received $10,000.
Champlain College in Burlington, Vermont, received $8,000.

Comments/Analysis

Higher education receives approximately 15 percent of the funds distributed by the foundation. The foundation prefers to support capital campaigns at colleges and universities rather than specific programs or departments, or operating expenses. Aid to higher education is also provided through grants to higher education related organizations and scholarship funds and employee matching gifts.

103
BankAmerica Foundation
PO Box 37000
Bank of America Center, Department 3246
San Francisco, CA   94137

Areas of Interest

Program Description: To support elementary, secondary, and higher education; community development and improvement; performing and visual arts; health and hospitals; United Way; and human services. Specific areas of interest in higher education include business, finance, economics, job training, and minority education.

Assistance Types: Annual campaigns, building funds, special projects, scholarship funds, employee-related scholarships, general purposes, continuing support, capital campaigns, emergency funds

Eligibility

Restrictions: No grants for religious groups, athletic events and programs, organizations where funding would primarily benefit membership, United Way-supported agencies, government funded programs, fund-raising events, advertising memorial campaigns, or endowments. No support for individuals, research, conferences, seminars, publications, or operating expenses. Giving mainly in areas of company operations including California, metropolitan areas nationwide, and foreign countries.

Personnel

Officers: Donald A. Mullane, Chair and Trustee; Caroline O. Boitano, President, Exec. Director, and Trustee; Joanne El-Gohary, VP; James S. Wagele, VP; Janet Nishioka, Treas.; Sandra Cohen, Secy.; Judy Tufo, Financial Officer
Trustees/Directors: Kathleen Burke, Lewis Coleman, Raymond McKee, Thomas E. Peterson, Richard Rosenberg, John S. Stephan
Staff: One full-time professional, one full-time support

Financial Profile

Assets: In 1993, $97,546
Total Grants: $14,854,325

Application Process

Contact: Caroline O. Boitano, President and Exec. Director, (415) 953-3175
Deadline: None, except for capital/major campaigns, July 31
Board Meeting: Annually and as necessary
Publications: Program policy statement, application guidelines, 990-PF

Guidelines: Application form is not required. Initial approach should be made by letter proposal including a statement of problem project will address; population and geographic area to be served by project; detailed description of project and amount of funding requested; list of additional sources and amount of support; copy of annual report or audited financial statement and 990; copy of IRS determination letter; list of board of directors, trustees, officers, and other key people and their affiliations.

Sample Grants

Citizens Scholarship Foundation of America in San Francisco, California, received three grants: $280,500 for its Achievement Awards Program, $52,800 for BankAmerica scholarship awards and management fees, and $15,000 for its California Project.

California Community College Foundation in Pasadena, California, received $33,750 for its Early Start project.

Santa Clara University in Santa Clara, California, received $100,000 for minority student aid and for its Institute for Agribusiness.

University of California, Los Angeles, received $50,000 for capital campaign for the Anderson Graduate School of Management Complex, which will include a Career Placement Executive Center.

National Hispanic Scholarship Fund in Novato, California, received $15,000 for general operating support.

Oregon Health Sciences University Foundation School of Nursing in Portland, Oregon, received $15,000 for a capital campaign.

University of Nevada in Las Vegas received $100,000.

Oregon Independent College Foundation in Portland, Oregon, received $20,000.   .

Comments/Analysis

The BankAmerica Foundation is primarily interested in supporting the following areas and programs: Bank of America Achievement Awards for outstanding high school students; California Educational Initiatives Fund (CEIF), aimed at encouraging local enterprise to improve the quality of public elementary and secondary education in California; Community Investment for projects that address the social and economic issues that face California communities; culture and art, particularly performing and visual arts organizations and programs that are aimed at audience development and increased access for the community at large; education that focuses on preparing people to become productive employees, knowledgeable customers, and participating citizens; and health and human services support made mainly through grants to United Way campaigns. Historically, community improvement and development has been the top subject area by dollar, followed by education. Colleges and universities generally account for the second largest recipient type, followed by educational support agencies, such as the Citizens Scholarship Foundation of America. The majority of higher education grants are awarded to institutions in California, Oregon, and Nevada.

104

Bechtel Foundation
50 Beale Street
San Francisco, CA   94105

Areas of Interest

Program Description: To support higher education, community funds, culture, public policy, health, and social services. Specific areas of interest in higher education include engineering and science and technology.
Assistance Types: General purpose, employee matching gifts

Eligibility

Restrictions: No grants for endowments, special projects, religious organizations, or individuals

Personnel

Officers: R.P. Bechtel, Chair and Director; C.W. Hull, Vice-Chair and Director; John Neerhout Jr., Vice-Chair and Director; J. W. Weiser, President and Director; W. L. Friend, Exec. VP and Director; D.J. Gunther, Exec. VP and Director; Adrian Zaccaria, Exec. V.P and Director; J.D. Carter, Senior VP, Secy., and Director; R. C. Johnstone, Senior V.P and Treas.; T.G. Flynn, Senior VP
Staff: One full-time professional, one part-time professional, one full-time support, one part-time support

Financial Profile

Assets: In 1992, $21,349,616
High Grant: $272,000
Low Grant: $75
Ave. Grant: $1,000-$20,000
Total Grants: 305 grants totaling $1,569,648; $169,573 in employee matching gifts
Total Grants Higher Ed.: 15 grants of $10,000 or more for a total of $213,250

Application Process

Contact: K.M. Bandarrae, Asst. Secy., (415) 768-5974
Deadline: None
Board Meeting: Annually
Guidelines: Applicants should submit a letter or a proposal and include a copy of their IRS determination letter and information describing their organization. Grants are made on a national or broad regional basis.

Sample Grants

National Society of Professional Engineers Educational Foundation in Alexandria, Virginia, received $20,000.
University of Washington in Seattle received $14,000.
California Polytechnic State University in San Luis Obisbo, California, received $10,000.
University of Maryland Foundation in Baltimore received $15,000.
Dominican College of Blauvelt in Blauvelt, New York, received $10,000.
Montana Tech University Foundation in Butte, Montana, received $10,000.

Comments/Analysis

Historically, education, including elementary, secondary, and higher education, has been the foundation's top subject area by dollars; while colleges and universities are the largest recipients by grant numbers and the second largest recipient type by dollars.

105

BellSouth Foundation
c/o BellSouth Corporation
1155 Peachtree Street NE, Room 7H08
Atlanta, GA   30367-6000

Areas of Interest

Program Description: To support elementary, secondary, higher, and minority education and science and technology.
Assistance Types: Seed money, program-related investments

Eligibility

Restrictions: No support for individuals; non-education-related programs; programs with local impact only; capital, building, or general endowment campaigns; general operating expenses; educational product development; equipment; scholarships; or fundraising events. Giving primarily in Alabama, Florida, Georgia, Kentucky, Louisiana, Mississippi, North Carolina, South Carolina, and Tennessee.

Personnel

Officers: H.C. Henry, Chair; Patricia L. Willis, President and Exec. Director; Charles W. Shewbridge III, VP; Leslie J. Graitcer, Secy. and Assoc. Director; Kincaid Patterson, Treas.
Trustees/Directors: D.M. Betz, O.C. Donald, R. Dunn, N.C. Humphries, R.L. McGuire, J.B. North
Staff: Two full-time professional, one part-time professional, one full-time support

Financial Profile

Assets: In 1992, $40,366,464; 1993, $40,793,093
High Grant: In 1992, $2,138,192; 1993, $240,000
Low Grant: In 1992, $75; 1993, $15,000
Ave. Grant: $10,000-$300,000
Total Grants: In 1992, 36 grants totaling $3,346,500; 1993, 42 grants totaling $4,310,232

Application Process

Contact: Leslie J. Graitcer, Assoc. Director, or Wendy L.K. Best, Grants Manager, (404) 249-2396, 249-2429, or 249-2428
Deadline: February 1 and August 1
Board Meeting: April and September
Processing Time: Notifications are made in April and September
Publications: Annual report, application guidelines
Guidelines: An application form is not required. Applicants should submit a letter proposal of not more than three pages that describes the project and the amount of the request; explains the results expected and how they will be evaluated; discusses why BellSouth is considered an appropriate donor; lists additional resources and amount of support; and provides a brief history of the organization and a description of its mission. The foundation also requires applicants to submit a copy of their organization's IRS determination letter and a list of their board of directors, trustees, officers, and other key people.

Sample Grants

Belmont Abbey College in Belmont, North Carolina, received a three-year, $150,000 grant to redesign an entire teacher preparation curriculum in response to new education needs.
Florida Institute of Technology in Melbourne, Florida, received a two-year, $120,000 grant for a technology apprentice program for teachers to develop a field-based teacher education program to ensure that preservice teachers are proficient technology users.
Southern Education Foundation in Atlanta, Georgia, received $200,000 to expand its Summer Scholars Program to change education curriculum at Historically Black Colleges and Universities.
University of Tennessee College of Engineering in Knoxville, Tennessee, received $60,000 toward developing two new courses designed to teach/stimulate creativity and creative problem-solving.

Comments/Analysis

The foundation is particularly interested in projects aimed at making lasting improvements in education in the South and addressing the inadequacy of the region's schools. The foundation supports three major education programs, including a program to encourage educational advances through information technology, a program linking educational policy with changing regional needs, and a program to help educators meet changing student needs. The foundation's emphasis is placed on expanding the role of information technology in education curriculum and practices; fostering new ideas and approaches within the educational public policy arena; enhancing the recruitment, training, and working conditions of teachers, administrators, and others involved in education; and creating opportunities to improve educational practices. The foundation favors projects that provide a model for the geographic region, include participation by multiple education groups, and involve local education stakeholders in implementing successful programs at the local level.

106
Bristol-Myers Squibb Foundation, Inc.
345 Park Avenue, 43rd Floor
New York, NY   10154

Areas of Interest

Program Description: To support secondary, higher, and minority education; community funds, services, and development; health and health care services, medical research, civic affairs, minorities, women, youth, international affairs, and arts and culture
Assistance Types: Employee-related scholarships, employee matching gifts, research, annual campaigns, general purposes

Eligibility

Restrictions: Giving primarily in areas of company operations and to national organizations. No grants to individuals; political, fraternal, social, or veterans organizations; religious or sectarian organizations not engaged in a project benefiting the entire community; or organizations receiving support through federated campaigns. No support for public broadcast programs or films or endowment funds. No loans.

Personnel

Officers: Richard L. Gelb, Chair; Patrick F. Crossman, President and Director; Marilyn L. Gruber, VP; Jonathan B. Morris, Treas.
Trustees/Directors: John Damonti, Charles A. Heimbold Jr., Florence McKenna
Staff: Four full-time professional, three full-time support

Financial Profile

Assets: In 1992, $2,841,710; 1993, $2,320,620
High Grant: In 1992, $1,000,000; 1993, $2,000,000
Low Grant: $25
Ave. Grant: $5,000-$35,000
Total Grants: In 1992, 1,262 grants totaling $11,091,523; 1993, 1,479 grants totaling $12,617,655

Application Process

Contact: Cindy Johnson, Grants Administrator, or John Damonti, Director
Deadline: October 1; submit proposal between February and September
Board Meeting: December, and as required
Processing Time: Two to three months
Publications: Informational brochure
Guidelines: An application form is not required. Initial approach should be made by proposal.

Sample Grants

Barnard College in New York City received $127,290.
Butler University in Indianapolis, Indiana, received $26,525.

Independent College Funds of America in New York City received $45,000.

George Mason University in Fairfax, Virginia, received $30,000.

Saint Meinrad College in Saint Meinrad, Indiana, received $16,860.

University of Redland in Redland, California, received $10,000.

Morehouse School of Medicine in Atlanta, Georgia, received $70,075.

Universite de Liege in Liege, Belgium, received $50,000.

University of Dayton in Dayton, Ohio, received $22,450.

University College in London, England, received $100,000.

Meharry Medical College in Nashville, Tennessee, received $10,180.

University of Evansville in Evansville, Indiana, received $134,268.

Rockfeller University in New York City received $271,000.

Comments/Analysis

Historically, the foundation directs its support of higher education to private colleges and universities; state associations of independent colleges; and graduate schools of business from which the company recruits. It is also interested in providing educational opportunities to minorities and women. The foundation is also interested in secondary education with a focus on programs and projects in the areas of high school drop-out prevention; math, science, and health education and the shortage of teachers in these disciplines; advancement and improvement of education; and the overall broadening of educational opportunities.

107
Burlington Northern Foundation
777 Main Street
3700 Continental Plaza
Fort Worth, TX   76102

Areas of Interest

Program Description: To support civic service, culture, education, faculty achievement, community funds, United Way, hospitals, human services, social services, youth, and recreation.
Assistance Types: Employee matching gifts, annual campaigns, building funds, equipment, and general purposes

Eligibility

Restrictions: Giving mainly in areas of company operations. No support for religious organizations; war veterans and fraternal service organizations; endowments; national health organizations and programs, including their local chapters; fund-raising events; corporate memberships; chambers of commerce; tax payer associations; state railroad associations; political organizations, campaigns, or candidates; computers or computers related projects. No grants or loans to individuals. Ordinarily educations grants will not be made to finance the expansion of a student body or the payment of scholarships.

Personnel

Officers: John N. Etchart, Chair; Ronald H. Reimann, VP; C. Ed Dagget, Secy.-Treas.; Beverly A. Edwards, Asst. Secy.
Staff: One full-time professional

Financial Profile

Assets: In 1992, $4,447,557
High Grant: $50,000
Low Grant: $100
Ave. Grant: $1,000-$25,000
Total Grants: 605 grants totaling $1,893,980, plus 176 employee matching gifts totaling $374,196
High Grant Higher Ed.: $25,000
Low Grant Higher Ed.: $1,000
Ave. Grant Higher Ed.: $2,500

Application Process

Contact: Pat Dickinson, Administrator, (817) 878-2265
Deadline: None
Board Meeting: Quarterly
Processing Time: Four-month evaluation cycle
Publications: Program policy statement, application guidelines
Guidelines: An application form is required as are the following attachments: general financial information including total current budget and the principal sources and amounts of ongoing annual support, copy of 501(c)3 tax-exempt letter, and a copy of latest IRS form 990 or 990PF. An original application form must be submitted. The foundation will not accept reproduced copies of the application form. In addition, applications should not be placed in a binder and no other type of cover should be used.

Sample Grants

Carroll College in Helena, Montana, received $2,500.

College of Saint Thomas in Saint Paul, Minnesota, received $2,500.

Gonzaga University in Spokane, Washington, received a grant for $25,000 and a grant for $2,500.

Southwest Missouri State University in Springfield, Missouri, received a grant for $5,000 and a grant for $2,500.

Iowa College Foundation in Des Moines, Iowa, received $15,000.

Associated Colleges of Illinois in Chicago received $20,000.

Nebraska Independent College Foundation in Omaha received $20,000.

Texas Christian University in Fort Worth, Texas, received $10,000.

Oklahoma State University in Stillwater received a grant for $5,000 and a grant for $2,500.

Comments/Analysis

Historically, education receives approximately 34 percent of the funds distributed by the foundation. The vast majority of these funds are awarded to public and private college and universities and higher education-related associations, organizations, and funds, for the improvement of the quality of education. Of the dollars given to education, approximately 33 percent is awarded to institutions of higher education for faculty achievement, 41 percent to educational institutions for other purposes, and 26 percent for employee matching gifts. Grants to higher education are made over a large geographic area with a concentration in (in order of funding amounts) Washington, Montana, Nebraska, Minnesota, Missouri, North Dakota, South Dakota, Colorado, Illinois, Arkansas, Alabama, Oregon, Oklahoma, Texas and Iowa.

108
Burlington Resources Foundation
999 Third Avenue
Seattle, WA   98104-4097

Areas of Interest

Program Description: To support federated organizations such as the United Way, Community Chest, and Red Cross; public and private higher education; youth organizations; hospitals and medical facilities and programs; culture; performing and visual arts; historical preservation; public and educational broadcasting; civic services and community development; conservation; crime prevention; parks and recreation; human services; chemical dependency treatment and prevention; senior citizens; runaway youth; spouse and child abuse; offender programs; and women's programs.
Assistance Types: Building funds, equipment

Eligibility

Restrictions: No grants to religious organizations for religious purposes; veterans or fraternal service organizations; national health organizations and programs, including their local chapters; Chambers of Commerce; taxpayer associations; corporate memberships; or political organizations, campaigns, and candidates. No support for endowment funds, fund-raising events, computers or computer-related projects. No grants or loans to individuals. Giving mainly in areas of company operations.

Personnel

Officers: Thomas H. O'Leary, Chair; Donald K. North, President; George E. Howison, VP; John E. Hagale, VP, Finance; Everett D. Dubois, Treas.; Leslie S. Leland, Secy.; L. David Hanover, Asst. Secy.

Financial Profile

Assets: In 1993, $1,602,614
High Grant: $200,000
Low Grant: $250
Ave. Grant: $5,000-$100,000
Total Grants: 247 grants totaling $6,708,498, plus $328,142 for 94 employee matching gifts
High Grant Higher Ed.: $200,000
Low Grant Higher Ed.: $2,000 (excluding matching gifts)
Ave. Grant Higher Ed.: $10,000-$100,000

Total Grants Higher Ed.: 1992, 43 grants totaling $1,665,000, plus $276,660 in matching gifts

Application Process

Contact: Donald K. North, President, (206) 728-8625
Processing Time: Approximately four months
Guidelines: Application form required. Proof of tax exemption should be submitted with application. No inquiries regarding status of application should be made during four-month evaluation cycle.

Sample Grants

Christian College Coalition in Washington, DC, received a $10,000 grant and a $50,000 grant.
Western Evangelical Seminary in Portland, Oregon, received two grants, one for $100,000 and one for $200,000.
Montana State University in Bozeman received $4,000.
Navajo Education and Scholarship Foundation in Window Rock, Arizona, received $50,000.
Seattle University in Seattle, Washington, received $53,500.
Louisiana State University in Baton Rouge received $100,000.
Arizona State University in Tempe, Arizona, was awarded $10,000.

Comments/Analysis

In the past, education received 40 percent of the dollars distributed by the foundation. This was followed by human services at 22 percent, culture at 18 percent, civic services at 8 percent, matching gifts at 6 percent, federated organizations at 4 percent, and youth at 2 percent. Higher education received 95 percent of the education dollars and 100 percent of the matching gifts. This is in accord with the foundation's strong commitment to support public and private institutions at the college level and to award a substantial amount of grant dollars for the improvement of the quality of education.

109
Burroughs Wellcome Fund
4709 Creekstone Drive, Suite 100
Morrisville, NC   27560-9771

Areas of Interest

Program Description: Primarily to provide support for the advancement of medical research. Areas of interest include medical education, medical research, basic medical sciences, pharmacology, experimental therapeutics, toxicology, microbiological sciences, life sciences, virology, allergic diseases, molecular parasitology, and clinical oncology.
Assistance Types: Scholarships, research, professorships, fellowships, lectureships

Eligibility

Restrictions: Grants restricted to organizations and institutions within the United States. No grants for building, endowments, equipment, operating budgets, continuing support, annual campaigns, deficit financing, publications, conferences, or matching gifts; no loans or grants to individuals

Personnel

Officers: Howard J. Schaeffer, President and Director; Martha G. Peck, Secy. and Exec. Director; Stephen D. Corman, Treas. and Director; Anne W. Alderson, Controller
Trustees/Directors: Dr. David W. Barry, Dr. Gertrude B. Elion, George H. Hitchings, Dr. Trevor M. Jones, Dr. Samuel L. Katz, Dr. Thomas Krenitsky, R. Tracy
Staff: Three full-time professional, one part-time professional, three full-time support

Financial Profile

Assets: For fiscal year ending August, 1993, $123,756,057
High Grant: $253,750
Low Grant: $420
Ave. Grant: $1,000-$50,000
Total Grants: 175 grants totaling $4,073,925

Application Process

Contact: Martha G. Peck, Exec. Director, (919) 991-5100
Deadline: Vary with the particular award and are noted in informational brochures
Board Meeting: Bimonthly beginning in February
Processing Time: Six weeks
Publications: Annual report, application guidelines, newsletters, informational brochures
Guidelines: Information on the competitive award programs is available upon request. An application form is required for the Wellcome Research Travel Grants Program only. Noncompetitive grant applications should be in letter form and include the following: a brief statement of the objectives of the project, its design, and time required for completion; the total budget with reference to any financial support already obtained or promised; qualifications of those undertaking the project; and certification of IRS tax-exempt status.

Sample Grants

University of Pennsylvania in Philadelphia received $60,000 for a new investigator award in molecular parasitology to study immune responses associated with parasite, Leishmania.
Michigan State University in East Lansing, Michigan, received $20,000 for a pilot study on pediatric cerebral malaria.
Washington University School of Medicine in Saint Louis, Missouri, received $350,000 for a scholar award in experimental therapeutics.
University of Kentucky in Lexington received $90,000 for a fellowship program for faculty at Appalachian colleges.

Harvard University in Cambridge, Massachusetts, received $350,000 for a scholar award in toxicology.
Oregon Health Sciences University in Portland, Oregon, was awarded $350,000 for a scholar award in molecular parasitology.
Northwestern State University in Natchitoches, Louisiana, was awarded $59,825 for its Advance Program for young scholars.
University of Alabama School of Medicine in Birmingham, Alabama, received $350,000 for a scholar award in immunopharmacology of allergic diseases.

Comments/Analysis

The major allocation of resources to institutions of higher education is made through the following annual competitive award programs: Experimental Therapeutics Scholar Award ($350,000 over five years); Toxicology Scholar Award ($350,000 over five years); Molecular Parasitology Scholar Award ($350,000 over five years); Wellcome Visiting Professorships in the Basic Medical Sciences; Wellcome Visiting Professorships in the Microbiological Sciences; Wellcome Research Travel Grants to Britain/Ireland; postdoctoral research fellowships; Immunopharmacology of Allergic Diseases Scholar Award ($350,000 over five years); New Investigator Awards in Virology ($90,000); and New Investigator Awards in Molecular Parasitology and Clinical Oncology ($60,000). Some support is also given to higher education institutions for science education and for specially talented investigators and innovative research projects in the basic medical sciences. Such support is awarded on a short-term basis as starter or bridging grants until funding from other sources becomes available.

110
Caterpillar Foundation
100 NE Adams Street
Peoria, IL　61629-1480

Areas of Interest

Program Description: To support community funds, higher education, culture, and youth agencies.
Assistance Types: Employee matching gifts, operating budgets, special projects, capital campaigns, annual support

Eligibility

Restrictions: No grants to individuals, for general operations or ongoing programs of agencies funded by the United Way, or for tickets or advertising for fundraising benefits. No support for fraternal organizations, religious organizations whose services are limited to one sectarian group, or political activities. Giving mainly in areas of company operations.

Personnel

Officers: H.W. Holling, VP; W.M. Zimmerman, VP; R.R. Atterbury, Secy.; T.R. Johnson, Asst. Secy.; R.D. Beran, Treas.

Trustees/Directors: D.V. Fites, G.S. Flaherty, T.N. Thompson

Financial Profile

Assets: In 1993, $21,665,500
High Grant: $620,000
Low Grant: $50
Ave. Grant: $1,000-$5,000
Total Grants: $5,302,462
High Grant Higher Ed.: $200,000
Low Grant Higher Ed.: $50
Ave. Grant Higher Ed.: $1,000-$25,000
Total Grants Higher Ed.: Approximately 146 grants totaling $1,321,914

Application Process

Contact: Maryann Morrison, Manager
Deadline: Applications are accepted at any time
Board Meeting: December 1
Processing Time: Approval or rejection usually in one month
Publications: Corporate giving report
Guidelines: Application form is not required. Initial approach should be by letter or proposal including the following support documentation: an annual report, audited financial statement, and 990 tax return; description of project and amount requested; IRS determination letter; list of board of directors, trustees, officers, and other key people and their affiliations; organizational budget and/or project budget; and list of additional funding sources and amount of support.

Sample Grants

South Dakota School of Mines and Technology in Rapid City received a grant for $750 and one for $25,000.
Northern Nevada Community College in Elko received $25,000.
Bradley University in Peoria, Illinois, received three grants totaling $213,350 and ranging from $400 to $200,000.
College of Saint Francis in Joliet, Illinois, received two grants: one for $7,050 and one for $25,000.
Ferris State University in Big Rapids, Michigan, received $25,000.
Illinois State University in Normal, Illinois, received five grants: $2,500, $4,000, $1,000, $45,000, and $2,000.
Purdue University in West Lafayette, Indiana, received seven grants totaling $77,100 and ranging $100-$70,000.

Comments/Analysis

The majority of grants awarded to colleges and universities by the Caterpillar Foundation are for capital, annual, or operating support.

111
Chrysler Corporation Fund
12000 Chrysler Drive
Highland Park, MI   48288-1919

Areas of Interest

Program Description: To support community funds, health and human services, education, civic affairs, and cultural programs. Specific areas of interest in higher education include automotive design, business administration, engineering, industrial design, minority education, minorities in engineering, management, and transportation design.
Assistance Types: Capital campaigns, employee matching gifts, employee related scholarships, operating budgets, scholarships

Eligibility

Restrictions: No grants to individuals; organizations without 501(c)3 IRS tax-exempt status; or organizations that discriminate by race, religion, color, creed, sex, age, or national origin. No support for endowment funds, equipment and materials, research, fellowships, primary or secondary schools, political organizations or campaigns, religious organizations for religious purposes, veterans and labor organizations, fraternal associations, athletic groups, social clubs, or similar organizations. No grants for courtesy advertising or for the support of conferences, seminars, or similar events. No support to local chapters of organizations receiving Chrysler Fund support, organizations or projects outside of the United States, or for the operating expenses of organizations supported by the United Way other than through the United Way. Giving primarily in areas where the company has a substantial number of employees.

Personnel

Officers: T.G. Denomme, President and Trustee; S.W. Bergeron, VP and Trustee; T. P. Capo, Asst. Treas; L.A. Feldhouse, Manager and Secy.; J.A. Koslowski, Asst. Secy.; R.M. Sherwood, Asst. Secy. and Trustee; C.A. Smith, Controller and Trustee; K.L. Trinh, Asst. Secy.
Trustees/Directors: W.J. O'Brien III, E.P. Pappert, L.C. Richie, G.C. Valade, F.J. Castaing, F.J. Farmer, M.J. Glusac
Staff: Two full-time professional, one full-time support

Financial Profile

Assets: In 1992, $15,732,389; 1993, $32,456,611
High Grant: $590,625
Low Grant: $500
Ave. Grant: $1,000-$50,000
Total Grants: 1,037 grants totaling $7,412,787
High Grant Higher Ed.: $475,000
Low Grant Higher Ed.: $50
Ave. Grant Higher Ed.: $50-$30,000
Total Grants Higher Ed.: In 1992, 665 grants totaling $3,595,308

Application Process

Contact: Lynn A. Feldhouse, Manager and Secy., (313) 956-5194
Deadline: None
Board Meeting: Board meets as required; usually quarterly
Processing Time: Educational grants approved at fall meeting; final notification in four months
Guidelines: All grant requests must be in writing and contain goals, objectives, and historical description of organization; amount requested together with a total budget or project cost amount; list of current contributors, particularly companies and foundations; explanation of relationship, if any, to a United Way organization or a governmental agency; list of officers and board of directors; copy of 501(c)3 tax-exemption letter; and copy of most recent audited financial statements.

Sample Grants

Ohio State University School of Engineering in Columbus, Ohio, received $5,000.

Northwood Institute in Midland, Michigan, received $10,000 for minority scholarships.

Carnegie Mellon University National Society of Black Engineers in Pittsburgh, Pennsylvania, received $1,500.

Consortium for Graduate Studies in Management in Saint Louis, Missouri, received $20,000.

University of Cincinnati Industrial Design Department in Cincinnati, Ohio, received $15,000.

Cleveland Institute of Art in Ohio received $15,000.

Howard University Society of Women in Engineering in Washington, DC, received $1,500.

SAE Foundation in Warrendale, Pennsylvania, received $50,000 for a Graduate Student Forgivable Loan Program.

Wayne State University School of Business in Detroit, Michigan, received $7,500.

Ohio Foundation of Independent Colleges in Columbus received $20,000.

Comments/Analysis

In the past, the fund awarded 36 percent of its total contributions, gifts, and grants paid to colleges, universities, and scholarship funds (higher education); 27 percent to community health, welfare, and social services; 16 percent to youth character and educational programs (non-higher education); 12 percent to civic and cultural betterment programs; and the remaining 9 percent to research regarding community, state, and national problems; groups combating bigotry and racial discrimination; tax and economic education programs; and public education regarding traffic safety. Historically the fund has focused its higher education support on colleges and universities with model schools of business or engineering or departments of automotive design, associations of independent colleges and universities located near where the corporation has a substantial number of employees, higher education institutions with a reputation for excellence in education, schools that consistently produce Chrysler recruits, and institutions that upgrade the quality of minority education in specific programs of interest to the Chrysler Corporation. For example, support has been provided for predominantly black schools that

are recognized nationally as resource centers for minorities in managerial careers. The fund has also been known to support national organizations that support higher education in general and affirmative action in particular. In addition, the fund supports an employee matching gift program for junior and community colleges, four-year colleges and universities, graduate and professional schools, and technical and specialized schools, and provides scholarship aid to the children of Chrysler employees.

112
CIGNA Foundation
One Liberty Place
Philadelphia, PA   19192-1540

Areas of Interest

Program Description: To support education, health and human services, civic affairs, and arts and culture. Specific areas of interest include public secondary education, minority higher education, maternal and infant health care, community economic development, literacy, career education, insurance education and business education. The foundation is also particularly interested in improving the understanding of societal issues significant to business and economic development in Philadelphia, Pennsylvania, and Hartford, Connecticut.
Assistance Types: General purposes, special projects, employee-related scholarships, scholarship funds, student aid, operating budgets, employee matching gifts, matching funds, fellowships, emergency funds, annual campaigns, seminars and conferences

Eligibility

Restrictions: No grants to religious organizations or religion, political organizations or campaigns, disease-specific research or treatment organizations, individuals, endowments, capital campaigns, or hospital capital improvements and expansions. No support for organizations receiving major support from United Way or other CIGNA-supported federated funding agencies. Giving primarily in Hartford, Connecticut, and Philadelphia, Pennsylvania, and to selected national organizations.

Personnel

Officers: Thomas J. Wagner, Chair; Barry F. Wiksen, President; Paul H. Rohrkemper, VP and Treas.; Arnold W. Wright Jr., VP and Exec. Director; Carol J. Ward, Secy.; John J. Corcoran, Asst. Secy.; Lee R. Hoffman, Asst. Secy.; David C. Kopp, Asst. Secy.; Michael Kuchs, Asst. Secy.
Trustees/Directors: Lawrence P. English, Gerald A. Isom, Donald M. Levinson, James G. Stewart, Thomas J. Wagner
Staff: Six full-time professional, one full-time support

Financial Profile

Assets: In 1993, $8,236,073
High Grant: $725,000

Low Grant: $50
Ave. Grant: $2,500-$10,000
Total Grants: $6,244,258
High Grant Higher Ed.: $208,000
Low Grant Higher Ed.: $500
Ave. Grant Higher Ed.: $1,000-$10,000
Total Grants Higher Ed.: Approximately 50 grants totaling $894,544, plus $839,442 in matching gifts to all categories of education

Application Process

Contact: Arnold W. Wright Jr., Exec. Director, (215) 761-6055
Deadline: None, but the foundation prefers to receive proposals by September
Board Meeting: Biennially
Processing Time: Six weeks
Publications: Corporate giving report, including application guidelines, annual report, grants list
Guidelines: In the greater Hartford, Connecticut, area requests should be directed to James N. Mason, Dir., Civic Affairs, CIGNA Foundation, W-A, Hartford, Connecticut 06152-5001. All other requests should be sent to the Philadelphia address. Application form is not required. Initial approach should be made by one- to two-page letter. Proposals should include a brief history of organization and description of its mission; list of board of directors, trustees, officers, and other key people and their affiliations; annual report/audited financial statement/990 tax return; IRS determination letter; detailed description of project and amount of request; organizational budget and/or project budget; and how the project will be sustained once foundation support is completed.

Sample Grants

Citizens' Scholarship Foundation of America in Saint Peter, Minnesota, received $208,000.

Hartford Consortium for Higher Education in Hartford, Connecticut, was awarded $20,000.

United Negro College Fund in Hartford, Connecticut, was awarded $1,000.

Moore College of Art in Philadelphia, Pennsylvania, received $10,000.

Pennsylvania State University Actuarial Program in University Park received $3,000.

Worcester Polytechnic Institute in Worcester, Massachusetts, received $7,500.

Trident Technical College in Charleston, South Carolina, received $1,000.

University of Chicago Graduate School of Business in Chicago, Illinois, received $5,000.

University of Connecticut Law School Foundation in Hartford, Connecticut, received $20,000.

University of Pennsylvania S.S. Huebner Foundation for Insurance Education in Philadelphia received $5,000.

Comments/Analysis

In 1993, health and human services was awarded the greatest proportion of the foundation's grant funds, receiving 38 percent of the total dollars distributed. This was followed by education at 37 percent, culture and arts at 14 percent and community and civic affairs at 11 percent. Higher education received approximately 62 percent of the funds awarded to education plus a significant portion of the $839,442 in matching gifts to education. The foundation operates the CIGNA Scholars/Fellows program, which supports academically talented students at institutions of higher education across the country where the foundation has a pre-existing recruiting relationship. The foundation also supports the study of actuarial sciences in colleges and universities where the foundation has pre-existing business relationships and special projects related to the insurance and financial service industry. The foundation is particularly interested in proposals to improve primary and secondary public education in Philadelphia as well as those aimed at helping schools in the Hartford and Bloomfield, Connecticut, areas enhance the quality and cost-effectiveness of education.

113
Coca-Cola Foundation, Inc.
One Coca-Cola Plaza NW
Atlanta, GA   30313-3009

Areas of Interest

Program Description: To support elementary, secondary, higher, minority, and adult education. Specific areas of interest in higher education include science and technology, health sciences, teacher education, international affairs, minority education, medical education for minorities, marketing, finance, and business.
Assistance Types: Scholarship funds, fellowships, internships, endowments, annual campaigns, capital campaigns, special projects, equipment, operating budgets, continuing support, general purposes, matching funds, student financial aid

Eligibility

Restrictions: No support for individuals, religious organizations or religious endeavors, veterans organizations, hospitals, or local chapters of national organizations. No grants for workshops, travel, conferences, seminars, building, operating budgets, charitable dinners, fund-raising events and related advertising publications, equipment, or land acquisition. No loans.

Personnel

Officers: Ingrid Saunders Jones, Chair and Director; Donald R. Greene, President and Director; Joseph W. Jones, Secy.; Jack L. Stahl, Treas.
Trustees/Directors: John Alm, Michelle Beale, R. Bruce Kirkman, Robert P. Wilkinson, Director
Staff: Six full-time professional, six full-time support

Financial Profile

Assets: In 1993, $21,118,000
Total Grants: 197 grants totaling $10,554,950

Application Process

Contact: Donald R. Greene, President, PO Drawer 1734, Atlanta, Georgia 30301, (404) 676-2568
Deadline: None
Board Meeting: March and August
Processing Time: 30 days
Publications: Annual report, application guidelines
Guidelines: A formal application form is required. Write or phone for guidelines and application.

Sample Grants

New York University in New York City received $100,000 for final payment for Project MUST, a mentoring program for New York City high school students interested in teaching careers.

Clark Atlanta University in Atlanta, Georgia, received $400,000 for teacher education and to develop its School of Public and International Affairs.

Interdemoninational Theological Center in Atlanta, Georgia, received $50,000 for student financial aid and foreign exchange program.

Benedict College in Columbia, South Carolina, received $100,000 for its After Program, encouraging persons from military service to pursue teaching as a second career.

Georgetown University School of Foreign Service in Washington, DC, received $100,000 for its international outreach programs focusing on government relations and business awareness.

Prairie View A & M University in Prairie View, Texas, received $10,000 for its scholarship fund and toward increasing the number of minority students studying science and technology.

Rice University in Houston, Texas, received $25,000 for marketing and finance programs.

Meharry Medical College in Nashville, Tennessee, received $25,000 for its Fisk-Meharry Joint Program, which helps increase the number of minority health care professionals.

Operation Smile International in Norfolk, Virginia, received $35,000 for medical education for health care professionals in Kenya, Africa.

Temple University in Philadelphia, Pennsylvania, received $20,000 for its Future Faculty Fellows Program and scholarship funds for minority graduate and undergraduate students.

United Negro College Fund in New York City received three grants totaling $550,000 for support of Historically Black Colleges and Universities and for Campaign 2000.

114

Cooper Industries Foundation
PO Box 4446
First City Tower, Suite 4000
Houston, TX   77210

Areas of Interest

Program Description: To support the United Way, higher education, vocational education, youth, art, performing arts, cultural programs, museums, health, conservation, and civic affairs.
Assistance Types: Employee matching gifts, employee related scholarships, special projects, building funds, capital campaigns, general purposes, operating budgets, continuing support, annual campaigns, seed money, matching funds

Eligibility

Restrictions: No support for religious organizations, national health and welfare organizations, fraternal or veterans organizations, political candidates or organizations, labor organizations, lobbying organizations, or private elementary and secondary schools. No grants for publications, conferences, seminars, or hospital capital fund drives or their operating campaigns. No loans. No grants to individuals. Giving mainly in Houston, Texas, and other communities with company operations.

Personnel

Officers: R. Cizik, Chair and Trustee; T. Campbell, President and Trustee; D. Cross, Treas. and Trustee; P. Meinecke, Secy.
Trustees/Directors: A. Riedel
Staff: None

Financial Profile

Assets: In 1993, $131,333
High Grant: $312,500
Low Grant: $175
Ave. Grant: $1,000-$5,000
Total Grants: 855 grants totaling $3,834,463, plus 3,125 employee matching gifts totaling $517,213
High Grant Higher Ed.: $1,250,000
Low Grant Higher Ed.: $200
Ave. Grant Higher Ed.: $1,000-$10,000
Total Grants Higher Ed.: In 1992, 98 grants totaling $2,397,760, plus $158,798 in employee matching gifts and $19,434 in special matching gifts

Application Process

Contact: Patricia B. Meinecke, c/o Cooper Industries, Inc., 1001 Fannin Street, Houston, Texas 77002, (713) 739-5617
Deadline: Fall for funding the following year

Board Meeting: February; distribution committee meets semiannually

Processing Time: Within 90 days

Publications: Application guidelines, annual report

Guidelines: Application form is not required. Initial approach should be by letter explaining the purpose of the organization, including its fund-raising goals. A copy of the letter granting the organization tax-exempt status should also be included. Requests from organizations within communities of company operations will be referred to the local operation for recommendation.

Sample Grants

Texas Southern University in Houston received two $3,000 grants.

Rice University in Houston, Texas, was awarded two $37,500 grants.

National Merit Scholarship Corporation in Evanston, Illinois, received $36,110 for employee-related scholarships.

Houston Community College System Foundation in Houston, Texas, received a grant for $5,000 and a grant for $2,000.

Wallace State Community College in Hanceville, Alabama, received two grants totaling $8,000.

Earlham College in Richmond, Indiana, received $100,000.

Ohio State University in Columbus received two $1,000 grants for it business office, $500,000 for the College of Engineering and Technology, and $2,500 for the Telecommunication Center.

South Carolina Foundation of Independent Colleges in Columbia received two grants totaling $2,800.

University of Wisconsin received eight $1,600 grants to be distributed among four of its campuses: Eau Claire, Madison, Milwaukee, and Oshkosh.

Illinois Benedictine College in Lisle received $9,000.

Comments/Analysis

In the past, higher education received approximately 59 percent of the dollars distributed by the foundation and was the recipient of the high award for a recent year: $1,250,000 to Harvard Business School for the Robert and Jane Cizik Endowment. Higher education recipients include four-year colleges and universities, community colleges, vocational and technical institutes, and state educational support agencies such as Independent College Funds and Foundations.

115
Deloitte & Touche Foundation
PO Box 820
10 Westport Road
Wilton, CT   06897-0820

Areas of Interest

Program Description: To support accounting and business education.

Assistance Types: Faculty development grants, professorships, research, fellowships, employee matching gifts, conferences, seminars

Eligibility

Restrictions: Grants given on a broad regional basis throughout the United States. No grants for general purposes, capital campaigns, matching funds, special programs, or publications. No loans.

Personnel

Officers: J. Michael Cook, Chair; Richard A. Shafer, President; D. Gerald Searfoss, Secy.-Treas.

Trustees/Directors: Randy Allen, Mark Chain, Michael J. Joyce, Andrew G. McMaster, David Passman

Staff: None

Financial Profile

Assets: For fiscal year ending August 1993, $132,309

High Grant: $161,662

Low Grant: $2,000

Ave. Grant: $5,000-$30,000

Total Grants: 25 grants totaling $591,674, 25 grants to individuals totaling $140,000, and $774,459 for employee matching gifts

Application Process

Contact: Stacy Van Steenwyk, Foundation Administrator, (203) 761-3424

Deadline: None, except for October 15 for the doctoral fellowship program

Board Meeting: Twice annually

Processing Time: Notification December 15 for the doctoral fellowship program

Publications: Informational brochure

Guidelines: Initial approach should be made by letter. Application form required for the doctoral fellowship program only; contact head of accounting department in educational institution for application information.

Sample Grants

American Accounting Association in Sarasota, Florida, received eight grants totaling $598,453 for various seminars, conferences, and consortium programs.

Consortium for Graduate Study in Management in Saint Louis, Missouri, received two grants totaling $27,500 for education in accounting.

Florida A&M University in Tallahassee, Florida, received two $20,000 grants for education in accounting.

Ohio State University in Columbus, Ohio, received two $25,000 grants for a Deloitte and Touche Accounting Professorship.

University of Nebraska in Lincoln received $15,000 for a Grant W. Gregory Chair in Accounting.

University of Notre Dame in Notre Dame, Indiana, received $21,000 for a Deloitte and Touche Endowed Fund in Accountancy.

University of Southern California in Los Angeles received $38,000 for an audit judgement symposium, $30,000 for an audit symposium, and $25,000 for tax scholarships and awards for aid of education in accounting.

Comments/Analysis

The foundation is particularly interested in furthering accounting education throughout the United States and supports a fellowship program for 10 accounting doctoral candidates each year. The foundation also supports an employee matching gifts program in education and matches gifts to four-year colleges and universities by full-time and retired partners, employees, and directors.

116

Walt Disney Company Foundation
500 S Buena Vista Street
Burbank, CA   91521

Areas of Interest

Program Description: To support the health and welfare of children, youth activities, higher education, community funds, medical and health services, and music and cultural arts.

Assistance Types: Scholarships funds, employee-related scholarships, general purposes, capital campaigns, annual campaigns, continuing support, operating budgets, special projects

Eligibility

Restrictions: Generally no grants to public agencies, educational institutions, or other nonprofits supported predominantly by tax dollars; agencies receiving funds from the United Way, permanent charities committees, or any other similar consolidated giving programs to which the foundation contributes; sectarian organizations; agency building campaigns; agency start-up campaigns or for seed purposes; medical research programs; or for individuals, except scholarships to children of company employees. Giving primarily in areas where the company's businesses are located, including central Florida and Los Angeles and Orange County, California.

Personnel

Officers: Michael D. Eisner, President and Trustee; Jack B. Lindquist, VP and Trustee; Roy E. Disney, VP and Trustee; Frank G. Wells, Treas.; Doris A. Smith, Secy.

Financial Profile

Assets: In 1993, $411,162
High Grant: $500,000
Low Grant: $200

Ave. Grant: $500-$500,000
Total Grants: 91 grants totaling $1,649,703, plus 53 grants to individuals totaling $179,089
High Grant Higher Ed.: $500,000
Low Grant Higher Ed.: $200
Ave. Grant Higher Ed.: $200-$10,000
Total Grants Higher Ed.: Approximately 33 grants totaling $935,972, plus 106 scholarships totaling $182,610

Application Process

Contact: Doris A. Smith, Secy., (818) 560-1006
Deadline: October 1 for scholarships; applications for other purposes received prior to December 31 are considered at the donations committee meeting held the following spring.
Board Meeting: Donations committee meets annually in the spring
Processing Time: 20 to 30 days after donations committee meeting
Publications: Application guidelines; annual report on file in the foundation office, but not available for distribution
Guidelines: Official application form must be obtained from the foundation for the scholarship program. Submit all other applications in letter format and include federal and state tax exemption letters, current financial statements (preferably audited), sources of income and major contributors, list of board of directors with their outside affiliations, and brief history of the organization.

Sample Grants

Endowment Association of William and Mary in Williamsburg, Virginia, received $1,000.

Florida Institute of Technology in Melbourne, Florida, received $1,250.

Florida Foundation of Future Scientists received $500.

Florida Independent College Fund in Lakeland, Florida, was awarded $1,250.

Rollins College in Winter Park, Florida, received $1,250.

University of Pennsylvania in Philadelphia received $7,173.

Stanford University in Stanford, California, received two grants for $5,034 each.

Comments/Analysis

In the recent past, the Walt Disney Company Foundation distributed approximately 65 percent of all its annual contributions, gifts, and grants paid to higher education. This included numerous scholarships to colleges, universities, and institutes of technology for children of employees of the Walt Disney Company and its subsidiaries and associated companies, and several awards ranging in size from $500-$500,000 to the California Institute of the Arts in Valencia.

117
Dow Chemical Company Foundation
1776 Building
Midland, MI   48674

Areas of Interest

Program Description: To support higher education and the field of chemistry.
Assistance Types: Scholarship funds, research

Eligibility

Restrictions: No grants to individuals

Personnel

Officers: Frank P. Popoff, Chair, President, and Trustee; F.P. Corson, VP; A.H. Jenkins, Secy.; Enrique C. Falla, Treas. and Director
Trustees/Directors: A.J. Butler, J.L. Downey, Paul F. Oreffice, E.J. Sosa, W.S. Stravropoulos

Financial Profile

Assets: In 1992, $1,404,955
High Grant: $150,000
Low Grant: $100
Ave. Grant: $5,000-$15,000
Total Grants: 741 grants totaling $5,061,867

Application Process

Contact: Theodore E. Tabor, Program Manager, (517) 636-0773
Deadline: None
Board Meeting: Usually four times per year
Processing Time: Two to three months
Publications: Informational brochure
Guidelines: Initial approach should be by brief letter.

Sample Grants

Michigan State University in East Lansing received a grant for $150,000, a grant for $11,000, and a grant for $10,000.

Massachusetts Institute of Technology in Cambridge received three grants totaling $48,000, ranging $10,000-$23,000.

Purdue University in West Lafayette, Indiana, received a $50,000 grant and a $15,000 grant.

Southwest Texas State University in San Marcos, Texas, received $18,500.

Southeastern Consortium for Minorities in Engineering in Atlanta, Georgia, received $10,000.

Virginia Polytechnic Institute and State University in Blacksburg, Virginia, received two $10,000 grants.

University of Texas in Arlington received four grants totaling $93,500 and ranging $10,000-$50,000.

Albion College in Albion, Michigan, received a $70,000 grant and a $18,500 grant.

Comments/Analysis

The Dow Chemical Company Foundation is committed to supporting programs at selected schools that encourage outstanding high school students to embark on a program leading to a career in chemistry.

118
Exxon Education Foundation
225 E John W. Carpenter Freeway
Irving, TX   75062-2298

Areas of Interest

Program Description: To support education by providing matching gifts, departmental grants to higher education, aid to education-related organizations and associations, and grants for projects related to mathematics education, elementary and secondary school restructuring, teacher education reform, and disadvantaged, minority education. Specific areas of interest in higher education include science and technology, chemistry, mechanical engineering, chemical engineering, industrial engineering, physics, polymer science, mathematics and statistics, business and industry, educational research, teacher education, and minority education.
Assistance Types: Employee matching gifts, general support, special projects, conferences, symposiums, lectures, and research

Eligibility

Restrictions: No grants for capital, building and renovation, land acquisition, equipment, endowments, or institutional scholarships or fellowships; no loans; no grants to individuals

Personnel

Officers: Elliot R. Cattarulla, Chair, President, and Trustee; A.W. Atkiss, VP; C.G. Korshin, Secy.; J.E. Bayne, Treas.; T.P. Notarainni, Controller; E.F. Ahnert, Exec. Director
Trustees/Directors: D.L. Guttormson, K.N. Robertson, E.A. Robinson, F.B. Sprow
Staff: Four full-time professional, two full-time support

Financial Profile

Assets: In 1992, $3,493,017; 1993, $3,998,013
High Grant: $1,200,000
Low Grant: $500
Ave. Grant: $5,000-$15,000
Total Grants: 193 grants totaling $7,711,867, plus 10,430 employee matching gifts totaling $12,134,719
High Grant Higher Ed.: $1,200,000
Low Grant Higher Ed.: $1,000
Ave. Grant Higher Ed.: $5,000-$15,000

Total Grants Higher Ed.: In 1992, approximately 135 grants totaling $5,744,673, plus $8,699,763 in employee matching gifts

Application Process

Contact: E.F. Ahnert, Exec. Director, (214) 444-1104
Publications: Annual report
Guidelines: The foundation strongly suggests that prospective applicants request guidelines for letters of inquiry before sending any information since applications for some of the foundation's programs are not encouraged.

Sample Grants

Stanford University in Stanford, California, received two $45,000 grants for an energy research program at its Center for Economic Policy Research.

University of Florida in Gainesville received $10,000 for its chemistry department's study of the synthesis of nitrogen heterocyclic compounds and $15,000 for a study on phase separation in polymer solutions.

American Association for Higher Education received $15,000 for general support.

The University of Chicago in Chicago, Illinois, received $10,000 for research on zeolite frameworks.

University of Nebraska in Lincoln received $233,000 for a project entitled Building a School Community to Support Children in Education.

Purdue University's chemical engineering department in West Lafayette, Indiana, received $7,500 for research related to catalysis on transient kinetics.

University of Washington in Seattle received $250,000 for its project, Education of Educators: Phase Two.

Princeton University's Mechanical and Aerospace Engineering Department in Princeton, New Jersey, received $10,000 for research related to infrared spectroscopy.

Baylor College of Medicine in Houston, Texas, received $49,800 for developing training for alternatively certified teachers.

University of Kentucky in Lexington received $30,000 for its K-3 Mathematics Specialist Program to improve math teaching in the early elementary grades.

Comments/Analysis

The foundation operates five education-related programs. In the past, its educational matching gifts program for colleges and universities, the United Negro College Fund, the American Indian College Fund, and the Hispanic Association of Colleges and Universities received 47 percent of all the dollars distributed by the foundation. Its organizational support program, aimed at assisting education associations and organizations address the needs of the education community, received 15 percent. Fourteen percent was given for projects falling under the foundation's elementary and secondary school improvement program; while its mathematics education program accounted for 7 percent, as did its research and training program to underwrite university-based research in science and engineering. The remainder of the foundation's funds were awarded for special projects and undergraduate general education. Over three-fourths of all the foundation's funds were given

to higher education with an emphasis on the sciences, engineering, mathematics, and the enhancement of the educational system through the restructuring of schools and the improvement of teacher education. The foundation's largest award went to the United Negro College Fund's Campaign 2000 in the form of two $1,200,000 grants. This is indicative of the foundation's strong support for minority education.

119
First Interstate Bank of California Foundation
633 W Fifth Street, T11-55
Los Angeles, CA   90071

Areas of Interest

Program Description: To support community funds, education, the performing arts, culture, hospitals, urban and civic affairs, social services, and youth. Specific areas of interest in higher education include business education and minority education.
Assistance Types: General purposes, capital campaigns, continuing support, operating budgets, annual campaigns, employee matching gifts, special projects, employee-related scholarships, scholarship funds, technical assistance, building, land acquisition, endowments, fellowships, matching funds

Eligibility

Restrictions: No grants to religious organizations for religious purposes, individuals, private foundations, or United Way-supported organizations. No equipment support for hospitals. No loans. No grants for research or conferences. Giving usually limited to California.

Personnel

Officers: Bruce Willison, Chair and Director; Ruth Jones-Saxy, Secy.-Treas.; Roger Molvar, CFO and Director
Trustees/Directors: Daniel Eitingon, Edward Garlock, David Holman, William Sudmann
Staff: Two full-time professional

Financial Profile

Assets: In 1992, $17,108,000
High Grant: $680,853
Low Grant: $500
Ave. Grant: $1,000-$25,000
Total Grants: 324 grants totaling $2,312,917, plus $222,952 in employee matching gifts

Application Process

Contact: Ruth Jones-Saxey, Secy.-Treas., (213) 614-3068 or (213) 614-3090
Deadline: July 1 for capital campaigns; none for other programs

Board Meeting: Quarterly
Processing Time: Six weeks to three months after board meeting
Publications: Informational brochure, including application guidelines
Guidelines: Prospective applicants should request application guidelines and an application. A formal application form is required. Receipt of proposals is not acknowledged and rarely are interviews granted. Applications must be accompanied by a copy of the applicant organization's IRS determination letter; a copy of the organization's current budget and the project budget; a copy of the organization's most recent annual report, audited financial statement, or 990 tax return; the organization's policy statement on nondiscrimination in employment and providing of services; and a list of contributors and potential donors.

Sample Grants

Citizens Scholarship Foundation of America in Saint Peter, Minnesota, received $37,500 for a First Interstate Scholarship Program.

Independent Colleges of Southern California in Los Angeles received $22,000 for general support.

Santa Clara University in Santa Clara, California, received $10,000 to establish the First Interstate Endowed Scholarship Fund for financially needy, underrepresented minority junior or senior year students majoring in business or liberal arts.

Stanford University Graduate School of Business in Stanford, California, received $35,000 for a First Interstate Bank of California Foundation Fellowship.

University of Southern California in Los Angeles received $50,000 for a campaign for unrestricted endowment.

Comments/Analysis

Historically, education has been the foundation's second largest subject area by dollars, and colleges and universities have been its second largest recipient type by dollars. Community improvement and development is traditionally its number one field of interest and as such, receives approximately 50 percent of all grant dollars annually distributed by the foundation. Much of this support is awarded to federated giving programs.

120
Ford Motor Company Fund
The American Road
Dearborn, MI   48121-1899

Areas of Interest

Program Description: To support arts and humanities, performing arts, museums, public television and radio, United Way, social welfare, hospitals and health, community improvement, employment, safety, public policy and research, US-international relations, social welfare, education, and youth organizations. Specific areas of interest in higher education include business, engineering and science, and state and national higher education-related associations.

Assistance Types: Employee matching gifts, employee student loans, employee-related scholarships, matching funds, research, annual campaigns, equipment, general purposes, publications, conferences, seminars, continuing support, capital

Eligibility

Restrictions: No grants to individuals or for scholarships or fellowships (except for employee-related scholarships). Giving mainly in areas of company operations with a concentration in Detroit, Michigan, and Michigan in general for higher education.

Personnel

Officers: Frank J. Darin, VP; David N. McCammon, Treas. and Trustee; Dennis A. Tosh, Asst. Treas.; John M. Rintamaki, Asst. Secy.
Trustees/Directors: Alfred B. Ford, Allan D. Gilmour, S.F. Hamp, John W. Martin Jr., Peter J. Pestillo, David W. Scott, Stanley A. Seneker, Alexander J. Trotman
Staff: Four full-time professional, one part-time professional, one full-time support, two part-time support

Financial Profile

Assets: In 1993, $8,954,670
High Grant: $665,000
Low Grant: $150
Ave. Grant: $1,000-$25,000
Total Grants: $16,804,535
High Grant Higher Ed.: $312,500
Low Grant Higher Ed.: $500
Ave. Grant Higher Ed.: $1,000-$10,000
Total Grants Higher Ed.: Approximately 213 grants totaling $3,231,450, plus $2,330,324 in matching gifts

Application Process

Contact: Leo J. Brennan Jr., Exec. Director, (313) 845-8711
Deadline: None
Board Meeting: April and October
Processing Time: Six months
Publications: Annual report, application guidelines, informational brochure
Guidelines: An application form is not required. Applicants should initially submit a proposal in brief narrative form. If the project interests the fund, further data and detailed exhibits will be requested.

Sample Grants

University of Pennsylvania in Philadelphia received four grants for its business programs: two for $5,000, one for $10,000, and one for $25,000.

Consortium of Graduate Study in Management in Saint Louis, Missouri, received $26,000 for its business program.

Michigan State University in East Lansing was awarded $312,500 for business capital.

Case Western Reserve in Cleveland, Ohio, received a grant for $5,000 and a grant for $10,000 for its engineering and science programs.

Georgia Institute of Technology in Atlanta received two $5,000 grants for engineering and science programs.

Howard University in Washington, DC, was awarded $200,000 for engineering and science programs.

University of California in Berkeley received four grants for engineering and science programs: one for $5,000, one for $8,000, one for $30,000, and one for $50,000.

University of Illinois in Urbana received six grants totaling $43,500 for engineering and science programs.

Michigan State University in East Lansing received $312,500 for an engineering and science capital grant.

Cleary College in Ypsilanti, Michigan, received $1,000 for general purposes.

Madonna University in Livonia, Michigan, received $5,000 for general purposes.

University of Nevada in Reno was awarded $20,000 for general purposes.

Alabama Association of Independent Colleges and Universities in Birmingham was awarded $500.

American Association of Community Colleges in Washington, DC, was awarded $7,500.

The United Negro College Fund in New York City received three grants totaling $145,000.

Comments/Analysis

In 1993, education received 44 percent of the dollars distributed by the fund, followed by health and welfare (22 percent), civic activities and public policy (18 percent), arts and humanities (12 percent), US-international relations (2 percent), and Directors Matching Gifts Program (2 percent). Of the $7.5 million given to education, approximately 74 percent went to higher education for business programs; business capital; engineering and science programs; engineering and science capital; general; general capital; state and national higher education-related associations; and employee matching gifts to colleges and universities, graduate and professional schools, and seminaries and theological schools.

121
GE Foundation
3135 Easton Turnpike
Fairfield, CT   06431

Areas of Interest

Program Description: To support education, community funds, arts and culture, public policy, civil rights, intercultural relations, and AIDS. Specific areas of interest in higher education include graduate-level research and teaching; the physical sciences; engineering; computer science; mathematics; industrial management; business administration; and minority education, particularly in the disciplines of engineering and business.

Assistance Types: Employee matching gifts, fellowships, research, scholarship funds, publications, special projects, seed money, general purposes, annual campaigns, continuing support

Eligibility

Restrictions: Giving on a broad national basis except for support for community funds which is limited to areas of significant company presence. No grants to individuals or religious or sectarian groups. No support for capital funds or endowments. No loans or equipment donations.

Personnel

Officers: Dennis D. Dammerman, Chair and Trustee; Clifford V. Smith, President; Michael J. Cosgrove, Treas.; Jane L. Polin, Comptroller
Trustees/Directors: James P. Baughman, Frank P. Doyle, Benjamin W. Heineman Jr., Joyce Hergenhan, Jack O. Pfeiffer, Lloyd G. Trotter
Staff: Seven full-time professional, four full-time support

Financial Profile

Assets: In 1992, $11,492,941
High Grant: $537,500
Low Grant: $250
Ave. Grant: $5,000-$100,000
Total Grants: 444 grants totaling $15,683,327, plus $7,683,327 in employee matching gifts

Application Process

Contact: Clifford V. Smith, President, (203) 373-3216
Deadline: None
Board Meeting: Quarterly
Processing Time: Varies
Publications: Annual report including application guidelines, informational brochure
Guidelines: An application form is not required. Proposals should include a brief history of the organization and a description of its mission; a detailed description of the project, the amount requested, and the project budget; an explanation of how the project results will be evaluated; qualifications of key project personnel; and a copy of the applicant organization's IRS determination letter; and current year's budget.

Sample Grants

Cornell University in Ithaca, New York, received a $159,220 and a $32,510 grant.

Financial Accounting Foundation in New York City received $50,000 for higher education program.

Purdue University in West Lafayette, Indiana, received $342,440.

National Conference on Undergraduate Research in Asheville, North Carolina, received $10,000.

Syracuse University in Syracuse, New York, received $165,000.

American Assembly of Collegiate Schools of Business in Saint Louis, Missouri, received $22,000.

American Association of Engineering Societies in New York City received $10,000 for a higher education program.

University of Iowa in Iowa City received $110,000.

Jackie Robinson Foundation in New York City received $65,000.

University of California in Irvine received $23,360.

University of Virginia in Charlottesville received $41,000.

National Consortium for Graduate Degrees for Minorities in Science and Engineering (GEM) in Notre Dame, Indiana, received $100,000.

National Action Council for Minorities in Engineering (NACME) in New York City received $275,000 for higher education program.

Society of Women Engineers in New York City received $14,000 for higher education program.

Franklin and Marshall College in Lancaster, Pennsylvania, received $25,000.

American Indian College Fund in New York City received $25,000.

Students in Free Enterprise in Bolivar, Missouri, received $50,000 for higher education program.

Comments/Analysis

In terms of higher education, the foundation is interested in programs that result in increases in the number of PhDs, particularly underrepresented minorities and women, who join faculties of engineering, physical sciences, and business. The foundation also favors projects and programs that improve the quality of engineering, science, and business curricula; provide undergraduate scholarships for minorities; and improve the retention of minority engineering students. Occasionally awards are made to universities overseas in the areas of engineering and business management.

122
General Mills Foundation
PO Box 1113
Minneapolis, MN   55440

Areas of Interest

Program Description: To support secondary, higher, and minority education, culture and art, social services, United Way, community funds, health, civic activities, the homeless, and the disadvantaged.

Assistance Types: Presidential discretionary funds, special projects, scholarships, employee-related scholarships, operating budgets, matching funds, employee matching gifts

Eligibility

Restrictions: Giving primarily in Minneapolis and other areas of major company operations. No grants for endowments, research, publications, films, conferences, seminars, advertising, athletic events, testimonial dinners, workshops, symposia, travel, fundrais-

ing events, deficit financing, religious activities, recreation, or national or local campaigns to eliminate or control specific diseases. No grants to individuals.

Personnel

Officers: H.B. Atwater Jr., Chair and Trustee; Reatha Clark King, President; D.A. Nasby, VP; C.L. Whitehill, Secy. and Trustee; D.B. Van Benschoten, Treas.; I.S. Bernardson, Asst. Secy.; C. Skaja, Asst. Treas.; J.R. Weddle, Asst. Treas.

Trustees/Directors: J.R. Lee, T.P. Nelson, S.W. Sanger, M.H. Willes

Staff: Two full-time professional, three full-time support

Financial Profile

Assets: In 1993, $59,466,476

High Grant: $1,472,086

Low Grant: $500

Ave. Grant: $5,000-$15,000

Total Grants: $17,206,533

High Grant Higher Ed.: $250,000

Low Grant Higher Ed.: $500

Ave. Grant Higher Ed.: $5,000-$25,000

Total Grants Higher Ed.: Approximately 70 grants totaling $2,195,848, plus $804,137 in matching gifts to all education

Application Process

Contact: Dr. Reatha Clark King, President, (612) 540-7891; fax: (612) 540-4925

Deadline: None, except for scholarship programs; check foundation guidelines

Board Meeting: Four times a year and as required

Processing Time: Four weeks

Publications: Corporate giving report (including application guidelines), informational brochure, annual report

Guidelines: Preliminary telephone calls and personal visits are discouraged. Application form is not required. Submit proposal with brief cover letter, including description of project and amount requested; population served; qualifications of key personnel; methods to be used to evaluate/measure project results; organizational budget and/or project budget; brief history of organization and description of its mission; list of board of directors, trustees, officers, and other key people and their affiliations; annual report, audited financial statement, and 990 tax return; IRS determination letter; and list of additional sources and amount of support.

Sample Grants

American Indian College Fund in New York City received $25,000 for operating support.

Augsburg College in Minneapolis, Minnesota, received four grants: $5,000 for an evaluation program, $80,000 for the Southeast Asian student program, $1,500 for student achievement of Native American youth, and $4,435 for the Youth and Family Institute.

College of Saint Benedict in Saint Joseph, Minnesota, received a $50,000 capital grant.

Valencia Community College Foundation in Orlando, Florida, received $25,000 for services for students with disabilities.

Reed College in Portland, Oregon, received a $25,000 presidential discretionary grant.

United Negro College Fund in Minneapolis, Minnesota, received $250,000 for a capital campaign for its member institutions, $80,000 for operating support, and $20,000 for a Martin Luther King Holiday Breakfast.

Mount Mercy College in Cedar Rapids, Iowa, received $5,000 for a Library Operations Through Automation project.

Citizens Scholarship Foundation of America in Saint Peter, Minnesota, received two scholarship stipends of $100,625 each for their Sons and Daughters Merit Scholarship Program.

Elgin Community College in Elgin, Illinois, received $2,000 for its music department.

Eisenhower Exchange Fellowships in Philadelphia, Pennsylvania, received $25,000.

Carleton College in Northfield, Minnesota, received $150,000 for its Excellence in Science Program.

Comments/Analysis

In the fiscal year ending May 1993, the foundation awarded 49 percent of its grant funds to health and social action, 26 percent to education, 21 percent to arts and culture, and 4 percent to other. Higher education received approximately 60 percent of all the education dollars distributed, plus a portion of the $804,137 awarded in education-related matching gifts. Recipients included junior and community colleges, four-year colleges and universities, graduate and professional schools, seminaries and theological schools, vocational and technical schools, and a variety of higher education-related fund-raising organizations such as the American Indian College Fund and the United Negro College Fund. Over $200,000 of the higher education money distributed was given through the foundation's Post-High School Scholarship Program, a program independently administered by the Citizens' Scholarship Foundation of America and aimed at helping the sons and daughters of employees obtain a postsecondary education.

123

General Motors Foundation, Inc.
3044 W Grand Boulevard
13-145 General Motors Building
Detroit, MI   48202-3091

Areas of Interest

Program Description: To support health and human services, United Way, education, culture and art, civic and community affairs, and public policy. Specific areas of interest in higher education include engineering, business, and minority education.

Assistance Types: Operating budgets, capital, capital campaigns, departmental grants, research, special projects, matching gifts, scholarships, fellowships

Eligibility

Restrictions: The foundation gives primarily within communities in which a significant number of General Motors employees work and live, and to national organizations that have a broad appeal and are recognized for their excellence. Generally no support for endowments, special interest groups or projects, hospitals or United Way-supported organizations. No grants to individuals or for deficit financing. No loans; no contributions of General Motors products.

Personnel

Officers: B.G. MacDonald, Chair; D.I. Dingell, President; G.D. Briggs, Treas.; W.W. Creek, Secy.; R.L. Theis, Director; E.P. Pasternak, Asst. Treas.

Trustees/Directors: W.E. Hoglund, L. Hughs, H. Pearce

Staff: One full-time professional, one full-time support

Financial Profile

Assets: In 1993, $113,458,520

Total Grants: $34,918,915

High Grant Higher Ed.: $500,000

Low Grant Higher Ed.: $1,000 (excluding matching gifts)

Ave. Grant Higher Ed.: $1,000-$50,000

Total Grants Higher Ed.: In 1992, approximately 138 grants totaling $7,268,284, plus $1,064,754 in matching gifts

Application Process

Contact: Ronald L. Theis, Director, (313) 556-4260

Deadline: None

Board Meeting: Contributions Committee meets annually

Processing Time: Two months

Publications: Informational brochure

Guidelines: Application form is not required. Requests should be made by letter and include a statement summarizing the expected use of the proposed grant, a copy of the organization's 501(c)3 IRS determination letter, historical organizational information, detailed budget information for the previous three years, a detailed budget proposal, a list of major annual contributions for the previous three years, and a brief description of the organization's activities and operations for the current year.

Sample Grants

Tennessee State University in Nashville received $20,000 for an unrestricted operating grant for minority engineering.

University of Wisconsin in Madison received $150,000 for a special projects grant.

Rose-Hulman Institute of Technology in Terre Haute, Indiana, received $40,000 for an unrestricted operating grant.

American Graduate School of International Management in Glendale, Arizona, received $10,000 for scholarships and fellowships.

Trustees of Purdue University in West Lafayette, Indiana, received $400,000 for an unrestricted operating grant for the business, engineering, and technology schools.

University of Michigan Law School in Ann Arbor received $20,000.

Grand Valley State College in Allendale, Michigan, received $20,000 for a capital campaign.

Comments/Analysis

Historically, education accounts for approximately half of all the grant dollars distributed by the foundation. Institutions of higher education receive approximately three-fourths of all the education dollars with the remainder going to precollege institutions and precollege minority education, Junior Achievement and other education-related organizations, education-related state and national fund-raising groups, and other minority education-related grants. Of the grants going to colleges and universities in the past, 27 percent was given for departmental grants to engineering, 27 percent for special projects and research, 13 percent for matching gifts, 9 percent for capital grants, 8 percent for departmental grants to business, 7 percent for unrestricted operating grants, 6 percent for departmental grants to minority engineering, 2 percent for scholarships and fellowships, and 1 percent for other.

124
Grace Foundation, Inc.
One Town Center Road
Boca Raton, FL   33486-1010

Areas of Interest

Program Description: To support education, urban and minority affairs, cultural programs, performing arts, community funds, civic affairs, minorities, handicapped, youth, social services, and health and hospitals. Specific areas of interest in higher education include business, chemistry, science and technology, environmental studies, and agricultural sciences.

Assistance Types: Employee matching gifts, employee-related scholarships, scholarship funds, fellowships, capital campaigns, annual campaigns, operating budgets, continuing support, building, equipment, matching funds

Eligibility

Restrictions: No support for individuals (except for employee-related scholarships), endowment funds, seed money, emergency funds, deficit financing, land acquisition, publications, demonstration projects, conferences, or specific research projects. Giving is primarily in areas in which W.R. Grace & Co. does business, with corporate locations in Florida, Connecticut, Iowa, Illinois, Massachusetts, Maryland, New Jersey, South Carolina, Texas, and Wisconsin.

Personnel

Officers: W. Brian McGowan, Chair; Brian J. Smit, President and Director; James P. Neeves, VP, Treas., and Director; Thomas M. Doyle, VP and Director; Robert B. Lamm, Secy. and Director

Trustees/Directors: J.P. Bolduc, James W. Frick, George P. Jenkins, Paul D. Paganucci, Eben W. Pyne, John R. Young
Staff: None

Financial Profile

Assets: In 1993, $15,092,484
High Grant: $200,000
Low Grant: $100
Ave. Grant: $1,000-$20,000
Total Grants: $2,299,810 for grants, plus $75,447 for 39 grants to individuals and $524,165 in employee matching gifts

Application Process

Contact: Susan Harris, Asst. Treas., (407) 362-1487
Deadline: None
Board Meeting: As required
Processing Time: Two to three months
Guidelines: An application form is not required. Applicants should submit a letter proposal and include a brief history of their organization and a description of its mission; a detailed description of the project and the amount requested; a list of additional sources and amount of support; a copy of their IRS determination letter; and a copy of their most recent annual report, audited financial statement, or 990 tax return.

Sample Grants

Boston College in Chestnut Hill, Massachusetts, received $125,000.

University of Rochester William E. Simon Graduate School of Business in Rochester, New York, received $125,000.

Comments/Analysis

Historically, the foundation awards approximately 25 percent of its annual grant dollars to community improvement and development; 19 percent to education; 14 percent to other; 8 percent to human services; 9 percent to medicine; 6 percent to international affairs, development, and peace; 6 percent to science; and 13 percent to employee matching gifts to US and Canadian secondary schools, community and junior colleges, and four-year colleges and universities. In terms of higher education, the foundation has historically preferred to support colleges and universities with exemplary schools and departments in their areas of interest (business, chemistry, environmental studies, agricultural studies, and science and technology), state associations of colleges and universities, national educational organizations supportive of the higher education system, and colleges and universities offering excellence in education on a continual basis.

125
GTE Foundation
One Stamford Forum
Stamford, CT   06904

Areas of Interest

Program Description: To support higher education, community funds, social services, literacy, substance abuse, and volunteerism. Specific areas of interest in higher education include minority education, science, technology, and mathematics.
Assistance Types: Scholarship funds, fellowships, student aid, employee-related scholarships, lectureships, operating budgets, special projects, program-related investments, emergency funds, employee matching gifts, continuing support

Eligibility

Restrictions: No grants for research or to individuals except for employee-related scholarships

Personnel

Officers: Maureen Gorman, VP and Secy.; Charles R. Lee, Chair and Trustee
Trustees/Directors: Bruce Carswell, Kent B. Foster, Edward C. MacEwen, Terry S. Parker, Edward Schmults, Nicholas Trivisonno, Bankers Trust Company
Staff: Five full-time professional, four full-time support, two part-time support

Financial Profile

Assets: In 1992, $25,858,569; 1993, $28,551,293
High Grant: In 1992, $2,138,192; 1993, $2,016,448
Low Grant: In 1992, $75; 1993, $1,000
Ave. Grant: $1,000-$10,000
Total Grants: In 1992, 1,869 grants totaling $16,699,582, plus $3,256,301 in employee matching gifts and $1,295,220 for in-kind gifts; 1993, 2,030 grants totaling $15,836,285, plus $3,244,487 in employee matching gifts, $1,150,088 for in-kind gifts, and $415,050 for grants to individuals

Application Process

Contact: Maureen Gorman, Foundation VP, Secy., and Director of Corporate Social Responsibility, GTE Corporation, (203) 965-3620
Deadline: Summer
Board Meeting: February, May, August, November, and as required
Processing Time: Notification after December 15
Publications: Informational brochure including application guidelines
Guidelines: Applicants should send for informational brochure and required application. The following attachments should be submitted with the application: copy of IRS determination letter; list of board of directorss, trustees, officers, and other key people; and copy of most recent annual report, audited financial statement, or 990 tax return.

Sample Grants

Woodrow Wilson National Fellowship Foundation in Princeton, New Jersey, received $25,000.
United Negro College Fund in New York City received two grants totaling $243,000 for its Black Teachers Program.
University of Massachusetts in Boston received $30,000.
Associated Colleges of Illinois in Chicago received $45,000.
National Consortium for Graduate Degrees for Minorities in Science and Engineering (GEM) in Notre Dame, Indiana, received $26,000.
University of Pennsylvania in Philadelphia received $70,000 for the Huntsman Center for Global Competition and Leadership and $20,000 for its Wharton School fellowship in business.
Eckerd College in Saint Petersburg, Florida, received $20,000.
Sacred Heart University in Fairfield, Connecticut, received $12,000 for teaching opportunities for paraprofessionals.
Henderson State University in Arkadelphia, Arkansas, received $30,000.

Comments/Analysis

Historically, education, not including employee matching gifts or employee-related scholarships, has received 22 percent of the foundation's grant dollars. Of these funds, 53 percent is given to higher education and graduate and professional schools in the form of grants of at least $10,000. Education is consistently the foundation's top subject area by dollars and also by number of grants. Giving for higher education is on a national basis with an emphasis on areas of company operations. Besides providing support for mathematics, science, technology, and the retention of minority students, the foundation also sponsors a scholarship program for children of GTE employees and an education employee matching gifts program. The foundation is also a supporter of state college funds, state college associations, and state independent colleges organizations.

126
HCA Foundation
c/o Hospital Corporation of America
PO Box 550, One Park Plaza
Nashville, TN   37202-0550

Areas of Interest

Program Description: To support health, higher education, culture, the arts, social services, civic affairs, community development, and the United Way. Specific areas of interest in higher education include nursing, physical therapy, occupational therapy, health administration, and allied health professions.

Assistance Types: General support, employee-related scholarships, special projects, capital campaigns, renovation, building, equipment, employee matching gifts

Eligibility

Restrictions: No grants for social, religious, fraternal, labor, athletic or veterans groups; schools below the college level, hospitals, private foundations, and United Way-supported agencies; endowment funds; biomedical or clinical research; dinners, tables, or tickets to fund-raising events; promotional materials; publications; trips or tours. No support for individuals except through employee-related scholarships. Giving mainly in Nashville, Tennessee, and communities with Hospital Corporation of America (HCA) facilities.

Personnel

Officers: Thomas F. Frist Jr., Chair and Director; Kenneth L. Roberts, President and Director; Peter F. Bird, Secy. and Senior Program Officer; Don Swain, Treas.
Trustees/Directors: Jack O. Bovender Jr., Robert C. Crosby, Helen K. Cummings, Frank F. Drowota III, Charles J. Kane, R. Clayton McWhorter
Staff: Three full-time professional, one full-time support, two part-time support

Financial Profile

Assets: In 1992, $57,818,155; 1993, $81,363,884
High Grant: In 1992, $150,000; 1993, $196,055
Low Grant: $750
Ave. Grant: $1,000-$20,000
Total Grants: 121 grants totaling $2,476,741, plus $141,236 in employee matching gifts

Application Process

Contact: Kenneth L. Roberts, President, (615) 320-2165; fax: (615) 320-2017
Deadline: None
Board Meeting: January, April, July, and October
Processing Time: Approximately one month
Publications: Annual report including application guidelines
Guidelines: Initial approach should be made by telephone or letter. Informational brochures on the foundation's major programs are available upon request. An application form is not required. However, application must be made through HCA-affiliated hospitals, and not the foundation directly.

Sample Grants

Association of University Programs in Health Administration in Arlington, Virginia, received $10,000 for general support.
Citizens Scholarship Foundation of America in Saint Peter, Minnesota, received $196,055 for scholarship program for children of employees of HCA and its affiliates.

John Tyler College Foundation in Chester, Virginia, received $10,000 for equipment for programs in nursing and physical therapy.
Kansas Newman College in Wichita, Kansas, received $10,000 for the development of a baccalaureate degree program in occupational therapy.
University of Kentucky in Lexington received $10,000 for a capital campaign for a building to house the College of Allied Health Professions.
United Negro College Fund in New York City received $15,000 for general support.

Comments/Analysis

The foundation awards grants in the following areas: HCA Awards of Achievement, employee matching gifts, HCA Fund for Collaboration, HCA recyling program, HCA teachers award, HCA Volunteer Involvement Program (VIP), Volunteer Service Awards, the Center for Nonprofit Management, Nashville Donors Forum, employee-related scholarships, the United Way, the Young Leaders Council, and other. Interested parties should contact the foundation for more information on these programs. Historically, community improvement and development receive the greatest amount of grant dollars distributed by the foundation, followed by education, arts and culture, other, employee matching gifts, and medicine. The majority of education funds are awarded for graduate and professional studies and scholarships and student services.

127
H. J. Heinz Company Foundation
PO Box 57
Pittsburgh, PA   15230

Areas of Interest

Program Description: To support community funds, higher education, hospitals, youth and social services, culture, medical and nutritional research, prevention of cruelty to animals and children, child welfare, and agriculture. Other areas of interest include religion, science, recreation, conservation, fine arts, and aid to indigent and handicapped persons.
Assistance Types: Employee matching gifts, general operating funds, capital funds, research, scholarships and fellowships

Eligibility

Restrictions: No grants to individuals; no loans; no support for deficit financing or land acquisition; giving mainly in areas of company operations.

Personnel

Officers: A.J.F. O'Reilly, Chair and Trustee; S. D. Wiley, Vice-Chair and Trustee
Trustees/Directors: D.R. Williams, K.A. Davis
Staff: One full-time professional, one full-time support

Financial Profile

Assets: In 1993, $3,213,400
Ave. Grant: $100-$1,000
Total Grants: $6,159,311
High Grant Higher Ed.: $165,000
Low Grant Higher Ed.: $50
Ave. Grant Higher Ed.: $100-$1,000
Total Grants Higher Ed.: Approximately 460 grants totaling $1.4 million

Application Process

Contact: Loretta M. Oken, Manager, (412) 456-5772
Deadline: None
Board Meeting: As required
Processing Time: Varies
Publications: Application guidelines
Guidelines: Interviews are sometimes granted at applicant's request. Application form is not required. Submit letter proposal including statement of problem to be addressed; population to be served; annual report, audited financial statement, and 990 tax return; budget; IRS determination letter; summary of additional sources and amount of support; and how the results will be evaluated or measured.

Sample Grants

Duquesne University in Pittsburgh, Pennsylvania, received $110,00 for scholarships and fellowships.

Community College of Allegheny County in Pittsburgh, Pennsylvania, received $10,000 for capital funding.

University of California in Oakland was awarded $25,000 for research.

College of Idaho in Caldwell was awarded $25,000 for scholarships and fellowships.

Westminster College in New Wilmington, Pennsylvania, received $100,000 for capital funding.

Tufts University School of Nutrition in Medford, Massachusetts, received $10,000 for research.

National Merit Scholarship Corporation in Evanston, Illinois, received $34,400 for scholarships for relatives of employees.

Hartburg Theological Seminary in Dubuque, Iowa, received $2,200 for general operating expenses.

Carnegie Mellon University in Pittsburgh, Pennsylvania, received $165,000 for general operating expenses.

Comments/Analysis

The majority of the foundation's support for higher education is in the form of matching gifts to junior and four-year colleges, graduate schools, seminaries, and technical schools. A limited number of larger grants are awarded to institutions of higher education for general operating expenses, capital funds, research, scholarship and fellowships, and scholarships for relatives of employees.

128
Hitachi Foundation
1509 22nd Street NW
Washington, DC   20037

Areas of Interest

Program Description: To support projects that help the underserved address the multicultural, community, and global issues facing them by building their problem-solving capacities and promoting a sense of empowerment and responsibility. Specific areas of interest include minority, elementary, and secondary education; community and economic development; global citizenship; US-Japan relations; civic affairs; leadership development; and culture.
Assistance Types: Program-related investments, seed money, special projects, technical assistance, continuing support, matching funds

Eligibility

Restrictions: Unsolicited proposals are accepted in the areas of community development and education only. Unsolicited proposals are not accepted in the area of global citizenship. No support for sectarian or religious organizations, health programs, or social organizations. No grants for fund-raising events, building funds, publications, conferences and seminars, endowments, advertising, capital campaigns, or research. Grants to individuals made only for Yoshiyama Awards for Exemplary Service to the Community, a foundation program that recognizes high school seniors who have distinguished themselves through extensive community service and leadership.

Personnel

Officers: Elliot Lee Richardson, Chair, Board of Directors; Delwin A. Roy, President and Director; Masayuki Yamada, Treas.; Soji Teramura, Secy.
Trustees/Directors: Katsushige Mita, Clara R. Apodaca, Patricia Albjerg Graham, Joseph P. Kasputys, Percy A. Pierre
Staff: Six full-time professionals, one part-time professionals, two full-time support

Financial Profile

Assets: For year ending March 1994, $26,624,349
High Grant: $175,900
Low Grant: $1,000
Ave. Grant: $1,000-$10,000
Total Grants: $2,347,364
High Grant Higher Ed.: $74,250
Low Grant Higher Ed.: $1,000
Total Grants Higher Ed.: Approximately four grants totaling $81,250

Application Process

Contact: Joseph P. Getch III, Operations Manager, (202) 457-0588
Deadline: Preliminary proposals must be postmarked by February 1 or October 1 to be considered for funding during the cycle.
Board Meeting: March, July, and October to review proposals
Processing Time: Within six weeks of submission of preliminary proposal
Publications: Annual report including application guidelines, grant application cover sheet, program policy statement, newsletter
Guidelines: A preliminary proposal, no longer than five pages, should be submitted. If a proposed project is of interest to the foundation, the applicant will be invited to submit a full proposal and foundation staff will confer with the applicant concerning issues to be addressed in the full proposal. Preliminary proposals should include a completed grant application cover sheet; statement of project need, specific purpose, and description of who the project will serve; summary of proposed project activities and anticipated outcomes; how the project seeks to improve on present practice and/or contribute to the knowledge base in the field; why the project is important to the community; description of applicant organization, its mission, objectives, activities, and scope; copy of IRS determination letter. No faxed preliminary proposals will be reviewed, and supplementary materials may not be submitted with preliminary proposals.

Sample Grants

University of Florida in Gainesville received $74,250.
Council for Aid to Education in New York City was awarded $1,000.

Comments/Analysis

The majority of the foundation's education dollars are distributed to precollegiate education, with support at the postsecondary level directed mainly toward helping institutions build collaborative and cooperative programs with communities and/or K-12 schools.

129
Honeywell Foundation
Honeywell Plaza
PO Box 524
Minneapolis, MN   55440-0524

Areas of Interest

Program Description: To support early childhood, elementary, secondary, and higher education; human services; United Way; community development; and art and civic activities. Specific areas of interest in higher education include engineering, minority engineering, business, business partnerships, and computer science.

Assistance Types: General support, special projects, scholarships, financial aid, capital, matching gifts, continuing support, seed money

Eligibility

Restrictions: No loans; no grants to political organizations, religious, organizations or individuals; no support for conferences, travel, general endowment funds, deficit financing, fund raising, research, demonstration projects, or public relations-related activities. Giving is limited to cities and states where company has major facilities with an emphasis on Minneapolis, Minnesota, and Arizona, Florida, Illinois, and New Mexico.

Personnel

Officers: R.K. Speed, President and Director; V.E. Bowen, VP and Director; M.P. Hoven, VP and Director; J.J. Brieson, Treas.; S. Ueland Jr., Secy.; I.A. Carlson, Asst. Secy. and Director
Trustees/Directors: K. Bachman, M. Bonsignore, M.L. Jackson, C.O. Larson, D.W. Devonshire, D.L. Moore, S.W. Emery, L.W. Knoblauch
Staff: Three full-time professional, two full-time support, five part-time support

Financial Profile

Assets: In 1993, $8,526,680
High Grant: $375,000
Low Grant: $150
Ave. Grant: $1,500-$35,000
Total Grants: 975 grants totaling $8,027,833, plus $255,168 for employee matching gifts and $130,828 for in-kind gifts
High Grant Higher Ed.: $175,000
Low Grant Higher Ed.: $1,000 (excluding matching gifts)
Ave. Grant Higher Ed.: $1,000-$10,000

Application Process

Contact: Laurisa Sellers, Director, (612) 951-2368
Deadline: None
Board Meeting: February and September; board committee meets quarterly
Processing Time: Two to three months
Publications: Corporate giving report, application guidelines, grants list, newsletter
Guidelines: An application form is not required. All grant requests should be written and sent to the nearest Honeywell facility. Proposals should include the following: brief history of organization, purpose, and governing board; statement of need for service; plan of operation; method of self-assessment; budget, including revenue sources, expenses, definition of use for funds requested and sources of financial support, committed and pending; copy of IRS tax-exempt ruling; and copy of organization's most recent 990 income tax return.

Sample Grants

Albuquerque Technical Vocational Institute in Albuquerque, New Mexico, received $1,000 for general support.

Arizona State University in Tempe received eight grants totaling $191,000 including $60,000 grant for an Engineering Excellence Program and $20,000 for undergraduate scholarships.

Boston College Center for Corporate Relations in Chestnut Hill, Massachusetts, received $10,000 for general support.

Drexel University in Philadelphia, Pennsylvania, received $5,500 for financial aid for women and minority engineering students.

Florida A&M University in Tallahassee received two $10,000 grants for its Life Gets Better Program.

Highland Community College in Freeport, Illinois, received two grants totaling $6,840 for scholarships.

Illinois Institute of Technology in Chicago received $2,000 for its minority engineering scholarship program and $2,500 in support of the department of computer science.

University of Minnesota Foundation in Minneapolis received $175,000 for its Commitment to Focus program.

Comments/Analysis

Historically, the foundation has awarded approximately 52 percent its grant dollars to education. Human services receive 18 percent, as do United Way campaigns. Art and civic activities receive 8 percent of the total amount distributed, while employee matching gifts to colleges and universities and public radio and television receive 4 percent. Higher education receives approximately one-fourth of the total dollars distributed to education. Of that money, the majority goes toward engineering scholarships, minority engineering programs, special projects, schools of business, and computer science.

130
Intel Foundation
3200 NE Elam Young Parkway, HF 3-50
Hillsboro, OR   97124-6497

Areas of Interest

Program Description: To support elementary, secondary, and higher education and computer science, engineering, graduate education, mathematics, science, science and technology, minority education, women in engineering, electronics technologies, and basic literacy.

Assistance Types: Conferences, educational television, employee matching gifts, equipment, fellowships, program support, scholarships, special projects, teleconferences

Eligibility

Restrictions: Grants only to tax-exempt, nonprofit organizations. The foundation does not entertain funding requests for direct grants, scholarships, or loans to individuals; endowment or capital improvement campaigns; general fund drives, annual appeals, or fund-raising events; or projects seeking to influence elections or

legislation. Proposals are not accepted from private foundations described under IRS Code Section 509(s); religious, sectarian, fraternal, or political organizations; or organizations that practice or promote discrimination or illegal acts. Proposals from organizations that are supported by United Way campaigns to which the foundation has already made a contribution are not normally favored. Giving primarily in corporation's major operating areas, including Santa Clara and Folsom, California; Phoenix, Arizona; Albuquerque, New Mexico; and Portland, Oregon.

Personnel

Officers: Margie Diaz Kintz, Exec. Director; Thomas R. Lavelle, Secy. and Director; Robert W. Reed, President and Director; Arvind Sodhani, Treas.
Trustees/Directors: Gordon E. Moore
Staff: One full-time professional, one full-time support

Financial Profile

Assets: In 1993, $7,487,911
High Grant: $325,000
Low Grant: $1,000
Ave. Grant: $1,000-$25,000
Total Grants: $2,614,304
High Grant Higher Ed.: $27,500
Low Grant Higher Ed.: $1,000
Ave. Grant Higher Ed.: $1,000-$10,000
Total Grants Higher Ed.: $1,022,045 in grants, plus $164,549 in matching gifts

Application Process

Contact: Margie Diaz Kintz, Exec. Director, (503) 696-2390
Deadline: None; proposals are accepted throughout the year
Board Meeting: Semiannually
Processing Time: Evaluation may take up to three months
Guidelines: Submit a one- to two-page description of the project for initial review. If interested, the foundation will encourage the submission of a formal application including a completed grant application cover sheet; brief description of applicant or organization, its history and purposes, and why it is appropriate to carry out the project it proposes; brief description of project, its significance, the need, and the relationship of the project to other activities in the field; project time-line, milestones, and how the project meets the foundation's priorities; qualifications of key staff; detailed budget and information on other sources of support; copy of the organization's most recent 990 IRS tax return; copy of tax-exemption; list of names and affiliations of the organization and its board of directors; and statement from the board supporting the project. Prospective applicants must send for the Intel Grant Application Cover Sheet.

Sample Grants

Stanford University in Stanford, California, received two grants for $27,500 each for its National Institute for Native Leadership in Higher Education.

Arizona State University Department of Industrial Engineering in Tempe, Arizona, received $5,000 for a research project on total quality learning.

Sacramento City College in Sacramento, California, received $3,000 for a conference entitled Expanding Your Horizons.

University of New Mexico Foundation in Albuquerque received $2,000 for a science and engineering fair.

Whitman College in Walla Walla, Washington, was awarded $5,000 for its I Have a Dream Partnership.

Carnegie Mellon University in Pittsburgh, Pennsylvania, received $5,000 for an undergraduate research initiative.

Purdue University Minority Engineering Program in Lafayette, Indiana, was awarded $2,500 for women's scholarships.

Massachusetts Institute of Technology in Cambridge received $1,000 for Corporate Development.

California State University in Sacramento received $1,000 for minority engineering program scholarships.

Johns Hopkins University in Baltimore, Maryland, received $10,000 for teleconference support.

Comments/Analysis

The Intel Foundation funds grants that fall in one or more of the following four subject areas: technology awareness, opportunities for women and targeted minorities, improving the quality of life in Intel communities, and science and engineering education. Projects that address more than one of these areas have a better chance of funding. The foundation funds national and local programs and supports approximately one-third of the grant requests it receives. In 1993 contributions and gifts were made in three categories: Noyce Fellowship payments, foundation grant payments, and higher education matching gifts. Of the $2,224,755 made in foundation grant payments approximately 46 percent was given in the area of higher education. This included $345,280 in science education graduate fellowship payments made to colleges and universities throughout the United States to departments of engineering, schools of computer science, microsystems and research centers, corporate development, and minority and women engineering students. The foundation grant awards also included 38 minority scholar awards for a total of $158,765. These awards were distributed primarily to women and minorities in engineering. Other higher education scholarships focusing on women in engineering were also awarded within the foundation grants category. Scholarships and fellowships were awarded to preselected colleges and universities and application was made to the schools rather than the foundation. The remaining higher education grants were given for special projects, summer programs and institutes, university foundations, conferences and fairs, minority engineering programs, undergraduate research initiatives, and teleconferences. The Intel Corporation operates an active equipment giving program for colleges and universities. Contributions are made primarily to computer science and engineering departments in the form of equipment grants, surplus equipment donations, and technical literature. For more information on the equipment program contact Intel Corporation's Academic Relations Department at (503) 696-5307.

131
Johnson & Johnson Family of Companies Contribution Fund
One Johnson & Johnson Plaza
New Brunswick, NJ   08933

Areas of Interest

Program Description: To support health and health care programs, higher education, family services, employment and training, public broadcasting, performing and visual arts, business management education for nurses and Head Start directors, substance and alcohol abuse prevention, federated drives, science and technology in medicine, and medical research. Specific areas of interest in higher education include business education, medical education, minority medical education, health sciences, and health policy and management.

Assistance Types: Fellowships, scholarships, research, special projects, general purpose, employee matching gifts, operating budgets, continuing support, annual campaigns, emergency funds, matching funds, seed money, conferences, seminars, technical assistance

Eligibility

Restrictions: No support for deficit financing, capital campaigns, endowments, or publications. No grants to individuals. No loans. The majority of gifts are awarded to established programs and unsolicited support is limited.

Personnel

Officers: Robert S. Fine, President and Trustee; F.A. Bolden, VP, Secy., and Trustee; Curtis G. Weeden, VP and Trustee; Andrew J. Markey, VP and Trustee
Staff: None

Financial Profile

Assets: In 1992, $2,258,305; 1993, $1,416,455
High Grant: In 1992, $1,320,000; 1993, $50,000
Low Grant: In 1992, $500; 1993, $30,000
Ave. Grant: $30,000-$50,000
Total Grants: In 1992, 320 grants totaling $10,513,607, plus $4,210,650 for employee matching gifts; 1993, two grants totaling $80,000, plus $3,613,044 in employee matching gifts

Application Process

Contact: Helen M. Hughes, Manager, Corporate Contributions, (908) 524-3255
Deadline: None
Board Meeting: March, June, September, and December
Processing Time: Two months
Publications: Application guidelines, program policy statement, corporate giving report, informational brochure
Guidelines: Initial approach should be by letter. An application form is not required. Video and cassette tapes are not accepted.

Sample Grants

Rutgers University Foundation in New Brunswick received $120,000 for predoctoral fellowships, $85,000 for its Discovery Research Fund, and $50,000 for a Discretionary Fund.

University of Medicine and Dentistry of New Jersey in Newark received three grants totaling $400,000.

University of Pennsylvania Wharton School of Business in Philadelphia, Pennsylvania, received $495,229.

Foundation for Independent Higher Education in Stamford, Connecticut, received $15,000.

George Washington University in Washington, DC, received $15,000 for a grant shared with the National Health Policy Forum.

Harvard University in Cambridge, Massachusetts, received a $10,000 grant for its medical school and a $50,000 grant for the School of Public Health, Department of Health Policy and Management.

Medical Education for South African Blacks in Washington, DC, received $40,000.

National Hispanic Scholarship Fund in Novato, California, received $15,000.

Fairleigh Dickinson University, College of Business Administration, in Teaneck, New Jersey, received $15,000.

University of California at Los Angeles Management Education Associates received $349,920 for its Entrepreneurial Study Center.

Comments/Analysis

As with all of the foundation's giving, support for higher education has been primarily concentrated in areas where the company has facilities, particularly New Jersey. Support for higher education has been project- or program-oriented and usually for the medical or health sciences fields. In the past education, excluding employee matching gifts, received 26 percent of the foundation's grant dollars with the majority of the education funds going to colleges and universities and graduate and professional schools. A few grants to institutions of higher education were also awarded under the foundation's health category for health research. In 1993, the majority of the foundation's support was awarded through employee matching gifts.

132
Johnson's Wax Fund, Inc.
1525 Howe Street
Racine, WI   53402

Areas of Interest

Program Description: To support scholarships and fellowships for children of company employees; welfare, cultural, and civic organizations; environmental protection; health; education; and human service programs. Specific areas of interest include chemistry, biology, marketing, and business scholarships and fellowships; and minority education.

Assistance Types: Seed money, building funds, equipment, scholarship funds, exchange programs, fellowships, research, employee matching gifts, employee-related scholarships, capital campaigns

Eligibility

Restrictions: No loans; no grants to individuals; national health organizations; religious or social groups; veterans, labor, or fraternal organizations; no support for organizations receiving United Way funds; no grants for operating budgets, emergency funds, deficit financing, demonstration projects, or conferences. Giving primarily in Wisconsin and the midwest in areas of company operations.

Personnel

Officers: William D. George Jr., Vice-Chair and Trustee; Reva A. Holmes, VP and Secy.; Samuel C. Johnson, Chair, President, and Trustee; Julie A. Rango, Asst. Secy.; John M. Schroeder, Treas.
Trustees/Directors: Darrell Campbell, Maria L. Campbell, James F. DiMarco, Roger H. Grothaus, Sue A. Holland
Staff: One full-time professional, one part-time professional, one part-time support

Financial Profile

Assets: In 1993, $3,116,818
High Grant: $584,873
Low Grant: $25
Ave. Grant: $500-$100,000
Total Grants: $2,471,549
High Grant Higher Ed.: $30,000
Low Grant Higher Ed.: $25,000
Total Grants Higher Ed.: $884,630

Application Process

Contact: Reva A. Holmes, VP and Secy., (414) 631-2267
Deadline: November 1, March 1, and July 1
Board Meeting: February, June, and October
Processing Time: Three to four months; applicants are usually notified whether their application has been approved or rejected
Guidelines: No formal procedure; applicants should submit a brief description of and purpose behind request.

Sample Grants

Carroll College in Waukesha, Wisconsin, received $10,000 for a non-scholarship grant.

Milwaukee School of Engineering in Wisconsin received $30,000 for a non-scholarship grant.

Dillard University in New Orleans, Louisiana, received $4,500 under the foundation's Historically Black Scholarship Program.

Western Michigan University in Kalamazoo received $6,500 for food industry scholarships.

Citizens Scholarship Foundation of America in Saint Peter, Minnesota, was awarded $404,020 for the foundation's Sons and Daughters Scholarship Program.

Comments/Analysis

Most of the foundation's funds are used for grants to educational institutions, matching gifts of employees, employee scholarships, and contributions to United Way funds serving communities in which S.C. Johnson and Son, Inc. employees live and work. Grants for other purposes are limited. In 1993, non-scholarship grants to colleges, universities, high schools, and education-related fundraising organizations accounted for approximately 10 percent of the total aid distributed by the foundation. Scholarships and fellowships received 25 percent with more than three-fourths of these dollars going toward the foundation's Sons and Daughters Scholarship Program. The majority of these scholarships and fellowships were awarded in the foundation's areas of interest including chemistry, biology, marketing, and business. The foundation also distributed two scholarships to universities for food industry and 10 scholarships through its Historically Black College Scholarship program. Matching gifts and grants accounted for 33 percent of the funds distributed by the foundation with United Way receiving 26 percent, postsecondary educational institutions 5 percent, and secondary schools 2 percent. Grant distributions for other purposes included 13 percent for environmental protection, 9 percent for social and community programs, 5 percent for culture, 3 percent for medicine and health, and 2 percent for new programs.

133
KPMG Peat Marwick Foundation
Three Chestnut Ridge Road
Montvale, NJ   07645

Areas of Interest

Program Description: To support education related to accounting, auditing, taxation, management, and middle marketing services. Areas of interest also include economics, business education, educational research, and minority education.
Assistance Types: Employee matching gifts, scholarship funds, special projects, lectureships, research, professorships, conferences and seminars, endowment funds, fellowships, publications, annual campaigns, matching funds, general purposes

Eligibility

Restrictions: No grants to individuals except through the foundation's competitive programs. No support for intercollegiate athletics.

Personnel

Officers: R.C. Barry Jr., Chair and Trustee; B.J. Milano, Secy.
Trustees/Directors: W.F. Blaufuss Jr., Anthony P.Dolanski, M.L. Dupont, T.E. Hanson, A.M. Richter, A.L. Stone

Staff: Two full-time support

Financial Profile

Assets: In 1993, $732,819
High Grant: $199,318
Low Grant: $250
Ave. Grant: $500-$40,000
Total Grants: 258 grants totaling $1,672,806, plus $3,259,065 for employee matching gifts and $429,838 for grants to individuals

Application Process

Contact: Elizabeth Burak, Foundation Administrator, (201) 307-7151
Deadline: Research Opportunities in Auditing Program (ROA), October 31; Tax Research Opportunities (TRO), October 31; doctoral scholarship and research fellowship, March 15
Board Meeting: January and September
Processing Time: Notification immediately after board meeting
Publications: Annual report, informational brochure including application guidelines
Guidelines: Prospective applicants should contact the operating office first and then submit a proposal. A formal application form is not required.

Sample Grants

American Assembly of Collegiate Schools of Business in Saint Louis, Missouri, received $19,000.
Bryant College of Business Administration in Smithfield, Rhode Island, received $10,000.
National Association of Black Accountants in Washington, DC, received $16,668.
Duke University in Durham, North Carolina, received $52,000.
Arizona State University in Tempe received $29,833.
Beta Alpha Psi in Sarasota, Florida, received $76,000.
Ohio State University in Columbus, Ohio, received $20,833.
United Negro College Fund in New York City received $10,000.
San Diego State University in San Diego, California, received $19,833.
University of Kansas in Lawrence received $56,000.

Comments/Analysis

KPMG Peat Marwick is an accounting, tax, and management consulting firm, and its company-sponsored foundation conducts programs to strengthen it professions' educational and research resources and awards grants in the company's main areas of practice. Besides supporting educational organizations related to its interests, awarding special grants aimed at creating new educational opportunities, and sponsoring an employee matching gifts program, the foundation operates six specific programs. They include an auditing practice and research seminars program designed to advance auditing education and research at select college and universities; a doctoral scholarship program that encourages individuals with at least two years of business or public accounting experience to return to doctoral programs that will prepare them to teach accounting; a faculty attendance program providing academics with the opportunity to keep abreast of current professional practice while exchanging ideas at seminars with others in the field; KPMG Peat Marwick Professorships, which support faculty leadership in research and training; a research fellowship program to assist outstanding members of accounting faculties to attain promotion, tenure, and national recognition; and a Research Opportunities in Auditing Program (ROA) and a Tax Research Opportunities Program (TRO), both of which provide funds, administrative support, aid in gaining access to empirical data and specialized knowledge skills, and help in developing research findings and publishing completed manuscripts through the distribution of grants of not more than $40,000.

134
Eli Lilly and Company Foundation
Lilly Corporate Center
Indianapolis, IN   46285

Areas of Interest

Program Description: To support health and welfare, education, culture, civics, and community improvement and development. Specific areas of interest in higher education include pharmacy, medical education, and minority (Hispanic) education.
Assistance Types: Operating expenses, capital campaigns, employee matching gifts, scholarship and fellowship funds, general purposes, building, land acquisition, matching funds, continuing support, equipment, annual campaigns

Eligibility

Restrictions: No grants for endowments, special projects, research, publications, or conferences; no loans or grants to individuals; giving mainly in Indianapolis, Indiana, and other areas of company operations.

Personnel

Officers: Mitchell E. Daniels, President; Michael S. Hunt, VP and Treas.; Carol A. Edgar, Secy.
Trustees/Directors: V.D. Bryson, J.M. Cornelius, E.B. Herr, M. Perelman, S.A. Stitle, S.A. Taurel
Staff: One full-time professional, three full-time support

Financial Profile

Assets: In 1993, $17,777,332
High Grant: $2,695,554
Low Grant: $500
Ave. Grant: $500-$150,000
Total Grants: $5,305,483 in grants, plus $5,170,949 in employee matching gifts
High Grant Higher Ed.: $100,000
Low Grant Higher Ed.: $200,000
Ave. Grant Higher Ed.: $2,500-$10,000

Total Grants Higher Ed.: In 1992, approximately 19 grants totaling $345,150, plus $3,480,766 in matching gifts

Application Process

Contact: Carol Edgar, Secy., (317) 276-5342
Deadline: None
Board Meeting: Quarterly
Processing Time: Three weeks to three months
Publications: Corporate giving report, application, guidelines
Guidelines: Application form is not required. Proposals should include a 501(c)3 letter, annual report, explanation of amount and purpose of request, and purpose of organization.

Sample Grants

Associated Colleges of Indiana in Indianapolis received $10,000 for capital programs.
Hispanic Association of Colleges and Universities in San Antonio, Texas, was awarded $2,500 for operating expenses.
Johns Hopkins University in Baltimore, Maryland, received $100,000 for community programs.
Purdue University and Purdue Foundation in West Lafayette, Indiana, received two grants for community programs: one for $44,650 and one for $4,500.
Rose-Hulman Institute of Technology in Terre Haute, Indiana, received $15,000 for capital programs.
Saint Louis College of Pharmacy in Saint Louis, Missouri, was awarded $5,000 for operating expenses.
Medical College of Wisconsin in Milwaukee received $10,000 for community programs.
National Medical Fellowships in New York City was awarded $36,000 for community programs.
University of Notre Dame in Notre Dame, Indiana, received $25,000 for capital programs.

Comments/Analysis

Historically, support for higher education has accounted for approximately one-third of the funds distributed by the foundation. Grant recipients include colleges and universities, higher education-related associations and organizations, and scholarship and fellowship funds. Awards are given for operating expenses, capital programs, community programs, and employee matching gifts. Higher education employee matching gifts, ranging $25-$15,000, are given to junior and community colleges, four-year colleges and universities, graduate and professional schools, seminaries and theological schools, and technical and specialized schools. Grants to higher education are concentrated primarily in Indiana.

135
Lockheed Leadership Fund
4500 Park Granada Boulevard
Calabasas, CA   91399-0214

Areas of Interest

Program Description: Primarily to support higher education with an emphasis on engineering, science, the aerospace industry, and minority education for Hispanics.
Assistance Types: Program support, program development, employee-related scholarships, scholarship funds, annual campaigns, capital campaigns, endowment funds, professorships

Eligibility

Restrictions: No support for special projects, individuals, or matching gifts. No loans. Giving primarily in areas of company facilities.

Personnel

Officers: Robert B. Corlett, President and Director; Vance Holley, VP; W.T. Vinson, Secy.; A.G. Van Schaick, Treas. and Director
Trustees/Directors: K.W. Cannestra, R.P. Caren, H.I. Fluornoy, D.C. Jones, C.R. Scanlan, J.G. Twomey
Staff: One part-time professional, one part-time support

Financial Profile

Assets: In 1993, $31,092
High Grant: $114,700
Low Grant: $250
Ave. Grant: $1,000-$100,000
Total Grants: 198 grants totaling $1,552,304

Application Process

Contact: Vance Holley, VP, (818) 876-2426
Deadline: September-October
Board Meeting: March, and as required
Publications: Program policy statement
Guidelines: An application form is not required. Initial approach should be made by telephone or letter. Selection of recipients are made by the organizations to which the fund donates.

Sample Grants

California Polytechnic State University in San Luis Obispo, California, received a $35,000 grant for excellence awards, a $17,000 grant, and a $14,000 grant.
Massachusetts Institute in Cambridge received $50,000 for excellence awards.
National Merit Scholarship Corporation in Evanston, Illinois, received $119,500.
Prairie View A&M University in Prairie View, Texas, received $60,000 for excellence awards.
San Jose State University in San Jose, California, received $30,500.

University of Houston in Houston, Texas, received $11,000.
University of Utah in Salt Lake City received $10,000.
United Negro College Fund in New York City received $17,500.
Stanford University in Stanford, California, received a $100,000 grant for excellence awards and a $16,000 grant.

Comments/Analysis

The Lockheed Leadership Fund is primarily interested in supporting higher education. It provides scholarships to children of employees as well as achievement scholarships and GI Forum scholarships for Hispanics. Grant support to higher education is aimed at training future engineers and scientists for the aerospace industry. Its primary recipients of grants of $10,000 or more are colleges and universities, educational support agencies, graduate schools, technical assistance centers, science organizations, and civil rights groups. The vast majority of its grants funds are awarded for program support and program development.

136
Merrill Lynch & Company Foundation, Inc.
South Tower, 6th Floor
World Financial Center
New York, NY   10080-0614

Areas of Interest

Program Description: To support education, higher education, arts and culture, health, civic affairs, social services, and AIDS. Specific areas of interest in higher education include business and management.
Assistance Types: General purposes, operating budgets, special projects, research, capital campaigns, continuing support, endowment funds, publications, renovation, scholarship funds

Eligibility

Restrictions: No loans. No grants for religious purposes, deficit financing, matching gifts, or conferences. No support for individuals or social, fraternal, or athletic organizations.

Personnel

Officers: John A. Fitzgerald, President and Trustee; Paul W. Critchlow, VP and Trustee; William A. Schreyer, VP and Trustee; Daniel P. Tully, VP and Trustee; Westina L. Matthews, Secy.; Thomas J. Lombardi, Treas.
Trustees/Directors: Mathew W. McKenna
Staff: Three full-time professional, one part-time professional, three full-time support, two part-time support

Financial Profile

Assets: In 1992, $29,670,819; 1993, $33,478,762
High Grant: $200,000
Low Grant: In 1992, $1,000; 1993, $500

Ave. Grant: $5,000-$50,000
Total Grants: In 1992, 368 grants totaling $4,563,000, plus $1,906,590 in employee matching gifts; 1993, 463 grants totaling $5,315,250, plus $2,018,465 in employee matching gifts

Application Process

Contact: Westina L. Matthews, Secy., (212) 236-4319
Deadline: None
Board Meeting: March, June, September, and December
Processing Time: Three months
Publications: Corporate giving report, 990-PF, application guidelines
Guidelines: A formal application form is not required. Initial approach should be made by letter or proposal. Proposal should include a brief history of the organization and a description of its mission; a detailed description of the project and the amount requested; a timetable for implementation and evaluation of the project; how the project results will be evaluated; a copy of the applicant organization's IRS determination letter; a list of board of directors, trustees, officers, and other key people; and a copy of the organization's most recent annual report, audited financial statement, or 990 tax return.

Sample Grants

University of Pennsylvania in Philadelphia received $10,000 for its Graduate School of Education and $100,000 for MBA fellowships for the Wharton School of Business.
Boston College in Chestnut Hill, Massachusetts, received $25,000 for Fulton Hall renovation.
Citizens Scholarship Foundation of America in Saint Peter, Minnesota, received $70,000.
Florida Southern College in Lakeland, Florida, received $10,000 for computer upgrade.
Guilford College in Greensboro, North Carolina, received $15,000 for general operating purposes.
New York University Stern School of Business in New York City received $50,000 for its Management Education Center.
Woodrow Wilson National Fellowship Foundation in Princeton, New Jersey, received $15,000 for a visiting fellows program.
Pennsylvania State University in University Park, Pennsylvania, received $100,000 for a William A. Schreyer Endowed Chair.
United Negro College Fund in New York City received $40,000 for general operating purposes.

Comments/Analysis

Historically, education receives approximately 30 percent of the foundation's grant dollars with the majority of the education funds going to colleges and universities for grants of $10,000 or more. The foundation also sponsors an employee matching gifts program for all levels of educational institutions with appropriate accreditation and provides scholarships for children of employees through the Citizens Scholarship Foundation of America.

137
Martin Marietta Corporation Foundation
6801 Rockledge Drive
Bethesda, MD   20817

Areas of Interest

Program Description: To support higher education, health, civic affairs, and culture. Specific areas of interest in higher education include engineering and science and technology.
Assistance Types: Employee-related scholarships, employee matching gifts, general purposes

Eligibility

Restrictions: No grants to individuals, except for employee-related scholarships; political groups; religious organizations; or United Way recipients. Giving mainly in areas of company operations.

Personnel

Trustees/Directors: Wayne A. Shaner, Peter F. Warren Jr., A. Thomas Young
Staff: One

Financial Profile

Assets: In 1992, $818,520
High Grant: $3,200
Low Grant: $895
Ave. Grant: $1,000-$3,000
Total Grants: 404 grants totaling $3,832,770, plus $532,622 for grants to individuals and $2,030,946 for employee matching gifts

Application Process

Contact: John T. de Visser, Director, Corporate Affairs, (301) 897-6863
Deadline: Scholarship deadline February 1; no deadline for other grants
Board Meeting: As needed
Processing Time: Two to three months; majority of commitments made in the fall
Publications: Application guidelines
Guidelines: An application form for scholarships is available. A formal application for other grants is not required.

Sample Grants

Accreditation Board for Engineering and Technology in New York City received $22,600.
Johns Hopkins University in Baltimore, Maryland, received $100,000.
Roane State Community College in Harriman, Tennessee, received $52,000.
University of Maryland in College Park received $200,000.

University of Colorado in Denver received $10,000 for minority engineering education.

University of Tennessee in Knoxville received $25,000 for Bridge to the Future Campaign.

University of Central Florida Foundation in Orlando received $270,000.

Comments/Analysis

The foundation's support of higher education is made through a scholarship fund for the children of the corporation's employees, employee matching gifts, and grants. In the past, education, excluding matching gifts and scholarships, received 14 percent of the grant dollars distributed by the foundation. Higher education received approximately 80 percent of the education dollars for grants of $10,000 or more.

138
MCI Foundation
1139 19th Street NW
Washington, DC   20036

Areas of Interest

Program Description: Primarily to support organizations that provide job training, education, and learning opportunities for the disadvantaged. Areas of interest in higher education include business education, minority education, engineering, and science and technology.

Assistance Types: Scholarships, program-related investments, general support, program support, fellowship

Eligibility

Restrictions: No grants to individuals; political, fraternal, or religious groups; or organizations having the primary purpose of promoting a particular ideological point of view. No support for capital or endowment campaigns.

Personnel

Trustees/Directors: Gary M. Parsons, John R. Worthington, John H. Zimmerman

Staff: One part-time professional

Financial Profile

Assets: In 1993, $5,292,081
High Grant: $100,000
Low Grant: $65
Ave. Grant: $1,000-$20,000
Total Grants: 369 grants totaling $2,228,665

Application Process

Contact: Dorothy Olley at (202) 887-2175 or Public Relations Office of the MCI Division Headquarters in Denver, Colorado; Saint Louis, Missouri; Atlanta, Georgia; San Francisco, California; Chicago, Illinois; Arlington, Virginia; or Rye Brook, New York
Deadline: None
Guidelines: A formal application form is not required. Initial approach should be made by proposal.

Sample Grants

California State University School of Business Administration in Long Beach received $10,000 for its minority business program.

Kings College in Wilkes-Barre, Pennsylvania, received $25,000 for general support.

Fordham University School of Law in New York City received $15,000 for an MCI fellowship program.

Howard University in Washington, DC, received $20,000 for its teacher enhancement program.

University of Alabama in Birmingham received $10,000 for scholarship support.

Leadership, Education, and Development (LEAD) Program in Business in New York City received $35,000 for minority college outreach program.

University of Colorado Institute for International Business in Denver received $10,000 for general program support.

Citizenship Foundation of America in Concord, New Hampshire, received six grants of $10,000 each for scholarship programs in Baltimore, Maryland; Harrisburg, Pennsylvania; Pittsburgh, Pennsylvania; Boston, Massachusetts; Hartford, Connecticut; and Richmond, Virginia.

Comments/Analysis

In the past, the foundation's grant dollars have been distributed as follows: 25 percent for the subject area entitled other; 22 percent for education; 11 percent for human services; 10 percent for community improvement and development; 8 percent for science; 6 percent for youth development; and 1 percent for employee matching gifts. Grants to colleges and universities occur in more categories than education, making institutions of higher education the top recipient type by dollars.

139
Mead Corporation Foundation
Courthouse Plaza NE
Dayton, OH   45463

Areas of Interest

Program Description: Support for community funds; civic affairs; elementary, secondary, and higher education; social and human services; the arts; and culture. Specific areas of interest in higher education include business administration, minority education, pulp and paper technology, and technical education.

Assistance Types: Building funds, emergency funds, employee matching gifts, equipment, matching funds, seed money, special projects

Eligibility

Restrictions: No grants to individuals, political parties or candidates, fraternal, labor or veterans organizations, or religious organizations for religious purposes; only corporations classified as public charities under IRS Section 501(c)3 can be considered for support; no grants for endowment funds, advertising, dinners, or tickets; no loans; normally no operating support for organizations already receiving substantial support through the United Way. Giving primarily in areas of company operations. National giving to institutions of higher education.

Personnel

Officers: R.F. Budzik, Exec. Director and Governing Committee Member; W.R. Graber, Treas.; F.A. Marcano, Asst. Secy.; E.L. Miller, Secy.; K.A. Strawn, VP and Administrative Officer
Trustees/Directors: Governing Committee Members: B.P. Bent, L.A. Horn, E.M. Karter, R.W. Lane, E.L. Russo
Staff: None

Financial Profile

Assets: In 1993, $23,828,538
High Grant: $215,000
Low Grant: $50
Ave. Grant: $200-$40,000
Total Grants: $2,545,163
High Grant Higher Ed.: $107,234
Low Grant Higher Ed.: $50
Total Grants Higher Ed.: 411 grants totaling $912,703 (includes employee matching gifts)

Application Process

Contact: Ronald F. Buzdik, Exec. Director, (513) 495-3428
Deadline: Requests accepted at any time
Board Meeting: Distribution Committee meets in April, August, and November
Processing Time: Applicants can expect a response one to two weeks after the Distribution Committee meeting
Guidelines: Request may be submitted in any format but must include purpose of the organization, audited financial statements, support base, governing board; copy of organization's 501(c)3 letter of exemption, need statement for and explanation of the project, budget and proposed funding sources, population and number of people served, and geographic area to be served.

Sample Grants

Northern Michigan University Foundation in Marquette received $22,602.
Sparks State Technical College in Eufaula, Alabama, received $45,000.

Rose-Hulman Institute of Technology in Terre Haute, Indiana, was awarded $4,800.
Berkshire Community College in Pittsfield, Massachusetts, received $500.
Miami University Pulp and Paper Foundation in Oxford, Ohio, received $6,900.
University of Georgia Foundation in Athens received $5,000.
Florida Agricultural and Mechanical University in Tallahassee received $2,000.

Comments/Analysis

The Mead Corporation Foundation's grants fell into five categories in 1993: health and human services, education, culture, civic, and miscellaneous. The high award of the year, $215,000, was given to the United Way of Dayton under the category of health and human services. Support for education accounted for approximately 36 percent of the foundation's total contributions, gifts, and grants paid. Of the 411 grants to education (including matching gifts), approximately 60 percent were given to institutions of higher education and related organizations and associations. The largest higher education grant was for $107,234 and was given to the Miami University Foundation in Miami, Ohio. Historically, education grants are distributed to institutions that produce trained business personnel and to those that train women and other minorities in technical education and the skills needed by the Mead Corporation. The foundation also supports institutions that develop technologies that may result in new corporate products or services or the improvement of the environment. The availability of educational facilities and continuing education for Mead employees and their families is of utmost importance to the management of local company operations, as is promoting a better understanding of our economic system.

140
Merck Company Foundation
PO Box 100
One Merck Drive
Whitehouse Station, NJ   08889-0100

Areas of Interest

Program Description: To support education; community programs; hospitals and health agencies; medical, biological, and physical sciences; public and civic organizations; public policy; the aged; environment; and the handicapped. Specific areas of interest in higher education include pharmacology, public health, medical education, and veterinary medicine.
Assistance Types: Employee matching gifts, fellowships, seed money, special projects, equipment

Eligibility

Restrictions: Grants are usually made at the initiative of the foundation. No grants for operating budgets, continuing support, annual campaigns, emergency funds, endowments, deficit financing, land acquisition, research, travel, conferences, publications, or media productions. No loans and no grants to individuals except for fellowships in clinical pharmacology.

Personnel

Officers: Dr. P. Roy Vagelos, Chair and Trustee; Albert D. Angel, President and Trustee; C. Robin Hogen Jr., Exec. VP; John R. Taylor, Senior VP; Shuang Ruy Huang, VP; Clarence A. Abramson, Secy.; Michael G. Atieb, Treas.
Trustees/Directors: H. Brewster Atwater Jr., William G. Bowen, Frank T. Cary, Carolyne K. Davis, Lloyd C. Elam, Charles E. Exley Jr, Jacques Genes, Marian S. Heiskell, John J. Horan, John E. Lyons, Albert W. Merck, Ruben F. Mettler, Paul G. Rogers, Richard S. Ross, Dennis Weatherstone
Staff: Three full-time professional, three full-time support

Financial Profile

Assets: In 1992, $7,691,983
High Grant: $500,000
Low Grant: $200
Ave. Grant: $10,000-$50,000
Total Grants: 334 grants totaling $12,747,290, plus $351,277 for grants to individuals and $1,310,757 for employee matching gifts

Application Process

Contact: John R. Taylor, Senior VP, (908) 423-2042
Deadline: August 31 for fellowships in clinical pharmacology; no deadline for other grants
Board Meeting: Semiannually and as required
Processing Time: Two months
Publications: Corporate giving report
Guidelines: An application form is not required. Initial approach should be by letter.

Sample Grants

American Foundation for Pharmaceutical Education in North Plainfield, New Jersey, received $40,000.
Boston University School of Public Health in Boston, Massachusetts, received $30,000.
Carnegie Mellon University in Pittsburgh, Pennsylvania, received $125,000.
Council for Undergraduate Research in Tucson, Arizona, received two grants totaling $25,000.
Duquesne University School of Pharmacology in Pittsburgh, Pennsylvania, received $35,000.
Tuskegee University School of Veterinary Medicine in Tuskegee, Alabama, received $22,000.
Johns Hopkins University in Baltimore, Maryland, received a $50,000 grant for its School of Hygiene and Public Health and a $100,000 grant for its School of Medicine.
Fordham University Joseph Martino Graduate School of Business Administration in New York City received $40,000.
University of Pennsylvania Wharton School of Finance and Commerce in Philadelphia received $40,000.

Council for Advancement and Support of Education in Washington, DC, received $12,000 for Professor of the Year Awards.
Independent College Fund of New Jersey in Summit, New Jersey, received seven grants totaling $232,200.
Rockfeller University in New York City received $200,000.

Comments/Analysis

The top recipients of the foundation's higher education funds are schools of veterinary medicine, schools of pharmacy, schools of medicine, and schools of public health. Support of education is primarily medical related and includes the Merck Sharp & Dohme International Fellowships in Clinical Pharmacology. Geographically, support is focused on colleges and universities located in areas of major company operations, with an emphasis in New Jersey and Pennsylvania. The foundation supports secondary schools, junior and community colleges, four-year colleges and universities, graduate and professional schools, the United Negro College Fund, and hospitals through its employee matching gifts program. In the past, education received 43 percent of the foundation's grant dollars, followed by other at 13 percent, medicine at 12 percent, community improvement and development at 12 percent, employee matching gifts at 10 percent, science at 6 percent, and research fellowships to individuals at 4 percent.

141
Mobil Foundation, Inc.
3225 Gallows Road
Fairfax, VA   22037

Areas of Interest

Program Description: To support arts and culture, higher education, community funds, civic affairs, social services, and health and hospitals. Specific areas of interest in higher education include disciplines related to the petroleum and chemical industries and the physical sciences.
Assistance Types: Research, general purposes, exchange programs, employee related scholarships, employee matching gifts

Eligibility

Restrictions: Giving primarily in the states of California, Colorado, Illinois, Florida, Louisiana, Michigan, New York, Ohio, South Carolina, Texas, and Virginia. No grants to individuals, local and national organizations concerned with specific diseases, or religious or fraternal organizations. No support for building, endowment funds, operating budgets, charity benefits, athletic events, or advertising. No loans.

Personnel

Officers: Ellen Z. McCloy, President and Director; Richard G. Mund, Secy. and Exec. Director; Anthony L. Cavaliere, Treas.; Richard H. Stock, Controller

Trustees/Directors: Donald J. Bolger, G. Broadhead, Harold B. Olsen, Barbara A. Patocka, Jerome F. Trautschold Jr., John J. Wise
Staff: Three full-time professional, eight full-time support

Financial Profile

Assets: In 1992, $7,610,494; 1993, $8,480,778
High Grant: $300,000
Low Grant: $100
Ave. Grant: $1,000-$25,000
Total Grants: In 1992, 829 grants totaling $9,920,031, plus $2,570,932 for employee matching gifts; 1993, 715 grants totaling $8,942,953, plus $2,260,330 for employee matching gifts

Application Process

Contact: Richard G. Mund, Secy., (702) 846-3381
Deadline: None
Board Meeting: Monthly
Processing Time: Six to eight weeks
Publications: Financial statement, application guidelines, grants list
Guidelines: Application form is not required. Initial approach should be by letter or proposal.

Sample Grants

Bucknell University in Lewisburg, Pennsylvania, received $36,000.
Colorado School of Mines Foundation in Golden, Colorado, received $178,000.
New Mexico Institute of Mining and Technology in Socorro, New Mexico, received $12,000.
Tufts University in Medford, Massachusetts, received $56,000.
University of Minnesota Foundation in Minneapolis received $30,000.
University of Wyoming Foundation in Laramie received $12,000.
Woodrow Wilson National Fellowship Foundation in Princeton, New Jersey, received $10,000.
University of Houston in Houston, Texas, received $33,000.
National Consortium for Graduate Degrees for Minorities in Science and Engineering (GEM) in Notre Dame, Indiana, received $30,000.
National Merit Scholarship Corporation in Evanston, Illinois, received $211,556.
Old Dominion University in Norfolk, Virginia, received $15,000.

Comments/Analysis

Education, excluding employee matching gifts, receives approximately one-fourth of the grant dollars distributed by the foundation. More than half of the funds awarded to education are given to higher education in the form of grants of $10,000 or more.

142
Monsanto Fund
800 N Lindbergh Boulevard
Saint Louis, MO   63167

Areas of Interest

Program Description: To support early childhood, elementary, and higher education; health services; arts and culture; social services and welfare; youth; disadvantaged; and the homeless. Specific areas of interest in education include math and science.
Assistance Types: Equipment, annual campaigns, fellowships, special projects, employee matching gifts, in-kind gifts, continuing support, employee-related scholarships

Eligibility

Restrictions: No grants to individuals or religious institutions. No support for endowment funds. Giving mainly in states with company operations, including Alabama, Florida, Georgia, Idaho, Illinois, Massachusetts, Michigan, Missouri, North Carolina, Ohio, South Carolina, Texas, and West Virginia.

Personnel

Officers: Francis A. Stroble, Chair; John L. Mason, President; Richard W. Duesenberg, VP and Director; J. Russell Bley, Secy.; Juanita H. Hinshaw, Treas.
Trustees/Directors: Peter Clarke, Norma J. Curby, Daniel J. Mickelson, Michael E. Miller, Larry W. Solley
Staff: Two full-time professional, two full-time support

Financial Profile

Assets: In 1992, $7,500,755; 1993, $6,274,340
High Grant: In 1992, $1,320,000; 1993, $200,000
Low Grant: $50
Ave. Grant: $100-$10,000
Total Grants: In 1992, 1,664 grants totaling $9,927,444; 1993, 1,411 grants totaling $8,004,821

Application Process

Contact: John L. Mason, President
Deadline: None
Board Meeting: Four times a year
Processing Time: Two to four months
Publications: Informational brochure, application guidelines
Guidelines: A formal application form is not required. Proposals should include a brief history of the organization, a description of its mission, and any pertinent literature about the organization; statement of problem project will address; detailed description of project and project budget; what distinguishes project from others in the field; results expected and how they will be evaluated or measured; how project will be sustained once foundation support is completed; list of additional sources and amount of support; copy of IRS determination letter, organization's budget, and most recent

annual report, audited financial statement, or 990 tax form; and additional materials and documentation.

Sample Grants

Council of Independent Colleges in Washington, DC, received $25,000.

University of Dayton in Dayton, Ohio, received $10,125.

United Negro College Fund in New York City received $28,835.

Mount Holyoke College in South Hadley, Massachusetts, received $11,850.

Fontbonne College in Saint Louis, Missouri, received $108,500.

Valparaiso University Association in Valparaiso, Indiana, received $17,900.

University of West Florida in Pensacola, Florida, received $22,285.

Lander College in Greenwood, South Carolina, received $25,700.

David Lipscomb University in Nashville, Tennessee, received $11,650.

Clark Atlanta University in Atlanta, Georgia, received $37,500.

Washington University in Saint Louis, Missouri, received $64,245.

Webster University in Saint Louis, Missouri, received $40,840.

Comments/Analysis

Education receives approximately one-third of the foundation's grant dollars. This includes grants of $10,000 or more to higher and other education, and contributions to education of under $10,000, many of which are employee matching gifts to junior colleges, community colleges, four-year colleges, and universities and graduate schools. Although grants to higher education are given to institutions located in various states, the foundation's primary higher education focus is on colleges and universities in the Saint Louis, Missouri area.

143
Nationwide Insurance Enterprise Foundation
One Nationwide Plaza
Columbus, OH   43216

Areas of Interest

Program Description: To support human and social services, culture, civic affairs, community funds, and higher education. Other areas of interest include the aged, the disadvantaged, family services, the handicapped, health, and the arts. Specific areas of interest in higher education include business, economics, minority education, education for the handicapped, insurance education, and support of education associations.

Assistance Types: Operating budgets, continuing support, annual campaigns, seed money, emergency funds, special projects, employee matching gifts, capital campaigns, matching funds, research, student financial aid, endowments

Eligibility

Restrictions: No support for public elementary and secondary schools, fraternal or veterans organizations, or for individuals. No building funds or loans. Giving primarily in Ohio, particularly Columbus, and in other communities where the company maintains offices.

Personnel

Officers: John E. Fisher, Chair; D. Richard McFerson, President, CEO, and Trustee; Robert A. Oakley, Senior VP and CFO; Gordon E. McCutchan, Exec. VP, General Counsel, and Secy.; Peter F. Frenzer, Exec. VP, Investments, and Trustee; Stephen A. Rish, VP; Robert Woodward Jr., Senior VP; Harry Scherner, VP; Dennis W. Click, Asst. VP and Asst. Secy.; Mark A. Folk, VP and Treas.; D.M. Campbell, Asst. Treas.

Trustees/Directors: Charles L. Fuellgraf Jr., David O. Miller, W. Barton Montgomery, Henry S. Holloway, Arden L. Schisler

Staff: One part-time professional, one full-time support

Financial Profile

Assets: In 1993, $35,636,478

High Grant: $3,013,766

Low Grant: $100

Ave. Grant: $1,000-$30,000

Total Grants: 230 grants totaling $9,886,180, plus $376,981 for 413 employee matching gifts

Application Process

Contact: S.A. Rish, VP, (614) 249-5095

Deadline: Submit request by September 1st of year prior to funding

Board Meeting: February, May, August, and November

Processing Time: Two weeks after trustees' annual meeting in February

Guidelines: Request a Guidelines for Grant Consideration brochure, which outlines the foundation's required format. In general, proposals will be required to include the following items: name, address, and phone number of the organization and the name of the person to whom correspondence should be directed; brief history of the organization; description of the organization's program activities and goals for the current year; names and addresses of the board of directors and members of the board associates with or employed by the organization; documentation that the request has been authorized by the board; names, titles, duties, and qualifications of the key staff involved in the project; most recent audited financial statement; letter certifying 501(c)3 tax-exempt status; most recent 990 income tax return; project title; project purpose—what it will accomplish, if the request is for a special project, operating support or capital fund drive, and whether the funds will be used for the continuation of an existing program or a new activity; budget, including the total cost and the amount being requested from Nationwide; description of the problems the project will attempt to solve—the immediate and long range results expected, who will benefit from the project, and how and to what extent; approach—how the project will be carried out, where, by whom, and how long it will take; support—what others are committed or being sought for commitment (list organizations and amounts); future support—if and how the project will continue after the funding period; coordination—how coordination will be accomplished with other organizations working on the project; evaluation—criteria for success or failure and methods and dates of evaluation; and letters of support, articles, and data relating to the project included in appendices. Grant requests will be evaluated based on the following criteria: if the organization is managed well enough to assure successful completion of the project; the organization's sources of support and if its resources are consistent with its programs; if and how the organization's programs benefit Nationwide employees and agents; if the organization's efforts can be conveniently monitored; why Nationwide should be interested in the proposed project; how the project addresses basic human needs; if the project's approach is designed to meet its objectives and if a foundation grant will really help to bring about the desired solution; broad community involvement as evidenced by cooperative planning, diversified funding, and commitments for future support; and if the project duplicates or counteracts public or private sector interests. The foundation may want to meet with representatives of the requesting organization or make a visit to the project site to get a more complete understanding of the project. Once funded, a brief report will be required at the end of each grant year. Grant renewals are not automatic and reports are an important factor in future funding decisions.

Sample Grants

Franklin University in Columbus, Ohio, received a $1,000 unrestricted operating grant and a $200,000 capital grant.
Lemoyne-Owen College in Memphis, Tennessee, and Virginia Union University in Richmond received $50,000 for minority scholarships.
Shawnee State University in Portsmouth, Ohio, received $5,000.
United Negro College Fund in Columbus, Ohio, received $10,000.
Kentucky Independent College Fund in Louisville was awarded $1,100.

Comments/Analysis

In 1993, the Nationwide Insurance Enterprise Foundation awarded grants in five broad categories: health and welfare, education, culture and art, civic and community, and other. Health and welfare was its biggest recipient of funds, receiving 62 percent of all grant dollars distributed. Education received 20 percent. Higher education received approximately 93 percent of the education funds distributed. This included 42 percent for capital grants, 25 percent for employee matching gifts, 12 percent for grants to state and national higher education- related fund raising groups, 7 percent for departmental and research grants, 6 percent for student financial aid, and 1 percent for unrestricted operating grants.

144
Norfolk Southern Foundation
Three Commercial Place
Norfolk, VA   23510-2191

Areas of Interest

Program Description: To support higher education, culture, museums, performing arts, and community funds.
Assistance Types: Operating budgets, endowments, in-kind gifts, employee matching gifts

Eligibility

Restrictions: No grants to individuals. Giving mainly in Atlanta, Georgia, and Hampton Roads and Roanoke, Virginia.

Personnel

Officers: Arnold B. McKinnon, Chair, President, and CEO; Joseph R. Neikirk, VP and Exec. Director; R.E.D. deButts, VP; David R. Goode, VP; Paul E. Rudder, VP; John S. Shannon, VP; Thomas C. Scheller, VP; John R. Turbyfill, VP; D.H. Watts, VP; Donald E. Middleton, Secy.; Thomas H. Kerwin, Treas.
Staff: None

Financial Profile

Assets: In 1993, $8,137,580
High Grant: $150,000
Low Grant: $100
Ave. Grant: $500-$30,000
Total Grants: 220 grants totaling $3,079,159, and $781,873 for employee matching gifts

Application Process

Contact: Joseph R. Neikirk, VP and Exec. Director, (804) 629-2650
Deadline: None
Board Meeting: As necessary
Processing Time: 60 days
Guidelines: Initial approach should be made by letter. Proposals should include a detailed description of the project and amount requested, as well as a list of additional sources and amounts and a copy of the applicant organization's IRS determination letter.

Sample Grants

Ohio Foundation of Independent Colleges in Columbus, Ohio, received $21,600 for operating support.
Duke University Fuqua School of Business in Durham, North Carolina, received $125,000 for endowment.
National Merit Scholarship Corporation in Evanston, Illinois, received $104,556 for National Merit Scholarships.
Roaknoke College in Salem, Virginia, received $25,000 for operating support.

Pikeville College in Pikeville, Kentucky, received $10,000 for operating support.

Virginia Foundation for Independent Colleges in Richmond, Virginia, received $100,000 for operating support.

Comments/Analysis

Historically, arts and culture receives approximately 30 percent of the foundation's grant dollars; community improvement and development receives 21 percent, other receives 15 percent, education receives 13 percent, and employee matching gifts to educational and cultural institutions receives 21 percent. The majority of education grants go to higher education. Higher education recipients include colleges and universities, independent college foundations, and scholarship funds.

145

NYNEX Foundation
1113 Westchester Avenue, 1st Floor
White Plains, NY   10604-3510

Areas of Interest

Program Description: To support education, economic and community development, culture, disadvantaged, youth, employment, minorities, and science and technology. Specific areas of interest in higher education include minority and disadvantaged education and teacher education.

Assistance Types: Special projects

Eligibility

Restrictions: No support for religious organizations; operating expenses of United Way-supported organizations; organizations that duplicate work of federal, state, or local public agencies; or individuals. No grants for advertising. Giving mainly in areas of company operations in New York and New England.

Personnel

Officers: Raymond F. Burke, President, Secy., and Director; William F. Heitmann, VP and Treas.; Patricia Gallatin, VP, Programs; A.J. Krzemienski, Comptroller; Geoffrey B. Cooke, Exec. Director

Trustees/Directors: William C. Ferguson, Frederic V. Salerno, Ivan G. Seidenberg

Staff: Two full-time professional, three part-time professional

Financial Profile

Assets: In 1993, $43,702,288
High Grant: $462,930
Ave. Grant: $10,000-$50,000
Total Grants: 51 grants totaling $2,752,962

Application Process

Contact: Patricia Gallatin, VP, Programs, (914) 644-7226
Deadline: None
Board Meeting: Contributions committee meets four times a year
Processing Time: Four to six months
Publications: Annual report including application guidelines and informational brochure
Guidelines: An application form is not required. Submit letter with proposal. Proposal should include brief history of organization and description of its mission; description of project and amount requested; need statement; results expected; timetable for implementation and evaluation; qualifications of key personnel; how results will be evaluated or measured; copy of IRS determination letter; copy of annual report, audited financial statement, or 990 tax return; and list of board of directors, trustees, officers, and other key people.

Sample Grants

State University of New York Empire State College in Saratoga Springs, New York, received $75,000.

Rose-Hulman Institute of Technology in Terre Haute, Indiana, received $62,500.

Lesley College in Cambridge, Massachusetts, received $90,000.

Consortium for Graduate Study in Management in Saint Louis, Missouri, received $10,000.

United Negro College Fund in New York City received $30,000.

Hartwick College in Oneonta, New York, received $25,000.

New York University in New York City received $60,000.

Council for Aid to Education in New York City received $15,000.

Comments/Analysis

The foundation is particularly interested in funding projects that address the teacher shortage and programs that help minority and disadvantaged students enter and graduate from accredited engineering schools or other scientific disciplines. Historically, education has received 36 percent of the foundation's grant dollars. Higher education receives approximately 28 percent of the education funds for grants of $10,000 or more. The remainder goes to elementary and secondary education, other, and for grants under $10,000.

146

PacifiCorp Foundation
700 NE Multnomah, Suite 1600
Portland, OR   97232-4116

Areas of Interest

Program Description: To support culture and the arts, civic and social improvement, community development, education and research, United Way, and health and welfare.

Eligibility

Restrictions: No support for religious organizations for religious purposes; political organizations, campaigns, or candidates; organizations that discriminate; veterans or fraternal organizations for operating purposes; or memberships in Chambers of Commerce, taxpayer associations, and other bodies whose activities directly benefit PacifiCorp or its operating companies. No grants to individuals or for endowments or coverage of operating deficits. Giving mainly in areas of major company operation in the west.

Personnel

Officers: Gerald K. Drummond, Chair; Ernest Bloch II, Exec. Director; Sally A. Nofziger, Secy.
Trustees/Directors: William J. Glasgow, Thomas J. Imeson, Paul G. Lorenzini, Theodore D. Berns, Verl R. Topham; Allocations Committee Members: John A. Bohling, William W. Lyons, Dave Mead, William E. Peressini, Brian M. Wirkkala

Financial Profile

Assets: In 1993, $13,750,797
High Grant: $130,062
Low Grant: $100
Ave. Grant: $250-$10,000
Total Grants: 480 grants totaling $2,420,700

Application Process

Contact: Ernest Bloch II, Exec. Director, 500 NE Multnomah, Suite 1500, Portland, Oregon 97232, (503) 731-6676
Guidelines: Submit letter or proposal including details of program and tax-exempt status verification.

Sample Grants

Oregon Health Sciences University Foundation in Portland, Oregon, received $25,000.
Clark Community College, District 14 Foundation in Vancouver, Washington, received $30,000.
Marylhurst College in Marylhurst, Oregon, received $20,000.
Oregon Independent College Foundation in Portland, Oregon, received four grants totaling $70,000, ranging $1,500-$51,000.
Independent Colleges of Washington in Seattle received $3,000.
University of Utah in Salt Lake City received four grants totaling $35,100.
United Negro College Fund in Seattle, Washington, received $1,000.
Westminister College, Office of the President, in Salt Lake City, Utah, received a grant for $7,000 and a grant for $5,000.
Willamette University in Salem, Oregon, received $16,666.
Wisconsin Foundation of Independent Colleges in Milwaukee, Wisconsin, received $1,000.

Comments/Analysis

Historically, federated funds are the foundation's top recipient type by dollars, followed by museums and historical societies and colleges and universities. However, it is not unusual for institutions of higher education, particularly in Oregon, Washington, and Utah, to receive the greatest number of the foundation's grants.

147
PepsiCo Foundation, Inc.
700 Anderson Hill Road
Purchase, NY   10577

Areas of Interest

Program Description: To support education, higher education, business education, and minority education; preventive medicine, health services, and medical sciences; culture; the arts and performing arts; international affairs; nonprofit organizations where employees volunteer; economics; youth; civic affairs; and community funds.
Assistance Types: Primarily employee matching gifts and employee-related scholarships

Eligibility

Restrictions: No grants to individuals. Giving mainly in areas of company operations including Irvine, California; Wichita, Kansas; Louisville, Kentucky; Somers, New York; and Plano, Texas.

Personnel

Officers: Donald M. Kendall, Chair and Director; Joseph F. McCann, President and Director; Jacqueline R. Millian, VP, Contributions; Douglas M. Cram, Secy.; Claudia Morf, Treas.
Trustees/Directors: D. Wayne Calloway, Robert G. Dettmer, Roger A. Enrico, Ronald E. Harrison, Steven S. Reinemund
Staff: Two full-time professional, two full-time support

Financial Profile

Assets: In 1993, $6,001,695
High Grant: $924,854
Low Grant: $69
Ave. Grant: $10,000-$50,000
Total Grants: 282 grants totaling $5,434,323, plus $1,887,460 for employee matching gifts

Application Process

Contact: Jacqueline R. Millan, VP, Contributions, (914) 253-3153
Deadline: None
Board Meeting: Annually at minimum
Processing Time: Within three months
Publications: Informational brochure including application guidelines

Guidelines: Initial approach should be made by proposal. Proposal should include a brief description of organization and its mission; detailed description of project and amount requested; list of board of directors, trustees, officers, and other key people; copy of IRS determination letter; copy of annual report, financial statement, or 990 tax return; and any additional materials and documentation.

Sample Grants

Arizona State University in Tempe received $197,000.
Manhattanville College in Purchase, New York, received $200,000.
Connecticut College in New London, Connecticut, received $36,000.
Texas Christian University in Fort Worth, Texas, received $13,000
United Negro College Fund in New York City received $200,000.
National Merit Scholarship Corporation in Evanston, Illinois, received $924,854.
Hispanic Association of Colleges and Universities in San Antonio, Texas, received $10,000.
University of Virginia in Charlottesville received $200,000.

Comments/Analysis

Giving for higher education is primarily through employee matching gifts, scholarships for employees' children administered through the National Merit Scholarship Corporation, and support of programs that foster opportunities for minorities through scholarships and leadership development programs. Education is the foundation's top subject area by dollars.

148
Phillips Petroleum Foundation, Inc.
16 C4 Phillips Building
Bartlesville, OK   74001

Areas of Interest

Program Description: To support youth, civic affairs, culture, education, health and social sciences. Specific areas of interest in higher education include business education, engineering, geophysics, mining and minorities in engineering.
Assistance Types: Employee matching gifts, general support, scholarships

Eligibility

Restrictions: Must be tax-exempt organization under IRS Section 501(c)3. Generally no grants to religious organizations or specialized health agencies. No grants to individuals, or for trips or fund-raising dinners; no loans. Overall giving is primarily in the areas of company operations, particularly Oklahoma, Texas, Colorado, and other states in the south and southwest.

Personnel

Officers: V. Edward Adams, Assistant Controller; R.C. Berney, Associate Tax Officer; Dale J. Billam, Secy. and Director; J.M. Bork, Controller; D.L. Cone, Asst. Secy.; W.F. Dausses, President and Director; J.F. Francis, Assistant General Tax Officer; R.W. Holsapple, VP, Director, and Treas.; J.W. O'Toole, General Tax Officer; J.C. West, Exec. Manager; J. Bryan Whitworth, VP and Director
Trustees/Directors: Stanley R. Mueller
Staff: One part-time professional, one part-time support

Financial Profile

Assets: In 1993, $496,876
High Grant: $100,000
Low Grant: $25
Ave. Grant: $1,000-$25,000
Total Grants: 629 grants totaling $3,959,891, plus 1,308 employee matching gifts totaling $1,880,680
High Grant Higher Ed.: $85,300
Low Grant Higher Ed.: $50
Ave. Grant Higher Ed.: $50-$11,500
Total Grants Higher Ed.: 199 grants totaling $1,794,049, plus $1,685,410 in matching gifts

Application Process

Contact: John C. West, Exec. Manager, (918) 661-6248
Deadline: None
Board Meeting: Board meets in March and as required
Processing Time: Final notification in eight to 12 weeks
Guidelines: Application form not required. Address letter to contact person stating detailed description of the project and amount of funding requested, a project budget, and listing of other sources of funding with a copy of tax-exempt certificate attached. Organizations must provide a statement indicating that funds will be used for tax-exempt purposes and that organizations will, upon request, provide periodic statements regarding the utilization of funds.

Sample Grants

American Indian College Fund in New York City received $1,000.
Colorado School of Mines Foundation in Golden was awarded $9,000.
Kansas University Endowment Association in Lawrence received $10,000.
National Hispanic Scholarship Fund in Novato, California, received $1,000.
New Mexico State University College of Engineering in Las Cruces received $9,000.
Odessa Junior College in Odessa, Texas, received $6,500.
Texas Tech University Foundation in Lubbock received $41,800.
Missouri Baptist College in Saint Louis received $2,000.
University of Oklahoma School of Electrical Engineering in Norman received $9,000.
Mt. Holyoke College in Hadley, Massachusetts, received $4,000.

Comments/Analysis

Recently, the Phillips Petroleum Foundation awarded over $5 million in grants in the following five categories: education, arts and humanities, health and welfare, youth, and civic. The foundation's largest grant was awarded in the civic category and was given to Ethics Resource Center Inc. in Washington, DC. Education awards totaled $3,644,958 and accounted for approximately 66 percent of the foundation's total contributions, gifts, and grants paid. This $3,644,958 included $1,685,410 in employee matching gifts to junior and community colleges, four-year colleges and universities, seminaries and theological schools, and technical and specialized schools, and $1,959,549 in grant expenditures. Approximately 92 percent of the education grants were awarded to colleges and universities and higher education-related organizations. Several large universities in the foundation's geographic preference areas received multiple grants totaling over $100,000. For example, Oklahoma State University was awarded five grants totaling $112,550, the University of Oklahoma received six grants for a total of $118,600, and the University of Texas campuses received 15 grants for a total of $142,550. The single largest higher education grant was awarded to the University of Oklahoma ($85,300). All of the foundation's grant awards were unrestricted and were to be used in the United States for the tax exempt purposes of the recipient. Based on the foundation's listing of recipients, Phillips Petroleum's support of engineering and minorities in engineering was apparent.

149
Potlatch Foundation II
c/o Potlatch Corporation
One Maritime Plaza, Suite 2400
San Francisco, CA　94111

Areas of Interest

Program Description: To support higher education, health, and civic affairs. Specific areas of interest in higher education include business and forestry.
Assistance Types: General support, targeted support, employee matching gifts

Eligibility

Restrictions: Grants are made on a national or broad regional basis.

Personnel

Officers: Hubert D. Travaille, President and Trustee; John M. Richards, VP and Trustee; Sandra T. Powell, Secy.-Treas.
Trustees/Directors: Ralph M. Davidson, Barbara M. Failing, George F. Jewett Jr., George F. Pfautsch, Charles R. Pottenger, L. Pendleton Siegel, Thomas J. Smerkar

Financial Profile

Assets: In 1992, $103,653
High Grant: $500,000
Low Grant: $25
Ave. Grant: $300-$25,000
Total Grants: 341 grants totaling $1,325,866, plus $84,278 in employee matching gifts

Application Process

Contact: Hubert D. Travaille, President, (415) 576-8826
Deadline: None
Guidelines: Application form is required.

Sample Grants

American Council on Education in Washington, DC, received $15,000 for a Business-Higher Education Forum.
College of Saint Scholastica in Duluth, Minnesota, received $25,000.
Lewis State College in Lewiston, Idaho, received $30,000 for targeted support of its library.
University of Washington in Seattle received $10,000 in targeted support for its College of Forestry Wood Use and Design Program.
North Carolina State University in Raleigh received $15,000 for targeted support of its Forest Biology Research Center.

Comments/Analysis

Education accounts for approximately 14 percent of grant dollars distributed by the foundation, with education grants generally ranging from $300 to $15,000. Colleges and universities were the third largest recipient type by dollars in the past for grants of $10,000 or more and the largest recipient type by number of $10,000 or more grants distributed.

150
Procter & Gamble Fund
PO Box 599
Cincinnati, OH　45201

Areas of Interest

Program Description: To support private higher education, public policy research organizations, community funds, hospitals, youth agencies, urban affairs, and the handicapped. Specific areas of interest in higher education include business administration, economic education, engineering, management, math, minorities in education, public policy research, and science.
Assistance Types: Annual campaigns, building funds, employee matching gifts, employee-related scholarships, equipment, land acquisition, scholarships

Eligibility

Restrictions: Grant requests from colleges and universities are discouraged, as most grants are initiated by the trustees within specified programs; no grants to individuals. Contributions limited to the United States and Canada; giving primarily in areas where the company and its subsidiaries have large concentrations of employees; national giving for higher education.

Personnel

Officers: R.L. Wehling, President and Trustee; R.A. Bachhuber, VP and Trustee; S. J. Fitch, VP and Trustee; R.R. Fitzpatrick, VP and Secy.; Raymond D. Mains, Treas.; R.M. Neago, Asst. Secy.; E.G. Nelson, VP and Trustee; Vicki F. Tylman, Asst. Treas.
Staff: Three full-time professional, one full-time support

Financial Profile

Assets: In 1993, $19,561,836
High Grant: $2,050,000
Low Grant: $50
Ave. Grant: $1,000-$50,000
Total Grants: 1,023 grants totaling $19,146,977
High Grant Higher Ed.: $824,785
Low Grant Higher Ed.: $50
Ave. Grant Higher Ed.: $50-$3,000
Total Grants Higher Ed.: 739 grants for $9,522,789

Application Process

Contact: R.R. Fitzpatrick, VP and Secy., (513) 983-2201
Deadline: None; requests may be submitted at any time and are reviewed upon receipt; contributions are reviewed for as soon as is practical
Processing Time: Final notification usually within one month
Guidelines: Formal application form not required; initial approach by proposal.

Sample Grants

University of Cincinnati Foundation in Ohio received $100,000.
Spalding University in Louisville, Kentucky, received $12,000.
Stephens College in Columbia, Missouri, was awarded $2,000.
National Hispanic Scholarship Fund in San Francisco, California, received $40,000.
United Negro College Fund in New York City received $200,000.
University of Tennessee in Knoxville was awarded $55,873.
Washington and Lee University in Lexington, Virginia, received $5,840.
Wesley College in Florence, Mississippi, received $1,000.
Ohio Foundation of Independent Colleges in Columbus was awarded $55,000.

Comments/Analysis

In 1993, the Procter & Gamble Fund gave in the following categories: health and social services, education, civic programs, culture, and environmental programs. The fund's largest grant was awarded in the area of health and social services: $2,050,000 to the United Way and Community Chest of Cincinnati, Ohio. Aid to education reached almost $11 million and accounted for approximately 57 percent of the fund's total contributions, gifts, and grants paid. Within the aid to education category, 814 grants were awarded (including employee matching gifts and scholarships) and four subcategories were identified. The subcategories included colleges and universities, state and regional associations, public policy research and economic education, and special events. Approximately 91 percent of the total number of aid to education grants were given to higher education institutions and associations. This equated to 50 percent percent of the fund's total dollars contributed. Of the 700 plus grants awarded to higher education only 20 were for over $100,000 and the majority of these went to large, well-known institutions or educationally related organizations in Cincinnati. The largest grant awarded in the field of higher education was for $824,785 and went to the National Merit Scholarship Corporation. The largest grant to an institution of higher education went to Cornell University ($229,808); with the second largest going to Xavier University of Cincinnati, Ohio ($222,478). As in previous years, the fund continued to provide support for colleges and universities under four main programs: departmental grants, employee matching gifts, plant city and Cincinnati Colleges, and special grants. Within the departmental grants program, the fund provided support for colleges and universities on the basis of their value as a continuing source of employees for the company. Departments within colleges and universities that rated highly in producing graduates working at Procter & Gamble received unrestricted departmental grants that could be used for such purposes as curriculum improvement or faculty development. The fund also focused support on higher education institutions located in Cincinnati and plant communities where there was a significant concentration of Procter & Gamble employees and where the institution played a significant role in community life. Aid to colleges and universities was also given in the form of employee matching gifts and special grants to national organizations that contributed significantly to the improvement of education and educational opportunities.

151
Prudential Foundation
751 Broad Street
Prudential Plaza
Newark, NJ   07102-3777

Areas of Interest

Program Description: To support early childhood, elementary, secondary, and higher education; urban and community development; civic affairs; health; AIDS; child development and welfare; arts and culture; youth; and United Way. Specific areas of interest in higher education include insurance education and minority education.
Assistance Types: Employee-related scholarships, employee matching gifts, special projects, seed money, equipment, matching funds, consulting services, technical assistance, conferences, seminars, internships, faculty development

Eligibility

Restrictions: Giving mainly in states where company operations are located including New Jersey, California, Florida, Minnesota, and Pennsylvania, with an emphasis in Newark, New Jersey. No grants to individuals; labor, religious, or athletic groups; or single disease health-related organizations for general operating funds. No support for endowments. No loans.

Personnel

Officers: Dorothy Kaplan Light, Chair and Trustee; Peter B. Goldberg, President; Paul G. O'Leary, VP; Barbara L. Halburda, Secy.; James J. Straine, Treas.; Eugene M. O'Hara, Comptroller
Trustees/Directors: Lisle C. Carter Jr., Carolyne K. Davis, James R. Gillen, Jon F. Hanson, Donald E. Procknow, Robert C. Winters, Edward D. Zinbarg
Staff: Seven full-time professional, seven full-time support

Financial Profile

Assets: In 1993, $131,705,000
Ave. Grant: $10,000-$75,000
Total Grants: 762 grants totaling $14,149,796, plus $2,449,355 for employee matching gifts

Application Process

Contact: Barbara L. Halaburda, Secy., (201)802-7354
Deadline: None
Board Meeting: April, August, and December
Processing Time: Four to six weeks
Publications: Annual report including application guidelines
Guidelines: First submit a letter with a brief description of the proposed program and the foundation will determine eligibility. An application form is not required.

Sample Grants

Citizens Scholarship Foundation of America in Saint Peter, Minnesota, received $92,040 for employees' children scholarship program.

Upsala College in East Orange, New Jersey, received $10,000 for strategic planning and fund-raising assistance.

New Jersey Institute of Technology in Newark, New Jersey, received $10,000 for student internship funding and $22,000 for precollege programs for urban youth.

University of Pennsylvania S.S. Huebner Foundation for Insurance Education in Philadelphia received $18,000 for insurance research and education.

Life Underwriter Training Council in Bethesda, Maryland, received $165,000 for insurance education.

Middlesex County College Foundation in Edison, New Jersey, received $15,000 for a Minority Access to the Professions (MAPS) program.

National Merit Scholarship Foundation Corporation in Evanston, Illinois, received $62,426 for an employees' children scholarship program.

United Negro College Fund in New York City received $100,000 for a UNCF/Prudential faculty development program.

Rutgers University Public Education Institute in New Brunswick, New Jersey, received $13,400 for New Jersey school district report card and gap analysis projects.

Essex County College in Newark, New Jersey, received $50,000 for precollege programs for Newark youth.

Comments/Analysis

In terms of education, the Prudential Foundation is particularly interested in supporting programs and projects that improve basic skills in mathematics, science, language arts, and computer literacy in public schools in disadvantaged urban communities; and enhance educational opportunities for the disadvantaged, minorities, the disabled, and women. Its focus in higher education is primarily directed toward programs related to the insurance and financial services industries and projects aimed at improving management capabilities. The foundation also provides scholarships for the sons and daughters of employees through the Citizens Scholarship Foundation of America and the National Merit Scholarship Foundation Corporation and sponsors an education employee matching gifts program for secondary schools, junior and community colleges, four-year colleges and universities, graduate schools, and seminaries and theological schools.

152
Rockwell International Corporation Trust
625 Liberty Avenue
Pittsburgh, PA   15222-3123

Areas of Interest

Program Description: To support education, culture, and health and human services. Specific areas of interest include higher education, engineering education, science education, and K-12 math and science education.
Assistance Types: Operating budgets, building funds, employee matching gifts, scholarship funds, fellowships, professorships

Eligibility

Restrictions: Grants are not made to individuals. No support for religious organizations or for religious purposes, hospital building campaigns, or general endowments. No loans. Giving mainly in areas of corporate operations except for selected national organizations and universities that are sources of recruits.

Personnel

Trustees/Directors: Trust Committee: Donald R. Beal, Chair; W. M. Barnes, Secy.; R.L. Cattoi; Richard R. Mau
Staff: Four

Financial Profile

Assets: For fiscal year ending September 1993, $3,565,068
Total Grants: $10,064,696

Application Process

Contact: William R. Fitz, (412) 565-5803
Deadline: None
Board Meeting: Monthly
Processing Time: 60 to 90 days
Publications: Informational brochure
Guidelines: Application form is not required. Submit a letter with any pertinent information, including a copy of IRS determination letter.

Sample Grants

Kirkwood Community College Foundation in Cedar Rapids, Iowa, received $40,000.

Milwaukee School of Engineering in Wisconsin received $10,000.

University of Southern California in Los Angeles was awarded $100,000.

University of Wisconsin in Madison received $23,995.

Massachusetts Institute of Technology in Cambridge received two grants: one for $77,512 and one for $25,000.

Southwest Missouri State University in Springfield received $3,000.

Stanford University in Stanford, California, received two grants: one for $76,924 and one for $100,000.

Texas A&M University in College Station was awarded $21,985.

United Negro College Fund in New York City received $29,000.

Walters State Community College in Morristown, Tennessee, received $3,000.

Comments/Analysis

Historically, education is the trust's top subject area by dollars, although United Way usually receives the highest award each year. In terms of higher education, Rockwell International Corporation Trust provides operating funds to many institutions, matches gifts from full-time employees, and awards scholarships to sons and daughters of Rockwell employees who qualify under the National Merit Scholarship competition. In addition, the trust awards fellowships to doctoral students in science and engineering. Institutions of higher education within the University of California system are normally recipients of numerous grants.

153
Schering-Plough Foundation, Inc.
PO Box 1000
One Giralda Farms
Madison, NJ   07940-1000

Areas of Interest

Program Description: The foundation's primary objective is to support programs, projects, and organizations that work toward improving the quality and delivery of health care services through medical and allied education. Other areas of interest include higher education, culture, biochemistry, science and technology, minority education, museums, performing arts, the Caribbean, safety, and environment. Pharmaceutical education is one of the foundation's specific areas of interest in higher education.
Assistance Types: Special projects, employee-related scholarships, scholarship funds, employee matching gifts, annual campaigns, seed money, building and renovation, equipment, internships, fellowships, general purposes, professorships, continuing support, operating budgets, capital campaigns, endowments

Eligibility

Restrictions: No support for individuals, deficit financing, publications, or conferences. No loans. Giving mainly in areas of company operations, particularly New Jersey and Tennessee.

Personnel

Officers: Allan S. Kushen, President and Trustee; Joseph S. Roth, Secy.; Jack Wyszomierski, Treas.
Trustees/Directors: David E. Collins, Donald R. Conklin, Hugh A. D'Andrade, Harold R. Hiser, Richard J. Kogan, Robert P. Luciano
Staff: One full-time professional, one part-time support

Financial Profile

Assets: In 1993, $18,294,715
High Grant: $100,000
Low Grant: $25
Ave. Grant: $10,000-$50,000
Total Grants: 118 grants totaling $2,520,301, plus $448,123 in employee matching gifts

Application Process

Contact: Rita Sacco, Asst. Secy., (201) 822-7412
Deadline: February 1 and July 1
Board Meeting: Spring and Fall
Processing Time: Six months
Publications: Corporate giving report including application guidelines
Guidelines: An application form is not required. Proposals should include brief history of organization, description of its mission, and literature about the organization; statement of problem project will address; copy of IRS determination letter; copy of annual report,

audited financial statement, or 990; and copy of organization's budget and project budget. Receipt of proposals is acknowledged by the foundation, and interviews are granted when deemed necessary.

Sample Grants

American Foundation for Pharmaceutical Education in North Plainfield, New Jersey, received $15,000.

Foundation for Independent Higher Education in New York City received $10,000.

LeMoyne-Owen College in Memphis, Tennessee, received $37,500.

National Merit Scholarship Corporation in Evanston, Illinois, received $68,397.

Rutgers University in New Brunswick, New Jersey, received three grants totaling $90,000.

Tennessee Foundation for Independent Colleges in Brentwood, Tennessee, received $22,000.

University of Cape Town Fund in New York City received $10,000.

Fordham University in Bronx, New York, received $50,000.

Occupational Physicians Scholarship Fund in New York City received $10,000.

Comments/Analysis

Education is the foundation's top subject area by dollars and also by number of grants. In addition, colleges and universities are its top recipients of funds. Generally, colleges of pharmacy at institutions of higher education receive grants.

154
Scott Paper Company Foundation
One Scott Plaza
Philadelphia, PA   19113

Areas of Interest

Program Description: To support education, health and human services, and arts and culture. Specific areas of interest include school reform, early childhood and secondary education, at-risk youth, volunteerism, literacy, and the disadvantaged.

Assistance Types: Employee-related scholarships, seed money, consulting services, continuing support, equipment, special projects, and technical assistance.

Eligibility

Restrictions: Giving limited to areas of major company operations in Pennsylvania, Washington, New York, Mississippi, Wisconsin, Alabama, Michigan, Arkansas, and Maine. No grants for endowments, deficit financing, land acquisition, goodwill advertising, research, or capital campaigns. No loans or grants to individuals. No support for government agencies; religious organizations for religious purposes; national health funds; entertainment groups; or veterans, labor, or fraternal organizations.

Personnel

Trustees/Directors: John J. Butler, Thomas P. Czepial, Phillip E. Lippincott, James A. Morrill, Paul N. Schregal

Staff: One full-time professional, one full-time support

Financial Profile

Assets: In 1993, $110,670
High Grant: $97,115
Low Grant: $200 (excluding Dollars for Doers)
Ave. Grant: $5,000-$10,000
Total Grants: $1,779,288
High Grant Higher Ed.: $97,115
Low Grant Higher Ed.: $5,000
Ave. Grant Higher Ed.: $5,000-$10,000
Total Grants Higher Ed.: Approximately seven grants totaling $226,685

Application Process

Contact: Fran Rizzardi Urso, Manager, Corporate Contributions, (215) 522-6160
Deadline: None
Board Meeting: June and December
Processing Time: Three months
Publications: Annual report
Guidelines: Send letter requesting guidelines. Application form is required.

Sample Grants

Citizens' Scholarship Foundation of America in Saint Peter, Minnesota, received three grants: one for $97,115, one for $11,850, and one for $89,625.

Muskegon Community College in Muskegon, Michigan, received $10,000.

United Negro College Fund in Philadelphia, Pennsylvania, received $7,000.

University of Pennsylvania University Museum in Philadelphia received $6,095.

University of Pennsylvania School of Medicine in Philadelphia received $5,000.

Comments/Analysis

Employee-related scholarships administered by the Citizens' Scholarship Foundation of America account for the vast majority of the foundation's support for higher education. A limited number of dollars are also distributed to higher education through the foundation's Dollars for Doers program in which gift eligibility is based on time volunteered by employees.

155
Shell Oil Company Foundation
PO Box 2099
Two Shell Plaza
Houston, TX   77252

Areas of Interest

Program Description: Primarily to support education and community funds (United Way organizations). Other areas of interest are the arts, performing arts, health, civic affairs, and public policy. Fields of interest in education include math, engineering, science, and career counseling.

Assistance Types: Student aid, faculty development, research, departmental grants, continuing support, matching gifts, fellowships, general purposes, operating budgets, professorships, publications, scholarship funds, employee-related scholarships, special projects, capital campaigns

Eligibility

Restrictions: No grants to individuals, or for endowment funds, capital campaigns of national organizations, or development funds. No support for special requests of colleges, universities, and college fund-raising associations, or hospital operating expenses. No loans. Giving mainly in areas of company operations with an emphasis in Texas for higher education.

Personnel

Officers: F.H. Richardson, President and Trustee; D.J. O'Connor, VP; L.E. Sloan, VP; B.W. Levan, VP; R.L. Kuhns, Secy.; T.J. Howard, Asst. Treas.; J.M. Bishop, Asst. Treas.; K.C. Clayton, Asst. Treas.; T.J. Howard, Asst. Treas.; J.M. Bishop, Asst. Treas., Asst. Secy.

Trustees/Directors: P.O. Carroll, J.B. Little, D.B. Richardson, J.M. Morgan, J.P. Parrish, R. L. Lopez, L.L. Smith, C.W. Wilson, B.L. Bernard

Staff: Five full-time professional, three full-time support

Financial Profile

Assets: In 1993, $48,317,126
Ave. Grant: $3,000-$30,000
Total Grants: $20,511,367
High Grant Higher Ed.: $200,000
Low Grant Higher Ed.: $200
Ave. Grant Higher Ed.: $1,000-$25,000
Total Grants Higher Ed.: In 1992, $7,566,974

Application Process

Contact: J.N. Doherty, VP, or R.L. Kuhns, Secy., (713) 241-3616
Deadline: August 31; submit proposal between January and August

Board Meeting: December, March
Processing Time: One month
Publications: Corporate giving report, including application guidelines
Guidelines: Application form not required. Prospective grantees should submit a letter proposal and include a history of the organization and a description of its mission, detailed description of project and amount requested, most recent annual report or audited financial statement, project budget, copy of IRS determination letter, and a list of corporate donors and their level of support.

Sample Grants

Colorado School of Mines in Golden received five departmental grants: $10,000 for chemical engineering, $5,000 for computer science, $2,000 for geological engineering, $10,000 for geology, and $7,000 for petroleum engineering.

Georgetown University in Washington, DC, received a $10,000 departmental grant for its tax program.

University of Delaware in Newark received $200 for career planning and placement.

Rice University in Houston, Texas, received $150,000 for a Shell Distinguished Chair in Environmental Science and Engineering.

Grambling State University in Grambling, Louisiana, received a $2,000 departmental grant for business administration.

Pennsylvania State University in University Park received $14,197 for Shell Doctoral Fellowships in chemistry and $17,300 for Shell Doctoral Fellowships in the geosciences.

The University of California in Berkeley received $25,000 for Shell Faculty Career Initiation Funds in chemical engineering.

Arizona State University in Tempe received three departmental grants: $2,000 for chemical engineering, $12,000 for chemistry, and $7,000 for the College of Business/Purchasing and Materials Management.

Mississippi State University in Mississippi State received $600 for its Career Services Center.

Comments/Analysis

In the past, 55 percent of the funds distributed by the foundation went to education, 32 percent to health and welfare, 7 percent to culture and art, 5 percent to civic affairs, and 1 percent to other. A substantial portion of the funds awarded to education went to higher education through a number of planned programs. For example, 23 percent of the education funds were awarded for departmental grants ranging $2,000-$12,000 and aimed at strengthening teaching and research in a number of specified areas including, but not limited to, chemical, petroleum, mechanical, mining, and civil engineering; polymer science; accounting, business, purchasing, materials management, and finance; occupational medicine, toxicology, and environmental health; tax programs; law; and human resource management. Twenty-two percent went to employee matching gifts to postsecondary institutions. Seven percent was awarded for Century III scholarships to high school students with outstanding leadership skills. Shell Doctoral Fellowships ranging $14,500-$37,600 accounted for 6 percent of the education funds. Scholarships to sons and daughters of employees administered through the National Merit Scholarship Corporation received 5 percent. Shell Faculty Initiation funds represented 4 percent, while Shell Distinguished Chairs in Environmental Science and Engineering and petroleum engineering accounted for another 4 percent. Other planned higher education-related programs included Shell Incentive Funds and Shell Career Counseling Grants.

156

SmithKline Beecham Foundation
PO Box 7929
One Franklin Plaza
Philadelphia, PA   19101

Areas of Interest

Program Description: To support education; health and hospitals; medical sciences; research and education; community funds; arts and fine arts; public policy; civic affairs; and South Africa. Specific areas of interest in higher education include pharmacology, osteopathic medicine, and optometry.
Assistance Types: General purposes, operating budgets, research, special projects, employee matching gifts

Eligibility

Restrictions: No grants to individuals. Giving to colleges and universities is primarily focused in Pennsylvania with an emphasis in the Philadelphia area.

Personnel

Officers: Albert J. White, Secy. and Director; Henry J. King, Treas. and Director
Trustees/Directors: Norman H. Blanchard, Ralph Christofferson, J.P. Garnier, Harry Groome, Tod R. Hullin, Frederick W. Kyle, John B. Ziegler
Staff: One full-time professional, one part-time professional, three full-time support

Financial Profile

Assets: In 1992, $1,509,345
High Grant: $500,000
Low Grant: $500
Ave. Grant: $2,000-$50,000
Total Grants: 125 grants totaling $3,648,280, plus $919,417 in employee matching gifts

Application Process

Contact: (215) 751-7024
Board Meeting: May and as required to review proposals
Publications: Annual report, 990-PF tax return
Guidelines: Initial approach should be made by proposal. Proposals should include a description of the project and the amount re-quested; statement of the problem the project will address; list of additional sources and amounts; copy of annual report, audited financial statement, or 990; and a copy of the applicant organization's IRS determination letter.

Sample Grants

American Association of Colleges of Osteopathic Medicine in Rockville, Maryland, received a grant for $121,000 and a grant for $28,900.
American Association of Colleges of Pharmacy in Bethesda, Maryland, received a $350,000 grant and a $50,000 grant.
Pennsylvania College of Pharmacy and Science in Philadelphia received $50,000.
Pennsylvania College of Optometry in Philadelphia received $10,000.
Gwynedd-Mercy College in Gwynedd Valley, Pennsylvania, received $10,000.
Swathmore College in Swathmore, Pennsylvania, received $10,000.
Temple University in Philadelphia, Pennsylvania, received $250,000.
United Negro College Fund in New York City received two $10,000 grants.
University of California in Berkeley received $10,000.
University of Cape Town Fund in New York City received a $53,000 grant and a $47,000 grant.
University of Pennsylvania in Philadelphia received a $500,000 grant and a $30,000 grant.

Comments/Analysis

Historically, education has received 32 percent of the grant dollars paid by the foundation. Arts and culture accounted for 16 percent; other, 16 percent; community improvement and development, 14 percent; medicine, 6 percent; and employee matching gifts, 16 percent. The vast majority of education grants are awarded to colleges and universities and higher education related associations and organizations.

157

Southwestern Bell Foundation
175 E Houston, Suite 200
San Antonio, TX   78205

Areas of Interest

Program Description: To support education, health, welfare, the arts, cultural programs, civic affairs, community development, United Way, and youth organizations.
Assistance Types: Employee matching gifts, lectureships, research, seed money, special projects, technical assistance, conferences, seminars, matching funds

Eligibility

Restrictions: No grants to individuals; religious organizations; or fraternal, veterans, or labor groups. No support for hospital operating funds, capital funds, or operating funds for United Way-supported organizations. No grants for special advertising, or ticket/dinner purchases. Giving mainly in Texas; Kansas; Missouri; Washington, DC; Arkansas; Oklahoma; and New York.

Personnel

Officers: Gerald D. Blatherwick, Chair; Larry J. Alexander, President; Robert W. Wohlert, VP and Treas.; Harold E. Rainbolt, VP and Secy.; Charles DeReimer, Exec. Director
Trustees/Directors: James R. Adams, Royce C. Caldwell, James D. Ellis, Charles E. Foster, Robert C. Pope,
Staff: Four full-time professional, one full-time support

Financial Profile

Assets: In 1993, $45,462,974
Total Grants: $17,674,280
High Grant Higher Ed.: $200,000
Low Grant Higher Ed.: $500 (excluding matching gifts)
Ave. Grant Higher Ed.: $1,000-$10,000
Total Grants Higher Ed.: In 1992, approximately 134 grants totaling $1,747,240

Application Process

Contact: Charles DeRiemer, Exec. Director, (201) 351-2208
Deadline: None; unsuccessful applications may not reapply in same calendar year
Processing Time: Four to six weeks
Publications: Annual report, informational brochure, application guidelines
Guidelines: Application form is not required. Request should include copy of IRS determination letter; brief statement of history and accomplishments; statement of objectives including problem being addressed, program budget, and amount sought; link between project's goal and foundation priorities; timetable for implementation and description of expected results; details of fund-raising plans, including sources, amounts, and commitments; plans for sustaining activities after conclusion of foundation support; annual report or budget for organization showing all income sources and objectives; list of board members; and list of accrediting agencies when appropriate.

Sample Grants

Brown University in Providence, Rhode Island, received three grants totaling $190,000.
Cameron University in Lawton, Oklahoma, received two grants: one for $3,000 and one for $25,000.
Kansas State University Endowment in Lawrence received $200,000.
Mineral Area College in Flat River, Missouri, received two grants: one for $2,000 and one for $1,500.

Texas A&M University in College Station received three grants totaling $74,000.
Texas Tech University in Lubbock received 14 grants totaling $411,250, ranging $500-$200,000.
Various branches of the University of Texas received 17 grants totaling approximately $159,175 and ranging $500-$100,000.
Central Methodist College in Fayette, Missouri, received $1,000.
Consortium for Graduate Study in Saint Louis, Missouri, received $2,000.
Hutchinson Community College in Hutchinson, Kansas, received $5,000.
Saint Louis University in Saint Louis, Missouri, was awarded $135,000.

Comments/Analysis

In the past, grants accounted for 92 percent of the funds distributed by the foundation, followed by matching gifts at approximately 7 percent and Volunteer Improvement Program (VIP) support at 1 percent. Under the VIP, an employee who volunteers at a tax-exempt organization for at least eight hours a month for six consecutive months is eligible to request grants for the organization for up to $250. Of the grant dollars distributed, education received 36 percent; United Way, 29 percent; culture and arts, 13 percent; health, hospitals, and human services, 7 percent; community development, 6 percent; civic and community, 6 percent; and youth organizations, 3 percent. Approximately 38 percent of the education grant dollars distributed supported higher education with an emphasis on public colleges and universities in Texas, Arkansas, Oklahoma, Missouri, and Kansas. Historically, the foundation prefers to support institutions that are a source of employees for the Southwestern Bell Companies and programs that build both enrollment and quality of education as well as those that develop quality teaching practices or recognize outstanding teachers. The foundation has also shown an interest in the development of quality economic education and programs aimed at retraining the economically displaced, the elderly, and/or the disadvantaged.

158
State Farm Companies Foundation
One State Farm Plaza
Bloomington, IL   61710

Areas of Interest

Program Description: To support civic affairs; health and human services; social services; United Way; and education, particularly insurance education, business education, and minority education.
Assistance Types: Professorships, fellowships, scholarship funds, employee-related scholarships, matching gifts, building funds, capital campaigns

Eligibility

Restrictions: Funds largely committed; no direct appeals accepted; no grants to individuals, except for employee-related scholarships, or to fraternal organizations or religious organizations for religious purposes. No support for dinners, special events, goodwill advertising, conferences, or seminars. Giving primarily in Bloomington, Illinois, and 27 regional sites.

Personnel

Officers: Edward B. Rust Jr., Chair, President, and Treas.; Laura P. Sullivan, VP, Secy., and Director; John Coffey, VP, Programs; Dave Polzin, Asst. VP, Programs; Vince Trevino, Asst. Secy.; Donna Vincent, Asst. Secy.; Roger Joslin, Asst. Treas.
Trustees/Directors: Charles O. Galvin, Robert Eckley,
Staff: Two full-time professional, two full-time support, one part-time support

Financial Profile

Assets: In 1993, $2,632,855
High Grant: $1,000,000
Low Grant: $13
Ave. Grant: $500-$15,000
Total Grants: 396 grants totaling $5,066,043, plus $1,470,550 for employee matching gifts and $230,000 for grants to individuals
High Grant Higher Ed.: $1,000,000
Low Grant Higher Ed.: $250
Ave. Grant Higher Ed.: $500-$15,000
Total Grants Higher Ed.: In 1992, approximately 165 for $2,976,079, plus $1,304,777 in matching gifts

Application Process

Contact: Dave Polzin, Asst. VP, Programs, (309) 766-2161
Deadline: December 31 for scholarships; February 15 for fellowships; March 31 for doctoral program; three weeks before quarterly board meetings for other grants
Board Meeting: March, June, September, and December
Publications: Informational brochure, application guidelines
Guidelines: Specific application form required for scholarship programs, fellowship program, doctoral program, and matching gift program.

Sample Grants

Hunter College of the City University of New York in New York City received $3,000 for an exceptional student fellowship.
University of Virginia School of Law in Charlottesville received $3,000 for an exceptional student fellowship.
Minnesota Private College Fund in Saint Paul received $5,000.
University of Georgia in Athens received $3,000.
University of Michigan in Ann Arbor received $25,000 for a Risk Management Professorship.
Illinois Wesleyan University Center for Natural Science Learning and Research in Bloomington received $1,000,000.
National Merit Scholarship Corporation in Evanston, Illinois, received $663,796.
Willamette University in Salem, Oregon, received $10,000 for Minority Opportunity scholarships.
American Indian College Fund in New York City received $10,000 for Native American scholarships.

National Hispanic Scholarship Fund in San Francisco, California, received $22,000 for scholarships for Hispanic college students.

Comments/Analysis

In the past, support for higher education accounted for approximately 74 percent of all the grant dollars distributed by the foundation. Sixty-one percent of support to higher education was given through the foundation's Doctoral Dissertation Award Program to stimulate research and the development of new knowledge in the insurance industry and through its various scholarship programs including an achievement scholarship program, a foundation scholarship program, a Hispanic scholarship program, the National Merit Scholarship Program, and a Native American scholarship program. Another 30 percent of the higher education funds was distributed through the foundation's employee matching gift program to four-year colleges, universities, and graduate schools. Five percent was given to colleges and universities for insurance education, while 4 percent was awarded through the foundation's Exceptional Student Fellowship Program for college juniors and seniors majoring in business-related studies to aid and encourage their preparation for leadership roles in industry and society.

159
Tektronix Foundation
PO Box 1000
Wilsonville, OR   97070-1000

Areas of Interest

Program Description: To support education, community funds, social services, health, and the arts. Specific areas of interest in education include the physical sciences and engineering.
Assistance Types: Employee matching gifts, employee-related scholarships, fellowships, equipment, building, operating budgets, continuing support, annual campaigns, seed money

Eligibility

Restrictions: Giving mainly in Oregon. No loans. No grants for emergency funds, endowments, demonstration projects, deficit financing, research, publications, or conferences. No matching or challenge grants, and no grants to individuals except for employee-related scholarships.

Personnel

Officers: Jean Vollum, Chair and Trustee; Charles H. Frost, Vice-Chair and Trustee; William Spivey, Secy.; Jill Kirk, Exec. Director
Trustees/Directors: Paul Bragdon, Richard S. Hill, William D. Walker
Staff: One part-time professional, one part-time support

Financial Profile

Assets: In 1992, $1,840,477
High Grant: $100,000
Low Grant: $250
Ave. Grant: $10,000-$25,000
Total Grants: 59 grants totaling $1,374,970

Application Process

Contact: Jill Kirk, Exec. Director, (503) 627-7084
Deadline: None
Board Meeting: February, May, August, and November
Processing Time: Following board meeting
Guidelines: An application form is not required. Initial approach should be made by letter. Proposals should include a copy of the applicant organization's IRS determination letter; list of the organization's board of directors, trustees, officers, and other key people; and copy of organizational budget and project budget.

Sample Grants

Oregon Independent College Foundation in Portland, Oregon, received $75,000.
Oregon State University in Corvallis received six grants totaling $290,415 and including two $100,000 grants.
Portland Community College in Portland, Oregon, received $12,000.
Portland State University in Portland, Oregon, received a $253,930 grant and a $50,000 grant.
Reed College in Portland, Oregon, received $120,000.
University of Portland in Portland, Oregon, received $27,334.

Comments/Analysis

Historically, education, excluding employee matching gifts, has received 35 percent of the grant dollars distributed by the foundation. Of the awards to education, higher education receives approximately 80 percent. Higher education grants are distributed to colleges and universities in Oregon only, with an emphasis in the Portland and Corvallis areas.

160
Texaco Foundation
2000 Westchester Avenue
White Plains, NY   10650

Areas of Interest

Program Description: To support arts and culture, education, higher education, social services, civic affairs, health and hospitals, environment, public policy, and youth. Specific areas of interest in education include engineering; computer science; geology; accounting; business; schools of public health; precollege and education reform in math, science, and technology; the environment; minority education; and educational opportunities for the disabled.

Assistance Types: Employee matching gifts, fellowships, research, employee-related scholarships, special project, scholarship funds

Eligibility

Restrictions: No support for individuals except for employee-related scholarships; religious organizations; private foundations; or fraternal, social, or veterans organizations. No grants for social functions, commemorative journals, meetings, political activities, endowments, general operating support, or capital funds, except to selected private nonprofit hospitals. Giving mainly to organizations located in areas of company operations and to some national organizations.

Personnel

Officers: J. Brademas, Chair and Director; Carl B. Davidson, President and Director; Maria Mike-Mayer, Secy.; Robert W. Ulrich, Treas.; George Eaton, Comptroller
Staff: Five

Financial Profile

Assets: In 1993, $14,910,571
High Grant: $500,000
Low Grant: $500
Ave. Grant: $5,000-$18,000
Total Grants: 617 grants totaling $10,024,979, plus $1,806,420 in employee matching gifts

Application Process

Contact: Maria Mike-Mayer, Secy., (914) 253-4150
Deadline: None
Board Meeting: March and September
Processing Time: Two months
Publications: Annual report including application guidelines
Guidelines: A formal application form is not required. Submit a proposal including the following: brief history of organization and description of its mission; detailed description of project, amount of request, and project budget; populations served by project and results expected; how results will be evaluated; timetable for implementation and evaluation of project; qualifications of project personnel; list of additional sources and amount of support; copy of IRS determination letter; copy of organization's budget; copy of annual report, audited financial statement, or 990; and list of organization's board of directors, trustees, officers, and other key people.

Sample Grants

Louisiana State University College of Engineering in Baton Rouge received $200,000.
Stanford University Graduate School of Business in Stanford, California, received $15,000.
Texaco Foundation Scholarship Program in White Plains, New York, received $880,743.

University of Pittsburgh College of Engineering in Pittsburgh, Pennsylvania, received $50,000.

University of Texas School of Public Health in Houston received $10,000.

Foundation for Management Education in Central America in Washington, DC, received $10,000.

Rogers State College in Claremore, Oklahoma, received $45,000.

University of Hawaii School of Public Health in Honolulu, Hawaii, received $15,000.

University of California School of Engineering and Applied Sciences in Los Angeles, California, received $10,500.

The United Negro College Fund in New York City received two grants totaling $240,000.

Comments/Analysis

In the past, the foundation distributed 17 percent of its dollars within its education category and another 11 percent for employee matching gifts to colleges, universities, and professional or graduate schools located in the United States. Forty percent of the foundation's education funds were awarded for scholarships and student services, 31 percent for graduate and professional programs, 16 percent for grants under $10,000, and 13 percent for other. The foundation is a strong supporter of scholarships for children of employees, and the Texaco Foundation Scholarship Program is generally the recipient of the foundation's high award each year.

161
TRW Foundation
1900 Richmond Road
Cleveland, OH   44124

Areas of Interest

Program Description: To support higher education, community funds, hospitals, welfare, youth, civic affairs, and culture. Other areas of interest include early childhood, elementary, and secondary education; the disadvantaged; and volunteerism. Specific areas of interest in higher education include business administration, engineering, minority education, science and technology, and computer science.

Assistance Types: Employee matching gifts, scholarships, fellowships, faculty assistanceships, research, employee-related scholarships, minority scholarships, faculty/staff development, program development

Eligibility

Restrictions: The foundation will not consider personal requests or requests from groups with unusually high fund-raising or administrative expenses or from fraternal, political, labor, or religious organizations; no grants to medical research organizations or private elementary or secondary schools; generally no support for endowments. Preference given to organizations with projects or programs in areas having a significant number of TRW employees and other significant TRW presence. Grants to higher education

awarded to colleges, universities, and professional associations in communities throughout 17 states, with an emphasis on Berkeley, Los Angeles, Orange, San Bernardino, San Diego, and Sunnyvale, California; and Cleveland, Ohio.

Personnel

Officers: H.V. Knicley, President and Trustee; R.M. Hamje, VP and Trustee; C.G. Miller, VP and Controller; J. Powers, VP; A.F. Senger, VP; W.A. Warren, VP; R.P. Vargo, VP and Treas.;. J.M. Schmidt, Asst. Secy.; E.L. Bennardo, Asst. Treas

Trustees/Directors: M.A. Coyle, E.D. Dunford, J.T. Gorman, P.S. Hellman

Staff: None

Financial Profile

Assets: In 1993, $26,642,281
High Grant: $328,000
Low Grant: $1,000
Ave. Grant: $5,000-$25,000
Total Grants: $6,440,906
High Grant Higher Ed.: $200,000
Low Grant Higher Ed.: $1,000
Ave. Grant Higher Ed.: $1,000-$25,000
Total Grants Higher Ed.: 95 grants totaling $1,734,500, plus $516,810 in matching gifts

Application Process

Contact: Alan F. Senger, VP, (216) 291-7160 or Laura L. Johnson, Contributions Manager, (216) 291-7166

Deadline: September 1 for organizations already receiving support from the foundation; grant requests from others accepted and reviewed throughout the year although the foundation's calendar budget year cycle begins in September of each year

Board Meeting: Board meets in December

Processing Time: 30 to 90 days

Guidelines: Colleges and universities should check with the foundation office to determine the potential level of interest before submitting a proposal. Approach should then be made by a brief letter. If the foundation is interested, additional documentation will be requested. However, the following information should be included in the original request: brief description of organization (history, mission, activities); purpose for which grant is requested with particular emphasis on the needs of the community, specific activities to meet those defined needs, time-lines, and plan for measurement and evaluation of results; itemized project/program budget; list of committed financial supporters of project; and how publicity for the project/program will be developed. If there is foundation interest in the project/program the following materials will also be required: evidence of the organization's IRS status as a nonprofit 501(c)3 organization, copy of most recent income tax return of organization exempt from income tax, and a list of the board of directors and officers and their affiliations.

Sample Grants

University of California at Berkeley received $75,000.

Cayuga County Community College Foundation in Auburn, New York, received $5,000.

John Carroll University in Cleveland, Ohio, received two grants for $8,000 each.

Ohio Foundation of Independent Colleges in Columbus received $25,000.

Weber State University in Ogden, Utah, was awarded $7,000.

California State University Dominguez Hills in Carson, California, received two grants: one for $100,000 and one for $12,500.

Purdue University in Lafayette, Indiana, received $30,000.

University of Michigan Graduate School of Business Administration in Ann Arbor was awarded $25,000.

George Mason University in Fairfax, Virginia, was awarded $37,500.

Cleveland Hispanic Scholarship Fund in Ohio received $3,500.

Comments/Analysis

The TRW Foundation makes grants in six categories: education; arts and culture; health, welfare, and youth; United Funds; hospitals; and national and international programs. In education, giving is focused on selected educational institutions with engineering, technical science, and/or business administration programs. In 1993, higher education received approximately 35 percent of the foundation's total contributions, gifts, and grants paid. Of the 95 grants awarded to higher education institutions and organizations, 79 percent was given within one of TRW's special program categories: 20 grants for Education Support Review; nine for TRW Augmentation Fellowships; six for TRW Faculty Assistanceships; 35 for Minority Scholars; and five for TRW Presidential Young Investigator Awards. TRW Foundation's second largest grant, $200,000, was given to CalTech in Pasadena, California, which also received another grant for $100,000. In general, the foundation was a strong supporter of colleges and universities in California and Ohio in 1993.

162
US WEST Foundation
7800 E Orchard Road, Suite 300
Englewood, CO   80111

Areas of Interest

Program Description: To support early childhood, elementary, secondary, and higher education; health and human services; rural and community development; culture; disadvantaged; leadership development; minorities; homeless; disadvantaged; Native Americans; youth; and AIDS.

Assistance Types: Operating budgets, general purposes, employee matching gifts, special projects, continuing support, matching funds, seed money, technical assistance

Eligibility

Restrictions: No grants for endowments, deficit financing, scholarships, athletic funds, trips, tours, goodwill advertising, or general operating budgets of United Way-supported organizations or pub-

lic educational institutions. No support for individuals, international organizations, religious organizations, national health agencies, grantmaking foundations, or school or fraternal organizations. Giving mainly in states served by US WEST calling areas, including Arizona, Colorado, Idaho, Minnesota, North Dakota, Nebraska, New Mexico, South Dakota, Oregon, Utah, Washington, and Wyoming.

Personnel

Officers: Richard D. McCormick, President and Director; Judith A. Servoss, VP and Director; Leon Marks, Secy.; James M. Osterhoff, Treas. and Director; Jane Prancan, Exec. Director and Treas.
Trustees/Directors: Gary A. Ames, Marsha Congdon, Joanne R. Crosson, Ron James, James Smith, Solomon Trujillo, Bud Wonsiewicz
Staff: Six full-time professional

Financial Profile

Assets: In 1993, $24,801,558
Ave. Grant: $5,000-$30,000
Total Grants: $23,673,008

Application Process

Contact: Janet Kalicki, Grants Manager, (303) 793-6648
Deadline: None
Board Meeting: February, May, August, and November
Processing Time: Most funds disbursed during fourth quarter each year
Publications: Multiyear report, newsletter
Guidelines: Application form is not required. Prospective applicants should contact their local US WEST Communications Public Relations Office for information on the foundation's general grants program. Information on the foundation's special initiatives is contained in the foundation's annual report. All applicants are notified of the foundation's decision.

Sample Grants

Saint Cloud State University in Saint Cloud, Minnesota, received two $10,000 grants for minority mentoring and recruitment.

Oregon Independent College Foundation in Portland, Oregon, received $80,000 for independent college minority scholarships.

Seattle Central Community College Foundation in Seattle, Washington, received $10,000 for general operating support.

University of Utah in Salt Lake City received $15,000 for program support.

San Juan College in Farmington, New Mexico, received $10,000 for its Possible Dream program.

Nebraska Independent College Foundation in Omaha, Nebraska, received $10,000 to lower tuition costs and operating expenses at independent colleges.

Comments/Analysis

The foundation sponsors an educational initiative program, a general grants program in education, and an outstanding teacher program. The educational initiative is designed to strengthen the education system by building coalitions, enhancing the teaching profession, building on existing strengths of institutions of higher education, expanding access to information and knowledge, and encouraging early childhood education by involving parents as first teachers. The general grant program in education favors projects that address the special needs of minority students, promote literacy, and help troubled youth develop skills to gain meaningful employment. The outstanding teacher program is designed to honor excellence in teaching at the elementary and secondary levels. Over 72 percent of the grants distributed to education in the past were less than $10,000. Higher education, however, received 53 grants of over $10,000, which equated to approximately 9 percent of the total grant dollars distributed by the foundation.

163

USX Foundation, Inc.
600 Grant Street
Pittsburgh, PA   15219-4776

Areas of Interest

Program Description: To support education; health and human services; and public, cultural, and scientific affairs. Areas of interest in higher education include marketing; business; accounting; minority programs; petroleum, mechanical, and electrical engineering; mineral science and technology; geology and geological science; law and paralegal programs; industrial relations; safety studies; and energy policy.
Assistance Types: Capital, special projects, operating expenses, renovation, minority scholarships, scholarship programs, equipment, salary supplements, professorships, endowments, research, matching gifts, employee-related scholarships

Eligibility

Restrictions: Support limited to organizations within the United States with preference to those in USX Corporation's operating areas. No grants to individuals or to religious organizations for religious purposes. No support for conferences, seminars, or symposia; travel; publication of papers, books, or magazines; or production of films, videotapes, or other audio-visual materials.

Personnel

Officers: C.A. Corey, Chair, Board of Trustees; P.B. Mulloney, President and Trustee; R.M. Hernandez, CFO; G.R. Haggerty, VP and Treas.; L.B. Jones, VP and Comptroller; G.A. Glynn, VP, Investments; J.L. Hamilton III, General Manager; D.D. Sandman, General Counsel, Secy., and Trustee; J.T. Mills, Tax Counsel; J.H. Fix, Asst. Comptroller; J.D. Richmond, Asst. Treas.; D.A. Lynch,

Asst. Secy.; J.A. Hammerschmidt, Asst. Secy.; M.B. Cassidy, Asst. Secy.
Trustees/Directors: V. G. Beghini, T.J. Usher, L. A. Valli
Staff: Two full-time professionals, two full-time support

Financial Profile

Assets: For fiscal year ending November, 1993, $6,346,806
High Grant: $350,000
Low Grant: $500 (excluding matching gifts)
Ave. Grant: $1,000-$25,000
Total Grants: $6,362,625
High Grant Higher Ed.: $300,000
Low Grant Higher Ed.: $1,000
Ave. Grant Higher Ed.: $1,000-$5,000
Total Grants Higher Ed.: Approximately 100 grants totaling $1,085,500, plus $1,008,490 in matching gifts

Application Process

Contact: James L. Hamilton III, General Manager, (412) 433-5237
Deadline: January 15, public, cultural, scientific affairs; April 15, education; July 15, health and human services
Board Meeting: Late April, late June, late October
Processing Time: Notification made following board meetings
Publications: Annual report, including application guidelines
Guidelines: Application form is not required. Submit a one- to two-page letter that describes the organization's mission and need, plus the following support documentation: a copy of IRS certification of tax-exempt status; copy of organization's most current budget and its most recent audited financial report; a full description of the project and its goals; the estimated cost of the project, the amount requested from USX, and an explanation of the need for funds in relation to the total requirements of the project and available resources; statement of sources in hand (if any) and the amount of committed support; statement of sources of anticipated aid; list of the organization's chief executives and members of the board of directors/trustees; signature of an authorized executive; and signed statement of approval by the chief executive of the parent organization if the application originates in a subdivision of such entity. Organizations seeking ongoing support must reapply each year in accordance with the deadlines. Requests for personal interviews and site visits are accommodated as foundation staff schedules permit.

Sample Grants

National Association of College and University Business Officers in Washington, DC, received $60,000 for a Cost Reduction Incentive Award.
Louisiana State University in Baton Rouge received $20,000 toward a professorship in energy policy.
University of Cincinnati College of Law in Ohio received $200,000 for an endowment.
University of Texas in Austin received $3,000 for minority scholarships for the minority engineering program, $11,000 for operating expenses for the engineering department, $2,000 for operating expenses in the law department, $5,000 in operating expenses for the Department of Geological Sci-

ences, $1,000 for the Pi Sigma Pi-Minority Engineering Association, $3,000 for the engineering department's scholarship program, and $5,000 for the Department of Geological Sciences' scholarship program.

Northwestern University's Department of Transportation in Evanston, Illinois, received $5,000 for operating expenses.

University of Pittsburgh Graduate School of Business in Pennsylvania received $300,000 for capital support.

Comments/Analysis

Higher education received approximately 33 percent of the funds distributed by the foundation in the fiscal year ending November, 1993. Of the funds awarded to higher education, 48 percent was given for employee matching gifts, 27 percent for capital support, 10 percent for endowments, 5 percent for operating support, 4 percent for scholarships and minority scholarships, 3 percent for special projects, and the remaining for professorships, salary supplements, equipment, and renovation. The greatest number of grants to colleges and universities was given in the area of operating support, with 42 awards made ranging $1,000-$30,000. The vast majority of these operating grants were for $1,000 and $2,000. Grants to higher education were geographically concentrated in Pittsburgh, Pennsylvania, and the following states: Indiana, Ohio, Texas, Colorado, Louisiana, Michigan, West Virginia, Kentucky, Virginia, North Carolina, Oklahoma, and Wyoming.

164
Wachovia Foundation, Inc.
c/o Wachovia Bank & Trust Company, NA
PO Box 3099
Winston-Salem, NC   27150-0001

Areas of Interest

Program Description: To support education, higher education, community development, community funds, libraries, crime and law enforcement, social services, child welfare, recreation, humanities, historic preservation, media and communications, performing arts, ecology, handicapped, health and hospitals, and substance abuse prevention.
Assistance Types: Renovation, building, capital campaigns, special projects, endowments, research, operating budgets, annual campaigns

Eligibility

Restrictions: No grants to individuals

Personnel

Officers: John G. Medlin Jr., Chair; L.M. Baker Jr., President; Anthony L. Furr, VP; Kenneth W. McAllister, Secy.; Robert S. McCoy, Treas.
Staff: None

Financial Profile

Assets: In 1993, $10,342,411
Ave. Grant: $2,000-$20,000
Total Grants: 366 grants totaling $4,602,590

Application Process

Contact: L.M. Baker Jr., President
Deadline: None
Board Meeting: Monthly
Guidelines: Prospective applicants should contact their local bank office to obtain grant application guidelines.

Sample Grants

Independent College Fund of North Carolina in Winston-Salem received $45,000.

North Carolina Community Colleges Foundation in Raleigh received $10,000.

University of North Carolina in Chapel Hill received $1,000,000.

A & T University Foundation in Greensboro, North Carolina, received $50,000.

Elon College in Elon College, North Carolina, received $125,000.

Elizabeth City State University in Elizabeth City, North Carolina, received $75,000.

Rowan-Cabarrus Community College Foundation in Salisbury, North Carolina, received $10,000.

Tulane Education Fund in New Orleans, Louisiana, received $15,000.

Comments/Analysis

Historically, education receives approximately 30 percent of the grant dollars paid by the foundation annually. The vast majority of grants to higher education are awarded to colleges and universities in North Carolina.

165
Warner-Lambert Charitable Foundation
201 Tabor Road
Morris Plains, NJ   07950

Areas of Interest

Program Description: To support higher education, community funds, hospitals, civil rights, social welfare, and youth. Specific areas of interest in higher education include medical research, medical education, and pharmacology.
Assistance Types: Professorships, medical research, equipment, annual campaigns, building, continuing support, operating budgets, emergency funds, employee matching gifts

Eligibility

Restrictions: No grants for endowments, demonstration projects, conferences or research other than medical research. No loans. No grants to individuals. Giving mainly in areas of company operations.

Personnel

Officers: Richard W. Keelty, Chair and Director; Ronald E. Zier, President and Director; Stanley D. Grubman, First VP; Raymond M. Fino, Second VP and Director; Lodewijk J.R. deVink, Third VP and Director; Ernest J. Larini, Fourth VP and Director; Evelyn Self, Secy.-Treas.
Staff: One full-time professional, one part-time professional, one part-time support

Financial Profile

High Grant: $500,000
Ave. Grant: $5,000-$50,000
Total Grants: 165 grants totaling $5,624,534

Application Process

Contact: Richard Keelty, Chair, (201) 540-3652
Deadline: Submit proposal between July and September
Board Meeting: Quarterly
Guidelines: A formal application form is not required. Submit a letter proposal and include a detailed description of the project and the amount of funding requested.

Sample Grants

American Academy of Family Physicians in Kansas City, Missouri, received $30,000 for teacher development awards.
Consortium for Graduate Students in Management in Saint Louis, Missouri, received $30,000.
County College of Morris in Randolph, New Jersey, received $45,000.
Duke University in Durham, North Carolina, received $12,500 for a Samuel J. Katz Professorship.
Rutgers University Graduate School of Management in Newark, New Jersey, received $10,000.
United Negro College Fund in New York City received $200,000.
University of Washington School of Medicine in Seattle received $60,000.
Woodrow Wilson National Fellowship Foundation in Princeton, New Jersey, received $10,000.
Oakland University in Rochester, Michigan, received $10,000.
University of Nebraska College of Pharmacy in Omaha received $100,000.
Seton Hall University in South Orange, New Jersey, received $25,000 for capital fund and $200,000 for a Peter Rodino Chair at its Law School.
Harvard University Medical School in Cambridge, Massachusetts, received $250,000.

Comments/Analysis

A priority area of funding is schools of pharmacy. In the past, grants ranging $10,000-$100,000 were awarded to schools and colleges of pharmacy at the University of Texas, University of Southern California, University of Nebraska, University of Minnesota, University of Michigan, University of Maryland, and the Philadelphia College of Pharmacy and Science. Higher education and graduate and professional education received approximately 41 percent of the grant dollars distributed by the foundation. Colleges and universities were the foundation's top recipients by dollars and also by number of grants. The majority of the foundation's funding for grants of $10,000 or more was for program support including professorships, faculty and staff development, and program development; followed by capital support and fellowship funds.

166
Westinghouse Foundation
c/o Westinghouse Electric Corporation
11 Stanwix Street
Pittsburgh, PA   15222-1384

Areas of Interest

Program Description: To support civic and social programs, culture and the arts, higher education, health and human services, youth and recreation, and United Way. Specific areas of interest include economic development, environment, government, public policy, disadvantaged, elderly, engineering, applied science, business, curriculum development, minority education, and the handicapped.
Assistance Types: Employee matching gifts, employee-related scholarships, in-kind gifts, matching funds, special projects, capital campaigns, seed money, and operating budgets.

Eligibility

Restrictions: No grants for hospitals, land acquisition, equipment, deficit financing, conferences, research, emergency funds, endowments, or fellowships. No scholarships or grants to individuals, except employee-related scholarships. No grants to religious organizations or for specific health campaigns. Giving mainly in areas of company operation.

Personnel

Officers: F.W. Hill, Chair and Trustee; G.M. Clark, President; G.R. Clark, Acting Treas.; C.L. Kubelick, Secy.
Trustees/Directors: L.W. Briskman, T.P. Costello, W.H. Hollinshead, R.A. Linder, J.S. Moore
Staff: Three full-time professional, three full-time support

Financial Profile

Assets: In 1993, $2,767,887
High Grant: $345,000

Low Grant: $1,0500
Ave. Grant: $1,000-$50,000
Total Grants: 75 grants totaling $5,638, plus $327,000 for grants to individuals and $335,263 for employee matching gifts

Application Process

Contact: G.R. Clark, Director and Acting Treas., (412) 642-5524
Deadline: None
Board Meeting: March, June, September, and December
Processing Time: Two months
Publications: Annual report, including application guidelines
Guidelines: Application form is not required. Submit proposal with description of project and population to be served, amount requested, copy of IRS determination letter, project budget, and list of board members and key people. The foundation grants interviews with prospective grantees when appropriate.

Sample Grants

Pennsylvania State University in University Park received $100,000.
University of Pittsburgh in Pennsylvania received $185,000.
South Carolina State College in Orangeburg received $100,000.
Bradley University in Peoria, Illinois, received $20,000.
Michigan Technological University in Houghton received $30,000.
Wheeling Jesuit College in Wheeling, West Virginia, received $50,000.
Southeastern Consortium for Minorities in Engineering in Atlanta, Georgia, received $20,000.

Comments/Analysis

Historically, private institutions of higher education are the foundation's top recipients with emphasis placed on engineering, applied science, and business programs. Foundation grants have also been made to private and public education for innovative curriculum and faculty development; projects aimed at enhancing teaching and learning; and programs striving to meet the educational needs of the young, older persons, gifted, handicapped, minorities, and women. The foundation also supports an employee matching gifts program on a one-to-one basis for educational institutions with a maximum contribution of $4,000 and a scholarship program for the children of Westinghouse employees, with scholarships ranging $3,000-$12,000.

167
Weyerhaeuser Company Foundation
CHIF 31
Tacoma, WA   98477

Areas of Interest

Program Description: To improve the quality of life where Weyerhaeuser Company has a major presence and to increase public understanding of the issues that intersect society's needs and the interests of the forest products industry. Areas of interest include environment, forest resources, community development, minority education, elementary and higher education, educational research, rural development, social services, the arts, industry and technology, and industrial relations.

Assistance Types: General purposes, capital campaigns, employee matching gifts, employee-related scholarships, technical assistance, special projects, research, operating budgets, renovation, lectureships, seminars and conferences, publications, land acquisition, equipment, building, emergency funds, seed money

Eligibility

Restrictions: No support for individuals, religious organizations for sacramental or theological functions, political or legislative campaigns, ticket purchases or tables at fund-raising events, or organizations that discriminate in any way. No grants for deficit financing, operating budgets for United Way-supported organizations, indirect costs, conferences outside of the forest products industry, endowments, or memorials. Giving primarily to areas of company operations, especially western Washington, western Oregon, southeastern Oklahoma, and Alabama, Arkansas, Mississippi, and North Carolina. Giving to national organizations in fields related to the forest products industry. Multiple year grants are discouraged.

Personnel

Officers: Charles W. Bingham, Chair and Trustee; Mary Steward Hall, President and Trustee; Elizabeth A. Crossman, VP; Connie A. Bergeron, Secy.; Karen L. Veiterhans, Asst. Secy.; Sandy D. McDade, Asst. Secy. for Legal Affairs; David R. Edwards, Treas.; Linda L. Terrien, Asst. Treas.; Kenneth J. Stancato, Controller; Mary L. Cabral, Asst. Controller
Trustees/Directors: John W. Creighton Jr., Fred R. Fosmire, Steven R. Hill, Norman E. Johnson, C. Stephen Lewis, W. Howarth Meadowcroft, Gence C. Meyer, William C. Stivers, John H. Waechter, George H. Weyerhaeuser, Robert B. Wilson
Staff: None

Financial Profile

Assets: In 1993, $14,356,779
High Grant: $215,617
Low Grant: $1,000
Ave. Grant: $5,000-$10,000
Total Grants: 649 grants totaling $5,454,426, plus $78,091 for employee matching gifts
High Grant Higher Ed.: $215,617
Low Grant Higher Ed.: $1,000
Ave. Grant Higher Ed.: $1,000-$15,000
Total Grants Higher Ed.: In 1992, approximately 83 grants totaling $968,012, plus $74,952 in matching gifts

Application Process

Contact: Elizabeth A. Crossman, VP, (206) 924-3159

Deadline: None; however the foundation operates on a calendar year, so requests submitted in the fall may not be considered until budgets are established the following year.
Board Meeting: January and mid-year
Processing Time: 60 to 120 days
Publications: Biennial report including application guidelines
Guidelines: Contact the foundation by phone or letter to request copies of guidelines and current priorities in specific geographical or program areas prior to submitting a request for funding. To apply, obtain an application form from the foundation or submit a brief letter that includes an introduction of program and sponsoring organization; explanation of how the project is consistent with the foundation's stated mission, priorities, and geographical interests; evidence of how the project addresses a community need; amount requested and additional funding sources, including future support; demonstration of leadership team's management competency; and verification of IRS tax exempt status.

Sample Grants

National Merit Scholarship Corporation in Washington, DC, received $215,617.

Citizens' Scholarship Foundation of America in Saint Peter, Minnesota, received three grants totaling $126,785.

Michigan State University School of Labor and Industrial Relations in East Lansing received $3,150.

University of Washington in Seattle received 14 grants totaling $201,500; recipients included the College of Forest Resources, Office of Minority Affairs, College of Engineering, School of Business Administration, University of Washington Press, Department of Political Science, Graduate School of Public Affairs, and the Institute for Public Policy and Management.

Western Kentucky University received four grants: $1,000 for its libraries, $5,000 for its Center for Industry and Technology, $1,000 for WKYU-TV, and $1,000 for WKYU-FM.

North Carolina State University in Raleigh received $10,000 for its College of Textiles and $5,000 for its College of Forest Resources.

Miami University Pulp and Paper Foundation in Oxford, Ohio, received $7,500.

Mississippi State University in Mississippi State received $5,000 for their Writing/Thinking Project and $5,000 for student financial aid.

Comments/Analysis

In the past, higher education received approximately 20 percent of the dollars distributed by the foundation. Much of these funds were distributed to preselected universities for fellowships, chairs, equipment, and capital. A substantial amount of support to higher education was also provided through employee-related scholarships administered by the Citizens' Scholarship Foundation of America and the National Merit Scholarship Corporation. In addition, several two-year colleges in Weyerhaeuser communities received grants for curriculum improvement and scholarships primarily in disciplines related to the forest products industry.

168
Whirlpool Foundation
400 Riverview Drive, Suite 410
Benton Harbor, MI   49022

Areas of Interest

Program Description: Primarily to support life-long learning, cultural diversity, contemporary family life, international education, international management, and technical education
Assistance Types: Employee-related scholarships and matching gifts, matching funds, operating budgets, equipment, research, scholarship funds, special projects, continuing support, program development, building and renovation, fellowship funds

Eligibility

Restrictions: No loans; no grants to individuals, except employee-related scholarships, or for endowment funds. Giving for higher education primarily limited to cities and states of company operations including Clyde, Findlay, Greenville, and Marion, Ohio; Evansville, Indiana; Fort Smith, Arkansas; Lavergne, Tennessee; Oxford, Mississippi; and Columbia, South Carolina

Personnel

Officers: James R. Samartini, Chair and Trustee; Bruce K. Berger, President and Trustee; Colleen D. Keast, Exec. Director; Bradley J. Bell, Treas.
Trustees/Directors: J.C. Anderson, Charles P. Miller, Jay P. Van Den Berg, Gloria A. Zamora
Staff: Two full-time professional, one full-time support

Financial Profile

Assets: In 1993, $20,027,479
High Grant: $1,030,385
Low Grant: $1,000
Ave. Grant: $1,000-$25,000
Total Grants: $4,602,228
High Grant Higher Ed.: $206,071
Low Grant Higher Ed.: $1,000 (not including matching gifts)
Ave. Grant Higher Ed.: $13,334
Total Grants Higher Ed.: 31 grants for $880,538, plus $297,000 for employee-related scholarships and $176,818 in employee matching gifts

Application Process

Contact: Colleen D. Keast, Exec. Director, (616) 923-4934
Deadline: January 3, April 1, July 1, October 1
Board Meeting: Board meets quarterly
Guidelines: Submit letter plus prescribed application form. Foundation acknowledges receipt of application and grants interviews with applicants.

Sample Grants

American Graduate School of International Management in Glendale, Arizona, received $5,000.

Indiana University Foundation in Bloomington received $42,000.

Marion Technical College Development Fund in Marion, Ohio, received $3,000.

Westark Community College Foundation in Fort Smith, Arkansas, received $21,700.

International School of Stuttgart in Germany received $20,000.

Lake Michigan College Educational Fund in Benton Harbor, Michigan, received $206,071.

University of Mississippi in University received $4,000.

City University in Bellevue, Washington, received $20,000.

Michigan Tech Fund in Houghton, Michigan, received $21,500.

Comments/Analysis

In 1993, this company-sponsored foundation awarded grants in the following categories: contemporary family life, cultural diversity, life-long learning, education, health and human services, arts and culture, civic and community, matching gifts, student scholarships, United Way, and other. Grants to the education category accounted for approximately 20 percent of the foundation's total contributions, gifts, and grants paid. Of the 56 grants within this category approximately one-half went to institutions of higher education and higher education-related associations for a total of $645,021. Higher education grants within this category ranged from $2,000 to $206,071 and were distributed within the states of Arizona, Michigan, Ohio, Indiana, Illinois, Missouri, Arkansas, and Tennessee. Two higher education grants were awarded to international management programs in Germany and in France. Six grants to colleges and universities totaling $115,834 were also awarded in the category of life-long learning with the largest going to the University of Notre Dame for $50,000. A $119,683 grant was given to Andrew University in Berrien Springs, Michigan, under the subject area of cultural diversity. Besides higher education grants falling within these categories, $297,000 was given in individual scholarship awards through colleges and universities to children of company employees and $176,818 in an employee matching gifts program to junior and community colleges, four-year colleges and universities, and graduate and professional schools. Contributions to higher education, including matching gifts and Whirlpool Sons and Daughters Scholarships, accounted for approximately 30 percent of all contributions.

169
Xerox Foundation
PO Box 1600
Stamford, CT 06904

Areas of Interest

Program Description: To support early childhood, secondary, and higher education; social services; civic affairs; culture; United Way; community funds; rural development; drug abuse prevention; public policy; international affairs; and foreign policy. The foundation also supports worldwide interests in Southern Africa, Asia, Canada, Latin America, the Caribbean, and the Middle East, and in leprosy. Specific areas of interest in higher education include minority and disadvantaged education; preparing students for careers in business, government, and education; and science and technology.

Assistance Types: Scholarship funds, fellowships, professorships, internships, exchange programs, research, employee-related scholarships, employee matching gifts, operating budgets, general purposes, annual campaigns, seed money, emergency funds, conferences and seminars, program-related investments, consulting services, publications

Eligibility

Restrictions: No support for individuals, community colleges, capital funds, endowments, United Way-supported organizations, religious groups, political organizations or candidates, or government agencies. No donations of machines or related services. No loans. Giving on both a national and international basis.

Personnel

Officers: Robert H. Gudger, VP; Martin S. Wagner, Secy.; Alan Z. Senter, Treas.

Trustees/Directors: Paul A. Allaire, David T. Kearns, Stuart B. Ross

Staff: One full-time professional, four full-time support

Financial Profile

High Grant: In 1992, $500,000
Low Grant: $900
Ave. Grant: $1,000-$10,000
Total Grants: 31 grants totaling $901,600

Application Process

Contact: Robert H. Gudger, VP, (203) 968-3306
Deadline: None
Board Meeting: Usually in December and as required
Processing Time: Three months
Publications: Application guidelines
Guidelines: An application form is not required. A brief letter proposal should be submitted including a description of the project and the amount of funding requested, an explanation of how the results will be evaluated, a copy of the project budget, a list of any additional sources and amounts, and a copy of the IRS determination letter.

Sample Grants

Rochester Institute of Technology in Rochester, New York, received three grants totaling $305,820 and ranging from $1,380 to $300,000.

Independent College Fund of New York in New York City received two grants for $15,000 each.

Worcester Polytechnic Institute in Worcester, Massachusetts, received $40,000.

Fund for Excellence in Education in Los Angeles, California, received $15,000.

Columbia University Teachers College in New York City received $20,000.

National Council on Economic Education in New York City received $10,000.

Comments/Analysis

Historically, education receives the largest proportion of the foundation's grant dollars as well as the greatest number of grants. Education has received 35 percent of grant dollars paid, while community improvement and development received 32 percent; human services, 16 percent; other, 12 percent; and arts and culture, 5 percent. Grants to higher education account for the majority of the dollars distributed to education. Although the foundation does give on a broad regional basis, its large higher education grants seem to be awarded to institutions located in cities with major company operations such as Rochester, New York. For example, in a recent year, the University of Rochester received the foundation's largest grant awarded for that year ($1,000,000), plus seven other grants, for a total of up to $1,134,853. The foundation also matches gifts of employees, nonemployee directors, retired employees, and spouses of employees to four-year colleges and universities. Note that in recent years, the foundation has significantly reduced its level of giving.

SECTION

IV

Sources of Government Funding for Higher Education

GOVERNMENT FUNDING FOR HIGHER EDUCATION

HOW TO MAXIMIZE YOUR SUCCESS IN ATTRACTING PUBLIC GRANTS

There are over 1,300 federal funding opportunities that provide over $80 billion in grants and billions more in contracts annually. Review Section I of this book to sharpen your knowledge of the government grants marketplace.

Choosing which government granting programs to include in this sourcebook was a difficult task since redefinition enables grantseekers to relate all or part of their projects to a great variety of programs. To simplify the task, only those programs that are closely related to higher education were included.

Attempts were made to contact each of the government funding sources contained herein to validate areas of interest, contact information, selection criteria, etc. Due to changes in appropriations and staff, and the reorganization of some federal agencies, we cannot be responsible for any inaccuracies reported. Think of the data presented in this sourcebook as "preliminary" and contact each of the programs you are interested in to verify information, uncover changes, and demonstrate your ability to "play the grants game."

In these changing times, there is much pressure to return the control of federal grant programs to states. Because of this, reconfirmation of the data in this section is even more critical. If several federal programs have been combined to form a block grant to the states, you must know this so that you can contact your state officials and conduct a realistic assessment of your grant opportunities by using the techniques outlined in Section I of this book.

The programs selected for this book have been taken from the *Catalog of Federal Domestic Assistance* (CFDA). The CFDA is published annually and can be found in most libraries, or accessed electronically through Internet. This sourcebook contains 89 of the 1,370 programs listed in the CFDA.

The data presented here is designed to provide the grantseeker with insight into and a historical perspective of the best government funding programs for higher education. By researching the higher education portion of the grants awarded by the federal marketplace, we have sought to provide information that will help you make a preliminary match between your proposal interests and those of a particular federal program.

To move from a preliminary match to a "bulls-eye," you *must* make pre-proposal contact. The information in this section will help you ask the program's contact person intelligent questions that demonstrate your knowledge of the program. For example, instead of asking when their deadline is, you can say, "My research indicates that in the past your deadline was in March. What do you anticipate it to be this year? Review "Questions to Ask a Program Officer" in Section I and tailor the questions you choose to the particular funding source you are approaching so that you will gain their respect while acquiring additional information from them.

HOW TO USE THIS SECTION

Each federal funding source description contains the following information:

1. CFDA Number: The entries are in numerical order according to their five-digit, Catalogue of Federal Domestic Assistance number. There are large gaps in the numbering sequence since this sourcebook contains only select programs from the CFDA and because some federal programs have been eliminated.

2. Program Title and Address: Be very precise when recording this information. When working with the federal government you must accurately record room numbers, letter codes, zip codes, etc.

3. Program Description: This information has been derived from the enabling legislation and program descriptions available from the funders and reflects their areas of interest. Once you have determined your key words, you can go to the index of this book (and other grant resource books) to match them with the areas of interest reported by the funding sources. This will lead you to specific grantors that may be interested in your project, research, etc. You may also use the information provided under this heading to help you consider how your idea or proposal could be slanted or redefined to fit the purpose of the program as stated by the funding source.

4. Assistance Types: This provides information on the types of support offered by the program: project grants, challenge grants, matching funds, contracts, continuing projects grants, formula or block grants to states, and so on. In program 10.200, while the program description refers to "research," the assistance type is listed as "project grants."

5. Applicants Eligible: This includes those eligible to receive the agency's funds. If you find that you are not an eligible recipient for a program you are interested in, consider developing a consortium or partnership effort with an organization that is eligible.

   Note that while this section allows you to ascertain eligibility, it does not tell you anything about how frequently each eligible recipient category is funded. For example, "individuals" are often listed as eligible recipients, but rarely is an individual awarded a grant. You must make pre-proposal contact with the granting agency to determine how likely their support is for some-

one in your eligibility category. In the 10.200 example, colleges and universities are listed as eligible recipients and the sample grants attest to the fact that institutions of higher education do receive grants from this source.

6. Restrictions: The restrictions area should be read carefully to be sure that the particular activities you want to carry out will not meet with problems later. In the 10.200 example, it is revealed that the funding source is only interested in supporting research for high-priority problem areas of a regional or national scope. An important question to ask the program officer would be which of the identified problem areas will receive the most emphasis and funding in the next grant cycle.

7. Financial Profile: This chronological history of obligations and number of awards provides insight into the program's growth (or reduction) over the years. The grant range allows you to determine if your project falls within the financial scope of the funding source. Contact the programs that appear to be a good match with your project to verify appropriation levels and average grant size for your type of project. And note that in some cases not all appropriations are expended. In the 10.200 example, pre-proposal contact is necessitated by the forecasted drop in obligations and the broad grant range of $3,320 to $360,000. It is quite possible that the funds may be utilized to phase out currently funded projects or that the average grant size will be reduced.

8. Application Process: This section of each entry will provide you with information on whom to contact, deadlines, and processing time. Review the suggestions in Section I before telephoning the program official. Even if you have missed the current deadline it pays to contact a funding official since you can

   • ask about becoming a reviewer,

   • inquire about unannounced or unsolicited proposals

   • discuss next year's funding cycle and their interest in your project

   Please note that some entries in Section IV contain phone numbers and names. Others just have phone numbers. In those cases, call the number listed and ask to speak to the program officer.

9. Review Process/Criteria: This section provides you with information on the selection process, and review criteria program staff and/or reviewers will apply in evaluating your proposal. Having access to this information will help you prepare a proposal with the reviewer's viewpoint in mind.

10. Project Period: This refers to the time frame or number of years that the agency considers a project supportable. If an agency funds proposals for one to five years (as in the case of program 10.200), do not assume it will fund your project for the maximum allowable time. Federal granting officials have been criticized for not awarding projects of varying duration, and it is best to ask the program official during pre-proposal contact what their most likely project period is for your type of proposal.

11. Sample Grants: A listing of sample grants can provide you with a sense of the type of recipient (educational institution) and project preferred by the funding source. Remember, the sample grants included with the entries represent only a few out of the many grants awarded by each program. Therefore, request a complete listing of grant recipients from those programs that you are interested in pursuing. Once you have this list, you can contact a past recipient to gather vital information concerning the funding agency and you can obtain a copy of a successful proposal (when you visit the federal agency) to help you develop your proposal.

12. Comments/Analysis: This section contains more in-depth information and insight into the program.

FEDERAL FUNDING SOURCES

170
10.200
Special Research Grants Program
Competitive Grants Program
Cooperative State Research Service
Department of Agriculture
Aerospace Center, Room 303
Washington, DC   20250-2200

Areas of Interest

Program Description: The objective of this program is to carry out research to facilitate or expand promising breakthroughs in areas of food and agricultural sciences of importance to the country. Program areas are aquaculture, water quality, and wood utilization.
Assistance Types: Project grants

Eligibility

Applicants Eligible: Colleges and universities, state experimental stations, research institutions and organizations, private organizations or corporations, and individuals
Restrictions: Basic and applied research limited to high-priority problems of a regional or national scope. Competitive research grants awarded for agriculture, water quality, rangeland research, and integrated pest management. Rangeland research grants require a 50 percent match.

Financial Profile

Obligations: Fiscal year 1994, $13,414,587
Grant Range: $4,000-$2,093,067; average, $181,271
Total Grants: In 1993, 558 applications received, 156 grants awarded; 1994, 235 applications received, 78 grants awarded

Application Process

Contact: (202) 720-4423; Internet: www.reeusda.gov
Deadline: December, March, and April

Processing Time: Four to six months
Review Process: USDA Uniform Federal Assistance Regulations apply. Proposals are reviewed by program staff and peer panels composed of groups of scientists, educators, and specialists from the field represented by the proposal.
Criteria: Proposals are evaluated on a point system, with a maximum of 100 points allotted as follows: overall scientific quality (40 points); relevance of project to area of inquiry (20 points); budget, resources, and personnel (20 points); multidisciplinary or multi-institutional collaboration (10 points); and application of results (10 points).
Project Period: One to five years

Sample Grants

The University of Maryland Eastern Shore at Princess Anne received a two-year aquaculture research grant for a project, Management of Phosphorus Discharge Through Alternative Fish Feed Technology.

The University of Georgia in Athens received a two-year water quality grant of $67,102 for the study, Evaluation of Tools for Assessing the Accuracy of Poultry Manure Applications on Agricultural Lands in the Southeast.

West Virginia University in Morgantown was awarded a two-year wood utilization grant of $55,996 for the study, A High Speed Non-Destructive Scanner for the Automated Lumber Processing System.

Comments/Analysis

Consideration will be given to proposals that address innovative as well as fundamental approaches to the research areas covered by the program.

171
10.206
National Research Initiative
Competitive Grants Program
Cooperative State Research Service

Department of Agriculture
Aerospace Center, Room 323, AG Box 2241
Washington, DC   20250-2241

Areas of Interest

Program Description: The initiative supports research projects intended to provide scientific and technological advances needed to meet major challenges facing agriculture in the United States. The six research divisions are natural resources and the environment; nutrition, food safety, and health; animals; plants; markets, trade, and rural development; and processing for added value or developing new products; in addition, proposals are accepted for cross-divisional topics. The initiative supports research that is fundamental, mission-linked or multidisciplinary, as well as for conferences, acquisition of equipment, and fellowships.
Assistance Types: Project grants

Eligibility

Applicants Eligible: Colleges and universities, state experimental stations, research institutions and organizations, private organizations or corporations, and individuals
Restrictions: Grantee institutions are expected to take responsibility for supervision of the grant, while the principal investigator is responsible for the scientific work.

Financial Profile

Obligations: Fiscal year 1994, $96,631,445; 1995, $96,688,989
Grant Range: $1,402-$786,450; average, $116,004
Total Grants: In 1994, 3,493 applications received, 833 grants awarded

Application Process

Contact: (202) 401-5022; Internet: www.reeusda.gov/topics/nri-home.htm
Deadline: Vary by program area but fall between November and March
Processing Time: 90 to 180 days
Review Process: USDA Uniform Federal Assistance Regulations apply. Proposals are reviewed by program staff and peer panels composed of groups of educators, administrators, industrialists, and specialists from the field represented by the proposal.
Criteria: Proposals are judged on the basis of scientific merit, the probability that the research will contribute to discoveries or breakthroughs in the field, qualifications of the principal investigator and research team, and the adequacy of the facilities.
Project Period: Up to three years

Sample Grants

Duke University in Durham, North Carolina, received a two-year grant of $127,000 for a forestry-related research project, Response of Western Montana Forest Ecosystems to Global Climate Change.

Auburn University in Auburn, Alabama, received a two-year grant for a water quality research project, Subsurf Transport and Mixing of Dense Leachates Near the Groundwater Table.
The University of Vermont in Burlington was awarded a two-year grant of $120,000 for a Human Nutrition research project, Energy Requirements in Young Children.

Comments/Analysis

The USDA encourages applications to this program that are innovative and high-risk as well as proposals with potential for immediate application. The program will give particular consideration to proposals that address fundamental questions in areas relevant to the Initiative and consistent with long-range missions of the USDA.

172
10.217
Higher Education Challenge Grants
Department of Agriculture
Aerospace Center, Room 310E
Washington, DC   20250-2200

Areas of Interest

Program Description: The objective of this program is to stimulate and enable colleges and universities to provide the kind of baccalaureate-level education necessary to produce graduates capable of strengthening the country's food and agricultural scientific and professional work force. Projects are supported in the areas of curricula design and materials development; faculty preparation and enhancement for teaching; instruction delivery systems; and student experiential learning. Projects supported by the program should address a regional, state, national, or international need; involve a creative or novel approach that can serve as a model or others; encourage and facilitate better working relationships in the university science and education community; and result in benefits that will extend beyond the grant period and support.
Assistance Types: Project grants

Eligibility

Applicants Eligible: Colleges and universities with the capacity to teach in the areas of food and agriculture sciences
Restrictions: Funds may only be used in approved curricular areas.

Financial Profile

Obligations: Fiscal year 1994, $1,422,076
Grant Range: $39,792-$130,000; average, $75,899
Total Grants: In 1994, 2,106 applications received, 24 grants awarded

Application Process

Contact: (202) 401-1799; Internet: www.reeusda.gov

Deadline: January
Processing Time: 90 to 180 days
Review Process: USDA Uniform Federal Assistance Regulations apply. Proposals are reviewed by program staff and peer panels composed of groups of educators, scientists, administrators, and specialists from the field represented by the proposal.
Criteria: Proposals are judged on the basis of scientific merit, qualifications of the personnel, relevance of the project to the goals of the program, and the estimate of expected results. In addition, proposals will be evaluated according to adequacy of financial resources and financial management system.
Project Period: One to three years

Sample Grants

Oregon State University in Corvallis received a two-year grant of $65,000 to support a project, Co-learning: An Educational Model in Agroforestry.

Utah State University in Logan received a two-year grant of $67,985 for the development of an international agribusiness internship center.

Virginia Polytechnic Institute and State University in Blacksburg received $64,568 for a two-year project, Valuing Diversity: Activities to Enhance Education.

Comments/Analysis

Priorities for funding are projects in the areas of ethics in agriculture, women and leadership, computer technology, and the multicultural environment.

173
10.219
Biotechnology Risk Assessment Research
Competitive Grants Program
Cooperative State Research Service
Department of Agriculture
Aerospace Center, Room 323, AG Box 2241
Washington, DC   20250-2241

Areas of Interest

Program Description: This program supports research into the effects of introducing genetically modified organisms, plants, and animals into the environment and to help regulators develop policies concerning such introduction. Proposals based upon field research and whole organism-population level studies are encouraged. Proposals should be applicable to current regulatory issues surrounding the ecological impacts of genetically modified organisms, with special emphasis on natural ecosystem consequences.
Assistance Types: Project grants

Eligibility

Applicants Eligible: Colleges and universities, public and private research institutions or originations
Restrictions: Research not supported by this program includes projects in greenhouses or controlled environments and surveys or inventories. Funds may not be used for renovation of facilities or acquisition of equipment.

Financial Profile

Obligations: Fiscal year 1994, $1,697,847; 1995, $1,713,340
Grant Range: $31,981-$266,050; average, $169,785
Total Grants: In 1994, 40 applications received, 10 grants awarded

Application Process

Contact: Dr. David MacKenzie, (202) 401-4892; Internet: www.reeusda.gov
Deadline: Contact program office
Processing Time: Four to six months
Review Process: USDA Uniform Federal Assistance Regulations apply. Proposals are reviewed by program staff and peer panels composed of groups of educators, administrators, industrialists, and specialists from the field represented by the proposal.
Criteria: Proposals are judged on the basis of scientific merit, qualifications of the principal investigator and research team, the adequacy of the facilities and related support, relevance of the project to solving biotechnology uncertainty, and the estimate of expected results. In addition, proposals are evaluated according to adequacy of financial resources and financial management systems.
Project Period: One to five years

Sample Grants

University of Arkansas in Fayetteville received a two-year grant of $100,000 for the project, Sexual Cycle and Potential for Gene Flow In Fungal Biological Control Agents.

Iowa State University in Ames received a three-year award of $160,000 for the project, Genetic Exchange Between Baccillus Thuringiensis and Other Microbes in Soil.

University of Idaho at Moscow was awarded $106,704 for a two-year study, Model for Dispersal and Epiphytic Survival of Bacteria Applied to Crop Foliage.

Comments/Analysis

Priorities for funding are projects in the areas of ethics in agriculture, women and leadership, computer technology, and the multicultural environment.

174
16.560
Justice Research, Development, and Evaluation Programs
National Institute of Justice
Department of Justice
Washington, DC   20531

Areas of Interest

Program Description: The purpose of the program is to encourage and support research, development, training, and evaluation to increase understanding of causes and control of crime, and to improve the criminal justice system. Proposals should address one or more of the institute's long-range goals: to reduce violent crimes and their consequences; reduce drug- and alcohol-related crime; reduce the consequences of crime for individuals, households, organizations, and communities; develop household, school, business, workplace, and community crime-prevention programs; improve the effectiveness of law enforcement, criminal justice, correctional, and service systems' responses to offenses, offending, and victimization; and develop, promote, and use criminal justice research, evaluation, and technology. Funded projects are expected to generate products of maximum benefit to criminal justice professionals, researchers, and policymakers.
Assistance Types: Project grants, cooperative agreements, and contracts

Eligibility

Applicants Eligible: Governments, profit, and nonprofit public and private organizations, institutions of higher education and individuals
Restrictions: Though there is no statutory match, recipients are expected to contribute funds, facilities, and/or services.

Financial Profile

Obligations: Fiscal year 1994, $23,098,316; 1995, $26,731,000
Grant Range: In amounts consistent with the institute's plans, priorities, and levels of financing
Total Grants: In 1993, 395 applications received, 80 grants awarded; 1994, 347 applications received, 135 grants awarded

Application Process

Contact: (202) 307-2942; NIJ electronic bulletin board: (301) 738-8895.
Deadline: Contact program office
Processing Time: 90 days
Review Process: Program managers and a review panel of experts evaluate proposals for general merit relevance to needs of the institute and the institute's research plan.
Criteria: See program solicitation
Project Period: Usually 24 months; however, applicants may request more time

Sample Grants

Temple University in Philadelphia, Pennsylvania, was awarded $205,814 for a project, Building a Culture and Climate of Safety in Public Schools: School-Based Management and Violence Reduction in Philadelphia.
The University of California at Berkeley was awarded $118,970 for the development of the project, An Extended Computer Sourcebook of Forensic Science Information.

Comments/Analysis

For detailed information, prospective applicants may request NIJ documents by calling (800) 851-3420. Available materials include the National Institute of Justice Research and Evaluation Plan, the National Institute of Justice Program Plan, and the bimonthly journal, NIJ Reports.

175
45.001
NEA Design Arts Program
National Endowment for the Arts
1100 Pennsylvania Avenue NW
The Nancy Hanks Ctr
Washington, DC   20506

Areas of Interest

Program Description: The Design Arts Program supports work that will advance the fields of architecture, landscape architecture, urban design and planning, historic preservation, interior design, costume and fashion design, industrial and product design, and graphic design on a local, state, regional, and national level. The program aims to create public awareness and recognition of good design as well as to improve practices and techniques and develop new talent. Organizations are eligible to apply under the categories of planning grants for rural and small communities, project grants for arts facilities design, design education, design history and documentation, and project grants for organizations.
Assistance Types: Planning and project grants

Eligibility

Applicants Eligible: Arts presenters, colleges and universities, state arts agencies, and local and regional arts agencies
Restrictions: Organizations must provide a one-to-one match.

Financial Profile

Obligations: Fiscal year 1994, $3,310,000
Grant Range: $10,000-$50,000
Total Grants: In 1994, 573 applications received, 96 grants awarded

Application Process

Contact: (202) 682-5437; fax: (202) 682-5669; TDD: (202) 682-5496
Deadline: Contact program to verify deadlines
Processing Time: Nine months
Review Process: Each application is evaluated by a panel. Panels are composed of rotating groups of professionally qualified experts and lay people knowledgeable about the arts, but not necessarily engaged in them as a profession. The panel's recommendations are reviewed by the National Council on the Arts, and the final decision is made by the chair of the National Endowment for the Arts. Council members and the chair of the Endowment are appointed by the president of the United States and confirmed by the Senate.
Criteria: Panelists will consider the following factors: potential of the project to advance the design field; national, regional, state, or local significance of the project; presentation and quality of written and visual materials; appropriateness of the budget; and the applicant's ability to accomplish the project.
Project Period: Up to 24 months

Sample Grants

Pennsylvania State University in University Park received a project grant of $39,650 to support research and production of two videotapes on the design of children's museums. The videotapes will disseminate research on the subject to both targeted and public television audiences.

The Rochester Institute of Technology in Rochester, New York, received a project grant for heritage conservation to support the next phases of the Graphic Design Archive Project, which will make thousands of historic images available on laserdisc.

The University of Southern California in Los Angeles was awarded a $25,000 project grant for design education to support a summer design studio and mentoring program to attract minority students to design careers.

Comments/Analysis

Collaborative projects are welcomed. To learn more about design activities, contact Design Access, an information database service provided by the Design Arts Program in cooperation with the National Building Museum. Abstracts of past projects are available free of charge from Design Access, The National Building Museum, Suite 322, 410 F Street NW, Washington, DC 20001, (202) 272-5247. Applicants are welcome to attend meetings of the National Council on the Arts, as well as open sessions of advisory panels. Persons who would like to be considered for service on an advisory peer-review panel should contact the Arts Endowment's Office of Panel Operations at the above address. You will be asked to complete a form for the automated data bank and to submit a resume.

176
45.002
NEA Dance Program
National Endowment for the Arts
1100 Pennsylvania Avenue NW
The Nancy Hanks Ctr
Washington, DC   20506

Areas of Interest

Program Description: The Dance Program's mission is to assist dance artists of national or regional significance to make, produce, and transmit their work, and to foster a climate of support and public appreciation for dance that enriches our nation. Categories of support to organizations and institutions include services to the field and special projects. Those interested in presenting dance performances are encouraged to apply to the Presenting and Commissioning Program, 45.011.
Assistance Types: Project grants

Eligibility

Applicants Eligible: Individual artists, arts organizations, arts presenters, colleges and universities, state arts agencies, local arts agencies, and regional arts organizations. A consortium of groups may apply.
Restrictions: Grants to organizations may be used to pay no more than half of project costs. The Dance Program does not fund scholarships; student, recreational, or nonprofessional dance activities; construction or renovation of buildings; dance training; or competitions.

Financial Profile

Obligations: Fiscal year 1994, $7,239,000; 1995, $6,890,000
Grant Range: $5,000-$300,000
Total Grants: In 1993, 809 applications received, 237 grants awarded; in 1994, 678 applications received, 200 grants awarded

Application Process

Contact: (202) 682-5435; TDD: (202) 682-5496
Deadline: Contact the program to verify deadline
Processing Time: Seven months
Review Process: Each application is evaluated by a panel. Panels are composed of rotating groups of professionally qualified experts and lay people knowledgeable about the arts but not necessarily engaged in them as a profession. The panel's recommendations are reviewed by the National Council on the Arts, and the final decision is made by the chair of the National Endowment for the Arts. Council members and the chair of the Endowment are appointed by the president of the United States and confirmed by the Senate.
Criteria: Merit and excellence of the project; applicant's ability to carry out the project; the quality, number, and diversity of artists and arts organizations served; and impact on the community.
Project Period: One to two years

Sample Grants

The Borough of Manhattan Community College Performing Arts Center in New York received $4,700 from the dance presenters category to support artists' fees and costs related to the Asian American Performance Initiative dance series.

University of Minnesota at Twin Cities was granted $10,500 from the dance presenters category to support the presentation of dance.

Comments/Analysis

The Dance Program is interested in projects that identify and respond in significant ways to vital issues affecting artists' creative activities and public understanding of their work. Priority will be given to projects that can demonstrate national or regional leadership in serving critical needs of the dance field and its communities. Applicants are welcome to attend meetings of the National Council on the Arts as well as open sessions of advisory panels. Persons who would like to be considered for service on an advisory peer review panel should contact the Arts Endowment's Office of Panel Operations at the above address. You will be asked to complete a form for the automated data bank and to submit a resume.

177
45.004
NEA Literature Program
National Endowment for the Arts
1100 Pennsylvania Avenue NW
The Nancy Hanks Ctr
Washington, DC   20506

Areas of Interest

Program Description: The Literature Program assists individual creative writers of excellence or promise, encourages wider audience for contemporary literature, and helps support nonprofit organizations that foster literature as a professional pursuit. Poetry, fiction, plays, and creative nonfiction by contemporary writers are included. Categories of the Literature Program open to organizations and institutions are literary publishing, including small press assistance, assistance to literary magazines, and distribution projects; audience development, including residencies for writers and reading series; and professional development.

Assistance Types: Project grants

Eligibility

Applicants Eligible: Individual artists, arts presenters, colleges and universities, state arts agencies, local and regional arts and literary organizations (those publishing primarily theater-related materials should apply to the Theater Program, 45.008).

Restrictions: Grants must be matched by the organization. Funds may not be used for construction or renovation; faculty salaries; publications by applicant organization's faculty, staff, students, or

board; regular curricula or scholarly writing. (Writers engaged in scholarly work should apply to the National Endowment for the Humanities.)

Financial Profile

Obligations: Fiscal year 1993, $4,340,000; 1994, $4,400,000
Grant Range: $2,000-$125,000
Total Grants: In 1993, 2,716 applications received, 228 grants awarded; 1994, 2,787 applications received, 215 grants awarded

Application Process

Contact: (202) 682-5451; TDD: (202) 682-5496
Deadline: Small press assistance, August 5; distribution projects, September 9; audience development, October 1; professional development, December 1.
Processing Time: Eight months
Review Process: Each application is evaluated by a panel. Panels are composed of rotating groups of professionally qualified experts and laypersons knowledgeable about the arts but not necessarily engaged in them as a profession. The panel's recommendations are reviewed by the National Council on the Arts, and the final decision is made by the chair of the National Endowment for the Arts. Council members and the chair of the Endowment are appointed by the president of the United States and confirmed by the Senate.
Criteria: Criteria include artistic excellence and literary merit of project as indicated by the clarity of editorial vision, potential for project to serve diverse audiences, and range of contributors; and ability to carry out the project including fiscal management.
Project Period: One year

Sample Grants

Arizona State University in Tempe received support of $10,000 for a series of public readings and speaking engagements in rural and urban areas featuring such writers as Judith Barrington, Lynn Collins Emmanuel, Martin Espada, and Marilynne Robinson.

San Francisco State University in California was awarded $25,000 to support The Poetry Center in recording, distributing, and archiving live literary performances on videotape.

Comments/Analysis

Applicants are welcome to attend meetings of the National Council on the Arts as well as open sessions of advisory panels. Persons who would like to be considered for service on an advisory peer review panel should contact the Arts Endowment's Office of Panel Operations at the above address. You will be asked to complete a form for the automated data bank and to submit a resume.

178
45.005
NEA Music Program
National Endowment for the Arts
1100 Pennsylvania Avenue NW
The Nancy Hanks Ctr
Washington, DC   20506

Areas of Interest

Program Description: The Music Program supports the creation and performance of music and places special emphasis on encouraging the growth of American music and musicians. The Music Program assists creative and performing artists of exceptional talent, as well as music performing and service organizations of regional or national significance. Service organizations, choruses, orchestras, and jazz or chamber music ensembles are supported. Colleges and universities are eligible to apply in the following categories: jazz services to the field/special projects, music professional training, music recording, services to composers, and special projects.

Assistance Types: One-to-one matching project grants; grants of $15,000 or more generally require a three-to-one match

Eligibility

Applicants Eligible: Colleges and universities, local and regional arts organizations, arts presenters, and individual artists.

Restrictions: Music presenters and festival producers are not eligible, but are encouraged to seek funding through the NEA Presenting and Commissioning Program (see 45.011). The Music Program does not fund general academic support, foreign travel, competitions, research, performance events, construction and renovation of facilities, summer camp, purchase of instruments, or publications.

Financial Profile

Obligations: Fiscal year 1994, $10,920,000

Grant Range: Individuals: $2,500-$20,000; organizations: $4,400-$236,000

Total Grants: In 1993, 1,609 applications received, 679 grants awarded; 1994, 1,395 applications received, 524 grants awarded

Application Process

Contact: (202) 682-5445; TDD: (202) 682-5496. Requests should specify category name.

Deadline: Music professional training, October 22; special projects, April 1; jazz services to the field/special projects, May 1; for all other categories, September 24. Prospective applicants to either the jazz special projects or special projects categories are encouraged to contact the Music Program before applying.

Processing Time: Six to eight months.

Review Process: Proposals are evaluated by panels composed of professional artists and knowledgeable lay persons. The panel's recommendations are reviewed by the National Council on the Arts, and the final decision is made by the chair of the National Endowment for the Arts. Council members and the chair of the Endowment are appointed by the president of the United States and confirmed by the Senate.

Project Period: One year

Sample Grants

The University of Massachusetts at Amherst received $6,500 from the music professional training category to support scholarship aid for the Jazz in July Workshop in Improvisation.

The University of Maryland at College Park was awarded $6,000 in the Music Festivals category for artists' fees for the Maryland Handel Festival.

The University of Idaho at Moscow received $18,000 from the Jazz Presenters category for guest artists' performances at the Lionel Hampton/Chevron Jazz Festival.

Leland Stanford Junior University in Stanford, California, was awarded $6,000 in the Special Projects category to support the International Digital Electroacoustic Music Archive.

Comments/Analysis

Applicants are welcome to attend meetings of the National Council on the Arts as well as open sessions of advisory panels. Persons who would like to be considered for service on an advisory peer review panel should contact the Endowment's Office of Panel Operations at the above address. You will be asked to complete a form for the automated data bank and to submit a resume.

179
45.006
NEA Media Arts Program: Film/Radio/Television
National Endowment for the Arts
1100 Pennsylvania Avenue NW
The Nancy Hanks Ctr
Washington, DC   20506

Areas of Interest

Program Description: The Media Arts Program aims to support new work by artists of exceptional talent; distribute that work through exhibition, broadcast, and cassette; and to preserve media heritage. The media arts include documentary, experimental, animated, and narrative film/video works, as well as radio/audio art. Institutional support is offered in the following categories: Film Preservation Program, The Arts on Radio, The Arts on Television, Film/Video and Radio/Audio Production, Media Arts Centers, National Services, and Special Projects.

Assistance Types: Project grants

Eligibility

Applicants Eligible: Colleges and universities, local and regional arts organizations, arts presenters, and individual artists.

Restrictions: Organizational grantees must match the funds on at least a one-to-one basis. The program does not fund university-based programs that serve primarily a university constituency as an extension of curriculum-related activities.

Financial Profile

Obligations: Fiscal year 1993, $10,675,000; 1994, $10,312,000
Grant Range: Individuals: $3,000-$35,000; organizations, $5,000-$500,000
Total Grants: In 1993, 831 applications received, 186 grants awarded; 1994, 808 applications received, 193 grants awarded

Application Process

Contact: (202) 682-5452; TDD: (202) 682-5496
Deadline: Media Arts Centers, early May; Film/Video Production, late October; Radio/Audio Production, mid-December; Art on Television or Radio, letter of intent by end of September; contact the program for all others
Processing Time: Seven months
Review Process: Proposals are evaluated by panels composed of professional artists and knowledgeable laypersons. The panel's recommendations are reviewed by the National Council on the Arts, and the final decision is made by the chair of the National Endowment for the Arts. Council members and the chair of the Endowment are appointed by the president of the United States and confirmed by the Senate.
Criteria: Applications are judged on the basis of the artistic excellence of the organization's programs, importance and/or uniqueness of the proposed project, capacity to advance the art and expand the audience for media arts, participation of individuals from diverse communities, and organizational stability.
Project Period: A project may extend beyond one year.

Sample Grants

Ohio State University in Columbus, Ohio, was awarded $10,000 from the Media Art Center category to support the film/video components of RE/VISIONS at the Wexner Center for the Arts.

The University of the District of Columbia received $10,000 to support the Black Film Institute's screenings and lecture presentations on black and Third World films.

Johns Hopkins University in Baltimore, Maryland, was awarded $60,000 to support Soundprint, a series of radio documentaries by independent producers.

Comments/Analysis

Applicants are welcome to attend meetings of the National Council on the Arts, as well as open sessions of advisory panels. Persons who would like to be considered for service on an advisory peer review panel should contact the Arts Endowment's Office of Panel Operations at the above address. You will be asked to complete a form for the automated data bank and to submit a resume.

180
45.009
NEA Visual Arts Program
National Endowment for the Arts
1100 Pennsylvania Avenue NW
The Nancy Hanks Ctr
Washington, DC   20506

Areas of Interest

Program Description: The Visual Arts Program aims to encourage professional artists in painting, sculpture, photography, works on paper, and experimental visual genres to pursue and develop their work. Special project and public project grants are awarded to organizations and institutions that serve visual artists and enhance public appreciation through opportunities to create or present new work or through residencies or conferences.
Assistance Types: Project grants

Eligibility

Applicants Eligible: Arts organizations, arts presenters, colleges and universities, state and local arts agencies, and regional arts organizations. Collaborative projects are encouraged, particularly those that involve the communities the project aims to serve.
Restrictions: Grants must be matched on at least a one-to-one basis by the organization. Projects for students pursuing degrees or nonprofessional artists are ineligible.

Financial Profile

Obligations: Fiscal year 1993, $5,196,000; 1994, $4,771,000
Grant Range: Individuals: $20,000; organizations: $5,000-$45,000
Total Grants: In 1993, 5,603 applications received, 316 grants awarded; 1994, 5,531 applications received, 260 grants awarded

Application Process

Contact: (202) 682-5448; TDD: (202) 682-5496
Deadline: Contact program for deadline
Processing Time: Seven months
Review Process: Proposals are evaluated by panels composed of professional artists and knowledgeable laypersons. The panel's recommendations are reviewed by the National Council on the Arts, and the final decision is made by the chair of the National Endowment for the Arts. Council members and the chair of the Endowment are appointed by the president of the United States and confirmed by the Senate.
Criteria: Applications are judged on the basis of the artistic excellence; merit, innovation, and timeliness of the proposed project; potential of the project to promote discussion or enhanced public appreciation of contemporary visual art; constituencies served; plans for informing the public; and plans for documenting and disseminating the documentation as well as the organization's ability to administer the project. For public art projects, additional criteria include appropriateness of site, plans for community participation, and involvement of the artist in all phases of the project.

Project Period: A project period of more than one year is allowed.

Sample Grants

Moore College of Art and Design in Philadelphia, Pennsylvania, received a $25,000 grant to support commissions to 10 artists for a series of new works at a long-abandoned prison in central Philadelphia as part of a city and community project, with an accompanying exhibit and a symposium to be held at Moore College.

Stanford University Museum of Art was granted $10,000 to support commissions to 10 visual artists and two landscape architects for the creation of a permanent sculpture garden on the university campus.

Rutgers University Center for Innovative Printmaking in New Brunswick, New Jersey, received $11,000 for two projects. Funds supported residencies for Native American artists to create new work for installation in public venues and collaborative residencies for visual artists to create new work and participate in a public series entitled Diverse Narratives: Inserting Other Stories into the American Mainstream Culture.

Comments/Analysis

Fewer than 5 percent of proposals received are funded in this competitive program. Applicants are welcome to attend meetings of the National Council on the Arts as well as open sessions of advisory panels. Persons who would like to be considered for service on an advisory peer review panel should contact the Arts Endowment's Office of Panel Operations at the above address. You will be asked to complete a form for the automated data bank and to submit a resume.

181
45.011
NEA Presenting and Commissioning Grants
National Endowment for the Arts
1100 Pennsylvania Avenue NW
The Nancy Hanks Ctr
Washington, DC 20506

Areas of Interest

Program Description: The Presenting and Commissioning Program encourages creation and presentation in the performing arts. Working in two principal ways, the program supports presenting organizations that offer events to broad audiences, and it assists artists who work in interdisciplinary or collaborative forms. The categories for which colleges and universities are eligible are Commissioning Projects, Dance Presenting, Music Presenting, Opera-Musical Theater Initiative, Presenting Development Initiative, Presenting Networks, Presenting Organizations, Regional Arts Organizations/Consolidated Presenting Support, and Theater Initiative.

Assistance Types: Project grants

Eligibility

Applicants Eligible: Arts presenters, colleges and universities, state arts agencies, local and regional arts organizations
Restrictions: A one-to-one match with nonfederal funds is required.

Financial Profile

Obligations: Fiscal year 1993, $3,928,000; 1994, $5,516,000
Grant Range: $5,000-$150,000; average, $10,000-$30,000
Total Grants: In 1993, 563 applications received, 220 grants awarded; 1994, 662 applications received, 316 grants awarded

Application Process

Contact: (202) 682-5444; TDD: (202) 682-5496
Deadline: Music Presenting, April; Presenting Organizations, May; Dance Presenters, May; Presenters Development Initiative, August; Commissioning, October
Processing Time: Approximately nine months depending upon scheduling of panel meetings
Review Process: Each application is evaluated by a panel. Panels are composed of rotating groups of professionally qualified experts and lay persons knowledgeable about the arts but not necessarily engaged in them as a profession. The panel's recommendations are reviewed by the National Council on the Arts, and the final decision is made by the chair of the National Endowment for the Arts. Council members and the chair of the Endowment are appointed by the president of the United States and confirmed by the Senate.
Criteria: Panelists will consider the following factors: potential of the project to advance the design field; national, regional, state, or local significance of the project; presentation and quality of written and visual materials; appropriateness of the budget and the applicant's ability to accomplish the project.
Project Period: One year

Sample Grants

Duke University in Durham, North Carolina, received a $5,000 Presenting Organization grant in support of the Global Perspectives in the Arts and Young Artists series.

Rensselaer Polytechnic Institute in Troy, New York, was awarded a $7,800 interdisciplinary project grant to fund a collaborative video/performance project.

The University of California at Berkeley, with the University of Washington and Portland State University, received a $17,500 Partnership in Commissioning Grant. A new work was created by Trisha Brown, Alvin Curran, and Spencer Brown.

Comments/Analysis

Prospective applicants are encouraged to discuss the proposed project with program staff. Applicants are welcome to attend meetings of the National Council on the Arts as well as open sessions of advisory panels. Persons who would like to be considered for service on an advisory peer review panel should contact the Endowment's Office of Panel Operations at the above address. You will be asked to complete a form for the automated data bank and to submit a resume.

182
45.012
NEA Museum Program
National Endowment for the Arts
1100 Pennsylvania Avenue NW
The Nancy Hanks Ctr
Washington, DC   20506

Areas of Interest

Program Description: The Museum Program helps art museums and related organizations make art an integral part of American cultural life. Funds train museum professionals and help museums exhibit art, preserve and care for art, and present information about art to the public in imaginative and instructive ways. Categories of support open to organizations are Museum Training, such as workshops and seminars, apprenticeships, undergraduate and graduate internships, and graduate-level training; Utilization of Museum Resources, which includes education, presentation of collections, and cataloging; Care of Collections, which includes conservation and maintenance; and Special Exhibitions.
Assistance Types: Planning and project grants

Eligibility

Applicants Eligible: Colleges and universities, state arts agencies, local and regional arts organizations, nonprofit museums
Restrictions: Grants of $50,000 or less require at least a one-to-one match. Grants over $50,000 require at least a two-to-one match. Funds may not be used for new construction or renovation of facilities.

Financial Profile

Obligations: Fiscal year 1993, $10,000,000; 1994, $9,439,000
Grant Range: Utilization of Museum Resources: $5,000-$125,000; Care of Collections, $5,000-$60,000; Special Exhibitions, $200,000 maximum
Total Grants: In 1993, 1,057 applications received, 458 grants awarded; 1994, 964 applications received, 438 grants awarded

Application Process

Contact: (202) 682-5442; TDD: (202) 682-5496
Deadline: Utilization of Museum Resources, early June; Care of Collections, mid-September; Special Exhibitions, early November; contact program to verify deadlines
Processing Time: Seven months
Review Process: Each application is evaluated by a panel. Panels are composed of rotating groups of professionally qualified experts and lay persons knowledgeable about the arts but not necessarily engaged in them as a profession. The panel's recommendations are reviewed by the National Council on the Arts, and the final decision is made by the chair of the National Endowment for the Arts. Council members and the chair of the Endowment are appointed by the president of the United States and confirmed by the Senate.
Criteria: The quality of the project, not the size or location of the applicant institution, is the major criterion used to evaluate applications. Each category has specific criteria and application requirements; however, panelists will consider the following criteria for all applications: artistic significance of collections and value for intended audience, qualifications of key personnel, appropriateness of programming and interpretive materials, and appropriateness of budget.
Project Period: Flexible, as needed to complete project

Sample Grants

The University of Kansas in Lawrence received a grant to support the Spencer Museum of Art's Museum Training Program, designed to complement the graduate degree programs in art history at the University of Kansas.

New York University in New York City received a museum conservation grant of $75,000 to support the establishment of a permanent curriculum providing specialized instruction in the conservation of ethnographic and archeological works of art at the Conservation Center of the university's Institute of Fine Arts.

The University of Arizona at Tucson's Center for Creative Photography was awarded $10,000 to support the production of an informational video to provide broader public access to the collections and programming at the center.

Comments/Analysis

Applicants who plan public programs are encouraged to consider a variety of media, including publications, lectures, film, video, and computer-based formats.

183
45.013
NEA Challenge Grants
National Endowment for the Arts
1100 Pennsylvania Avenue NW
The Nancy Hanks Ctr
Washington, DC   20506

Areas of Interest

Program Description: Challenge Grants are intended to provide a special opportunity for arts institutions to strengthen long-term institutional capacity and to enhance artistic quality and diversity. The Challenge Program is an important complement to other Endowment programs that provide project or seasonal support. A key factor in awarding a Challenge Grant will be whether the Challenge effort can be expected to have significant, long-term impact. The two categories of support are Institutional Stabilization and Project Implementation.

Assistance Types: Project grants

Eligibility

Applicants Eligible: Arts institutions, state and local arts agencies, arts service organizations, colleges and universities, and consortia of such organizations and institutions

Restrictions: Challenge Grants must be matched three-to-one; four-to-one for construction, renovation, purchase of facilities, equipment, or fixtures

Financial Profile

Obligations: Fiscal year 1993, $13,435,000; 1994, $13,148,000
Grant Range: $75,000-$1,000,000
Total Grants: In 1993, 274 applications received, 61 grants awarded; 1994, 206 applications received, 51 grants awarded

Application Process

Contact: (202) 682-5436; TDD: (202) 682-5496
Deadline: A preapplication must be received in March; the application package is due in May.
Processing Time: Nine months
Review Process: Each application is evaluated by a panel. Panels are composed of rotating groups of professionally qualified experts and lay persons knowledgeable about the arts but not necessarily engaged in them as a profession. The panel's recommendations are reviewed by the National Council on the Arts, and the final decision is made by the chair of the National Endowment for the Arts. Council members and the chair of the Endowment are appointed by the president of the United States and confirmed by the Senate.
Criteria: Applications are considered on the basis of artistic quality, impact, nature, and clarity of the proposal; relationship with the community; ability to meet the match; and stability and past performance of the organization.
Project Period: The grant period begins March 1 and concludes at the end of the grantee's third full fiscal year.

Sample Grants

Howard University College of Fine Arts in Washington, DC, received $100,000 to establish residency appointments at selected historically black colleges and universities for internationally acclaimed African American visual, performing, and literary artists.

Cooper Union for the Advancement of Science and Art in New York received $250,000 to increase national recruitment of minority students and to expand School of the Arts facilities, student services, and community outreach programs.

Comments/Analysis

In developing a Challenge application, applicants are strongly advised to discuss the proposal with Challenge staff as well as with staff in the Arts Endowment program to which the applicant most directly relates. Great importance is placed on the formulation and implementation of long-range artistic and financial plans. The applicant's board is considered a significant factor in the success of the Challenge grant. All applicants must involve the boards in the development and ongoing review of artistic and financial plans. Evidence of plan approval and support by the applicant's board must accompany the application.

184
45.015
NEA Folk Arts Program
National Endowment for the Arts
1100 Pennsylvania Avenue NW
The Nancy Hanks Ctr
Washington, DC   20506

Areas of Interest

Program Description: The Folk Arts Program aims to honor and promote the folk, traditional, and community-based arts. Objectives are to identify traditional artists, support cultural activities or traditional communities, and to make this multicultural artistic heritage available to the wider public. Organizations are eligible in the categories of Media Documentation, Presentation of Traditional Arts, Services to the Field, and the State Apprenticeship Program.

Assistance Types: Project grants

Eligibility

Applicants Eligible: Arts presenters, colleges and universities, state arts agencies, local and regional arts organizations

Restrictions: Grants must be matched by the organization. Funds cannot be used for general operating expenses, research, foreign travel, construction or renovation, equipment purchase, nor can they support interpretations of traditional music or dance or reproductions of crafts or antiques.

Financial Profile

Obligations: Fiscal year 1993, $2,965,000; 1994, $3,333,000
Grant Range: Individuals, $10,000; organizations, $3,600-$50,000
Total Grants: In 1993, 516 applications received, 146 grants awarded; 1994, 506 applications received, 149 grants awarded

Application Process

Contact: (202) 682-5449; TDD: (202) 682-5496
Deadline: Optional proposal letter, January 1; application deadline, March 1
Processing Time: Six months
Review Process: Each application is evaluated by a panel. Panels are composed of rotating groups of professionally qualified experts and lay persons knowledgeable about the arts but not necessarily engaged in them as a profession. The panel's recommendations are

reviewed by the National Council on the Arts, and the final decision is made by the chair of the National Endowment for the Arts. Council members and the chair of the Endowment are appointed by the president of the United States and confirmed by the Senate.

Criteria: Traditionality of the artists and art forms, excellence of artists, feasibility of project plans, participation in the planning and commitment to the project by members of the cultural group whose traditions are to be presented, and potential benefit to the field as a whole.

Project Period: The grant period is generally up to one year; however, some projects, such as film or video, may require a longer time for completion. Estimate ample time to complete the proposed project.

Sample Grants

The University of Maine in Orono was awarded $26,700 to support the exhibition, Remnants of Our Lives: Maine Women and Traditional Textile Arts.

The University of South Carolina at Columbia received $27,000 to support an exhibition and accompanying interpretive material on the impact of the founding of Jugtown Pottery in 1921 by Jacques and Juliana Busbee.

Niagara University, New York, was awarded $27,400 to support field research on Catholic folk art traditions among Puerto Ricans in western New York State.

Comments/Analysis

The Folk Arts Program looks for demonstrations of community support, including financial assistance and contributions of cultural and/or technical expertise. The program urges that proposed projects include the expertise of persons with professional knowledge such as folklorists, anthropologists, or ethnomusicologists. Costs for involving such experts in training for local cultural workers, may be included in the grant request. Applicants are welcome to attend meetings of the National Council on the Arts as well as open sessions of advisory panels. Persons who would like to be considered for service on an advisory peer review panel should contact the Arts Endowment's Office of Panel Operations at the above address. You will be asked to complete a form for the automated data bank and to submit a resume.

185
45.022
NEA Advancement Program
National Endowment for the Arts
1100 Pennsylvania Avenue NW
The Nancy Hanks Ctr
Washington, DC   20506

Areas of Interest

Program Description: The Arts Advancement Program is designed to help organizations of the highest quality improve finan-

cial and managerial stability by developing specific strategies to eliminate deficiencies in organizational management practice and taking carefully planned steps toward the achievement of long-range goals. This program consists of two phases: Phase I, Planning and Technical Assistance; and Phase II, Advancement Grants for multiyear implementation. During Phase I the Endowment provides a consultant for a 15-month period to assess goals and address organizational needs impeding the organizations progress toward meeting its goals. A multiyear artistic and management plan is developed. Organizations can then apply for funds to implement the plan through an Advancement Grant.

Assistance Types: Planning and project grants

Eligibility

Applicants Eligible: Arts organizations, arts presenters, colleges and universities

Restrictions: Applicants must have a minimum of three years of artistic programming and a minimum operating budget of $100,000. Consortiums or groups of organizations are not eligible to apply. Phase II grants must be met with at least a three-to-one match.

Financial Profile

Obligations: Fiscal year 1994, $3,189,000
Grant Range: $25,000-$75,000
Total Grants: In 1993, 143 applications received, 90 grants awarded; 1994, 112 applications received, 76 grants awarded

Application Process

Contact: (202) 682-5436; TDD: (202) 682-5496
Deadline: Contact program to verify deadlines.
Processing Time: Eight months
Review Process: The Advancement review process involves two levels of panel review: one panel specific to each eligible discipline and one multidisciplinary panel composed of members of each of the discipline panels. The final list of applicants is forwarded to the National Council on the Arts, and the final decision is made by the chair of the National Endowment for the Arts. Council members and the chair of the Endowment are appointed by the president of the United States and confirmed by the Senate.

Criteria: Phase I applications will be considered on the basis of excellence, impact and potential benefit, capacity of organization to implement change, sustained performance, outreach to underserved areas, and demonstrated partnerships with the community, as well as the clarity and completeness of the application package.

Sample Grants

North Carolina University at Raleigh was awarded an Advancement Grant in the Presenting and Commissioning category.

The University of Arizona Museum of Art at Tucson was awarded an Advancement Grant in the Museum category.

Ferrum College and the Blue Ridge Institute in West Virginia received an Advancement Grant in the Folk Arts category.

Comments/Analysis

The Advancement Program has a two year cycle of eligibility. In the first year applications are accepted from Arts in Education, Design Arts, Museum, Music, Presenting and Commissioning, and Theater programs. The following fiscal year, Dance, Expansion Arts, Folk Arts, Literature, Media Arts, Opera-Musical Theater, and Visual Arts applications are accepted.

186
45.104
NEH Humanities Projects in Media
Division of Public Programs
National Endowment for the Humanities
1100 Pennsylvania Avenue NW
The Nancy Hanks Ctr
Washington, DC 20506

Areas of Interest

Program Description: The Media Program supports projects that use television, film, and radio programming to present important work in scholarship and learning in the humanities. Humanities disciplines include history; philosophy; languages; linguistics; literature; archaeology; jurisprudence; comparative religion; and the history, theory, and criticism of the arts. Projects involve collaboration between humanities scholars and experienced producers, directors, and scholars at every stage, from planning through production. The Media Program supports historical and cultural documentaries, dramatizations, talk shows, animation, or combinations of these formats. All television projects must have demonstrable value for a national audience, either adult or youth.
Assistance Types: Planning grants, scripting grants, and production grants are awarded as outright funds, matching funds, or combined funds

Eligibility

Applicants Eligible: Nonprofit organizations, institutions, and public television and radio stations
Restrictions: The Endowment's contribution to a project normally will not exceed 80 percent of project cost. The Endowment does not support research undertaken in the pursuit of a degree, the preparation or publication of textbooks, projects that are directed at persuading an audience to a particular point of view or that advocate a particular program of social action or change, projects that examine controversial issues without taking into account competing perspectives, or computer hardware or equipment costs. The Endowment does not support literary works for television or radio or projects designed to preserve information for deposit in archives. Applicants planning projects designed primarily for classroom use should consider applying to the Elementary and Secondary Education in the Humanities Program, 45.127.

Financial Profile

Obligations: Fiscal year 1993, $11,084,000; 1994, $10,345,000
Grant Range: $4,000-$2,500,000; average, $244,203
Total Grants: In 1993, 200 applications received, 43 grants awarded; 1994, 213 applications received, 49 grants awarded

Application Process

Contact: (202) 606-8278
Deadline: September and March
Processing Time: Five months
Review Process: Applications are reviewed by scholars and professionals in the humanities. Panelists represent a diversity of disciplinary, institutional, regional, and cultural backgrounds. The recommendations of panels and outside reviewers, as well as Endowment staff, are presented to the National Council on the Humanities, a board of 26 citizens who are nominated by the president of the United States and confirmed by the Senate. The National Council meets four times a year to advise the chair of the Endowment. The chair, appointed for a four-year term by the president with the consent of the Senate, makes the final decision about funding.
Criteria: NEH panelists will consider the following questions: How significant is the project? Does the project promise to advance scholarship in the humanities? What audience will benefit, and will the project increase the audience's understanding of the humanities? How appropriate is the methodology? How appropriate are the qualifications and expertise of those directing or contributing to the project? How clear, thorough, and realistic is the work plan? Is the medium appropriate for the subject matter?

Sample Grants

Dateline 1787, a series of fourteen half-hour weekly radio episodes, each summarizing one week's activities of the Constitutional Convention, was supported by an NEH grant.
The Homefront, a ninety-minute documentary film, used archival footage, photographs, and interviews to examine the impact of World War II on the lives of ordinary people.
Out of Time, a media program for youth, depicted life in nineteenth-century America as seen through the eyes of two children who are transported back in time to the Baltimore harborfront of 1851.

Comments/Analysis

Those interested in participating on Endowment panels may request an application from the above address. Applicants are urged to begin the preparation of proposals early so there is sufficient time for preliminary discussions with the NEH staff. Once the Endowment has received a formal application, however, staff will not comment on the status of that application except with respect to questions of completeness or eligibility.

187
45.113
NEH Public Humanities Projects
Division of Public Programs
National Endowment for the Humanities
1100 Pennsylvania Avenue NW
The Nancy Hanks Ctr
Washington, DC   20506

Areas of Interest

Program Description: The Public Humanities Program supports nationally significant projects and model programs designed to increase public understanding of the humanities and awareness of cultural works. Works such as poetry, drama, fiction, biography, essays, and philosophy as well as painting, sculpture, architecture, music, or dance may be the focus. The approach of one humanities discipline might be explored in depth, or the perspectives of several disciplines could be brought to bear on a specific topic. Applicants should consider a variety of formats that will reach the general public, including public symposia, community forums, lectures, interpretive exhibitions, or radio and television programs. The program invites proposals in the following three areas: Interpretation and Appreciation of Cultural Works; Illumination of Historical Ideas, Figures, and Events; and Understanding the Disciplines of the Humanities.

Assistance Types: Planning grants are awarded to support collaborative efforts of scholars, public programming specialists, and an institution's staff in conceiving and planning programs on a particular theme or topic in the humanities. Implementation grants support the presentation of fully developed public programs in the humanities. Grants may be in the form of outright funds, which are not contingent on additional fundraising by grantees, or matching funds, which require grantees to secure funds from a third party before federal funds are awarded. Applicants may also request a combination of outright and matching funds.

Eligibility

Applicants Eligible: Any state or public agency, and any nonprofit society, institution, organization, association, or museum, is eligible.

Restrictions: The following types of projects are ineligible: artistic or media productions, research projects, projects focused on the organization or exhibition of collections, publication costs for materials intended for scholarly audiences, stipends or fellowships, workshops, vocational or continuing education courses, or projects intended to persuade an audience to a particular point of view without provision for competing perspectives.

Financial Profile

Obligations: Fiscal year 1993, $2,118,622; 1994, $2,384,000
Grant Range: $15,000-$250,000; average, $70,000
Total Grants: In 1993, 80 applications received, 21 grants awarded; 1994, 85 applications received, 23 grants awarded

Application Process

Contact: (202) 786-0271
Deadline: Mid-March and mid-September
Processing Time: Projects begin October 1 and April 1. Before developing a final proposal, applicants should submit a preliminary proposal at least 10 weeks before the deadline for formal applications. The preliminary proposal should include a five-page statement describing the project and its humanities themes, a general implementation plan, and an estimate of the total budget.

Review Process: Applications are reviewed by scholars and professionals in the humanities. Panelists represent a diversity of disciplinary, institutional, regional, and cultural backgrounds. In some cases supplementary reviews are solicited from specialists.

Criteria: Of highest priority is the quality of the content to be communicated to public audiences. Evaluators consider the following questions when assessing proposals: Does the project advance public understanding and appreciation of significant ideas in the humanities? Does the proposal fall within one or more of the three areas of interest to the Public Humanities Projects program? To what degree are the objectives and plan of work clearly defined and capable of realization by the applicant? Do the staff and consultants have the requisite experience and qualifications to successfully complete the project? Will written or electronic products be created as part of the project to extend its life and scope? The recommendations of panels and outside reviewers, as well as Endowment staff, are presented to the National Council on the Humanities, a board of 26 citizens who are nominated by the president of the United States and confirmed by the Senate. The National Council meets four times a year to advise the chair of the Endowment. The chair, appointed for a four-year term by the president with the consent of the Senate, makes the final decision about funding.

Project Period: Planning grant periods are usually under six months; implementation grant periods are usually one to three years.

Sample Grants

Delaware County Community College was awarded funds to support conferences, lectures, tours, and workshops and to mount an exhibition and compile a publication on the development of manufacturing from the colonial period to 1876.

Southwest Texas State University received a grant to support a public lecture series, book discussion groups, a film series, and an exhibit on the Native American Southwest.

Virginia Polytechnic Institute and State University was awarded a grant to support forums and community discussions and to produce videotapes focusing on ethical issues in modern medicine and technology.

Comments/Analysis

Of the 21 grants awarded in 1993, four colleges or universities were selected. Collaborations between scholars and individuals with public programming expertise, such as exhibition designers or filmmakers, or collaborations between institutions, are encouraged. Those interested in participating on Endowment panels may request an application from the above address.

188
45.125
NEH Humanities Projects in Museum and Historical Organizations
Division of Public Programs
National Endowment for the Humanities
1100 Pennsylvania Avenue NW
The Nancy Hanks Ctr
Washington, DC   20506

Areas of Interest

Program Description: This program offers grants to museums and similar institutions for projects designed to increase understanding of the humanities. Projects may include planning and implementation of temporary, traveling, and permanent exhibitions and development of related materials.

Assistance Types: The program offers outright, matching, and combination grants in four categories: planning grants are used to develop the themes and ideas underlying an exhibition as well as to develop installation plans; implementation grants support the final production of a project; humanities self-study grants allow museums to work with subject experts to craft a long-range plan; and professional development in the humanities grants fund seminars, conferences, or publications directed towards improving abilities of museum staff to present public humanities programs.

Eligibility

Applicants Eligible: History, art, anthropology, and natural history museums; historical societies; historic sites; university museums and galleries; youth museums; science and technology centers; and zoos and botanical gardens

Restrictions: The program does not fund acquisition of artifacts, research undertaken in the pursuit of a degree, the preparation or publication of textbooks, projects that are directed at persuading an audience to a particular point of view or that advocate a particular program of social action or change, projects that examine controversial issues without taking into account competing perspectives, or computer hardware or equipment costs.

Financial Profile

Obligations: Fiscal year 1993, $9,217,000; 1994, $9,953,000
Grant Range: $10,000-$500,000; average, $100,000
Total Grants: In 1993, 240 applications received, 92 grants awarded; 1994, 224 applications received, 72 grants awarded

Application Process

Contact: (202) 606-8284
Deadline: June and December. All applicants, particularly first-time applicants, are encouraged to call the office to discuss the project, and to submit preliminary drafts of proposals at least six weeks in advance of deadline dates to allow time for consultation with program staff.

Processing Time: Five months
Review Process: Applications are reviewed by scholars and professionals in the humanities. Panelists represent a diversity of disciplinary, institutional, regional, and cultural backgrounds. The recommendations of panels and outside reviewers, as well as Endowment staff, are presented to the National Council on the Humanities, a board of 26 citizens who are nominated by the president of the United States and confirmed by the Senate. The National Council meets four times a year to advise the chair of the Endowment. The chair, appointed for a four-year term by the president with the consent of the Senate, makes the final decision about funding.
Criteria: Evaluators consider the following factors, depending on the category: conceptual framework, intellectual content of project, format, resources for planning and plan of work, personnel, and budget.
Project Period: Up to three years

Sample Grants

The State University of New York at Binghamton's University Art Museum received a $50,000 planning grant to plan an exhibition to examine the concept of insanity in America from the late 18th through the 19th century, emphasizing its depiction in the fine and popular arts.

The Maxwell Museum of Anthropology at the University of New Mexico received an implementation grant to develop a permanent exhibition, People of the Southwest.

The Brown County Historical Society in Minnesota, with collections documenting local history and Native American and European ethnic traditions, received a humanities self-study grant to reassess the humanities interpretation of its exhibitions and public programs.

Through a Professional Development grant, the Valentine Museum in Richmond, in collaboration with the Chicago Historical Society and the American Association of State and Local History, organized a three-day conference to explore the role of museums in advancing public understanding of urban history.

Comments/Analysis

The program urges applicants to clearly describe how their project relates to the disciplines of the humanities, to the mission of their institution, and to their intended audiences. For planning and implementation applications, applicants should describe any evaluation activities that will occur, include visual material with the application, and remember that the walk through is central to implementation applications and should provide readers with a clear idea of the visitor's experience of the exhibitions. Applicants are urged to begin the preparation of proposals early so there is sufficient time for preliminary discussions with the NEH staff. Once the Endowment has received a formal application, however, staff will not comment on the status of that application except with respect to questions of completeness or eligibility. Those interested in participating on Endowment panels may request an application from the above address.

189
45.127
NEH Elementary and Secondary Education in
the Humanities
Division of Education Programs
National Endowment for the Humanities
1100 Pennsylvania Avenue NW
The Nancy Hanks Ctr
Washington, DC   20506

Areas of Interest

Program Description: The program promotes a central role for the humanities in the school curriculum and in professional development activities of educators. The program supports a variety of projects that involve the serious study of history, literature, foreign languages, and other humanities fields. National and regional categories include Institutes for Teachers and Administrators; Special Projects, including conference grants; and Collaborative Projects, partnerships between schools and institutions of higher education.

Assistance Types: Project grants in the form of outright grants, matching funds, and combined funds

Eligibility

Applicants Eligible: Schools and school systems, nonprofit organizations, two- and four-year colleges, universities, libraries, museums, educational associations, professional organizations, research centers, state or local government units, and educational and cultural consortia are eligible. When two or more institutions collaborate on an application, one of them should serve as the lead applicant and administer the project.

Restrictions: Contributions by the Education Division will not exceed 70 percent. The Endowment does not support research undertaken in the pursuit of a degree, the preparation or publication of textbooks, projects that are directed at persuading an audience to a particular point of view or that advocate a particular program of social action or change, projects that examine controversial issues without taking into account competing perspectives, or computer hardware or equipment costs.

Financial Profile

Obligations: Fiscal year 1993, $7,251,000; 1994, $6,871,111
Grant Range: Institute grants, $140,000-$180,000; collaborative project grants will not generally exceed $250,000; humanities focus grants, $10,000-$25,000
Total Grants: In 1993, 142 applications received, 62 grants awarded; 1994, 132 applications received, 48 grants awarded

Application Process

Contact: (202) 606-8377
Deadline: December 15, March 15
Processing Time: Approximately six months. Applicants should initiate contact by telephone or by sending a brief description of the proposed project to the program for an assessment of eligibility. Approximately two months before the formal application deadline, the applicant should submit a draft of the full proposal for further review by the program officer.

Review Process: Applications are reviewed by scholars and professionals in the humanities and educators knowledgeable about the pertinent level of instruction. Panelists represent a diversity of disciplinary, institutional, regional, and cultural backgrounds. In some cases supplementary reviews are solicited from specialists. The recommendations of panels and outside reviewers, as well as Endowment staff, are presented to the National Council on the Humanities, a board of 26 citizens who are nominated by the president of the United States and confirmed by the Senate. The National Council meets four times a year to advise the chair of the Endowment. The chair, appointed for a four-year term by the president with the consent of the Senate, makes the final decision about funding.

Criteria: Reviewers evaluate proposals by answering the following general questions: is the project rooted in texts and topics of central importance to the humanities, and is it likely to result in better humanities instruction? Is the intellectual rationale for the proposed project clear and persuasive? Does the proposal include academically rigorous syllabi or reading lists? Is the schedule of activities well planned and feasible? Are project personnel well qualified to carry out the proposed duties? Do letters from visiting scholars, consultants, or prospective participants demonstrate sufficient interest and commitment? Are the plans for project administration sound? Is the budget reasonable? Is the level of institutional cost sharing adequate? Where appropriate, does the institution possess the resources and commitment to maintain the program once it is in place? Are plans for project evaluation reasonable? Where appropriate, are follow-up activities likely to improve teaching and learning in the humanities?

Project Period: One to three years

Sample Grants

The George Washington University in Washington, DC, received NEH support for a national institute for elementary and secondary teachers: America in World Affairs Since 1945.

Columbia University in New York received NEH support for a regional institute for elementary and secondary teachers: Project Pluma: Writing through Content in the 4th-12th Grade Spanish Class.

The University of Illinois, Urbana-Champaign, received NEH support for a state institute for elementary and secondary teachers: The African American Experience: A Framework for Integrating American History.

Comments/Analysis

Those interested in participating on Endowment panels may request an application from the above address. Applicants are urged to begin the preparation of proposals early so there is sufficient time for preliminary discussions with the NEH staff. Once the Endowment has received a formal application, however, staff will not comment on the status of that application except with respect to questions of completeness or eligibility.

190

45.130

NEH Challenge Grants
National Endowment for the Humanities
1100 Pennsylvania Avenue NW
The Nancy Hanks Ctr
Washington, DC   20506

Areas of Interest

Program Description: NEH Challenge Grants assist nonprofit institutions interested in developing new sources of long-term support for educational, scholarly, preservation, and public programs in the humanities. Funds may be used to establish or increase institutional endowments and thus guarantee long-term support for a variety of humanities needs. Funds may also be used for construction, renovation, equipment purchases, and retirement of debt, where such needs are clearly related to improvements in the humanities. Proposals are reviewed in one of three NEH divisions: education programs, public programs, and research programs.
Assistance Types: Challenge grants

Eligibility

Applicants Eligible: Nonprofit postsecondary, educational, or cultural institutions and organizations working within the humanities
Restrictions: Grantees must raise three or four dollars for each federal dollar offered

Financial Profile

Obligations: Fiscal year 1993, $14,228,000; 1994, $14,426,000
Grant Range: Applicants may request up to $1,000,000 over three years; range $137,500-$1,000,000; average, $467,000
Total Grants: In 1993, 121 applications received, 26 grants awarded; 1994, 141 applications received, 36 grants awarded

Application Process

Contact: Division of Education Programs, (202) 606-8380; Division of Public Programs, (202) 606-8267; Division of Research Programs, (202) 606-8358
Deadline: May
Processing Time: Six months
Review Process: Applications are reviewed by scholars and professionals in the humanities. Panelists represent a diversity of disciplinary, institutional, regional, and cultural backgrounds. The recommendations of panels and outside reviewers, as well as Endowment staff, are presented to the National Council on the Humanities, a board of 26 citizens who are nominated by the president of the United States and confirmed by the Senate. The National Council meets four times a year to advise the chair of the Endowment. The chair, appointed for a four-year term by the president with the consent of the Senate, makes the final decision about funding.
Criteria: Evaluators consider the following criteria: the intellectual significance and potential contribution to scholarship in the hu-

manities; the appropriateness of project and of the methods by which these will be addressed; the quality and expertise of project staff and contributors; the quality and usefulness of the product or outcome; and the potential for success, including appropriateness of the budget.
Project Period: Not applicable

Sample Grants

A Challenge Grant enabled a private university to acquire holdings to expand its humanities collections in areas where the curriculum has expanded. Grant funds also supported the purchase of library materials and the addition of two library staff members.

Comments/Analysis

Those interested in participating on Endowment panels may request an application from the above address. Applicants are urged to begin the preparation of proposals early so there is sufficient time for preliminary discussions with the NEH staff. Once the Endowment has received a formal application, however, staff will not comment on the status of that application except with respect to questions of completeness or eligibility.

191

45.132

NEH Scholarly Publications: Editions, Translations, and Subventions
Division of Research Programs
National Endowment for the Humanities
1100 Pennsylvania Avenue NW
The Nancy Hanks Ctr
Washington, DC   20506

Areas of Interest

Program Description: Scholarly Publications grants provide support for the preparation for publication of texts that promise to make contributions to the study of humanities. Projects may explore the disciplines of history; philosophy; languages; linguistics; literature; archaeology; jurisprudence; ethics; comparative religion; and the history, theory, and criticism of the arts. There are three categories in the program: Editions grants, which support various stages in the preparation of authoritative and annotated editions of works and documents of value to humanities scholars and general readers; Translations grants, which support individual or collaborative projects to translate into English works that provide insight into the history, literature, philosophy, and artistic achievements of other cultures and that make available the thought and learning of those civilizations; and Subventions grants to scholarly presses and publishing entities to support the publication and dissemination of excellent books in all fields of the humanities.
Assistance Types: Project grants

Eligibility

Applicants Eligible: Individuals and nonprofit institutions and organizations

Restrictions: Applications from individuals are not accepted for Subvention grants. The Endowment does not support research undertaken in the pursuit of a degree, the preparation or publication of textbooks, projects that are directed at persuading an audience to a particular point of view or that advocate a particular program of social action or change, projects that examine controversial issues without taking into account competing perspectives, or computer hardware or equipment costs.

Financial Profile

Obligations: Fiscal year 1994, $6,700,000

Grant Range: Editions and Translations, $7,000-$25,000; average $100,000; Subventions, $7,000, a fixed amount per volume

Total Grants: In 1994, Editions: 79 applications received, 34 grants awarded; Translations: 112 applications received, 24 grants awarded; Subventions: 108 applications received, 48 grants awarded

Application Process

Contact: (202) 606-8207

Deadline: Editions and Translations: Those desiring staff comment should send draft proposals in April; the deadline for formal applications is in June. Subventions: Those desiring staff comment should send draft proposals in January; deadline for formal proposals is March.

Processing Time: Six months

Review Process: Applications are reviewed by scholars and professionals in the humanities. Panelists represent a diversity of disciplinary, institutional, regional, and cultural backgrounds. The recommendations of panels and outside reviewers, as well as Endowment staff, are presented to the National Council on the Humanities, a board of 26 citizens who are nominated by the president of the United States and confirmed by the Senate. The National Council meets four times a year to advise the chair of the Endowment. The chair, appointed for a four-year term by the President with the consent of the Senate, makes the final decision about funding.

Criteria: Evaluators consider the following criteria: the intellectual significance and potential contribution to scholarship in the humanities; the appropriateness of the research questions posed in the project and of the methods by which these will be addressed; the quality and expertise of project staff and contributors; the quality and usefulness of the product or outcome; and the potential for success, including appropriateness of the budget.

Sample Grants

George Washington University in Washington, DC, was awarded $1,920 to support the preparation of a documentary history of the first US Congress, 1789-91.

Rutgers University in Newark, New Jersey, received a two-year grant of $100,000 to support the preparation of microfilm and book editions of the papers of Thomas A. Edison.

University of Washington at Seattle received a grant of $6,500 to support the translation of Nietzche's works, with annotations, postscripts on the individual texts, and indices.

Rice University in Houston, Texas, was awarded $76,897 to support the collection, transcription, and translation of Ju/'hoan Namibian Bushman texts, which include folktales, oral histories, environmental knowledge accounts, healing narratives, and political oration.

University of North Carolina Press in Chapel Hill received a grant to support the publication of a history of the Cherokee nation from its westward removal to the end of its sovereign status.

University of California Press at Oakland received a grant to support the publication of a cross-cultural study of a 16th-century Venetian madrigal.

Comments/Analysis

Those interested in participating on Endowment panels may request an application from the above address. Applicants are urged to begin the preparation of proposals early so there is sufficient time for preliminary discussions with the NEH staff. Once the Endowment has received a formal application, however, staff will not comment on the status of that application except with respect to questions of completeness or eligibility. The Endowment encourages proposals related to the important historical and literary materials in the collections of historically black colleges and universities texts and documents pertaining to Native American and Hispanic American history and culture.

192
45.140
NEH Interpretive Research: Collaborative Projects, Archaeology Projects, Humanities, Science and Technology, and Conferences
Division of Research Programs
National Endowment for the Humanities
1100 Pennsylvania Avenue NW
The Nancy Hanks Ctr
Washington, DC   20506

Areas of Interest

Program Description: Interpretive Research grants provide support for scholarly research that will advance knowledge and enhance understanding of topics, themes, or issues of central importance to the humanities. Projects may explore the disciplines of history; philosophy; languages; linguistics; literature; archaeology; jurisprudence; ethics; comparative religion; and the history, theory, and criticism of the arts. Four categories are included in this program. Collaborative Projects: Grants are intended to support collaborative research that will have a significant impact on scholarship in the humanities. The Endowment encourages collaborative projects that provide synthesis of scholarly and intellectual issues. The collaboration may involve two or more scholars from the same or different disciplines, from one or more institu-

tions. Consultants and research assistants may supplement the team. Archaeology Projects: The Endowment supports archaeology projects with the potential to enhance scholarly knowledge and understanding of history and culture. Although the priority is for projects that focus on preparing the results of excavations for scholarly and popular publications, support is also available for work in survey, excavation, materials analysis, laboratory research, artifact preservation and field reports for work on US or foreign sites. Humanities, Science, and Technology: Grants in this category support research that brings to bear the knowledge, methods, and perspectives of the humanities on the subjects of science, technology, and medicine. Both historical studies and studies of current topics are eligible. Collaborative or coordinated research involving humanities scholars and scientists are encouraged. All projects are expected to lead to major publications. Conferences: The Conferences program supports opportunities for the exchange of ideas to advance the state of research in a field or topic of major importance to one or more disciplines in the humanities. A proposed conference may be motivated by the availability of new data or materials, recent developments that may affect future directions of the field, or by a critical juncture in research on a particular topic. All projects should be organized around a specific set of research objectives, and applicant must demonstrate that a conference is the appropriate method of realizing these objectives.
Assistance Types: Outright grants, matching funds, combined funds

Eligibility

Applicants Eligible: Individuals and nonprofit institutions and organizations
Restrictions: The Endowment generally does not fund more than 70 percent of eligible expenses. The Endowment does not support research undertaken in the pursuit of a degree, the preparation or publication of textbooks, projects that are directed at persuading an audience to a particular point of view or that advocate a particular program of social action or change, projects that examine controversial issues without taking into account competing perspectives, or computer hardware or equipment costs.

Financial Profile

Obligations: Fiscal year 1993, $4,100,000; 1994, $4,090,000
Grant Range: $15,000-$305,000; average, $66,000
Total Grants: In 1994, 328 applications received, 62 grants awarded

Application Process

Contact: (202) 606-8210
Deadline: In all but the Conferences program categories, draft proposals due by mid-August. For the Conferences program, deadlines are January, October, and April; applicants are encouraged to submit a draft of the narrative and budget sections of the proposal at least eight weeks before the deadline. All applicants are encouraged to consult with the NEH staff by telephone or letter well in advance of the deadline. To receive advice about the eligibility of a project, the applicants should send a brief (one- to five-page) description of the project

Processing Time: Nine months
Review Process: Applications are reviewed by scholars and professionals in the humanities. Panelists represent a diversity of disciplinary, institutional, regional, and cultural backgrounds. The recommendations of panels and outside reviewers, as well as Endowment staff, are presented to the National Council on the Humanities, a board of 26 citizens nominated by the president of the United States and confirmed by the Senate. The National Council meets four times a year to advise the chair of the Endowment. The chair, appointed for a four-year term by the president with the consent of the Senate, makes the final decision about funding.
Criteria: Evaluators consider the following criteria: intellectual significance and potential contribution to scholarship in the humanities; the appropriateness of the research questions posed in the project and of the methods by which these will be addressed; the quality and expertise of project staff and contributors; the quality and usefulness of the product or outcome; and the potential for success, including appropriateness of the budget.
Project Period: Up to three years

Sample Grants

Collaborative Projects:
The University of Tennessee at Knoxville received a three-year award of $119,885 to support a comparative history of food riots in Britain, France, and Germany between 1750 and 1850, which will illustrate the transformation of agrarian practices in the 18th and 19th centuries.
Indiana University in Bloomington received $10,000 to support a study of how Arapaho Indian age groups and genders in the southern Plains have responded to rapid social changes and maintained traditions in the late 19th and early 20th centuries.
Archaeology Projects:
The University of Florida at Gainesville received a two-year grant of $105,000 to support the analysis and publication of work at two island sites of the Middle and Late Archaic periods off the Florida coast.
The University of Arizona at Tucson received $15,000 to support a final six-month interpretive study before publication of the excavations at Naukratis, Egypt, integrating the findings from five seasons of work at this Greek trading post in the Nile Delta, ca. 800 BC to 300 A.D.
Humanities, Science, and Technology:
The University of California at Los Angeles was awarded a three-year grant of $110,000 to support a study of the 16th-century encounter between Spain and the Americans, focusing on the Spanish physician Francisco Hernandez and his accounts of Aztec customs and descriptions of Mexican plants and animals in the 1570s.
Villanova University in Pennsylvania was granted $63,500 to support the preparation of a history of the chemistry profession and how the interactions of academic and industrial chemists and society in Germany from 1865 to 1935 forged that nation's powerful science-based industry.
Conferences:
Tulane University in New Orleans, Louisiana, received $29,904 support of a conference, European Nationalism Revisited: An

Interdisciplinary, Cross-Cultural Approach to Conceptual Classification.

Yale University in New Haven, Connecticut, received $20,530 to support an international conference, The Age of Giorgio Vasari: Art, Literature, and History at the Medicean Court.

Comments/Analysis

The Endowment solicits reviews of applications to the Interpretive Research program. Applicants are asked to suggest six persons who can provide impartial evaluations of the proposal. Also, those interested in participating on Endowment panels may request an application from the above address. Applicants are urged to begin the preparation of proposals early so there is sufficient time for preliminary discussions with the NEH staff. Once the Endowment has received a formal application, however, staff will not comment on the status of that application except with respect to questions of completeness or eligibility.

193
45.145
NEH Reference Materials Program
Division of Research Programs
National Endowment for the Humanities
1100 Pennsylvania Avenue NW
The Nancy Hanks Ctr
Washington, DC   20506

Areas of Interest

Program Description: The Reference Materials Program provides support for the preparation of reference works that will enhance the availability of information and research materials. Support is available for the creation of dictionaries, historical or linguistic atlases, encyclopedias, databases, textbases, and other projects that will provide essential scholarly tools for the advancement of research or for general reference purpose. Grants may also support projects that help researchers locate information about humanities documentation and produce scholarly guides. Planning efforts or feasibility studies are eligible. Humanities disciplines include history; philosophy; languages; linguistics; literature; archaeology; jurisprudence; comparative religion; and the history, theory, and criticism of the arts.

Assistance Types: Project grants in the form of outright, matching, and combined funds

Eligibility

Applicants Eligible: Individuals and nonprofit organizations and institutions

Restrictions: The Endowment's contribution to a project normally will not exceed 80 percent of project cost. The Endowment does not support research undertaken in the pursuit of a degree, the preparation or publication of textbooks, projects that are directed at persuading an audience to a particular point of view or that advocate a particular program of social action or change, projects

that examine controversial issues without taking into account competing perspectives, computer hardware, or equipment costs.

Financial Profile

Obligations: Fiscal year 1993, $5,000,000; 1994, $3,431,000
Grant Range: $5,000-$300,000; average, $130,000
Total Grants: In 1993, 160 applications received, 38 grants awarded; 1994, 188 applications received, 37 grants awarded

Application Process

Contact: (202) 606-8358
Deadline: Draft proposals due, July; postmark deadline for formal applications, September
Processing Time: Nine months
Review Process: Applications are reviewed by scholars and professionals in the humanities. Panelists represent a diversity of disciplinary, institutional, regional, and cultural backgrounds. The recommendations of panels and outside reviewers, as well as Endowment staff, are presented to the National Council on the Humanities, a board of 26 citizens who are nominated by the president of the United States and confirmed by the Senate. The National Council meets four times a year to advise the chair of the Endowment. The chair, appointed for a four-year term by the president with the consent of the Senate, makes the final decision about funding.
Criteria: NEH panelists will consider the following questions: How significant is the project? Does the project promise to advance scholarship in the humanities? What audience will benefit? How appropriate is the methodology? How appropriate are the qualifications and expertise of those directing or contributing to the project? How thorough and realistic is the work plan? Will the project result in a significant publication? How strong is the case for the form (e.g. print volume, microform, CD-ROM, database) of the product?
Project Period: Up to three years

Sample Grants

University of Wisconsin at Madison was awarded a two-year grant of $600,000 to support the preparation of the Dictionary of American Regional English, a reference work describing regional and folk varieties of American English.

University of Arizona at Tucson was awarded a two-year grant toward the creation of a comprehensive dictionary of Hopi, a language of the Southwest Pueblo Indians.

Georgetown College in Georgetown, Kentucky, received $91,455 for a two-year project resulting in a computerized first-line index and bibliography of approximately 20,000 Elizabethan poems.

Catholic University in Washington, DC, received an award of $10,000 to support the creation of indices for manuscripts of Gregorian chants to be added to existing indices and distributed in printed or electronic format.

Comments/Analysis

Those interested in participating on Endowment panels may request an application from the above address. Applicants are urged to begin the preparation of proposals early so there is sufficient time for preliminary discussions with the NEH staff. Once the Endowment has received a formal application, however, staff will not comment on the status of that application except with respect to questions of completeness or eligibility.

194
45.150
NEH Higher Education in the Humanities
Division of Education Programs
National Endowment for the Humanities
1100 Pennsylvania Avenue NW
The Nancy Hanks Ctr
Washington, DC   20506

Areas of Interest

Program Description: Humanities disciplines include history; philosophy; languages; linguistics; literature; archaeology; jurisprudence; comparative religion; and the history, theory, and criticism of the arts. The Higher Education program assists institutions that are trying to provide students with a coherent and rigorous introduction to the humanities by establishing liberal arts core curricula. The program seeks projects that are aimed at expanding and enriching the humanities content in the undergraduate and graduate preparation of elementary and secondary school teachers and college faculty. In addition, the program supports faculty study projects and curricular revision projects in two-year colleges. To assist in the development of broad-based humanities courses, the program supports summer institutes for college and university faculty.

Eligibility

Applicants Eligible: Nonprofit organizations, two- and four-year colleges, universities, libraries, museums, educational associations, professional organizations, research centers, state or local government units, and educational and cultural consortia are eligible. When two or more institutions collaborate on an application, one of them should serve as the lead applicant and administer the project.
Restrictions: Contributions by the education division will not exceed 70 percent. The Endowment does not support research undertaken in the pursuit of a degree, the preparation or publication of textbooks, projects that are directed at persuading an audience to a particular point of view or that advocate a particular program of social action or change, projects that examine controversial issues without taking into account competing perspectives, or computer hardware or equipment costs.

Financial Profile

Obligations: Fiscal year 1993, $7,100,000; 1994, $6,777,663
Grant Range: The maximum grant for complex one-year projects is $250,000. Humanities focus grants range from $10,000-$25,000
Total Grants: In 1993, 150 applications received, 50 grants awarded; 1994, 137 applications received, 51 grants awarded

Application Process

Contact: (202) 606-8380
Deadline: October and April
Processing Time: Five to eight months. Applicants should initiate contact by telephone or by sending a brief description of the proposed project to the program for an assessment of eligibility. Two months before the formal application deadline, the applicant should submit a draft of the full proposal for further review by the program officer.
Review Process: Applications are reviewed by scholars and professionals in the humanities and educators knowledgeable about the pertinent level of instruction. Panelists represent a diversity of disciplinary, institutional, regional, and cultural backgrounds. In some cases supplementary reviews are solicited from specialists. The recommendations of panels and outside reviewers, as well as Endowment staff, are presented to the National Council on the Humanities, a board of 26 citizens who are nominated by the president of the United States and confirmed by the Senate. The National Council meets four times a year to advise the chair of the Endowment. The chair, appointed for a four-year term by the president with the consent of the Senate, makes the final decision about funding.
Criteria: Reviewers evaluate proposals by answering the following general questions: Is the project rooted in texts and topics of central importance to the humanities, and is it likely to result in better humanities instruction? Is the intellectual rationale for the proposed project clear and persuasive? Does the proposal include academically rigorous syllabi or reading lists? Is the schedule of activities well planned and feasible? Are project personnel well qualified to carry out the proposed duties? Do letters from visiting scholars, consultants, or prospective participants demonstrate sufficient interest and commitment? Are the plans for project administration sound? Is the budget reasonable? Is the level of institutional cost sharing adequate? Where appropriate, does the institution possess the resources and commitment to maintain the program once it is in place? Are plans for project evaluation reasonable? Where appropriate, are follow-up activities likely to improve teaching and learning in the humanities?
Project Period: One to three years

Sample Grants

The NEH supported a five-week institute for undergraduate faculty members to study primary sources bearing on the cultural background and world view of Christopher Columbus.
The NEH supported the development of a new year-long course in world literature, including a six-week faculty workshop for those teaching the course.
The NEH supported a collaboration between a museum and a university, including an exploration of ways that existing

courses could benefit for using the museum's resources, the development of an internship program for advanced art history students, and design of a new team-taught course involving faculty and museum staff.

Comments/Analysis

Those interested in participating on Endowment panels may request an application from the above address. Applicants are urged to begin the preparation of proposals early so there is sufficient time for preliminary discussions with the NEH staff. Once the Endowment has received a formal application, however, staff will not comment on the status of that application except with respect to questions of completeness or eligibility.

195
45.158
NEH/NSF Leadership Opportunity in Science and Humanities Education
National Endowment for the Humanities
1100 Pennsylvania Avenue NW
The Nancy Hanks Ctr
Washington, DC   20506

Areas of Interest

Program Description: This joint program of the National Endowment for the Humanities (NEH), the Fund for the Improvement of Postsecondary Education (FIPSE), and the National Science Foundation (NSF) was created in 1992 to encourage the integration of science, social science, and humanities education in the undergraduate curriculum. The program supports the development of courses, course sequences, or curricula that go beyond the boundaries of a single discipline and promote scientific and humanistic literacy. Projects should be based on a close collaboration of faculty in sciences and the humanities and should have potential for replication and leadership at the national level.
Assistance Types: Project grants

Eligibility

Applicants Eligible: Two- and four-year colleges, universities, libraries, museums, educational associations, professional organizations, research centers, state and local governments, and educational and cultural consortia are eligible. When two or more institutions or organizations collaborate on an application, one serves as the lead applicant.
Restrictions: Substantial cost sharing is expected of participating institutions; Leadership Opportunity contributions will not exceed 70 percent of total project costs. In general, institutions are expected to provide most of the equipment needed for project activities.

Financial Profile

Obligations: Fiscal year 1993, $1,700,000; 1994, $1,700,000
Grant Range: $31,000-$219,132
Total Grants: In 1994, 14 grants awarded

Application Process

Contact: NEH Division of Education Programs, (202) 606-8380; NSF Division of Undergraduate Education, (703) 306-1666; FIPSE, (202) 708-5750
Deadline: Applicants are encouraged to call a program officer or to send a preliminary description of the proposed project. Final proposals are due in March.
Processing Time: Six months
Review Process: Since reviewers from various disciplines will participate in the evaluation, applicants should write proposals without technical language or jargon.
Criteria: Proposals will be evaluated according to the following NEH, NSF, and FIPSE criteria: merit of the idea, including a sound rationale and demonstration that the project will examine significant relations among the sciences and the humanities and will result in improvements in instruction and learning; quality of the educational activities; feasibility and quality of planning and administration; and potential for impact.
Project Period: One to three years

Sample Grants

Nassau Community College in Garden City, New Jersey, was awarded a grant for Education in the 21st Century: Multidisciplinary General Education Liberal Arts Project in Science and the Humanities, an integrative five-course sequence. The new courses created are the Making of the Modern Mind I and II, World Cultures, Major Ideas in the Post-Modern World, and Issues in Science and Society.

Skidmore College in Saratoga Springs, New York, received funds for capstone courses in Science and the Humanities. An interdisciplinary liberal studies core program was followed by four new team-taught courses: The New Reproductive Technology: Science, Law, and Ethics; Scientific Discovery and Societal Choices; Construction of the Individual: Mind/Brain/Consciousness/Culture; and the Global Village: Information Revolution and the Twenty-First Century.

Worcester Polytechnic Institute in Massachusetts was awarded a grant to create a capstone seminar for science and engineering students: Light, Vision, and Understanding.

Comments/Analysis

Humanities disciplines include history; philosophy; languages; linguistics; literature; archaeology; jurisprudence; comparative religion; and the history, theory, and criticism of the arts. Social sciences, including education and behavioral and economic sciences; biological, computer, engineering, and geosciences; mathematics; and physical sciences are eligible. Projects should make use of significant texts and topics from the sciences and humanities; should include field experiences, laboratory activities, and mathematics, as appropriate; and should demonstrate excellent pedagogy. Projects may initiate comprehensive reform of general education programs or core curricula, develop new interdisciplinary majors or minors, or develop introductory or capstone courses. Projects that would increase the participation of qualified women, minorities, and persons with disabilities or strengthen the preparation of prospective elementary and secondary teachers are especially encouraged. Applicants are urged to begin the preparation of proposals early so there is sufficient time for preliminary discussions with the NEH staff. Once the Endowment has received a formal application, however, staff will not comment on the status of that application except with respect to questions of completeness or eligibility. Those interested in participating on Endowment panels may request an application from the above address.

196
45.301
Institute of Museum Services Grants
Institute of Museum Services
1100 Pennsylvania Avenue NW
Washington, DC   20506

Areas of Interest

Program Description: The institute seeks to increase and improve museum services, to encourage and assist museums in their educational role, and assist museums in modernizing methods and facilities so that they can conserve the nation's cultural, historic, and scientific heritage. Both competitive and non-competitive grants are awarded through the following programs: General Operating Support (GOS), Conservation Project (CP), Museum Assessment Program (MAP), Conservation Assessment Program (CAP), Technical Assistance Grants (TAG), the Professional Services Program (PSP), and Museum Leadership Initiatives (MLI).
Assistance Types: Competitive and noncompetitive project grants

Eligibility

Applicants Eligible: Museums organized as public or private non-profit institutions
Restrictions: GOS grants are two-year awards. MAP grants are awarded on a one-time first-come, first-served basis. MAP I grants fund an independent professional assessment of the institution's programs and operations. MAP II grants fund an independent professional assessment of collection care and maintenance; MAP III grants fund an assessment of the public dimensions of a museum's work. Applications for MAP I, II, or III include a self-study questionnaire by the American Association of Museums.

Financial Profile

Obligations: Fiscal year 1993, GOS: $22,103,000; CP: $3,064,000; CAP: $966,000; MAP I: $200,000; MAP II: $100,000; MAP III: $100,000. Fiscal year 1994, GOS: $22,052,000; CP: $2,501,000; CAP: $915,000; MAP I: $298,225; MAP II: $122,450; MAP III: $100,000; PSP: $199,500; MLI: $498,000; TAG: $499,000

Grant Range: GOS: $5,000-$112,000, average $73,000; CP: average $15,000; CAP: average $6,000; MAP I, II, and III: average $2,000; MIL: average $30,000
Total Grants: In 1994: GOS, 1,158 applications received, 300 grants awarded; CP, 297 applications received, 154 grants awarded; PSP, 27 applications received, nine grants awarded; CAP, 358 applications received, 155 grants awarded; MAP, 252 applications received, 231 grants awarded; TAG: 238 applications received, 167 grants awarded; MLI: 314 applications received, 13 grants awarded

Application Process

Contact: Mamie Bittner, (202) 606-8536
Deadline: GOS: January; CP: December; MAP I: April; MAP II: January; MAP III: February
Processing Time: Four to six months
Review Process: Applications are evaluated by a panel from the appropriate professional field, the National Museum Services Board, and the Director of the Institute of Museum Services.
Criteria: Proposals are evaluated by whether the project addresses problems general to a large number of museums and represents a model approach to the problem, the quality of the project, and the institution's resources to complete the project.
Project Period: One- and two-year grants

Sample Grants

The Peabody Museum at Harvard University in Cambridge, Massachusetts, was awarded $13,826 for the treatment of nitro-cellulose-based photographic images; the rehousing of photographs, glass plate negatives, and archival photograph maps; and the purchase of three hygrothermographs.

The Museum of Art at the Rhode Island School of Design in Providence received $2,500 for an environmental survey of the storage areas for prints, drawings, and photographs.

The Irvine Arboretum at the University of California at Irvine was awarded $22,278 to survey and assess the condition of non-Iridaceae petalloid monocots in the collections.

197
47.041
NSF Engineering Grants
Directorate for Engineering
National Science Foundation
4201 Wilson Boulevard
Arlington, VA   22230

Areas of Interest

Program Description: Through its Directorate for Engineering, the National Science Foundation promotes the progress of engineering and technology and provides broad, long-range support. Goals for the program are to ensure that the United States stays in the forefront of technology, to improve national prosperity and quality of life, to contribute to national security, and to respond to future technological opportunities and needs. The directorate's seven divisions are Biological and Critical Systems, Mechanical and Structural Systems, Chemical and Thermal Systems, Design and Manufacturing Systems and Industrial Innovation Interface, Electrical and Communications Systems, and Engineering Education and Centers.

Assistance Types: Project grants and continuing project grants

Eligibility

Applicants Eligible: Awards are primarily granted to academic institutions, but individuals and profitmaking organizations are eligible to apply.

Restrictions: NSF does not support technical assistance pilot efforts, the development of products for commercial marketing, or research requiring security classification. There is no match required for funds utilized for conferences, education and training, equipment, facilities, or travel.

Financial Profile

Obligations: Fiscal year 1993, $296,877,000; 1994, $296,726,000
Grant Range: $1,000-$5,000,000; average, $102,000
Total Grants: In 1994, 8,761 applications received, 2,894 grants awarded

Application Process

Contact: (703) 306-1300; e-mail: firstop@nsf.gov; TDD: (703) 306-0090; voice mail: (703) 306-0214; Internet: stis.nsf.gov or www.nsf.gov
Deadline: Rolling
Processing Time: Four to eight months
Review Process: NSF staff review proposals with the assistance of specialists in the same field as the applicant as well as prospective users of the research.
Criteria: The NSF evaluates projects according to the following: competent performance of the research, including capability of the investigator(s), technical soundness of the approach, and adequacy of institutional resources available; intrinsic merit of the project, including the likelihood that the research will lead to new discoveries or advances within its field or have substantial impact on the progress in other scientific and engineering fields; utility of relevance of research and the likelihood that the research can serve as the basis for a new or improved technology or assist in the solution of a societal problem; and effect of the research on the infrastructure of science and engineering, including research, education, and human resources in the field.
Project Period: Six months to three years

Sample Grants

A cooperative project between United States and Japan to provide workshops in ocean engineering research.

Development of mechanical engineering curricula for the 1990s, Implementing Change and Documenting Experience.

The Engineering Program funded a project, Signal Processing for Acoustic Emission and Ultrasonic Testing.

Comments/Analysis

Applicants may include a list of suggested reviewers they believe are especially qualified to review the proposal. Additional funds are available for planning, research, and career advancement grants to women, minority, and disabled engineers. As the program prepares for the 21st century, it aims to work toward the following goals: to improve the quality of engineering education and preparation of engineers who can assume broad leadership roles in society; to foster intellectual growth and technological advances supporting research in multidisciplinary areas; to encourage integration and synergy between education, research, and practical applicants; to capitalize on diversity of human resources by increasing representation of women and minorities in engineering research, education, and practice; and to promote new partnerships among engineering constituencies including academe, industries, other federal agencies, and other nations.

198
47.049
NSF Mathematical and Physical Sciences Grants
Directorate for Mathematical and Physical Sciences
National Science Foundation
4201 Wilson Boulevard
Arlington, VA   22230

Areas of Interest

Program Description: The program supports efforts to increase the knowledge base in the mathematical and physical sciences, improve the quality of education in the mathematical and physical sciences, increase the rate at which advances are translated into societal benefits, and to increase the diversity of people and approaches in the mathematical and physical sciences. Support may take the forms of standard research projects; research centers; and workshops, symposia, and conferences that disseminate results and address directions for future work. Major facilities supported by the program are open to scientists and researchers. Categories include astronomy, mathematical sciences, physics, chemistry, and materials research.
Assistance Types: Project grants

Eligibility

Applicants Eligible: Colleges and universities; nonprofit, nonacademic institutions; for-profit organizations; state and local governments; and unaffiliated scientists, engineers, or science educators
Restrictions: NSF does not support technical assistance pilot efforts, the development of products for commercial marketing, or research requiring security classification. There is no match required for funds utilized for conferences, education and training, equipment, facilities, or travel.

Financial Profile

Obligations: Fiscal year 1993, $619,940,000; 1994, $617,880,000
Grant Range: $10,000-$15,900,000; average, $115,000
Total Grants: In 1994, 1,500 applications received, 4,700 grants awarded

Application Process

Contact: Division of Astronomy, (703) 306-1820; Division of Mathematics, (703) 306-1870; Division of Physics, (202) 357-7939; Division of Chemistry, (202) 357-7947; Division of Materials Research, (202) 357-9794; TDD: (703) 306-0090; voice mail: (703) 306-0214; e-mail: firstop@nsf.gov; Internet: stis.nsf.gov or www.nsf.gov
Deadline: Astronomy, May; mathematics, October and November. For some categories, proposals may be submitted at any time; in other cases deadlines are observed. Contact the program category for more information.
Processing Time: Six to nine months
Review Process: Each proposal is reviewed by a scientist, engineer, or science educator and three to 10 other experts in the particular field represented by the proposal. Proposals may include a list of suggested reviewers.
Criteria: The general areas that will be examined in each application are research performance and competency, intrinsic merit of the research, utility or relevance of the research, and effect of the research on the infrastructure of sciences and engineering.
Project Period: Three to five years

Sample Grants

Major projects supported by the Division of Astronomy include the National Astronomy and Ionosphere Center, managed by Cornell University, with observing facilities in Puerto Rico; the National Optical Astronomy Observatories, managed by the Association of Universities for Research in Astronomy, Inc.; and the National Radio Astronomy Observatory. Facilities and instrumentation at a variety of observing and research sites are available to scientists based on the merit of proposals and time available.

National facilities supported by the Division of Materials Research include the High-Energy Synchrotron Source at Cornell University, the Synchrotron Radiation Center at the University of Wisconsin-Madison, and the National Magnet Laboratory at the Massachusetts Institute of Technology. These facilities are available to the scientific research community.

Comments/Analysis

Contact with NSF program personnel prior to proposal preparation is encouraged to help determine if preparation of a formal submission is appropriate. General information about NSF programs may be found in the Guide to Programs. For more information about the NSF grant process, applicants may refer to the NSF Grant Policy Manual (NSF 95-26). The Manual is available by subscription from the Superintendent of Documents, Government Printing Office, Washington, DC 20402, (202) 783-3238, or from NSF's gopher or web site: stis.nsf.gov or www.nsf.gov.

199
47.050
NSF Geosciences Grants
Directorate for Geosciences
National Science Foundation
4201 Wilson Boulevard
Arlington, VA   22230

Areas of Interest

Program Description: Research in the geosciences is supported to advance the state of knowledge about the earth, including its atmosphere, continents, oceans, sun and interior, and the processes that modify them and link them together. The four divisions of the program are atmospheric sciences, earth sciences, ocean sciences, and polar programs.
Assistance Types: Project grants

Eligibility

Applicants Eligible: Academic institutions, nonacademic and nonprofit research organizations, profitmaking and private research organizations, and individuals. Some programs accept proposals for collaborative efforts of associated researchers working on coordinated projects.
Restrictions: NSF does not support technical assistance for pilot efforts, the development of products for commercial marketing, or research requiring security classification. There is no match required for funds utilized for conferences, education and training, equipment, facilities, or travel.

Financial Profile

Obligations: Fiscal year 1993, $430,430,000; 1994, $456,160,000
Grant Range: $1,000-$3,000,000; average, $80,500
Total Grants: In 1994, 6,300 applications received, 3,026 grants awarded

Application Process

Contact: Atmospheric Sciences, (703) 306-1520; Earth Sciences, (703) 306-1550; Ocean Sciences, (703) 306-1576; and Polar Programs, (703) 306-1030, e-mail: firstop@nsf.gov; TDD: (703) 306-0090; voice mail: (703) 306-0214; Internet: stis.nsf.gov or www.nsf.gov
Deadline: Generally on a rolling basis, but applicants should check with program
Processing Time: 90 to 180 days
Review Process: NSF staff review proposals with the assistance of specialists in the same field as the applicant as well as prospective users of the research.
Criteria: The NSF evaluates projects according to the following criteria: competent performance of the research, including capability of the investigator(s), technical soundness of the approach, and adequacy of institutional resources available; intrinsic merit of the project, including the likelihood that the research will lead to new discoveries or advances within its field or have substantial

impact on the progress in other scientific and engineering fields; utility of relevance of research and the likelihood that the research can serve as the basis for a new or improved technology or assist in the solution of a societal problem; and effect of the research on the infrastructure of science and engineering, including research, education, and human resources in the field.

Project Period: The NSF encourages proposals of a duration of between three to five years.

Sample Grants

The Atmospheric Sciences Program has funded studies of the physical behavior of climate and the weather. The program supports several centers that are accessible to qualified scientists, including the National Center for Atmospheric Research in Boulder, Colorado.

The Earth Sciences Program has funded research on the structure; history; and physical, chemical, and biological processes that affect the earth.

The Ocean Sciences Program has funded research of the physical, chemical, geological, and biological processes of the ocean.

The Polar Program has supported investigations of the atmosphere, earth, and ocean science and glaciology in the Arctic and Antarctic. The program maintains research facilities, including the McMurdo Station in Antarctica.

Comments/Analysis

Applicants may include a list of suggested reviewers they believe are especially qualified to review the proposal. The NSF particularly encourages Arctic proposals from women, minorities (including Native Americans), and persons with disabilities.

200
47.070
NSF Computer and Information Science and Engineering Grants
Computer and Information Science and
    Engineering Directorate (CISE)
National Science Foundation
4201 Wilson Boulevard
Arlington, VA   22230

Areas of Interest

Program Description: The Computer and Information Science and Engineering Directorate supports efforts to improve fundamental understanding of computing and information processing. CISE supports training of scientists and engineers, encourages and facilitates state-of-the-art computational techniques and provides access to advanced networking and computing capabilities at national supercomputing centers. CISE is inherently multidisciplinary, supporting not only computer and information scientists but also electrical engineers; mathematicians; artificial intelligence and cognitive scientists; and behavioral, economic, and social

scientists. CISE's divisions are Computer and Computation Research; Information, Robotics, and Intelligent Systems; Microelectronic Information Processing Systems; Advanced Scientific Computing; Networking and Communications Research and Infrastructure; and Cross-Disciplinary Activities.

Assistance Types: Project grants

Eligibility

Applicants Eligible: Awards are primarily granted to academic institutions, but individuals and profit-making organizations are eligible to apply.

Restrictions: No fellowships or scholarships, no new product development or marketing can be funded with grant funds. Cost sharing is expected, but there is no formula for match.

Financial Profile

Obligations: Fiscal year 1993, $215,600,000; 1994, $239,525,000
Grant Range: $15,000-$5,000,000; average, $155,000
Total Grants: In 1993, 3,552 applications received, 1,394 grants awarded; 1994, 3,148 applications received, 1,498 grants awarded

Application Process

Contact: (703) 306-1900; e-mail: firstop@nsf.gov; TDD: (703) 306-0090; voice mail: (703) 306-0214; Internet: stis.nsf.gov or www.nsf.gov

Deadline: Rolling

Processing Time: 90 to 180 days

Review Process: NSF staff review proposals with the assistance of specialists in the same field as the applicant as well as prospective users of the research.

Criteria: The NSF evaluates projects according to the following criteria: competent performance of the research, including capability of the investigator(s), technical soundness of the approach, and adequacy of institutional resources available; intrinsic merit of the project, including the likelihood that the research will lead to new discoveries or advances within its field or have substantial impact on the progress in other scientific and engineering fields; utility of relevance of research and the likelihood that the research can serve as the basis for a new or improved technology or assist in the solution of a societal problem; and effect of the research on the infrastructure of science and engineering, including research, education, and human resources in the field.

Project Period: Six months to three years

Comments/Analysis

Prospective applicants are strongly urged to discuss possible proposals with the program director. Additional support is available for activities to expand opportunities for women, minorities, and persons with disabilities. Support is also provided for special workshops, symposia, and analytical studies of interest to the CISE Directorate. Applicants may include a list of suggested reviewers they believe are especially qualified to review the proposal.

201
47.074
NSF Biological Sciences Grants
Directorate for Biological Sciences
National Science Foundation
4201 Wilson Boulevard
Arlington, VA 22230

Areas of Interest

Program Description: The Directorate for Biological Sciences promotes the progress of science through programs designed to strengthen scientific understanding of biological phenomena. It accomplishes this mission through programs in four divisions: Molecular and Cellular Sciences, Integrative Biology and Neuroscience, Environmental Biology, and Biological Instrumentation and Resources. Support is provided for research, conferences, and symposia, as well as the acquisition of equipment, the operation of facilities, and the improvement of facilities.
Assistance Types: Project grants

Eligibility

Applicants Eligible: Public and private institutions of higher education, nonprofit research groups
Restrictions: NSF does not support technical assistance for pilot efforts, the development of products for commercial marketing, or research requiring security classification. There is no match required for funds utilized for conferences, education and training, equipment, facilities or travel. Funds may not be used for purposes not approved in project budget.

Financial Profile

Obligations: Fiscal year 1994, $287,880,000
Grant Range: $4,000-$3,500,000; average, $90,000
Total Grants: In 1994, 7,100 applications received, 2,900 grants awarded

Application Process

Contact: (703) 306-1040; e-mail: firstop@nsf.gov; TDD: (703) 306-0090; voice mail: (703) 306-0214; Internet: stis.nsf.gov or www.nsf.gov
Deadline: Proposals may be submitted at any time. However, prospective applicants should contact the program for target dates.
Processing Time: Five to nine months
Review Process: NSF staff review proposals with the assistance of specialists in the same field as the applicant as well as prospective users of the research.
Criteria: The NSF evaluates projects according to the following criteria: competent performance of the research, including capability of the investigator(s), technical soundness of the approach, and adequacy of institutional resources available; intrinsic merit of the project, including the likelihood that the research will lead to new discoveries or advances within its field or have substantial impact on the progress in other scientific and engineering fields;

utility of relevance of research and the likelihood that the research can serve as the basis for a new or improved technology or assist in the solution of a societal problem; and effect of the research on the infrastructure of science and engineering, including research, education, and human resources in the field.
Project Period: Up to five years

Sample Grants

Projects funded include The Role of Membrane Lipids in Paramecium Behavioral Mutants; Structure, Regulation, and Mechanisms of Action of Mitochondrial Enzymes; and Photosynthetic Adaptation of Higher Plants to Ecologically Diverse Environments.

Comments/Analysis

Support may be provided for projects involving a single scientist or a number of scientists. Awards are made for projects confined to a single disciplinary area and for those that cross or merge disciplinary interests.

202
47.075
NSF Social, Behavioral, and Economic Sciences Grants
Directorate for Social, Behavioral, and
    Economic Sciences
National Science Foundation
4201 Wilson Boulevard
Arlington, VA 22230

Areas of Interest

Program Description: The Social, Behavioral, and Economic Sciences division supports research in a broad range of disciplines and in interdisciplinary areas. The division is divided into five clusters, each of which includes two or more programs. Each program considers proposals for research projects, conferences, and workshops; some support large-scale data collection projects and the acquisition of specialized equipment. The clusters are anthropological and geographic sciences; cognitive, psychological, and language sciences; economic, decision, and management science; science, technology, and society; and social and political sciences. The division also supports science resource studies and international science and engineering.
Assistance Types: Project grants

Eligibility

Applicants Eligible: Public and private institutions of higher education
Restrictions: NSF does not support technical assistance for pilot efforts, the development of products for commercial marketing, or research requiring security classification. There is no match re-

quired for funds utilized for conferences, education and training, equipment, facilities, or travel.

Financial Profile

Obligations: Fiscal year 1993, $98,960,000; 1994, $98,210,000
Grant Range: $1,000-$9,000,000; average, $57,458
Total Grants: In 1993, 1,724 grants awarded; 1994, 1,553 grants awarded

Application Process

Contact: E-mail: firstop@nsf.gov; TDD: (703) 306-0090; voice mail: (703) 306-0214; Internet: stis.nsf.gov or www.nsf.gov
Deadline: Proposals may be submitted at any time. However, prospective applicants should contact the program for target dates.
Processing Time: Five to nine months
Review Process: NSF staff review proposals with the assistance of specialists in the same field as the applicant as well as prospective users of the research.
Criteria: The NSF evaluates projects according to the following criteria: competent performance of the research, including capability of the investigator(s), technical soundness of the approach, and adequacy of institutional resources available; intrinsic merit of the project, including the likelihood that the research will lead to new discoveries or advances within its field or have substantial impact on the progress in other scientific and engineering fields; utility of relevance of research and the likelihood that the research can serve as the basis for a new or improved technology or assist in the solution of a societal problem; and effect of the research on the infrastructure of science and engineering, including research, education, and human resources in the field.
Project Period: Up to five years

Sample Grants

Projects supported by the program include Political Economy of Regulation and Public Policy; and Higher Education Quick Response Survey.

Comments/Analysis

The program also supports international and collaborative efforts. Prospective applicants should contact the appropriate division for more information.

203
47.076
NSF Education and Human Resources Grants
Directorate for Education and Human Resources
National Science Foundation
4201 Wilson Boulevard
Arlington, VA   22230

Areas of Interest

Program Description: The Education and Human Resources division provides leadership and support for education at all levels in science, engineering, mathematics, and technology. The division is comprised of six divisions/offices: Office of Systemic Reform; Elementary, Secondary, and Informal Education; Undergraduate Education; Graduate Education and Research Development; Human Resource Development; and Research, Evaluation, and Dissemination
Assistance Types: Project grants

Eligibility

Applicants Eligible: Public and private institutions of higher education
Restrictions: NSF does not support technical assistance for pilot efforts, the development of products for commercial marketing, or research requiring security classification. There is no match required for funds utilized for conferences, education and training, equipment, facilities, or travel.

Financial Profile

Obligations: Fiscal year 1993, $487,500,000; 1994, $569,033,000
Grant Range: $7,500-$2,000,000; average, $104,500
Total Grants: In 1993, 16,800 applications received, 2,550 grants awarded; 1993, 17,692 applications received, 2,573 grants awarded

Application Process

Contact: (703) 306-1600; e-mail: firstop@nsf.gov; TDD: (703) 306-0090; voice mail: (703) 306-0214; Internet: stis.nsf.gov or www.nsf.gov
Deadline: Proposals may be submitted at any time. However, prospective applicants should contact the program for target dates.
Processing Time: Five to nine months
Review Process: NSF staff review proposals with the assistance of specialists in the same field as the applicant as well as prospective users of the research.
Criteria: The NSF evaluates projects according to the following criteria: competent performance of the research, including capability of the investigator(s), technical soundness of the approach, and adequacy of institutional resources available; intrinsic merit of the project, including the likelihood that the research will lead to new discoveries or advances within its field or have substantial impact on the progress in other scientific and engineering fields; utility of relevance of research and the likelihood that the research can serve as the basis for a new or improved technology or assist in the solution of a societal problem; and effect of the research on the infrastructure of science and engineering, including research, education, and human resources in the field.
Project Period: Five years

Sample Grants

Projects funded include an Ocean Science Institute for young scholars, Waves and Vibrations: An Exhibit, and research courses in physical sciences for minority scholars.

204
47.077
Academic Research Infrastructure Program
National Science Foundation
4201 Wilson Boulevard
Arlington, VA 22230

Areas of Interest

Program Description: The purpose of the program is to improve the nation's research infrastructure through focused investment in the revitalization of equipment and facilities for research and research training. The program responds to needs identified by the academic science and engineering community for research instrumentation that is not routinely available through NSF programs. The two categories of grants offered are the Facilities Modernization program and the Instrumentation Development and Acquisition program.
Assistance Types: Project grants

Eligibility

Applicants Eligible: Institutions of higher education, independent nonprofit research institutions, research museums, and consortia of the above
Restrictions: Matching or cost sharing at the level of at least 50 percent of total eligible project costs from PhD granting institutions or 20 percent to 50 percent from non-PhD granting institutions.

Financial Profile

Obligations: Fiscal year 1993, $54,700,000; 1994, $105,380,000
Grant Range: Facilities: $100,000-$2,000,000, average $765,000; instrumentation: $100,000-$2,000,000, average $236,000
Total Grants: In 1994, facilities: 285 applications received, 69 grants awarded; instrumentation: 429 applications received, 182 grants awarded

Application Process

Contact: (703) 306-1040; e-mail: firstop@nsf.gov; TDD: (703) 306-0090; voice mail: (703) 306-0214; Internet: stis.nsf.gov or www.nsf.gov
Deadline: Facilities, April; instrumentation, March
Processing Time: Six months
Review Process: Proposals are evaluated by panels, mail review, and site visits. External reviewers will be broadly representative of the various types of eligible organizations.

Criteria: Proposals are evaluated in terms of research and research training merit, infrastructure need, project impacts, plans, and funding.
Project Period: Up to five years

Sample Grants

Roanoke College in Virginia received $233,783 for renovation of its science center complex.
The University of Puerto Rico was awarded $199,562 for renovation of research laboratories in biology, geology, and chemistry.
Case Western University in Ohio received $1,985,000 to revitalize its department of physics.

Comments/Analysis

The percentage of matching funds will be an explicit criterion used in evaluating proposals, as well as the equitable distribution of funds among institutions of different sizes and geographic locations, and whether the project addresses themes of priority to the program, such as advanced materials and processing, biotechnology, global change, high-performance computing/communication, advanced manufacturing technology, human resources, information infrastructure, and environmental research. Contact with NSF program personnel prior to proposal preparation is encouraged to help determine if preparation of a formal submission is appropriate. General information about NSF programs may be found in the Guide to Programs. For more information about the NSF grant process, applicants may refer to the NSF Grant Policy Manual (NSF 95-26). The Manual is available by subscription from the Superintendent of Documents, Government Printing Office, Washington, DC 20402, (202) 783-3238; or from NSF's gopher and web sites: stis.nsf.gov or www.nsf.gov.

205
66.500
Consolidated Research Programs
Office of Research and Development
Environmental Protection Agency
Washington, DC 20460

Areas of Interest

Program Description: The program supports fundamental research aimed at developing a better basic understanding of the environment and its inherent problems as well as research to determine environmental effects and control requirements regarding air quality, acid deposition, drinking water, water quality, hazardous waste, toxic substances, and pesticides. In addition, the program supports development and demonstration of pollution control and consequences of alternative strategies.
Assistance Types: Project grants

Eligibility

Applicants Eligible: State governments, institutions of higher education, or individuals are eligible to apply. A minimum of 5 percent cost sharing by recipients is required.

Financial Profile

Obligations: Fiscal year 1993, $56,404,800; 1994, $65,795,515
Grant Range: $5,748-$2,000,000; average, $239,013
Total Grants: In 1993, 153 grants awarded; 1994, 208 grants awarded

Application Process

Contact: (202) 260-2090
Deadline: None
Processing Time: 180 days
Review Process: Administrative evaluation determines the adequacy of the proposal in relationship to regulations; technical and extramural review determines the relevance and technical merit of the proposal.
Criteria: Scientific merit is evaluated in terms of strength and weaknesses of proposals, adequacy of design, competency of staff, available resources, appropriate project period and budget, and probable accomplishments in relation to the program objectives. In addition, the proposal is evaluated in terms of the need for the proposed research and relevance of objectives in an approved work plan.
Project Period: Projects are funded on a 12-month basis for up to five years

Comments/Analysis

Prospective applicants may want to contact the EPA office in their area of interest: Office of Health Research, (202) 382-5900; Office of Environmental Processes and Effects Research, (202) 382-5959; Office of Exploratory Research, (202) 382-5750; Office of Environmental Processes and Effects Research, (202) 382-5950. In addition, documents including the EPA and the Academic Community Solicitations for Grant Proposals, the EPA Research Program Guide, and the Technical Assistance Directory can be obtained from the Center for Environmental Research Information, Cincinnati, Ohio 45268, (513) 569-7391.

206
81.036
Energy-Related Inventions
Office of Technology Evaluation and Assessment
National Institute of Standards and Technology
Department of Commerce
Gaithersburg, MD   20899

Areas of Interest

Program Description: The purpose of this program is to select promising energy-related inventions for recommendation to the Department of Energy (DOE) for government support. The DOE will determine the amount and kind of support to be provided for the selected inventions. Any new concept, device, product, material, or industrial process can qualify. The invention may be at any stage of development, from concept to production.
Assistance Types: Referral to DOE Project grants

Eligibility

Applicants Eligible: Individuals or institutions may apply
Restrictions: Inventions concerned with the production or use of nuclear energy are not eligible.

Financial Profile

Obligations: Fiscal year 1993, $6,200,000; 1994, $6,040,000
Grant Range: Average, $83,000
Total Grants: In 1994, 648 inventions recommended to the DOE and 505 grants awarded

Application Process

Contact: George Lewett, (301) 975-5500
Deadline: Rolling
Processing Time: Notice that submission is acceptable for review, four weeks; first-stage evaluation, 16 to 20 weeks; second-stage evaluation, eight to 11 weeks
Review Process: First, submissions are reviewed to determine whether they are acceptable for evaluation. Next, technical opinions are obtained from scientists and experts inside and outside of the agency. Opinions are reviewed and integrated by a staff evaluator and a decision is made regarding the invention's potential. If the invention is rated as "promising," a second-stage evaluation is initiated. In the second-stage evaluation, a more in-depth analysis is conducted and a formal report prepared. If, during the second-stage evaluation, the finding of "promising" is confirmed, the disclosure and evaluation results are forwarded with a recommendation of government support to DOE Invention and Innovation Division.
Criteria: An invention must be technically feasible, have significant energy conservation or supply potential, and be economically and commercially practical.
Project Period: Two years

Sample Grants

Inventions supported by the program include a heat-pipe dehumidification for air conditioners, a method for cleaning condenser tubes at utility plants, and a molded pulp products dryer.

Comments/Analysis

Inventions are evaluated on the basis of the written submission. No testing or laboratory experimentation will be performed; models or samples are not needed.

207
81.049
Basic Energy Science: University and Science Education
Office of Energy Research
Department of Energy
Mail Stop G-236
Washington, DC   20545

Areas of Interest

Program Description: The program supports research and training in the following categories: high energy and nuclear physics, fusion energy, scientific computing, health and environmental research, program analysis, field operations management, and the Superconducting Supercollider.
Assistance Types: Project grants, cooperative agreements

Eligibility

Applicants Eligible: Institutions of higher education, industry (particularly small businesses), and nonprofit institutions
Restrictions: Restrictions depend on grant provisions

Financial Profile

Obligations: Fiscal year 1993, $432,795,853; 1994, $454,000,000
Grant Range: $10,000-$2,000,000; average, $200,000

Application Process

Contact: William Burrier, (301) 903-5541
Deadline: None
Processing Time: Six months
Review Process: After an initial review by program staff to determine that the proposed effort is technically sound and feasible, the proposal is subjected to a peer review by internal and external reviewers.
Criteria: Scientific merit, relevance to research priorities, possible contribution to knowledge and the field, background and experience of principle investigators, and facilities and environment.
Project Period: Arranged at time of award

Comments/Analysis

Informal communication should be made with the program office before submission of a detailed application.

208
84.003
Bilingual Education Programs
Office of Bilingual Education and Minority Languages Affairs
Department of Education
600 Independence Ave SW
Washington, DC   20202

Areas of Interest

Program Description: The program provides assistance projects that research, demonstrate, or train personnel in effective bilingual education practices or train limited English proficiency students. Categories include Transitional Bilingual Education (84.003A), Special Developmental Bilingual Education Program (84.003C), Alternative Instructional Program (84.003E), Academic Excellence Program (84.003G), Family Literacy Program (84.003J), and Special Populations Program (84.003L).
Assistance Types: Project grants

Eligibility

Applicants Eligible: Local educational agencies, institutions of higher education, including community or junior colleges, and nonprofit organizations applying separately or jointly
Restrictions: Grantees may only use funds for obligations it makes during the grant period.

Financial Profile

Obligations: Fiscal year 1994: 84.003A, $16,000,000; 84.003C, $1,000,000; 84.003E, $8,000,000; 84.003G, $1,800,000; 84.003J, $3,300,000; 84.003L, $3,000,000
Grant Range: 84.003A, $75,000-$300,000, average $174,000; 84.003C, $75,000-$300,000, average $167,000; 84.003E, $75,000-$300,000, average $174,000; 84.003G, $100,000-$200,000, average $150,000; 84.003J, $50,000-$100,000, average $125,000; and 84.003L, $130,000-$250,000, average $176,000
Total Grants: In 1994, 84.003A, 92 grants awarded; 84.003C, six grants awarded; 84.003E, 46 grants awarded; 84.003G, 12 grants awarded; 84.003J, 26 grants awarded; 84.003L, 17 grants awarded

Application Process

Contact: (202) 205-9700; TDD: (800) 877-8339; electronic bulletin board: (202) 260-9950; Internet: gopher.ed.gov.
Deadline: Vary by program from October through January
Processing Time: 180 days
Review Process: The Education Department General Administrative Regulations (EDGAR) apply. Proposals are evaluated by outside experts and internal reviewers. Criteria common in all categories are need for project, expected impact, plan of operation, evaluation plan, quality of personnel, adequacy of budget and cost-effectiveness, and commitment to building capacity to continue efforts after federal funding has ended.
Project Period: 36 months

Comments/Analysis

The program identifies priorities for each fiscal year in order to address specific problems or program areas. Each state has an office that is the single point of contact for the program, which in some cases also houses a clearinghouse. Applicants are encouraged to approach their respective contacts to discuss potential projects.

209
84.015
National Resource Centers and Foreign
Language and Area Studies Fellowships Programs
Center for International Education
Department of Education
400 Maryland Avenue SW
Washington, DC   20202

Areas of Interest

Program Description: These programs make awards to institutions of higher education for general assistance in strengthening nationally recognized centers of excellence in foreign language and area or international studies and for fellowship assistance to meritorious students undergoing advanced training in modern foreign languages and related area or international studies.
Assistance Types: Project grants

Eligibility

Applicants Eligible: Institutions of higher education or combinations of institutions. Students eligible for fellowships are US citizens or permanent residents enrolled in a program that combines foreign language training with area studies.
Restrictions: Equipment costs may not exceed 10 percent of the grant. Funds for undergraduate travel are allowable only in conjunction with a formal program of supervised study.

Financial Profile

Obligations: Fiscal year 1994, National Resource Centers Program (NRC), $17,575,000 for new awards; Foreign Language and Area Studies Fellowships Program (FLAS), $12,767,000
Grant Range: NRC awards: $87,000-$235,000; average, $167,000
Total Grants: In 1994, 105 awards for NRC; approximately 1,050 individual fellowships allocated by grantee institutions

Application Process

Contact: (202) 708-7283; fax: (202) 708-6286; TDD: (800) 877-8339
Deadline: Applications are available in September and due in January
Processing Time: Three months
Review Process: The Education Department General Administrative Regulations (EDGAR) apply.

Criteria: The Office of the Assistant Secretary for Postsecondary Education evaluates each application on a point system based on the following criteria: quality of the instructional program (20 points maximum for NRC; 40 points maximum for FLAS), quality of the center or program's relationships within the institution (10 points maximum for NRC; 5 points for FLAS), strength of the library (10 points maximum for NRC; 15 for FLAS), quality of key personnel (15 points), commitment to the subject area (5 points), overseas activities (5 points), plan of operation (10 points), need and potential impact (10 points), and evaluation plan (5 points). Additional points are given when the proposal meets stated priorities (20 points). Additional criteria for NRC applicants: budget and cost effectiveness (5 points) and outreach activities (5 points).
Project Period: 36 months

Sample Grants

Howard University in Washington, DC, received a one-year NRC award of $50,000 for studies of Africa.
Emory University in Atlanta, Georgia, received a three-year NRC award of $329,136 for studies of Eastern Europe.
Columbia University was awarded a three-year FLAS grant for fellowships to Latin America.
The University of Utah at Salt Lake City was awarded a three-year FLAS grant for fellowships to the Middle East.

Comments/Analysis

Applicants are encouraged to contact the program staff to discuss their applications. NRC priorities: Projects that initiate or expand training for elementary and secondary school teachers; projects that focus on a specific area or country or focus on issues of global importance; summer intensive language programs conducted in cooperation with other institutions; special library projects; and developing new courses or curriculum disciplines. FLAS priority: Programs that award fellowships to students in a variety of social science and humanities disciplines.

210
84.016
Undergraduate International Studies and
Foreign Language
Center for International Education
Department of Education
400 Maryland Avenue SW
Washington, DC   20202

Areas of Interest

Program Description: The program provides grants to strengthen and improve undergraduate instruction in international studies and foreign languages in the United States.
Assistance Types: Project grants

Eligibility

Applicants Eligible: Institutions of higher education, combinations of institutions of higher education, and public and private non-profit agencies and organizations, including professional and scholarly associations

Restrictions: Grantees must pay a minimum of 50 percent of project costs each fiscal year.

Financial Profile

Obligations: Fiscal year 1993, $4,180,500; 1994, $3,794,333
Grant Range: $40,000-$120,000; average, $63,000
Total Grants: In 1993, 29 grants and 37 continuations awarded; 1994, 60 grants awarded for undergraduate programs

Application Process

Contact: Christine Corey, (202) 732-6076; fax: (202) 732-1464, TDD: (800) 877-8339; Internet: gopher.ed.gov or www.ed.gov
Deadline: Applications available late August; deadline, early November
Processing Time: 150 days
Review Process: The Education Department General Administrative Regulations (EDGAR) apply. The Secretary evaluates each application on a point system.
Criteria: The criteria for this program are: plan of operation, quality of key personnel, budget and cost effectiveness, evaluation plan, adequacy of resources, need for the project, usefulness of expected results, development of new knowledge, formulation of problems and knowledge of related research theories and hypotheses, specificity of statement of procedures, and adequacy of methodology and scope of the project. In addition, applicants requiring students participating in funded projects to have completed at least two years of secondary school foreign language instruction and to earn two years of postsecondary credit may be eligible for an award of additional points.
Project Period: 24 to 36 months

Sample Grants

Kalamazoo Valley Community College received a three-year grant to create a consortium of 17 community colleges in Michigan and Michigan State University to design, establish, and operate an International Studies and Foreign Languages Institute for Community Colleges.

The South Asia Studies Department of the University of Iowa was awarded support to consolidate and strengthen undergraduate curriculum over two years including developing new courses, strengthening library services, and acquiring new materials.

Comments/Analysis

Applicants are encouraged to contact the program staff to discuss their applications.

211
84.017
International Research and Studies Program
Center for International Education
Department of Education
400 Maryland Avenue SW
Washington, DC   20202

Areas of Interest

Program Description: The program provides grants to conduct research and studies to improve and strengthen instruction in modern foreign languages, area studies, and other international fields to provide full understanding of the places in which modern foreign languages are commonly used. Projects may include studies and surveys to determine needs in the field of language and area studies, research on more effective instructional methodologies for language learning, developing and publishing specialized instructional materials, or comparative studies of the effectiveness of strategies to provide international capabilities at institutions of higher education.
Assistance Types: Project grants

Eligibility

Applicants Eligible: Public and private agencies, organizations, institutions of higher education, and individuals
Restrictions: Funds granted by this program cannot be used for the training of students and teachers.

Financial Profile

Obligations: Fiscal year 1993, $2,250,000; 1994, $2,999,123
Grant Range: $30,241-$217,968; average, $103,692
Total Grants: In 1994, 19 new grants and 12 continuations awarded

Application Process

Contact: Jos Martinez, (202) 708-9297; (800) 877-8339; fax: (202) 732-1464; electronic bulletin board: (202) 260-9950; Internet: gopher.ed.gov or www.ed.gov
Deadline: Applications available early September; deadline, early November
Processing Time: 18 months
Review Process: The Education Department General Administrative Regulations apply.
Criteria: The secretary evaluates each application on a point system based on the following criteria: plan of operation (maximum 10 points), quality of key personnel (maximum 10 points), budget and cost effectiveness, evaluation plan, and adequacy of resources. Criteria applied to this program are need for the project (maximum 10 points), usefulness of expected results (maximum 10 points), development of new knowledge (maximum 10 points), formulation of problems and knowledge of related research theories and hypotheses (maximum 10 points), specificity of statement of procedures (maximum 10 points), and adequacy of methodology

and scope of the project (maximum 10 points). In addition, applications for assistance to develop specialized materials will be evaluated by the following criteria: need for proposed materials and the priority and national significance of the languages or issues to be studied (maximum 10 points), potential use of materials by other programs (maximum 10 points), account of related materials (maximum 10 points), likelihood of achieving results (maximum 10 points), and expected contributions to other programs (maximum 10 points).

Project Period: 12 to 36 months

Sample Grants

MIT in Cambridge, Massachusetts, was awarded a one-year grant of $179,969 to create an interactive documentary for Japanese language and culture.

Georgetown University in Washington, DC, received a new grant to examine and develop learning strategies in language immersion programs. The award was granted over a three-year period: fiscal year 1993, $91,432; 1994, $183,122; 1995, $191,654.

Emory University in Atlanta, Georgia, received an award to develop elementary and secondary school instructional materials on the Middle East.

Comments/Analysis

Increased attention is being given to research in testing foreign language proficiency, teaching methodologies, and the development of materials for foreign language instruction in the uncommonly taught modern foreign languages. Applicants are encouraged to contact the program staff to discuss their applications.

212
84.021
Fulbright-Hays Group Projects Abroad
Center for International Education
Department of Education
Seventh and D Streets SW
Washington, DC　20202

Areas of Interest

Program Description: The Group Projects Abroad program assists eligible institutions to improve their programs in modern foreign languages and area studies through overseas projects in research, training, or curriculum development. Groups of teachers, students, and faculty may engage in a common endeavor such as short-term seminars, group research, or study.

Assistance Types: Project grants.

Eligibility

Restrictions: Language training projects must offer an advanced level of training; participants must have completed at least two academic years of language study. The language to be studied must be indigenous to the host country and maximize involvement of local institutions and personnel. Participants must be citizens or permanent residents of the United States and either a faculty member in modern foreign languages or area studies or an experienced educator at the elementary, secondary, or postsecondary levels or a graduate or upper class student who plans a teaching career in modern foreign languages or area studies. The program pays only part of the total project cost, including a maintenance stipend, round-trip air travel, local travel within the country of study, and rent of instructional facilities. The grant does not provide funds for project-related expenses within the United States.

Financial Profile

Obligations: Fiscal year 1994, $2,191,600 and 8,463,780 Indian rupees

Grant Range: $40,000-$165,000; average, $52,000

Total Grants: In 1994, 24 grants awarded; in addition, five projects were supported by rupees from the US/India Fund

Application Process

Contact: Dr. Lungching Chiao, (202) 708-7292; TDD: (800) 877-8339

Deadline: Applications available early September; deadline, October

Review Process: The Education Department General Administrative Regulations (EDGAR) apply. The secretary evaluates and awards 90 possible points to each proposal. If priority criteria are used, up to 105 points are possible. The Board of Foreign Scholarships gives final approval to the secretary's recommendations.

Criteria: Plan of operation, including high quality of project design, effective management plan, a clear description of how objectives will be met, and a description of how the project will provide equal access for eligible participants from traditionally underrepresented groups (maximum 25 points), quality of key personnel (maximum 20 points), budget and cost effectiveness (maximum 10 points), evaluation plan (maximum 10 points), adequacy of resources (5 points), and specific program criteria, including demonstration of the impact of the project on the development of study in modern foreign languages and area studies and the project's relevance to the applicant's educational goals (maximum 20 points). Short-term seminars designed to develop foreign language and area studies at elementary and secondary schools received priority in 1994 and earned up to an additional five points for an effective plan to meet this objective. In addition, the secretary established a hierarchy of priorty geographic areas as follows: sub-Saharan Africa, Latin America and the Caribbean, East Asia, Southeast Asia and the Pacific, East Central Europe, the Near East and North Africa, and South Asia.

Project Period: Five weeks for short-term seminar projects, six to eight weeks for curriculum development projects, and two to 12 months for group research of study projects.

Sample Grants

Manchester College, Indiana, received $62,000 for The Social Impact of Urbanization in Africa, Two Case Studies: Malawi and Zimbabwe. Thirteen faculty from the Indiana Consortium for International Programs from Indiana, Kentucky, and Ohio were participants. A five-week research project was followed by a series of workshops and conferences to disseminate teaching materials developed by participants.

University of Maryland Foundation received $72,000 for Japan Society from Inside/Out, which involved 14 teachers from three countries. The three-phase project included a course in Japanese culture and education at the University of Maryland, a five-week intensive seminar in Japan, and follow-up workshops for which teachers produced a curriculum unit or design for a teacher or community workshop.

Yale University was awarded $55,000 for an advanced intensive Swahili course in Tanzania.

Comments/Analysis

In fiscal year 1993, 95 applications were received, and 40 projects were funded.

213
84.023
Research in Education of Individuals with Disabilities
Office of Special Education and Rehabilitative Services
Special Education Programs
Department of Education
400 Maryland Avenue SW
Washington, DC   20202

Areas of Interest

Program Description: The program supports efforts to advance and improve the knowledge base and improve the practice of professionals, parents, and others providing early intervention, special education, and related services to children with disabilities. Categories include Advancing and Improving the Research Knowledge Base (84.023A), Student-Initiated Research Projects (84.023 B), Field-Initiated Research Projects (84.023C), School-Linked Services (84.023D), Synthesize and Communicate a Professional Knowledge Base (84.023E), Center for Policy Research (84.023H), and Initial Career Awards (84.023N).

Assistance Types: Project grants, contracts, and cooperative agreements

Eligibility

Applicants Eligible: State and local educational agencies, institutions of higher education, nonprofit private organizations
Restrictions: Cost sharing is expected.

Financial Profile

Obligations: Fiscal year 1993, $20,634,695; 1994, $20,635,000
Grant Range: $4,000-$700,000
Total Grants: In 1994, all categories, 55 awards made

Application Process

Contact: (202) 205-8156; electronic bulletin board: (202) 260-9950; Internet: gopher.ed.gov or www.ed.gov
Deadline: Contact program office
Processing Time: 90 to 180 days
Review Process: The Education Department General Administrative Regulations (EDGAR) apply. A panel of three reviewers, including one repeat reviewer and one director or key staff member of a current federally funded project, evaluates applications. Recommendations are made to the secretary who makes the final determinations.
Criteria: Plan of operation (10 points), qualifications of key personnel (10 points), budget and cost effectiveness (10 points), evaluation plan (5 points), resources (5 points), potential importance of project (15 points), impact of project (15 points), and technically sound (30 points).
Project Period: 36 months to 60 months

Sample Grants

Projects in the category of Advancing and Improving the Knowledge Base were awarded $1,527,000 for 23 new grants. Participating institutions include Vanderbilt University in Nashville, Western Michigan University in Kalamazoo, Northeastern University in Boston, Massachusetts, and Arizona State University in Tempe.

In the category of Student-Initiated Research Projects, 17 new grants were awarded to support student researchers at institutions including the University of North Carolina at Chapel Hill, the University of Oregon at Eugene, and the University of California at Los Angeles.

Comments/Analysis

Applicants are encouraged to contact program staff prior to submitting an application. Program proposals that cut across competition categories should be submitted under the most specific of the applicable areas. Questions about the most appropriate category should be directed to program staff. Potential new nonfederal reviewers will be selected separately for each competition. A database of eligible reviewers is maintained by the program. Those interested in being considered as panelists should contact the program.

214
84.025
Services for Children with Deaf-Blindness
Office of Special Education and Rehabilitative
　Services
Special Education Programs
Department of Education
400 Maryland Avenue SW
Washington, DC   20202

Areas of Interest

Program Description: The program supports research, development, replication, preservice and inservice training, and other activities to improve services to children who are deaf-blind. Program categories are: State/MultiState Pilot Projects, Model Demonstration Projects, Transitional Services, research projects, and Clearinghouse Projects.
Assistance Types: Project grants

Eligibility

Applicants Eligible: Public and private nonprofit agencies, institutions, or organizations
Restrictions: A minimum of 10 percent of project costs must be contributed by recipient.

Financial Profile

Obligations: Fiscal year 1994, $12,832,000
Grant Range: $28,000-$979,000; average, $200,000
Total Grants: In 1993, 24 applications received, six grants awarded; 1994, three new and 59 continuation grants awarded

Application Process

Contact: Charles Freeman, (202) 205-8165; TDD: (202) 205-8169; electronic bulletin board: (202) 260-9950; Internet: gopher.ed.gov or www.ed.gov
Deadline: Program announcement is available in September, deadline, December.
Processing Time: Eight to 10 weeks
Review Process: The Education Department General Administrative Regulations (EDGAR) apply. Proposals are reviewed by a panel of outside experts and staff who make recommendations to the secretary. The secretary makes the final decision.
Criteria: Importance and impact of program, technical soundness, plan of operation, personnel, and evaluation plan.
Project Period: Awards are usually made on a competitive basis the first year, and renewed on a noncompetitive basis for two succeeding fiscal years.

Sample Grants

Georgia State University in Atlanta was awarded funds to continue the project, Utilization of the Best Educational Practices for Children with Deaf-Blindness.
Indiana State University received a grant to encourage comprehensive, coordinated, and longitudinal service plans and a state training system for staff.
Five Model Demonstration Projects were awarded a total of $665,000 to develop, improve, or demonstrate new or existing approaches for service to deaf-blind students. The projects are based at San Francisco University in California, Oregon Research Institute in Eugene, University of Washington at Seattle, California State University at Northridge, and Perkins School for the Blind at Watertown, Massachusetts.

Comments/Analysis

Applicants are encouraged to contact program staff prior to submitting an application. Program proposals that cut across competition categories should be submitted under the most specific of the applicable areas. Questions about the most appropriate category should be directed to program staff. Potential new nonfederal reviewers will be selected separately for each competition. A database of eligible reviewers is maintained by the program. Those interested in being considered as panelists should contact the program.

215
84.029
Training Personnel for the Education of
Individuals with Disabilities
Office of Special Education and Rehabilitative
　Services
Special Education Programs
Department of Education
400 Maryland Avenue SW
Washington, DC   20202

Areas of Interest

Program Description: The program aims to increase the quantity and improve the quality of personnel available to serve infants, toddlers, children, and youth with disabilities through support for training programs. Categories include training personnel to serve low-incidence disabilities (84.029A), preparation of personnel for careers in special education (84.029B), preparation of leadership personnel (84.029D), minority institutions (84.029E), preparation of related services personnel (84.029F), special projects (84.029K), training educational interpreters (84.029L), and training early intervention and preschool personnel (84.029Q).
Assistance Types: Project grants and cooperative agreements

Eligibility

Applicants Eligible: Institutions of higher education, state educational agencies, public and nonprofit agencies
Restrictions: Cost sharing is expected, although there is no formal match.

Financial Profile

Obligations: Fiscal year 1994, $104,074,000
Grant Range: $30,000-$1,376,000; average, $100,000
Total Grants: In 1994, 257 new awards and 669 continuations were awarded

Application Process

Contact: Max Mueller, (202) 205-9554; TDD: (202) 205-9999; fax: (202) 205-9070; electronic bulletin board: (202) 260-9950; Internet: gopher.ed.gov or www.ed.gov
Deadline: Applications for 84.029 B, D, and F are due in September; applications for 84.029A and Q are due in October; the deadline for 84.029K is in November; and applications for 84.029E and L are due in January.
Processing Time: Three to six months
Review Process: The Education Department General Administrative Regulations (EDGAR) apply. A panel of three reviewers, including one repeat reviewer and one director or key staff member of a current federally funded project, evaluates applications. Recommendations are made to the secretary who makes the final determinations. In addition to the following criteria, the secretary seeks to ensure that projects are geographically dispersed throughout the country in urban and rural areas.
Criteria: Impact on critical present and projected need (30 points), capacity of the applicant to carry out proposed training (25 points), plan of operation (25 points), evaluation plan (10 points), and budget and cost-effectiveness (10 points). Additional points are awarded for annually determined priority areas.
Project Period: Up to 60 months

Sample Grants

Under the category of Preparation of Personnel for Careers in Special Education, 73 new grants and 171 continuation grants received a total of $22,626,000 to provide preservice training.

Under the category of Preparation of Leadership Personnel 25 new and 86 continuation grants were awarded at a total of $10,689,000 for preparation of doctoral and postdoctoral personnel.

Comments/Analysis

Applicants are encouraged to contact program staff prior to submitting an application. Program proposals that cut across competition categories should be submitted under the most specific of the applicable areas. Questions about the most appropriate category should be directed to program staff. Potential new nonfederal reviewers will be selected separately for each competition. A database of eligible reviewers is maintained by the program. Those interested in being considered as panelists should contact the program.

216
84.031
Higher Education Institutional Aid
Office of Postsecondary Education
Department of Education
400 Maryland Avenue SW
Washington, DC   20202

Areas of Interest

Program Description: The program aims to strengthen management and fiscal operations and to provide assistance to planning and implementation activities to increase academic quality of higher education. Within this category are the Strengthening Institutions Program and the Strengthening Historically Black Colleges and Universities (HBCUs), both assisting eligible institutions of higher education to become self-sufficient by providing funds to improve and strengthen their academic quality, planning, management, and fiscal capabilities. Funds may be used for faculty development, funds and administrative management, development and improvement of programs, acquisition of equipment, joint use of facilities, and student services.

Eligibility

Applicants Eligible: All programs: institutions of higher education; Strengthening HBCUs: historically black colleges and universities established before 1964
Restrictions: Grants over $500,000 must be matched one-to-one; Endowment grants must be matched $1 institutional funds to $2 federal funds.

Financial Profile

Obligations: Fiscal year 1994: Strengthening Institutions, $88,585,000; Strengthening HBCUs, $116,719,000; Endowment Challenge Grants, $5,750,000
Grant Range: Strengthening Institutions development grants: $76,000-$500,000; Strengthening HBCUs: undergraduate, $500,000-$2,171,419, graduate, $500,000-$5,725,088; Endowment Challenge Grants: $50,000-$500,000
Total Grants: In 1994, Strengthening Institutions, 61 development grants, 14 planning grants, and 186 continuation grants; Strengthening HBCUs, 116; Endowment Challenge Grants, 16

Application Process

Contact: (202) 708-8866; electronic bulletin board: (202) 260-9950; Internet: gopher.ed.gov or www.ed.gov
Deadline: Contact program office or see Federal Register
Processing Time: Six months
Review Process: The Education Department General Administrative Regulations (EDGAR) apply. Proposals are reviewed by a

panel of staff and outside experts who make recommendations to the secretary.

Criteria: See regulations for each program.

Project Period: Strengthening Institutions: one-year planning grants and five-year development grants; Strengthening HBCUs: up to five years

Comments/Analysis

On a yearly basis the program sets priorities and solicits applications for research, demonstration, and training activities. Prospective applicants are encouraged to contact the program office to determine funding prospects, procedures, and schedules.

217
84.039C
Library Research and Demonstration Program: Statewide Multitype Library Network and Database
Office of Educational Research and
    Improvement
Department of Education
555 New Jersey Avenue NW
Washington, DC   20208

Areas of Interest

Program Description: The Library Research and Demonstration Program provides grants related to the improvement of libraries, including the promotion of economical and efficient delivery of information, cooperative efforts, developmental projects, education in library and information science, and dissemination of information derived from such projects.

Assistance Types: Grants, contracts

Eligibility

Applicants Eligible: Institutions of higher education, public or private agencies

Restrictions: No match required

Financial Profile

Obligations: Fiscal year 1994, $2.5 million
Grant Range: $2.5 million
Total Grants: One

Application Process

Contact: Neal Kaske, (202) 219-1315; fax: (202) 219-1725; TDD: (800) 877-8339; and e-mail: nkaske@inet.ed.gov; electronic bulletin board: (202) 260-9950; Internet: gopher.ed.gov or www.ed.gov

Deadline: Contact program office

Processing Time: 60 to 90 days

Review Process: The Education Department General Administrative Regulations (EDGAR) apply. Proposals are reviewed by a panel of staff and outside experts who make recommendations to the secretary.

Criteria: Plan of operation, budget, evaluation plan, resources, significance of project, dissemination, and likelihood of continuation beyond the grant period.

Project Period: One to five years

218
84.042
Student Support Services, Federal TRIO Programs
Division of Student Services
Office of Postsecondary Education
Department of Education
400 Maryland Avenue SW
Washington, DC   20202

Areas of Interest

Program Description: The program supports projects that provide supportive services to disadvantaged college students to enhance their potential for successfully completing the education program in which they are enrolled and to facilitate their transition to the next higher level of higher education. Services may include tutorial services; instruction in reading, writing, study skills, mathematics, and other subjects necessary for success beyond high school; academic, financial, or personal counseling; exposure to cultural events; and assistance in securing admission and financial assistance for enrolling in two- or four-year graduate or professional programs.

Assistance Types: Project grants

Eligibility

Applicants Eligible: Institutions of higher education

Restrictions: Applying institutions must be prepared to demonstrate that the full financial needs of each participant will be met. Student participants must be enrolled, or accepted for enrollment, in a program of postsecondary education at a sponsoring institution and have an established need for academic assistance.

Financial Profile

Obligations: Fiscal year 1993, $131,300,000; 1994, $140,135,000
Grant Range: $54,000-$354,000; average, $185,000
Total Grants: In 1994, seven new and 707 continuation grants awarded

Application Process

Contact: May Weaver, (202) 708-4804; electronic bulletin board: (202) 260-9950; Internet: gopher.ed.gov or www.ed.gov

Deadline: Applications for programs 1997-2001, fall 1996
Processing Time: 90 to 180 days
Review Process: The Education Department General Administrative Regulations (EDGAR) apply. Each application is reviewed by a panel of experts. Each reviewer prepares a written evaluation of the application and assigns points on the basis of criteria. In addition, the applicant's prior experience and the geographic distribution of all projects is reviewed. Program staff of the Division of Student Services make recommendations to the Assistant Secretary for Postsecondary Education who authorizes final funding decisions.
Criteria: A maximum of 100 points are awarded according to the following criteria: plan of operation (10 points), quality of key personnel (10 points), budget and cost effectiveness (5 points), evaluation plan (10 points), adequacy of resources (5 points), demonstrated need for services at institution (25 points), likelihood of success (20 points), and institutional commitment (15 points).
Project Period: Four years

Comments/Analysis

Programs designed for students with limited English proficiency are eligible. See Upward Bound, 84.047; Educational Opportunity Centers, 84.066; Training Program for Federal TRIO Programs, 84.103; and School, College, and University Partnerships, 84.204.

219
84.047

Upward Bound, Federal TRIO Programs
Division of Student Services
Office of Postsecondary Education
Department of Education
400 Maryland Avenue SW
Washington, DC 20202

Areas of Interest

Program Description: The Upward Bound program attempts to generate skills and motivation necessary for success in education beyond high school among low-income and potential first generation college students who are enrolled in high schools. Services may include instruction in reading, writing, study skills, mathematics, and other subjects necessary for success beyond high school; academic, financial, or personal counseling; exposure to cultural events; exposure to the range of career options where disadvantaged persons might be underrepresented; and assistance in securing admission and financial assistance for enrolling in college programs. Through Upward Bound Math/Science Centers, the program seeks to strengthen the education of participating students and to encourage them to pursue postsecondary degrees in math and science.
Assistance Types: Project grants

Eligibility

Applicants Eligible: Institutions of higher education, public and private nonprofit agencies
Restrictions: Applying institutions must be prepared to demonstrate that the full financial needs of each participant will be met. Student participants must be enrolled, or accepted for enrollment, in a program of postsecondary education at a sponsoring institution and have an established need for academic assistance.

Financial Profile

Obligations: Fiscal year 1993, $142,691,000; 1994, $162,500,000. Math/Science Centers: 1994, $156,000,000
Grant Range: $190,000-$610,000; average, $321,053
Total Grants: In 1994, 534 continuation grants, 75 Math/Science Center grants awarded

Application Process

Contact: Prince O. Teal Jr., (202) 708-4804; electronic bulletin board: (202) 260-9950; Internet: gopher.ed.gov or www.ed.gov
Deadline: Competitions for new awards are not held every year. Contact the program office for information about the next competition.
Processing Time: 90 to 180 days
Review Process: The Education Department General Administrative Regulations (EDGAR) apply. Each application is reviewed by a panel of experts. Each reviewer prepares a written evaluation of the application and assigns points on the basis of criteria. In addition, the applicant's prior experience and the geographic distribution of all projects is reviewed. Program staff of the Division of Student Services make recommendations to the Assistant Secretary for Postsecondary Education, who authorizes final funding decisions.
Criteria: A maximum of 100 points are awarded evaluation according to the following criteria: plan of operation (10 points), quality of key personnel (10 points), budget and cost effectiveness (5 points), evaluation plan (10 points), adequacy of resources (5 points), demonstrated need for services at institution (25 points), likelihood of success (20 points), and institutional commitment (15 points).
Project Period: Four years

Comments/Analysis

Programs designed for students with limited English proficiency are eligible. See Student Support Services, 84.042; Educational Opportunity Centers, 84.066; Training Program for Federal TRIO Programs, 84.103; and School, College, and University Partnerships, 84.204

220
84.055

Cooperative Education Program
Office of Postsecondary Education
Division of Higher Education Incentive Programs

Department of Education
400 Maryland Avenue SW
Washington, DC   20202

Areas of Interest

Program Description: The Cooperative Education Program supports the efforts of institutions to make available to their students work experiences that will aid the students in their future careers and enable them to support themselves financially while in school. The program is administered in the following categories: Administration, Part A, Projects (84.055A) for grants for new projects; Demonstration Projects (84.055B) for grants to demonstrate the feasibility or value of innovative cooperative education projects as well as to disseminate information about effective innovative projects; Research Projects (84.055C) for grants to conduct studies to improve, develop, or evaluate methods of cooperative education for the benefit of the cooperative education community; Training and Resource Center Projects (84.055D) to train and assist individuals who participate in planning, establishment, and administration of cooperative education projects; and Administration, Part B, Projects (84.055E) for grants for existing cooperative education projects.
Assistance Types: Project grants

Eligibility

Applicants Eligible: Institutions of higher education and combinations of such institutions, public and nonprofit private agencies and organizations
Restrictions: Funds may not be used to compensate students for cooperative education work experiences, teaching salaries, admissions activities, or indirect costs in excess of 8 percent.

Financial Profile

Obligations: Fiscal year 1993, $13,749,000; 1994, $13,749,000
Grant Range: $2,000-$253,298; average, $81,030
Total Grants: In 1994, 203 grants awarded

Application Process

Contact: Dr. John Bonas, (202) 708-9407: electronic bulletin board: (202) 260-9950; Internet: gopher.ed.gov or www.ed.gov
Deadline: February
Processing Time: Six months
Review Process: The Education Department General Administrative Regulations (EDGAR) apply.
Criteria: Proposals are evaluated according to the following criteria, and scored numerically with a maximum of 100 points. 84.055A and E: Institutional commitment, plan of operation, quality of key personnel, evaluation plan, and budget. Up to 20 additional points may be assigned based on the following factors: the extent of public and private-sector employers support, the applicant's plan for continuation cooperative education beyond the grant period, the extent of the applicant's plan to serve all eligible students, and the institution's demonstrated commitment to servicing special populations. 84.055B: Purposes and objectives

of the project, project design and plan, quality of key personnel, evaluation plan, and budget. 84.055C: Relevancy of research, design of research, plan of operation, adequacy of resources, dissemination of results. 84.055D: Needs assessment, purpose and scope of training, plan of operation, quality of key personnel, adequacy of resources, evaluation plan, and budget.
Project Period: 84.055A, up to 60 months; 84.055B, up to 36 months; 84.055C, up to 36 months; 84.055D, up to 36 months; 84.055E, up to 60 months

Sample Grants

San Francisco University in California received an Administrative Award to expand a cooperative education program from its original base in the School of Science to an institution-wide program.

Highline Community College in Des Moines, Washington, received a Training and Resource Center Award to provide training, technical assistance, and information needs of personnel who plan, implement, and administer cooperative education programs in Washington, Idaho, Oregon, Montana, and Alaska.

The North Dakota Network of Two-Year Public and Tribal Colleges and North Dakota State University received a Demonstration award to establish a statewide network of cooperative education programs in all two-year colleges in rural North Dakota.

Comments/Analysis

Program priorities include model cooperative education projects in the fields of science, mathematics, and technical skills for nontraditional students and populations underrepresented in those fields; cooperative arrangements between secondary and postsecondary institutions; and research projects that assess the impact of cooperative education programs.

221
84.066
Educational Opportunity Centers
Division of Student Services
Office of Postsecondary Education
Department of Education
400 Maryland Avenue SW
Washington, DC   20202

Areas of Interest

Program Description: The Educational Opportunity Centers Program aims to increase educational opportunities for adults. The program supports projects designed to provide information regarding financial and academic assistance available for individuals who desire to pursue a postsecondary education, to assist individuals to apply for admissions to institutions that offer programs of postsecondary education, or to improve academic competency of program participants.
Assistance Types: Project grants

Eligibility

Applicants Eligible: Institutions of higher education, public and private agencies and organizations, and combinations of organizations and institutions

Restrictions: At least two-thirds of the persons participating in supported projects must be low-income individuals who are first generation college students over the age of 19. Program funds may not be used for direct financial support for participants, research not directly related to the evaluation or improvement of the project, or construction or renovation of facilities.

Financial Profile

Obligations: Fiscal year 1993, $20,500,000; 1994, $23,934,000
Grant Range: $190,000-$761,760; average, $142,000
Total Grants: In 1994, 65 grants awarded

Application Process

Contact: Margaret Wingfield, (202) 708-4804; TDD (800) 877-8339; electronic bulletin board: (202) 260-9950; Internet: gopher.ed.gov or www.ed.gov
Deadline: Applications are available in January; deadline, March
Processing Time: 90 to 180 days
Review Process: The Education Department General Administrative Regulations (EDGAR) apply.
Criteria: Applications are evaluated based on the need for the project, clear and measurable objectives that address needs of the target area, plan of operation, applicant and community support, quality of personnel, and evaluation plan.
Project Period: Four years

Comments/Analysis

Priority is given to applicants that have conducted effective and well-administered projects within the three years prior to the fiscal year for which the applicant is applying. The Educational Opportunity Centers Program is one of six programs under the umbrella of the federal TRIO programs that provide services for students from disadvantaged backgrounds. See Upward Bound, 84.047; Student Support Services, 84.042; Training Program for Special Programs Staff and Leadership Personnel, 84.103; and School, College, and University Partnerships, 84.204.

222
84.078
Postsecondary Education Program for Persons with Disabilities
Office of Special Education and Rehabilitative
  Services
Special Education Programs
Department of Education
400 Maryland Avenue SW
Washington, DC   20202

Areas of Interest

Program Description: The program provides assistance for the development, operation, and dissemination of specially designed model programs of postsecondary, vocational, technical, continuing, or adult education for individuals with disabilities. Legislation requires that a certain amount of funds be awarded to four institutions to develop statewide, regional, and national programs. The remaining funds are allocated to other applicants. Categories include Regional Programs for Children and Youth with Deafness, Career Placement Opportunities for Students with Disabilities in Postsecondary Programs, Evaluation and Dissemination of Effective Practices, and Field Reviewers.
Assistance Types: Project grants and contracts

Eligibility

Applicants Eligible: Institutions of higher education, junior and community colleges, vocational and technical institutions, and other nonprofit educational agencies
Restrictions: Recipients of program funds must coordinate their efforts with and disseminate information about their activities to the National Clearinghouse for Individuals with Disabilities.

Financial Profile

Obligations: Fiscal year 1994, $8,839,000
Grant Range: $1,000,000; model programs: $100,000; regional centers for the deaf: $1,000,000
Total Grants: In 1994, 14 new grants and 38 continuations awarded

Application Process

Contact: Joseph Clair, (202) 205-9503; TDD: (202) 205-8170; electronic bulletin board: (202) 260-9950; Internet: gopher.ed.gov or www.ed.gov
Deadline: The program announcement is available in September, with a February deadline.
Processing Time: 150 days
Review Process: The Education Department General Administrative Regulations (EDGAR) apply. Proposals are reviewed by a panel of outside experts and staff who make recommendations to the secretary. The secretary makes the final decision.
Criteria: Plan of operation, quality of key personnel, budget and cost-effectiveness, evaluation plan, adequacy of resources, impact, importance, and continuation of funded program. Additional criteria for centers include progress reports, strength of proposal, and site visits.
Project Period: Grants are made for 12 months, with continuations possible up to 36 months.

Sample Grants

Projects at the college level on the topic of Career Opportunities for Students with Disabilities in Postsecondary Programs received $4,609,000 for 15 new grants and 30 continuation grants. The University of Mississippi, Florida State University at Tallahassee, Springfield Technical Community College in

Massachusetts, and Utah Valley Community College in Orem are among the recipients.

Comments/Analysis

Applicants are encouraged to contact program staff prior to submitting an application. Potential new nonfederal reviewers will be selected separately for each competition. A database of eligible reviewers is maintained by the program. Those interested in being considered as panelists should contact the program.

223
84.083
Women's Educational Equity Act Program
Office of Elementary and Secondary Education
Department of Education
600 Independence Avenue SW
Washington, DC   20202

Areas of Interest

Program Description: The program aims to promote educational equity for women and girls at all levels of education, particularly those who suffer multiple discrimination, bias, or stereotyping based on sex and on race, national origin, disability, or age. The program supports efforts of educational agencies and institutions to meet the requirements of Title IX of the Educational Amendment of 1972, which prohibits discrimination on the basis of sex in educational programs receiving federal assistance. Two categories of grants are General Significance Grants (84.083A) for projects with national or statewide significance, and Challenge Grants (84.083B) for projects designed to develop innovative approaches to achieving the purposes of the Act.
Assistance Types: Project grants

Eligibility

Applicants Eligible: Public and private nonprofit agencies, institutions, and organizations; student and community groups; and individuals are eligible. A consortium of these entities is eligible to receive a Challenge Grant.

Financial Profile

Obligations: Fiscal year 1993, $1,984,000; 1994, $1,984,000
Grant Range: Grants: $60,000-$310,000; contracts: $650,000
Total Grants: In 1994, one contract continued, five new grants and 17 continuations awarded

Application Process

Contact: Alice Ford, (202) 732-4351; Internet: gopher.ed.gov or www.ed.gov
Deadline: Applications are available in January and are due in March.

Processing Time: Four months from receipt of application
Review Process: The Education Department General Administrative Regulations (EDGAR) apply.
Criteria: Proposals are evaluated according to the following criteria and awarded up to 100 points: need (20 points), impact (24 points), plan of operation (40 points), and qualifications of staff (16 points). Challenge Grants are also rated on innovative of approach (5 points). In addition, consideration is given to the geographic distribution of awards.
Project Period: Up to 24 months

Comments/Analysis

For either category, preference is given to applications that meet the following priorities: projects that develop and test model programs and materials that could be used by local educational agencies in meeting the requirements of Title IX; applications that propose projects to prevent the sexual harassment of students; and projects to develop new educational, training, counseling, or other programs designed to increase interest and participation of women in instructional courses in mathematics, science, and computer science.

224
84.086
Program for Children with Severe Disabilities
Office of Special Education and Rehabilitative
   Services
Special Education Programs
Department of Education
400 Maryland Avenue SW
Washington, DC   20202

Areas of Interest

Program Description: The program supports efforts to address the needs of infants, children, and youth with severe disabilities and their families. Categories are Research Projects for Educating Children with Severe Disabilities in Inclusive Settings (84.086D), Model Inservice Training Projects to Prepare Personnel to Educate Students with Severe Disabilities in General Education Classrooms and Community Settings (84.086R), Statewide Systems Change (84.086J), and Institute on Implementing Inclusive Education for Children with Severe Disabilities (84.086V).
Assistance Types: Project grants

Eligibility

Applicants Eligible: Public and private nonprofit agencies, institutions, or organizations
Restrictions: No financial match is required. The secretary may require recipients to prepare reports to disseminate procedures and findings through electronic clearinghouses and resource centers.

Financial Profile

Obligations: Fiscal year 1994, $2,470,000
Grant Range: $135,000-$700,000; average, $190,000
Total Grants: In 1994, 10 grants awarded

Application Process

Contact: Dawn Hunter, (202) 205-5809; TDD: (202) 205-8169; electronic bulletin board: (202) 260-9950; Internet: gopher.ed.gov or www.ed.gov
Deadline: Applications are available in October; the deadlines for 84.086D and 84.086V are in December; for 84.086J, January; for 84.086R, February
Processing Time: Two to three months
Review Process: The Education Department General Administrative Regulations (EDGAR) apply. Proposals are reviewed by a panel of outside experts and staff who make recommendations to the secretary. The secretary makes the final decision.
Criteria: Importance and expected impact of the research (20 points), technical soundness of the project (15 points), plan of operation (15 points), quality of key personnel (20 points), budget and cost-effectiveness (10 points), evaluation plan (10 points), adequacy of resources (5 points), and dissemination plan (5 points).
Project Period: 84.086D and 84.086R, up to 36 months; 84.086J and 84.086V, up to 60 months

Sample Grants

The State University of New York at Albany received a grant for the project, Enhancing Communication Skills with Assistive Technology.

San Francisco State University in California received support for a project, Development of Optimal Learning and Social Environments in Full Inclusion Settings. The collaborative project will involve three local elementary schools, as well as other projects in teacher and doctoral training at the university.

The University of Kansas at Lawrence received funds for a project, ABLE Inservice Project (Analyzing Behavior States in Learning Environments). The university developed inservice materials using computer software and videodisc technology to provide teachers of students with profound disabilities the best-practice training.

Comments/Analysis

Each year, the program announces priorities within each program category.

225
84.091
Improving Access to Research Library Resources Program
Library Programs
Office of Educational Research and
    Improvement
Department of Education
555 New Jersey Avenue NW
Washington, DC   20208

Areas of Interest

Program Description: The program aims to promote high-quality research and education nationwide by providing funds to major research libraries to preserve and strengthen their collections, to make their resources accessible to researchers and scholars outside their primary clientele, and to make the collections available to other libraries and patrons via national networks and databases.

Eligibility

Applicants Eligible: A major research library is defined as broadly based, recognized as having national or international significance for scholarly research, and containing unique resources. Such institutions include public and private nonprofit institutions, independent research libraries, state or public libraries, or a consortium of such institutions.
Restrictions: Applicants eligible for payments from other federal programs will not be granted duplicate awards.

Financial Profile

Obligations: Fiscal year 1993, $5,808,160; $1994, $5,808,160
Grant Range: $41,000-$475,000; average, $126,265
Total Grants: In 1994, 77 applications received, 38 grants awarded to major research libraries

Application Process

Contact: Linda Miles, (202) 219-1315; fax: (202) 219-1725; e-mail: lmiles@inet.ed.gov; electronic bulletin board: (202) 260-9950; Internet: gopher.ed.gov or www.ed.gov
Deadline: The program has a two-stage application process: for institutions without current eligibility status, Part I establishes status of the applicant as a major research library; the deadline is in October. All applicants submit Part II in December.
Processing Time: Six months. Applicants submitting Part I may not be notified of status prior to the Part II deadline. Such applicants should prepare both Parts I and II by the deadlines listed.
Review Process: The Education Department General Administrative Regulations (EDGAR) apply.
Criteria: A panel of experts reviews and evaluates each proposal and assigns a numerical score according to the program criteria. Description of the project (5 points), significance of the project (45 points), plan of operation (20 points), budget and cost-effective-

ness (10 points), adequacy of resources (3 points), and institutional commitment (5 points). After evaluating the applications according to these criteria, the secretary considers the geographic distribution of projects funded under this program during the preceding five years and the impact of that distribution on the needs of the research community.

Project Period: One to three years

Sample Grants

Harvard University was awarded $358,000 to increase accessibility to 347,177 machine-readable records representing the Widener and Houghton Libraries, Harvard's research collections in the humanities. These records will be entered into OCLC, RLIN, and Harvard's HOLLIS.

Ohio State University in Columbus was awarded $60,500 to provide online bibliographic access to the 15th-20th century plays and festival books on microform in the library of the Jerome Lawrence and Robert E. Lee Theatre Research Institute.

The University of Kansas in Lawrence received $135,000 to provide national access to the imperial Russian collection of social history encompassing books on history, literature, philosophy, geography, government, and religion.

Comments/Analysis

Authorized activities may include, but are not limited to, acquiring books and other materials; preserving special materials; cataloging and creating indices for distribution; distribution of materials and information by mail, electronic mail, or other means; acquiring staff, equipment, and supplies to carry out the project; and performing evaluations and dissemination.

226
84.103
Training Program for Federal TRIO Programs: Upward Bound, Talent Search, Student Support Services, Educational Opportunity Centers
Division of Student Services
Office of Postsecondary Education
Department of Education
400 Maryland Avenue SW
Washington, DC   20202

Areas of Interest

Program Description: The program provides financial assistance to train the staff and leadership personnel employed in, or preparing for employment in, federal TRIO Programs. Priority is given to applications that provide training in the subjects of student financial aid, project management for new directors, and legislative and regulatory requirements for the operation of TRIO programs.

Assistance Types: Project grants

Eligibility

Applicants Eligible: Institutions of higher education and public and private nonprofit agencies and organizations

Restrictions: Costs for research not directly related to the evaluation or improvement of the project, construction or renovation of facilities, or stipends and other financial assistance to trainees other than those participating in internships may not be charged against a grant.

Financial Profile

Obligations: Fiscal year 1993, $1,867,000; 1994, $2,018,000
Grant Range: $90,000-$260,000; average, $142,857
Total Grants: In 1994, 12 continuation grants awarded

Application Process

Contact: May Weaver, (202) 708-4804; electronic bulletin board: (202) 260-9950; Internet: gopher.ed.gov or www.ed.gov
Deadline: Applications are available in February; deadline in March
Processing Time: 90 to 180 days
Review Process: The Education Department General Administrative Regulations (EDGAR) apply. Each application is reviewed by a panel of experts. Each reviewer prepares a written evaluation of the application and assigns points on the basis of criteria. In addition, the applicant's prior experience and the geographic distribution of all projects is reviewed. Program staff of the Division of Student Services make recommendations to the Assistant Secretary for Postsecondary Education who authorizes final funding decisions.
Criteria: A maximum of 100 points are awarded according to the following criteria: plan of operation (20 points), quality of key personnel (20 points), budget and cost effectiveness (10 points), evaluation plan (10 points), adequacy of resources (15 points), and need (25 points).
Project Period: Up to 24 months

Comments/Analysis

Training programs may take the forms of conferences, internships, seminars, workshops, and the publication of manuals designed to improve operation of training programs. See Upward Bound, 84.047; Student Support Services, 84.042; and Educational Opportunity Centers, 84.066.

227
84.116
Fund for the Improvement of Postsecondary Education: FIPSE
Department of Education
Seventh and D Streets SW
Washington, DC   20202

Areas of Interest

Program Description: The broad purposes of FIPSE encompass encouraging reform, innovation, and improvement in postsecondary and graduate education; career and professional training, including the areas of faculty recruitment and retention; equal educational opportunity for all; instructional innovation; and improved institutional management. FIPSE conducts a Comprehensive Program, an annual grants competition that supports a variety of efforts throughout the range of postsecondary education, is action-oriented, takes risks by supporting new approaches, is responsive, and invites applicants to be creative in addressing problems identified in an annual agenda for improvement.
Assistance Types: Project grants

Eligibility

Applicants Eligible: Newly formed and established agencies, including two- and four-year colleges and universities, trade and technical schools, community organizations, libraries, museums, unions, consortia, student groups, nonprofit corporations, associations, and local government agencies

Financial Profile

Obligations: Fiscal year 1993, $15,872,000; 1994, $16,872,000
Grant Range: $5,000-$150,000; average, $70,000
Total Grants: In 1994, 1,895 applications received, 72 new grants and 119 continuations awarded

Application Process

Contact: (202) 708-5750 or 205-0082; electronic bulletin board: (202) 260-9950; Internet: gopher.ed.gov or www.ed.gov
Deadline: January
Processing Time: Four to six months
Review Process: The Education Department General Administrative Regulations (EDGAR) apply. FIPSE has a two-stage application process. A preapplication, including a five-page narrative and a budget and budget narrative, is required. Applicants are encouraged to contact program staff by telephone to discuss project ideas before the preapplication stage. Once the preapplications have been examined by an external review panel, selected applicants are invited to submit a final proposal. The final proposal includes a 25-page narrative and a budget and budget narrative. Final proposals are also evaluated by outside reviewers, including specialists in the subject area.
Criteria: When evaluators consider preapplications, the criteria in the category of significance are more important than those in the categories of feasibility and appropriateness. For final proposals, the three areas are equally important. Significance is determined by the extent to which the project addresses the following concerns: an important problem or need, in both local and national contexts; an improvement upon existing practice; leaner-centered improvements; a far-reaching impact; and cost-effectiveness of services. Feasibility is determined by the extent to which the project represents an appropriate response to the problem or need identified, the applicant is capable of carrying out the proposed project, the applicant and other participating organizations are committed to the success of the proposed project, and the project demonstrates potential for dissemination to or adaptation by other organizations. Appropriateness for funding includes a review of availability of other funding sources for the proposed project.
Project Period: One-, two-, or three-year periods

Sample Grants

Boise State University in Idaho received an award in support of a two-year project, In the Spirit of Collaboration: Curriculum Reform in the Preparation of Elementary Teachers. Faculty from the academic disciplines, education faculty, and public school teachers worked together to design and deliver integrated coursework and field experience for prospective teachers.

The New School for Social Research in New York was awarded a grant for a three-year pilot project to develop, deliver, assess, and disseminate three interdisciplinary core courses in the humanities and social sciences designed especially for adult baccalaureate students.

Princeton University in New Jersey received an award to develop software for a project, Teaching Art History with Interactive Three-Dimensional Computer Graphics.

Comments/Analysis

FIPSE is an extremely competitive program; however, almost half of the current project directors have never before directed a federal grant, one in ten has been in charge of a FIPSE project before, and about 25 percent of each year's awards go to applicants who did not receive a FIPSE grant on their first attempt. Most funded projects are local improvements that continue beyond the period of federal support; however, successful projects are generally designed to influence practice elsewhere.

228
84.117
Field-Initiated Studies Program
Office of Educational Research and
     Improvement
Department of Education
555 New Jersey Avenue NW
Washington, DC   20208

Areas of Interest

Program Description: This program supports field-initiated studies designed to advance educational theory and practice. Part of the mission of the Office of Educational Research and Improvement is to support basic and applied research on the teaching and learning process and the economic, social, and policy contexts of education. This includes such aspects of education as improving student achievement, promoting equity in schools, conducting studies in specific subject areas such as science and foreign language instruction, conducting research on adult and postsecondary education, and advancing educational practice in the United

States. A Field-Initiated Studies application should focus on activities designed to accomplish one or more of the following: educational research, dissemination of educational research, and/or training of individuals in educational research.

Assistance Types: Project grants

Eligibility

Applicants Eligible: Institutions of higher education, public and private organizations or agencies, and individuals

Restrictions: The secretary may restrict the amount of funds awarded under this program used to purchase equipment.

Financial Profile

Obligations: Fiscal year 1994, $958,272

Grant Range: $50,000-$90,000; average, $80,000

Total Grants: In 1993, 246 applications received, 11 grants awarded; 1994, approximately 12 grants awarded

Application Process

Contact: Delores Monroe, Program Coordinator, (202) 219-2223; TDD: (800) 877-8339; electronic bulletin board: (202) 260-9950; Internet: gopher.ed.gov or www.ed.gov

Deadline: December

Processing Time: Awards announced in June

Review Process: Proposals are reviewed and evaluated by scholars and practitioners from outside of the federal government. The Education Department General Administrative Regulations (EDGAR) apply.

Criteria: Applications are ranked on the basis of the following criteria: plan of operation (10 points), quality of key personnel (10 points), budget and cost effectiveness (5 points), evaluation plan (5 points), adequacy of resources (5 points), significance (15 points), technical soundness (15 points). Further review includes consideration to determine whether the proposed activities would address educational problems of national importance.

Project Period: Up to 18 months

Sample Grants

Northern Arizona University received a grant to refine a teacher education program within a school-university partnership to assist educators to work productively with all students, regardless of gender or ethnicity. The study will also focus on recruitment of qualified teachers from Latino communities and the Hopi and Navajo Nations.

Johns Hopkins University received funds to examine tracking alternatives and to evaluate effects on student self-confidence and academic satisfaction as well as on academic performance.

Montana State University was awarded a grant to develop a set of recommendations for state and local policy makers that will strengthen, increase, and support parent and community involvement in the education of school-aged children.

Comments/Analysis

In fiscal year 1993, nine out of 11 grants were awarded to colleges or universities.

229
84.120
Minority Science Improvement Program
Office of Postsecondary Education
Department of Education
400 Maryland Avenue SW
Washington, DC   20202

Areas of Interest

Program Description: The program provides support to effect long-range improvement in science education at predominantly minority institutions and to increase the flow of underrepresented ethnic minorities, particularly minority women, into careers in the sciences and engineering. The program provides grants for design projects, institutional projects, cooperative projects, and special projects.

Assistance Types: Project grants

Eligibility

Applicants Eligible: Institutions of higher education whose enrollment of a single ethnic minority group or a combination of minority groups exceeds 50 percent of the total enrollment, nonprofit science-oriented organizations, and professional scientific societies

Restrictions: Cost sharing is expected; however, there is no statutory formula.

Financial Profile

Obligations: Fiscal year 1993, $5,892,480; 1994, $5,839,000

Grant Range: $24,084-$295,653; institutions: $149,986; cooperative: $217,924; special projects: $30,284

Total Grants: In 1994, 53 grants awarded

Application Process

Contact: Argelia Velez-Rodriguez, (202) 708-4662; electronic bulletin board: (202) 260-9950; Internet: gopher.ed.gov or www.ed.gov

Deadline: December

Processing Time: Three to six months

Review Process: The Education Department General Administrative Regulations (EDGAR) apply. Proposals are reviewed by a panel of staff and outside experts who make recommendations to the secretary.

Criteria: Proposals are evaluated on the basis of scientific and educational merit. Consideration is given to creating equitable distribution by geographical region, discipline, and type.

Project Period: One to three years

Sample Grants

The program supported the development of 18 mobile science laboratories for use in teaching basic science courses on Indian reservations.

The program supported the development of a mentoring and apprenticeship program for Hispanic students at the University of Texas.

230
84.129
Rehabilitation Long-Term Training
Office of Developmental Programs
Rehabilitation Services Administration
Department of Education
Washington, DC   20202

Areas of Interest

Program Description: The program is intended to increase the supply of personnel involved in vocational rehabilitation, independent living rehabilitation, and supported employment of individuals with physical and mental disabilities and maintain and upgrade basic skills of those employed as providers of services to individuals with disabilities. The program supports training, technical assistance, and demonstration projects.

Assistance Types: Project grants, cooperative agreements, or contracts

Eligibility

Applicants Eligible: State agencies and public or nonprofit private agencies and organizations, including institutions of higher education

Restrictions: Cost sharing is expected, although there is no formula match. Any advisory committee to the proposed project must include individuals with disabilities. Any training materials developed must be submitted to a clearinghouse as designated by the secretary.

Financial Profile

Obligations: Fiscal year 1994, $25,532,339
Grant Range: $36,000-$300,000; average, $100,577
Total Grants: In 1994, 243 grants awarded, including 89 new and 154 continuations

Application Process

Contact: (202) 732-1282. For each category, see Comments. Department of Education electronic bulletin board: (202) 260-9950; Internet: gopher.ed.gov or www.ed.gov
Deadline: November
Processing Time: Six months
Review Process: The Education Department General Administrative Regulations (EDGAR) apply. Proposals are reviewed by a panel of outside experts and staff who make recommendations to the secretary. The secretary makes the final decision.

Criteria: Plan of operation (30 points), quality of key personnel (10 points), budget and cost-effectiveness (10 points), evaluation plan (5 points), adequacy of resources (5 points), evidence of need (10 points), relevance to state-federal rehabilitation service program (10 points), and nature and scope of curriculum (20 points). In addition to these criteria, the secretary considers the geographic distribution of projects in each category and the past performance of the applicant in carrying out similar training activities.

Project Period: One to three years

Sample Grants

The University of Georgia in Athens received a 60-month grant in the rehabilitation counseling category to support scholarships to students planning to work in state rehabilitation agencies.

Hunter College in New York City was awarded a 36 month grant in the Rehabilitation of the Blind category for a collaborative project by the college's Department of Special Education and Graduate Program in Rehabilitation Counselor Education to train teachers to serve blind and visually impaired students.

The New Jersey Institute of Technology in Newark received a 36-month grant from the rehabilitation technology category to support an academic certificate program for high school graduates designed to prepare paraprofessionals to work as rehabilitation technicians.

Comments/Analysis

Contacts by Program Area: Rehabilitation Medicine, Rehabilitation Nursing, Rehabilitation Psychology, and Rehabilitation Technician Training: Beverly Brightly, (202) 205-9561; Rehabilitation of Individuals Who Are Mentally Ill, Specialized Personnel for Supported Employment, and Rehabilitation Counseling: Ellen Chesley, (202) 205-9481; Prosthetics and Orthotics, Occupational Therapy, Physical Therapy, and Rehabilitation Technology: Sylvia Johnson, (202) 205-9312; Community Rehabilitation Administration, Community Rehabilitation Personnel, Vocational Evaluation and Work Adjustment, Rehabilitation Job Development and Placement, and Independent Living: Beverly Steburg, (202) 205-9817; Rehabilitation Administration, Rehabilitation of Individuals Who are Blind, Rehabilitation of Individuals Who are Deaf, Undergraduate Education in Rehabilitative Services, and Speech Pathology and Audiology: Robert Werner, (202) 205-8291. Applicants are encouraged to contact program staff prior to submitting an application. Potential new nonfederal reviewers are continuously recruited. A database of eligible reviewers is maintained by the program. Those interested in being considered as panelists should contact the program.

231
84.133
National Institute on Disability and
Rehabilitation Research (NIDRR)
Department of Education
400 Maryland Avenue SW
Washington, DC   20202

Areas of Interest

Program Description: The institute supports and coordinates research and its utilization to contribute to the independence of persons of all ages who have disabilities by seeking improved systems, products, and practices in the rehabilitative process. Programs include rehabilitation research and training centers, rehabilitation engineering centers, field initiated research, research and demonstration projects, research fellowships, research training and career development grants, dissemination and utilization grants, technology assistance, Small Business Innovative Research (SBIR) grants, international program, innovation grants, and Regional Disability and Business Technical Assistance Centers.

Assistance Types: Grants, contracts, and cooperative agreements

Eligibility

Applicants Eligible: Institutions of higher education, Native American tribes, research groups, nonprofit organizations, some for-profit organizations and individuals, and consortia of institutions and organizations

Restrictions: Grants are awarded for programs of national significance, which must meet high standards of excellence.

Financial Profile

Obligations: Fiscal year 1993, $67,238,000; 1994, $63,734,000
Grant Range: Grants and Contracts: $10,000-$750,000; individual project grants: average, $150,000 per year
Total Grants: In 1994, nine fellowships; 37 continuations and 19 new field-initiated grants; 38 rehabilitation and training centers and 10 new centers funded; 15 Rehabilitation Engineering Centers were maintained and one new center funded; 16 research and development grants continued and 6 new grants awarded; 13 spinal cord model systems projects continued; 18 utilization projects continued and five new projects funded; eight research traning grants continued and four new grants awarded

Application Process

Contact: David Esquith, (202) 205-9151; TDD: (202) 205-9136; Grant Information Line: (202) 205-8207; electronic bulletin board: (202) 260-9950; Internet: gopher.ed.gov or www.ed.gov
Deadline: Contact program
Processing Time: Minimum three months
Review Process: A panel of peer reviewers makes recommendation to NIDRR senior staff. The director, with the assistant secretary for the Office of Special Education and Rehabilitative Services, makes the final decision.

Criteria: Proposals are rated by the following point system: relevance and importance of the research program (20 points), quality of the research design (35 points), quality of the training and dissemination program (25 points), and quality of the organization and management (20 points).

Project Period: Awards are made on a 12-month basis; support beyond that period is contingent on progress of the program, to a maximum of five years

Sample Grants

The Virginia Commonwealth University in Richmond was awarded an innovative research one-year grant of $48,527 for a project, Employer Attitudes Toward Job Accommodation: A Multinational Perspective, to compare the effectiveness of Japanese and American approaches to promoting the employment of persons with disabilities.

Suffolk University in Boston, Massachusetts, was awarded a three-year Field-Initiated research grant of $149,192 for a project, The Americans with Disabilities Act: Implementation and Evaluation.

The University of Arizona in Tucson was awarded a 60-month grant of $1,574,851 for a project, Native American Research and Training Center: Improving Rehabilitation of American Indians.

Comments/Analysis

Programs are not funded in every category every year. Applicants are encouraged to contact program staff prior to submitting an application. Potential new nonfederal reviewers will be selected separately for each competition. A database of eligible reviewers is maintained by the program. Those interested in being considered as panelists should contact the program.

232
84.153
Business and International Education Program
Center for International Education
Department of Education
600 Independence Ave SW
Washington, DC   20202

Areas of Interest

Program Description: The program provides grants to enhance international business education programs and to expand the capacity of the business community to engage in international economic activities.

Assistance Types: Project grants

Eligibility

Applicants Eligible: Institutions of higher education that have entered into agreements with business enterprises, trade organizations, or associations engaged in international business activity. Each project must be carried out in an active partnership, and each project's application must be accompanied by a copy of an agreement between an institution of higher education and an appropriate organization or business.

Restrictions: A minimum 50 percent match of project cost for each fiscal year is required.

Financial Profile

Obligations: Fiscal year 1993, $3,180,525; 1994, $3,481,000
Grant Range: $45,000-$90,000; average, $77,573
Total Grants: In 1994, 47 grants awarded

Application Process

Contact: Susanna C. Easton, (202) 708-7283; TDD: (800) 877-8339; electronic bulletin board: (202) 260-9950; Internet: gopher.ed.gov or www.ed.gov
Deadline: Applications available early September; deadline, late November
Processing Time: 120 days
Review Process: The Education Department General Administrative Regulations (EDGAR) apply.
Criteria: Criteria applied to this program are need for the project (maximum 10 points), usefulness of expected results (maximum 10 points), development of new knowledge (maximum 10 points), formulation of problems and knowledge of related research theories and hypotheses (maximum 10 points), specificity of statement of procedures (maximum 10 points), and adequacy of methodology and scope of the project (maximum 10 points). In addition, applications for assistance to develop specialized materials will be evaluated by the following criteria: need for proposed materials and the priority and national significance of the languages or issues to be studied (maximum 10 points), potential use of materials by other programs (maximum 10 points), account of related materials (maximum 10 points), likelihood of achieving results (maximum 10 points), and expected contributions to other programs (maximum 10 points).
Project Period: 24 months

Comments/Analysis

Increased attention is being given to research in testing foreign language proficiency, teaching methodologies, and the development of materials for foreign language instruction in the uncommonly taught modern foreign languages. Applicants are encouraged to contact the program staff to discuss their applications.

233
84.180
Technology, Educational Media, and Materials for Individuals with Disabilities
Office of Special Education and Rehabilitative Services
Special Education Programs
Department of Education
400 Maryland Avenue SW
Washington, DC   20202

Areas of Interest

Program Description: The program supports projects and centers for the advancement of the availability, quality, use, and effectiveness of technology, educational media, and materials in the education of children and youth with disabilities and provision of early intervention services to infants and toddlers with disabilities. Categories include technology in the arts, innovations using technology, software/courseware, research programs that support literacy, demonstration programs that support literacy, application of assistive technology, and practice improvement centers.
Assistance Types: Project grants, cooperative agreements, contracts

Eligibility

Applicants Eligible: Institutions of higher education, state and local educational agencies, public agencies, and private nonprofit or for-profit organizations.
Restrictions: No matching requirements

Financial Profile

Obligations: Fiscal year 1993, $10,862,400; 1994, $10,862,000
Grant Range: $100,000-$500,000; average, $250,000
Total Grants: In 1994, 17 new grants awarded

Application Process

Contact: Ellen Schiller, (202)-205-8123; fax: (202) 205-8105; electronic bulletin board: (202) 260-9950; Internet: gopher.ed.gov or www.ed.gov
Deadline: Program announcements are available in August; the deadline is in November.
Processing Time: 90 to 180 days
Review Process: Proposals are evaluated by outside experts and staff; recommendations are made to the secretary, who makes the final decision.
Criteria: Criteria for each program is presented in requests for proposals and applications for grants or cooperative agreements.
Project Period: 12 to 24 months

Sample Grants

In the category of innovative applications of technology to enhance experiences in the arts for children with disabilities, five continuation grants with a total of $891,000 were awarded to institutions, including Western Illinois University in Macomb, Ohio State University in Columbus, and Foothill-DeAnza Community College in Los Altos, California.

In the category of demonstrating and evaluating the benefits of educational innovations using technology, 10 new grants, one continuation grant, and 10 grants forward funded in the previous year received a total of $4,392,000. Institutions included the Valdosta State College in Georgia, the University of Minneapolis in Minnesota, and the University of Kansas at Lawrence.

Comments/Analysis

Applicants are encouraged to contact program staff prior to submitting an application.

234
84.197
College Library Technology and Cooperation
Grants Program
Library Programs
Office of Educational Research and
    Improvement
Department of Education
555 New Jersey Avenue NW
Washington, DC   20208

Areas of Interest

Program Description: The program assists college and university libraries in acquiring technological equipment and in conducting research in information technology.

Assistance Types: Networking grants, combination grants, services to institutions grants, and research and demonstration grants

Eligibility

Applicants Eligible: Institutions of higher education, combinations of institutions, and public and private nonprofit organizations that provide library and information services to institution of higher education

Restrictions: Institutions must contribute at least one-third of total project costs.

Financial Profile

Obligations: Fiscal year 1994, $3,872,786
Grant Range: $25,000-$350,000; average grants: networking, $113,200; combination, $212,300; services to institutions, $282,700; research and demonstration, $128,500

Total Grants: In 1994, approximately 37 grants awarded

Application Process

Contact: Neal Kaske, (202) 219-1315; fax: (202) 219-1725; e-mail: nkaske@inet.ed.gov; electronic bulletin board: (202) 260-9950; Internet: gopher.ed.gov or www.ed.gov
Deadline: December
Processing Time: Nine months
Review Process: The Education Department General Administration Regulations (EDGAR) apply to this program.
Criteria: Priority will be given to institutions of higher education seeking assistance for projects that assist developing institutions of higher education in linking one or more institutions to resource sharing networks. Applicants may receive up to 60 points in the following criteria: project description (10 points), plan of operation (15 points), quality of key personnel (15 points), budget and cost-effectiveness (10 points), adequacy of resources, and evaluation plan (10 points). An additional 40 points are allocated according to special criteria for each category: networking—need and commitment (15 points), impact (25 points); combination grants—need and commitment (15 points), impact (25 points); services to institutions—need and commitment (20 points), impact (20 points); research and demonstration—need (5 points), innovative utilization of technology (10 points), consultation and dissemination (15 points), impact (10 points).
Project Period: One to three years

Sample Grants

Shawnee Community College in Ullin, Illinois, received a $49,690 networking grant for a three-year project to allow rural, isolated libraries to network with the regional Shawnee Library System and two area community colleges.

The Alabama Commission on Higher Education in Montgomery, Alabama, received a combination grant of $225,000 to establish a statewide online library network enabling students, faculty, and researchers to access academic library resources throughout the state.

The University of Illinois received a research and demonstration grant of $641,866 for the first year of a two-year grant to create a virtual electronic library among 13 major research libraries.

235
84.198
National Workplace Literacy Program
Office of Vocational and Adult Education
Department of Education
600 Independence Avenue SW
Switzer Bldg
Washington, DC   20202

Areas of Interest

Program Description: The National Workplace Literacy Program makes demonstration grants for job-related programs of literacy and basic skills that result in new employment, continued employment, career advancement, or increased productivity for workers. Eligible projects may meet the literacy need of adults with limited English proficiency; upgrade or update basic skills of adult workers in accordance with changes in workplace requirements, technology, products, or processes; or improve the competency of adult workers in speaking, listening, reasoning, and problem-solving.

Assistance Types: Project grants

Eligibility

Applicants Eligible: Applications must be submitted from a partnership including at least one partner from each of the following groups: a business, industry, labor organization, or private industry council; an institution of higher education, state or local educational agency, or school.

Restrictions: Projects must benefit adults whose basic skills are inadequate to their jobs. A maximum of 70 percent of project costs can be paid with federal funds.

Financial Profile

Obligations: Fiscal year 1993, $40,656,536; 1994, $19,017,000
Grant Range: $90,274-$1,003,407; average, $398,547
Total Grants: In 1994, 46 grants awarded

Application Process

Contact: Jeanne Williams, (202) 205-5977; electronic bulletin board: (202) 260-9950; Internet: gopher.ed.gov or www.ed.gov
Deadline: Contact program office
Processing Time: Eight months
Review Process: The Education Department General Administrative Regulations (EDGAR) apply. Proposals are reviewed by a panel of staff and outside experts who make recommendations to the secretary.
Criteria: Relevance of skills to requirements of job, need, quality of training, plan of operation, experience of personnel, evaluation plan, budget, and cost effectiveness. Also, the secretary may consider geographic distribution of funded projects.
Project Period: 36 months

Sample Grants

Funded proposals have included projects to increase math and literacy skills for masonry and construction workers, to teach basic skills to health care workers, and to teach English language basics to hotel workers.

Comments/Analysis

Prospective applicants may want to contact the National Center for Research in Vocational Education, which provides research dissemination and training through regional centers. For more information contact the Center at 1995 University Avenue, Suite 375, Berkeley, California 94704-1058, (800) 762-4093; fax: (510) 642-2124; e-mail: ncrve@cmsa.berkeley.edu. Those interested in serving as field readers for this program should send a resume or vita to the program office or call (202) 205-9249 for more information. Note: It has been proposed to consolidate adult education programs into one unified state grant and national authority in 1996.

236
84.202
Grants to Institutions to Encourage Women and Minority Participation in Graduate Education
Office of Postsecondary Education
Department of Education
400 Maryland Avenue SW
Washington, DC 20202

Areas of Interest

Program Description: The program provides grants to institutions of higher education and consortia of such institutions to enable them to identify and recruit talented undergraduate students who demonstrate financial need and are individuals from minority groups underrepresented in graduate education and to provide such students with an opportunity to participate in a program of research and scholarly activities designed to prepare students for graduate study.

Assistance Types: Project grants

Eligibility

Applicants Eligible: Institutions of higher education and consortia of institutions
Restrictions: Fellowships created under this program must include need-based stipends.

Financial Profile

Obligations: Fiscal year 1993, $5,845,856; 1994, $37,730,000
Grant Range: $28,600-$100,000; average, $87,253
Total Grants: In 1994, 18 continuation and 53 new grants awarded

Application Process

Contact: (202) 708-7127; electronic bulletin board: (202) 260-9950; Internet: gopher.ed.gov or www.ed.gov
Deadline: Contact program office
Processing Time: Six months
Review Process: The Education Department General Administrative Regulations (EDGAR) apply. Proposals are reviewed by a panel of staff and outside experts who make recommendations to the secretary.
Criteria: Degree to which the project meets the purposes of the program, need, plan of action, quality of personnel, budget and cost effectiveness, evaluation plan, and adequacy of resources.
Project Period: Six weeks to two years

Sample Grants

The program has funded summer institutes and research internships.

237
84.203

Star Schools Program
Department of Education
555 New Jersey Avenue NW
Washington, DC   20208

Areas of Interest

Program Description: The purpose of the program is to encourage improved instruction in mathematics, science, foreign languages, and other subjects, such as literacy skills and vocational education. The three program categories are Distance Education Projects (84.203A), Special Statewide Projects (84.203B), and Dissemination Grants (84.203C).

Assistance Types: Project grants

Eligibility

Applicants Eligible: For 84.203A and 84.203C, telecommunications partnerships must be organized on a statewide or a multistate basis. Partnerships should include a state or local educational agency and two or more of the following: an institution of higher education, a public or private entity with experience in the planning and operation of a telecommunications network, or a public broadcasting entity. For 84.203B, one statewide project will be funded to demonstrate the delivery of instructional programming by linking public and private institutions of higher education and secondary schools.

Restrictions: Grants may not exceed 50 percent of costs each fiscal year. 84.203A: projects must demonstrate the use of a fiber-optic telecommunications network to carry two-way interactive voice, video, and data transmissions; 84.203C: projects must provide services nationwide and provide technical assistance to state and local education agencies to plan and implement technology-based systems.

Financial Profile

Obligations: Fiscal year 1994: 84.203A, $20,096,800; 84.203B, $4,000,000; 84.203C, $1,297,200

Grant Range: 84.203A, $1,500,000; 84.203B, $4,000,000; 84.203C, $205,000-$350,000

Total Grants: In 1994: 84.203A eight grants awarded; 84.203B, one grant awarded; 84.203C, four grants awarded

Application Process

Contact: Deborah Williams, (202) 219-1770; TDD: 800-877-8339; electronic bulletin board: (202) 260-9950; Internet: gopher.ed.gov or www.ed.gov

Deadline: April

Processing Time: Three months

Review Process: The Education Department General Administrative Regulations (EDGAR) apply. Proposals are evaluated by outside experts and internal reviewers.

Criteria: Meeting the purposes of the program (30 points), extent of the need for the program (20 points), plan of operation (20 points), quality of key personnel (10 points), budget and cost effectiveness (5 points), evaluation plan (10 points), and adequacy of resources (5 points).

Project Period: Up to 24 months

Sample Grants

Statewide network grant to provide two-way, full-motion interactive video and audio communications that link together public colleges, universities, and secondary schools throughout the State of Iowa.

Comments/Analysis

Areas of priority are identified for each funding round. For example, in fiscal year 1994, proposals needed to meet at least two of the secretary's priorities in order to receive funding. Of overall priority are projects that support achievement of the National Education Goals, that prepare secondary students for work, and projects that develop and deliver programming to preservice teachers.

238
84.204

School, College, and University Partnerships
Division of Student Services
Office of Postsecondary Education
Department of Education
400 Maryland Avenue SW
Washington, DC   20202

Areas of Interest

Program Description: The program encourages partnerships between institutions of higher education and secondary schools serving low-income students. The program supports efforts to improve the academic skills of secondary students and thereby increase their opportunities to continue their education after secondary school, as well as to improve their prospects for employment after secondary school.

Assistance Types: Project grants

Eligibility

Applicants Eligible: Institutions of higher education in partnership with local educational agencies which may include business, labor organizations, professional associations, community-based organizations, public television, and others

Restrictions: Grants must be matched 30 percent the first year, 40 percent the second year, and 50 percent the third year. The program must serve low-income populations, educationally disadvantaged students, students with disabilities, potential drop-outs, pregnant teens or teenage mothers, or children of migrant workers.

Financial Profile

Obligations: Fiscal year 1993, $3,928,000; 1994, $3,928,000
Grant Range: $250,000-$400,000; average, $285,000
Total Grants: In 1994, 12 grants awarded

Application Process

Contact: May Weaver, (202) 708-4804; electronic bulletin board: (202) 260-9950; Internet: gopher.ed.gov or www.ed.gov
Deadline: Contact program
Processing Time: 90 to 180 days
Review Process: The Education Department General Administrative Regulations (EDGAR) apply. Each application is reviewed by a panel of experts. Each reviewer prepares a written evaluation of the application and assigns points on the basis of criteria. In addition, the applicant's prior experience and the overall geographic distribution of projects are reviewed. Program staff of the Division of Student Services make recommendations to the Assistant Secretary for Postsecondary Education, who authorizes final funding decisions.
Criteria: Plan of operation, quality of key personnel, budget and cost effectiveness, evaluation plan, adequacy of resources, demonstrated commitment by institutions, and likelihood of success.
Project Period: Three years

Sample Grants

The program supported a project to ensure that secondary students have marketable skills upon graduation. The project was a collaboration that included educational institutions, local businesses, and industry.

The program supported a project where college students, under the supervision of faculty, tutored and encouraged secondary students in preparation for higher education.

Comments/Analysis

See Upward Bound, 84.047; Student Services, 84.042; Educational Opportunity Centers, 84.066; and Training for Federal TRIO Programs, 84.103.

239
84.215C
Fund for Innovation in Education: Technology Education Program
Fund for the Improvement and Reform of School and Teaching
Department of Education
555 New Jersey Avenue NW
Washington, DC   20208

Areas of Interest

Program Description: The aim of the program is to provide assistance for model projects using advanced technologies. Project areas include support for developing materials for educational television and radio for programming for use in elementary and secondary education, programs that use telecommunications and video resources for the instruction of students, and for teacher training and teacher networking programs.
Assistance Types: Project grants

Eligibility

Applicants Eligible: State and local educational agencies, institutions of higher education, and other public and private agencies.
Restrictions: Grantees can only use funds for obligations it makes during the grant period.

Financial Profile

Obligations: Fiscal year 1994, $1,000,000
Grant Range: $5,000-$200,000; average, $50,000
Total Grants: In 1994, 20 grants awarded

Application Process

Contact: Beverly Coleman, (202) 219-2116; TDD: (800) 877-8339; electronic bulletin board: (202) 260-9950 Internet: gopher.ed.gov or www.ed.gov
Deadline: Applications are available in March and due in April
Processing Time: Three to four months
Review Process: The Education Department General Administrative Regulations (EDGAR) apply. Proposals are evaluated by outside experts and internal reviewers.
Criteria: Need for project, expected impact, plan of operation, evaluation plan, quality of personnel, adequacy of budget and cost-effectiveness, and commitment to building capacity to continue efforts after federal funding has ended.
Project Period: Up to 36 months

Comments/Analysis

Areas of priority are identified for each funding round. For example, in fiscal year 1994, the secretary awarded up to 10 additional points to the evaluation of applications that proposed to use electronic networks to provide professional development opportunities for teachers in schools and classrooms with high concentrations of students from low-income families.

240
84.248
Demonstration Projects for the Integration of Vocational and Academic Learning Program
Office of Vocational and Adult Education
Department of Education
600 Independence Avenue SW
Switzer Bldg
Washington, DC   20202

Areas of Interest

Program Description: Projects funded by this program develop, implement, and operate programs using different models of curricula that integrate vocational and academic learning by designing integrated curricula and courses, providing inservice training for teachers of vocational education students and administrators of integrated curricula, and disseminating information regarding effective integrative strategies to other school districts through the National Diffusion Network.
Assistance Types: Project grants

Eligibility

Applicants Eligible: Institutions of higher education, state boards of vocational education, public or private nonprofit organizations, local educational agencies, and consortia composed of these entities
Restrictions: Grantees must provide and budget for an independent evaluation of grant activities.

Financial Profile

Obligations: Fiscal year 1994, $15,000,000; 1995, $10,000,000
Grant Range: $127,523-$501,073; average, $361,612
Total Grants: In 1994, 11 grants awarded

Application Process

Contact: Patriece Wilkins, (202) 205-9673; electronic bulletin board: (202) 260-9950; Internet: gopher.ed.gov or www.ed.gov
Deadline: Contact program office
Processing Time: 120 to 180 days
Review Process: The Education Department General Administrative Regulations (EDGAR) apply. Proposals are reviewed by a panel of staff and outside experts who make recommendations to the secretary.
Criteria: Program factors, educational significance, plan of operation, evaluation plan, dissemination, quality of personnel, budget and cost-effectiveness, adequacy of resources, and institutional commitment.
Project Period: Up to four years

Sample Grants

The 11 demonstration projects funded in 1994 conducted independent evaluations of their programs and provided technical assistance to help others replicate successful integration programs and projects.

Comments/Analysis

Prospective applicants may want to contact the National Center for Research in Vocational Education, which provides research dissemination and training through regional centers. For more information contact the center at 1995 University Avenue, Suite 375, Berkeley, California 94704-1058, (800) 762-4093; fax: (510) 642-2124; or e-mail: ncrve@cmsa.berkeley.edu. Those interested in serving as field readers for this program should send a resume or vita to the program office or call (202) 205-9249 for more information.

241
84.252
Urban Community Service
Office of Postsecondary Education
Department of Education
400 Maryland Avenue SW
Washington, DC   20202

Areas of Interest

Program Description: The Urban Community Service Program provides grants to urban institutions of higher education to assist projects designed to encourage the use of such institutions as sources of skills, talents, and knowledge that can serve urban areas in which they are located. Grants are made for planning activities, applied research, training, resource exchanges or technology transfers, delivery of services, and other activities to design and implement programs to assist urban communities to meet and address pressing and severe problems. Priority is given to applications proposing joint projects with existing local, state, and federal programs.
Assistance Types: Project grants

Eligibility

Applicants Eligible: Urban institutions of higher education or a consortia of institutions
Restrictions: Applicants must contribute at least 25 percent of project costs in cash or in-kind. Grant funds may be used to support cooperative projects that provide urban areas with applied research and services.

Financial Profile

Obligations: Fiscal year 1993, $9,424,000; 1994, $10,606,000
Grant Range: $150,000-$1,200,000; average, $500,000

Total Grants: In 1994, three new grants and 23 continuations awarded

Application Process

Contact: W. Stanley Kruger, (202) 708-7389; electronic bulletin board: (202) 260-9950; Internet: gopher.ed.gov or www.ed.gov
Deadline: Contact program office
Processing Time: Four months
Review Process: A peer panel composed of representatives of public and private sectors, including higher education, labor, business, and government agencies make recommendations.
Criteria: Proposals are evaluated on the following criteria: need for project, organization of operation, quality of objectives, implementation strategy, evaluation plan, quality of personnel, budget and cost-effectiveness, and institutional commitment.
Project Period: Up to five years

Sample Grants

Crime prevention, youth safety, neighborhood revitalization, and improving student retention and performance.

242
93.118
AIDS Activity
Centers for Disease Control and Prevention
Public Health Service
Department of Health and Human Services
255 E Paces Ferry Road NE
Atlanta, GA   30305

Areas of Interest

Program Description: The program supports the development and implementation of HIV prevention, education, and public information efforts.
Assistance Types: Cooperative agreements

Eligibility

Applicants Eligible: Both profit and nonprofit public and private organizations, institutions of higher education, governments, and businesses. No match is required.

Financial Profile

Obligations: Fiscal year 1994, $25,236,115
Grant Range: $20,000-$2,750,000; average, $300,000

Application Process

Contact: Clara Jenkins, (404) 842-6575; publications and applications: Internet: gopher.nih.gov or www.nih.gov
Deadline: Contact program

Processing Time: Contact program
Review Process: Contact program
Criteria: Proposals should document the need for health education and risk reduction, involvement of health and educational agencies and organizations, and current activities in the area.
Project Period: One to five years

Sample Grants

1,400 labs performing tests for the HIV antibody participated in the CDC Model Performance Evaluation Program.
The program supported school/college partnership prevention education programs.
The program supported the identification and tracking of new HIV related developments and issues and facilitated exchange of information at the state and local levels.

243
93.173
Deafness and Communications Disorders Grants
Division of Communicative Sciences and
    Disorders
National Institute of Deafness and Communications Disorders
9000 Rockville Pike, Federal Bldg
Bethesda, MD   20892

Areas of Interest

Program Description: The institute supports research and projects designed to increase knowledge and demonstrate new approaches related to hearing, speech language, chemical senses, and balance. Funding mechanisms include research project grants, research program grants, research center grants, Independent Scientist Awards, National Research Service Awards (NRSAs), Mentored Clinical Scientist Development Awards, research and development contracts, Small Business Innovation Research Awards (SBIR), and academic research enhancement awards.
Assistance Types: Project grants, cooperative agreements, and contracts

Eligibility

Applicants Eligible: Public and private institutions, universities, medical schools, profit and nonprofit organizations
Restrictions: No statutory formula or matching requirements. Restrictions may vary depending on type of award. Contact the institute for details.

Financial Profile

Obligations: Fiscal year 1993, $129,503,000; 1994, $134,791,000
Grant Range: $72,486-$458,342; average, $186,000
Total Grants: In 1994, 1,113 applications received, 635 grants awarded

Application Process

Contact: Dr. Ralph Naunton, (301) 496-1804; publications and applications: Internet: gopher.nih.gov or www.nih.gov
Deadline: February, May, and September
Processing Time: Nine months
Review Process: Proposals are initially reviewed for relevance to the overall mission of the National Institutes of Health (NIH). Each proposal is subjected to a two-step scientific peer review. The review process may include a site visit. Institute staff conducts the final evaluation and makes recommendations for awards.
Criteria: Proposals are evaluated for scientific merit and significance, technical adequacy of design, competence of investigators, adequacy of budget, and relevance of objectives to anticipated outcomes.
Project Period: The usual period is 12 months, with four years of additional support possible.

Sample Grants

Research funded by the program includes the projects, Spatial Processing in the Auditory Cortex, Electrophysiology of Olfactory Discrimination, and Encoding of Vocal Systems in the Auditory System.

Comments/Analysis

The most common reasons that proposals are not recommended for further consideration are lack of original ideas, unfocused research plan, lack of knowledge of published relevant work, lack of experience in the essential methodology, uncertainty concerning future directions, questionable reasoning in experimental approach, absence of an acceptable scientific rationale, unrealistic work load, and an uncritical approach. Reviewers are active and productive researchers who have demonstrated scientific expertise; possess a doctoral degree or equivalent; have the ability to work effectively in a group context; and have a balanced, objective perspective. Contact the NIH if you are interested in serving as a reviewer.

244
93.192
Interdisciplinary Training for Health Care for Rural Areas
Bureau of Health Professions
Public Health Service
Department of Health and Human Services
5600 Fishers Lane, Parklawn Bldg
Rockville, MD   20857

Areas of Interest

Program Description: The program provides support for new and innovative interdisciplinary training of health care professionals to prepare them to enter into and/or to remain in rural areas to provide health care services.

Assistance Types: Project grants

Eligibility

Applicants Eligible: Two or more organizations must apply conjointly to foster collaborative efforts; applicants may include academic institutions, rural health care agencies, health departments, and health professionals who practice in a rural area.
Restrictions: Ninety percent of the training is to be directed toward health professionals other than physicians.

Financial Profile

Obligations: Fiscal year 1994, $3,698,558
Grant Range: $146,558-$282,250; average, $194,661
Total Grants: In 1994, 11 new and eight continuation grants awarded

Application Process

Contact: (301) 443-6763; fax: (301) 443-1164; Internet: gopher.nih.gov or www.nih.gov
Deadline: February
Processing Time: Five to six months
Review Process: Applications are initially reviewed by nonfederal consultants whose recommendations are considered by the secretary, who will approve projects.
Criteria: Proposals are evaluated according to the following criteria: potential effectiveness of the proposed project in carrying out the training purposes of the program, extent to which the project explains and documents need for the project in rural areas, degree to which the proposed project adequately provides for the interdisciplinary training of health professionals to practice in the rural area to be addressed in the project, degree to which the applicant offers appropriate clinical training, degree to which the applicant demonstrates a commitment to establishing and maintaining continuing collaborative relationships, effectiveness of the organizational arrangements, capability of applicant to carry out and manage project, quality of staff and faculty, extent of trainee recruitment, budget justification and institutional and community support, and plan for efficient utilization of grant funds.
Project Period: Three years

Sample Grants

The University of Maine in Orono, the Central Maine Indian Association, University of New England, Maine AHEC, and Kinnebec Valley Technical College and Medical Care Development received a three-year grant of $633,268 for a project designed to increase the number of qualified health professionals in rural Maine, as well as to increase the minority and low-income representation from underserved areas.

The Morehouse School of Medicine in Atlanta, Georgia; Georgia AHEC; and Georgia Southern University received a three-year grant of $543,944 to support a project designed to enroll and graduate students and increase the number of health professionals practicing in underserved communities, particularly in south Georgia.

Comments/Analysis

Preference will be given to interdisciplinary training involving practitioners, faculty, or students representing three or more disciplines. In addition, priority will be given to academic institutions that demonstrate either substantial progress over the last three years or a significant experience of 10 or more years in enrolling and graduating trainees from those minority or low-income populations identified as at risk of poor health outcomes. Note: This program is proposed for consolidation into the Enhanced Area Health Education Centers Initiative Performance Partnership in fiscal year 1996.

245
93.226
Health Service Research and Development
Agency for Health Care Policy and Research
Public Health Service
Department of Health and Human Services
Rockville, MD 20852

Areas of Interest

Program Description: This program supports efforts to study the ways health care is organized, delivered, and financed and focuses on basic research in the areas of quality of care, health status measurement, primary care, cost-effectiveness of interventions, and access to appropriate care. The program conducts the AIDS Cost and Service Utilization Survey, a national examination of how persons with AIDS use and pay for health and social services.
Assistance Types: Project grants and contracts

Eligibility

Applicants Eligible: Public and private institutions, universities, medical schools, and nonprofit organizations
Restrictions: No match is required.

Financial Profile

Obligations: Fiscal year 1993, $21,731,900; 1994, $25,990,446
Grant Range: $18,000-$900,000; average, $200,000
Total Grants: In 1994, 107 grants awarded

Application Process

Contact: (301) 227-8447; publications and applications: Internet: gopher.nih.gov or www.nih.gov
Deadline: February, June, and October; AIDS projects, May, September, and January
Processing Time: Six to nine months
Review Process: Upon receipt, applications are reviewed by completeness. Applications are reviewed for scientific and technical merit by an initial review group composed primarily of nonfederal scientific experts. The final review is conducted by the National Advisory Council.

Criteria: Proposals are evaluated for significance and originality from a scientific and technical viewpoint, availability of data or plan to collect data, qualifications and experience of the principal investigator and staff, adequacy of plan for carrying out the project, reasonableness of budget, and adequacy of resources.
Project Period: Five years; awards are made annually.

Sample Grants

The University of Alabama at Birmingham received a one-year grant of $71,000 for a project, Follow-up After Discharge from an Urban Public Hospital.

The University of Arizona at Tucson was awarded a two-year grant of $396,693 for a project, Community Physician's Diagnostic Accuracy on Colposcopy.

The University of Pennsylvania at Philadelphia received a one-year award of $81,250 for a project, Adolescents' Access to Health Care: the Teen's Perspective.

New York University in New York City received $382,275 for a two-year project, Determinants of Physician AIDS-Related Practice Behavior.

Comments/Analysis

The Agency for Health Care Policy and Research sponsors numerous collaborative projects with other agencies and short-term special initiatives on topics such as rural health services, public policy implications of AIDS and care of persons with AIDS, and cost-effectiveness of health reform. Potential applicants are encouraged to contact the agency for information about current announcements of requests for applications.

246
93.242
Mental Health Research
Division of Extramural Activities
National Institute of Mental Health
5600 Fishers Lane, Parklawn Bldg
Rockville, MD 20857

Areas of Interest

Program Description: Increase knowledge and research methods on mental and behavioral disorders and improvement of mental health services.
Assistance Types: Project grants, contracts, and cooperative agreements

Eligibility

Applicants Eligible: Public and private institutions, universities, medical schools, profit and nonprofit organizations
Restrictions: No match required

Financial Profile

Obligations: Fiscal year 1993, $377,507,000; 1994, $406,816,049
Grant Range: $8,686-$4,425,699; average, $270,310
Total Grants: In 1993, 1,455 grants awarded; 1994, 1,505 grants awarded

Application Process

Contact: (301) 443-3367; publications and applications: Internet: gopher.nih.gov or www.nih.gov
Deadline: February, May, and September
Processing Time: 240 to 270 days
Review Process: Proposals are initially reviewed for relevance to the overall mission of the National Institutes of Health (NIH). Each proposal is subjected to a two-step scientific peer review. The review process may include a site visit. Institute staff conducts the final evaluation and makes recommendations for awards.
Criteria: Proposals are evaluated for scientific merit and significance, technical adequacy of design, competence of investigators, adequacy of budget, relevance of objectives to National Institute of Mental Health objectives, and anticipated outcomes and implications for the mental health field.
Project Period: Up to five years

Sample Grants

Research projects funded by the program have included: Genetic Studies of Depressive Disorders, Processes in Learning and Behavioral Change, and Basic Social Psychology in Inherent Senile Dementia.

Comments/Analysis

Prospective applicants should discuss proposals with program staff. The most common reasons that proposals are not recommended for further consideration are lack of original ideas, unfocused research plan, lack of knowledge of published relevant work, lack of experience in the essential methodology, uncertainty concerning future directions, questionable reasoning in experimental approach, absence of acceptable scientific rationale, unrealistic work load, and an uncritical approach. Reviewers are active and productive researchers who have demonstrated scientific expertise; possess a doctoral degree or equivalent; have the ability to work effectively in a group context; and have a balanced, objective, perspective. Contact the NIH if you are interested in serving as a reviewer.

247
93.273
Alcohol Research Programs
Office of Scientific Affairs
National Institute on Alcohol Abuse and Alcoholism
5600 Fishers Lane, Parklawn Bldg
Rockville, MD   20857

Areas of Interest

Program Description: The program supports research to develop a fundamental knowledge base and to develop improved methods of prevention and treatment of alcoholism and related problems.
Assistance Types: Project grants

Eligibility

Applicants Eligible: Public and private institutions, universities, medical schools, profit and nonprofit organizations. No match required.

Financial Profile

Obligations: Fiscal year 1993, $109,671,000; 1994, $115,217,000
Grant Range: $5,000-$1,052,392; average, $210,081
Total Grants: In 1993, 471 grants awarded; 1994, 492 grants awarded

Application Process

Contact: Joseph Weeda, (301) 443-4703; publications and applications: Internet: gopher.nih.gov or www.nih.gov
Deadline: February, June, and October
Processing Time: 240 to 270 days
Review Process: Proposals are initially reviewed for relevance to the overall mission of the National Institutes of Health (NIH). Each proposal is subjected to a two-step scientific peer review. The review process may include a site visit. Institute staff conducts the final evaluation and makes recommendations for awards.
Criteria: Proposals are evaluated for scientific merit and significance, technical adequacy of design, competence of investigators, adequacy of budget, and relevance of objectives to anticipated outcomes.
Project Period: Three to five years

Sample Grants

Research supported by the program has included Alcohol Use During Pregnancy and Pregnancy Outcomes, Studies of Alcohol and Hepatitis, and Alcohol and Drug Interactions.

Comments/Analysis

Preapplication consultation with program staff is encouraged. The most common reasons that proposals are not recommended for further consideration are lack of original ideas, unfocused research plan, lack of knowledge of published relevant work, lack of experience in the essential methodology, uncertainty concerning future directions, questionable reasoning in experimental approach, absence of an acceptable scientific rationale, unrealistic work load, and an uncritical approach. Reviewers are active and productive researchers who have demonstrated scientific expertise; possess a doctoral degree or equivalent; have the ability to work effectively in a group context; and have a balanced, objective perspective. Contact the NIH if you are interested in serving as a reviewer.

248
93.279
Drug Abuse Research Programs
Office of Extramural Programs
National Institute on Drug Abuse
5600 Fishers Lane, Parklawn Bldg
Rockville, MD 20857

Areas of Interest

Program Description: The program supports research to develop new knowledge and approaches related to prevention, treatment, and consequences of drug addictions, including AIDS.
Assistance Types: Project grants, cooperative agreements, and contracts

Eligibility

Applicants Eligible: Public and private institutions, universities, medical schools, profit and nonprofit organizations
Restrictions: No match required

Financial Profile

Obligations: Fiscal year 1993, $288,407,000; 1994, $307,191,000
Grant Range: $27,000-$3,500,000; average, $310,939
Total Grants: In 1994, 971 grants awarded

Application Process

Contact: Shirley Penney, (301) 443-6710; publications and applications: Internet: gopher.nih.gov or www.nih.gov
Deadline: February, June, and October; January, May, and September for AIDS research
Processing Time: 240 to 270 days; 180 days for AIDS research
Review Process: Proposals are initially reviewed for relevance to the overall mission of the National Institutes of Health (NIH). Each proposal is subjected to a two-step scientific peer review. The review process may include a site visit. Institute staff conducts the final evaluation and makes recommendations for awards.
Criteria: Proposals are evaluated for scientific and technical merit and significance, feasibility, potential contribution to the field, and relevance of objectives to institute priorities.
Project Period: Up to five years

Sample Grants

The program has supported research such as the following projects: Kinetics of Morphine and Derivatives, Epidemiology of Drug Abuse Among Minority Populations, Studies of AIDS and IV Drug Abusers, Biological and Behavioral Mechanisms of Addictive and Compulsive Behaviors, and Maternal and Paternal Effects of Drug Abuse.

Comments/Analysis

Prospective applicants should discuss their proposals with program staff. The most common reasons that proposals are not recommended for further consideration are lack of original ideas, unfocused research plan, lack of knowledge of published relevant work, lack of experience in the essential methodology, uncertainty concerning future directions, questionable reasoning in experimental approach, absence of an acceptable scientific rationale, unrealistic work load, and an uncritical approach. Reviewers are active and productive researchers who have demonstrated scientific expertise; possess a doctoral degree or equivalent; have the ability to work effectively in a group context; and have a balanced, objective perspective. Contact the NIH if you are interested in serving as a reviewer.

249
93.298
Nurse Practitioner and Nurse-Midwifery Grants
Bureau of Health Professions
Advanced Nursing Education Branch
Department of Health and Human Services
5600 Fishers Lane, Parklawn Bldg
Rockville, MD 20857

Areas of Interest

Program Description: Grants are awarded to plan, develop and operate, or significantly expand in nurse practitioner and nurse-midwifery programs to prepare nurses to provide primary health care.
Assistance Types: Project grants and contracts

Eligibility

Applicants Eligible: Public and nonprofit collegiate schools of nursing.
Restrictions: No statutory formula or matching requirements

Financial Profile

Obligations: Fiscal year 1993, $15,443,000; 1994, $16,884,000
Grant Range: $35,408-$369,430; average, $238,840
Total Grants: In 1993, 36 continuations, 16 new awards, and 10 renewals awarded; 1994, 42 continuations and 15 new grants awarded

Application Process

Contact: (301) 443-6333; publications and applications: Internet: gopher.nih.gov or www.nih.gov
Deadline: Contact program office
Processing Time: Six months
Review Process: Proposals are evaluated by a peer review process to conduct a thorough technical review and evaluation of each application. The panel consists of seven to 15 nurse educators,

administrators, clinicians, and other professionals. Recommendations are made, and the Public Health Services awarding official makes the final decision.

Criteria: Proposals are evaluated according to the national or special local need that the project proposes to serve, the potential effectiveness of the project, the managerial and administrative capability of the applicant to conduct the project, the adequacy of the facilities and resources available, the qualifications of the project director and key staff, budget, and the potential of the project to continue on self-sustaining basis after the period of grant support.

Project Period: Three years, with possible renewal of two years

Sample Grants

The Virginia Commonwealth University in Richmond was awarded a grant from the Nurse Practitioner and Nurse-Midwifery program to implement a weekend outreach family nurse practitioner option aimed at nurses in medically underserved areas.

The University of Hawaii in Honolulu received a grant to initiate primary care nurse practitioner programs in three specialty areas of pediatrics, women's health, and family health.

Comments/Analysis

Persons interested in serving as reviewers should contact the program office. Note: This program is proposed for consolidation into the Nurse Education/Practice Initiative Cluster in fiscal year 1996.

250
93.299
Advanced Nurse Education
Bureau of Health Professions
Advanced Nursing Education Branch
Department of Health and Human Services
5600 Fishers Lane, Parklawn Bldg
Rockville, MD   20857

Areas of Interest

Program Description: Grants are awarded to plan, develop, and operate, or significantly expand programs in the areas of advanced nurse education, at a master's or doctoral level, to prepare nurses to serve as educators or public health nurses.

Assistance Types: Project grants and contracts

Eligibility

Applicants Eligible: Public and nonprofit collegiate schools of nursing.

Restrictions: No statutory formula or matching requirements

Financial Profile

Obligations: Fiscal year 1993, 12,000; 1994, $11,884,000
Grant Range: $39,049-$364,567; average, $191,287
Total Grants: In 1994, 60 grants awarded

Application Process

Contact: (301) 443-6333; publications and applications: Internet: gopher.nih.gov or www.nih.gov
Deadline: Contact program office
Processing Time: Six months
Review Process: Proposals are evaluated by a peer review process to conduct a thorough technical review and evaluation of each application. The panel consists of seven to 15 nurse educators, administrators, clinicians, and other professionals. Recommendations are made, and the Public Health Services awarding official makes the final decision.
Criteria: Proposals are evaluated according to the national or special local need which the project proposes to serve, the potential effectiveness of the project, the managerial and administrative capability of the applicant to conduct the project, the adequacy of the facilities and resources available, the qualifications of the project director and key staff, budget, and the potential of the project to continue on self-sustaining basis after the period of grant support.
Project Period: Five years

Sample Grants

Howard University in Washington, DC, received a grant from the Advanced Nurse Education Program for an expansion of its master's program to include a subspecialty in HIV/AIDS nursing.

The University of Utah at Salt Lake City was awarded a grant from the Advanced Nurse Education program for an expansion of its master's program to include a specialty in community health nursing that focuses on the care of at-risk populations living in urban, rural, and frontier areas of Utah.

Comments/Analysis

Persons interested in serving as reviewers should contact the program office. Note: This program is proposed for consolidation into the Nurse Education/Practice Initiative Cluster in fiscal year 1996.

251
93.306
Comparative Medicine Program
National Center for Research Resources (NCRR)
5333 Westbard Avenue, Westwood Bldg
Bethesda, MD   20892

Areas of Interest

Program Description: The Comparative Medicine Program (CMP) helps to meet the needs of the biomedical and health research community in the general area encompassing laboratory animal science and medicine. The CMP aims to be of assistance in meeting the animal resource needs of investigators and to be responsive to the public demand and legal requirements assuring that animals are properly cared for and used. The CMP is comprised of three sub-programs: the Laboratory Animal Sciences Program, the AIDS Animal Models Program, and Regional Primate Research Centers.

Assistance Types: Project grants, cooperative agreements, and contracts

Eligibility

Applicants Eligible: Public and private institutions, universities, medical or veterinary schools, profit and nonprofit organizations

Restrictions: Research projects for the characterization and development of animal models are limited to those that span the interests of two or more categorical institutes of the NIH. Costs for pilot studies using an animal model that has been developed may be supported only to the extent that such studies may be useful in defining the animal's value as a research subject.

Financial Profile

Obligations: Fiscal year 1993, $72,188,000; 1994, $67,285,000

Grant Range: Regional Primate Centers: $4,587,000-$7,541,000, average $6,085,000; laboratory animals grants: $36,089-$651,572, average $354,235

Total Grants: In 1994, support provided for 14 animal resource grants, 11 animal resource cooperative agreements, seven Regional Primate Research Centers, five small research grants, four FIRST awards, 27 individual research project grants, three research program project grants, 16 special emphasis research career awards, five conference grants, 16 institutional postdoctoral training grants, three individual postdoctoral fellowships, two professional student short-term research training grants, seven resource-related project grants, and 27 animal facility improvement grants

Application Process

Contact: (301) 496-5175; fax: (301) 480-0868; publications and applications: Internet: gopher.nih.gov or www.nih.gov

Deadline: For new grants, the deadlines are in February, June, and October. For continuing grants, March, July, and November.

Processing Time: Seven to eight months

Review Process: Upon receipt, applications are reviewed for completeness. Acceptable applications will be assigned to the Comparative Medicine Review Committee and evaluated for responsiveness to guidelines. Responsive applications will be further evaluated through NIH peer review procedures. Site visits may take place as part of the review process.

Criteria: Proposals are evaluated based on the scientific, technical, or medical significance of the project; appropriateness of experimental approach and models; qualifications of principal investigator and staff; availability of resources; reasonableness of budget;

and adequacy of means for protecting against adverse effects upon humans, animals, and the environment.

Project Period: Five years

Sample Grants

Seven Regional Primate Research Centers are supported to provide special environments in which multidisciplinary health-related research is conducted with nonhuman primate models.

Institutional animal resource improvement projects are supported to assist institutions in upgrading and developing centralized animal resource programs. Projects in this area included funds for animal cages, cage washes, etc., and renovations of existing facilities.

Comments/Analysis

Potential applicants should contact program staff to discuss their projects to determine whether plans for the project conform with CMP policies. Applicants should submit a letter of intent at least three months prior to submission of the formal application. The letter should not exceed two pages. The most common reasons that proposals are not recommended for further consideration are lack of original ideas, unfocused research plan, lack of knowledge of published relevant work, lack of experience in the essential methodology, uncertainty concerning future directions, questionable reasoning in experimental approach, absence of an acceptable scientific rationale, unrealistic work load, and an uncritical approach. Reviewers are active and productive researchers who have demonstrated scientific expertise; possess a doctoral degree or equivalent; have the ability to work effectively in a group context; and have a balanced, objective perspective. Contact the NIH if you are interested in serving as a reviewer.

252
93.337
Minority Initiative: K-12 Teachers and High School Students
Biomedical Research Support Program
National Center for Research Resources (NCRR)
5333 Westbard Avenue, Westwood Bldg
Bethesda, MD   20892

Areas of Interest

Program Description: The program aims to increase the pool of underrepresented minority high school students who are interested and academically prepared to pursue careers in biomedical/behavioral research and health professions. The program supports both K-12 inservice and preservice for teachers and structured summer science research experiences for both teachers and minority students.

Assistance Types: Project grants

Eligibility

Applicants Eligible: Public and private for-profit and nonprofit organizations, such as universities, colleges, hospitals, and laboratories; units of state and local governments

Restrictions: Salaries and wages for teachers and students are eligible, but stipends are not. Costs, such as research supplies and equipment, can be requested as a lump sum of up to $250 per participant per year.

Financial Profile

Obligations: Fiscal year 1994, $2,500,000
Grant Range: Average, $30,000
Total Grants: In 1994, 75 grants awarded

Application Process

Contact: (301) 594-7947; applications may be requested at (301) 594-7248; Internet: gopher.nih.gov or www.nih.gov
Deadline: Letter of intent should be submitted in January; deadline for applications, February
Processing Time: Three months
Review Process: Applications will be reviewed to determine administrative and programmatic response to the goals of the program. Those applications considered complete and responsive will be subjected to a triage review by a peer review panel and staff review committees to determine scientific and technical merit.
Criteria: Proposals are evaluated based on overall scientific quality and educational content of the programs, appropriateness of plans considering characteristics of the institution, qualifications of the program director and proposed mentors, evaluation plans, institutional commitment, prior accomplishments in precollege education, impact of the proposal in meeting program goals. In addition, NCRR reviewers will consider program balance among types of institutions and geographic distribution of awards.
Project Period: Up to three years

Comments/Analysis

Written and telephone inquiries are encouraged. The NCRR staff welcomes the opportunity to clarify issues or questions from potential applicants. Prospective applicants are requested to submit a letter of intent in January. Although the letter is not required, is not binding, and does not enter into the review of subsequent applications, the information is helpful for the program in terms of planning for the review of applications. The letter should be addressed to Dr. Marjorie A. Tingle, at the listed address.

253
93.375
Minority Biomedical Research Support
National Institutes of Health
9000 Rockville Pike, Bldg 31
Bethesda, MD   20892

Areas of Interest

Program Description: These grants are intended to strengthen the research and research training capability of colleges and universities that have significant enrollments of ethnic minority groups.
Assistance Types: Project grants

Eligibility

Applicants Eligible: Public and private institutions, universities, medical schools, profit and nonprofit organizations
Restrictions: No statutory formula or matching requirements

Financial Profile

Obligations: Fiscal year 1993, $32,795,000; 1994, $34,795,000
Grant Range: $100,000-$1,500,000 per year for three to four years
Total Grants: In 1993, 98 grants awarded; 1994, 98 grants awarded

Application Process

Contact: (301) 594-7955; publications and applications: Internet: gopher.nih.gov or www.nih.gov
Deadline: February, June, and October
Processing Time: Five to nine months
Review Process: Proposals are initially reviewed for relevance to the overall mission of the National Institutes of Health (NIH). Each proposal is subjected to a two-step scientific peer review. The review process may include a site visit. Institute staff conducts the final evaluation and makes recommendations for awards.
Criteria: Proposals are evaluated based on scientific merit and significance, technical adequacy of design, competence of investigators, adequacy of budget, and relevance of objectives to anticipated outcomes.
Project Period: Three to four years

Comments/Analysis

The most common reasons that proposals are not recommended for further consideration are lack of original ideas, unfocused research plan, lack of knowledge of published relevant work, lack of experience in the essential methodology, uncertainty concerning future directions, questionable reasoning in experimental approach, absence of an acceptable scientific rationale, unrealistic work load, and an uncritical approach. Reviewers are active and productive researchers who have demonstrated scientific expertise; possess a doctoral degree or equivalent; have the ability to work effectively in a group context; and have a balanced, objective perspective. Contact the NIH if you are interested in serving as a reviewer.

254
93.390
NIH Academic Research Enhancement Awards
National Institutes of Health
9000 Rockville Pike, Bldg 31
Bethesda, MD   20892

Areas of Interest

Program Description: This award is directed toward public and private colleges and universities that are not research intensive, but that provide undergraduate training to a significant number of research scientists. Grants create a research opportunity for scientists and institutions, otherwise unlikely to participate extensively in NIH programs, to participate in biomedical research efforts. Support is provided for small-scale, new, or expanded health-related projects.
Assistance Types: Project grants

Eligibility

Applicants Eligible: Public and private institutions, universities, medical schools, profit and nonprofit organizations
Restrictions: Research must be conducted at grantee's institution.

Financial Profile

Obligations: Fiscal year 1993, $12,860,908; 1994, $13,234,000
Grant Range: Up to $75,000
Total Grants: In 1993, 127 grants awarded; 1994, 130 grants awarded

Application Process

Contact: Publications and applications, (301) 594-7248; fax: (301) 594-7045; Internet: gopher.nih.gov or www.nih.gov
Deadline: June
Processing Time: Eight to nine months
Review Process: Proposals are initially reviewed for relevance to the overall mission of the National Institutes of Health (NIH). Each proposal is subjected to a two-step scientific peer review. The review process may include a site visit. Institute staff conducts the final evaluation and makes recommendations for awards.
Criteria: Proposals are evaluated based on scientific merit and significance, technical adequacy of design, competence of investigators, adequacy of budget, and relevance of objectives to anticipated outcomes.
Project Period: Five years

Comments/Analysis

The most common reasons that proposals are not recommended for further consideration are lack of original ideas, unfocused research plan, lack of knowledge of published relevant work, lack of experience in the essential methodology, uncertainty concerning future directions, questionable reasoning in experimental approach, absence of an acceptable scientific rationale, unrealistic work load, and an uncritical approach. Reviewers are active and productive researchers who have demonstrated scientific expertise; possess a doctoral degree or equivalent; have the ability to work effectively in a group context; and have a balanced, objective perspective. Contact the NIH if you are interested in serving as a reviewer.

255
93.608
Child Welfare Research and Development
Children's Bureau
Administration for Children, Youth, and Families
Department of Health and Human Services
PO Box 1182
Washington, DC   20013

Areas of Interest

Program Description: The program supports research and development related to child and family development and welfare. Funded projects show national or regional significance and demonstrate new methods or ideas. Research and development in the areas of adoption, rural families, military families, leadership development, and training have received support.
Assistance Types: Project grants

Eligibility

Applicants Eligible: Public and private organizations, institutions of higher education, government and nonprofit agencies

Financial Profile

Obligations: Fiscal year 1993, $6,466,744; 1994, $6,466,744
Grant Range: $10,000-$250,000

Application Process

Contact: Penny Maza, (202) 205-8172; publications and applications: Internet: gopher.nih.gov or www.nih.gov
Deadline: Contact program office
Processing Time: 90 to 180 days
Review Process: Proposals are evaluated by staff and a peer review panel.
Criteria: Proposals are evaluated on the basis of cost effectiveness, staff qualifications, and methodology, as well as to determine whether they meet the objectives established in the program announcement.
Project Period: Indicated in program announcement

Sample Grants

Promoting Permanence in Kinship Care, a collaborative project between Western Michigan University School of Social Work and the Michigan Department of Social Services received a three-year grant.

The University of Hawaii School of Social Work received a three-year grant for a public child welfare traineeship project.

The Institute for Child and Family Services in Houston, Texas, received the three-year grant for a project, African-American Adoption: Gender Preference and Parental Coping Strategies.

Comments/Analysis

Priorities and programs vary each year; prospective applicants should consult the Federal Register or contact the program office for current program announcements.

256
93.647

Social Services Research and Demonstration
Administration for Children, Youth, and Families
Department of Health and Human Services
330 C Street SW, Switzer Bldg
Washington, DC   20201

Areas of Interest

Program Description: The program aims to promote the ability of families to be financially self-sufficient and promote the healthy development and greater social well-being of children and families. Projects funded under this program are designed to test new approaches to solving human services problems through research and demonstration grants; collect data for policy, management, and analytical purposes; evaluate programs for efficiency and effectiveness; replicate exemplary projects; and develop commercially viable products for the human services area through the small business innovation research (SBIR) program.

Assistance Types: Project grants, cooperative agreements, contracts

Eligibility

Applicants Eligible: Government entities, colleges and universities, nonprofit and for-profit organizations (if fee is waived)

Restrictions: Recipients of grants and cooperative agreements are expected to contribute at least 25 percent of the project costs; recipients of contracts are not expected to share in the project cost. All applications must meet standards of excellence in research, demonstration, or evaluation design. Applicants must present written evidence of other agencies' willingness to cooperate when the project involves the use of their facilities of services. Eligible beneficiaries include low-income individuals, children, youth, families, individuals with developmental disabilities, and Native Americans.

Financial Profile

Obligations: Fiscal year 1993, $13,828,000; 1994, $13,828,000

Grant Range: $30,000-$1,000,000

Application Process

Contact: (202) 205-8347; publications and applications: Internet: gopher.nih.gov or www.nih.gov

Deadline: Contact program office

Processing Time: 60 to 365 days. Generally, solicited proposals will be acted upon within 120 days.

Criteria: Criteria for selecting projects to be funded are published in the Federal Register grant announcement and in the solicitation for proposals and contracts.

Project Period: Funds are granted on a one- to three-year basis, with support beyond the first year contingent upon acceptable evidence of satisfactory progress, continued program relevance, and availability of funds.

Sample Grants

The program has funded projects that demonstrate the use of technology to benefit children with disabilities in the Head Start program, study juvenile sex offenders, and transfer international innovations.

Comments/Analysis

On a yearly basis, the program sets priorities and solicits applications for research, demonstration, and training activities. Prospective applicants are encouraged to contact the program administration to determine funding prospects, procedures, and schedules.

257
93.864

Population Research
National Institute of Child Health and Human
   Development
9000 Rockville Pike, Bldg 31
Bethesda, MD   20892

Areas of Interest

Program Description: The program supports research into solutions for problems of reproduction and how population structure and change affects health and well-being of the individual and society.

Assistance Types: Project grants, contracts, cooperative agreements

Eligibility

Applicants Eligible: Public and private institutions, universities, medical and nursing schools, and individuals

Restrictions: No statutory match required

Financial Profile

Obligations: Fiscal year 1993, $122,476,000; 1994, $119,385,000
Grant Range: $16,300-$4,000,000; average, $183,600
Total Grants: In 1994, 470 grants awarded

Application Process

Contact: Hildegard Topper: (301) 496-1848; publications and applications: Internet: gopher.nih.gov or www.nih.gov
Deadline: February, June, and October
Processing Time: Six to nine months
Review Process: Proposals are initially reviewed for relevance to the overall mission of the National Institutes of Health (NIH). Each proposal is subjected to a two-step scientific peer review. The review process may include a site visit. Institute staff conducts the final evaluation and makes recommendations for awards.
Criteria: Proposals are evaluated based on scientific merit and significance, technical adequacy of design, competence of investigators, adequacy of budget, and relevance of objectives to anticipated outcome.
Project Period: Five years

Sample Grants

The program has supported research projects such as Determinants of Adolescent Pregnancy and Child Bearing; and Psychosocial Determinants of Adolescent Contraceptive Use

Comments/Analysis

The most common reasons that proposals are not recommended for further consideration are lack of original ideas, unfocused research plan, lack of knowledge of published relevant work, lack of experience in the essential methodology, uncertainty concerning future directions, questionable reasoning in experimental approach, absence of an acceptable scientific rationale, unrealistic work load, and an uncritical approach. Reviewers are active and productive researchers who have demonstrated scientific expertise; possess a doctoral degree or equivalent; have the ability to work effectively in a group context; and have a balanced, objective perspective. Contact the NIH if you are interested in serving as a reviewer.

258
93.879
Medical Library Assistance Grants
Division of Extramural Programs
National Library of Medicine (NLM)
Bldg 38A
Bethesda, MD   20894

Areas of Interest

Program Description: The NLM awards grants for research, development, and demonstration projects. In addition, the NLM assists health science libraries in building basic library collections and in making existing science information resources available to users. Program categories are research, development, and demonstration grants; training in medical informatics; special scientific projects; medical library resources; and biomedical publications.
Assistance Types: Project grants

Eligibility

Applicants Eligible: Public and private institutions, universities, medical schools
Restrictions: Grants funds may not support audiovisual production, construction, binding, or acquisition of health science information source material; indirect costs; depreciation; or foreign travel. No statutory formula or matching requirements.

Financial Profile

Obligations: Fiscal year 1993, $21,050,000; 1994, $22,742,000
Grant Range: $12,000-$1,800,000; average, $225,000
Total Grants: In 1994, 121 grants awarded

Application Process

Contact: (301) 496-4621; publications and applications: Internet: gopher.nih.gov or www.nih.gov
Deadline: February, June, and October
Processing Time: Nine months
Review Process: Proposals are initially reviewed for relevance to the overall mission of the National Institutes of Health (NIH). Each proposal is subjected to a two-step scientific peer review. The review process may include a site visit. Institute staff conducts the final evaluation and makes recommendations for awards.
Criteria: Scientific merit and significance, technical adequacy of design, competence of investigators, adequacy of budget, and relevance of objectives to anticipated outcomes.
Project Period: One to five years, depending on category

Sample Grants

Funded projects included an information systems grant to link by electronic network several health science libraries, and a training grant supporting a program that offered computer science training in health areas for persons entering research careers.

Comments/Analysis

The most common reasons that proposals are not recommended for further consideration are lack of original ideas, unfocused research plan, lack of knowledge of published relevant work, lack of experience in the essential methodology, uncertainty concerning future directions, questionable reasoning in experimental approach, absence of an acceptable scientific rationale, unrealistic work load, and an uncritical approach. Reviewers are active and productive researchers who have demonstrated scientific expertise; possess a doctoral degree or equivalent; have the ability to work effectively in a group context; and have a balanced, objective perspective. Contact the NIH if you are interested in serving as a reviewer.

APPENDIXES

APPENDIX A

FOUNDATION CENTER COOPERATIVE COLLECTIONS

REFERENCE COLLECTIONS OPERATED BY THE FOUNDATION CENTER

The Foundation Center
8th Fl., 70 Fifth Ave.
New York, NY 10003
(212) 620-4230

The Foundation Center
312 Sutter St., Rm. 312
San Francisco, CA 94108
(415) 397-0902

The Foundation Center
1001 Connecticut Ave., NW, Ste. 938
Washington, DC 20036
(202) 331-1400

The Foundation Center
Kent H. Smith Library
1422 Euclid, Ste. 1356
Cleveland, OH 44115
(216) 861-1933

The Foundation Center
Ste. 150, Grand Lobby
Hurt Bldg., 50 Hurt Plaza
Atlanta, GA 30303
(404) 880-0094

Because the collections vary in their hours, materials, and services, it is recommended that you call the collection in advance. To check on new locations or current information, call toll-free 1-800-424-9836.

Alabama

Birmingham Public Library
Government Documents
2100 Park Pl.
Birmingham, AL 35203
(205) 226-3600

Huntsville Public Library
915 Monroe St.
Huntsvile, AL 35801
(205) 532-5940

University of South Alabama
Library Bldg.
Mobile, AL 36688
(205) 460-7025

Auburn University at Montgomery Library
7300 University Dr.
Montgomery, AL 36117-3596
(205) 244-3653

Alaska

University of Alaska at Anchorage Library
3211 Providence Dr.
Anchorage, AK 99508
(907) 786-1848

Juneau Public Library
292 Marine Way
Juneau, AK 99801
(907) 586-5267

Arizona

Phoenix Public Library
Business and Sciences Unit
1221 N. Central Ave.
Phoenix, AZ 85004
(602) 262-4636

Tucson Pima Library
101 N. Stone Ave.
Tucson, AZ 87501
(520) 791-4010

Arkansas

Westark Community College—Borham Library
5210 Grand Ave.

Ft. Smith, AR 72913
(501) 785-7133

Central Arkansas Library System
700 Louisiana
Little Rock, AR 72201
(501) 370-5952

Pine Bluff-Jefferson County Library System
200 E. Eighth
Pine Bluff, AR 71601
(501) 534-2159

California

Ventura County Community Foundation
Funding and Information Resource Center
1355 Del Norte Rd.
Camarillo, CA 93010
(805) 988-0196

California Community Foundation
Funding Information Center
606 S. Olive St., Ste. 2400
Los Angeles, CA 90014-1526
(213) 413-4042

Community Foundation for Monterey County
177 Van Buren
Monterey, CA 93940
(408) 375-9712

Grant & Resource Center of Northern California
2280 Benton Dr., Bldg. C, Ste. A
Redding, CA 96003
(916) 244-1219

Riverside City & County Public Library
3581 Seventh St.
Riverside, CA 92502
(714) 782-5201

Nonprofit Resource Center
Sacramento Public Library
828 I St., 2nd Fl.
Sacramento, CA 95812-2036
(916) 552-8817

San Diego Community Foundation
Funding Information Center
101 W. Broadway, Ste. 1120
San Diego, CA 92101
(619) 239-8815

Nonprofit Development Center Library
1762 Technology Dr., Ste. 225
San Jose, CA 95110
(408) 452-8181

Peninsula Community Foundation
Funding Information Library
1700 S. El Camino Real, R301

San Mateo, CA 94402-3049
(415) 358-9392

Volunteer Center of Greater Orange County
Nonprofit Management Assistance Center
1000 E. Santa Ana Blvd., Ste. 200
Santa Ana, CA 92701
(714) 953-1655

Santa Barbara Public Library
40 E. Anapamu St.
Santa Barbara, CA 93101
(707) 545-0831

Santa Monica Public Library
1343 Sixth St.
Santa Monica, CA 90401-1603
(310) 458-8600

Sonoma County Library
3rd & E St.
Santa Rosa, CA 95404
(707) 545-0831

Colorado

Pikes Peak Library District
20 N. Cascade
Colorado Springs, CO 80901
(719) 531-6333

Denver Public Library
Social Sciences & Genealogy
1357 Broadway
Denver, CO 80203
(303) 640-8870

Connecticut

Danbury Public Library
170 Main St.
Danbury, CT 06810
(203) 797-4527

Hartford Public Library
500 Main St.
Hartford, CT 06103
(203) 293-6000

DATA
70 Audubon St.
New Haven, CT 06510
(203) 772-1345

Delaware

University of Delaware
Hugh Morris Library
Neward, DE 19717-5267
(302) 831-2432

Florida

Volusia County Library Center
City Island
Daytona Beach, FL 32014-4484
(904) 255-3765
Nova University
Einstein Library
3301 College Ave.
Ft. Lauderdale, FL 33314
(305) 475-7050

Indian River Community College
Charles S. Miley Learning Resource Center
3209 Virginia Ave.
Ft. Pierce, FL 34981-5599
(407) 462-4757

Jacksonville Public Libraries
Grants Resource Center
122 N. Ocean St.
Jacksonville, FL 32202
(904) 630-2665

Miami-Dade Public Library
Humanities/Social Science
101 W. Flagler St.
Miami, FL 33130
(305) 375-5015

Orlando Public Library
Social Sciences Department
101 E. Central Blvd.
Orlando, FL 32801

Selby Public Library
1001 Blvd. of the Arts
Sarasota, FL 34236
(813) 951-5501

Tampa-Hillsborough County Public Library
900 N. Ashley Dr.
Tampa, FL 33602
(813) 273-3628

Community Foundation of Palm Beach & Martin Counties
324 Datura St., Ste. 340
West Palm Beach, FL 33401
(407) 659-6800

Georgia

Atlanta-Fulton Public Library
Foundation Collection—Ivan Allen Department
1 Margaret Mitchell Sq.
Atlanta, GA 30303-1089
(404) 730-1900

Dalton Regional Library
310 Cappes St.
Dalton, GA 30720
(706) 278-4507

Hawaii

University of Hawaii
Hamilton Library
2550 The Mall
Honolulu, HI 96822
(808) 956-7214

Hawaii Community Foundation
Hawaii Resource Center
222 Merchant St., Second Fl.
Honolulu, HI 96813
(808) 537-6333

Idaho

Boise Public Library
715 S. Capitol Blvd.
Boise, ID 83702
(208) 384-4024

Caldwell Public Library
1010 Dearborn St.
Caldwell, ID 83605
(208) 459-3242

Illinois

Donors Forum of Chicago
53 W. Jackson Blvd., Ste. 430
Chicago, IL 60604-3608

Evanston Public Library
1703 Orrington Ave.
Evanston, IL 60201
(708) 866-0305

Rock Island Public Library
401-19th St.
Rock Island, IL 61201
(309) 788-7627

Sangamon State University Library
Shepherd Rd.
Springfield, IL 62794-9243
(217) 786-6633

Indiana

Allen County Public Library
900 Webster St.
Ft. Wayne, IN 46802
(219) 424-0544

Indiana University Northwest Library
3400 Broadway
Gary, IN 46408
(219) 980-6582

Indianapolis-Marion County Public Library
Social Sciences
40 E. St. Clair

Indianapolis, IN 46206
(317) 269-1733

Iowa

Cedar Rapids Public Library
Foundation Center Collection
500 first St., SE
Cedar Rapids, IA 52401
(319) 398-5123

Southwestern Community College
Learning Resource Center
1501 W. Townline Rd.
Creston, IA 50801
(515) 782-7081

Public Library of Des Moines
100 Locust
Des Moines, 50309-1791
(515) 283-4152

Kansas

Topeka and Shawnee County Public Library
1515 SW 10th Ave.
Topeka, KS 66604-1374
(913) 233-2040

Wichita Public Library
223 S. Main St.
Wichita, KS 67202
(316) 262-0611

Kuntucky

Western Kentucky University
Helm-Cravens Library
Bowling Green, KY 42101-3576
(502) 745-6125

Louisville Free Public Library
301 York St.
Louisville, KY 40203
(502) 574-1611

Louisiana

East Baton Rouge Parish Library
Centroplex Branch Grants Collection
120 St. Louis
Baton Rouge, LA 70802
(504) 389-4960

Beauregard Parish Library
205 S. Washington Ave.
De Ridder, LA 70634
(318) 463-6217

New Orleans Public Library
Business & Science Division
219 Loyola Ave.

New Orleans, LA 70140
(504) 596-2580

Shreve Memorial Library
424 Texas St.
Shreveport, LA 71120-1523
(318) 226-5894

Maine

University of Southern Maine
Office of Sponsored Research
246 Deering Ave., Rm 628
Portland, ME 04103
(207) 780-4871

Maryland

Enoch Pratt Free Library
Social Science & History
400 Cathedral St.
Baltimore, MD 21201
(410) 396-5430

Massachusetts

Associated Grantmakers of Massachusetts
294 Washington St., Ste. 840
Boston, MA 02108
(617) 426-2606

Boston Public Library
Social Science Reference
666 Boylston St.
Boston, MA 02117
(617) 536-5400

Western Massachusetts Funding Resource Center
65 Elliot St.
Springfield, MA 01101-1730
(413) 732-3175

Worcester Public Library
Grants Resource Center
Salem Sq.
Worcester, MA 01608
(508) 799-1655

Michigan

Alpena County Library
211 N. First St.
Alpena, MI 49707
(517) 356-6188

University of Michigan—Ann Arbor
Graduate Library
Reference & Research Services Department
Ann Arbor, MI 48109-1205
(313) 764-9373

Battle Creek Community Foundation
Southwest Michigan Funding Resource Center

2 Riverwalk Centre, 34 W. Jackson St.
Battle Creek, MI 49017-3505
(616) 962-2181

Henry Ford Centennial Library Adult Services
16301 Michigan Ave.
Dearborn, MI 48126
(313) 943-2330

Wayne State University
Purdy/Kresge Library
5265 Cass Ave.
Detroit, MI 48202
(313) 577-6424

Michigan State University Libraries
Social Sciences/Humanities
Main Library
East Lansing, MI 48824-1048
(517) 353-8818

Farmington Community Library
32737 W. 12 Mile Rd.
Farmington Hills, MI 48018
(313) 553-0300

University of Michigan—Flint Library
Flint, MI 48502-2186
(313) 762-3408

Grand Rapids Public Library
Business Dept., 3rd Fl.
60 Library Plaza NE
Grand Rapids, MI 49503-3093
(616) 456-3600

Michigan Technological University
Van Pelt Library
1400 Townsend Dr.
Houghton, MI 49931
(906) 487-2507

Sault Ste. Marie Area Public Schools
Office of Compensatory Education
460 W. Spruce St.
Sault Ste. Marie, MI 49783-1874

Northwestern Michigan College
Mark & Helen Osterin Library
1701 E. Front St.
Traverse City, MI 49684
(616) 922-1060

Minnesota

Duluth Public Library
520 W. Superior St.
Duluth, MN 55802
(218) 723-3802

Southwest State University
University Library

Marshall, MN 56258
(507) 537-6176

Minneapolis Public Library
Socialogy Department
300 Nicollet Mall
Minneapolis, MN 55401
(612) 372-6555

Rochester Public Library
11 First St., SE
Rochester, MN 55904-3777
(507) 285-8002

St. Paul Public Library
90 W. Fourth St.
St. Paul, MN 55102
(612) 292-6307

Mississippi

Jackson/Hinds Library System
300 N. State St.
Jackson, MS 39201
(601) 968-5803

Missouri

Clearinghouse of Mindcontinent Foundations
University of Missouri
5315 Rockhill Rd.
Kansas City, MO 64110
(816) 235-1176

Kansas City Public Library
311 E. 12th St.
Kansas City, MO 64106
(816) 221-9650

Metropolitan Association for Philanthropy, Inc
5615 Pershing Ave., Ste. 20
St. Louis, MO 63112
(314) 361-3900

Springfield-Greene County Library
397 E. Central
Springfield, MO 65802
(417) 869-9400

Montana

Eastern Montana College Library
Special Collections—Grants
1500 N. 30th St.
Billings, MT 59101-0298
(406) 657-0298

Bozeman Public Library
220 E. Lamme
Bozeman, MT 59715
(406) 586-4787

Montana State Library
Library Services
1515 E. 6th Ave.
Helena, MT 59620
(406) 444-3004

University of Montana
Maureen & Mike Mansfield Library
Missoula, MT 59812-1195
(406) 243-6800

Nebraska

University of Nebraska—Lincoln Love Library
14th & R St.
Lincoln, NE 68588-0410
(402) 472-2848

W. Dale Clark Library
Social Sciences Department
215 S. 15th St.
Omaha, NE 68102
(402) 444-4826

Nevada

Las Vegas-Clark County Library District
833 Las Vegas Blvd., N.
Las Vegas, NV 89101
(702) 382-5280

Washoe County Library
301 S. Center St.
Reno, NV 89501
(702) 785-4010

New Hampshire

New Hampshire Charitable Foundation
One South St.
Concord, NH 03302-1335
(603) 225-6641

Plymouth State College
Herbert H. Lamson Library
Plymouth, NH 03264
(603) 535-2258

New Jersey

Cumberland County Library
New Jersey Room
800 E. Commerce St.
Bridgeton, NJ 08302
(609) 453-2210

Free Public Library of Elizabeth
11 S. Broad St.
Elizabeth, NJ 07202
(908) 354-6060

County College of Morris
Learning Resource Center

214 Center Grove Rd.
Randolph, NJ 07869
(201) 328-5296

New Jersey State Library
Governmental Reference Services
185 W. State St.
Trenton, NJ 08625-0520
(609) 292-6220

New Mexico

Albuquerque Community Foundation
3301 Menual NE, Ste. 16
Albuquerque, NM 87176-6960
(505) 883-6240

New Mexico State Library
Information Services
325 Don Gaspar
Santa Fe, NM 87503
(505) 827-3824

New York

New York State Library
Humanities Reference
Cultural Education Center
Empire State Plaza
Albany, NY 12230
(518) 474-5355

Suffolk Cooperative Library System
627 N. Sunrise Service Rd.
Bellport, NY 11713
(516) 286-1600

New York Public Library
Fordham Branch
2556 Bainbridge Ave.
Bronx, NY 10458
(718) 220-6575

Brooklyn-In-Touch Information Center, Inc
One Hanson Pl., R. 2504
Brooklyn, NY 11243
(718) 230-3200

Buffalo & Erie County Public Library
History Department
Lafayette Square
Buffalo, NY 14203
(716) 858-7103

Huntington Public Library
338 Main St.
Huntington, NY 11743
(516) 427-5165

Queens Borough Public Library
Social Sciences Division
89-11 Merrick Blvd.

Jamaica, NY 11432
(718) 990-0761

Levittown Public Library
1 Bluegrass Ln.
Levittown, NY 11756
(516) 731-5728

New York Public Library
Countee Cullen Branch Library
104 W. 136th St.
New York, NY 10030
(212) 491-2070

Adriance Memorial Library
Special Services Department
93 Market St.
Poughkeepsie, NY 12601
(914) 485-3445

Rochester Public Library
Business, Economics, & Law
115 South Ave.
Rochester, NY 14604
(716) 428-7328

Onondaga County Public Library
447 S. Salina St.
Syracuse, NY 13202-2494
(315) 448-4700

Utica Public Library
303 Genesee St.
Utica, NY 13501
(315) 735-2279

White Plains Public Library
100 Martine Ave.
White Plains, NY 10601
(914) 422-1480

North Carolina

Asheville-Buncombe Technical Community College
Learning Resources Center
14 College St., PO Box 1888
Asheville, NC 28801
(704) 254-4960

Duke Endowment
200 S. Tryon St., Ste. 1100
Charlotte, NC 28202
(704) 376-0291

Durham County Public Library
301 N. Roxboro
Durham, NC 27702
(919) 560-0110

State Library of North Carolina
Government and Business Services
Archives Bldg., 109 E. Jones St.

Raleigh, NC 27601
(919) 733-3270

Winston-Salem Foundation
310 W. 4th St., Ste. 229
Winston-Salem, NC 27101-2889
(919) 725-2382

North Dakota

North Dakota State University Library
Fargo, ND 58105
(701) 237-8886

Ohio

Stark County District Library
Humanities
715 Market Ave. N
Canton, OH 44702
(216) 452-0665

Public Library of Cincinatti & Hamilton County
Grants Resource Center
800 Vine St., Library Sq.
Cincinatti, OH 45202-2071
(513) 369-6940

Columbus Metropolitan Library
Business and Technology
96 S. Grant Ave.
Columbus, OH 43215
(614) 645-2590

Dayton & Montgomery County Public Library
Grants Resource Center
215 E. Third St.
Dayton, OH 45402
(513) 227-9500, ext. 211

Toledo-Lucas County Public Library
Social Sciences Department
325 Michigan St.
Toledo, OH 43624-1614
(419) 259-5245

Youngstown & Mahoning County Library
305 Wick Ave.
Youngstown, OH 44503
(216) 744-8636

Muskingum County Library
220 N. 5th St.
Zanesville, OH 43701
(614) 453-0391

Oklahoma

Oklahoma City University
Dulaney Browne Library
2501 N. Blackwelder
Oklahoma City, OK 73106
(405) 521-5072

Tulsa City-County Library
400 Civic Center
Tulsa, OK 74103
(918) 596-7944

Oregon

Oregon Institute of Technology Library
3201 Campus Dr.
Klamath Falls, OR 97601-8801
(503) 885-1773

Pacific Non-Profit Network
Grantsmanship Resource Library
33 N. Central, Ste. 211
Medford, OR 97501
(503) 779-6044

Multnomah County Library
Government Documents
801 SW 10th Ave.
Portland, OR 97205
(503) 248-5123

Oregon State Library
State Library Building
Salem, OR 97310
(503) 378-4277

Pennsylvania

Northampton Community College
Learning Resources Center
3835 Green Pond Rd.
Bethlehem, PA 18017
(215) 861-5360

Erie County Library System
27 S. Park Row
Erie, PA 16501
(814) 451-6927

Dauphin County Library System
Central Library
101 Walnut St.
Harrisburg, PA 17101
(717) 234-4976

Lancaster County Public Library
125 N. Duke St.
Lancaster, PA 17602
(717) 394-2651

Free Library of Philadelphia
Regional Foundation Center
Logan Sq.
Philadelphia, PA 19103
(215) 686-5423

Carnegie Library of Pittsburgh
Foundation Collection
4400 Forbes Ave.

Pittsburgh, PA 15213-4080
(412) 622-1917

Pocono Northeast Development Fund
James Pettinger Memorial Library
1151 Oak St.
Pittston, PA 18640-3755
(717) 655-5581

Reading Public Library
100 S. 5th St.
Reading, PA 19602
(215) 655-6355

Martin Library
159 Market St.
York, PA 17401
(717) 846-5300

Rhode Island

Providence Public Library
150 Empire St.
Providence, RI 02906
(401) 521-7722

South Carolina

Charleston County Library
404 King St.
Charleston, SC 29403
(803) 723-1645

South Carolina State Library
1500 Senate St.
Columbia, SC 29211
(803) 734-8666

South Dakota

Nonprofit Grants Assistance Center
Business & Education Institute
Washington St., East Hall
Dakota State University
Madison, SD 57042
(605) 256-5555

South Dakota State Library
800 Governors Dr.
Pierre, SD 57501-2294
(605) 773-5070
(800) 592-1841 (SD residents only)

Sioux Falls Area Foundation
141 N. Main Ave., Ste. 310
Sioux Falls, SD 57102-1132
(605) 336-7055

Tennessee

Knox County Public Library
500 W. Church Ave.

Knoxville, TN 37902
(615) 544-5700

Memphis & Shelby County Public Library
1850 Peabody Ave.
Memphis, TN 38104
(901) 725-8877

Nashville Public Library
Business Information Division
225 Polk Ave.
Nashville, TN 37203
(615) 862-5843

Texas

Community Foundation of Abilene
Funding Information Library
500 N. Chestnut, Ste. 1509
Abilene, TX 79604
(915) 676-3883

Amarillo Area Foundation
700 First National Pl.
801 S. Fillmore
Amarillo, TX 79101
(806) 376-4521

Hogg Foundation for Mental Health
Will C. Hogg Blg., Rm. 301
Inner Campus Dr.
University of Texas
Austin, TX 78713
(512) 471-5041

Texas A&M University at Corpus Christi
Library, Reference Department
6300 Ocean Dr.
Corpus Christi, TX 78412
(512) 994-2608

Dallas Public Library
Urban Information
1515 Young St.
Dallas, TX 75201
(214) 670-1487

El Paso Community Foundation
1616 Texas Commerce Bldg.
El Paso, TX 79901
(915) 533-4020

Funding Information Center of Fort Worth
Texas Christian University Library
2800 S. University Dr.
Ft. Worth, TX 76129
(817) 921-7664

Houston Public Library
Bibliographic Information Center
500 McKinney

Houston, TX 77002
(713) 236-1313

Longview Public Library
222 W. Cotton St.
Longview, TX 75601
(903) 237-1352

Lubbock Area Foundation, Inc
502 Texas Commerce Bank Bldg.
Lubbock, TX 79401
(806) 763-8061

Funding Information Center
530 McCullough, Ste. 600
San Antonio, TX 78212-8270
(210) 227-4333

North Texas Center for Nonprofit Management
624 Indiana, Ste. 307
Wichita Falls, TX 76301
(817) 322-4961

Utah

Salt Lake City Public Library
209 E. 500 S.
Salt Lake City, UT 84111
(801) 524-8200

Vermont

Vermont Department of Libraries
Reference & Law Information Services
109 State St.
Montpelier, VT 05609
(802) 828-3268

Virginia

Hampton Public Library
4207 Victoria Blvd.
Hampton, VA 23669
(804) 727-1312

Richmond Public Library
Business, Science, and Technology
101 E. Franklin St.
Richmond, VA 23219
(804) 780-8223

Roanoke City Public Library System
Central Library
706 S. Jefferson St.
Roanoke, VA 24016
(703) 981-2477

Washington

Mid-Columbia Library
405 S. Dayton
Kennewick, WA 99336
(509) 586-3156

Seattle Public Library
Science, Social Science
1000 4th Ave.
Seattle, WA 98104
(206) 386-4620

Spokane Public Library
Funding Information Center
W. 811 Main Ave.
Spokane, WA 99201
(509) 838-3364

United Way of Pierce County
Center for Nonprofit Development
734 Broadway, P.O. Box 2215
Tacoma, WA 98401
(206) 597-6686

Greater Wenatchee Community Foundation at the
    Wanatchee Public Library
310 Douglas St.
Wanatchee, WA 98807
(509) 662-5021

West Virginia

Kanawha County Public Library
123 Capitol St.
Charleston, WV 25301
(304) 343-4646

Wisconsin

University of Wisconsin-Madison Memorial Library
778 State St.
Madison, WI 53706
(608) 262-3242

Marquette University Memorial Library
Funding Information Center
1415 W. Wisconsin Ave.
Milwaukee, WI 53233
(414) 288-1515

University of Wisconsin—Stevens Point
Library—Foundation Collection
99 Reserve St.
Stevens Point, 54481-3897
(715) 346-3826

Wyoming

Natrona County Public Library
307 E. 2nd St.

Casper, WY 82601-2598
(307) 237-4935

Laramie County Community College
Instructional Resource Center
1400 E. College Dr.
Cheyenne, WY 82007-3299
(307) 778-1206

Campbell County Public Library
2101 4-J Rd.
Gillette, WY 82716
(307) 682-3223

Teton County Library
320 S. King St.
Jackson, WY 83001
(307) 733-2164

Rock Springs Library
400 C St.
Rock Springs, WY 82901
(307) 362-6212

Puerto Rico

University of Puerto Rico
Ponce Technological College
Library
Box 7186
Ponce, PR 00732
(809) 844-8181

Universidad del Sagrado Corazon
M.M.T. Guevara Library
Santurce, PR 00914
(809) 728-1515, ext. 4357

Participants in the Foundation Center's Cooperating Collections Network are libraries or nonprofit information centers that provide fund-raising and other funding-related technical assistance in their communities. Cooperating Collections agree to provide free public access to a basic collection of Foundation Center publications during a regular schedule of hours, offering free funding research guidance to all visitors. Many also provide a variety of services for local nonprofit organizations, using staff or volunteers to prepare special materials, organize workshops, or conduct orientations. (Reprinted with permission from the Foundation Center.)

APPENDIX B
ADDITIONAL RESOURCES

You may wish to look at copies of these recommended grant tools before you purchase them. Many of the resource listings include locations where you can find the materials and get assistance from helpful staff. Many institutions have developed joint or cooperative grants libraries to reduce costs and encourage consortium projects.

The list of resources is divided into the following sections:

- Government Grant Research Aids
- Foundation Grant Research Aids
- Corporate Grant Research Aids
- Government, Foundation, and Corporate Grant Resources
- Computer Research Services and Resources

GOVERNMENT GRANT RESEARCH AIDS
Tips

1. Each congressional district has at least two federal depository libraries. Your local college librarian or public librarian will know where the designated libraries are and will advise you on the availability of the resources listed in this section.

2. Many federal agencies have newsletters or agency publications. You can ask to be placed on their mailing lists to receive these publications.

3. Contacting federal programs to get the most up-to-date information is recommended.

4. All of the government grant publications listed here are available through your congressperson's office.

Government Publications

Catalog of Federal Domestic Assistance (CFDA)

The *Catalog* is the government's most complete listing of federal domestic assistance programs, with details on eligibility, application procedures, and deadlines, including the location of state plans. It is published at the beginning of each fiscal year, with supplementary updates during the year. Indexes are by agency program, function, popular name, applicant eligibility, and subject. The *Catalog* comes in loose-leaf form, punched for a three-ring binder.
Price: $50.00 per year
Order from:
Superintendent of Documents
U.S. Government Printing Office
Washington, DC 20402
(202)783-3238

Commerce Business Daily

The government's contracts publication, published five times a week, the *Daily* announces every government Request for Proposal (RFP) that exceeds $25,000, as well as upcoming sales of government surplus.
Price: $275.00 per year
Order from:
Superintendent of Documents
U.S. Government Printing Office
Washington, DC 20402
(202)783-3238

Congressional Record

The *Congressional Record* covers the day-to-day proceedings of the Senate and House of Representatives.

Price: $30.00 hardcover; $20.00 softcover
Order from:
Superintendent of Documents
U.S. Government Printing Office
Washington, DC 20402
(202)783-3238

Federal Register

Published five times a week (Monday through Friday), the *Federal Register* supplies up-to-date information on federal assistance and supplements the *Catalog of Federal Domestic Assistance (CFDA)*. The *Federal Register* includes public regulations and legal notices issued by all federal agencies and presidential proclamations. Of particular importance are the proposed rules, final rules, and program deadlines. An index is published monthly.

Price: $490.00 per year
Order from:
Superintendent of Documents
U.S. Government Printing Office
Washington, DC 20402
(202)783-3238

National Science Foundation Bulletin

Provides monthly news about NSF programs, deadline dates, publications, and meetings as well as sources for more information. The material in the print version of this publication is also available electronically on STIS, NSF's science and technology Information System. There is no cost for this service.

For information contact:
National Science Foundation
Office of Legislative and Public Affairs
Arlington, VA 22230
(703)306-1070

NIH Guide for Grants and Contracts

NIH Guide is published weekly and there is no subscription fee. Electronic access to the *Guide* is now available. For information contact:

The Institutional Affairs Office
National Institutes of Health
Building 1, Room 328
Bethesda, MD 20892
(301)496-5366

United States Government Manual

This paperback manual gives the names of key personnel, addresses, and telephone numbers for all agencies, departments, etc., that constitute the federal bureaucracy.

Price: $30.00 per year
Order from:
Superintendent of Documents
U.S. Government Printing Office
Washington, DC 20402
(202)783-3238

Commercially Produced Publications

Academic Research Information System (ARIS)

ARIS provides timely information about grant and contract opportunities, including concise descriptions of guidelines and eligibility requirements, upcoming deadline dates, identification of program resource persons, and new program policies for both government and nongovernment funding sources.

Price: Biomedical Sciences Report: $210.00; Social and Natural Science Report: $210.00; Arts and Humanities Report: $125.00; all three ARIS Reports and Supplements: $495.00
Order from:
Academic Research Information System, Inc.
The Redstone Building
2940 16th Street, Suite 314
San Francisco, CA 94103
(415)558-8133

Education Daily

Price: $581.00 for 250 issues
Order from:
Capitol Publications, Inc.
P.O. Box 1453, 1101 King Street
Alexandria, VA 22313-2053
(800)655-5597

Education Grants Alert

Price: $299.00 for 50 issues
Order from:
Capitol Publications, Inc.
P.O. Box 1453, 1101 King Street
Alexandria, VA 22313-2053
(800)655-5597

ERC Newsbriefs (Ecumenical Resource Consultants)

Geared to providers of human services and designed for keeping up-to-date on government grant deadlines, this 30-page bulletin covers resource material for program development in over 28 subject areas as well as for resource development in general.

Price: $75.00 per year
Order from: *ERC Newsbriefs*
P.O. Box 21385
Washington, DC 20009-0885
(202)328-9517

Federal Executive Directory

The *Directory* includes names, addresses, and phone numbers of federal government agencies and key personnel.

Price: $197.00 per year
Order from:
Federal Executive Directory
1058 Thomas Jefferson Street, NW
Washington, DC 20007
(202)333-8620

Federal Grants and Contracts Weekly

This weekly contains information on the latest Requests for Proposals (RFPs), contracting opportunities, and upcoming grants. Each 10-page issue includes details on RFPs, closing dates for grant programs, procurement-related news, and newly issued regulations.

Price: $369.00 for 50 issues
Order from:
Capitol Publications, Inc.
P.O. Box 1453, 1101 King Street
Alexandria, VA 22313-2053
(800)655-5597

Federal Yellow Book

This directory of the federal departments and agencies is updated quarterly.

Price: $225.00
Order from:
Monitor Leadership Directories, Inc.
104 Fifth Avenue
New York, NY 10011
(212)627-4140

Health Grants and Contracts Weekly

Price: $349.00 for 50 issues
Order from:
Capitol Publications, Inc.
P.O. Box 1453, 1101 King Street
Alexandria, VA 22313-2053
(800)655-5597

1995 Federal Funding Guide

Programs that provide grants and/or loans to local, county, and state government, nonprofit organizations, and community and volunteer groups are described in this guide.

Price: $349.95, plus $14.95 shipping and handling
Order from:
Government Information Services
4301 N. Fairfax Drive, Suite 875
Arlington, VA 22203
(703)528-1082

Washington Information Directory, 1994/1995

This directory is divided into three categories: agencies of the executive branch; Congress; and private or "nongovernmental" organizations. Each entry includes the name, address, telephone number, and director of the organization, along with a short description of its work.

Price: $94.95
Order from:
Congressional Quarterly Books
1414 22nd Street, NW
Washington, DC 20037
(800)638-1710

FOUNDATION GRANT RESEARCH AIDS
Tips

Many of the following research aids can be found through the Foundation Center Cooperating Collections Network. If you wish to purchase any of the following Foundation Center publications contact:

The Foundation Center
79 Fifth Avenue, Dept. ME
New York, NY 10003-3076
(800)424-9836 or (212)620-4230
Fax: (212)807-3677

AIDS Funding: A Guide to Giving by Foundations and Charitable Organizations, 3rd edition, 1993, 196 pp.

Over 450 grantmakers who have stated or demonstrated a commitment to AIDS-related services and research are identified here.

Price: $75.00
Order from: The Foundation Center

Corporate Foundation Profiles, 8th edition, 1994, 716 pp.

A Foundation Center publication, this book contains detailed analyses of 228 of the largest corporate foundations in the United States. An appendix lists financial data on an additional 1,000 smaller grantmakers.

Price: $145.00
Order from: The Foundation Center

Directory of Foundation and Corporate Members of the European Foundation Centre, 1993/1994 edition, 192 pp.

Data on a wide range of European and international foundations currently making grants in Europe are provided in this directory.

Price: $88.00
Order from: The Foundation Center

Directory of Operating Grants, 2nd Edition, February 1995, 156 pp.

Profiles on more than 640 foundations receptive to proposals for operating grants are provided.

Price: $58.50
Order from:
Research Grant Guides
P.O. Box 1214
Loxahatchee, FL 33470
Fax: (407)795-7794

Education Funding News

This weekly report provides funding information.

Price: $287.00 for 50 issues
Order from:
Government Information Service
4301 North Fairfax Drive, Suite 875
Arlington, VA 22203
(703)528-1082

Foundation and Corporate Grants Alert

Price: $227 for 50 issues
Order from:
Capitol Publications, Inc.
P.O. Box 1453, 1101 King Street
Alexandria, VA 22313-2053
(800)655-5597

The Foundation Directory, 16th edition, 1994, 1702 pp.

The most important single reference work available on grant-making foundations in the United States, this directory includes information on foundations having assets of more than $2 million or annual grants exceeding $200,000. Each entry includes a description of giving interests, along with address, telephone numbers, current financial data, names of donors, contact person, and IRS identification number. Six indexes are included: index to donors, officers, and trustees; geographic index; types of support index; subject index; foundations new to edition index; and foundation name index. The index to donors, officers, and trustees is very valuable in developing links to decision makers.

> Price: $195.00 hardcover; $170.00 softcover
> Order from: The Foundation Center

The Foundation Directory Part 2, 1994, 1016 pp.

This directory provides information on over 4,000 mid-size foundations with grant programs between $50,000 and $200,000. Published biennially.

> Price: $170.00 *Part 2*; $435.00 hardcover *Directory, Supplement,* and *Part 2*; $410.00 softcover *Directory, Supplement,* and *Part 2*
> Order from: The Foundation Center

The Foundation Directory Supplement, 1994, 523 pp.

The *Supplement* updates the 1994 edition of the *Directory,* so that users will have the latest addresses, contacts, policy statements, application guidelines, and financial data.

> Price: $110.00 *Supplement*; $285.00 hardcover *Directory* and *Supplement*; $260.00 softcover *Directory* and *Supplement*
> Order from: The Foundation Center

Foundation Giving Watch

News and the "how-to's" of foundation giving, are provided in this monthly newsletter, along with a listing of recent grants.

> Price: $139.00 for 12 issues
> Order from:
> Taft Group
> 835 Penobscot Building
> Detroit, MI 48226
> (800)877-8238

The Foundation Grants Index, 22nd edition, 1994, 2012 pp.

This is a cumulative listing of over 65,000 grants of $10,000 or more made by over 950 major foundations. A recipient name index, a subject index, a type of support/geographic index, a recipient category index, and an index to grants by foundation are included.

> Price: $135.00
> Order from: The Foundation Center

Foundation Grants to Individuals, 8th edition, 1993, 536 pp.

This directory provides a comprehensive listing of over 2,250 independent and corporate foundations that provide financial assistance to individuals.

> Price: $55.00
> Order from: The Foundation Center

Foundation News

Each bimonthly issue of the *News* covers the activities of private, company-sponsored, and community foundations, direct corporate giving, and government agencies and their programs, and includes the kinds of grants being awarded, overall trends, legal matters, regulatory actions, and other areas of common concern.

> Price: $35.50 per year or $65.00 for 2 years
> Order from:
> Foundation News
> P.O. Box 96043
> Washington, DC 20090-6043
> (301)853-6590

The Foundation 1,000, 1993/1994 edition, 2870 pp.

The 1,000 largest U.S. foundations are profiled by foundation name, subject field, type of support, and geographic location in this research aid. There is also an index that allows you to target grantmakers by the names of officers, staff, and trustees.

> Price: $225.00
> Order from: The Foundation Center

Foundation Reporter

This annual directory of the largest private charitable foundations in the United States supplies descriptions and statistical analyses.

> Price: $365.00
> Order from:
> Taft Group
> 835 Penobscot Building
> Detroit, MI 48226
> (800)877-8238

Grant Guides

There are a total of 30 *Grant Guides* available from the Foundation Center in a variety of areas such as children and youth, alcohol and drug abuse, mental health, addictions and crisis services, minorities, the homeless, public health and diseases, and social services. Each guide provides descriptions of hundreds of foundation grants of $10,000 or more recently awarded in its subject area. Sources of funding are indexed by type of organization, subject focus, and geographic funding area.

Of the 30 guides, eight are in the field of education including elementary and secondary education, higher education, libraries and information services, literacy, reading and adult/continuing education, scholarships, student aid and loans, science and technology programs, and social and political science programs.

> Price: $65.00 each
> Order from: The Foundation Center

Guide to Funding for International and Foreign Programs, **2nd edition, 1994, 356 pp.**

The guide includes over 650 funding sources that award grants to international nonprofit institutions and projects, as well as over 5,600 grant descriptions.

Price: $85.00
Order from: The Foundation Center

Guide to U.S. Foundations, Their Trustees, Officers, and Donors, **1994 edition, 4416 pp.**

Includes information on over 35,700 U.S. private, corporate, and community foundations and an index to the individuals who establish, manage, and oversee these foundations.

Price: $195.00
Order from: The Foundation Center

National Guide to Funding for Elementary and Secondary Education, **2nd edition, 1993, 589 pp.**

Over 2,000 sources of funding for elementary and secondary education and over 4,700 grant descriptions listing organizations that have successfully approached these funding sources are included in this guide.

Price: $135.00
Order from: The Foundation Center

National Guide to Funding for the Environment and Animal Welfare, **2nd edition, 1994, 322 pp.**

Includes over 1,100 sources of funding for environment- and animal welfare–related nonprofit institutions and projects, as well as over 2,700 grant descriptions.

Price: $85.00
Order from: The Foundation Center

National Guide to Funding in Arts and Culture, **3rd edition, 1994, 1035 pp.**

This guide includes over 4,000 sources of funding for arts- and culture-related nonprofit organizations and projects, as well as over 9,000 grant descriptions.

Price: $135.00
Order from: The Foundation Center

National Guide to Funding in Health, **3rd edition, 1993, 971 pp.**

This guide includes over 3,300 funding sources for health-related projects and institutions and over 9,000 grant descriptions.

Price: $135.00
Order from: The Foundation Center

National Guide to Funding in Higher Education, **3rd edition, 1994, 1012 pp.**

Over 3,600 sources of funding for higher education projects and institutions and over 10,000 grant descriptions are included in this source.

Price: $135.00
Order from: The Foundation Center

National Guides from The Foundation Center are also available in the following areas:

Aging, 1992, $80.00

Children, Youth and Families, 1993, $135.00
Economically Disadvantaged, 1993, $85.00
Library and Information Services, 1993, $85.00
Religion, 1993, $135.00
Women and Girls, 1993, $95.00

Who Gets Grants/Who Gives Grants, **2nd edition, 1994, 1353 pp.**

This book includes over 18,400 nonprofit organizations and descriptions for more than 54,500 foundation grants they received. The introduction also lists the 1,000 largest recipients of foundation grant dollars and the 50 largest recipients in each of the 19 subject fields tested.

Price: $95.00
Order from: The Foundation Center

Private Foundation IRS Tax Returns

The Internal Revenue Service requires private foundations to file income tax returns each year. Form 990-PF provides fiscal details on receipts and expenditures, compensation of officers, capital gains or losses, and other financial matters. Form 990-AR provides information on foundation managers, assets, and grants paid or committed for future payment.

The IRS makes this information available on aperture cards that may be viewed for free at the reference collections operated by the Foundation Center (New York, San Francisco, Washington, DC, Cleveland, and Atlanta) or at the Foundation Center's regional cooperating collections (see Appendix A). You may also obtain this information by writing to the appropriate IRS office (see accompanying list). Enclose as much information about the foundation as possible, including its full name, street address with zip code, employer identification number if available, and the year or years for which returns are requested. It generally takes four to six weeks for the IRS to respond, and the IRS will bill you for all charges, which vary depending on the office and length of the return.

Internal Revenue Service Center Regional Offices

- **Central Region** (Indiana, Kentucky, Michigan, Ohio, West Virginia):
  Public Affairs Officer
  Internal Revenue Service Center
  P.O. Box 1699
  Cincinnati, OH 45201

- **Mid-Atlantic Region** (District of Columbia, Maryland, Virginia, Pennsylvania [zip codes starting with 150-168 and 172]):

Public Affairs Officer
Internal Revenue Service Center
11601 Roosevelt Boulevard
Philadelphia, PA 19154

- **Midwest Region** (Illinois, Iowa, Minnesota, Missouri, Montana, Nebraska, North Dakota, Oregon, South Dakota, Wisconsin):
  Public Affairs Officer
  Internal Revenue Service Center
  P.O. Box 24551
  Kansas City, MO 64131

- **North Atlantic Region** (Connecticut, Delaware, Maine, Massachusetts, New Hampshire, New York, New Jersey, Rhode Island, Vermont, Pennsylvania [zip codes 169-171 and 173-196]):
  Public Affairs Officer
  Internal Revenue Service Center
  P.O. Box 400
  Brookhaven, NY 11742

- **Southeast Region** (Alabama, Arkansas, Georgia, Florida, Louisiana, Mississippi, North Carolina, South Carolina, Tennessee):
  Public Affairs Officer
  Internal Revenue Service Center
  P.O. Box 47-421
  Doraville, GA 30362

- **Southwest Region** (Arizona, Colorado, Kansas, New Mexico, Oklahoma, Texas, Utah, Wyoming):
  Public Affairs Officer
  Internal Revenue Service Center
  P.O. Box 934
  Austin, TX 78767

- **Western Region** (Alaska, California, Hawaii, Idaho, Nevada, Washington):
  Public Affairs Officer
  Internal Revenue Service Center
  P.O. Box 12866
  Fresno, CA 93779

Directories of State and Local Grant Makers

The number of directories made available by the Foundation Center is significant and, therefore, cannot all be listed here. Visit the Foundation Center cooperating collection (see Appendix A) closest to you to determine what directories are available for your state and surrounding region.

CORPORATE GRANT RESEARCH AIDS

Corporations interested in corporate giving often establish foundations to handle their contributions. Once foundations are established, their Internal Revenue Service returns become public information, and data are compiled into the directories previously mentioned under Foundation Grant Research Aids.

Corporate contributions that do not go through a foundation are not public information, and research sources consist of

- information volunteered by the corporation
- product information
- profitability information

Annual Survey of Corporate Contributions
Sponsored by the Conference Board and the Council for Financial Aid to Education, this annual survey of corporate giving includes a detailed analysis of beneficiaries of corporate support but does not list individual firms and specific recipients.
Price: $25.00 for associates; $100.00 for non-associates
Order from:
The Conference Board
845 Third Avenue
New York, NY 10022
(212)759-0900

Corporate Giving Watch
This newsletter reports on corporate giving developments.
Price: $139.00 for 16 issues
Order from:
Taft Group
838 Penobscot Building
Detroit, MI 48226
(800)877-8238

Directory of Corporate Affiliations, six volumes
This six-volume directory lists divisions, subsidiaries, and affiliates of thousands of companies with addresses, telephone numbers, key persons, employees, etc.
Price: $950.00, plus shipping and handling
Order from:
Reed Reference Publishing
P.O. Box 31
New Providence, NJ 07974
(800)323-6772

Dun and Bradstreet's Million Dollar Directory, five volumes
The five volumes list names, addresses, employees, sales volume, and other pertinent data for 160,000 of the largest businesses in the United States.
Price: $1,395.00
Order from:
Dun and Bradstreet Information Services

3 Sylvan Way
Parsippany, NJ 07054
(800)526-0651

National Directory of Corporate Giving, 3rd edition, 1993, 956 pp.

Information on over 1,700 corporate foundations, plus an additional 600 direct-giving programs, is provided in this directory. An extensive bibliography and six indexes are included to help you target funding prospects.

Price: $195.00
Order from:
The Foundation Center
79 Fifth Avenue, Dept. ME
New York, NY 10003-3076
(800)424-9836 or (212)620-4230
Fax: (212)807-3677

Standard and Poor's Register of Corporations, Directors and Executives, three volumes

This annual register is made up of three volumes (volume 1, *Corporations*; volume 2, *Directors and Executives*; and volume 3, *Indexes*). These volumes are available on a lease basis only. The volumes provide up-to-date rosters of over 400,000 executives of the 46,000 nationally known corporations they represent, along with their names, titles, and business affiliations.

Price: $595.00 per year, includes 3 supplements
Order from:
Standard and Poor's Corporation
Attn: Sales
25 Broadway, 17th Floor
New York, NY 10004
(212)208-8786

Standard Industrial Classification Manual

Developed for use in the classification of establishments by type of activity in which they are engaged. Published every 10 years.

Price: $30.00 plus $4.00 for handling
Order from:
National Technical Information Service
5285 Port Royal Road
Springfield, VA 22161
(703)487-4028

Taft Corporate Giving Directory, 16th edition, 1995

This directory provides detailed entries on 1,000 company-sponsored foundations. Included are nine indexes.

Price: $365.00 plus shipping and handling
Order from:
Taft Group
838 Penobscot Building
Detroit, MI 48226
(800)877-8238

Who's Who in America, 1995, 49th edition

Known for its life and career data on noteworthy individuals. The 48th edition has three volumes and more than 82,500 biographies.

Price $449.95
Order from:
Marquis Who's Who
121 Chanion Road
New Providence, NJ 07974
(800)521-8110

GOVERNMENT, FOUNDATION, AND CORPORATE GRANT RESOURCES

Many of the following research aids can be purchased from Oryx Press, 4041 N. Central Avenue, Suite 700, Phoenix, AZ 85012-3397, (800)279-6799, fax: (800)279-4663, Internet: info@oryxpress.com.

Administering Grants, Contracts, and Funds

Provides information on the roles and responsibilities of an effective grants office. Particularly useful for those in the process of setting up a new grants office or evaluating an existing one.

Price: $36.95
Order from: Oryx Press

Directory of Biomedical and Health Care Grants

This directory provides information on over 3,182 biomedical and health care–related programs sponsored by the federal government, corporations, professional associations, special interest groups, and state and local governments. Published annually.

Price: $84.50
Order from: Oryx Press

Directory of Building and Equipment Grants, 2nd edition

Aimed at aiding in the search for building and equipment grants, this directory profiles more than 900 foundations and also includes federal sources of support.

Price: $49.50
Order from:
Research Grant Guides
P.O. Box 1214
Loxahatchee, FL 33470
Fax: (407)795-7794

Directory of Computer and High Technology Grants, 2nd edition

This directory provides 3,000 funding entries, including profiles on 600 foundation and 33 federal programs, to help organizations obtain software and computer and high-tech equipment.

Price: $52.50
Order from:
Research Grant Guides
P.O. Box 1214
Loxahatchee, FL 33470
Fax: (407)795-7794

Funding Sources for Community and Economic Development

Descriptions of over 2,000 programs that offer funding opportunities for quality-of-life projects at the community level are included. Funding programs sponsored by both local and national sources are listed, including state, local, and federal government sources, nonprofit and corporate sponsors, foundations, and advocacy groups. Published annually.

Price: $49.95
Order from: Oryx Press

Directory of Grants for Organizations Serving People with Disabilities, 8th edition

Profiles on more than 1,000 foundations, 29 federal sources of support, and 4,100 funding entries are included. Foundations listed in the directory have a history of awarding grants that help organizations serving people with disabilities.

Price: $47.50
Order from:
Research Grant Guides
P.O. Box 1214
Loxahatchee, FL 33470
Fax: (407)795-7794

Directory of Grants in the Humanities

Nearly 4,000 programs sponsored by corporations, foundations, professional associations, and special interest groups are covered. Also included are programs funded by the National Endowment for the Arts, the National Endowment for the Humanities, and state and local arts and humanities councils. Published annually.

Price: $84.50
Order from: Oryx Press

Directory of Research Grants

Information on over 6,000 government, corporate, organizational, and private funding sources supporting research programs in academic, scientific, and technology related subjects is included. Published annually.

Price: $135.00
Order from: Oryx Press

Giving USA 94

Annual report on philanthropy for the year 1993.
Price: $45 without *Giving USA Update* newsletter;
$75 annual report plus newsletter
Order from:
AAFRC Trust for Philanthropy
25 W. 43rd Street, Suite 820
New York, NY 10036
(212)354-5799

Grantseeking Primer for Classroom Leaders, Scholastic, Inc.

Systematic guide providing classroom leaders with a step-by-step approach to preparing a proposal and locating likely funders.

Price: $19.95
Order from: David G. Bauer Associates, Inc.
(800)836-0732

The Principal's Guide to Grant Success, Scholastic, Inc.

Practical techniques for developing an efficient and successful grant system and for helping teachers and staff produce on-target applications for grants.

Price: $24.95
Order from: David G. Bauer Associates, Inc.
(800)836-0732

Successful Grants Program Management, Scholastic, Inc.

Valuable tool for superintendents or central office administrators interested in evaluating the grants system in their districts and developing a grants program that saves time and produces needed funding.

Price: $29.95
Order from: David G. Bauer Associates, Inc.
(800)836-0732

COMPUTER RESEARCH SERVICES AND RESOURCES

There is a wealth of information available through databases and information retrieval systems. Check with your librarian and your grants office to locate those databases you may already have access to. Most large libraries and many smaller ones offer Knight-Ridder searches as part of their reference service for a fee.

Congressional Information Service Index (CIS Index)

CIS Index covers congressional publications and legislation from 1970 to date. Hearings, committee prints, House and Senate reports and documents, special publications, Senate executive reports and documents, and public laws are indexed. *CIS Index* includes monthly abstracts and index volumes. Hard copies of grant-related materials are also available from *CIS*, including *CIS Federal Register Index,* which covers announcements from the *Federal Register* on a weekly basis.

Price: $1,145.00 hardcover annual edition; monthly service (including hardcover annual edition) is on a sliding scale ranging from $1,145.00 to $4,845.00 depending on your library's annual book, periodical, and microform budget
Order from:
Congressional Information Services, Inc.
4520 East West Highway, Suite 800
Bethesda, MD 20814
(800)638-8380

Knight-Ridder Information Services

A commercial organization which provides access to 500 databases in a range of subject areas, Knight-Ridder has a one-time set-up fee of $290.00, which includes one day of training, and an annual fee of $75.00. Knight-Ridder Information Services also provides a CD-ROM version of the *Federal Register*. The price for this service is $750.00 annually, plus an additional $750.00 for a basic Local Area Network subscription.

For more information contact:
Knight-Ridder Information Services
3460 Hillview Avenue
Palo Alto, CA 94304
(800)334-2564

KR Information OnDisc: The GRANTS Database

The CD-ROM version of *The GRANTS Database* describes nearly 10,000 funding programs in more than 90 different areas and subjects, including grants from private and commercial organizations, as well as federal, state, and local governments. Updated bimonthly.

Price: $850.00 yearly subscription fee (without CD-ROM drive); $1,500.00 (with CD-ROM drive)
Order from:
Knight-Ridder Information Services
3460 Hillview Avenue
Palo Alto, CA 94304
(800)334-2564
Fax: (415)858-7069

For more information:
Oryx Press
4041 North Central Avenue, Suite 700
Phoenix, AZ 85012-3397
(800)279-6799
Fax: (800)279-4663
Internet: info@oryxpress.com

Federal Assistance Programs Retrieval System (FAPRS)

The *FAPRS* lists more than 1,250 federal grant programs. All states have *FAPRS* services available through state, county, and local agencies, as well as through federal extension services. For further information, call (202)708-5126 or write to your congressperson's office; he or she can request a search for you, in some cases at no charge.

For more information:
Federal Domestic Assistance Catalog Staff
GSA/IRMS/WKU
300 Seventh Street, SW
Reporters Building, Room 101
Washington, DC 20407

Foundation Center Databases

The Foundation Center offers the public two online computer databases—*The Foundation Directory* file and *The Foundation Grants Index* file. Both databases are available online through DIALOG. The cost for this service is $1.20 per connect minute and $.45 for each record printed.

Contact:
The Foundation Center
79 Fifth Avenue
New York, NY 10003-3076
(800)424-9836

In NY State: (212)620-4230
Fax: (212)807-3677

Grant Winner

Four diskettes designed to make the busy grantseeker more efficient by organizing the process. Contains many of the forms and letters in David Bauer's *The "How To" Grants Manual,* published by ACE/Oryx Press.

Price: $215.00
Order from: David G. Bauer Associates, Inc. at (800) 836-0732 or
Bauer and Ferguson
2225 Elevado Road
Vista, CA 92084
(619) 758-5213

The GRANTS Subject Authority Guide, 1991, 88 pp.

This guide includes 2,421 subject terms used to index *The GRANTS Database* and features "see" and "see also" references to help users target the most appropriate files.

Price: $29.50
Order from:
Oryx Press
4041 N. Central Avenue, Suite 700
Phoenix, AZ 85012-3397
(800)279-6799
Fax: (800)279-4663
Internet: info@oryxpress.com

GrantSearch CFDA

This is an electronic edition of the *Catalog of Federal Domestic Assistance,* including the full text of all federal grant programs included in the *CFDA.*

Price: $375.00
Order from:
Capitol Publications, Inc.
1101 King Street, Suite 444
Alexandria, VA 22314
(800)847-7772

The Sponsored Programs Information Network (SPIN)

SPIN is a database of federal and private funding sources. A microversion is available as well as an online version.

Price: Online: $500.00 annually, plus $10.00 per search, or $3,500.00 annually with unlimited searches; microversion: $2,995.00 for biweekly updates, $1,995.00 for monthly updates, or $1,195.00 for quarterly updates
Order from:
InfoEd
453 New Karner Road
Albany, NY 12205
(800)727-6427

Winning Links

Software for recording information on links to funding sources provided by your board members, staff members, and volunteers.

Price $139.00

Order from:
David G. Bauer Associates at (800)836-0732 or
Bauer and Ferguson
2225 Elevado Road
Vista, CA 92084
(619) 758-5213

INTERNET SOURCES

The explosive growth of the Internet has created many new sources of information for funding programs. There is an especially large wealth of information on federal grant programs. The following is a sampling of gopher and World Wide Web sites containing grant information. Internet searches will produce many more.

List of federal government agency www pages:

www.lib.lsu.edu/gov/fedgov.html

Department of Education:

gopher.ed.gov
www.ed.gov

Department of Health and Human Services:

www.os.dhhs.gov

National Institutes of Health:

gopher.nih.gov
www.nih.gov

National Science Foundation:

stis.nsf.gov
www.nsf.gov

The Foundation Center:

http://fdncenter.org

Knight-Ridder Information Inc:

www.rs.ch

Oryx Press:

www.oryxpress.com

The MacArthur Foundation:

gopher.macfdn.org

The Alfred P. Sloan Foundation

www.sloan.org

INDEXES

SUBJECT INDEX

This index is arranged by subject and then by title. It includes the type of grantor (C = corporate foundation, Fo = foundation, Fe = federal). Foundations that begin with a personal name are sorted by last name. The accession number refers to numerical listing in text.

CURRICULUM DEVELOPMENT

DANCE

DENTAL EDUCATION

DENTISTRY

DESIGN

DISABLED

DISABLED CHILDREN

DISABLED IN EDUCATION

DISABLED IN ENGINEERING AND SCIENCE

HEALTH ADMINISTRATION

HEALTH CARE POLICY AND RESEARCH

HEALTH SCIENCES LIBRARIES

HEALTH SERVICES

HEART DISEASE

HIGHER EDUCATION

HISTORIC PRESERVATION

HISTORICAL PROGRAMS

HISTORICALLY BLACK COLLEGES AND UNIVERSITIES

HISTORY

Pew Charitable Trusts, Fo, 71
Tinker Foundation, Inc., Fo, 87

IMMUNIZATIONS

Aetna Foundation, Inc., C, 92

INDUSTRIAL DESIGN

Chrysler Corporation Fund, C, 111
NEA Design Arts Program, Fe, 175

INDUSTRIAL ENGINEERING

Exxon Education Foundation, C, 118
NSF Engineering Grants, Fe, 197

INDUSTRIAL RELATIONS

Alfred P. Sloan Foundation, Fo, 81
USX Foundation, Inc., C, 163
Weyerhaeuser Company Foundation, C, 167

INFORMATION SYSTEMS

W.K. Kellogg Foundation, Fo, 51

INSURANCE EDUCATION

CIGNA Foundation, C, 112
Nationwide Insurance Enterprise Foundation, C, 143
Prudential Foundation, C, 151
State Farm Companies Foundation, C, 158

INTERCULTURAL RELATIONS

Nathan Cummings Foundation, Inc., Fo, 19
GE Foundation, C, 121
Florence Gould Foundation, Fo, 34
Harry Frank Guggenheim Foundation, Fo, 36
Hitachi Foundation, C, 128
James Irvine Foundation, Fo, 44
Joyce Foundation, Fo, 48
Rockefeller Brothers Fund, Fo, 76
Whirlpool Foundation, C, 168

INTERNATIONAL AFFAIRS

Archer-Daniels-Midland Foundation, C, 99
AT&T Foundation, C, 101
Bristol-Myers Squibb Foundation, Inc., C, 106
Carnegie Corporation of New York, Fo, 11
Coca-Cola Foundation, Inc., C, 113
Compton Foundation, Inc., Fo, 16
Earhart Foundation, Fo, 25
Ford Foundation, Fo, 29
Joyce Mertz-Gilmore Foundation, Fo, 33
Harry Frank Guggenheim Foundation, Fo, 36
John D. and Catherine T. MacArthur Foundation, Fo, 58
PepsiCo Foundation, Inc., C, 147
Pew Charitable Trusts, Fo, 71
Rockefeller Foundation, Fo, 77
Sarah Scaife Foundation, Inc., Fo, 78
Tinker Foundation, Inc., Fo, 87
Xerox Foundation, C, 169

INTERNATIONAL BUSINESS EDUCATION

Business and International Education Program, Fe, 232

INTERNATIONAL EDUCATION

Whirlpool Foundation, C, 168

INTERNATIONAL ENGINEERING AND SCIENCE

NSF Social, Behavioral, and Economic Sciences Grants, Fe, 202

INTERNATIONAL EXCHANGE PROGRAMS

Fulbright-Hays Group Projects Abroad, Fe, 212
Max Kade Foundation, Inc., Fo, 49

INTERNATIONAL LAW

Joyce Mertz-Gilmore Foundation, Fo, 33
Sarah Scaife Foundation, Inc., Fo, 78

INTERNATIONAL MANAGEMENT

Whirlpool Foundation, C, 168

INTERNATIONAL RELATIONS

Ford Motor Company Fund, C, 120
Hitachi Foundation, C, 128
Rockefeller Brothers Fund, Fo, 76
Florence and John Schumann Foundation, Fo, 79
Tinker Foundation, Inc., Fo, 87

INTERNATIONAL STUDIES

Fulbright-Hays Group Projects Abroad, Fe, 212
William and Flora Hewlett Foundation, Fo, 41
International Research and Studies Program, Fe, 211
Henry Luce Foundation, Inc., Fo, 56
National Resource Centers and Foreign Language and Area Studies
        Fellowships Programs, Fe, 209
John M. Olin Foundation, Inc., Fo, 68
Sarah Scaife Foundation, Inc., Fo, 78
Undergraduate International Studies and Foreign Language, Fe, 210

INTERNATIONAL TRADE

Rockefeller Brothers Fund, Fo, 76

JAPAN

Hitachi Foundation, C, 128

JEWISH WELFARE

Nathan Cummings Foundation, Inc., Fo, 19

JOB TRAINING

Bank of Boston Corporation Charitable Foundation, C, 102
BankAmerica Foundation, C, 103
CIGNA Foundation, C, 112
Commonwealth Fund, Fo, 15
Cooperative Education Program, Fe, 220
Johnson & Johnson Family of Companies Contribution Fund,
    C, 131

Star Schools Program, Fe, 237

Technology, Educational Media, and Materials for Individuals with Disabilities, Fe, 233

Wachovia Foundation, Inc., C, 164

MEDICAL EDUCATION

Burroughs Wellcome Fund, C, 109

Charles E. Culpeper Foundation, Inc., Fo, 18

Ira W. DeCamp Foundation, Fo, 23

Higher Education Institutional Aid, Fe, 216

Interdisciplinary Training for Health Care for Rural Areas, Fe, 244

Johnson & Johnson Family of Companies Contribution Fund, C, 131

Robert Wood Johnson Foundation, Fo, 45

Eli Lilly and Company Foundation, C, 134

Merck Company Foundation, C, 140

Schering-Plough Foundation, Inc., C, 153

SmithKline Beecham Foundation, C, 156

Warner-Lambert Charitable Foundation, C, 165

E.L. Wiegand Foundation, Fo, 91

MEDICAL RESEARCH

Amoco Foundation, Inc., C, 97

Arnold and Mabel Beckman Foundation, Fo, 4

Corella and Bertram Bonner Foundation, Inc., Fo, 6

Bristol-Myers Squibb Foundation, Inc., C, 106

Burroughs Wellcome Fund, C, 109

Edna McConnell Clark Foundation, Fo, 14

Comparative Medicine Program, Fe, 251

Charles A. Dana Foundation, Inc., Fo, 20

Ira W. DeCamp Foundation, Fo, 23

Sherman Fairchild Foundation, Inc., Fo, 28

Francis Families Foundation, Fo, 30

H. J. Heinz Company Foundation, C, 127

Johnson & Johnson Family of Companies Contribution Fund, C, 131

W. M. Keck Foundation, Fo, 50

J.E. and L.E. Mabee Foundation, Inc., Fo, 57

John D. and Catherine T. MacArthur Foundation, Fo, 58

G. Harold and Leila Y. Mathers Charitable Foundation, Fo, 60

John Merck Fund, Fo, 62

Ambrose Monell Foundation, Fo, 63

M.J. Murdock Charitable Trust, Fo, 65

Samuel Roberts Noble Foundation, Inc., Fo, 67

Seaver Institute, Fo, 80

SmithKline Beecham Foundation, C, 156

Thrasher Research Fund, Fo, 86

Warner-Lambert Charitable Foundation, C, 165

Del E. Webb Foundation, Fo, 90

E.L. Wiegand Foundation, Fo, 91

MEDICAL SCIENCES

Ahmanson Foundation, Fo, 1

Arnold and Mabel Beckman Foundation, Fo, 4

Burroughs Wellcome Fund, C, 109

Coca-Cola Foundation, Inc., C, 113

Arthur Vining Davis Foundation, Fo, 22

Johnson & Johnson Family of Companies Contribution Fund, C, 131

Merck Company Foundation, C, 140

PepsiCo Foundation, Inc., C, 147

Pew Charitable Trusts, Fo, 71

Seaver Institute, Fo, 80

SmithKline Beecham Foundation, C, 156

Thrasher Research Fund, Fo, 86

MEDICINE

Max Kade Foundation, Inc., Fo, 49

MENTAL HEALTH

Ahmanson Foundation, Fo, 1

Charles A. Frueauff Foundation, Inc., Fo, 31

Robert Wood Johnson Foundation, Fo, 45

John D. and Catherine T. MacArthur Foundation, Fo, 58

Mental Health Research, Fe, 246

Ambrose Monell Foundation, Fo, 63

Pew Charitable Trusts, Fo, 71

MEXICO

William and Flora Hewlett Foundation, Fo, 41

MICROBIOLOGICAL SCIENCES

Burroughs Wellcome Fund, C, 109

MINERAL SCIENCE AND TECHNOLOGY

Phillips Petroleum Foundation, Inc., C, 148

USX Foundation, Inc., C, 163

MINORITIES

Archer-Daniels-Midland Foundation, C, 99

Bristol-Myers Squibb Foundation, Inc., C, 106

Carnegie Corporation of New York, Fo, 11

Ford Foundation, Fo, 29

Grace Foundation, Inc., C, 124

Hearst Foundation, Inc., Fo, 38

William Randolph Hearst Foundation, Fo, 39

James Irvine Foundation, Fo, 44

Robert Wood Johnson Foundation, Fo, 45

W.K. Kellogg Foundation, Fo, 51

NYNEX Foundation, C, 145

Pew Charitable Trusts, Fo, 71

US WEST Foundation, C, 162

MINORITIES IN ENGINEERING AND SCIENCE

Amoco Foundation, Inc., C, 97

Chrysler Corporation Fund, C, 111

GE Foundation, C, 121

William Randolph Hearst Foundation, Fo, 39

Honeywell Foundation, C, 129

Minority Science Improvement Program, Fe, 229

NSF Computer and Information Science and Engineering Grants, Fe, 200

NSF Engineering Grants, Fe, 197

NSF Geosciences Grants, Fe, 199

Phillips Petroleum Foundation, Inc., C, 148

SCIENCE AND TECHNOLOGY

SCIENCE EDUCATION

SCULPTURE

SECONDARY EDUCATION

INDEX OF FOUNDATIONS AND CORPORATE FOUNDATIONS BY STATE

This index is arranged alphabetically by state and then by name of funding source. It includes foundation and corporate foundation grantors (C = corporate foundation, Fo = foundation). Foundations beginning with personal names are sorted by the last name. Numbers refers to numerical listing in text.

INDEX OF FOUNDATION AND CORPORATE FOUNDATION NAMES

This index is arranged alphabetically by foundation or corporate foundation name (Fo = foundation, C = corporate foundation). Foundations beginning with personal names are sorted by the last name. Numbers refers to numerical listing in text.

INDEX OF FEDERAL PROGRAMS BY TITLE

![black square]

This index is arranged alphabetically by federal grant program title. Numbers refer to numerical listing in text.

INDEX OF FEDERAL PROGRAMS BY CFDA NUMBER

This index lists federal programs numerically by CFDA (Catalog of Federal Domestic Assistance) number. Numbers refer to numerical listing in text.

INDEX OF ADDITIONAL FOUNDATIONS

This index lists additional foundations, not included in the sourcebook, that you may want to research as potential funding sources for your project. Entries are arranged alphabetically by state and then by funding source.

Alabama

J.L. Bedsole Foundation
c/o AmSouth Bank, N.A.
PO Box 1628
Mobile, Alabama 36629
205-432-3369

Comments: The foundation supports higher education and social services in Alabama. An application form is required.

The Comer Foundation
PO Box 302
Sylacauga, Alabama 35150
205-249-2962

Comments: The foundation supports higher and other education, health, and cultural programs. Initial approach should be by letter.

The Daniel Foundation of Alabama
820 Shades Creek Parkway, Suite 1200
Birmingham, Alabama 35209
205-879-0902

Comments: The foundation supports higher education, health, cultural programs, and youth agencies. Initial approach should be by letter; an application form is not required.

Alaska

The Doyon Foundation
201 First Avenue
Fairbanks, Alaska 99701
907-452-4755

Comments: Giving focuses on higher education, libraries, and Native Americans in Alaska. An application form is required.

Arizona

The Flinn Foundation
3300 North Central Avenue, Suite 2300

Phoenix, Arizona 85012
602-274-9000

Comments: The foundation is interested in health, education, and cultural arts in Arizona. Initial approach by letter or telephone; application form not required.

The Margaret T. Morris Foundation
PO Box 592
Prescott, Arizona 86302
602-445-4010

Comments: The foundation gives to the arts, cultural programs, and education in Arizona. Initial approach is by letter or proposal; an application form is not required.

Arkansas

The Winthrop Rockefeller Foundation
308 East Eighth Street
Little Rock, Arkansas 72202
501-376-6854

Comments: The foundation's priorities are education and economic development. Initial approach by letter or telephone; no application form is required.

Walker Charitable Foundation Trust
117 Rogueries Circle Drive
Springdale, Arkansas 72764
501-751-9083

Comments: The foundation's primary interest is higher education. An application form is not required.

California

Fritz B. Burns Foundation
4001 West Alameda Avenue, Suite 201
Burbank, California 91505
818-840-8802

Comments: Giving primarily in the Los Angeles area for education, medical research, and social welfare. Initial approach should be by letter.

Community Foundation of Santa Clara
960 West Hedding, Suite 220
San Jose, California 95126-1215
408-241-2666
Comments: Giving for scholarship funds, consulting, technical assistance, and matching funds in Santa Clara County. An application form is not required; initial approach should be by telephone or letter.

The Thomas and Dorothy Leavey Foundation
4680 Wilshire Boulevard
Los Angeles, California 90010
213-930-4252
Comments: Giving primarily in Southern California for hospitals and medical research.

The Koret Foundation
33 New Montgomery Street, Suite 1090
San Francisco, California 94105-4509
415-882-7740
Comments: Giving primarily to the Bay Area for education and social welfare through operating budgets, special projects, and fellowships. An application form not required; initial inquiry should by letter.

The McCone Foundation
PO Box 1499
Pebble Beach, California 93953
Comments: Giving for higher education and hospitals in California and Washington.

San Diego Community Foundation
Wells Fargo Bank Building
101 West Broadway, Suite 1120
San Diego, California 92101
619-239-8815
Comments: Giving in San Diego County for education and social services through seed money, building or endowment funds, and general purposes. Application form required.

Colorado

The Boettcher Foundation
600 17th Street, Suite 2210 South
Denver, Colorado 80202
303-534-1937
Comments: Interests include higher education, arts, and ecology; support provided for scholarships, general purposes, and building.

The El Pomar Foundation
Ten Lake Circle

Colorado Springs, Colorado 80906
719-633-7733
Comments: The foundation is interested in higher education. Application form not required, initial approach should be by letter.

Connecticut

The Dibner Fund, Inc.
44 Old Ridgefield Road
PO Box 7575
Wilton, Connecticut 06897
Comments: Giving primarily in Connecticut, Massachusetts, and New York. The foundation's interests are in science and technology. Application form not required.

The Lawson Valentine Foundation
988 Farmington Avenue, Suite 123
West Hartford, Connecticut 06107
203-521-3108
Comments: The foundation is interested in education, civil and human rights, race relations, peace, and the environment. Initial approach should be by letter.

Delaware

The Milton and Hattie Kutz Foundation
101 Garden of Eden Road
Wilmington, Delaware 19803
302-478-6200
Comments: The foundation gives for scholarships, buildings, and emergency funds in Delaware. Application form is required.

The Longwood Foundation, Inc.
1004 Wilmington Trust Center
Wilmington, Delaware 19801
302-654-2477
Comments: The foundation gives to higher education. Initial approach should be by letter.

District of Columbia

The Morris and Gwendolyn Cafritz Foundation
1825 K Street, NW, 14th Floor
Washington, DC 20006
202-223-3100
Comments: Interests include education, arts and cultural programs, health, and AIDS. Application form not required.

The James M. Johnston Trust for Charitable and Educational Purposes
1101 Vermont Avenue, NW, Suite 403
Washington, DC 20005
202-289-4996
Comments: The foundation gives to higher education. Application form not required; initial approach should be by letter.

Mary and Daniel Loughran Foundation, Inc.
c/o Security Trust Co. NA
15th Street and Pennsylvania Avenue, NW
Washington, DC 20013
202-624-5744
Comments: The foundation gives in Washington, DC; Virginia; and Maryland and has an interest in youth, social services, education, and the arts. Application form not required.

Florida

The Dade Community Foundation
200 South Biscayne Boulevard, Suite 4770
Miami, Florida 33131-2343
305-371-2711
Comments: The foundation makes awards to higher education in Dade County. Application form not required; initial approach should be by letter.

M.E. Rinker, Sr. Foundation, Inc.
310 Okeechobee Boulevard
West Palm Beach, Florida 33401-6432
Comments: Giving primarily for higher education in Florida.

Georgia

The Callaway Foundation, Inc.
209 Broome Street
PO Box 790
La Grange, Georgia 30241
706-884-7348
Comments: The foundation gives to libraries and health through continuing support, aid to annual campaigns, matching funds, building, and equipment. Application form not required; initial approach should be by letter.

John H. and Wihelmina D. Harland Charitable Foundation, Inc.
Two Piedmont Center, Suite 106
Atlanta, Georgia 30305
404-264-9912
Comments: Support for arts, culture, education, and youth development projects aimed at increasing the long-term effectiveness of the grantee.

Hawaii

Atherton Family Foundation
c/o Hawaiian Trust Co., Ltd.
PO Box 3170
Honolulu, Hawaii 96802
808-521-6286
Comments: Giving to education, arts, cultural programs, the environment, and health in Hawaii, through building funds, student aid, annual campaigns, and continuing support. Application form not required; initial approach by telephone or proposal.

Samuel N. and Mary Castle Foundation
222 Merchant Street
Honolulu, Hawaii 96813
808-521-6286
Comments: The foundation gives primarily to private higher and secondary education in Hawaii.

Idaho

Laura Moor Cunningham Foundation, Inc.
519 Main Street
Boise, Idaho 83702-5932
208-347-7852
Comments: The foundation gives to higher education and business scholarship funds in Idaho. Application form is required.

Ray Foundation
PO Box 2156
Ketchum, Idaho 83340
Comments: The foundation gives to higher education in Idaho, Arizona, Oregon, and Washington. Application form is required.

Illinois

Beloit Foundation
11722 Main Street
Roscoe, Idaho 61703
815-623-6600
Comments: The foundation makes grants in Illinois and Wisconsin. Application form is required.

The Gary K. and Carlotta J. Bielfeldt Foundation
124 S. W. Adams, Suite 340
Peoria, Illinois 61602
Comments: Grants to higher education are given in Illinois. Application form is required.

The Butz Foundation
c/o the Northern Trust Co.
50 South La Salle Street
Chicago, Illinois 60675
312-444-3788
Comments: The foundation gives to higher education and for medical research and projects that benefit the disabled in Illinois.

Indiana

The John W. Anderson Foundation
402 Wall Street
Valparaiso, Indiana 46383
219-462-4611
Comments: The foundation is particularly interested in education, youth, libraries, and the disabled. Giving primarily in

northwest Indiana. Application form is not required; approach by letter first.

The Ball Brothers Foundation
222 Mulberry Street
PO Box 1408
Muncie, Indiana 47308
317-741-5500

Comments: The foundation supports the humanities, cultural programs, health, and medical education in Indiana. Application form is not required, approach first by letter and proposal.

The Foellinger Foundation
520 East Berry Street
Fort Wayne, Indiana 46802
219-422-2900

Comments: The foundation's interests include leadership development, cultural programs, literacy, education, AIDS, and health services.

Iowa

The Gardner and Florence Call Cowles Foundation, Inc.
715 Locust Street
Des Moines, Iowa 50309
515-284-8116

Comments: The foundation gives primarily to four-year private colleges in Iowa. Application form not required; initial contact should be by letter or proposal.

The Des Moines Community Foundation
601 Locust Street
Des Moines, Iowa 50309
515-245-3766

Comments: The foundation provides seed money to projects in human services and the arts. Application form is required.

The R.J. McElroy Trust
KWWL Building, Suite 318
500 East Fourth Street
Waterloo, Iowa 50703
319-291-1299

Comments: The foundation gives to higher education through scholarships, fellowships, and student loan programs.

Kansas

Dane Hansen Foundation
PO Box 187
Logan, Kansas 67646
913-689-4832

Comments: The foundation is interested in higher education, including postsecondary vocational education in northwestern Kansas. Application form is required.

The Julia Mingenback Foundation, Inc.
c/o Bank IV Kansas, NA
One Main Place
McPherson, Kansas 67460

Comments: Giving primarily in McPherson County, Kansas, for building, renovation, and capital funds. Initial approach by letter.

Kentucky

James Graham Brown, Inc.
132 East Gray Street
Louisville, Kentucky 40404
502-583-4085

Comments: The foundation supports higher education in Kansas, particularly annual and capital campaigns, endowment funds, scholarship funds, and building funds.

C.E. and S. Foundation, Inc.
3300 First National Tower
Louisville, Kentucky 40202

Comments: The foundation gives primarily to higher education in Kentucky, through building, endowment, and scholarship funds. Application form required.

Louisiana

Coughlin-Saunders Foundation, Inc.
c/o Adler and Pias
1412 Centre Court, Suite 202
Alexandria, Louisiana 71301-3406
318-442-9642

Comments: The foundation supports higher education, the arts, health, and youth services in Louisiana. Application form not required; initial approach should be by letter.

Edward G. Schlieder Educational Foundation
431 Gravier Street, Suite 400
New Orleans, Louisiana 70130
504-581-6179

Comments: The foundation gives to educational institutions in Louisiana. Support is provided for research and medical research. Application form not required; initial approach should be by letter.

Maryland

The Abell Foundation
1116 Fidelity Building
210 North Charles Street
Baltimore, Maryland 21201

Comments: The foundation primarily supports projects in Maryland that benefit children and youth, and also provides support for health, homeless, hunger, education, the arts, and culture. Application form required, initial approach by letter; application guidelines should be requested.

The Jacob and Hilda Blaustein Foundation, Inc.
Blaustein Building
PO Box 238
Baltimore, Maryland 21203
Comments: Giving primarily in Maryland and New York for higher education and Jewish welfare. Initial approach should be by letter.

The Jacob and Annita France Foundation, Inc.
The Exchange, Suite 118
1122 Kenilworth, Suite 118
Baltimore, Maryland 21204
Comments: The foundation gives to higher education, social services, health, historic preservation, arts and culture, conservation, and civic projects. Application form not required; initial approach should be by letter.

Massachusetts

L.G. Balfour Foundation
c/o Fleet Bank of Boston, NA
28 State Street
Boston, Massachusetts 02109
617-573-6415
Comments: The foundation gives in Massachusetts and New England for scholarships and projects designed to increase access to higher education. Application form required; initial approach should be a letter of inquiry.

The Fred Harris Daniels Foundation, Inc.
c/o The Mechanics Bank, Trust Department
PO Box 15073
Worcester, Massachusetts 01615-0073
508-798-6467
Comments: The foundation supports science, marine and medical science, libraries, health, mental health, music, and libraries primarily in the Worcester area. Application form is not required; initial approach should be by letter.

The Amelia Peabody Foundation
c/o Hale and Dorr
60 State Street
Boston, Massachusetts 02109
617-742-9100
Comments: The foundation gives to education, culture, and youth. Application form is not required; initial approach should be by letter.

Michigan

Dorothy U. Dalton Foundation, Inc.
c/o Arcadia Bank
PO Box 50566
Kalamazoo, Michigan 49005
Comments: The foundation primarily gives to higher education, mental health, youth agencies, and cultural programs in Kalamazoo County. Application form not required, submit proposal.

The Herbert H. and Grace A. Dow Foundation
PO Box 2184
Midland, Michigan 48641-2184
517-631-3699
Comments: The foundation supports the arts and sciences and research, primarily in Midland County. Application form not required, submit proposal.

The McGregor Fund
333 West Fort Street, Suite 1380
Detroit, Michigan 48226
313-963-3495
Comments: The foundation supports education, welfare, youth, and private colleges and universities in Michigan, Ohio, and Indiana. Application form is not required; initial approach should be by letter.

Minnesota

The Charles and Ellora Alliss Educational Foundation
c/o First Trust, NA
Three West, PO Box 64704
St. Paul, Minnesota 55164
612-291-5158
Comments: The foundation supports scholarships and undergraduate aid in Minnesota. Application form is not required; initial letter should include background information.

F.R. Bigelow Foundation
600 Norwest Center
St. Paul, Minnesota 55101
612-224-5463
Comments: The foundation gives to higher education, arts, humanities, and health in the St. Paul area. Application form required; initial approach can be made by telephone, letter, or proposal.

The Curtis L. Carlson Foundation
12755 State Highway 55
Minneapolis, Minnesota 55441
Comments: The foundation supports education, youth, and the arts in Minnesota. Initial approach should be the submission of a proposal.

Missouri

The Hall Family Foundations
Charitable & Crown Investment - 323
PO Box 419580
Kansas City, Missouri 64141-6580
816-274-8516
Comments: Giving for the arts, youth, economic development, and the elderly in Missouri and Kansas. Application form is not required; initial approach should be by letter.

The Webb Foundation
232 Kings Highway, Suite 205
St. Louis, Missouri 63108
314-367-0232

Comments: Giving in the midwest is focused on children, the disabled, the indigent, and higher education. Application form required; initial approach may be by telephone, letter, or proposal.

Montana

W.J. Gallagher Foundation
c/o First Trust Company of Montana, NA
PO Box 4787
Missoula, Montana 59807-7969

Comments: Giving through annual campaigns in Montana. Applicants should approach the foundation by letter.

Nebraska

The Peter Kiewit Foundation
900 Woodmen Tower
17th and Farnam Street
Omaha, Nebraska 68102
402-344-7890

Comments: The foundation provides support for challenge and matching funds to higher education, the arts, health, and youth in Nebraska, Iowa, and Wyoming. Application form is required; request by letter or telephone.

Lied Foundation Trust
10050 Regency Circle, Suite 200
Omaha, Nebraska 68114
702-878-1559

Comments: Giving for youth and higher education in Nebraska and Las Vegas, Nevada. Application form is not required.

Nevada

The Cord Foundation
200 Court Street
Reno, Nevada 89501
702-323-0373

Comments: Giving to higher education, youth, and culture.

New Hampshire

The Cogwheel Benevolent Trust
875 Elm Street
Manchester, New Hampshire 03101
603-622-4013

Comments: Giving for higher education and youth in New Hampshire. Application form is not required.

Agnes M. Lindsay Trust
95 Market Street

Manchester, New Hampshire 03101
603-669-4140

Comments: The foundation supports higher education, with an emphasis on scholarship funds in New Hampshire, Maine, Massachusetts, and Vermont. Initial approach by proposal.

New Jersey

The Hyde and Watson Foundation
437 Southern Boulevard
Chatham, New Jersey 07928
201-966-6024

Comments: The foundation supports capital projects in New Jersey and New York. Application form is required; submit preliminary letter of appeal and request application guidelines.

The Turrell Fund
111 Northfield Avenue
West Orange, New Jersey 07052
201-325-5108

Comments: The foundation's emphasis is on projects that benefit New Jersey.

The Victoria Foundation, Inc.
40 South Fullerton Avenue
Montclair, New Jersey 07042
201-783-4450

Comments: The foundation supports projects that provide solutions to urban problems in New Jersey. The foundation is particularly interested in the areas of education, leadership development, and the environment.

New Mexico

The Frost Foundation, Ltd.
314 McKenzie Street
Santa Fe, New Mexico 87501
505-986-0208

Comments: The foundation gives primarily in the southwest for higher education, including medical education and business education. Other areas of interest include health, youth, and social services. Application form is not required; initiate contact with the foundation by letter or telephone.

J.F. Maddox Foundation
PO Box 5410
Hobbs, New Mexico 88241
505-393-6338

Comments: The foundation gives to higher education through student loans and building funds. It also supports the arts and projects that benefit youth and elderly in New Mexico and west Texas. Application form is not required; initiate contact with the foundation by letter.

New York

Altman Foundation
220 East 42nd Street, Suite 411
New York, New York 10017
212-682-0970
Comments: Giving in New York City for education, the arts, AIDS, and projects that benefit the disadvantaged and youth.

Booth Ferris Foundation
c/o Morgan Guaranty Trust Co. of New York
60 Wall Street
New York, New York 10260-0001
Comments: The foundation supports smaller colleges in the New York metropolitan area. Application form not required; submit proposal.

Carnahan-Jackson Foundation
Fourth and Pine Building
Jamestown, New York 14701
716-483-1015
Comments: The foundation gives to higher education, libraries, and youth-related projects in western New York State. Application form is required; in initial letter outline needs and use of grant.

The Rosamond Gifford Charitable Corporation
731 James Street, Room 404
Syracuse, New York 13203
315-474-2489
Comments: The foundation gives to higher education and to projects that benefit youth and elderly in central New York. Application form not required.

North Carolina

Z. Smith Reynolds Foundation, Inc.
101 Reynolds Village
Winston-Salem, North Carolina 27106-5199
919-725-7541
Comments: The foundation gives to education, community development, and social services in North Carolina. Application form is required; contact by telephone or letter.

Weaver Foundation
324 West Wendover, Suite 300
Greensboro, North Carolina 27408
919-275-9600
Comments: The foundation gives to higher education and the arts in North Carolina. Application form not required; submit proposal.

Ohio

The Cleveland Foundation
1422 Euclid Avenue, Suite 1400
Cleveland, Ohio 4415-2001
216-861-3810

Comments: The foundation supports education and economic and community development in the greater Cleveland area. Contact the foundation by letter; application form is not required.

The GAR Foundation, Inc.
50 South Main Street
PO Box 1500
Akron, Ohio 44309
216-376-5300
Comments: The foundation gives to education, youth, and civic affairs in northeastern Ohio. Application form is required.

The Iddings Foundation
Kettering Tower, Suite 1620
Dayton, Ohio 45423
513-224-1773
Comments: The foundation supports precollege and higher education, mental health, youth, and cultural programs in the Dayton area. Application form is not required; approach by telephone or letter.

The Kettering Fund
1440 Kettering Tower
Dayton, Ohio 45423
513-228-1021
Comments: The foundation makes grants for research in science, medicine, and the social sciences and also supports the performing arts in Ohio. Application form is not required; initial submission should be a brief outline of proposal.

Oklahoma

The H.A. and Mary K. Chapman Charitable Trust
One Warren Place, Suite 1816
6100 South Yale
Tulsa, Oklahoma
918-496-7882
Comments: The foundation gives to higher education in the Tulsa area. Application form is required.

The Cuesta Foundation, Inc.
One Williams Center, Suite 4400
Tulsa, Oklahoma 74172
918-584-7266
Comments: The foundation gives to higher education and the arts in Oklahoma. Applicant form is not required; submit letter.

McCasland Foundation
McCasland Building
PO Box 400
Duncan, Oklahoma 73534
405-252-5580

Comments: The foundation gives to higher education and social services in Oklahoma and the Southwest. Initial approach should be made by letter.

Oregon

The Chiles Foundation
111 S.W. Fifth Avenue, Suite 4050
Portland, Oregon 97204-3643
503-222-2143

Comments: The foundation gives to higher education in the areas of business and medicine in Oregon and the Pacific Northwest. Application form is required.

The Collins Foundation
1618 S.W. First Avenue, Suite 305
Portland, Oregon 97201
503-227-7171

Comments: The foundation gives to higher education, youth, and the arts in Oregon. An application form is not required; submit a letter.

Meyer Memorial Trust
1515 SW Fifth Avenue, Suite 500
Portland, Oregon 97201
503-228-5512

Comments: The foundation makes grants for education, the arts and humanities, and health and social welfare in Oregon, and for social projects in the Pacific Northwest. An application form is required; initial approach by proposal.

Pennsylvania

The Buhl Foundation
Four Gateway Center, Room 1522
Pittsburgh, Pennsylvania 15222
412-566-2711

Comments: The foundation has a special interest in innovative regional projects, and primarily makes grants in the Pittsburgh area. An application form is not required.

Conelly Foundation
One Tower Bridge, Suite 1450
West Coshoken, Pennsylvania 19428
215-834-3222

Comments: The foundation supports education and social services in the Philadelphia area. An application form is not required; submit a proposal.

The Eden Hall Foundation
Pittsburgh Office and Research Park
5500 Corporate Drive, Suite 210
Pittsburgh, Pennsylvania 15237
412-364-6670

Comments: The foundation supports higher education, health, and programs for the disadvantaged in western Penn-

sylvania. An application form is not required; initial approach by letter.

The Whitaker Foundation
4718 Old Gettysburg Road, Suite 405
Mechanicsburg, Pennsylvania 17055-8411

Comments: Giving primarily for biomedical research in the United States and Canada, and to service and educational organizations in the Harrisburg, Pennsylvania area.

Rhode Island

Chace Fund, Inc.
731 Hospital Trust Building
Providence, Rhode Island 02903

Comments: The foundation provides support for higher education in Rhode island, New York, and Massachusetts. Initial approach should be by letter.

The Champlin Foundations
410 South Main Street
Providence, Rhode Island 02903
401-421-3719

Comments: The foundation supports conservation, higher education, and libraries in Rhode Island. An application form is not required; first contact should be a one-page letter.

South Carolina

The Abney Foundation
PO Box 1138
Greenwood, South Carolina 29648-1138
803-229-5777

Comments: The foundation supports higher education in South Carolina. An application form is not required; first contact should be by letter.

The Fullerton Foundation, Inc.
515 West Buford Street
Gaffney, South Carolina 29340
803-489-6678

Comments: The foundation supports health care, hospitals, and higher education in North and South Carolina. Initial approach should be by letter.

South Dakota

South Dakota Community Foundation
207 East Capitol
PO Box 296
Pierre, South Dakota 57501
605-224-1025

Comments: The foundation supports education, citizenship, and community development in South Dakota. An application form is required.